Steely Dan
FAQ

Steely Dan FAQ

All That's Left to Know About This Elusive Band

Anthony Robustelli

Backbeat
Books

An Imprint of Hal Leonard LLC

Published in 2017 by Backbeat Books
An Imprint of Hal Leonard LLC
7777 West Bluemound Road
Milwaukee, WI 53213

Trade Book Division Editorial Offices
33 Plymouth St., Montclair, NJ 07042

All photos are from the author's collection unless otherwise noted.

The FAQ series was conceived by Robert Rodriguez and developed with Stuart Shea.

Printed in the United States of America

Book design by Snow Creative

Library of Congress Cataloging-in-Publication Data

Names: Robustelli, Anthony.
Title: Steely Dan FAQ : all that's left to know about this elusive band / Anthony Robustelli.
Description: Montclair, NJ : Backbeat Books, 2016. | Includes bibliographical references and index.
Identifiers: LCCN 2016046726 | ISBN 9781495025129 (pbk.)
Subjects: LCSH: Steely Dan (Musical group) | Rock musicians—United States—Biography.
Classification: LCC ML421.S76 R63 2016 | DDC 782.42166092/2 [B]—dc23
LC record available at https://lccn.loc.gov/2016046726

www.backbeatbooks.com

This book is dedicated to the two most important people in my life: my wife, Sharon, who has not only supported my myriad endeavors for twenty years, but has also been a steadfast sounding board for my various ideas and ramblings; and my daughter, Ella, whose huge heart, humor, and inner light has gotten me through any tough days I've encountered.

Contents

Foreword

I had my Steely Dan epiphany in 1975 as a sixteen-year-old. Music never mattered to me until that one day my friend's brother put *Katy Lied* on his turntable. "Bad Sneakers" started spinning, and from that moment on, I was never the same. I had to know everything about these guys. Was I totally obsessed? You bet I was. I scoured every music rag for articles, pictures, or any blurb I could find on the notoriously reclusive band. When *Aja* came out in 1977, I held listening parties that became so popular, people made appointments to come over. Needless to say, I was pretty bummed when the band broke up in 1980. Deep down inside I knew this couldn't be the end, and if it was, I was personally going to change it.

In October 1984, I decided to move to Manhattan after living in Oceanside on Long Island, New York, for twenty-five years. Typically, people who make the move to the city have job opportunities or are working on a degree. I had a different plan. I was moving to New York City on a mission to reunite Walter Becker and Donald Fagen. The task ahead of me was more daunting than I realized. It had been four years since Steely Dan announced they were breaking up and two since Fagen's debut as a solo artist. Steely Dan's albums remained extremely popular with audiophiles, and with the new compact disc format, their catalog was being purchased all over again. They lacked the impetus to create new material and remained as reclusive as ever.

I began bartending at the Mayflower Hotel on Central Park West, which, at the time, was the preferred hotel for the movie and music industries. I would tell anybody and everybody of my plans to reunite the founders of Steely Dan. Eventually, I made friends with a guitarist who would later play a major role in helping me to fulfill my goal, Jimmy Vivino.

Steely Dan was never known for their live performances, although their shows in the early '70s were some of the best of the decade. By 1974 they had broken up their "band," stopped touring, and focused solely on recording. So, it was a welcome surprise when I found out that Fagen was performing at the Lone Star Roadhouse in the fall of 1989. I eagerly picked up tickets for the show and thoroughly enjoyed the night of soul songs written by the Brill Building songwriting team of Bert Berns and Jerry Ragovoy. Although I can't say I wasn't disappointed that no Steely Dan material was played and that Fagen refused to sing.

However, after sixteen years, Fagen had apparently caught the bug for playing live again, and he put the word out to a small circle of musicians. Jimmy Vivino had a Tuesday night residency with his Little Big Band at Hades on the Upper East Side, a dive bar that maybe held a hundred people. Fagen began showing up to these gigs with sometimes only a few hours' notice to the band. Vivino would call me at the Mayflower whenever Fagen was going to show up, and I would do whatever it took to get out of work. I'd set up my stereo tape recorder on the table directly in front of the former Steely Dan singer. The set lists consisted mostly of soul and R&B covers, but eventually, they started adding a few Steely Dan songs. In the beginning, there were hardly any people in the place, so I'm sure it seemed odd to him that I was running around taking pictures and recording the shows. Fagen often slipped out immediately after through the back door to avoid any contact with the few people left in the bar.

By this point, I was publishing the Steely Dan fanzine *Metal Leg* and had the phone numbers of the hundreds of Steely Dan fans in the area that subscribed. I began to let them know whenever Fagen was performing, and the crowds grew quickly. Libby Titus, Fagen's girlfriend at the time, was going to start producing shows at the Lone Star Roadhouse that featured Donald and special guests. The shows would be called "Libby Titus's New York Nights." The Lone Star was having a problem with promotion because, for a number of reasons, Fagen didn't want his name advertised. One afternoon, I walked into the club to inquire about the upcoming show, and the owner, Mort Cooperman, approached me. He had heard from a fan that I published *Metal Leg* and explained his dilemma. I suggested to Mort that I could promote the shows directly to my subscribers as I had been doing for Hades. He loved the idea and asked me how I wanted to be compensated. To his amazement I told him I didn't want to be paid; all I was interested in was running the floor and seating my friends at the best tables. I was given an office at the venue to make my phone calls, and it immediately paid off. With no mention of Fagen's name in the advertising, the New York Nights shows were selling out the five-hundred-capacity room.

One day, during a rehearsal, Libby informed me that Walter Becker was going to be attending the next show, but he had absolutely no intention of playing. I told her that I would make it happen; I was not going to let this opportunity slip away. She assured me that it would never happen. Not in a million years.

I wasted no time in getting the word out to Steely Dan fans. This was the moment I had been waiting for: the opportunity to reunite these two on stage playing Steely Dan songs. I spoke with Jimmy Vivino, and we devised a plan. At a certain point during the show he would give me a signal before announcing that Becker was in the audience. When I made my phone calls to the *Metal Leg* subscribers, I already had my spiel. It went something like this:

Me: Donald's playing the Lone Star again and Walter's going to be there.

Fan: Wow, that's incredible!

Me: But he's not going to perform.

Fan: What?!? @#%!

Me: Well, we have a plan. When Jimmy Vivino announces that he's in the audience, you need to go absolutely berserk. Yell, scream, stomp your feet. Make more noise than you've ever made so that there is no way he can refuse to play.

Fan: Okay! How can I get tickets?

When Vivino gave me the signal, I knew it was time. After his announcement, the eruption from the crowd blew the roof off of the place and the room was literally shaking. The response was so overwhelming that Becker had no choice but to go on stage. On October 22, 1991, several hundred ecstatic Steely Dan fans got to hear Becker and Fagen perform "Josie," "Chain Lightning," and "Black Friday" live for the first time ever. Apparently, Walter had so much fun, he decided to join Donald for the *New York Rock & Soul Revue* tour the next year, followed by what would be the first of many Steely Dan tours. Mission accomplished.

Pete Fogel is a music promoter who has booked many of New York's iconic venues over the past 25 years, including the Lone Star Roadhouse, Le Bar Bat, and Kenny's Castaways. He was the editor of the award winning Steely Dan fanzine Metal Leg and is also a part-time photographer whose photos have appeared on Steely Dan albums and documentaries, as well as in Rolling Stone magazine. An avid baseball fan, he was a freelance photographer for the New York Mets in 2000. Pete is the current weekend booking agent at the legendary venue the Bitter End in New York's Greenwich Village. He lives in Manhattan with his girlfriend.

Introduction
Hot Licks and Rhetoric

When Steely Dan's *Aja* was released on September 23, 1977, I had just started second grade. By that point I was heavily into the Beatles and had all of their records due to a monthly trip to E. J. Korvette's with my father where I would always pick a Beatles album. My brother, seven years my elder, already had an extensive record collection and introduced me to the group via *The Beatles' Second Album* and I was hooked. I had been playing piano for a couple of years and was constantly listening for new sounds. My father, who was a part-time singer and had led a big band in the late '40s under the pseudonym Tony Randall, had a massive collection of albums with artists ranging from Frank Sinatra and Ella Fitzgerald to Miles Davis and John Coltrane to Vic Damone and Louis Prima.

I had been attending jazz concerts from a young age and had seen Ahmad Jamal, Buddy Rich, Maynard Ferguson, Anita O'Day, and others before I had ever heard of Steely Dan. One day I was looking through my brother Fred's collection and found a curious-looking black record cover with a hint of a woman's face highlighted with red and white. Always a fan of a gatefold sleeve, I opened it up and saw a photo of a shirtless, skinny, smiling man with dark sunglasses and a Siberian Husky and another photo of a long-haired, bearded man, also with dark sunglasses playing a Fender Mustang guitar.

I was a voracious reader as a child, so I always found album liner notes to be fascinating. My tastes, however, were odd; my favorite book in second grade was *The Lincoln Conspiracy*. Although the book was met with disdain from academic historians, who derided the sensationalist theories, it certainly piqued the interest of a seven-year-old who would write his bachelor's thesis on the assassination of President John F. Kennedy. But I digress. The first half of the liner notes told the story of how journalist Michael Phalen was invited to the early sessions for the album by ABC Records to write an article for a European magazine that would fold long before the album was released. He attended a dozen sessions and attempted to interview the duo twice, but both tapes were confiscated, presumably by someone in the employ of Becker and Fagen. He was called a year later to write the liner notes for the album.

His descriptions of the seven songs made me even more curious as to what this band with the weird name sounded like. That was something else that seemed odd—an album with only seven songs? Even the bastardized Capitol Records Beatles albums had eleven or twelve songs. What could be said in seven songs?

Apparently quite a lot. The second half of the liner notes was written by the man who originally called Phalen for the press coverage a year earlier, Steve Diener, the major difference being that he was now president of ABC Records. His glowing review of the album was in a way hyperbole to sell more records, but it wasn't untrue.

After I placed the needle on the vinyl, I set up my *Peanuts* Colorforms set, the collection where they each had instruments. As soon as "Black Cow" started, something made me stop in my tracks. This album sounded different than anything I'd ever heard. It blended the jazz my father played with the rock sensibility and superior songwriting of the Beatles and an R&B flavor I had heard on the radio. It made an indelible mark and influenced me as a musician long before I realized that music was my calling.

By 1983, my monthly record-buying excursion had expanded from Korvette's in Port Chester, New York, ten minutes from my childhood home in Mamaroneck, to Tower Records on East 4th Street and Broadway, six blocks and five years from my future freshman NYU dormitory. It was there that I purchased *The Nightfly*, my next step in the journey to complete Steely Dan fandom. Was this the same skinny figure that crouched with a Siberian husky on the inside cover of *Aja*? The black-and-white photo featured a short-haired man with a tie, smoking a cigarette while sitting in a disc jockey booth in a 1950s-era radio station. The album was another jazzy slice of funk-and-soul-influenced rock, and the record was constantly on the turntable.

A few years later I had a job at one of the first CD stores in Westchester County, New York. It was here that I purchased the entire Steely Dan catalog, including some titles that I had never owned. Although some of the albums I bought were nearly fifteen years old, they sounded fresh and sonically superior to many artists of the day. At the time I didn't know of the countless stories detailing their quest for sonic, as well as instrumental, perfection, but it had definitely paid off.

Their musical style was so unconventional that they've even had two chords credited to them, the Steely Dan chord and the mu-major chord. The first, heard extensively in "Peg," is so immediately recognizable that professional musicians call it the Steely Dan chord rather than what it actually is, a minor seventh chord with a sharp five. Even Becker and Fagen were impressed by the fact that their music has been so inspirational, with Fagen stating in a 2000 interview with *The Guardian*, "I don't know if it's the greatest chord in the world, but it's not bad. It's a pretty good chord, a pretty neat chord . . . it has the stability of a tonic chord, but the cool satisfying quality that a true minor seventh has, in the sense of being . . . Bartókian. Or Copelandian."

The second, the mu-major, or μ major, is basically a major chord with an added ninth, but the way Becker and Fagen use the chord, as well as their inversions, make it unique to their music. It is one of their most frequently used stylistic devices and appeared on every album from "Dirty Work" from *Can't Buy a Thrill* to "Things I Miss the Most" from *Everything Must Go*.

Steely Dan influenced not only their contemporaries, but countless artists that followed. Their brand of jazz-infused, R&B-flavored rock sounds like nothing else, and when musicians and songwriters are inspired by the band, it is apparent. They have had songs from every album sampled by over seventy artists, including Kanye West, Beyoncé, Rakim, De La Soul, the Art of Noise featuring Tom Jones, Super Furry Animals, Ice Cube, Naughty by Nature, and countless others from every different musical genre. In addition to their countless sampled appearances, their songs have been covered by dozens of performers in myriad musical styles from straight-ahead jazz to country to alternative rock.

While their prominent stature among rock 'n' roll acts is apparent, there has been a dearth of books written about the elusive duo. With *Steely Dan FAQ* I've not only delved deep into each song recorded by Steely Dan as well as Becker and Fagen's solo albums, but taken the opportunity to discuss rare recordings, projects the duo worked on outside of Steely Dan, their countless tours including the three with the original lineup, Dan songs covered by other artists, television appearances, the numerous musicians used on their albums, and the different characters that helped the band achieve their goals.

Although fans and critics alike saw Steely Dan as being innovative not only lyrically but also musically, Becker and Fagen disagreed. Fagen put it best when he stated in a 2013 interview for *Keyboard* magazine, "We always felt a little deficient for not being innovators, in our own minds at least. We loved certain traditions in jazz and R&B, and we used those as our foundation. Maybe what we tried to do was combine some things that weren't usually combined. But we never thought of ourselves as innovative. I find that ninety-five percent of what people call 'innovative' or 'experimental' is just pure B.S. Most such things are forgotten a year later, because it's often just someone being self-conscious in an attempt to be different. And it usually ends up being really bad." Becker and Fagen always wrote music to entertain themselves first. They weren't concerned with being pioneers; they were just trying to keep things fresh so that, as Fagen noted, they "wouldn't fall asleep." Luckily for us their need to create music that appealed to their own sensibilities produced a wealth of material that is just as entertaining today as it was when it was originally released.

These Suburban Streets

The Childhood Years of Becker and Fagen

Neither Walter Becker nor Donald Fagen grew up in Manhattan, but they were both raised in the tri-state area, Becker in the Borough of Queens and then in the tony suburb of Scarsdale, New York, and Fagen in Passaic, New Jersey, and then in Kendall Park in Central New Jersey. Even as children, they both felt somewhat alienated from mainstream culture and lived along the outer fringes of society. They were drawn to the mysticism of Manhattan and the music that emanated from the New York City jazz radio stations. As Fagen said in a 1981 interview with *Musician, Player and Listener*, "New York City is the depository for misfit Americans—there's a reason why we're here . . . You walk down the street and think: Hmmm, something about all these folks is just a little off-center." From a young age they both desired to be a part of that scene.

Donald Fagen's Early Years

Donald Jay Fagen was born on January 10, 1948, in Passaic, New Jersey, to Jewish parents, Joseph "Jerry" Fagen, an accountant, and his wife, Elinor, a homemaker. His sister Susan was born six years later. When Donald was between the ages of twelve and sixteen, his mother performed in the predominantly Jewish resort area known as the Borscht Belt in the Catskill Mountains. Each summer she would sing the popular songs of the day until stage fright finally forced her to stop performing. In addition to his mother's musical talent, Fagen would also inherit this fear of performing live.

Although his mother's singing career was over before Fagen was born, music was constantly playing around the house. His mother would sing along to the hits of the '50s from her vast record collection, and Fagen has said that he developed his uncommon vocal phrasing and natural swing feel from hearing his mother sing.

He got along with his parents, but was disappointed by their desire to assimilate into mainstream America. Fagen was aware of the fact that in comparison to his parents, he looked distinctly Jewish. When his father was a child, Fagen's grandfather's paint store was burned down by white supremacists. In order to blend in with their surroundings, Fagen's father decided that Donald needed a crew-cut, the typical haircut of the day for American males. When he was ten years old, the family moved deeper into New Jersey to Fair Lawn, but this brief layover didn't upset the preteen nearly as much as the next decision: the move to a ranch-style home on Bedford Road in the South Brunswick neighborhood of Kendall Park near Princeton, New Jersey. Although young Donald thought his parents tried too hard to "fit in," his father did help to establish a brand new synagogue in Kendall Park where Fagen had the first bar mitzvah, the rabbi's only student in 1961.

Kendall Park gets its name from its builder, Herbert Kendall, who built the planned community in three stages between 1956 and 1961. The development doubled the population of South Brunswick Township and was an early sign of its transformation from a rural farming area to a suburban community, but the Fagen family moved in at a relatively early stage, and much of the land was still undeveloped. They also had moved from fifteen miles outside of Manhattan to forty-five miles from the city to a development with identical houses that still had dirt for lawns and twigs for trees. Fagen described it as one of the worst suburbs he'd ever seen. Given that it was a new development, it was quite deserted, and for the first time he began to doubt his parents' judgment, realizing that he had his own views that were not in tune with theirs.

The feeling of alienation multiplied once they moved to Kendall Park, and Fagen sought solace in music and reading. He quit Little League and the Boy Scouts because of his allergic reaction to poison ivy. He was, however, an accomplished swimmer and enjoyed the pool in his backyard. He was a member of the Stamp Club and Science Fiction Book Club and elaborated on his and Becker's love of science fiction in a 2011 interview with Marc Myers for *JazzWax*. "Walter and I enjoyed reading science fiction as kids. Writers like Alfred Bester, Fredric Brown, and Robert Heinlein. They were mainly writing satire under the guise of science fiction. They created this alternate reality that's sort of like this one. They all had a sense of humor. . . . They got you to think expansively. . . . Being an outcast is secondary. The primary motive is the music and freedom." Many of these writers came from the socialist movement of the '30s, and Bester, a New Yorker who understood the fast pace of the city, wrote prose that affected the way Becker and Fagen would write lyrics in a significant way.

The first instrument Fagen played was the guitar. At the age of seven, his parents rented one for him and he took a few lessons, but because the strings were rusted and the action made them too far above the frets, his fingers hurt and he quickly gave it up. As a child, he was a fan of early rock 'n' roll musicians like Fats Domino and Chuck Berry, whose "Reelin' and Rockin'" was the first record that he bought. But as the raucous sound of real rock 'n' roll was replaced by the lightweight fare of pop idols like Fabian, Frankie Avalon, and Bobby Rydell, Fagen knew that he needed to find a new musical outlet. When he was eleven years old, he discovered jazz at a time when rock 'n' roll was losing its vitality and bland, white, middle-of-the-road acts like Pat Boone, the Crew Cuts, and the Diamonds were continuing their chart success singing watered-down versions of songs by black artists. A new generation of singers such as Paul Anka, Bobby Vee, and Ricky Nelson provided safe, formulaic music for the teenybopper crowd. This type of music would dominate the charts until the Beatles landed in America on February 7,

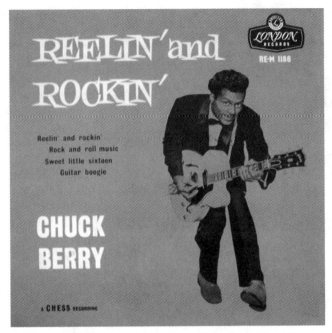

The first record that Donald Fagen ever bought was Chuck Berry's *Reelin' and Rockin'*, a 1958 EP originally released in the U.K. on London Records, the label that distributed Chess Records in England.

1964, and started the British Invasion, something that would rekindle Becker and Fagen's love of rock 'n' roll and affect their identities as musicians and songwriters.

As his musical tastes were transitioning from rock 'n' roll to jazz, Fagen became aware of the late-night jazz radio shows broadcast from New York City that became his "lifeline to urban life." He gave all of his rock 'n' roll records to his younger sister, Susan, and began to listen to jazz exclusively. The first jazz LP he purchased was *Dave Brubeck at Newport, 1958*. Fagen began to listen to Miles Davis, John Coltrane, Sonny Rollins, Thelonious Monk, and Charles Mingus, and his interest in music grew exponentially.

Donald Fagen, Pianist

When Fagen was twelve, his grandmother bought a piano for the family, and although his sister was the first to take lessons, he showed an immediate interest in the instrument. He began to figure out songs by ear and learned "Exodus," the theme from the Otto Preminger film that was a hit for Ferrante & Teicher in 1960. Donald's younger sister studied piano first, but Fagen's parents saw the inherent musical talent that he had and brought him to the Princeton New School of Music, assuming he would want to take formal lessons. The teacher was impressed but said that he wouldn't develop unless he was prepared to learn to sight-read

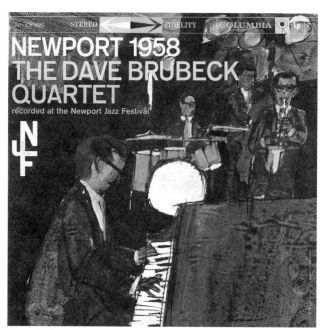

Fagen's first jazz record was also released in 1958, *The Dave Brubeck Quartet Newport 1958* on Fontana Records.

and begin his formal study from scratch. Fagen wasn't interested in that kind of training and decided that he would teach himself how to play piano.

He practiced diligently each day after school and began to toy with the idea of composing his own songs. The only lessons he received were from a family friend who taught him a few jazz chords, something that would provide a foundation for his quest to become a jazz pianist. He slowed down jazz records and played along until he figured out what they were playing. After hearing pianist Red Garland on Symphony Sid's jazz radio show, he went to E. J. Korvette's and bought the pianist's *Jazz Junction* LP and tried to imitate his style, but never felt that he had the technique to be a straight-ahead jazz musician. Besides Red Garland, who played with Miles Davis's first great quintet, he began to listen to bebop pianist extraordinaire Bud Powell, as well as Bill Evans, who along with Miles Davis would introduce modal jazz to the masses with 1959's *Kind of Blue*.

Even when it came to jazz, Fagen was a snob, his anti-social personality forming quickly and at a young age. Even though Becker and Fagen would quote Horace Silver's "Song for My Father" (whether it was intentional or not is up for debate), Fagen was very aware of the piano–playing leader and composer. But he has stated that he didn't like his style that much, or any of the backbeat-embracing funky players heard primarily on Alfred Lion's Blue Note records. He also thought that Lion had too much influence on the jazz scene, given that the records released on his label were so successful. He has since wisely embraced the beauty of the music that came from this progressive, forward-thinking record label.

One pianist in particular who not only influenced Fagen musically but also personally was Thelonious Monk. To Fagen, Monk was otherworldly as a musician, and as a person, yet jazz touched Fagen in a way that made it seem more realistic and grounded than his own environment in a suburb of New York City. He subscribed to *Down Beat* magazine, and when he was a teenager he began to take the one-and-a-half-hour journey into New York City's Port Authority Bus Depot with his older cousins Mike and Jack, who were jazz enthusiasts and managed to get him into the Village Vanguard to see Miles Davis, Thelonious Monk, Coleman

Donald Fagen was a lifelong fan of Thelonious Monk and would perform a duet with guitarist Steve Khan of Monk's "Reflections" for the 1984 tribute album *That's the Way I Feel Now*, released two years after the pianist-composer's death.

Hawkins, Charles Mingus, Sonny Rollins, Count Basie, and a number of other famous jazz musicians. Although he was underage, the owner, Max Gordon, realized his enthusiasm for jazz music and often let him sit near the drums while he sipped his Coca-Cola. For Fagen, jazz was an escape from the suburban pallor of Kendall Park and the sensibilities of the typical American's Cold War mentality of the 1950s. To be cool in the late '50s you needed to be underground, and Fagen had no problem with that premise.

Donald Fagen: The High School Years

Fagen continued to be a voracious reader in high school, absorbing the works of W. B. Yeats, William Blake, and the beat poets, including Lawrence Ferlinghetti, co-founder of City Lights Booksellers & Publishers, whose slim books of poetry he'd cop from his older cousins who were jazz fans and aspiring beatniks. When Fagen was in high school, there was a minority of kids who listened to jazz, and those same kids had a lot of other interests that were different from the majority of their classmates. Fagen has said that it was all about the types of books that you read and the "hipster ethic." His identity was formed by his obsession with jazz, beat writers, science fiction, and an inescapable desire to leave the doldrums of the New Jersey suburbs for good.

Donald Fagen
"Don" . . . individualist . . . phys ed major . . . the thinker . . . journalist extraordinaire . . . jazz enthusiast . . . quotations for all occasions . . . "Harry the Horse."

Fagen's senior photo from South Brunswick High School's 1965 yearbook.

Fagen never had much of a social life at South Brunswick High School and was described by those who knew him as anti-social, eccentric, and aloof. He

To this day Fagen is an adept table tennis player. His love of the sport began as a teenager.

did, however, participate in some extracurricular activities and was a staffer for the school newspaper, where he shined as a journalist. He also played baritone horn in the school marching band until the director, Chauncey Chatten, advised him that he'd have to spend every Saturday marching during half-time at the school's football games. He formed a jazz trio before graduating, and under his yearbook portrait it stated that he was a "jazz enthusiast, an individualist, and a thinker." He's also shown in a few candid shots playing ping-pong and a couple of photos related to his journalistic bent. In the class photo he didn't look so dour resting a shoulder on a fellow student in typical high school fashion, but he was extremely shy with girls and didn't attend the school proms or graduation. With not much of a social life, all of his time was spent reading, playing table tennis, playing the piano, listening to jazz records, and heading into Manhattan to see the jazz masters live. He hadn't watched much television since he was thirteen, but he did enjoy detective shows and loved Henry Mancini's "fake jazz" score for *Peter Gunn*. At age seventeen, Fagen's rapier wit was already apparent as documented by his class will, where he wrote, "I, Donald Fagen, leave seven barrels of steaming, fetid boredom."

Walter Becker's Early Years

Walter Carl Becker was born in the Forest Hills section of Queens, New York, on February 20, 1950. Like Fagen, he also has one sister, Wendy, born in 1953. Becker's father sold paper-gutting machinery that was imported from Germany for a company that had offices in Manhattan, near the city's printing district. When Becker was a young boy, his parents separated, and his mother, who is British, moved to England. With his mother absent, he was raised by his father and paternal grandmother. They lived in Queens for a number of years, then relocated to the upscale suburb of Scarsdale, New York. After a few years, the commute to Manhattan became too time consuming for his father, and the family moved back to Forest Hills. Becker enrolled at the prestigious Stuyvesant High School in Manhattan and worked at his father's shop on Canal Street. If one thought that

Fagen the writer hard at work.

Fagen was voted class wit in his senior year.

the teenage Fagen was anti-social and aloof, he was practically Mr. Popularity in comparison to Becker. Not only was Becker listed as "camera shy" in his senior class yearbook, that is the only mention of his name in the entire book. He listed no hobbies, clubs, or interests, solely his name.

Like Fagen, the teenage Becker began to frequent jazz concerts and was overwhelmed by how different musicians could express themselves in such diverse ways on the same instrument. He attended a concert at Hunter College that showcased three piano players, Billy Taylor (who was also a promoter and disc jockey), Mary Lou Williams, and Thelonious Monk. Although they all played the same piano, each artist interpreted music in a different way, and when Monk played, it hardly sounded like a piano at all, his interpretation being so otherworldly. It made a lasting impression on the young musician.

Becker's father would spend one month per year in Germany for his job, and when Becker was sixteen his father had a heart attack, but survived. Becker has said that this brought them closer together, and they often spoke of future plans. Soon after, he brought his father to the airport for one of his trips overseas, and one month later on the return trip, he died on the plane. Becker reacted badly to his father's death, as any teenager would, and it took quite a while before he would find something that could capture his imagination.

Walter Becker, Musician

Walter Becker's earliest musical memories are of hearing Rosemary Clooney while driving on the West Side Highway in Manhattan. Like Fagen, he was a jazz fan at an early age and listened to many of the same late-night jazz programs broadcast from Manhattan radio stations. As a child, Becker's first instrument was one that Donald Fagen would play when the duo began performing live again in the '90s: the melodica. The melodica, also known as the pianica, blow-organ, key harmonica, or melodyhorn, is a reed instrument similar to the pump organ and harmonica. It has a two- or three-octave keyboard on top, and is played by blowing air through a mouthpiece that fits into a hole in the side of the instrument. In the 1950s, Hohner produced a modern form of the melodica, although similar instruments have been known in Italy since the 1800s.

Soon after, he switched to the saxophone inspired by one of his idols, Charlie Parker. However, the amount of practice needed to master the instrument proved too much for him and he dropped it. It's interesting to note that Becker began his musical exploration with two instruments that Fagen would end up playing, and Fagen's first instrument would become one of Becker's main axes.

For Becker, third time's the charm, as his third choice of instrument, the guitar, would be the one that he would eventually master. Once he decided that he was better suited to play guitar than saxophone, he began taking lessons from a neighbor in his building, The Balfour, named Randy Wolfe. The two shared the same birthday, although Wolfe was a year younger. In the summer of '66, Wolfe relocated to Queens from Los Angeles, where he had studied various musical styles at his family's folk club, the world-famous Ash Grove. The club, which was founded by his uncle, Ed Pearl, was a perfect place for a young guitarist to learn his craft. The artists who performed there ranged from blues legends Mississippi John Hurt, Son House, Earl Hooker, and Muddy Waters to young artists who were a part of the '60s music revolution, including Pete Seeger, June Carter, Johnny Cash, José Feliciano, Phil Ochs, Joan Baez, Johnny Otis, Lightnin' Hopkins, Arlo Guthrie, Howlin' Wolf, Willie Dixon, Lonnie Mack, and Kris Kristofferson. Wolfe began playing guitar at the age of eight when his mother taught him some chords, and by fifteen he was able to teach others.

The move was imperative because his mother, Bernice Pearl, had recently gotten remarried to jazz drummer Ed Cassidy, and Cassidy had a number of gigs lined up on the East Coast. He lived in a basement flat with his mother, stepfather, and three sisters. Soon after arriving in New York, Wolfe met Jimi Hendrix at Manny's Music and played some slide guitar for him. Hendrix was impressed, and they both realized that there was a true musical connection between them. Hendrix invited him to join his band Jimmy James and the Blue Flames on stage at the Café Wha? for their first gig at the venue that night. Since the bass player was named Randy Palmer, Hendrix began calling Palmer "Randy Texas" and Wolfe "Randy California" after their home states. In 1967, Randy California would found the band Spirit with his stepfather, Ed Cassidy.

Becker took some lessons from Randy, but once again he became frustrated at the amount of work necessary to master the technique and decided to temporarily switch to bass guitar because learning a four-string instrument would be less complicated. When they played with other local musicians, California played guitar and Becker would play bass, although he continued to play guitar as well, which in the long run would be a wise choice. When Fagen first met Becker at Bard College a few years later, it was Becker's blues-guitar playing, much of which he gleaned from Randy California, that would initially impress Fagen and be the foundation of a long and fruitful musical relationship that would change the face of rock music.

I'm Never Going Back to My Old School

The Bard College Years

In 1965, Donald Fagen enrolled at Bard College in Annandale-on-Hudson to study English literature, having been influenced by the beat writers of the '50s. He originally considered theater as a major but realized that he was too self-conscious for the types of exercises that they did, such as lying on their backs and yelling. He planned on driving himself to college that fall, but his father steadfastly refused to allow that, so father and son made the three-hour trip together.

Instead of settling into one of the two remarkable riverside manor houses that had been converted into dormitories, Fagen ended up in Stone Row, a group of buildings in the center of campus that were rather run down. His roommates were Chester Brezniak, a clarinetist; artist Lonnie Yongue, a senior with an extensive record collection and an even more extensive collection of marijuana; and a gay dancer named Alan.

Fagen didn't consider being a musician as a profession until he was at Bard, because he didn't think he had the technique. Although he was quite talented and had played piano as well as saxophone, he was a jazz fan, and that was the type of musician he wanted to be. He eventually realized that technique wasn't everything and that he brought something original to the table. His roommate Yongue recognized his talent and questioned why he was studying English literature rather than music. Fagen eventually questioned his decision as well.

College proved to be quite a different experience for Fagen in comparison to high school. He hadn't had much of a social life as a

Stone Row, where Fagen lived in the Potter dormitory during his freshman year.

teenager in Kendall Park, but at Bard he actually had friends, as he would recall somewhat facetiously, the only time in his life that he did. But when he first arrived he was still somewhat shy, so the idea of attending a Tequila mixer at Sottery Hall was a bit ambitious. That night he watched two bands perform. The first, the Group Image, was a pre-hippie band whose female frontwoman eventually stopped singing and danced alongside the band as strobe lights flickered along with the music. After too much tequila, Fagen drunkenly considered ditching college and jumping in the van with the Group Image to travel the country as a dropout. The second group had a more lasting effect on the freshman musician. The Ginger Men was a talented group led by two Bard students, the Boylan brothers. Both Becker and Fagen would play on Terence Boylan's debut LP, *Alias Boona*, in 1969.

Donald Fagen's Friends and Love Interests

In his first year at Bard, the self-proclaimed anti-social Fagen actually made friends, some that he would keep in touch with to this day. These included his roommate Yongue, who like Fagen was attempting to teach himself how to play saxophone; a group of stoned hipsters from Washington, D.C.; a philosophy major from Harlem; a couple of sardonic prep school graduates from Pennsylvania; and a few students from the class of '68, one of whom named Bexley would teach Fagen proper musical notation.

He continued to admire at least one different Bard beauty, usually from afar, every semester until he met girlfriend Dorothy White in 1968. Each one seemed more insane than the last, which Fagen attributes to his

Fagen used to walk down a long, wooded path behind his dorm to this hidden, one-room, octagonal stone building, The Observatory, to practice piano.

desire to be with someone who was crazier than he was. He also was attracted to what he described as "damaged, incandescent originals who . . . out of necessity, created themselves from scratch." At one point he worked himself into such frenzy for a woman that he stopped eating and sleeping and developed walking pneumonia. He ended up knocking on the co-ed's dorm window in the dead of winter until she let him in.

During his time at Bard, he also developed a crush on a professor's wife, future novelist Rikki Ducornet, born Erica DeGre. She would be the subject of Steely Dan's best-selling single "Rikki Don't Lose That Number." Fagen would also first set eyes upon his future wife Libby Titus while she was visiting friends. Titus was a student at Bard the year before Fagen enrolled, but in her sophomore year, she got pregnant, left school, and married novelist Barry Titus, grandson of Helena Rubinstein. Their son Ezra Titus was born on July 23, 1966, but the couple separated two years later. He was raised by Titus and Levon Helm, drummer and singer for the Band, and later became an author. Tragically, Ezra Titus committed suicide on his forty-third birthday on July 23, 2009.

The Summer of '66—Boston Bound

In the summer of 1966, Fagen went to the Berklee College of Music in Boston, but he was never one to embrace music as a course of study and spent most of the summer hanging out in the city and smoking pot. His teacher had been offered a gig that he couldn't refuse, so he gave Fagen three months of instruction in one afternoon.

He has stated that while he isn't a fan of formal music tuition, he did learn quite a bit that summer. In 1992, he was interviewed by Steve Morse of the *Boston Globe* about the *New York Rock and Soul Revue* tour and spoke of his summer in Boston. "I lived on Symphony Road and it was a foul summer. I had almost no money and was eating a lot of brown rice. But I picked up a lot of good stuff from the Berklee course. I remember the practice rooms at Berklee were always being used, so I'd take the bus up to MIT and use their practice rooms. Amazingly, MIT has these great practice rooms with little pianos in them. The pianos were tuned up really nicely and I'd just play scales all day . . . But I never had the patience to be a professional musician. There are great gaps in my musical knowledge. I'm mostly self-taught."

That summer did, however, have a lasting effect on Fagen. When he returned to Bard rather than continue with his degree in English literature, he switched his major to music. In the late '60s, the music department at numerous liberal arts universities focused on both classical music and contemporary avant-garde composers such as Stockhausen, Cage, Boulez, and Berio. Unlike a full-time music school such as Berklee whose curriculum was more varied, with classes offered in jazz, world music, fusion, and, by the end of the decade, rock, liberal arts schools had a stricter focus. It's a bit surprising that after Fagen's disillusionment with the premise of music education, he would become a music major. As a child, his parents brought him to the Princeton New School of Music, but he decided that formal training wasn't for him. He quit the high school band when he realized that he'd have to spend every Saturday afternoon marching around a football field with his baritone horn, and while he gained some essential knowledge and practice time at Berklee during the summer, it wasn't a typical semester with his professor AWOL. So the fact that he embraced music as a major, especially classical and avant-garde music, is more than a little surprising.

Drug Use on Campus

The summer before Fagen left for college, he had his first LSD experience with a friend who had just returned from his freshman year at Brandeis University in Massachusetts. He arrived in Kendall Park, New Jersey, with a satchel of sugar cubes laced with five hundred micrograms of lysergic acid diethylamide, still legal in 1965. Like so many others at the time, his friend Pete was also in possession of the book *The Psychedelic Experience: A Manual Based on The Tibetan Book of the Dead*. The book, published a year earlier in August 1964, served as a guide to tripping written by three Harvard professors—Ralph Metzner, Richard Alpert, and the infamous Timothy Leary. While *The Tibetan Book of the Dead* was written as a guide for death and rebirth, the purpose of *The Psychedelic Experience* was to guide people through their experiences of the death of the ego while undergoing the psychedelic experience. The book was dedicated to author Aldous Huxley and includes a short introductory citation from his revolutionary book *The Doors of Perception*. John Lennon used part of the text from *The Psychedelic Experience* in his lyrics for the 1966 *Revolver* track "Tomorrow Never Knows."

Pete's parents were rather forward thinking for this New Jersey enclave. They were both intellectual actors, and his father taught history at Rutgers University. They were so hip that Pete's mother, well aware of what her son and the young Donald Fagen were taking on a sunny Sunday afternoon, continued with her kitchen chores as the two teenagers had their psychedelic experience.

At Bard, Fagen smoked a fair amount of marijuana until anxiety attacks sidelined him for a time in the winter of his third year in '67. That winter he also experimented with dimethyltryptamine, better known as DMT, which would produce a full acid-like experience immediately and last for fifteen minutes. After a quick jaunt in the upstate New York cold, Fagen and Pete would return to their parsley-soaked bowls to get one more hit and experience another quick hallucination.

Becker and Fagen Meet

The summer before his sophomore year, Fagen headed to San Francisco looking for summer work, but had no luck. Lacking funds, he only attended one concert, Big Brother and the Holding Company and Jimi Hendrix at Winterland. He had met some people he became friendly with and went to Big Sur to camp. Fagen, not an outdoorsy type, contracted poison oak and as his father Joseph stated, "blew up like you couldn't recognize who he was. In fact, coming home on the plane, one of his cousins was on the plane with him, and she didn't recognize him."

Becker recalls that when they first met, Fagen was still suffering from the effects of poison oak.

Once he returned to school in the fall of '67, he began to play in a number of bands on campus including the Leather Canary and the Don Fagen Trio. All of his musical tastes were displayed, spread out amongst these different bands. One played Chicago blues, one was more of a free jazz experimental group, and the third was, as Fagen described it, "a sort of satirical pop group" that he'd put together in order to showcase material he had begun writing. Little did he know that within a year he would meet the one person who had such similar tastes in music, literature, and humor that they would create a band that was an amalgamation of all of the different styles that influenced their music, lyrics, and lifestyles.

In 1967, Walter Becker graduated from New York City's prestigious Stuyvesant High School and in the fall enrolled at Bard. Becker stated that one of the reasons he went to Bard was because "a good folk picker from my high school went there." He reminisced in a 1993 VH1 special about how he met Fagen. "I went to Bard College under the delusion that because there was [sic] a lot of people with long hair smoking dope on campus that there would be a lot of musicians only to find when I got there most of the people at Bard, and I was there on a scholarship, right, it was a very expensive school and most of the people at the school were rich ne'er do wells who couldn't even be bothered to learn how to play the guitar or the harmonica or anything."

When Becker arrived, he noticed that there were a few bands playing around the campus and they all had something in common. Fagen was the leader of every one of them. Becker approached the keyboard player to offer his services as a bassist, but unfortunately for Becker, the bass player in these bands owned all of the equipment and was also on the entertainment committee at Bard. So not only

Fagen rehearsed with Terence Boylan at this small practice space called Bard Hall.

did he own the gear, he booked the gigs. His position was secure, so for the time being Becker sat on the sidelines and watched.

Soon after, Fagen was walking past the Red Balloon, one of the buildings on campus that was used as an on-campus music venue for the student body, and he heard an unreal guitarist who sounded like Howlin' Wolf. Fagen was used to hearing, and playing with, guitarists around campus who had embraced the trebly surf sound that was prevalent in many of the white bands of the day. This was something different. A bluesy, vibrato-laden, sustain-inducing sound that was full of soul. He walked in and found a baby-faced Becker playing his red Epiphone hollow-body guitar. They immediately realized that they had a lot in common. Both were into jazz and blues as kids in the late '50s and early '60s, which was quite unusual at the time, and listened to many of the same jazz radio shows that emanated from New York City. Although they were more akin to beatniks than hippies, they were fans of the Beatles' music and Bob Dylan's lyrics, something that would play a significant role in their songwriting and the creation of Steely Dan.

They were also both interested in literature and were avid readers possessing a dark sense of humor, something that was typical of some of their favorite authors such as Kurt Vonnegut, Bruce Jay Friedman, and Vladimir Nabokov. They were interested in nonconformity and enjoyed being bookish, snarky members of this subculture. Although Fagen was unable to offer Becker a position as a bass player, he did bring him on as a guitarist, and soon after, the other three guitarists, who Becker described as "really bad," were let go.

It comes as no surprise that both Becker and Fagen's attitudes toward rock 'n' roll would change when they heard the Beatles. Becker's first exposure to the group came in a Woolworth's when he heard "No Reply" from the group's seventh release in the U.S., *Beatles '65* (the song was originally from their fourth LP in the U.K., *Beatles for Sale*). That song convinced him that there was more to rock 'n' roll music than three chords. For Fagen, the song that changed his perspective was their number one single from 1965, "Ticket to Ride," heard on his radio one summer evening. Becker, however, is still prejudiced against rock and doesn't like it if there aren't enough chord changes, unless it's played extremely well.

The Beatles, Bob Dylan, and the Rolling Stones helped to realign Becker and Fagen with rock music, and while they consider the '60s to be the most creative period for the genre, they also understood the significance and influence that the original rock 'n' roll and R&B music, played predominantly by African Americans, had on the bands from the UK. Although there was something exciting about the music of the British Invasion, they also realized that it was initially derived from these deep-rooted American genres. The inspiration for much of Steely Dan's music would come from a similar avenue, but with the important addition of another musical influence not commonly heard in rock music: jazz.

Even at this early age Becker was an audiophile, with two huge Altec speakers connected to his stereo where he and Fagen would spend countless hours listening to their favorite jazz, blues, and rock records and gleaning everything they could from the shared experience. Their tastes ran the gamut from Charlie Parker to Frank Zappa's Mothers of Invention, who they had both seen at the Garrick

Theater on Bleecker Street in Manhattan. Fagen has stated that Becker introduced him to music as old as Howlin' Wolf and as new as Laura Nyro.

Becker and Fagen: Songwriters, Bandmates, and Dropouts

Becker and Fagen had such an instant rapport that they immediately began writing songs together at an upright piano in a sitting room in the lobby of a building known as The Manor. Their similar tastes in music, literature, and humor created songs that would leave them in hysterics. It was almost as if they were trying to outdo each other with sheer absurdity, something that would make their early material hard to sell once they left Bard and began careers as professional songwriters. They incorporated science fiction, black humor, and the influence of novels by Thomas Berger, Terry Southern, Philip Roth, Vladimir Nabokov, and Kurt Vonnegut. They also admired the comic compositions of writers like Tom Lehrer, a piano player and songwriter who wrote dark yet humorous tunes.

They played a number of gigs on campus, some odder than others. They performed at a student art show opening at the Procter Art Center for which Fagen borrowed a Fender Rhodes electric piano. After a few songs, the heavy instrument crashed to the floor, and Fagen, afraid of the reaction of its owner (a rather large blond named Dinah), left Becker to finish the show on his own. Unfortunately for Becker, he had decided to prime himself for the gig by taking LSD, something that would prove to be a bit hazardous. They also had LSD-taking drummers who would disrupt their set, as well as a future comedy star who would prove to be a consummate professional. In October 1967, they played the Ward Manor Halloween party with future *Saturday Night Live* star Chevy Chase on drums. Fagen thought that he "looked like a frat boy who'd wandered onto the wrong campus," but he kept a steady groove and was a proficient drummer.

When the fall semester began in 1968, Becker had already shown a lack of interest in his academic studies and was asked to leave. With no guidance from anybody remotely related to jazz, Fagen began to skip classes as well, and although he had a good relationship with his composition professor, Jacob Druckman, his poor attendance and general attitude forced the hand of the department head and he was asked to leave the program. He resumed his study as an English literature major and scheduled his classes so that they were all on Thursday and Friday. By doing this he was able to move to Brooklyn with his girlfriend Dorothy White and begin pedaling the songs he and Becker had been writing to publishers in Manhattan.

The Big Bust

In May 1969, Fagen was at Bard for the weekend at an off-campus house he rented with other students working on his final draft of his senior thesis. At four in the morning, his house, as well as several other men's dorms, was raided by deputies of the local sheriff's department, along with a number of New York State police officers. The man who led the raid was a politician running for assistant DA, G. Gordon Liddy. Within a few years, Liddy

Becker and Fagen played the 1967 Halloween Party at Ward Manor with Chevy Chase on drums. The duo also wrote songs on an old upright piano in a sitting room inside the lobby.

would be convicted of conspiracy, burglary, and illegal wiretapping for his role in the Watergate scandal. He was sentenced to a twenty-year prison term and was ordered to pay $40,000 in fines. He began serving his sentence on January 30, 1973, but President Jimmy Carter commuted Liddy's sentence to eight years on April 12, 1977. Liddy was eligible for parole on July 9, 1977, and was released on September 7, 1977, after serving a total of four and a half years.

Fagen hadn't smoked marijuana since his panic attacks, but for some reason his landlord, Beau Coggins, had testified that Fagen sold him marijuana. Fagen never met the man since one of his roommates had rented the apartment and took care of the monthly payments, but this falsified information led to his arrest, as well as that of Walter Becker and Dorothy White, who were guests at the time. Actually, the school had placed an undercover agent among the students disguised as a janitor who helped to orchestrate these undercover operations. The male guests of the state were shorn of their long locks, and students were left in jail for a day or two until the university finally bailed out their current and past students, so for the time being Dorothy White was out of luck and left in jail.

Fagen called his father in Ohio, who arranged bail for White and hired an attorney to deal with the Peter Maroulis, the school's lawyer, who would later represent Liddy during the Watergate case. Fagen never got over this disservice, and while he returned to Bard for graduation day, he refused to sit with his class and watched his graduation from afar.

Stompin' on the Avenue by Radio City

Meeting and Working with Kenny Vance

During his final semester at Bard in 1969, Donald Fagen took an apartment on President Street in Brooklyn with his then-girlfriend Dorothy White and a medical student named Richard Ransohoff. Walter Becker dropped out of school and moved in with his sister and grandmother in Queens temporarily as the duo tried to sell their songs door to door, even then an outdated approach to breaking into the music business. In hindsight they realized that this was the way songwriters peddled their wares in the 1930s, but at the time they didn't see anything wrong with this method.

The business of music publishing had its origins in Boston in the late 19th century, but moved to Philadelphia, Chicago, and Cincinnati before settling in New York. Most publishers had initially set up shop around Union Square, but when the entertainment industry began moving uptown, one of the leading publishing companies, M. Witmark & Sons, moved to West 28th Street between Fifth and Sixth Avenues. It wouldn't be long before other publishers followed, and with that, Tin Pan Alley was born.

The Brill Building, located at 1619 Broadway in Manhattan, was completed in 1931 and was named after the Brill Brothers, whose clothing store originally occupied the ground floor and who would later buy it. During the Great Depression, there was a shortage of tenants, so a number of spaces were rented to music publishers. This began the shift farther uptown for more entertainment businesses, and by 1962, the Brill Building contained 165 music companies. Songwriters Jerry Leiber and Mike Stoller, Burt Bacharach and Hal David, Tommy Boyce and Bobby Hart, Neil Diamond, Paul Simon, Phil Spector, and Sonny Bono all worked at the Brill Building at one point or another. Two blocks away, 1650 Broadway was also a hub of the music business and was home to one of the most successful music publishers of the late '50s and early '60s, Aldon Music founded by Don Kirshner and Al Nevins in 1958. Aldon signed countless songwriters including Neil Sedaka, Howard Greenfield, Barry Mann, Cynthia Weil, Gerry Goffin, and Carole King.

Kenny Vance Meets Donald Fagen and Walter Becker

While peddling their songs, Becker and Fagen met Kenny Vance of the group Jay and the Americans. For all intents and purposes, Vance should be credited as the man who discovered the core of Steely Dan. Without him they wouldn't have met Gary Kannon, later Gary Katz, who would hire them as songwriters for ABC Dunhill. This situation in turn would lead to them being signed as artists and the formation of Steely Dan. They had been to multiple publishers, but many weren't willing to sit and listen to them play their songs live in their offices. By 1969, most songwriters approached things differently. Rather than play live, they would cut a demo tape that they could drop off to the different publishers with the hope that something would click and the publisher would place their song with an established artist. Unfortunately, Becker and Fagen didn't have the necessary funds to book a studio to record a demo, so they had no choice but to revert to the way song pluggers did it earlier in the decade. Fagen, however, remembered their situation differently when they were interviewed for *MOJO* magazine in 1995. "This was before cassettes, so we would just play and sing. We met a lot of people in the Brill Building. We met Jerry Leiber, which was great, because he was an idol of ours: and there were still some other great songwriters there, like Jeff Barry. We knew about the scene and we were into the craft of the thing. We wanted to become great songwriters. It was almost over then, but at 1650 Broadway there were still some things happening."

Although they weren't trying to imitate any of the top songwriters at the time, they were influenced by Burt Bacharach, especially the songs he had written for Dionne Warwick. They were impressed by how he could compose complex compositions but still stay in the pop realm. At one point after their demo was made it was played for Leiber and Stoller, and Leiber commented that it reminded him of German art songs written in a contemporary style. They knew that their songs didn't really fit in the musical landscape of the day and were well aware that there weren't many artists looking for their brand of pop music, but they continued to push them and eventually wrote some songs with a more commercial appeal.

Ready for yet another day of rejections, the duo entered the Brill Building and as they always did, started at the top floor. That day there was a music convention taking place, and there was hardly anybody in the building, so the duo didn't expect much for their efforts. Luckily for them, when they reached the fourth-floor offices of JATA Enterprises (an acronym for Jay and the Americans), their luck changed.

The Origins of JATA Enterprises

In 1959, a vocal group named the Harborlites was formed in Belle Harbor in Queens, New York, by Sandy Yaguda (Deanne), Sydelle Sherman, Kenny Rosenberg (Vance), Gail Sherman, Ritchie Graff, and Linda Kahn. After a failed audition for Stan Feldman, one of the owners of Ivy Records, Gail, Ritchie, and Linda quit the group, and the remaining trio worked on their sound and returned to Feldman when they felt they were ready. This time Feldman liked what he heard and signed them to a recording contract. The group released a song written by Sandy called "Is That Too Much to Ask," featuring Sydelle on lead vocals and Kenny and Sandy providing the background vocals. Although they had a minor hit with Sydelle singing, Sandy and Kenny decided that they wanted an all-male vocal group and recruited Sandy's boyhood friend from Brooklyn, Howie Kirschenbaum (Kane), and former Brooklynite John "Jay" Traynor.

In 1960, the group auditioned for two of the most popular songwriters and producers at the time, Jerry Leiber and Mike Stoller. Initially, they were critical of the group's material, but the next day Kenny Vance returned to the office and after a rather heated conversation, left with a record deal. While the group refused the name Leiber and Stoller had chosen for them, Binky Jones and the Americans, they did keep the second half, naming themselves Jay and the Americans.

Since Leiber and Stoller had a production deal with United Artists, it was no surprise that Jay and the Americans' first record would be "Tonight" released to promote the new musical *West Side Story*. The single was a local hit, selling forty-thousand copies around the New York area, but their second single, "Dawning," initially did nothing on the charts. But when a West Coast D.J. flipped it over six months after its release and played the B-side, "She Cried," for six hours straight, the audience responded. Jay and the Americans had their first big hit, reaching number five on the *Billboard* Hot 100. After months of touring and the failure of their next two singles, Jay Traynor left the group to pursue what would become an unsuccessful solo career.

Singer/guitarist Marty Sanders had been playing with the Americans live while Traynor was still in the group and had also played on their debut LP, but his most important contribution was recommending singer David Blatt to replace Jay Traynor. He auditioned for the group at Sandy's parents' home with the song "Cara Mia." The group was floored, and David Blatt became the second "Jay" for Jay and the Americans using the stage name Jay Black.

Although they were still working with Leiber and Stoller, they felt that they weren't being offered the duo's best material. The Drifters and the Coasters were having a great deal of success at the time, and the songwriters often offered them their choice compositions. The fact that the song "Only in America," which was co-written with Barry Mann and Cynthia Weil, was given to the Drifters rather than the Americans

Jay and the Americans' number five hit "She Cried" from 1962. The band at this time was comprised of original singer Jay Traynor along with Kenny Vance, Sandy Deanne, and Howard Kane.

was a particular sore spot. They felt that given the title and sentiment of the song, it was a perfect fit for them—after all, they were Jay and the Americans. The song was originally written about racism in America, and the original chorus was quite different than the one we've come to know with references to seats in the back of the bus and marches that occurred when schools attempted to end segregation. Atlantic Records was concerned about releasing a record with such overt political views and recommended that the songwriters rewrite the chorus. The Drifters recorded the song with the new lyrics, but were disappointed they had to be changed, thereby altering the original sentiment of the song, and refused to release it. "Only in America" was now available, and Jay and the Americans entered Atlantic Studios and recorded their vocals on the original backing track. Although the song only reached number twenty-five, Jay and the Americans were back on the charts.

In 1964, they would score their biggest hit with "Come a Little Bit Closer," written by Tommy Boyce and Bobby Hart, who would later write and produce some of the Monkees' most popular songs. It reached number three on the *Billboard* Hot 100 chart and opened many doors for the group. On February 11, 1964, they would be one of the four opening acts for the Beatles' first live show in the U.S. at the Washington Coliseum in Washington, D.C. Jay and the Americans had already performed with a number of the Beatles' favorite groups including Smokey Robinson and the Miracles, the Supremes, and the Temptations and were good friends with the Ronettes, who had just toured England, so the Beatles were aware of them. This experience was new for the group. They had never seen rock 'n' roll musicians interviewed on a dais and were also influenced by the fact that the Beatles wrote their own material. This inspired Kenny Vance to buy a guitar and try his hand at songwriting.

Jay and the Americans also opened for another British group on their first tour of the United States. They were hired by WINS D.J. Murray the K. to open for the Rolling Stones at the last date of their tour on June 20, 1964, at Carnegie Hall; a show he was emceeing. The experience, however, was memorable for a different reason than the Beatles concert. Two shows were booked for the day, and Jay and the Americans opened the first show. The reaction that the Rolling Stones induced was so great that Murray the K. asked Jay and the Americans to close the show instead for fear of a riot. During the group's first song, "Only in America," the entire audience began filing out in order to catch the Stones before they left. By the end of the song, Carnegie Hall was empty, and it was apparent that vocal groups were on their way out and rock 'n' roll bands were here to stay.

Their career changed course yet again with the 1968 release of a 1960 Ben E. King and the Drifters song, "This Magic Moment," which became a number six hit for the group. Jay and the Americans would have their last top forty hit in 1969 with "Walkin' in the Rain," a song written by Phil Spector, Barry Mann, and Cynthia Weil that was originally recorded by the Ronettes in 1964.

With the hits waning, the group started JATA Enterprises, the production and publishing company on whose door Becker and Fagen knocked in 1969. The office manager, Eddie Chorane, was face to face with a disheveled duo that didn't look like typical song peddlers. Becker and Fagen were used to dismissals by music publishers and producers by now, but Chorane actually took their proposal seriously and after speaking with two other employees, went to Kenny Vance to see if he was interested in meeting the two. Vance decided to take a break from his more mundane tasks of the day and listen to what they had to offer.

Kenny Vance Signs a Contract with Becker and Fagen

They entered his office, and Fagen sat down at the piano and opened their book of compositions and played him a number of their early songs including "Tell It to the Fat Man," "Number One," "Shuffling Up Your Downs," "Charlie Freak," "Brain Tap Shuffle," and "Parker's Band." Vance had the foresight to see something special in the songs, and in Becker and Fagen, although he didn't fully understand the nuances musically. He recommended that they return a few days later to record some demos on a two-track recorder that music company Peer Southern had in the same building. Vance offered them a management contract and suggested that he produce the duo. Since they had not had any success with any other publishers at that point, they accepted.

The initial plan was twofold. Vance would shop their demos to prospective record labels in the hope of finding artists to record them, and Becker and Fagen would put together a band to showcase their original material. Unfortunately, Vance was having the same problem that Becker and Fagen faced when peddling their songs; they were too strange and esoteric for the pop and rock world.

In order to give the duo a regular paycheck, Vance hired them to arrange strings and horns for Jay and the Americans' 1969 LP, *Sands of Time*. Soon after, the duo were on the road providing bass and keyboards for the singing group and would play and arrange strings and horns for their two 1970 releases, *Wax Museum* and *Capture the Moment*.

With the piano/vocal demos of Becker and Fagen's songs falling flat on the record labels Vance approached, he decided to produce four songs with the band that Becker and Fagen had assembled. The duo entered the studio along with

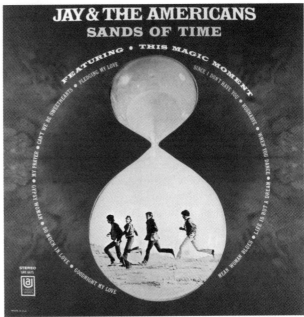

Becker and Fagen arranged strings and horns for Jay and the Americans' seventh studio album, 1969's *Sands of Time*. They were credited as "You know who you are . . . thanks."

Jay and the Americans circa 1970.

Jay and the Americans' drummer John Discepolo, future Steely Dan guitarist Denny Dias, and singer Keith Thomas to record "Brain Tap Shuffle," "Mock Turtle Song," "Let George Do It," and "The Old Regime."

Another project Vance was working on at the time was a group called the Kings County Carnival, which was actually the Americans minus Jay Black. They went into the studio with Becker and Fagen and recorded rhythm tracks for a number of their tunes including "Shuffling Up Your Downs," "Tell It to the Fat Man," and "Number One." What happened to these tapes is a mystery, but there was an upside. United Artists was interested in the publishing rights and paid Becker and Fagen for their songs, yet another way that Kenny Vance kept money in their pockets.

Vance also had the duo write and record the soundtrack to the low-budget film *You've Got to Walk It Like You Talk It or You'll Lose That Beat*. Although the film was made in 1969, it was not released until 1971. Written and directed by Peter Locke, the film starred Zalman King as Carter Fields, a hippie who has a number of misadventures while searching for the meaning of life in New York City. King had already appeared in a number of television shows such as *The Alfred Hitchcock Hour*, *The Munsters*, *Bonanza*, *Gunsmoke*, and *The Man from U.N.C.L.E.* and would go on to appear in dozens more including *Ironside*, *The F.B.I.*, and *Charlie's Angels*. He would also direct and produce more than thirty movies and television shows over four decades. Director Peter Locke would start a production company. the Kushner-Locke Company, with partner Donald Kushner in 1983 that would produce hundreds of movies and television shows. Peter Locke is also the father of guitarist Taylor Locke, a founding member of the Power Pop band Rooney, whose other founding members include Robert Schwartzman (son of Talia Shire and nephew of Francis Ford Coppola). *You've Got to Walk It Like You Talk It or You'll Lose That Beat* is noted as featuring one of the earliest Richard Pryor film performances and also starred actor/director Robert Downey Sr., father of Robert Downey Jr.

At this point, Vance set up a meeting with Richard Perry, who was producing Barbra Streisand for Clive Davis. They played him "Charlie Freak," which didn't go over so well, but they were asked to write a song for "Babs." They were working on a record for singer Linda Hoover at the time, and one of the songs, "I Mean to Shine," was presented to Perry. He decided to include it on the album with Fagen playing organ on the track, but by this time Becker and Fagen were done with Kenny Vance and Jay and the Americans and were ready to work with Vance's friend, and future Steely Dan producer, Gary Katz, still going by the pseudonym Gary Kannon.

Vance had been the only person in the music business to understand where they were coming from until Gary Katz, so Vance was understandably devastated about losing Becker and Fagen to his close friend. He had truly believed in them and had the foresight to see what they would become. He spent four years trying to sell their songs, had paid for demo sessions, secured a movie soundtrack for them, got a song placed on a Barbra Streisand album, and gave them a steady paying gig with Jay and the Americans. And now they were telling him, "We want to go to someone who understands what we're doing." Katz wouldn't fare much better placing their songs with other artists; he knew that they needed their own band to realize the genius of their songwriting.

After Becker and Fagen

Vance's career did not end once the duo stopped working with him. He released two solo albums; would become the music supervisor for *American Hot Wax*, *Animal House* (which sold over one million copies), and *Eddie and the Cruisers*; write the theme for the score of *American Hot Wax*, and produce the soundtrack album, which reached #31 on the *Billboard* charts. Vance's input on *Eddie and the Cruisers* was invaluable, relating his experiences on the road to director Martin Davidson and finding John Cafferty and the Beaver Brown Band to provide the soundtrack. When the movie was originally released in theaters, it was a flop at the box office and was pulled from theaters three weeks after its release on September 23, 1983. At this point, all involved believed that that was the end of the story. Six months later, *Eddie and the Cruisers* made its debut on HBO, and when the soundtrack album was rereleased in the fall of 1984 it went quadruple platinum, with the main song from the film, "On the Dark Side," reaching number one on *Billboard's* Mainstream, Rock, and Heatseeker charts and number seven on the *Billboard* Hot 100 chart.

Kenny Vance continued to contribute music for other films and TV shows, and after being a guest singer on *Saturday Night Live* in 1977, he served as the show's musical director from 1980 to 1981. Vance booked Aretha Franklin, Prince, and James Brown who during his only appearance on the show performed for far longer than his fixed time slot, which forced the producers to go to a commercial in the middle of his performance. Vance also became a favorite character actor of Woody Allen's and would appear in *Manhattan*, *Stardust Memories*, *Crimes and Misdemeanors*, *Husbands and Wives*, *Everyone Says I Love You*, and *Deconstructing Harry*. His group, Kenny Vance and the Planotones, were inducted into the Vocal Group Hall of Fame in 2002 and in the Long Island Music Hall of Fame in 2007.

Brooklyn Owes the Charmer Under Me

Becker and Fagen in Brooklyn

In late 1969, Walter Becker and Donald Fagen were living in New York City, Becker in Queens with his sister and grandmother and Fagen in Brooklyn with his girlfriend, Dorothy White, and a medical student named Richard Ransohoff. The Park Slope neighborhood in Brooklyn was quite different in 1969 than it is now. Today houses go for millions, but in the '60s Fagen compared it to the working-class Queens neighborhood made famous in Norman Lear's controversial television series *All in the Family*. The duo spoke of their stint in Brooklyn on a 1993 VH1 special.

> Becker: "After Donald . . . graduated from, actually before you even graduated, your last semester at Bard, and I kind of had been asked to leave for reasons of academic non-performance, and we ended up moving out here to Brooklyn where at that time . . . life was good, rents were low, $80–$90 a month range."

> Fagen: "My girlfriend and I found an apartment, $85 for the apartment . . . on 904 President St."

> Becker: "Pretty soon the building and the neighborhood started to get colonized with would-be hipsters, Donald's circle of acquaintance, and I moved in."

They had two separate notebooks filled with songs. The first contained more esoteric compositions that they intended to be performed by a band that would eventually be formed. The other book contained songs that were more straight ahead. These simpler pop songs were written with the intention of shopping them around for other artists to record.

Richard Lifschutz and the Aborted Steely Dan Musical

At the time, their social life was virtually nonexistent, as was their income. In New York, the two often go hand in hand. Once Kenny Vance became interested in their music, things changed financially and to an extent, socially. As a teenager in Belle Harbor, Queens, Richard Lifschutz met Vance and the other members of

Jay and the Americans, so when Vance began peddling Becker and Fagen's songs, would-be writer Lifschutz was introduced to the duo at JATA's office in the Brill Building.

Lifschutz had written for the *Daily News*, for some trade magazines, and was also involved with public relations firms that were trying to get press for films and documentaries. He lived on Union Street in Park Slope, Brooklyn, one block away from Fagen's apartment. Becker and Lifschutz would spend time together playing chess and cards and talking about music and literature. Although he was eight years Becker's senior, Lifschutz learned quite a bit about writing from both him and Fagen. Although he had no musical training, he began to learn about chord changes from Becker, took piano lessons, and started to write songs. He eventually co-wrote a song with Vance for a Jay and the Americans album and another that was recorded by Linda Hoover, a singer whose unreleased album was produced by future Steely Dan producer Gary Katz and featured Becker, Fagen, and Denny Dias.

After hearing some of Becker and Fagen's early material, he decided that he would write a musical based on their compositions. Although it sounds a bit outrageous today, it was actually an idea of the times. The musical *Hair* had moved from off-Broadway to Broadway in April 1968 and was a huge success, running for four years and 1,750 performances. The show was so successful that soon after there were nine simultaneous productions in cities across the United States. The show also had an extremely successful run at the Shaftesbury Theater in the London Borough of Camden that ran from September 1968 until July 1973, surpassing the Broadway production by running for 1,997 performances. The various cast members around the world included future stars such as Diane Keaton, Ben Vereen, Keith Carradine, Tim Curry, Donna Summer, Meat Loaf, Joe Mantegna, Barry McGuire, Ted Lange, Philip Michael Thomas, Melba Moore, Vicki Sue Robinson, Jennifer Warnes, Dobie Gray, Marsha Hunt, and Alex Harvey.

Hair wasn't the only vehicle melding rock music and theatrics. Although not a fully realized "musical" until its movie release in 1975, the Who's rock opera *Tommy* first made headlines in May 1969 and proved that rock music could be presented in an extended form. The album was commercially successful, reaching number two in the U.K. album charts and number four in the U.S. It sold two hundred thousand copies in the first two weeks in the U.S. alone, and was awarded a gold record for sales of five hundred thousand on August 18. A number of singles from the double LP were extremely successful including "Pinball Wizard," which reached the top twenty in the U.S. and the top five in the U.K., "See Me, Feel Me," which also reached the top twenty in the U.S.; and "I'm Free," which reached the top forty. The group would go on to perform a slightly abridged version of their rock opera during their 1969 and 1970 tours, at the Woodstock Festival, at the second Isle of Wight Festival, and at New York's Metropolitan Opera House. Subsequently, *Tommy* would also be transformed into a Seattle Opera production in 1971, an orchestral piece by Lou Reizner in 1972, and a Broadway musical in 1992.

In 1969, Andrew Lloyd Webber and Tim Rice were hard at work creating the rock opera *Jesus Christ Superstar*, originally conceived as a concept album released in 1970 before debuting on Broadway in '71. The same year, *Godspell*, written by

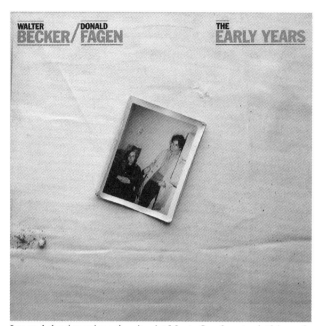

Jay and the Americans' guitarist Marty Sanders took this early photo of Becker and Fagen used for the album *The Early Years*, credited by his real name Marty Kupersmith. The LP was originally released in 1983 by Kenny Vance and included ten of the songs the duo demoed with Vance.

Stephen Schwartz and John-Michael Tebelak, would also open on Broadway, and the musical would spawn the number thirteen hit "Day by Day." So in a way Lifschutz was ahead of the pack attempting to create a story around the characters from Becker and Fagen's songs.

The musical was entitled *Ego—The Making of a Musical.* Lifschutz had read the play *Hair* and wasn't very impressed. The music didn't seem very advanced either, so the idea of writing a play based on eighteen of Becker and Fagen's compositions seemed like a phenomenal idea. Kenny Vance, who had signed a publishing deal with the duo, gave his blessing, and Lifschutz spent a few months locked in his apartment writing the book for the musical.

The songs that were to be used included "Parker's Band," "Number One," "Android Warehouse," "Charlie Freak," "Take It Out on Me," "Stone Piano," "Yellow Peril," "Soul Ram," "Horse in Town," "Let George Do It," "The Old Regime," "Brain Tap Shuffle," "Tell It To the Fat Man," "Mock Turtle Song," "Oh Wow It's You Again," "Undecided," "The Roaring of the Lamb," and "More to Come." Both Becker and Fagen read the play once it was finished, and they were neither overenthusiastic nor damning of the finished product. Needless to say, the play never got produced. Lifschutz ended up becoming deeply involved in the Jewish community in Brooklyn and embraced the Hasidic lifestyle. He's worked on numerous movies as a technical consultant and actor including *The Chosen*, *A Price Above Rubies*, *Over the Brooklyn Bridge*, and π.

He's a Crowd-Pleasing Man: Denny Dias

Although Becker and Fagen had a notebook filled with pop songs that they hoped would be performed by other artists, they continued to write songs with the intention of forming a band to perform them. By this time, the two had moved in together with Fagen's then-girlfriend Dorothy White and found a larger apartment than the one Fagen was living in on President Street. In the summer of 1970, they saw an ad in the *Village Voice* that read: "Looking for keyboardist and bassist. Must have jazz chops! Assholes need not apply." They called the number and spoke to Denny Dias of Hicksville, Long Island, who had a gigging band named Demian.

Early Years

Dias was born in Philadelphia, Pennsylvania, on December 12, 1946. While still a baby, his family moved to Brooklyn, New York, and when he was eight years old settled in Hicksville, Long Island. When he was twelve, he got his first guitar, a cheap model with only three strings. He initially showed little interest until a cousin of his started studying guitar. He ended up taking lessons with jazz guitarist, and the 1946 Metronome Poll winner, Billy Bauer. Bauer had played with Benny Goodman, Lenny Tristano, Dizzy Gillespie, and Lee Konitz, and was part Woody Herman's First Herd in 1944. Ironically, Herman would release an album in 1978 entitled *Chick, Donald, Walter & Woodrow* that contained five Steely Dan songs and a three-part suite by Chick Corea.

Fagen's first apartment after college was at 904 President Street in Brooklyn. His bedroom window juts out on the right side of the second floor.

Bauer was hired to replace guitarist Johnny Smith at NBC in 1950 and worked there as house guitarist for nine years. While working for NBC, he continued to do session work and in 1951 founded the William H. Bauer Publishing Co. in order to preserve transcriptions of recorded solos and works of great jazz artists for future generations. Always interested in education, in 1970 he established the Billy Bauer Guitar School in Albertson, New York, and spent thirty-five years developing his Guitar Instructor Series. He moved the studio to Roslyn Heights on Long Island, where Dias studied with him, as did guitarist Joe Satriani.

Hicksville was home to numerous musicians who would be incredibly successful. Dias attended Hicksville High School and played in a battle of the bands opposite another Hicksville musician, Billy Joel. He also graduated with some musicians who were in a band with drummer Mitch Mitchell, Jimi Hendrix's drummer.

When Dias first enrolled in junior college, it was as a music major, but he soon switched to engineering and then to math. When he graduated, he began to study computer science as it related to medicine at SUNY Downstate College of Medicine, but music was now his passion, and he only stayed in school for one semester before leaving to see if he could make it as a professional musician. As Becker and Fagen were getting acquainted at Bard College in 1967, Dias was starting his career as a professional guitarist.

Dias was always a jazz aficionado and was a diligent disciple of the recordings of Miles Davis, John Coltrane, Dizzy Gillespie, Hampton Hawes, and Thelonious Monk. He appreciated the music of the '50s, more for jazz than for rock 'n' roll, but still was a huge fan of the Beatles and their songwriting chops, something that was true for Becker and Fagen as well. When he saw Monk at Queens College, he was floored, but his style was always a blend of jazz and rock, and his musical sensibilities were quite similar to both Becker's and Fagen's. This was the reason that he would be the only original member of Steely Dan to contribute to six of their seven albums released before Becker and Fagen's reunion for 2000's *Two Against Nature*.

He played in a number of bands around Long Island including the Saints and the Grapevine. By 1969, he had settled into the band Demian, named after the Hermann Hesse novel. Along with Dias, the four-piece band consisted of drummer Mark Leon, bassist Jimmy Signorelli, and vocalist Keith Thomas, who Dias had known since they were children. They had been playing gigs in clubs around Long Island, their typical set list a mix of top forty covers and soul tunes by artists such as Otis Redding, James Brown, the Four Tops, and Sam and Dave. Although both Dias and Thomas were writing original material, the patrons of the clubs in Long Island were only interested in cover songs, so their own songs would rarely get played at their live shows. When the band's original bassist Jimmy Signorelli quit to return to college, Dias was prompted to put the ad in the *Village Voice*. They thought that by adding a keyboard player they would develop a fuller sound and possibly have more options for new material.

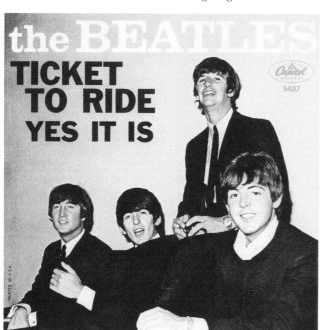

Fagen's introduction to the Beatles came when he heard the 1965 single "Ticket to Ride" from the *HELP!* LP and feature film. Their influence can be heard in some of the songs they were writing while living in Brooklyn in the late '60s.

Dias Meets Becker and Fagen

Walter Becker made the initial call to Denny Dias when he saw his advertisement for a bass player and keyboard player in *The*

Village Voice. Dias was interested in having Becker come out to Long Island for an audition, but told him they weren't sure if they still wanted to add a keyboard player. Becker convinced him that once he heard Fagen play he would change his mind. A date was set, and Becker and Fagen packed up their gear and headed out to Hicksville.

Since neither Becker nor Fagen owned a car, they had to first get their gear to the Long Island Railroad station in Brooklyn and then transfer in Jamaica, Queens, before landing in Hicksville. Although the train ride was only fifty minutes, Fagen's Fender Rhodes electric piano weighed 130 pounds, making train travel troublesome. Fagen and his Rhodes and Becker with his Dan Armstrong plexiglass bass arrived at the Hicksville train station, where Dias and Thomas were waiting to pick them up.

Their audition was held in Denny Dias's parents' kitchen, and after so many dismal applicants, Becker and Fagen made an immediate impression. They played many of the same songs that had impressed Kenny Vance the year before, and these songs had a similar effect on Dias and Thomas. They recognized their genius immediately, understanding that these were complex compositions, not a variation of a twelve-bar blues.

Although the duo seemed aloof, they were asked to join the band based on their songwriting prowess. Their songwriting might have been advanced, but they had virtually no experience playing live in clubs. They had played gigs while at Bard, but had never played bars and had no desire to. Their set lists would have to cater to an audience that wanted to hear the hits of the day and not unknown originals, and Becker and Fagen didn't see any point in pursuing this aspect of the music business. Even at this early stage, their sole aspiration was to get a record deal and spend time in the studio perfecting their craft. They also weren't that keen to put themselves in a situation that could at times be violent. They made it clear from day one that they wouldn't perform live, and Dias and Thomas begrudgingly gave in.

Becker and Fagen Hijack Demian

Dias and Thomas had been writing songs for about a year, but Dias was never happy with the lyrics. Once Becker and Fagen joined, it was obvious that their songs were far superior, and the founders of Demian gave up writing for the group. There were also personnel problems from the beginning, something that would plague Steely Dan throughout their career.

While Dias and Thomas were impressed with their new band members, the drummer from Demian, Mark Leon, didn't like them at all and made no attempt to hide it. At the same time, Becker and Fagen thought that Leon's playing was too busy and preferred more straightforward grooves that were heavy with the kick and the snare. This wasn't necessarily a new problem. Thomas had noticed that during many of their live shows the audience wasn't always responsive to Leon's playing because he would switch gears from a funk groove to a jazz drum solo that at times would clear the room. Becker and Fagen were willing to continue with the band, but only if Dias and Thomas would fire Leon. Leon, who was known to

The original soundtrack album *You Gotta Walk It Like You Talk It (Or You'll Lose That Beat)*, released in 1971 on Spark Records.

have a temper, initially took the news badly and exploded, but he eventually realized he had no say in the matter and left without much of a scene.

Becker and Fagen already had a replacement in mind. They were never too fond of the musicians in Jay and the Americans' road band, but they were impressed by drummer John Discepolo, who as Becker put it, "[was a] drummer who didn't find us totally repugnant." They were soon rehearsing as a newly formed five-piece unit, but Becker and Fagen soon tired of the expensive and exhaustive commute to Long Island due to their lack of funds and heft of equipment. Dias, who realized the potential of the band since the duo joined, began to chauffer them from Brooklyn to Keith Thomas's Ellwood Avenue home on Long Island twice a week for rehearsals. Although it would require Dias to drive for approximately four hours for each rehearsal, as a would-be songwriter he felt that their provocative compositions were worth the inconvenience.

The crux of the rehearsals would be spent working on Becker and Fagen's compositions, with Fagen, the reluctant vocalist, teaching Thomas the melody. As Thomas recalled, they were looking for a soulful voice with a lot of character, or in other words "a fuckin' impossible voice!" Dias was optimistic, but in many ways there was no reason to call it a proper band since no money was earned due to Becker and Fagen's refusal to play live. Regardless of the band's potential, there was quite a bit of frustration. Becker and Fagen had hijacked a local Long Island band, and although they were unwilling to hit the clubs, they had a plan. Not only were they ready to record more fleshed-out demos of their compositions, they had been hired to produce the music for the soundtrack of a forgotten film, *You've Got to Walk It Like You Talk It or You'll Lose That Beat*. These are, for all intents and purposes, the first Steely Dan recordings and need their own chapter for discussion. For more information on these, and all other rare recordings, see chapter eleven.

5

A Man of My Mind Can Do Anything

Enter Producer Gary Katz

hrough Kenny Vance, Becker and Fagan met a man who would eventually change their lives: Gary Kannon, better known as future Steely Dan producer Gary Katz. Katz grew up in a musical environment where his mother played piano and music was constantly in the house. Frankie Laine was Katz's first favorite singer, long before the advent of rock 'n' roll. But at age thirteen, while sitting on the roof of his building smoking a cigarette, something came on his transistor radio that changed everything. The artist: Chuck Berry. Katz spent most days after that on the roof smoking cigarettes and listening to New York disc jockey Alan Freed's show on WINS where he was exposed to Fats Domino, Little Richard, Ruth Brown, and countless other rock 'n' roll and rhythm and blues artists.

In the late '50s, there were Christmas shows at the Brooklyn Paramount Theater with all of the great rock 'n' roll artists including Chuck Berry, Little Richard, Buddy Holly, Bo Diddley, and others. For an entire week there would be eight shows a day, and since Katz's father was good friends with the manager of the Paramount Theater Gene Pleshette, father of actress Suzanne Pleshette, Katz and Suzanne would stay for the entire day and see every show for the whole week.

Growing up in Brooklyn, Gary Katz's closest friends were Jay and the Americans. This relationship opened doors for him, and he was brought to recording sessions to which he otherwise would not have had access. It was during these sessions that he was introduced to the songwriting production team of Jerry Leiber and Mike Stoller, who were working with Jay and the Americans. Katz had an epiphany when he realized that although lyricist Jerry Leiber knew what sounded good on a record, he knew nothing about music but could relate an idea to musician Mike Stoller. That's when Gary Katz decided he had enough knowledge to become a producer.

In 1965, after finishing college with a physical education degree, Katz founded Cloud Nine Productions with producer Richard Perry. A mutual friend from the Jay and the Americans camp had introduced the two, and although they had nothing in common, they decided to work together. The venture was funded by a $4,000 investment from each of their parents, and they set up shop in the same building on Broadway as Jay and the Americans. They produced a version of the Van McCoy song "Doin' Things Together with You" sung by Barbara Mercer; songs for the original "Jay" from Jay and the Americans, John "Jay" Traynor; a Bob Dylan cover for the Vassals; as well as a few singles for the Kama Sutra label, but their money soon ran out, and in 1968 Cloud Nine Productions folded. The fact that the two were, as Katz put it, "like oil and water" didn't help the situation. Although they didn't argue, their musical tastes and production styles were too different to work as a team. At this point, Gary Katz was using the pseudonym Gary Kannon for his production work and would continue to do so until the first Steely Dan LP.

Soon after, Katz landed a publishing job with Bobby Darin. Darin's career took off when he formed a songwriting partnership in 1955 with fellow Bronx High School of Science student Don Kirshner, who would eventually be known as "The Man with the Golden Ear." Darin signed with Decca Records in 1956 as a solo artist, but the records weren't successful, so he left for Atlantic Records' subsidiary ATCO. There, under the guidance of star-maker Ahmet Ertegun, he recorded his own first million-seller, "Splish Splash," in 1958. He followed with a string of hits including "Dream Lover," "Mack the Knife," and "Beyond the Sea," which brought him world fame. In 1962, he won a Golden Globe Award for his first film *Come September*, co-starring his first wife, Sandra Dee.

In the '60s, Darin founded TM Music Inc. with Doris Day's son, Terry Melcher, and settled in the Brill Building at 1619 Broadway. After working as a song runner, Katz went into production along with another employee at TM Music, Eddie Lambert, when Darin wanted to expand the company to include production. Darin had been working on Bobby Kennedy's presidential campaign and was at the Ambassador Hotel in Los Angeles on June 5, 1968, when Kennedy was assassinated. He had also recently found out that the woman who had raised him as her own was actually his grandmother and the girl he had known as his sister was, in fact, his mother. These events had a profound effect on him; TM Music folded and Darin disappeared from the public eye, spending the next year in a trailer near Big Sur.

With the job at TM Music at its end, Katz's next move was to create a production company with Eddie Lambert. They produced one single by J. R. Bailey, an R&B number entitled, "Hold Back the Dawn" b/w "Too Late" released on Mala records in 1968. The team split up when Lambert moved across the country to Los Angeles for a job at ABC Dunhill Records, a move that proved to be very fruitful for both Katz and Steely Dan.

With the failure of his second production team, Katz soon found a job at AVCO Embassy Records, founded by music producers/composers Hugo Peretti and Luigi Creatore along with film and television producer Joseph E. Levine in 1968. Katz signed and produced artists the Bead

The letterhead for TM Music Inc., Bobby Darin and Terry Melcher's publishing and production company that Gary Kannon (Katz) worked for in 1968 with Eddie Lambert.

Courtesy of Linda Hoover

Game, with future Steely Dan drummer Jim Hodder handling vocals and drumming duties, and Canadian singer Eric Mercury. Although Katz signed Bead Game first, in 1968, Mercury's LP *Electric Black Man*, released in 1969, would be the first full-length album that he would produce.

Eric Mercury

Eric Mercury performed in his hometown of Toronto, Ontario, in his family's band from a very young age. He played local social functions at churches and schools. Throughout the '60s, Mercury performed with groups including the Pharaohs, as a member, and Eric Mercury and the Soul Searchers, as a front man. They opened for Tiny Tim, the Doors, the Chambers Brothers, and others around Ontario, Nova Scotia, and in New York. After a number of personnel changes, the band officially split up after an argument at, ironically, the Mercury Club.

With the Soul Searchers' demise in 1968, Eric Mercury made a bold decision to move to New York to pursue a solo career. His debut LP, *Electric Black Man*, was produced by Gary Katz, using the pseudonym Gary Kannon, and was released on the AVCO Embassy label. The opening song, "Long Way Down," was co-written by Katz and Shelly Weis and would be sampled by A Tribe Called Quest on the song "Rap Promoter" from the LP *The Low End Theory*. Five out of six of the session musicians used on the album have direct Steely Dan connections. Guitarists Elliott Randall and Rick Derringer (credited by his real name Rick Zehringer) would play on Steely Dan albums, guitarist Marty Kupersmith was a member of Jay and the Americans (using the pseudonym Marty Sanders) when Becker and Fagen worked with them, bassist Harvey Brooks would play with the New York Rock and Soul Revue band when they toured in August 1992, and keyboardist Paul Harris would record with Terence Boylan, the artist who in 1969 brought Becker and Fagen into the studio for the first time to record his debut LP, *Alias Boona*. The album, recorded at the Record Plant in New York, was a mix of soul, country, and rock with a bit of a psychedelic bent. His voice, a blend of Teddy Pendergrass and Jeffrey Osborne, was expressive and suited the various styles he covered over his five solo LPs and two singles well.

After recording four additional albums, he continued to pen songs for other artists including Roberta Flack and Donny Hathaway, for whom he also produced; Thelma Houston; and Dionne Warwick. He also took part in the stage production of *Jesus Christ Superstar* and had roles in two films: *The Fish That Saved Pittsburgh* as Rudy/League Commissioner and *American Hot Wax* as Tyrone Blackwood.

Bead Game

The band Bead Game was formed in Cambridge, Massachusetts, in the late '60s, and included future Steely Dan member Jim Hodder on lead vocals and drums, as well as Kenny Westland-Haag on rhythm guitar and vocals, Robert Gass on organ and keyboards, Lassie Sachs on bass, and John Sheldon on lead guitar. After a number of personnel changes, this final rhythm section was in place, and the band began auditioning vocalists, but none of them felt quite right. Drummer

Bead Game's debut album *Welcome*. It was produced by Gary Kannon (Katz), and future Steely Dan member Jim Hodder was their lead singer and drummer.

Jim Hodder took on the role solely because they couldn't find anybody else, ironically quite similar to the way Donald Fagen would become the vocalist for Steely Dan only four years later.

The band built up a local following in the Boston clubs, and record companies began to take notice. They eventually signed with AVCO Embassy Records, who released their debut album *Welcome* in 1970 with Gary Katz, still using the pseudonym Kannon, in the producer's chair. AVCO did not release a single from the album, and it was not a success. This was a common practice in the '60s and '70s when record labels were dealing with unknown acts. They would press singles for regional promotional use and try to garner interest that way, something that rarely worked. Soon after, they contributed two songs to the AVCO Embassy–financed anti-drug film *The People Next Door* starring Eli Wallach and Julie Harris and appeared as a band in the film as well.

Bead Game began working on their self-produced sophomore LP, *Baptism*, in 1970, but the band was having major problems. Although they were financing the album themselves, they still needed distribution. When they were unable to secure a label, the group broke up and their second album wouldn't be released until 1996.

Katz Moves to Los Angeles

Katz would work with Becker and Fagen on two projects, singer Linda Hoover's unreleased album and a one-off track entitled "Cody Canyon" (see chapter twenty), before deciding in November 1971 that he needed a change. His friend and former production partner Eddie Lambert had been working for ABC Dunhill Records' publishing department for over a year and had been singing Katz's praises to Jay Lasker, the president of ABC Dunhill, and the head of A&R Steve Barri. A producer had just been fired, so he suggested to Katz that he write a letter to Lasker introducing himself and he'd see what he could do to help. Although Katz's work situation was virtually nonexistent at this point, he had no desire to write a cold letter to a label head asking for work. One night while watching Monday Night Football, his wife convinced him to write the letter, but it wouldn't be a typical letter sent to a prospective employer. As Katz recalled in a 2014 interview with Jason Wilber for the podcast *In Search of a Song,* the letter read, "Dear Jay. Writing this letter to you right now is a much bigger pain in the ass for me than it is for you sitting in your chair reading it. This is my name, this is what I do and if you have any interest call me. Thanks a lot." Three days later, Lasker called Katz and said, "I don't know who you are. I'm still laughing at your letter. There's a ticket at the airport. Be here in the morning at 11:00." By noon he was offered the job of staff producer at ABC Dunhill Records.

Katz wasted no time in playing them Becker and Fagen's material and insisted that the two be hired as staff writers at ABC. They were looking for something fresh, and for the third time (the first two being with Kenny Vance and then Katz) the quirkiness of their songs proved to be to their benefit. Steve Barri thought that their compositions were unique and believed that the fact that they were different from what he'd heard before was a positive. So, at his first meeting, Katz had secured himself a job as staff producer and a job as staff writers for Becker and Fagen.

There was, however, one problem; the duo were still signed to Kenny Vance's Red Giant Music. They had already made it quite apparent that they were no longer interested in working with Vance, and he was tired of their unappreciative attitude and their constant mocking of him, so he let them out of their contract. There was, however, one stipulation; that he would share half of the publishing royalties from their first album. Although they arrived at this agreement, Vance was unhappy that the duo were leaving him and that his friend seemed to be the cause of the split. In all fairness to Becker and Fagen, they had had little success with Vance, and Katz was offering them a full-time job with a major record company. With this obstacle out of the way, the duo were prepared to move to the West Coast to begin their new jobs as staff writers for ABC Dunhill Records.

Once working for the label, Katz would produce myriad artists, and in some way Becker, Fagen, and the countless musicians that would work on Steely Dan's records would be involved in the majority of the resulting records. These artists include Navasota, Thomas Jefferson Kaye, Marc Jordan, Eye to Eye, Diana Ross, and Rosie Vela. Ironically, the last project that Becker and Fagen worked on with Katz was the one that would reunite the duo in the studio: Rosie Vela's first and only release, *Zazu.* For more info on these productions, see chapter twenty. Of all the albums produced by Katz while working with Becker and Fagen, only three were made without any contribution from them.

Dirk Hamilton

In 1976, a young singer-songwriter named Dirk Hamilton was discovered and signed by Gary Katz to ABC Dunhill Records. He was compared to Bob Dylan, Van Morrison, and John Hiatt, and most people who heard him were certain he would be a star. His debut album, *You Can Sing on the Left or Bark on the Right,* was produced by Katz, engineered by Roger Nichols, who would engineer all of Steely Dan's albums, and featured a who's who of Steely Dan alumni including drummer Jeff Porcaro; bassist Chuck Rainey; guitarists Dean Parks, Larry Carlton, and Elliott Randall; keyboardist David Paich; percussionist Victor Feldman; and background vocalists Shirley Matthews (listed as Sherlie Matthews) and Venetta Fields. His style was hard to pigeonhole, so he was described as alt-rock, country-rock, indie-rock, Americana, and folk-rock.

He released one more album for ABC before moving to Elektra for his next two. His 1978 release *Meet Me at the Crux* was getting rave reviews with *Rolling Stone* calling it a "hidden gem." Elektra didn't give the record much of a push, so sales were disappointing. Hamilton went on an East Coast college tour opening for Warren Zevon to support his fourth album, *Thug of Love*, when things went seriously wrong. On the third night of the tour, Hamilton and Zevon both retired early to take care of their voices, but unfortunately for Hamilton their band members had a long night of drinking. As they lost their inhibitions, Hamilton's lead guitar player and his road manager began to mock the fact that Zevon's show was too staged and theatrical. In an interview with Mark McDermott for *Easy Reader News*, Hamilton recalled the situation. "Zevon had this choreographed wildness, I-don't-give-a-shit thing and he was wild and don't-give-a-shit exactly at the same place; every show he did exactly the same thing. And it was, like . . . showbiz, y'know? Bullshit. But I knew it wasn't my place to be badmouthing him—to him. They started spouting about his theatrical bent and Warren's guys were offended. My guys got really drunk and caused all sorts of trouble." The next day Zevon knocked on Hamilton's hotel door and kicked him off the tour. Hamilton explained that he had nothing to do with the situation and even offered to fire his lead guitarist and manager, but Zevon refused stating, "Man, I can't have these bad vibes."

Hamilton's fear that Elektra would drop him from the label if he lost this tour was turned into a reality when he returned to L.A. He quit the music business for nearly a decade before an Italian record executive named Franco Ratti, from the Milan-based independent label Appaloosa Records, tracked him down. While the singer was trying to revive his career in Los Angeles, he'd been a cult star for over a decade in Italy. Hamilton continues to tour and has released a total of seventeen albums since that first one produced by Gary Katz in 1976.

Root Boy Slim and the Sex Change Band with the Rootettes

Root Boy Slim and the Sex Change Band with the Rootettes was started by Foster MacKenzie III, a Yale graduate who had been fraternity brothers at Delta Kappa Epsilon with future president George W. Bush. After graduating from Yale, he returned with his band to play at DKE, but Bush, who was then president, kicked them out, and they were banned from the house. After graduation, MacKenzie drove an ice cream truck in Washington, D.C., and suffered a psychotic breakdown during an LSD trip. He climbed over the White House fence and told Secret Service officers that he was "looking for the center of the universe." He was admitted into St. Elizabeth's Hospital and was diagnosed with schizophrenia, for which he was medicated for the rest of his life.

While in Baltimore, Becker and Fagen caught Root Boy Slim and the Sex Change Band with the Rootettes in a nightclub and found the scene hilarious. A pudgy white blues singer performing songs with titles such as "Bride of the Burro," "Christmas at K-Mart," and "Too Sick to Reggae" was too much, and they convinced Gary Katz, who was also a fan, into signing and producing Root Boy Slim for Warner Bros. Records in 1978.

The band included saxophone great Ron Holloway; Miles Davis's keyboard player Winston Kelly; Joe Cocker/Dave Mason percussionist Felix Falcon; steel guitarist Walt Andrews (aka Cosmo Creek, who would play on Steely Dan's "FM (No Static at All)"); Tommy Ruger on drums; and gifted blues guitarist Ernie "Sex Ray" Lancaster, who co-wrote most of the music with bassist Bob Greenlee. While vacationing in Florida, Walter Becker attended some sessions and later noted, "This is a real laugh." They released their most popular song that year, "Boogie 'Till You Puke," from their eponymous debut LP produced by Gary Katz, who shockingly declared that it was his favorite album that he produced in his career and is one of the only ones that he listens to because it makes him "feel good."

Joe Cocker

In 1984, Gary Katz produced the first side of Joe Cocker's ninth studio album, *Civilized Man*. The album was recorded during two different sessions. Side A was recorded in Los Angeles at the Village Recorder, and Side B was recorded in Nashville and was produced by Stewart Levine, who had worked with Lionel Richie, Boz Scaggs, Sly Stone, B. B. King, Huey Lewis and the News, Aaron Neville, and countless others.

For his side, Stewart used some of Nashville's top session men, and Katz once again employed a number of musicians who had graced the records of Steely Dan and Donald Fagen including drummers Jim Keltner and Jeff Porcaro (who also played guitar on one track); guitarist Dean Parks; keyboard players David Paich, Greg Phillinganes, and Rob Mounsey; trumpet player Randy Brecker; trombonist Dave Bargeron; percussionist Starz Vanderlockett; and background vocalists Zachary Sanders and Frank Floyd. While the album only reached number 133 on the U.S. album charts, it peaked at number five in both Switzerland and Norway; reached the top ten in Germany and the Netherlands; and made the top twenty in Austria and Sweden.

Other Projects

Katz would continue to produce a variety of different musical styles including pop, rock, rap, and acid jazz throughout the '80s and '90s, with dozens of credits to his name. His diversity as a producer was evident by the acts he worked with and grew over the decades with albums by Love and Money, the Alarm, 10cc, Laura Nyro, Tupac Shakur, Digital Underground, Groove Collective (with future Steely Dan vibraphonist Bill Ware), and Peter Tosh topping the list. His career as an A&R man is also quite impressive, with a roster of artists signed by Katz that topped the charts including Rickie Lee Jones, Dire Straits, Christopher Cross, Jimmy Buffett,

and others. Katz always had a good ear; after all, he saw Becker and Fagen's potential when so many others didn't, and he also saw the potential of an extraordinary musician/singer/songwriter named Prince Rogers Nelson. Prince had been sending Warner Bros. demos for quite a while, yet for some reason they kept rejecting them. Luckily, Katz had the foresight to see his genius and signed him in 1977. The next year he released his debut album *For You,* on which he played every instrument, quite a feat at the time.

Katz not only produced Fagen's *Nightfly* LP in 1982 and "Century's End" from the *Bright Lights, Big City* soundtrack in 1988 (see chapters seventeen and twenty), he also worked with him on the soundtrack albums for *The King of Comedy* and *The Gospel at*

Most of the record-buying public never knew what the producer of an album looked like because photos of anybody but the artists were rarely found on the record cover. This practice has continued to this day, but for 1975's *Katy Lied* there is not only a photo of Gary Katz on the back cover, but also one of engineer Roger Nichols.

Colonus. But 1995's Raw Stylus album *Pushing Against the Flow* would be the last time he worked with Fagen and therefore would be his last project related to Steely Dan.

6

Daddy Don't Live in That New York City No More

Becker and Fagen Move to Los Angeles and Form Steely Dan

With Gary Katz in place as staff producer, Jay Lasker, president of ABC Dunhill, and Steve Barri, head of A&R, were convinced that Becker and Fagen's songs were extremely original, and since ABC was trying to branch out into the underground LP market, the duo were hired at $125 per week. The salary was an advance against future song royalties.

Walter Becker had never been to California, and neither he nor Fagen had a driver's license. (Fagen had one at some point, but he let it expire). Gary Katz had settled in Encino with his wife and two children, so when Becker and Fagen arrived, they found apartments in a new development and until they got their driver's licenses, were picked up by Katz each day and driven to ABC Dunhill's offices in West Hollywood. The duo reacted to the L.A. lifestyle as so many transplants from New York do. In a 1995 interview for *MOJO* magazine Becker recalled his initial impression of Los Angeles. "For cynical wiseass kids from New York like us, going to Los Angeles was an endless source of amusement. I'm sure you're familiar with the characterization: so sunny, air-headed optimism in glitzy LA and dense, rye-bread, cynical, intellectual New Yorkers." Fagen agreed with his partner, stating rather bluntly, "L.A. was certainly a lot of laughs. Neither of us really liked it, because we just weren't L.A.-type people. We called it Planet Stupid. Nobody seemed to understand us there. Our first manager made me buy a pair of green velour pants."

As staff writers, they were expected to write material for the acts that were currently signed to the label including Three Dog Night, the Grassroots, John Kay from Steppenwolf, and Denny Doherty from the Mamas and the Papas. Their songs were too esoteric for most artists to cover, with cryptic lyrics and sophisticated chord changes, so they found themselves in the same predicament they had been in with Kenny Vance in New York.

A staff writer's job is twofold. They should be creative, but they should also be aware of what's successful on the radio. In order to write songs for established artists, the composer needs to imitate, to a certain degree, what's on the radio. Although Becker and Fagen could write songs with hooks, their lyrics were too obscure, their wit too sardonic. They attempted to "dumb down" their songs for the masses, but as Becker stated, "we wrote some of the cheesiest songs you ever heard. But . . . they were so cheesy they were laughable." They wrote a song for the Grass Roots entitled "Tell Me a Lie," but the group never recorded it. The duo had no respect for the band, and it was obvious to all.

Denny Doherty from the recently disbanded Mamas and the Papas recorded demos of their songs "Sail the Waterway," which would become the B-side of "Dallas," Steely Dan's first single, and "Giles of the River," with the intention of shopping them for a solo record deal, but that never happened, and they weren't released. John Kay of Steppenwolf would record "Giles of the River" for his second solo album, *My Sportin' Life,* in 1973, but this was 1971, and Becker and Fagen were having no luck placing songs.

It was obvious that Becker and Fagen had infiltrated a major record label posing as staff writers when their true ambition was to start a band that could do their songs justice. Becker and Fagen realized early on that they would need to record their songs with their own band. Lyrically, they were too obtuse for the mainstream, and although there were rock elements, musically the songs were harmonically perplexing for the artists that they were supposed to be writing for. When musicians tried to cover their compositions after they found success, many of them had a hard time navigating through the jazzier chord changes and the difficult-to-sing melodies. Fagen explained their intentions in a 1973 interview for *Rolling Stone.* "We weren't too successful because the lyrics always turned left in the middle of the song. We knew they were conceptual songs for a group, so Gary found us a group."

Within six months, Becker and Fagen convinced the powers that be that they weren't cut out for the position of staff writers, and since ABC was unable to place their songs with their artists, they gave the go-ahead for the duo to put together their own group. Head of A&R Steve Barri was so impressed with the duo that he compared them to the Beatles and gave them more leeway than most newcomers would get, letting them rehearse in the accounting department after the staff would leave at 6:00. Amps and instruments were hauled in, the band tuned up, and Steely Dan was born.

Becker and Fagen were true to their word when they told Denny Dias that they would call for him when they were settled on the West Coast. Dias had been working odd jobs since quitting college with the hope that the duo would indeed call from California. He was about to give up when he got the call. Unfortunately, Dias was broke, so he couldn't afford a plane ticket and drove cross-country. Although he was the first called, he was the last to arrive, missing the sessions for Steely Dan's first single "Dallas" b/w "Sail the Waterway." It didn't really matter much because the single was withdrawn shortly after it was released. Their other guitarist, however, Jeff "Skunk" Baxter, did make it to the Steely Dan sessions for their debut single, and his pedal steel guitar played a significant role on the recording. It gave their first release a country feel, a major reason why it was withdrawn so quickly.

Jeffrey Allen "Skunk" Baxter

Baxter would play an integral role on the first three Steely Dan albums, contributing some of the hottest guitar leads and adding pedal steel guitar to countless tracks, a texture that enhanced every song on which it appeared.

Early Years

Jeffrey Allen Baxter was born on December 13, 1948, in Washington, D.C. He was originally a classically trained pianist, studying from the age of five to fifteen. His father, Loy Baxter, was the boss of future White House Chief of Staff to President Richard Nixon, H. R. Haldeman, best known for his consequent involvement in the Watergate scandal. When he was nine years old, his father was promoted to head of Latin American public relations for the J. Walter Thompson advertising agency, and the family relocated to Mexico City for six years. While there, Baxter bought a cheap guitar and started teaching himself how to play. His first band was Larry and the Escorts, a surf band that was heavily influenced by the music of Mexico City.

In 1964, at the age of fifteen, the Baxters returned to the U.S. and settled in New York City. Baxter knew that he needed to upgrade his guitar, and when he went to purchase a Fender Jazzmaster at Jimmy's Music Shop on New York City's music row, W. 48th St., he also ended up with a job unloading gear. His love of guitars and electronics led him to the repair shop, and soon he was working on guitars. Down the street, Dan Armstrong, future designer of the clear plexiglass guitars and basses distributed by Ampeg, also had a repair shop, and when he noticed that Jimmy's wasn't sending him work anymore, he investigated. What he found was Jeff Baxter, and he quickly hired him.

Baxter became Armstrong's apprentice and learned more about electronics as he built and customized guitars, something that would come in handy in the future. While delivering an amp to a record company, he filled in for a guitarist who was late for a demo session, and although he wasn't paid, the producer bought him a beer and a career was born. Before leaving Jimmy's, he made another acquaintance that would prove to be an important one. Jimi Hendrix was just beginning his career as a front man, and he befriended Baxter while visiting the shop. Baxter would sometimes sit in for their bass player Randy Palmer in Hendrix's first band as a leader called Jimmy James and the Blue Flames. The band began as a trio but would soon become a quartet after Hendrix met guitarist Randy Wolfe at Manny's Music, where Wolfe worked.

Randy recalled their first meeting in a 1994 interview with Steven Roby from the International Jimi Hendrix Fanzine, *Straight Ahead*. "I met Jimi in Manny's Music store. He was in the back of the store playing a Strat. Our eyes caught each other and I asked him if I could show him some things I learned on the guitar. He then gave me the Strat and I played him slide guitar. He really liked it and invited me down that night, which I believe was his first night of this gig at the Cafe Wha? I'll never forget that moment our eyes met and froze on each other. Some type of real spiritual affinity or connection happened between us."

Hendrix wasn't the only guitarist that was learning new techniques from California. At the time Walter Baker was also under his tutelage. So in 1966, a year before Becker had met Fagen, there was only one degree of separation between himself and Jeff "Skunk" Baxter.

The Boston Years

Baxter attended the prestigious Taft preparatory school in Watertown, Connecticut, and took part in the exchange program with Uppingham School in Rutland, England. After he graduated in 1967, he enrolled at the School of Public Communication (now College of Communication) at Boston University, where he studied journalism and worked with countless local Boston bands. He took a job at Frank's Drum Shop and recalled how he joined the Ultimate Spinach in 1968 in a 1980 interview with *Guitar Player* magazine. "A guy in a long robe came in and asked me if I knew any guitarists. I said 'Sure,' hopped over the counter, and became a member of Ultimate Spinach, joining in time to play on their third album, *The Ultimate Spinach*. Man, were we psychedelic!" Although they were one of the most famous, and the most infamous, groups to be marketed as being a part of the "Bosstown Sound," the movement gained little momentum once the audience realized that the bands were merely second-rate versions of the psychedelic bands that had created the "San Francisco Sound." As Baxter put it, they were a horrible band with a huge following.

After Ultimate Spinach, Baxter began to learn how to play pedal steel guitar and performed with the Holy Modal Rounders from 1969 until 1971. Unfortunately for a band that was quite prolific, releasing four albums in a five-year period, they were apparently on a recording moratorium. During Baxter's tenure with them, they didn't record any albums, so sadly there is no record of his early pedal steel performances from this period. He continued to do session work in Boston, played bass for singer-songwriter Tim Buckley, and began to commute to New York for some of the better sessions. One in particular did very well on the charts, Carly Simon's first top ten hit, 1971's "That's the Way I've Always Heard It Should Be." Another, however, was a far less successful project initially, yet the sessions for it changed Baxter's career path significantly.

Back to New York City

Baxter first met Gary Katz when he was producing Jim Hodder's band Bead Game for Avco/Embassy. Many Boston bands had the same manager, rehearsal studio owner Ray Paret, so when Baxter was doing a session at Intermedia Sound, he met the fledgling producer. Katz heard his guitar playing and was impressed. Baxter met Becker and Fagen while they were working on a Katz-produced album by singer Linda Hoover that was never released. Although he didn't play on the album, he did embark on their next project, a strange one indeed. Fagen, Becker, Dias, Baxter, Katz, and Hoover drove to Boston to record a song that Becker and Katz wrote called "Cody Canyon." They named their band after the song, but the strangest aspect of the group was that its lead vocalist was producer Katz. The group played a showcase for Warner Bros. Records with the hopes of scoring a deal, but nothing transpired, and for the time being the musicians and producer parted ways, but not for long.

Los Angeles

In Chris Briggs's 1974 interview for *Zig Zag*, Baxter spoke of the formation of Steely Dan. "Don and Walter had been writing tunes for a long time, bringing them to record companies. They'd get laughed at. They were good friends with Gary Katz, so they became house writers for a while. I knew Gary from the Boston days because he had produced a band with Jim Hodder. . . . We decided that when the time was right we would form a band with Donald and Walter . . . when I was gigging with Buzzy [Linhart] I got a call from Gary. He said the time was right. So I went back to L.A. and the band was formed."

When Baxter arrived on the West Coast, he immediately used his skills as a highly accomplished guitar technician and began customizing guitars at Valley Sound in L.A. while performing with the country act Sammy Masterson and the Country Gentlemen. In addition to his day gig at Valley Sound, he found the time to play live dates and recording sessions with numerous musicians. He contributed heavily to Buzzy Linhart's fourth LP, *Buzzy*, and played pedal steel guitar on two songs from the Gary Katz–produced act Navasoto's only LP, *Rootin'*. The LP included a Becker and Fagen composition, "Canyon Ladies," and also featured Fagen on keyboards on five tracks as well as horn arrangements by Becker and Fagen on four songs and a string arrangement for another. Those sessions coincided with the sessions for Steely Dan's first single, "Dallas" b/w "Sail the Waterway."

Steely Dan, the Doobie Brothers, and More

Baxter would play on Steely Dan's first three albums, *Can't Buy a Thrill*, *Countdown to Ecstasy*, and *Pretzel Logic*, and would embark on three tours as a full member of the group until July 1974. While still a member of Steely Dan, Baxter did sessions for other musicians and also performed live with a number of acts. Steely Dan had opened for the Doobie Brothers on some dates, and Baxter would sit in with the band almost every night. They formed a close relationship, and he played pedal steel guitar on the Doobie Brothers' albums *The Captain and Me* and *What Were Once Vices Are Now Habits*. After Linda Ronstadt saw him perform at the Palomino Club, she recruited him for her tour, and he even appeared on *Midnight Special* playing congas on an early version of "You're No Good" in 1973, two years before Ronstadt would have a number one hit with the song originally recorded by Betty Everett. Baxter always wanted to stay busy, feeling that the more people he played with, the more his technique would develop and his versatility as a player would increase exponentially.

In 1974, Becker and Fagen decided that they would no longer tour and would focus solely on making records. The group subsequently folded, and the duo and Baxter amicably parted ways. Financially, Becker and Fagen's situation differed from the rest of the band from the very beginning. They had money coming in from their publishing, but the band needed to be on the road in order to make a living. Baxter enjoyed touring, as did Hodder and, to a lesser extent, Dias, but it was no surprise that Becker and Fagen disliked the whole juvenile, frat-party atmosphere. So after the tour promoting *Pretzel Logic*, Baxter joined the Doobie Brothers as a full member and toured to support *What Were Once Vices Are Now Habits*. He also toured with Elton John that year and was offered a full-time gig but declined, preferring to stay with the Doobie Brothers.

He played a significant role on the Doobies' fifth LP, 1975's *Stampede*, although he doesn't appear on the record cover, having joined after the photo was taken. The same year, he played on Joni Mitchell's "In France They Kiss on Main Street" from her groundbreaking album *The Hissing of Summer Lawns*. He would continue to juggle session work with his position as a Doobie Brother. In 1976, he played on Carly Simon's *Another Passenger*, John Sebastian's *Welcome Back*, Flo and Eddie's *Moving Targets*, Richie Havens's *The End of the Beginning*, as well as the Doobie's sixth album, *Takin' It to the Streets*. Baxter should be credited as saving the Doobie Brothers from failure once founding member Tom Johnston had to temporarily leave the group due to his ulcers. On the eve of the tour to promote *Stampede*, Johnston became severely ill and required emergency hospitalization for a bleeding ulcer. Baxter recommended his fellow Steely Dan alum Michael McDonald as a replacement for the tour, and McDonald added keyboards and sang a number of Johnston's songs.

Although McDonald was originally hired as a vocalist and keyboard player, when the band entered the studio to record their next album, *Takin' It to the Streets*, it was apparent that he was also a gifted songwriter. He contributed three songs, including the title track, "Losin' End," and "It Keeps You Runnin'," and co-wrote the album's closer, "Carry Me Away," with guitarist/vocalist Patrick Simmons and Baxter. Baxter also co-wrote the opening track, "Wheels of Fortune," with Simmons and drummer John Hartman. Johnston only contributed one original song to *Takin' It to the Streets*, "Turn It Loose," and added vocals to the opener, "Wheels of Fortune." He also played live with the band in 1976, but by the fall he was sidelined again due to exhaustion.

Although the band recorded five of Johnston's compositions for the group's next LP, *Livin' on the Fault Line*, none of his songs appeared on the album. Johnston felt that the musical direction of the Doobie Brothers had strayed so far from their original sound, he had his songs removed, and he left the band that he co-founded.

Baxter co-wrote the opener, "You're Made That Way," for this album as well, this time with McDonald and drummer Keith Knudsen. McDonald sang lead on five songs, Simmons on three, and bassist Tiran Porter on one, but McDonald's background vocals were so strong they were almost as prominent as the lead vocal on Simmons's tunes.

The band's next album, *Minute by Minute*, spent five weeks at number one, won four Grammys, and contained their biggest hit, the Michael McDonald/Kenny Loggins–penned "What a Fool Believes." Although the album was a huge success, it would be Baxter's last with the group. Unfortunately, McDonald, who Baxter had brought to the group, heard his songs a certain way, and although

Baxter respected his song-writing ability, he insisted on changing the guitar parts. McDonald was looking for a straighter R&B feel, but Baxter was more eccentric and wanted to stretch out. They toured Japan in early 1979 to promote the album, but tensions were running high. When they returned, the band split up, but once "What a Fool Believes" hit number one, it was apparent that the band had to get back together, but with one less Brother. McDonald felt that he could no longer work with Baxter, and being the voice of their number one hit he wasn't going anywhere, so Baxter left the Doobie Brothers in a similar

The last Doobie Brothers record that Baxter would play on would be 1978's *Minute by Minute*.

manner as he had done five years earlier with Steely Dan. It was stated at the time that it was a mutual decision, but for all intents and purposes, Baxter had been let go by the man that he introduced to the Doobies, and to the world at large.

Session Musician and Military Advisor

After the Doobie Brothers, Baxter continued to work as a session guitarist for a diverse group of artists, including Eric Clapton, Joni Mitchell, Rod Stewart, Barbra Streisand, Dolly Parton, Carly Simon, Ringo Starr, Freddie Hubbard, Harry Nilsson, Willy DeVille, Bryan Adams, Hoyt Axton, Gene Clark, Rick Nelson, Gene Simmons, and Donna Summer, playing the famous lead guitar solo on "Hot Stuff." He played pedal steel with Billy Vera and the Beaters and produced their first album, recorded live at the Roxy in L.A., that contained the number one single "At This Moment." He also produced albums for the hard rock band Nazareth, the Stray Cats, Carl Wilson, the Ventures, Nils Lofgren, and Bob Welch's 1982 album, "Eye Contact." In 1990, Baxter formed a band called the Best with the Who's bassist John Entwistle, James Gang and Eagles guitarist Joe Walsh, ELP keyboard player Keith Emerson, singer Rick Livingstone, and drummer Simon Phillips for a one-time tour of Japan, after which the group released a live performance video.

Baxter's oddest gig of his career, however, has nothing to do with music. In the mid-1980s, his interest in music recording technology led him to specu-late about data-compression algorithms and large-capacity storage devices that were originally developed for military use. His next-door neighbor was a retired engineer who had worked on the Sidewinder missile program, and after Baxter helped him clean out his garage after the neighborhood had a number of mudslides, he bought Baxter a subscription to an aviation magazine, leading him to explore other facets of the military including missile defense systems. As he had done before with the guitar, he became a self-taught expert on the subject and wrote a paper that proposed converting the ship-based anti-aircraft Aegis system into a rudimentary missile defense system. When he gave the paper to California Republican congressman Dana Rohrabacher, his career as a defense consultant began.

Baxter elaborated on his popularity inside the beltway in a 2001 interview with Jon Weiderhorn for MTV News. "Some of these people who are generals now were listening to my music when they were lieutenant colonels or lieutenant commanders, so there was a bond there. But what they realized is that they're looking for people who think out of the box, who approach a problem with a very different point of view because we're talking about asymmetrical warfare here."

He was nominated to chair the Civilian Advisory Board for Ballistic Missile Defense in 1995, which led to consulting contracts with the Pentagon's Missile Defense Agency and National Geospatial-Intelligence Agency. He now consults for the U.S. Department of Defense and the U.S. intelligence community, as well as for private defense-oriented companies. Baxter always looked at things in an unconventional way, and this has been the main reason that he has been so successful in his second career. He compared music to defense strategies in an intriguing way in Thomas Quiggin's 2007 book *Seeing the Invisible: National Security Intelligence in an Uncertain Age.* "We thought turntables were for playing records until rappers began to use them as instruments, and we thought airplanes were for carrying passengers until terrorists realized they could be used as cruise missiles. Among other things, what I do is look at existing technologies and hypothesize how they might be applied in non-traditional ways, something that happens in music all the time and also happens to be something that terrorists are incredibly good at."

Jim Hodder

While Hodder originally seemed like the ideal drummer for the ill-fated original lineup of Steely Dan, he would be the first musician to be sidelined in favor of session musicians. He was the sole drummer for the Dan's first two albums, but by their third he had been replaced, although he appeared in the band photo for the album and was still part of the touring ensemble.

Early Years

Jim Hodder was born on December 17, 1947, in Bethpage, New York, on Long Island, a year and five days after Denny Dias was born. Bethpage was also only a few miles from Hicksville, where Dias's family would settle in 1954, but being from different towns, the two musicians went to different schools and didn't meet until they joined Steely Dan in Los Angeles in 1972.

As a child he began playing the accordion but soon found his true calling as a drummer and began playing in local bands around Long Island at the age of fifteen with a fake ID. When he graduated from Plainedge High School in 1965, he relocated to Boston to attend the Berklee College of Music and to begin his career as a musician.

Boston Years and Bead Game

Soon after arriving, he began playing around town, and after three years he joined the band Bead Game. Bead Game was formed in Cambridge, Massachusetts, in the late '60s and consisted of Jim Hodder on lead vocals and drums, Kenny Westland-Haag on rhythm guitar and vocals, Robert Gass on organ and keyboards, Lassie Sachs on bass, and John Sheldon on lead guitar. Like their contemporaries Steppenwolf, Bead Game was named after a novel by German writer Hermann Hesse, *The Glass Bead Game*. Ironically, Denny Dias's band that Becker and Fagen ambushed was also named after a Hesse novel, *Demian*.

Bead Game was originally comprised primarily of Harvard students and was formed by Robert Gass and lead singer and harp player John Leone. Their first gig was at the New York offices of *Vogue* magazine, but Leone, who was initially the driving force of the band, was disillusioned by the New York music scene. Bassist Lassie Sachs was part of this early lineup, and Jim Hodder was the next to join after original drummer, Joe D'Amico, left. The band was quickly changing, and soon after John Leone would quit the band as well.

After guitarist Will Dick's departure, John Sheldon auditioned for the band, but initially Jim Hodder and Robert Gass were the only ones who liked his playing. Sheldon was an inventive guitarist who learned how to play guitar at age thirteen from family friend James Taylor. After a self-proclaimed "mental breakdown," he auditioned for Van Morrison in the spring of 1968 and played with him until October of the same year, although he didn't appear on *Astral Weeks* which was recorded during his tenure, but primarily featured jazz musicians who hadn't played with Morrison before.

With the rhythm section in place, the group auditioned several vocalists, one of whom came back to their rehearsal space and stole

(From left to right: Robert Gass, Will Dick, Lassie Sachs, Jim Hodder & John Leone)

An early band photo of Bead Game. Jim Hodder is second from the right.

their equipment, but none of them felt right. Drummer Jim Hodder became the lead vocalist by default, similar to the way Donald Fagen would become the vocalist for Steely Dan four years later. The band lived like so many other bands in the late '60s—together in one house where they hardly rehearsed and at initial shows could play quite sloppily. But they improved, and Bead Game managed to build up a local following on the Boston club circuit, and their live performances garnered positive reviews including one in the *Harvard Crimson* on May 9, 1969: "Very few rock groups, and even fewer American ones, manage to make music that is not only complex in its musical structure but at the same time retains the visceral, frantic dynamism that one associates with true rock and roll. The Bead Game is one of the finest rock groups in the country precisely because its music is just such an extraordinary synthesis of complexity and dynamics."

Record companies began to take notice, and they landed a record deal with AVCO Embassy Records, who released their Gary Katz (Kannon)-produced debut album, *Welcome*, in March 1970. The album was recorded at the Record Plant East in New York in late 1969, with four songs written by Haag, three written by Haag and Sachs, and one written by Haag and Gass. It received a favorable review in *Billboard* magazine: "This New England quintet has an auspicious disk debut here with soft rock well done. All the material here is original and it's all good, including the opening rocker "Judy" and a good blended folk rock "Country Girls.'"

AVCO did not release a single from the album, and although the LP sold approximately fifty thousand copies, they were all East Coast sales, and the album stalled. This was the case with many lesser-known bands of the '60s and '70s. Record labels would press singles for regional promotional use and try to break bands that way. It rarely worked, and Bead Game is a perfect example of this. The group next contributed two songs to the AVCO Embassy–financed anti-drug film *The People Next Door* starring Eli Wallach and Julie Harris. They appeared as a band in the film as well.

The group also took part in the recording of an album by Buddy Miles's horn section, the Freedom Express. The resulting album, *Easy Ridin'*, was a jazz/soul/rock fusion album released on Mercury Records in late 1970, and although the horn section is clearly the focus, the members of the Bead Game are given enough space to shine as soloists and as a rhythm section. With Buddy Miles currently riding the wave of fame with Jimi Hendrix's Band of Gypsies, he did not take part in the sessions, and the album came and went with little fanfare.

While Bead Game was working on their second album, *Baptism*, in 1970, the band fell apart. Their sophomore effort had been financed by the band, and with no record label behind them, it was shelved. It eventually was released a full twenty-six years later. Today, the band is primarily remembered as the first professional band of drummer/vocalist Jim Hodder. For fanatics, there's also a non-LP single, "Sweet Medusa" b/w "Country Girls."

Meeting Baxter, Becker, and Fagen

Before Bead Game broke up, Hodder met Jeff Baxter while rehearsing at the studio of Ray Paret, who managed both Bead Game and Ultimate Spinach.

The two musicians got along well and played some gigs together while in Boston. Hodder also met Becker and Fagen before Steely Dan was formed to showcase the duo's material. During a Bead Game session at the Record Plant in Manhattan, Gary Katz brought Becker and Fagen along to hear the band and to introduce them to Hodder. Hodder wasn't impressed and initially thought Fagen was a "creep." At this point, he was the one who was the lead singer and drummer of a signed band and Becker and Fagen were still pedaling their songs and making demos, so he didn't give the duo much thought.

While Bead Game never became successful in its own right, it was the turning point for Hodder's career. Gary Katz was impressed with his drumming and thought that his ability as a vocalist could be utilized as well, so when it was time to find a drummer for the soon-to-be-assembled band that would perform the songs of Becker and Fagen, Katz recommended Hodder. Katz had played him some of their demos when working with Bead Game, and Hodder was familiar with Baxter's playing. He was also broke. After Bead Game, he continued to play gigs and do session work, but there wasn't enough available to make a living. So when the call came to relocate to Los Angeles and record with the band that would become Steely Dan, Hodder didn't hesitate.

Los Angeles and Steely Dan

Hodder arrived on the West Coast prepared to be the drummer and background vocalist, but when Steely Dan recorded their debut single, "Dallas" b/w "Sail the Waterway," his role was more prominent. The A-side was originally entitled "Bye, Bye, Dallas" and was sung by Fagen when they wrote it in New York, but when they recorded it in the spring of 1972, Hodder was handed the role of lead vocalist. He would sing lead on one other song while with Steely Dan, "Midnight Cruiser" from their debut LP, *Can't Buy a Thrill*. When asked about his function as a drummer in Steely Dan, he stated in their 1972 press release, "I like what I play in this band. I like to play strong rhythms, nothing too fancy, but strong. I like to make things go."

Hodder would play drums and contribute background vocals on their first two albums, but for their third, *Pretzel Logic*, he was demoted and session drummer extraordinaire Jim Gordon was brought in to play on all but one song, "Night by Night," which drummer Jeff Porcaro handled. Porcaro would also play alongside Gordon on the dual-drum track "Parker's Band." Although Hodder was in the band photo on the inner gatefold sleeve, his sole contribution to the album would be background vocals on "Parker's Band." Before production began, Becker and Fagen met with Hodder and informed him of their plan to use Jim Gordon to record the album. Hodder had attempted to record "Night by Night," but they felt that they wanted something different for this record; something Hodder couldn't offer. At the same time, he was approached by one of the Doobies' co-founders, guitarist/vocalist Patrick Simmons, and his Steely Dan bandmate Jeff Baxter, who asked him to tour with them; but Hodder still had faith in Becker and Fagen and declined. Keith Knudsen took the job and contributed background vocals to *What Were Once Vices Are Now Habits* and drums and vocals to *Stampede, Takin'*

It to the Streets, Livin' on the Fault Line, Minute by Minute, One Step Closer, and *Sibling Rivalry* and benefited significantly from his position in a successful touring band that continued to use their musicians in the studio. Hodder had apparently had too much faith in the songwriters.

It was difficult to accept his new position in the band, especially since he was still the band's official "live" drummer. After recording sessions during the day, which Hodder would often attend, the "band" would rehearse at night; not a pleasant situation for the drummer. This embarrassed Hodder, and when *Pretzel Logic* came out, he had the tough job of telling people that he didn't play on the album when they complimented the drumming.

Although Hodder was the only drummer for Steely Dan's first two tours, for the third drummer Jeff Porcaro as well as keyboardist Michael McDonald and vocalist Royce Jones, who had toured with the Dan along with two female vocalists on the second tour, augmented their sound. Initially, Hodder wasn't pleased with the new scenario, but he dealt with it in the same fashion as he had dealt with his sidelining on the *Pretzel Logic* LP; he went along with the plan. When interviewed about this in 1974 for *Melody Maker* magazine, he seemed content with the new expanded band. "I like having the two of us drumming. It doesn't always work in groups and both of you have to forget about your ego. With us it sounds like one guy playing at times, but it makes for a better combination of sounds. From the time the band was put together, Donald wanted two drummers. I was against it at first, but we had two guitarists and two keyboard players, so why not two drummers? And my favorite band has two drummers—Frank Zappa and the Mothers. It can work like a locomotive, especially on tunes like 'Do It Again.'" It worked well because it gave him time to relax during certain sections, and Porcaro's precise playing created a massive drum sound that moved forward like a locomotive.

By the end of the tour, it was apparent that Becker and Fagen were ready to transform Steely Dan into the band they always imagined: a studio band. Hodder had seen the writing on the wall from the very beginning. Regardless of how well the band recorded a take, the duo would constantly contemplate how the song would sound with an assortment of studio musicians. Hodder resented this at the time, but eventually understood their intention as songwriters.

After being let go from Steely Dan, Hodder continued to work as a session musician, but work was scarce. In 1976, he played on certain tracks on both Sammy Hager's *Nine on a Ten Scale* and *Sibling Rivalry* by the Rowans. He later appeared as the sole drummer on David Soul's *Playing to an Audience of One* and Rocky Sullivan's *Caught in the Crossfire* record. Hodder's career, however, had a heartbreaking ending. On June 5, 1990, he drowned in the swimming pool of his Point Arena, California, home at the age of forty-two.

David Palmer

David Palmer was brought in toward the end of the recording of Steely Dan's debut album once Becker and Fagen realized they would have to support the LP with a tour.

Early Years and Myddle Class

David Palmer was born in Warren Township, Watchung, New Jersey. He sang from a young age and participated in choir and folk groups, but once he heard the Rolling Stones, he was captivated by rock 'n' roll and formed his first group in 1964 while he was still attending Watchung Hills Regional High School. The group was founded by Palmer, his friend guitarist Rick Philp, bassist Charles Larkey, drummer Myke Rosa, and organist Danny Mansolino and was originally named the Kingbees after the Rolling Stones' cover of Slim Harpo's 1957 song "I'm a Kingbee." They were discovered by *New York Post* columnist Al Aronowitz at a concert at the Berkeley Heights Catholic Youth Organization in December 1964 after hearing of the band through his babysitter. They changed their name to the Myddle Class in the fall of 1965 to distinguish themselves from Danny Kortchmar's King Bees, who had recently released an album on RCA Victor and continued to perform around New Jersey. On December 11, 1965, the group played a show organized by Aronowitz at the Summit High School Auditorium with a curious opening act, the Velvet Underground. It was their first gig, and the band shocked the audience with their out-of-the-ordinary sound and stage presence.

Aronowitz became the Myddle Class's manager, although he had no experience representing acts, and introduced the band to Gerry Goffin and Carole King, aware of the fact that they were looking for rock bands to sign to their newly formed record label, Tomorrow Records. The band procured a record contract with Tomorrow, and Goffin and King served as songwriters and producers. They also secured a publishing deal for Palmer with Colgems Music, the same company that published their hit material and used them as a backing band for some of the other artists they were working with. Ironically, after King divorced Goffin, bassist Charles Larkey would become her second husband from 1970 to 1976. In October '65, Goffin and King signed a production deal for Tomorrow Records with Atlantic-Atco, specifically to release the first Myddle Class single.

That first single, released in December 1965, was "Free as the Wind," written by Goffin, King, Philp, and Palmer with the flip side containing a garage rock cover of Bob Dylan's "Gates of Eden."

An advertisement for Gerry Goffin and Carole King's record label, Tomorrow Records, and for the Myddle Class's debut single "Free as the Wind."

Billboard reviewed the record in December 1965: "New label, new group and new Goffin-King material has smash hit possibilities. Folk rocker is a powerhouse!" Despite the positive review and heavy rotation on New York radio stations, the single failed to chart nationally, but did chart at number twelve in Albany, New York, in March 1966.

Their second single, "Don't Let Me Sleep Too Long" b/w "I Happen to Love You," peaked at number two on WPTR in Albany during the summer of '66. In 1967, the B-side, written by Goffin and King, was recorded by a revamped version of Them without Van Morrison as well as by the Electric Prunes. Although the A-side was credited as a band composition, the song was actually the group's appropriation of the Blues Project's "Wake Me, Shake Me," an essential song from their live sets. The Blues Project's organist Al Kooper confirmed this when he stated in an interview with Lyn Nuttal, "The Blues Project let the Myddle Class open for them as a favor and in return, they stole their closing song! Nobody really even heard the Myddle Class theft in the U.S. outside of New York City. The Blues Project's version of "Wake Me, Shake Me" was the big version in the U.S. and influenced a lot of young bands." Ironically, the song wasn't an original for the Blues Project either, having adapted the song from traditional African American spirituals from the early 20th century. The Blues Project recorded a demo in January 1966 and then returned to the studio in August for their album *Projections*, released in November of the same year. When this Myddle Class 45 was reissued on the Buddah label, Al Kooper and the Blues Project were credited for the arrangement.

Fourteen months passed before the Myddle Class's third and final single was released. Goffin and King's distribution deal with Atlantic-Atco fell apart after only three singles, two by Myddle Class and one by King as a solo artist, so they moved to Cameo-Parkway. The self-produced "Don't Look Back" was originally the B-side of the Temptations' top twenty hit "My Baby," released in 1965, and was often their closing song live. Although it was a B-side, it reached number fourteen on the R&B charts. The Myddle Class version was more of a folksy take on a funkier original, but it did show that they could interpret a song in a completely original manner. The B-side, "Wind Chime Laughter," written by Philp and Palmer and produced by the band with Goffin, was an extremely mid-60s-sounding pop tune with thick harmonies and a Beach Boys-esque vibe to it and demonstrates the creative harmonic and melodic approach of their songwriting. Unfortunately, Allen Klein took over Cameo-Parkway and fired the band's representatives at the label, leaving their new single without any promotion.

Working with Gerry Goffin and Carole King After Myddle Class

Palmer and Philp wrote the song "You Go On" for one of Goffin and King's groups, Bach's Lunch, a girl group with singer Darlene McCrea of the Cookies and the Raelettes. The A-side of their debut single was a remake of Goffin and King's "Will You Still Love Me Tomorrow," but the B-side, "You Go On," was the highlight.

At this point, some band members were attending college and others were working with other artists, so the group rarely performed live anymore. Their main source of income came from recording demos for Goffin and King including "Goin' Back," a single for the Byrds in October '67; "I Can't Make It Alone," which would turn up on Dusty Springfield's 1969 classic *Dusty in Memphis*; and the Monkees' number three hit "Pleasant Valley Sunday."

Palmer also collaborated with King on a song called "Paradise Alley," named after a section of the Lower East Side in Manhattan and covered by '60s London singer Billy Fury in 1970 and by actress Sally Kellerman in 1972. When King and Goffin split up in 1967, she moved to Laurel Canyon in Los Angeles and formed the band the City with her boyfriend, bassist Larkey, and guitarist Danny Kortchmar, who had played with James Taylor in another Greenwich Village group, the Flying Machine. The City quickly signed a record deal with Lou Adler's Ode Records, his first record label since selling Dunhill Records (Steely Dan's future label) to ABC in 1967. They entered the studio with Adler in the producer's chair and future Steely Dan session drummer Jim Gordon and cut *Now That Everything's Been Said*, an album that was equal parts pop-rock of the day and the singer-songwriter sound that King would popularize with her 1971 release *Tapestry*, which would win four Grammy Awards in 1972. Rick Philp helped with the arrangements for the album, and aside from "Paradise Alley," Palmer also co-wrote "Victim of Circumstance" with King.

Boston and Jake and the Family Jewels

In the fall of 1968, David Palmer, Rick Philp, and organist Danny Mansolino relocated to Boston and collaborated with pianist Lloyd Baskin on a number of compositions. In March 1969, they recorded these songs in the studio, including a new Goffin and King composition, "Mr. Charlie," as well as two written by Palmer and Philp, "Redbeard" and "Keys to the Kingdom." They planned on reuniting with bassist Charles Larkey and drummer Myke Rosa to record an album in the summer of 1969, but their story was cut short when guitarist Rick Philp was murdered by his former roommate in Boston in May 1969.

Danny Mansolino and Myke Rosa joined Jake and the Family Jewels for two albums on Polydor in 1969 and 1970 and added David Palmer as vocalist for a 1971 album on Elektra as the Quinaimes Band. The group included guitarist Kenny Pine, who had played with Larkey in the Fugs, and Carole King's bandmate Danny Kortchmar, listed as Danny Kootch. Rosa later became a house producer for Elektra Records, and Larkey was a member of the Fugs, the City, and Jo Mama.

Los Angeles and Steely Dan

Palmer was working in a plastics factory in New Jersey when he got the call from Los Angeles. Jeff Baxter, who he knew from his days in Boston, had recommended him to Becker, Fagen, and Katz as a lead vocalist when the record label started talking about touring behind the album. This came as a surprise to Becker and Fagen, who assumed that they wouldn't have to go out and perform in public. Fagen had reluctantly agreed to be the band's lead vocalist in the studio, but was terrified of singing live and was averse to being the front man for a touring rock band. They had already recorded three-quarters of the album with Fagen singing lead, but with the prospect of going out on the road to support their debut LP, they knew they needed to find a suitable lead vocalist regardless of the pleas of Gary Katz and the other members for Fagen to sing their songs live. The band had a conflict about the situation because on one hand they knew that Fagen as a songwriter would convey the right attitude for the songs, but on the other hand Fagen's vocal range was somewhat small and they thought somebody with a bigger voice could possibly do the song's justice. Katz wasn't happy with the choice to hire Palmer and made it clear to Becker and Fagen that he thought it was the wrong decision.

Palmer arrived a week after he got the offer and was there in time to contribute lead vocals to two Steely Dan classics, "Dirty Work" and "Brooklyn (Owes the Charmer Under Me)," as well as background vocals on "Reelin' in the Years," "Only a Fool Would Say That," and "Change of the Guard." When *Can't Buy a Thrill* was mixed, he visited Carole King, who was enjoying the success of her *Tapestry* record, and played King the album. She was sure it would be a hit. Although Palmer played a minor role on *Can't Buy a Thrill*, his position on the road would be much greater. Not only did he sing the songs on which he originally handled lead vocals, he sang lead on their hit single "Do It Again" as well as numerous songs that Becker and Fagen had written to showcase his vocals, including "Megashine City," "Take My Money," and "Hellbound Train"; songs that would never be released on record.

Palmer had been brought into the band without anybody really knowing if he would fit in and interpret the material correctly, and although they told the press at the time that it was working out, it apparently was not. During their first tour of the U.S., they were also recording their second album, *Countdown to Ecstasy*, which credits Palmer with background vocals, although Becker and Fagen in the liner notes for the 1998 remastered CD stated that Palmer had left "for greener pastures without having sung a note on the actual *Countdown* recording."

The writing was on the wall, and by April 1973, toward the end of their first U.S. tour, Palmer was fired. Katz was right when he told Becker and Fagen that it was a mistake to bring Palmer into the band because he couldn't translate the songs the way that Fagen could. The singer was also drinking heavily on the road, and it is quite likely that a show at the Spectrum in Philadelphia on April 13, 1973, was the last straw. Not only did Palmer split his tight pants, he was wearing no undergarments; and he was so inebriated that he sang the entire show a half step down from the correct key. Although Fagen was originally unwilling to front the band, it was apparent that he had no choice, so in April '73 Fagen became the sole lead singer of Steely Dan. Palmer understood the decision, and in a 1997 interview with Bob DiCorcia he spoke of the way he felt about the situation. "When you have a singer as great as Donald Fagen was and is, you don't need another lead singer in the band.

After Steely Dan

It didn't take long for Palmer to find his feet. He had kept in touch with Carole King since joining Steely Dan, and when she began working on a new album in 1974, she called Palmer to work on a few songs. She had written all of the songs on her previous album, *Fantasy*, by herself, the first time she had done so, and decided she wanted to work with a lyricist for the next one. Palmer ended up writing the lyrics for the twelve songs on *Wrap Around Joy*, which hit number one on the *Billboard* albums chart in late 1974, was certified gold by the RIAA, and spun off two successful singles, "Jazzman," which peaked at number two on the pop charts, and "Nightingale," a number nine pop hit that reached number one on the adult contemporary chart.

Palmer's next band was Wha-Koo, a soft-rock group formed in 1977 by guitarist and singer-songwriter Danny Douma. He put the band together in a manner that was similar to the formation of Steely Dan. Besides Palmer he recruited guitarist Nick Van Maarth, from the post–Buddy Holly's Crickets; drummer/vocalist Don Francisco, formerly of the bands Crowfoot and Atlee; and bassist Andy Silvester, formerly of Savoy Brown. For their 1977 debut album, *The Big Wha-Koo* on ABC Records, L.A. session musician Reinie Press, bass player on many of Neil Diamond's most successful recordings, played bass and saxophone on two tracks. Andy Silvester was replaced by Peter Freiberger for the band's sophomore release, *Berkshire*, produced by Ken Caillat. It was Caillat's first album as a producer, but later that year he would gain fame as the co-producer of Fleetwood Mac's number one LP *Rumours*. For Wha-Koo, *Berkshire* proved to be the band's most successful release, featuring the single "You're Such a Fabulous Dancer," a top ten hit in some international markets that only reached number 101 on the U.S. charts.

In 1978, founder Danny Douma left Wha-Koo to pursue a solo career. Chuck Cochran replaced Douma on vocals and lead guitar and participated in two of Wha-Koo's most important performances: the Canada Jam festival near Toronto, Ontario, to an audience of 110,000; and on the steps of the Sydney Opera House in Sydney, Australia, before a crowd of 100,000 with the band Thin Lizzy.

Cochran left the band after the tour to work with Robb Royer of Bread; Jim Messina; Crosby, Stills & Nash; and others. Although he was no longer with the band, his lead guitar, background vocals, and compositions are heard on Wha-Koo's third and final album, *Fragile Line*, from 1979. The album was more rock-oriented, and Palmer was now the official leader of the band. Palmer wrote four of the songs on the LP and co-wrote the rest. Although pop critics thought the album was "tasty," it did little on the charts, and soon after the group disbanded.

Palmer continued to compose songs covered by the Pointer Sisters; Gladys Knight and the Pips; the Neville Brothers; Blood, Sweat & Tears; Richie Havens; Anne Murray; Randy Travis; Laura Branigan; and various other artists and contributed the song "Silhouette" to the 1985 film *Teen Wolf*. Since 2002, Palmer embraced one of his other passions and has been a professional digital photographer specializing in landscapes and fine art images.

Palmer Sues Becker and Fagen

In 2014, David Palmer sued his former bandmates with claims of being cheated on digital performance royalties. According to his lawsuit, he was contacted by AFTRA (American Federation of Television and Radio Artists), who wanted to know whether he was merely a "side man" or a royalty participant. In 1972, he signed an agreement that established Steely Dan Inc. (SDI) and was given a one-sixth percentage share of all royalties earned from songs on which he performed. The way that royalties are paid by SoundExchange could be difficult for former band members because when money derived from sources like Sirius XM and Pandora is distributed, the featured artist is paid directly rather than band entities.

When AFTRA approached, Palmer made it clear that he was a royalty participant. He was told to go to SoundExchange to resolve the issue. When SDI was contacted, the band allegedly told SoundExchange that all Steely Dan royalties were administered through SDI, but that didn't help Palmer. Palmer says he eventually got a royalty "going forward," and that "perhaps out of guilt over its outright deception and concealment of these royalties in the past," he was written a check from SDI for more than $8,000, which was his one-sixth share from a nine-month period up to March 31, 2013. But he is still concerned about all of the past royalties he believes he should have been getting since SoundExchange's inception in 2000.

Roger Nichols (Recording Engineer)

While working on songwriting demos for ABC Dunhill's artists, Becker and Fagen met engineer Roger Nichols. Like so many children in the '50s, Nichols spent his allowance buying records, but unlike his peers, he was interested not only in the music, but in the sound quality of the recordings. He was annoyed by the surface noise, clicks, and pops inherent to vinyl records, so he decided that he needed to start doing recordings of his own. He bought a stereo quarter-inch reel-to-reel tape recorder and began recording with high school classmate Frank Zappa, experimenting with multiple takes and bouncing tracks. He would also go out to underage clubs and record bands so that he had something pristine to listen to at home.

After graduating from high school, Nichols attended Oregon State University, where he studied nuclear physics. From 1965 to 1968, he was a nuclear operator at the San Onofre Nuclear Generating Station, but continued to record bands at clubs on the weekends. In 1965, while working at the power plant, he and a few friends built a four-track recording studio in a garage in Torrance, California, called Quantum Studios and founded a hi-fi supply store. His contacts through that business led the studio to start recording commercials, where he met future pop stars Karen and Richard Carpenter and future Steely Dan session guitarist Larry Carlton.

In 1971, Nichols met Gary Katz, who introduced him to Becker and Fagen, and there was instant chemistry between the newly minted staff writers and the genius engineer. In an interview with Brian Sweet for the fanzine *Metal Leg*, Nichols recalled, "The strive for true hi-fi was common ground with Donald and Walter and Gary—we're all perfectionists, especially Walter with his quad electrostatic speakers at home and the latest tone arm. It wasn't a drag for me to do things over and over until it was perfect, as here it would have driven a lot of other engineers up the wall. In my own way, I'm just as crazy as they are."

When it came time to record their debut LP, *Can't Buy a Thrill*, it was apparent that only one man could do the job, Roger Nichols. The sessions were due to start in the summer of 1972, but this conflicted with Nichols's summer vacation, so sessions were postponed until he returned, something that annoyed ABC Dunhill's president, Jay Lasker, who had already felt duped by Becker, Fagen, and Katz. He was nicknamed Roger "The Immortal" Nichols early on by Becker and Fagen because he was doing session work with Steve Barn during the day, Steely Dan at night, and Johnny Winter on the weekends, and somehow he kept going. Although he was a workaholic, the nickname can also be attributed to the time he was working at Cherokee Studios and two of the tape machines were grounded improperly. Nichols touched both of the machines and shorted out the whole system. Although the faceplate on one of the machines was completely melted, Nichols escaped unscathed. Something that to this day is inexplicable.

Nichols would be the sole engineer on their first four albums and would continue to work with Steely Dan, Donald Fagen, and Walter Becker on all of their projects until 2003's *Everything Must Go*; he would also continue to engineer the majority of Gary Katz's productions. Nichols always thought outside of the box, whether he was creating an eight-bar twenty four-track tape loop for "Show Biz Kids"; identifying a flaw on the master tape of "Rikki Don't Lose That Number" (when that part of the tape was sent back to the manufacturer, a workman's gob of mustard was discovered to be the culprit); recovering the sound on their fourth album, *Katy Lied*, which had suffered significantly when the master tape was processed through a faulty dbx noise reduction system; inventing the Wendel sampling computer, a new technique of digital drum replacement that was used on *Gaucho* and is now the norm in music production; or inventing a rubidium nuclear clock to more successfully synchronize digital recording equipment in the studio. His role as Steely Dan's engineer had a huge effect on the sound of their records, and he proved to be the perfect partner in the group's quest for perfection.

Nichols has won eight Grammy Awards, including four for "Best Engineered Recording, Non-Classical" for *Aja* in 1977, "FM (No Static At All)" (the only time the award was given for a single song) in 1978, *Gaucho* in 1981, and *Two Against Nature* in 2000. *Two Against Nature* gave him two more wins for Best Pop Vocal Album and Album of the Year. He won his only Grammy Award as a producer in 1997 for Best Children's Album for John Denver's *All Aboard!* and received a Special Merit/Technical Grammy Award for "contributions of outstanding technical significance to the recording field" in 2012.

In May 2010, Nichols was diagnosed with stage 4 pancreatic cancer and passed away less than a year later on April 9, 2011. His *New York Times* obituary was titled "Roger Nichols, Artist Among Sound Engineers, Dies at 66." Nichols had been a columnist for *EQ* magazine for a number of years and had written material to be used as a master class textbook, but he didn't live to see his work published. However, in 2013, *The Roger Nichols Recording Method* was published by Alfred Music Publishing, whose CEO, Ron Manus, was once Nichols's second engineer.

In 2011, Marc Myers interviewed Donald Fagen for *JazzWax*, and although they had fired engineer Roger Nichols unceremoniously, and hadn't checked on his health issues, Fagen was complimentary when speaking of his talents and what he brought to the Steely Dan sound. "Roger was able to execute the kind of production we were looking for in terms of sound. From the beginning . . . Walter and I were looking for the hi-fidelity sound that you didn't hear too much in rock music at the time. Roger was familiar with the jazz records that Walter and I used to listen to growing up . . . and taught us about recording. . . . The ideal engineer for all of us was Rudy Van Gelder. The technique he used was simple but not that easy to get down in a studio. A studio isn't live. It's kind of dry and clear."

Fagen Has the Last Words

In the 1974 *Rolling Stone* cover story on the band Fagen stated, "What I like about our group . . . outside of our technical accomplishments . . . our music scares me more than anybody else's. The combination of the words with the music—like a cheerful lyric and a sad or menacing melody, or vice versa—I find the irony frightening, the idea that somebody would think of recording that. I am attracted to music that frightens me. Not music about doom and melodrama—that kind of stuff isn't really frightening. What's really frightening is mediocrity. The mediocrity of everyday life, the mediocrity we see around us. That frightens me."

7

A Wailin' Combo

The First Two Steely Dan Albums

While Denny Dias was still making his way across the country, ABC Dunhill president Jay Lasker had realized that Becker and Fagen were not meant to be staff writers, although he and A&R man Steve Barri thought that a Carole King-type song entitled "Proud to Be Your Slave" had potential and could work for one of their artists. Eddie Lambert, who worked for the publishing department at ABC Dunhill and had been responsible for bringing Katz to L.A., considered it the best song that Steely Dan never recorded, but unfortunately for Becker and Fagen, Lambert was unable to place it, so it wasn't recorded by anybody else at the time either. It was, however, covered in 1975 by a group based in Hawaii named Diamond Head produced by Lambert's brother Dennis and Brian Potter for their Haven label, distributed by Capitol Records. It was released as the B-side to "All for the Love of Music" but didn't have much success, and the band never recorded a full album.

Another song that caught the ears of Lasker and Barry was "Dirty Work." They thought it would be perfect for either the Grass Roots or Three Dog Night. They also believed it could be a huge hit for the band that was forming around their two headstrong staff writers. Lasker and Barri were now aware that Katz, Becker, and Fagen always thought that they needed their own band to interpret their material successfully and that this had been the plan from the minute they stepped foot in L.A. Becker and Fagen had been renting and buying equipment for their new band and charging it to ABC Dunhill, but once the powers that be were aware of their intentions, and indiscretions, rather than fire the two renegade composers, they decided to back the band that was being formed—renegade style.

Critics and fans alike have often spoke of the "Steely Dan Sound," but the band would reinvent itself, to a certain degree, from one album to the next. It's possible to divide their recording career into four distinct periods: the band years (*Can't Buy a Thrill*, *Countdown to Ecstasy*, and *Pretzel Logic*), the workshop years (*Katy Lied* and *The Royal Scam*), the jazzy platinum years (*Aja* and *Gaucho*), and the comeback years (*Two Against Nature* and *Everything Must Go*). Like any band, the lead vocalist has quite a lot do to with their sound, and while one might perceive that Steely Dan was always a jazz-rock group, Becker and Fagen developed not only their songwriting over time, but the presentation of their compositions. It's impossible to compare a song like "Reelin' in the Years" to "Babylon Sisters" without noting the major stylistic differences, and overall production, between the two. Although *Pretzel Logic* is technically a "band" album, it was the first LP where Becker and

Fagen began to move toward using the studio as a workshop and hired more session musicians than ever before. So this chapter will cover the true "band" albums from the first period with a detailed discussion of each song from their debut single and first two albums.

The First Single—"Dallas" b/w "Sail the Waterway"

Although Lasker and Barri were behind the project, the contract stipulated that a single needed to be released before the album. Becker, Fagen, Baxter, Hodder, and background vocalist Tim Moore entered the studio to cut their first single, "Dallas" b/w "Sail the Waterway," a single that would sound like no other Steely Dan record. The A-side is almost a simpler, less successful version of "Any Major Dude Will Tell You" from their third LP, *Pretzel Logic*. Fagen's Wurlitzer electric piano and Baxter's pedal steel guitar are the highlights, and while Hodder's vocals are acceptable, one could only imagine how much better it would have sounded with Fagen singing. The addition of congas played by Baxter halfway through the song lifts it significantly and helps the song cruise to its ending, but the powers that be realized that it may have been too country sounding for the group's initial release, and the song disappeared quickly.

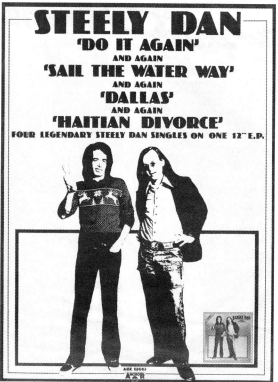

Steely Dan's debut single "Dallas" b/w "Sail the Waterway" got a limited release in 1972 and was quickly withdrawn. Five years later, a 12″ EP was released in the U.K. with the A-side of their 1976 U.K.-only single "Haitian Divorce" along with "Do It Again" and the two rarely heard songs from their first single.

Fagen took over lead vocal duties on the B-side, "Sail the Waterway," a ballad that contains some Steely Danish chord changes and melodic content. Baxter's short double-tracked solo is quite effective, and the background vocals on the chorus add significantly to the simple yet catchy hook. The song would definitely have fit on *Can't Buy a Thrill* better than the A-side, and it's a shame that Becker and Fagen consider it "stinko" and haven't allowed the song to be released on CD.

When Dias finally arrived in Los Angeles, he was surprised to hear their first single as well as the songs slated for inclusion on their debut album. He was used to the odder, more eccentric compositions he had recorded in New York City as demos, for the *You Gotta Walk It Like You Talk It* soundtrack, and even for Linda Hoover, and was shocked that the duo, in his opinion, had changed gears so drastically. By the time he had arrived, the single had already been withdrawn, and the Dan were ready to begin work on their debut LP in the summer of 1972. Make no mistake, as everything else had been for Becker and Fagen, this was a calculated move.

Can't Buy a Thrill

Becker, Fagen, and Katz had finally assembled what they thought was the perfect team to fully realize the obscure, esoteric compositions that were written with the express intention of being recorded by a "band." Engineer Roger Nichols was such an important piece of the puzzle that the sessions were postponed until he returned from his vacation, something that annoyed ABC Dunhill's president Jay Lasker to no end. A&R man Steve Barri, who had helped to secure Steely Dan's deal, advocated for the group and assured Lasker that they were worth the time and expense. They entered the Village Recorder in West Los Angeles and began recording the tracks for their debut LP with producer Gary Katz and engineer Roger Nichols, but from day one Becker and Fagen knew what they wanted from the music. Nichols was astonished at how well they worked together. In a 1993 interview with Brian Sweet for the *Metal Leg* fanzine he elaborated on the duo's working relationship and how it was a fifty-fifty operation. "Either one of them could've done the records alone, but you can tell there is a difference when both of them bounce ideas off each other. They seem to know what's going to fill a little hole in a chorus that won't be recorded for a year. We never have to do things over again because of arrangement problems or because one instrument conflicts with another. Stuff will get done over again because a player's style won't match the tune, or a player's execution isn't good enough, or the horn section is out of tune, or something like that."

So with Becker and Fagen taking such a hands-on role in the producer's chair, what was Gary Katz's function in the studio? Nichols's somewhat tongue-in-cheek opinion: hiring and firing musicians. In a more serious tone, Nichols believed that Katz was best at getting the most out of Fagen as a vocalist. Since Becker and Fagen would lead the musicians for the most part, Katz's role was more as an executive producer. He was the third opinion that might break a tie, if one came up.

Session bass player Chuck Rainey, who began playing with Steely Dan on *Pretzel Logic*, spoke of Katz's role as producer on the Steely Dan sessions on his website. "Gary Katz . . . was indeed the most important person in the success of Steely Dan recordings. He was the continuity director of personnel and held everything together with a watchful eye representing the record company . . . Although the songs written by Donald and Walter were exceptional in their apparent value as songs, Gary's experience with and knowledge of the ability, success and prominence of valued studio players hired, was the link that tied the project together." But this was still 1972, and Steely Dan was, for all intents and purposes, a five-piece rock band, so Katz's expertise as a wrangler of session musicians was not as important at this stage of the game.

The album allegedly took its title from the opening lines of Bob Dylan's "It Takes a Lot to Laugh, It Takes a Train to Cry" from his sixth studio album, the 1965 masterpiece *Highway 61 Revisited*. The line reads, "Well, I ride on a mail train, baby/Can't buy a thrill." However, another explanation came from Fagen, who attributes the title to a conversation he had with Becker, who stated, "You can't buy a thrill in California." Their debut was quite eclectic, with a clever blend of rock, jazz, and Latin-tinged grooves, and although Becker and Fagen's lyrics weren't as obtuse as the ones from the majority of songs they were pedaling in New York, they were still enigmatic and introduced the types of desperate, sordid characters that live on the fringes of society yet still deal with the heartbreak and frustration that most people can relate to.

The original idea for the record cover was a young girl looking into a pornographic shop as the owner leers at her from inside. They did a photo shoot with Katz's daughter, but luckily, greater heads prevailed and the idea was scrapped. Their second choice was a still from Billy Wilder's 1963 *Irma La Douce* starring Jack Lemmon and Shirley MacLaine, but due to copyright issues, their plan B was abandoned as well. The cover ended up being a somewhat tacky collage of prostitutes, a shirtless man, a nude woman cowering, and a pair of large lips conceived by Robert Lockart. The band immediately disliked it, but due to time constraints, it would be the way that Steely Dan would be visually introduced to their audience. In the liner notes for the reissue of their fifth album, 1976's *The Royal Scam*, the duo

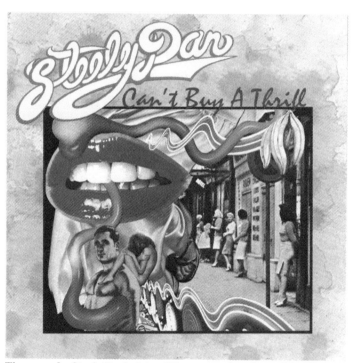

The cover for Steely Dan's debut LP was not what they originally envisioned, and they have called it one of the worst record covers of the '70s.

expressed their dislike for that cover as well, stating that it was "the most hideous album cover of the '70s, bar none (excepting perhaps *Can't Buy a Thrill*)." Becker and Fagen wrote the cryptic liner notes under the pseudonym Tristan Fabriani, Fagen's stage name during the Jay and the Americans years.

Reviews were generally favorable, but in hindsight it's odd to see what groups they were compared to by rock critics. James Isaacs's November 23, 1972, review for *Rolling Stone* was one of the first and noted, "many of the idiosyncratic touches of Fagen and Becker were scrapped in favor of a more salable songbook." He went on to compare the group to Crosby, Stills, Nash & Young; Procol Harum; Spirit; the Band; Moby Grape; and Motown and praised "Do It Again," "Dirty Work," and "Reelin' in the Years," but felt that as a whole the album wasn't consistent. Infamously tough critic Robert Christgau initially gave the album a B+ for *Creem* magazine when it was released but in 1981 changed his rating to an A, stating rather verbosely, "Think of the Dan as the first post-boogie band: the beat swings more than it blasts or blisters, the chord changes defy our primitive subconscious expectations, and the lyrics underline their own difficulty—as well as the difficulty of the reality to which they refer—with arbitrary personal allusions, most of which are ruses."

Interestingly, Isaacs was a drummer friend of Becker and Fagen's from their years at Bard College, and overall his *Rolling Stone* review was not very flattering. The duo were upset and even mentioned it in an interview:

> Donald Fagen: We got a terrible review in *Rolling Stone* today. A friend of ours, too.

> Walter Becker: You wanna dig it? That guy used to play with us. Jim Isaacs is a drummer we went to college with. We go back years and years.

The next year, Isaacs reviewed *Countdown to Ecstasy* for *Down Beat* magazine, giving it four-and-a-half stars out of a possible five and stated that the album was, "a consistently engaging, meticulously produced set that coheres beautifully."

Some critics also noticed that David Palmer's vocals didn't really fit in with the rest of the band, and although his voice sweetly sang the darker, misogynistic lyrics of "Dirty Work," somehow his approach wasn't entirely convincing. The album peaked at number seventeen on the *Billboard* Top Pop Album chart and spawned two hit singles, "Do It Again," which reached number six on the *Billboard* Hot 100, and "Reelin' in the Years," which peaked at number eleven in the *Billboard* charts. So Steely Dan had a top twenty album along with two singles that reached the top ten and top twenty respectively, but what did this debut sound like?

The Songs

Steely Dan's debut is arguably their most rock 'n' roll album, and while the songs hint at their jazz leanings, it is the work of a band still trying to find itself. The songs are eclectic, with Latin-flavored rhythms, all-out rockers, ballads, and bluesy workouts, but they only show a glimpse of what's to come in the future.

"Do It Again" (Traditional)

Becker and Fagen wrote all of the material for their debut album, but on the liner notes, "Do It Again" is listed as a "trad" (for traditional) song, the first of many fabrications that the two would put on liner notes and tell in interviews, constantly keeping fans, critics, and reporters on their feet. As Fagen has said, "You should never believe anything it says on a Steely Dan record." The song is one of their simplest harmonically, with only five chords that all fall within one key, something that is quite rare for a Becker and Fagen composition.

The almost six-minute song, with an intro that is over a minute long, was edited by one minute and forty-two seconds for single release by shortening the intro and outro and cutting out Fagen's organ solo played on a rented Yamaha YC-30, something that Becker and Fagen agreed to reluctantly. The YC-30 was an odd instrument because it was an organ with a felt strip used to bend notes, hence the strange sound of the keyboard solo. Another instrument of note was the electric sitar played by Denny Dias for the first solo of the song. The band allegedly wanted to rent an acoustic sitar for the song but couldn't procure one, so they settled for an electric sitar. It would be hard to imagine such a fluid solo played on an acoustic sitar by somebody who had never had one in his hands. Dias's solo is truly a highlight.

The Latin-flavored tune was accentuated by Victor Feldman's percussion and grooves effortlessly with Becker's pulsing bass line, Fagen's Wurlitzer electric

The German picture sleeve for the "Do It Again" single.

piano, and Baxter and Dias providing rhythm guitars while Hodder holds it down behind the kit. "Do It Again" tells the story of a murderer who should be hung for his crime but is let go instead. He continues to live life as a degenerate gambler and a sex addict, and Becker and Fagen tell the story of each facet of his personality over three verses, with a hook that proves that he can't change his ways. The song presented a truer essence of Steely Dan's sound and proved to be a much better introduction to the band than their aborted single "Dallas." The songwriters were proud of the song at the time but believed that it was only a starting point and that the band could only grow from there.

For a band that was so meticulous in the studio, there is a glaring mistake in Becker's bass part at the beginning of the second chorus (2:28). Rather than play the Cm7 chord, Becker continues to play the Gm7 chord from the verse for the first two beats before realizing his error. The song peaked at number six on the U.S. charts in 1973, the second-highest-charting single that Steely Dan would ever release.

"Dirty Work" (How's my little girl?)

One of the two songs that were given to last-minute addition, vocalist David Palmer, was "Dirty Work." The song actually suited his voice well and his smooth delivery made the dour lyrics that much more striking against the mellow groove. The main character of the song is so obsessed with another man's partner that he is willing to be humiliated and "come running" whenever this femme fatale's husband is away. A true tale of self-loathing if there ever was one. Becker and Fagen weren't too fond of the song and didn't want to include it on the album, but they realized its commercial potential, and it became one of their most well-known compositions.

The song's intro is sublime with a blend of Hammond B3 organ, Wurlitzer electric piano, rhythm guitar, and Steely Dan's first use of a horn section to create a moody tapestry for the sordid tale that follows. The simple two-part harmony of tenor saxophonist Jerome Richardson and flügelhorn player Snooky Young fit the mood of the song perfectly, and the darker tone of the flügelhorn works much better than the brighter-sounding trumpet would have.

Richardson was already an established jazz musician who had played with Charles Mingus, Dizzy Gillespie, Lionel Hampton, the Thad Jones/Mel Lewis Big Band, Kenny Burrell, Sarah Vaughn, Cannonball Adderley, Quincy Jones, Harry Belafonte, and countless others before he entered the studio for this Steely Dan session. Not only did he play the horn section parts, he laid down a superbly executed solo for the only song on the Dan's debut album with horns. During the solo section, the groove changes suddenly, and a new chord progression is introduced, building to a climax with the Hammond B3's spinning Leslie speaker switching gears from slow to fast, leading us into a final chorus.

Snooky Young was also a veteran jazz player, having done sessions and live dates with Count Basie, Lionel Hampton, the Thad Jones/Mel Lewis Big Band, Ray Charles, Charles Mingus, Jimmy Smith, and Tony Bennett, to name a few. His longest gig, however, was in Doc Severinsen's *Tonight Show* band, which he joined in 1967 and left in 1992 when Jay Leno took over for Johnny Carson and hired a new, smaller band led by saxophonist Branford Marsalis.

The chorus emphasizes a brash acoustic guitar part, rare for a Steely Dan song, that lifts the song to a higher level at the ideal moment as the Hammond B3 organ re-enters and the double-tracked background vocals soar. These subtle nuances are apparent even at this early juncture and show how Becker and Fagen knew exactly what each song needed to create the perfect sonic landscape and how Katz and Nichols could help to bring their ideas to fruition. From the very beginning, Becker and Fagen followed the lead of Lennon and McCartney, and even in the simplest of songs, they would inject at least one non-diatonic chord, a chord that was foreign to the key of the song. "Dirty Work" is a good example of that technique, something that would develop and be used in later compositions.

The song appeared in the first episode of the third season of *The Sopranos*, entitled "Mr. Ruggerio's Neighborhood" in an entertaining scene where Tony Soprano sings along to the song while driving his SUV. It also appeared in one of the key opening scenes in the movie *American Hustle*, but when the songwriters were approached about having the song on the soundtrack, they refused, even though Elton John, Paul McCartney, ELO, America, and Donna Summer signed off on the soundtrack.

"Kings" (No political significance)
The story of the death of King Richard the 1st of England in 1199 and the political turmoil that followed before his brother John Lackland ascended to the throne is hardly subject matter for a pop song, but Becker and Fagen thought it was fair game and composed "Kings." Apparently singer-songwriter Al Stewart, best known for his hit "Year of the Cat," thought that Richard the 1st was an interesting character as well. He included a line about him in the song "Soho" from his album *Past, Present, and Future* released the same year as *Can't Buy a Thrill*. Becker and Fagen's humor is also apparent in the disclaimer for "Kings" on the back cover: "No political significance," possibly in order to keep listeners from thinking that they were singing about Richard Nixon and John F. Kennedy.

The song is one of the more rock 'n' roll moments on the album and again borrows chords from other keys, creating an ambiguous mood. The song features deft piano playing by Fagen, double-tracked on the arpeggios at the top of the verses; heavy rhythm guitar playing by Baxter and Dias; percussion by Victor Feldman; and a smoking, schizophrenic solo by session guitarist Elliott Randall that he attributed to the personal troubles he was experiencing at the time. His first marriage had broken up earlier that year, and Randall let his feelings guide him through an emotional rollercoaster that begins melodically and ends up in cacophony with a second guitar overdubbed at a crucial moment in its development.

"Kings" is the first Steely Dan song to shine the spotlight on female background vocalists Clydie King, Shirley Matthews, and Venetta Fields, singers who had been used on numerous Gary Katz productions before and after Steely Dan. Interestingly, Steely Dan would add two female background vocalists and one male background vocalist to augment the sound on their second tour in 1973, but dropped the female vocalists for their third and final tour of the '70s because they thought it was too showbiz-like. Female background vocalists would be used on every Steely Dan album except for *Pretzel Logic* and on every tour they would embark on from the '90s onward.

"Midnight Cruiser" (The cruiser and his cronie out for a last fling)
"Midnight Cruiser" is a tale of two friends reminiscing about how they've become somewhat obsolete in this ever-changing world. The image of driving, the use of the term "gentleman loser," and the destination of Harlem make the song a precursor to "Deacon Blues" and visits numerous themes that would be explored in later Steely Dan songs. Fagen believed that while the song set a mood, it didn't actually say much. Drummer Jim Hodder had already sung the quickly withdrawn A-side of their first single "Dallas," and when he offered to sing "Midnight Cruiser," Becker and Fagen were immediately responsive to the idea.

The song was one of their earlier compositions that they thought could work along with some of the newer ones for their debut LP. The song's sections are quite distinct, beginning with a verse that glides along easily with a laid-back sidestick drum groove, a lilting bass line similar to "Deacon Blues," delicate piano playing, and a jazzy guitar part. The pre-chorus builds into the harmony-heavy chorus where the guitar gets heavier, and an added bar of two beats adds to the anticipation of a section that kicks into full gear. Baxter's double-tracked guitar lead adds another dimension to the song and builds into a solo that takes the song into the final chorus, which has a melody that sounds extremely similar to the Hollies' "Dear Eloise," the lead-off track from their second album, *Butterfly*, released in 1967.

"Only a Fool Would Say That" (A message cha-cha)
The Latin flavor of "Do It Again" returns with the A-side closer, "Only a Fool Would Say That," the B-side of "Reelin' in the Years." This time the song is less of a Latin-tinged rock 'n' roll number like the album's first single and is more of a lightweight samba/rock tune used to close the first side of the album.

The song's imagery paints a picture of two disparate characters, one for each verse; the first, a more optimistic hippie-like character, the second a downtrodden working stiff. The cynicism comes each time the narrator reminds the characters that their dreams are unrealistic by stating the title of the song. The bridge adds another level of misanthropic paranoia with the opening line, "Anybody on the street has murder in his eyes," and the unexpected change of key.

"Only a Fool Would Say That" is a perfect example of dark lyrics with a light tune. The soothing rhythm guitar, doubled on acoustic, gives the listener a false sense of security with its laid-back West Coast vibe. Jeff Baxter plays some tasty melodic licks during the intro and throughout the song, but adds some fire and gets a slightly more aggressive tone for the short solo after the bridge, a perfectly executed companion to the somewhat dire sentiment of the previous section. The song concludes with the title spoken in Spanish by Baxter. Bookending the first side of the album with two Latin-flavored tunes is a brilliant way to sequence the Dan's introduction to the record-buying public.

"Reelin' in the Years" (How's my little girl?)

Side B begins with the group's second top twenty hit, "Reelin' in the Years." The song is a conversation between a man and a woman who were once romantically involved, but have now split up due to the fact that the woman has found another partner that she believes can give her the life that she craves. The narrator is heartbroken, but expresses this by belittling his old flame and putting himself on a pedestal. The line "The weekend at the college didn't turn out like you planned" is possibly a veiled reference to the drug bust at Bard College that involved Becker, Fagen, and Fagen's girlfriend, Dorothy White (see chapter two).

Once again Elliott Randall comes through with some stinging guitar work. Randall knew Becker and Fagen from New York and had played some gigs with Jay and the Americans and on some of their early demos. Jeff Baxter also knew Randall, and when he was unable to nail a satisfactory guitar lead for the song, he invited Randall in to take a stab at it. His first pass, which some at the session say was better, wasn't recorded. He took a second pass, and the song was complete with no editing or punch-ins. Jimmy Page of Led Zeppelin has stated that it is his favorite guitar solo of all time.

The song bounces along nicely with Hodder's groovy shuffle, Becker's bubbling bass line, Fagen's syncopated piano part, and Baxter and Dias laying down some chunky rhythm guitars. Baxter's alternate take on a swampy blues riff during the intro and chorus is ingenious and adds a gutbucket quality to the proceedings. During their early tours, Fagen would sing the song live, rather than passing it over to David Palmer, and all six members of the band would contribute vocals. The quadraphonic mix of the song has some extra guitar fills played by Randall during the first half of the choruses not heard on the more familiar stereo version.

"Fire in the Hole" (How's my little girl?)

Fagen's piano is the star here and shows how talented he was as a player while also indicating his limitations. As Becker and Fagen's material developed, they realized that they were looking for a more fluid playing style and enlisted keyboard players such as Michael Omartian, David Paich, Victor Feldman, Paul Griffin, Don Grolnick, and others to achieve this on certain tracks. However, Fagen could definitely groove, and his mix of bluesy, Thelonious Monk–like playing with the more cascading, flowery choices on the bridges make "Fire in the Hole" one of the keyboard high points of the album.

Baxter's pedal steel playing throughout the song provides a pad-like quality behind Fagen's strident piano, but the solo he plays that closes the song is unforgettable and is yet another moment that shows how important his pedal steel was to Steely Dan's early sound. His approach to pedal steel was quite unusual and doesn't necessarily evoke a country flavor. Rather it brings together the bluesy elements of his lead guitar work when soloing along with a subtle melodicism used when playing behind a vocalist.

The title of the song was a phrase originally used by miners, and later by soldiers, to warn others that a charge had been set. The song tells the story of a man, possibly a veteran, whose life is spiraling out of control as he loses himself to madness. It was one of their earlier compositions, written before they arrived in Los Angeles, but is harmonically elaborate, moving through different keys before the listener can get grounded. This complements the mysterious, ominous nature of the lyrics; and the stark production of drums, bass, piano, pedal steel guitar, and solo vocal provides the perfect vehicle to showcase this underrated Steely Dan gem. It was another one of their older songs resurrected for the album, not written for commercial appeal, and therefore is rather involved, with chord changes that weave in and out of keys in an abrupt, yet never jarring manner. The song would also be the B-side to "Do It Again."

"Brooklyn (Owes the Charmer Under Me)" (President Street Pete is the beneficiary here)
This song served as David Palmer's second, and last, lead vocal on a Steely Dan album. As with "Dirty Work," his voice suits the gentler nature of the song, and his approach works well. "Brooklyn" was another old song demoed during the Kenny Vance years. The demo of the song originally included an additional verse (the second) not heard in the final released version and was sung by Fagen, with Becker taking over the vocals on the third verse.

For *Can't Buy a Thrill*, Fagen's organ intro heard on the demo is played by Dias on guitar, but the majority of the melody was already in place. The demo even has the double-time percussion, although it would be toned down on the final recording. The addition of Baxter's pedal steel guitar plays a big role in the creation of the melancholy vibe of the song, and his simple solo (double-tracked at times) is exquisite. Dias adds flavor with tasteful rhythm playing, lead riffs, as well as the aforementioned intro and outro. Hodder and Becker provide a rock-solid groove that adds the funk to what is essentially a ballad. Becker shows how adept he is, with some clever fills and octave work during the solo. It is the second of two songs from the album with female vocals courtesy of Clydie King, Shirley Matthews, and Venetta Fields, something that would become an increasingly important element of their later songs.

The song was written about "President Street Pete," the tenant who lived under Fagen's apartment at 904 President Street in the Park Slope neighborhood of Brooklyn. It tells the tale of what they imagined Pete was owed, as Becker stated, "for the indignities that they suffered living in Brooklyn, sitting on the stoop and just shooting the shit about the Mets and that kind of thing for 20 years." The lyrics list some of the perks he could have including money, lavish hotel rooms, Hollywood starlets, and gambling prowess as well as a verse about his wife, who has never been happy with their social position, or lack thereof.

The chord progression and melody of the beginning of the verse are similar to Bob Dylan's "Queen Jane Approximately" from 1965's *Highway 61 Revisited*, but the similarities stop after the first eight bars. The song's harmonic content and melody stretch far beyond Dylan's as it moves into the pre-chorus. The chordal twists that occur leading into the chorus add an unexpected tension that highlights the lyrical content before coming back to earth for a chorus that is more grounded, but still harmonically ambiguous. The song was never released as a single, but has proved to be a favorite among Steely Dan's fans.

"Change of the Guard" (Remember this one from college?)
"Change of the Guard" is one of the simplest songs on Steely Dan's debut album melodically, harmonically, and lyrically. The melody of the verse is similar to Crosby, Stills & Nash's 1969 song "Pre-Road Downs," but is such a typical melody that it is entirely possible that it's a coincidence. The song is a subtle hippie anthem that serves as notice to the "straights" that times are changing and they need to accept the inevitable. Harmonically, it contains only one true "surprise" for the ear when they reach the pre-chorus. The groove is fairly straightforward as well, with a simple drumbeat, a clever bass line, a groovy Wurlitzer electric piano part, appropriately placed guitar stabs and rhythmic playing, and a wordless "Na na na" hook, something that would never be done in another Steely Dan song. Once again, however, Baxter steals the show with his lead guitar work. After the relative tameness of the song, Baxter enters with a fierce solo, playing double time over Wurlitzer stabs and a fluid bass line accenting the hits. He concludes with a two-bar, overdubbed, distorted slide that moves from the right channel to the left; a perfect ending to an exceptional solo.

"Turn That Heartbeat Over Again" (A solemn prayer for peace)
We move from what is the simplest song on the album to what is arguably the most complex, with a plethora of key changes and a challenging arrangement. From a songwriting perspective, it seems as if Becker and Fagen took a page from the Lennon and McCartney playbook of combining a number of unfinished ideas to create a complete song. The lyrics cover several popular Steely Dan themes that would consistently be revisited throughout their career: thievery, drinking, literature, paranoia, etc. The song tells the story of a heist gone wrong and the problems that ensue, but the imagery afforded various interpretations including patricide, child abuse, and myriad religious connotations. The song also contains a sly reference to Mark Twain with the lyric, "We warned the corpse of William Wright, not to cuss and drink all night." Wright was the actual name of Dan De Quille, a fellow reporter of Twain's on the *Virginia City Enterprise* in the 1860s.

"Turn That Heartbeat Over Again" is a curious track for many reasons. The first: the vocals are shared by Fagen, Hodder, and Becker, the only time Becker would sing lead on a Steely Dan track until "Slang of Ages" from 2003's *Everything Must Go* LP. Listen for him during the "Love your mama" section. The song begins with a verse featuring country-like guitar picking prominently, but after four bars they switch gears for an accent-filled section before moving to a full-on groove. The sudden key changes and quick movement from one feel to another are quite sophisticated for early Dan and an indication of what Becker and Fagen would accomplish as composers later in their career.

The extended middle section sounds simple yet is quite complicated, introducing new melodic and harmonic content, with a few time signature curveballs, only heard during this thirty-bar instrumental section. It had definitely been worked on in advance, with Baxter and Fagen harmonizing during the second half of the section. Many have disregarded this early foray into the extended form, but it is a true testament to the ingenuity of Becker and Fagen as songwriters, even at this early juncture of their career. The wind chimes that close the song, and hence the album, aren't too bad either.

Conclusion

Denny Dias summed up his opinion of the album succinctly in a 1973 interview with Penny Valentine for *Sounds*. "I guess the people who say it sounds thrown together are right . . . Equally the ones who like it . . . it's fairly decent by any standards. Really we had just started learning to play together at that time. I guess I am a perfectionist but *Can't Buy a Thrill* is the worst album we'll ever make. Some of the songs on the album were written years ago and I think the older stuff tended to be stronger. I think Donald and Walter wrote the other numbers—the more commercial stuff—to get the record companies interested. I've always felt the writing was better on the more sophisticated numbers like 'Turn That Heartbeat' and 'Fire in the Hole.' That's going to be the bone of tone of the next album." Noting that Becker and Fagen have since considered the album "juvenile," it seems that Dias's take on their debut LP was on point.

Countdown to Ecstasy

For Steely Dan's second album, they decided to stretch a bit, something that resulted in longer songs and fewer sales. Whereas *Can't Buy a Thrill*'s songs were typically three to four minutes long, with only the album version of "Do It Again" reaching almost six minutes, the majority of the songs on their sophomore release were over five minutes long, with "Your Gold Teeth" clocking in at over seven minutes.

Fagen thought that they had possibly been typecast from *Can't Buy a Thrill*, but he and Becker still weren't sure that they knew what type of group Steely Dan was. Fagen in particular found it peculiar that their audience could find a particular theme to the songs that was never intended. In addition, many fans were unsure of how to label their music, as were Becker and Fagen.

Their second album was recorded in between tour dates, something that was not ideal for the writing partners. It left them little time to work, and often lyrics were devised at the last minute. They wouldn't be billed as headliners until after *Countdown to Ecstasy* was released, so their status as the second- or third-billed act didn't make the touring process any easier. A number of the headlining acts were rather juvenile and often wouldn't let opening bands sound check for fear that they might actually sound better than them. As Becker and Fagen would state themselves in the liner notes to the 1998 reissue of the album, "Public humiliation of the type we were subjected to as a result of some of our appearances during this period . . . while in the long run perhaps a powerful character-building element in the young lives of the authors, in the short term proved disruptive and generally detrimental to the creative process."

Baxter stated that Becker and Fagen had intended to write a mini-opera about a marine, and the final song was about his quest to find female companionship, which would suggest the title of the album, but they were worried about the problems that could arise from the State Department, so the idea was dropped.

Countdown to Ecstasy was the only Steely Dan album that was written with the members of the band in mind. Generally Becker and Fagen would come up with the basic idea for the song and play it for the band in rehearsal. They would then work together to develop the arrangement, with Baxter in particular contributing essential parts for each composition. This environment led to a true "band" sound and gives the album a unique flavor in the Steely Dan canon.

It was also the only album recorded as a five piece with the departure of singer David Palmer. Becker and Fagen recalled one of the last gigs of their first tour in Phoenix, Arizona, as one of the moments that they realized they should revert to their original concept of a five-man band. The extreme Arizona heat caused many of the band members to overindulge in the local beer for fear of dehydration. The resulting show was not to Becker and Fagen's standards, but as they stated in the liner notes for the remastered version of *Countdown to Ecstasy*, "The upshot of this soul-rattling experience was that the six-man configuration inaugurated towards the end of the recording of *Can't Buy a Thrill* was deemed obsolete: the band reverted to its original five-man lineup, with David Palmer departing for greener pastures without having sung a note on the actual *Countdown* recording." Although he is credited with background vocals, it seems as if his parts never made the final cut. Fagen was still hesitant about being a full-time vocalist and he and Becker considered both Gerry Rafferty, then of Stealers Wheel, and Elliott Lurie, the singer from Looking Glass, who had a number one hit with "Brandy (You're a Fine

Steely Dan's *Countdown to Ecstasy* cover was a painting by Fagen's then-girlfriend Dorothy White, credited as Dotty from Hollywood.

Girl)," for the lead vocal position. But nothing came of these far-fetched plans, and Donald Fagen would become the lead vocalist for Steely Dan.

Although the album was a true band recording, they used more session musicians for *Countdown to Ecstasy* than they had for *Can't Buy a Thrill*. Victor Feldman returned on percussion and also added vibraphone and marimba, and background vocalist Shirley Matthews (listed as Sherlie Matthews) was the only singer from their debut album to sing on their second. Matthews's cousin Myrna was added to the larger stable of background vocalists that included Patricia Hall, Royce Jones, James Rolleston, and Michael Fenelly. Legendary jazz bassist Ray Brown played acoustic bass on "Razor Boy"; guitarist, and old friend Rick Derringer added slide guitar to "Show Biz Kids." Ben Benay played acoustic guitar; and saxophonists Bill Perkins, Ernie Watts, John Rotella, and Lanny Morgan were brought in to played Jimmie Haskell's arrangement for "My Old School."

Becker and Fagen had been unhappy with the artwork for *Can't Buy a Thrill*, so for their second album, Fagen's girlfriend Dorothy White painted a surreal watercolor of three naked aliens. This time it was ABC Dunhill Records president Jay Lasker who had an issue with the cover art. He wondered why there were only three aliens when there were five band members. Although she explained that it wasn't a depiction of the band, Lasker had her add two figures standing behind the others. She was credited on the album as Dotty of Hollywood.

The reviews were again favorable, for the most part, and critics seemed to "get" what Steely Dan was about. *Billboard* stated in their July 14, 1973, review, "It's delightful to hear an LP by an act which has had a hit single and discover how much musical ability the act has. That's the end result of this LP: there's lots of music, vocal and instrumental from these five players. A number of influences run through this material—from the 1950's runs of 'Bodhisattva'; to the jazz-oriented electric piano runs on 'Your Gold Teeth' to the full richness of controlled rock." *Rolling Stone*'s David Logan stated in the August 16, 1973, issue, "It is this ability to play four- to five-minute rock songs in a jaunty, up-tempo fashion without becoming redundant or superfluous that may well make Steely Dan the American dance-band alternative to Slade. *Countdown to Ecstasy* is far from an ambitious statement of a progressive musical philosophy; in fact, one could perhaps argue that the Steelies have found a formula and are exploiting it. Well, for my part, if it takes exploitation of a formula to get the dilettantes and the glitter boys back to playing rock, then I'll go back, Jack, and do it again, with Steely Dan."

Even the reviews that weren't stellar still recommended the album. Steven X Rea's review from November 1973's issue of Music World focused on one song, "The Boston Rag," stating, "I recommend this LP wholeheartedly to anyone. Steely Dan isn't one of my favorite groups, but this is a good album with one triple A special deluxe number, penned by Walter Becker and Donald Fagen, as was the rest of the LP. Denny Dias, Jeff 'Skunk' Baxter, and Jim Hodder round out the band. Bring back that Ol' Boston Rag, just one more time, anytime." Mick Gold from *Let It Rock* wasn't impressed by the first side of the album but still wasn't that negative: "I don't feel like recommending an album with eight songs on it, four of which managed to pass through my head without producing any noticeable effect.

But 'Show Biz Kids' really is a great song and there's a lot of low-key intelligence at work on this record. Look for the single, or pick up the album cheap."

The Songs

Steely Dan's second LP would be the only one recorded with the original five members of the band and shows more interplay between the players musically. The songs are longer, with more solos that shine the spotlight not only on Baxter and Dias but Fagen as well. There are still the all-out rockers that fans had grown to love, but there are also jazzier moments that were missing from their debut LP.

"Bodhisattva" (Dias the Bebopper meets Baxter the skunk beneath the Bo Tree in this altered blues)
Steely Dan's sophomore LP opens with a parody of the way Westerners considered Eastern religion at the time and how they often oversimplified Eastern ideals. After the Beatles' experience with the Maharishi Mahesh Yogi in 1968, it became trendy for middle-class dropouts to embrace eastern religion, but few found the "instant karma" they were looking for. Written by Fagen the night before the session, he thought himself quite clever with references to "the shine in your Japan" and "the sparkle of your China," but in his and Becker's opinion most people didn't get it. The song has some of the heaviest-sounding guitars in their canon, rock-solid drumming from Hodder, and served as a powerful opener to their live shows.

The original liner notes included wisecracking asides for each song, as had been done for *Can't Buy a Thrill*, and Becker and Fagen captured the essence of "Bodhisattva" in one sentence: "Dias the Bebopper meets Baxter the skunk beneath the Bo Tree in this altered blues." From the intro, the song blends swinging drums, heavy guitars, and syncopated piano to set up an album that explores myriad styles over the course of only eight songs. Fagen adds horn-like pads on the choruses and outro as well as the synthesizer riffs during the instrumental section, a part that was far more difficult to record than one would think.

The synthesizer Fagen used was the same one heard on "King of the World" and is a monophonic keyboard, meaning that it could only play one note at a time. For "Bodhisattva," Fagen wrote a four-part saxophone-like section, so he needed to play each note separately on different tracks. The problem was the synthesizer was prone to pitch problems and would go out of tune frequently. In order to complete the part, they had to stop every few notes, and Fagen needed to retune the keyboard with a tiny plastic knob before they could punch in. Fagen's fingers were hurting and his patience was wearing thin, which affected his performances. Denny Dias recalled in an essay entitled "Steely Dan, Men and Machines," from his column "Denny's Corner" on the official Steely Dan website, "He began saying 'I'm gonna kill this thing' every time he had to retune. Then he started saying it whenever the tape stopped rolling. Then it was done. The last part had been played and played back. The look on Donald's face was one I will never forget. He yanked the wires out of that Arp Soloist and headed for the door. . . . Donald threw the synthesizer down the stairs as hard as he could. He then chased after it and started jumping up and down on it. . . . Roger got some alcohol from the studio and we proceeded to set the thing on fire!" Since the studio was in the same building as

A promotional poster for Steely Dan's second album.

ABC Dunhill headquarters. the next morning a number of executives came across the wreckage. Rather than chastise them for destroying equipment, they had the twisted lump of burnt plastic and metal framed and mounted on a wall with an inscription about Steely Dan, men, and machines.

The synthesizer part was an incredible addition to an already rocking song, but Dias and Baxter steal the show with their diametrically opposed solos; Dias's distorted bebop-style solo halfway through and Baxter's bluesy rocking solo that closes the song. The perfect ending to the song was Fagen's discordant piano chords, a moment that foreshadowed the ending of the *Katy Lied* LP played by pianist Michael Omartian.

"Razor Boy" (The legendary "Giant Girlfriend" of the Camden, New Jersey, area sees the specter of Benny King as a child in a nightmare of cosmic proportions) It's hard to imagine that at one time a reggae beat anchored the first Steely Dan song to use a bass player other than Walter Becker. After the song is almost completed, the drums were rerecorded with a jazzier cha-cha groove and was graced by the elegant acoustic bass playing of jazz legend Ray Brown and the perfectly executed vibraphone of Victor Feldman. His licks in between the verses and choruses lead nicely from the minor sound of the former to the major sound of the latter in an uplifting manner. Fagen's syncopated rhythmic piano playing is the perfect foil to yet another example of Baxter's innovative use of the pedal steel guitar. Add congas, shaker, and an energetic triangle performance, and you have a compelling production that is quite impressive for the time, and also a harbinger of what was to come on later albums.

The lyrics are abstract, but the general feeling of loss and desperation is apparent. It can be interpreted as the story of drug addiction, spousal abuse, or simply a tumultuous breakup. Regardless of the intent, the images conjured by the lyrics fit the melancholy mood of the music, something that isn't always the case in the world of Steely Dan. "Razor Boy" is allegedly Baxter's favorite Steely Dan song and would be the B-side of their first single from the album, "Show Biz Kids."

"The Boston Rag" (Enervated after an attack of unrelieved nostalgia, Jeff "Skunk" Baxter sheds his outer skin and stands revealed as a Wild Boy)
Baxter explained how he was teaching himself to play Bach's Toccata and Fugue on the guitar while the band was recording *Countdown to Ecstasy* and suggested to Fagen that they should try to incorporate a particular chord pattern from Bach's piece into one of the songs. The resulting song, "The Boston Rag," contained that particular chord change in it, and Baxter recalled, "It thrilled me to death, Donald listening to my ideas."

"The Boston Rag" is a curious song because it is written about living in Bayside, Queens, and incorporates a number of real characters, including "Lady Bayside," that Becker knew while living in the borough as well as one of Fagen's first roommates at Bard College, Lonnie Yongue. Fagen and Yongue kept very different schedules in college, with Yongue, an art major, painting all night and sleeping all day. He was also a heavy drinker and experimented with a variety of drugs, quite normal in the '60s, and in his own words, "blacked out almost every night," a line later used in "Daddy Don't Live in That New York City No More" from 1975's *Katy Lied* album.

The chorus of the song was primarily written by Fagen, with Becker composing the majority of the verses. The song begins with a guitar intro by Denny Dias, doubled and harmonized by Fagen on piano, played over a series of intricate chord changes that are never heard again in the song, a Tin Pan Alley tradition not used frequently in the '70s. The intro wasn't as easily executed as it should have been. As they worked on the intro melody, they attempted to punch-in a section, and no matter how many times they tried to fix it, the same three notes of Dias's guitar line would not record properly. Engineer Roger Nichols found a go-around, but they were curious about this recording anomaly, so they sent a piece of the defective tape back to the manufacturer, 3M. A few months later, they found out that there was a blister on the tape where the oxide had bubbled up from the backing because one of the workers had dropped mustard on that section of tape when the tape was being made. Becker's humorous take in 1998 was that their "efforts had been sabotaged in advance by a careless worker. This was to haunt us over and over in the years to come."

The verses are mainly acoustic, showcasing Fagen's piano and the acoustic guitar of session player Ben Benay. Baxter adds some lead licks at the end of the verses and pedal steel guitar to the second verse. His distorted rhythm guitar playing on the chorus gives the song a kick at the perfect moment. One of the highlights of the song is the solo section. It begins quietly with Fagen's piano and Hodder's hi-hat as Baxter adds a vibrato-laden melody that heavily relies on delay and volume manipulation. After twelve bars of this mysterious, eerie vibe, the drums and bass kick in, and Baxter begins to let loose over the same chord progression. After another twelve bars, all hell breaks loose as the acoustic guitar re-enters and the band preps for the outro choruses.

Baxter recalled the process of working on a solo that would satisfy the demanding duo in a 1980 interview with *Guitar Player* magazine. "My frame of mind during most of those solos was an extremely emotional emotionlessness. I was very into the music, but to get too involved would have been dangerous, because the idea was that nobody got that personally involved. Usually Donald would say, 'Bend a lot of strings' and 'Go fast.'" Becker and Katz would often push him to the brink of exhaustion, but Baxter never complained, always a professional striving for the best take possible.

"Your Gold Teeth" (In this number, several members of the Dan get to "Stretch Out")
"Your Gold Teeth" is another Latin jazz–influenced Dan song, but this one is quite different from the others; it's actually an extended jam. After a somewhat arresting introduction, Fagen and Dias play an angular, dissonant melody on Wurlitzer electric piano and guitar respectively. The band then settles in with a sold groove by Hodder, top-notch bass work from Becker, rhythm guitars by Dias (left channel) and Baxter (right channel through a Leslie speaker), Fagen's Wurlitzer, and congas by Victor Feldman.

Fagen's Wurlitzer electric piano and Denny Dias's lead guitar share the spotlight with two solos by Fagen and one by Dias. Fagen's first solo demonstrates his love of the dissonance of Thelonious Monk, and while it might not be at the level of a bona fide jazz pianist, it shows imagination and the creative nature of Fagen as a player. Dias follows with a slightly distorted bebop-inflected solo that goes outside of the key almost as much as it stays inside. The coup de grâce is the double-time outro featuring another Fagen solo that proves he could keep up with the manic playing of the rhythm section behind him.

Lyrically, the song has quite a few obscure references. Drummer Jim Hodder recalled where the song lyric originated in a 1985 interview with Dave DiMartino. "[Singer David Palmer] came back from the dentist one day with a bridge on. And Donald sang the fucking song, 'Do you throw out your gold teeth,' and the whole band got paranoid. Everybody but Donald and Walter. Literally, this is true . . . I remember when the axe came down on him. . . it did strike almost terror into Baxter and I and Denny." Their 1972 press release had short, comedic bios of all of the band members and in Palmer's Becker stated, "We saw his teeth and then we knew. Anyone with six eye teeth is OK with us." Most people only have four.

The song also contains the line, "Even Cathy Berberian knows there's one roulade she can't sing," followed by the dissonant flat seventh over a major seventh chord. At the time, many fans thought that she was a made-up character, but the in-joke was that Berberian was an avant-garde singer who was quite popular in those circles from the late '50s until her death in 1983, hence the dissonant note played by Fagen on the Wurlitzer. She even recorded an album of Beatles songs entitled *Beatles Arias* in 1967. She was quite flattered by the name check and sent copies of the record to her friends and family. They also pinch a line from the opposite end of the musical spectrum, "There ain't nothing in Chicago for a monkey woman to do" from Count Basie and Joe Williams's version of "Going to Chicago Blues" from 1959. "Your Gold Teeth" encapsulates what the Dan could accomplish as a working, playing, jamming band and has a grit that could only be accomplished by a true "band."

"Show Biz Kids" (The Dan moves to L.A. and is forced to give an oral report)
In 1973, you didn't usually hear the word "fuck" on the radio. While Lucille Bogan's 1935 "Shave 'Em Dry" contains not only that word but a number of others that many would find offensive, the song "Nothing" by the Fugs from their 1965 album *The Village Fugs Sing Ballads of Contemporary Protest, Point of Views, and General Dissatisfaction* is probably the first pop/rock record to throw caution to the wind with the lyric, "Fucking nothing/Sucking nothing/Flesh and sex nothing."

In 1969, MC5's vocalist Rob Tyner introduced their song "Kick Out the Jams," from the album of the same name, by shouting, "And right now . . . right now . . . right now it's time to . . . kick out the jams, motherfuckers!" Elektra Records executives were offended and had it edited out of the album. The band and their manager, John Sinclair, were not happy with this decision. The original release had "Kick Out The Jams, Motherfuckers!" printed on the inside album cover, but was pulled from stores soon after its release. Two versions were then released, both with censored album covers, with the uncensored audio version sold behind record counters. One particular department store, Hudson's, refused to carry either version, so MC5 took out a full-page ad that showed a picture of vocalist Rob Tyner with the quote "Fuck Hudson's." This caused the store to reject every album released on Elektra until they dropped MC5 from their label. The Jefferson Airplane also used the forbidden word in the phrase "Up against the wall, motherfucker" on "We Can Be Together," the B-side of the "Volunteers" single, which was also the first track on 1969's *Volunteers* LP. While the word wasn't censored on the single, it was mixed lower in the mix as compared to the LP version.

Steely Dan, however, put the word front and center at a pivotal point in the song where the vocals harmonize on the relatively dissonant flattened seventh and ninth following Rick Derringer's smoking slide-guitar solo. Although the song is based on a loop, there is movement between two chords throughout, but at the ideal moment, Feldman's marimba settles on an ominous single note roll on the fifth of the chord, and the tambourine adds some furious sixteenth notes that contributes to the weight of the lyrics and heightens the effectiveness of the moment. There is no denying Becker and Fagen's disgust with the L.A. lifestyle after hearing the lines "Show biz kids making movies of themselves/You know they don't give a fuck about anybody else." They even sang the "fuck" with extra gusto. Needless to say, radio stations weren't apt to play a single with the F-bomb, and it disappeared without a trace.

Becker and Fagen were looking for a rock-steady groove for the song that they couldn't accomplish with a live rhythm section, so they decided to create a four-bar, thirty-foot-long loop that was spooled into the hall and back into the studio to create the perfect backing track. A drone is odd for a Steely Dan song, but it creates a hypnotic groove of drums, bass, piano, and the background vocal mantra

"You're goin' to lost wages, lost wages, you're goin' to lost wages" that works as the ideal bed for the overdubs. The "lost wages" pronunciation of Las Vegas was part of one of comedian Lenny Bruce's monologues, and Becker and Fagen stated in an interview that the background vocalists were singing "Las Vegas" but at times mispronouncing it as Lenny Bruce did, "lost wages." Another example of the duo trying to baffle the media. Since the background vocals were part of the loop, they are consistent throughout singing "lost wages." Interestingly, it sounds like Fagen's background vocal sings the word "Las Vegas" over the third "lost wages," another attempt to throw listeners off.

The overdubs include Feldman's marimba, Derringer's slide guitar, male and female background vocals, handclaps, tambourine, harmonica, and Fagen's scathing lead vocal that rips apart the Hollywood scene in an unorthodox way, comparing the have-nots of the first verse, mentioning the Guernsey Fair, a county fair that has been held in Old Washington, Ohio, since 1847 as well as the Washington Zoo, with the haves of the second verse, the Hollywood crowd that has "all that money could buy." The chorus also cleverly juxtaposes the way poor people end a hardworking day as wealthy stars just begin their evening of expected debauchery.

Derringer recorded his slide guitar at Caribou Ranch, a recording studio built by producer James William Guercio in 1972 in a converted barn in the Rocky Mountains, while working on his 1973 LP *All American Boy*, which included the hit single "Rock and Roll, Hoochie Koo." Guercio was the manager and producer of Chicago and also produced numerous award-winning acts including the Buckinghams; Blood, Sweat & Tears; and the Beach Boys. The studio was a popular retreat in the '70s and early '80s, and records by Elton John, Earth, Wind & Fire, Michael Jackson, Rod Stewart, Frank Zappa, Joe Walsh, Supertramp, and others were recorded there until a fire in 1985 in the control room caused $3 million in damages. His licks throughout the song are marvelous, including a "Reelin' in the Years" reference after the self-deprecating line "They got the Steely Dan T-shirt" line, but the solo is the standout moment, building fiercely over a loop and creating a tension that explodes once the infamous vocal line enters.

The outro of the song includes a number of jumbled voices, at least two of whom were road-crew members Warren Wallace, credited on the record as "Grunt," and John Famular, credited as "Pilot." One line that you can hear if you listen closely enough is, "Hey, is this the band that's looking for a lead singer?" It also showcases Becker's bluesy, yet discordant, harmonica that increases the sense of tension and cacophony of the outro. "Show Biz Kids" was the first single from the album and unfortunately did not chart nearly as well as their two top twenty hits from their debut album, peaking at number sixty-one on *Billboard*'s Hot 100.

"My Old School" (A poignant memoire inspired by the "Giant Girlfriend," sometimes referred to as the "Anima Camden")

"My Old School" was one of the first Steely Dan songs that used Becker and Fagen's experiences at Bard College to comic, yet sarcastic, effect. The train "the Wolverine" ran from New York City to Boston and passed through Annandale-on-Hudson, the town where Bard College was located. Rather than mention Bard specifically, William and Mary, one of the oldest colleges in America, is used instead.

The song is a pastiche of life at the college, both factual and fictionalized. The first verse alludes to the big drug bust on campus led by a future politician running for assistant DA, G. Gordon Liddy. Liddy would be convicted of conspiracy, burglary, and illegal wiretapping for his role in the Watergate scandal a few years later. The line, "When your daddy was quite surprised to find you with the working girls in the county jail," is a reference to Fagen's girlfriend, Dorothy White, being arrested while visiting and not being released when the university bailed out their students. While her father didn't show up, Fagen's did, along with a lawyer to bail her out.

The song is simple harmonically, but contains a fabulous melody and a tight arrangement that came together after playing the song numerous times on the road before stepping into the studio. Fagen's piano is appropriately bluesy from the intro on and works as a rhythmic counterpart against Baxter's choppy rhythm guitar and Becker's R&B-infused bass line. Listen in particular to how his licks fall in the ideal spots throughout the song.

The song is the only one on the album with horns, and the saxophone chart written by Jimmie Haskell is an early example of the significant role horns would play on Steely Dan's later work. The beginning of the horn break is quite similar to the horn chart for Van Morrison's number nine hit, "Domino," from his fourth album, 1970's *His Band and the Street Choir*, on which future Steely Dan engineer Elliot Scheiner would serve as production coordinator. Steely Dan's section does, however, take it further, with a unison line that adds complexity to a rather straight song that in actuality has more in common with

A Japanese picture sleeve for the "My Old School" single.

Morrison's song than just the horn line. The overall feel is reminiscent of "Domino," but "Domino" itself is derivative of countless soul songs of the '60s.

Once again Jeff Baxter's guitar licks and solos add a discordant element while still remaining blues-like and catchy. Baxter built the Stratocaster that he played on the track the afternoon of the session. He cut the body from a piece of maple, cut the neck and fretted it, and even wound the pickups himself. He finished assembling it three hours before the session in the parking lot of Valley Sound where he still worked customizing guitars. It was built to be plugged directly into the console, and that was how the guitar on "My Old School" was recorded. And who doesn't love the cowbell and female background vocals, the second and last appearance of them on the album.

"Pearl of the Quarter" (Oh Lah Lah)
The tale of a New Orleans prostitute actually has a tender sentiment told by the man who truly loves his "pearl of the quarter." It's interesting that the narrator chooses not to judge her choice of profession, but acknowledges that she always has a "place to go" when she needs it, a rare instance of true love in a Steely Dan song. "Pearl of the Quarter" was written before *Can't Buy a Thrill* and was played live on some very early gigs, but it didn't fit the mood of their debut album and would be held back until *Countdown to Ecstasy*.

While the verses are harmonically simple, the chorus is anything but, with myriad non-diatonic (out of the key) chords creating an unsettling mood that echoes the sentiment of the lyrics. The beginning of the melody of the verse is extremely similar to that of the Band's "In a Station" from their debut LP, 1968's *Music from Big Pink*, but the song develops from there, and what follows doesn't mimic any elements of the folksy tune written by pianist Richard Manuel. Curiously, Becker and Fagen had played on a version of the song by singer Linda Hoover for an album produced by Gary Katz in 1970 that was never released (see chapter twenty).

The gentle lilt of "Pearl of the Quarter" is achieved by light drums, a groovy bass part, piano, acoustic guitar, and a beautiful pedal steel guitar part by Baxter. Fagen sings the first two verses solo, but for the third verse a single harmony is added, and by the fourth verse the vocals are sung in three-part harmony. The delicate atmosphere of the tune is temporarily suspended for Baxter's pedal steel solo, with the entire band kicking into high gear momentarily, an effective and unexpected change.

"King of the World" (I think my face is on fire)
Becker and Fagen were science fiction fans as children, and "King of the World" is one of their earliest songs to demonstrate this. The song about the aftermath of a nuclear holocaust was written after watching the 1962 movie *Panic in the Year Zero!*, directed by and starring Ray Milland.

The song is quite a departure on the album, and the musical pieces fit together like a jigsaw puzzle. Hodder and Becker lay down what is arguably the funkiest groove on the album, Fagen bangs out a slightly distorted Wurlitzer electric piano part played low on the keyboard, Baxter uses his Echoplex delay on his intriguing part, and Dias not only plays a wah-wah rhythm guitar but also adds bebop guitar

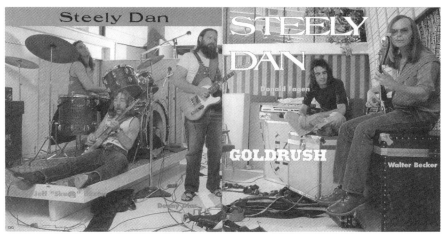

This photo of Steely Dan "rehearsing" was part of the same shoot that produced the back cover, and promotional poster, for *Countdown to Ecstasy*. It was used for the cover of the bootleg *Goldrush*.

leads during the verses. Fagen also plays a simple synthesizer lead that serves as an instrumental break before all hell breaks loose. The groove changes, and the listener can hear Becker saying lines such as "I think my face is on fire," recorded while lying under the drum set.

Fagen sings the verses solo but the choruses and middle section expands to three-part harmony. The song also features an outstanding solo by Dias on the outro. After Fagen returns to the synthesizer melody heard earlier in the song, Dias kicks in with an expertly played jazz guitar solo that plays over Fagen's synthesizer. Dias also played another role on "King of the World" that would give him the title "Stereo Mixmaster General." One night after the band had left, engineer Roger Nichols and Dias attempted to mix the song. Gary Katz had fallen asleep on the studio floor, and Dias came up with the idea of mixing each section separately, then splicing the two-track master tape together. They were still working when the next band came in for their 10:00 a.m. session, but the mix wasn't used. As Roger Nichols recalled, the mix was like sonic wallpaper; it was so perfect that after you heard it, you couldn't recall what you just heard. Dias never mixed all night again.

Conclusion

When *Countdown to Ecstasy* was completed, the executives and promotion staff of ABC Dunhill Records gathered to hear the album that was supposed to build on the success of their debut. Their response was underwhelming, and as Becker stated, "The confusion and disappointment that filled the room was thick and nasty." The fact that they chose a song that contained the F-bomb in the lyrics made it a hard sell to radio stations, which added to the trepidation of the powers that be at the label.

The Dan's first album hadn't gotten much attention in the U.K., so in the summer of 1973, Probe Records, as part of an aggressive publicity campaign for their second album, sponsored a Steely Dan Balloon Race at a Radio Luxembourg motor-racing event at Brand's Hatch. They also ran a series of advertisements on Radio Luxembourg, took full-page ads in music magazines, and distributed display cards to retailers to no avail. *Melody Maker* magazine had gone as far as stating, "If they don't happen here this time, there's something drastically wrong with this country's ears."

The album failed to crack the Top 30 in the U.S. and the two singles released from the album, "Show Biz Kids" and "My Old School," failed to chart well, peaking at sixty-one and sixty-three respectively, although "My Old School" and "Bodhisattva" became minor FM Radio staples in time. It is arguably the most underrated Steely Dan album and simultaneously harkens back to the rock and Latin grooves of *Can't Buy a Thrill* while foreshadowing the jazzier leanings and expanded song forms of their later works. The use of session musicians would exponentially multiply with each album, and *Countdown to Ecstasy* would be the last time that drummer Jim Hodder would play on a Steely Dan album.

8

Night by Night

The Early Tours of Steely Dan

Walter Becker and Donald Fagen were never that fond of life on the road, beginning with their days with Jay and the Americans to the tours that the Dan undertook in the early '70s. For this reason, after 1974, Steely Dan would not tour again for nearly twenty years. However, during that time in the early '70s they did embark on three tours in the U.S. and one very short tour in the U.K. At the time, Becker and Fagen didn't openly disparage the idea of touring as they later would, as evidenced by several interviews they gave once they stopped. When asked by journalist Chris Van Ness about the live experience after the band played their first show at Under the Ice House in Glendale, California, in October 1972, their response was surprisingly upbeat.

Do you feel the group is better represented in live performance?

Fagen: It will be very shortly, if it isn't now. I can see the way it's going, and it's growing very satisfactorily into what we'd like it to be.

Becker: There's a certain excitement that's in the live performance visually—especially because Dave (Palmer) is the singer on stage, whereas he only sang two cuts on the album. I think that gives it a different appeal. We're just starting to experiment, but I like it.

The First Tour

In October 1972, Steely Dan set out on their first tour, the only one they would ever do without additional musicians. They had released a single, "Dallas" b/w "Sail the Waterway," in January, but it had a limited release, and although promo copies were sent to disc jockeys, the song made no impression and disappeared quickly. Their debut LP, *Can't Buy a Thrill*, as well as the first single from it, "Do It Again" b/w "Fire in the Hole," wouldn't be released until November, so most of their audiences would hear their music for the first time in a live setting.

Becker and Fagen were quite surprised when ABC Dunhill advised them that they would have to tour to support the album; otherwise they would provide no promotion. The problem was they didn't have any experience playing as a live band. In reality they hardly knew each other. They had also never truly rehearsed with Fagen as the lead singer. They treated each song as a studio recording, laying down the basic tracks live with Fagen overdubbing his vocals afterward. After the success of "Do It Again," the dates multiplied; and as Becker recalled in a 2000 interview with *Rolling Stone*, they were sent on "a long, depressing march through Middle America, and ended with our being snowed in at the airport in Lincoln, Nebraska, with Frank Zappa and his band of the day, whose show we had opened the night before."

The shows were scattered from October through early December in smaller venues, but soon after they were booked to open for the Kinks, Elton John, the Beach Boys, Chuck Berry, Uriah Heep, the James Gang, ELO, the Guess Who, Bread, Black Oak Arkansas, Focus, and Slade. During the so-called first half of the Steely Dan tour, the band played twenty-one shows, yet they only played ten venues. They did one-off dates in Glendale, California; San Antonio, Texas; Houston, Texas; Chicago, Illinois; Philadelphia, Pennsylvania; Milwaukee, Wisconsin; St. Louis, Missouri; and two nights in Kansas City, Missouri. For New York City and Los Angeles, they played multiple dates at the same venue. In New York, they played a six-song, forty-five-minute set for a full week at Max's Kansas City in Union Square; and in Los Angeles, they played five nights in a row at the Whisky A Go-Go on Sunset Strip, three of them on a double bill with drummer Buddy Miles.

Van Ness described the show as "more pure rock and roll energy than the J. Geils Band and the Faces put together." They resumed the tour on January 28, 1973, and continued as an opening band in the second or third slot. In February, March, and April, the group would play between seven and eleven dates per month, leaving them time to begin work on their next album at the Village Recorder in West Los Angeles. May, the last month of the tour, was a bit busier, with sixteen shows in fifteen cities.

Since neither Becker nor Fagen was interested in being the lead singer, David Palmer was hired to sing lead vocals on two songs at the end of the *Can't Buy a Thrill* sessions and would become the lead singer for the live shows. In order to showcase Palmer's vocals, Becker and Fagen wrote a number of songs including "Megashine City," "Take My Money," and "Hellbound Train" that would never be released on a Steely Dan studio recording. Fagen elaborated on his thoughts on touring and being a lead vocalist to Mary Turner in 1992 for the *Off the Record* radio show. "I don't like to front a band. You know—you have to talk to the audience, tell jokes. I don't like the jock atmosphere of the traveling rock and roll band, either—it's corny, and it's boring, and it's silly." In hindsight Fagen would, however, share his true feelings about the fact that Baxter, Dias, and Hodder enjoyed the "perks" of touring life more than he or Becker. "It was a combination of envy and moral outrage."

Initially, the group seemed happy with the arrangement, with Fagen going so far as stating that had they been aware of David Palmer earlier, they would have tried to incorporate his vocal style into the sound of Steely Dan in a more seamless way. But by the end of their first tour, Palmer was fired due to his misinterpretation of the material, a propensity for the drink, as well as an unfortunate incident that resulted in the splitting of his tight pants. It is possible that a show at the Spectrum in Philadelphia might have contributed to his departure, with an extremely inebriated Palmer singing the entire show a half-step down from the correct key with a split in his pants that gave the audience full view of his nether region sans undergarments. A show in Phoenix five weeks later was another one that suffered due to Palmer's imbibing.

The tour wrapped up on May 27, 1973, in Atlanta, Georgia, and the band took a two-and-a-half-month break from the road to put the finishing touches on their sophomore LP, *Countdown to Ecstasy*. Fagen was still hesitant about being the lead vocalist, and he and Becker considered finding a replacement for Palmer. At this point it proved to be a futile search, so after years of consternation, Donald Fagen was forced to take over the lead vocals not only on record, as he had before, but on tour as well. Fagen somewhat unconvincingly told reporters that Palmer was a good singer for them in the beginning, but that he didn't have the right attitude for the songs. Although it was difficult for Fagen to sing lead in front of an audience night after night, he was forced to summon the courage to do it and began to enjoy it, to a certain extent, as he gained confidence as a front man.

In a 2012 interview with David Yaffe of Tabletmag.com, Fagen told a bit of a different story regarding David Palmer's tenure with the band. "Walter and I wanted a real singer for the band. Jeff Baxter, who was in the band, said he knew this guy David Palmer from Boston and he said, 'Hey, he looks like Roger Daltrey.' So, he came out to California and we rehearsed with him. But after a few songs, we realized that he didn't have the attitude. We didn't like him that much anyway. We didn't like the sound of his voice that much." According to that account, Palmer was never considered the right singer for Steely Dan, but Fagen's fear of singing live forced them to bring him on the first tour.

Although Fagen knew that he could convey the sentiment of the songs correctly, he didn't feel adept technically, nor did he feel comfortable fronting a band. He actually found it ironic that he became the singer in the band rather than Becker. When he first met his partner at Bard College, Becker had been singing and playing harmonica in front of blues bands since high school. Fagen only sang to demonstrate his songs.

Fagen was also a fan of soul singers like Marvin Gaye, Ray Charles, Joe Tex, and Wilson Pickett as well as jazz vocalists who had incredible chops such as Ella Fitzgerald. When the duo began composing together, Becker originally sang more because he enjoyed it and was confident with a louder voice, but he always sang a bit flat. He remembered Fagen hunched over the piano singing softly, so he didn't realize what a great singer he was until they recorded some of their songs. Becker recalled in a 2011 interview for *Time Out New York*, "I saw that Donald had a really cool style, and that he could do all kinds of fancy intervallic things, and as we later discovered a little further down the line, he could create these stacks of harmonies that really added a lot to what we were doing. And not everybody can do that; he can do it partially because of the precision and repeatability of what he does. He can double his own voice because he basically sings the song the same way every time: He has a perfect picture in his mind of what the song is going to be."

A pair of 1973 photos of Steely Dan taken during the shoot for *Countdown to Ecstasy* but used for a bootleg of a Memphis show from April 1974.

The Second Tour

After the July release of *Countdown to Ecstasy*, Steely Dan went back on the road as an opening act in August 1973, but headlining status was only nine shows away. On September 1, the band played their last gig as an opener at the Balboa Stadium in San Diego, California, supporting Elton John. The next day they were headliners for the first time at a large venue, the Civic Auditorium in Santa Monica, California. The tour was not only different because they were headliners for the majority of it; also, three vocalists were added to the fold. Royce Jones played percussion and took over lead vocals from Palmer on "Brooklyn (Owes the Charmer Under Me)," "Dirty Work," and "Change of the Guard," and two female background vocalists named Gloria Granola and Jenny Soule, nicknamed "Porky" and "Bucky," were added as well. On September 2, 1973, at the Santa Monica Civic Center, the two female vocalists had a bit of a showcase spot. For the encore, the group performed an improvised version of the Angels' 1963 hit "My Boyfriend's Back," and it was occasionally added to the set. Ironically, Becker and Fagen had played some shows with the Angels when they were members of Jay and the Americans' touring band.

Fagen had already shown signs of fatigue early in 1973. Their manager at the time was Joel Cohen, who used to road manage Three Dog Night. His approach was typical for the times: make an album, release singles from it, and tour constantly to support them. Fagen never felt that the band was well rehearsed and didn't think that the tours were well organized, which was extremely frustrating. In the end, the band played only twenty-two shows with this configuration before the year was out and the tour was finished. In some ways, the performances could hardly be considered a tour, with eight shows as an opening act in August, one date as an opening act in September, eleven headlining dates in September, and two headlining dates in December. Although they were out on the road, as leaders

This photo of Palmer, Hodder, and Dias was from the 1973 tour but used for another bootleg of the 1974 show in Memphis titled *Memphis Blues Again*.

Becker and Fagen had already begun to reveal their priority for the band: writing and recording new material. On February 20, 1974, Steely Dan released their third album in just fifteen months.

The Third Tour

On March 1, 1974, Steely Dan was ready to hit the road again to promote their third album, *Pretzel Logic*, but this time the band was augmented with additional musicians for the first time. In addition to the five members of Steely Dan and Royce Jones on percussion and vocals, Michael McDonald played Wurlitzer electric piano and provided lead and background vocals and Jeff Porcaro, who had recently played on two songs from *Pretzel Logic*, "Night by Night" and "Parker's Band" along with drummer Jim Gordon, played drums alongside Jim Hodder. At this point "Porky" and "Bucky" were dismissed due to the fact that Becker and Fagen thought it was a bit too "showbiz." When the Dan would return to touring in 1993, however, they were never without female background vocalists.

This tour was much more grueling than the previous ones, with the group playing fifty-three dates in the U.S. and five dates in the U.K. from March 1, 1974, until July 5, 1974. They were originally supposed to play an additional seven dates in England and Scotland, but these were cancelled due to a supposed throat infection that Fagen had developed. It was the first time the band appeared outside of

Photos from the 1973 tour with female vocalists Gloria "Porky"
Granola and Jenny "Bucky" Soule and male vocalist Royce Jones.
Although the touring ensemble had changed significantly by April
1974, the photos were used for a bootleg of the April 29th show in
St. Louis.

the U.S., and sadly, would be the last until 1993's U.S. tour in support of Fagen's
second solo album, *Kamakiriad*, which was produced by Becker.

The addition of a second drummer, second keyboard player, and additional
male vocalists gave the band a full sound, and Fagen continued to have the luxury
of having other singers to take the lead on a few songs. Fagen sang "Boston Rag,"
"Do It Again," "King of the World," "Rikki Don't Lose That Number," "Barrytown,"
"Pretzel Logic" with Michael McDonald singing lead on the break," "Reelin' in
the Years," and "This All Too Mobile Home."; Royce Jones took over lead vocals
on "Brooklyn (Owes the Charmer Under Me)," "Any Major Dude Will Tell You,"
and "Dirty Work." McDonald sang lead on "Show Biz Kids," and the three lead
vocalists shared the spotlight for the opening song, "Bodhisattva." The surprise
vocalist for many shows was Jeff Baxter, who would often take the lead vocals for
"My Old School," with Jones, McDonald, and Fagen providing the background
vocals with aplomb.

This was the tightest band they had ever had, and the audience response was
staggering. The sound on this tour was unparalleled for a number of reasons, not
the least of which were the additional musicians and the new vocal combinations.
When opening for the Kinks, they met sound engineer Stuart "Dinky" Dawson,
the first engineer to mix sound from the audience, a revolutionary move in the
'60s. The Kinks had a rather obnoxious practice of not letting the opening act get

After touring as an opening act for a year, Steely Dan became headliners. From September 2, 1973, Steely Dan was no longer an opening act. This poster from April 1974 lists Montrose as the opener.

a sound check, but Dawson didn't care. He thought every band deserved to have proper sound and gave Steely Dan the chance to sound check before the gig, although his bosses were apparently against it.

One of the gigs that was instrumental in changing the way live sound is experienced by an audience had Dawson behind the mixing board. He had been mixing the original Fleetwood Mac with Peter Green from the side of the stage, as was the common practice of the time, when he came up with the idea to mix from the front of house. This way of mixing immediately became the standard for live sound. After Peter Green left Fleetwood Mac, the band needed to regroup, so Dawson began working with the Byrds and would relocate to L.A. in 1970 to be closer to the group. In May 1972, after two years in their employ, Dawson left the Byrds to begin his own sound company.

His system was so game-changing that his company, Dawson Sound, would provide their state-of-the-art equipment and expertise for guitarist John McLaughlin's Mahavishnu Orchestra and Lou Reed the year prior to Steely Dan's 1974 tour. His custom acoustic suspension P.A., which was separate from the stereo speakers on the side of the stage, impressed Walter Becker so much when they opened for the Kinks in '72 that he told Dawson that once they were in better financial shape, they would hire him for their tours, and in the spring of 1974 they did. They played shows in California, Nevada, Arizona, Hawaii, and New York in March before reaching out to Dinky to handle sound for the majority of their third tour supporting *Pretzel Logic*; the last one for nineteen years.

He explained what was different about his system in a 1974 interview for *Rolling Stone*. "In effect, it is a huge home stereo set. It's nothing like the usual horn-loaded speaker system, which is a way of amplifying sound that is descended from PA systems. The name says it—public address. They were designed for speaking to crowds, not for reproducing music, so you have all sorts of jangling and head rattling when you try to play loud music on them. But with a system like this you can stand in front of a speaker for an hour and your ears won't even ring."

Dinky's first gig with Steely Dan was on April 4, 1974, at the University of North Carolina in Cullowhee, but it almost didn't happen. Dawson's truck full of equipment showed up that afternoon as scheduled, and his crew was set up and ready to go, but Steely Dan's truck with their instruments and amplifiers was nowhere to be found. Management had been calling the hotel and truck rental company all afternoon looking for the gear and the driver. The driver? The infamous Jerome Aniton, the man who would introduce the band as "Mr. Steely Dan or whatever" at numerous shows. So, in their best the-show-must-go-on spirit, they had the opening band play an extra-long set. When the truck still hadn't shown up by 9:00 p.m., Dawson and his crew frantically searched the college campus for instruments to augment the ones they were borrowing from the opening act. At the eleventh hour, Aniton came crashing into the garage door of the venue to the audience's amusement, and the crowd exploded into applause. Miraculously, none of the gear was damaged (even though it wasn't strapped down), and the show was a huge success.

The road crew also had another colorful character, monitor engineer Jim Jacobs. Jeff Baxter elaborated in an interview with Mary Turner for *Off the Record*. "The guy who mixed our monitors was interesting, too. He would set up the monitors so he could hear real well, and he'd get a nice sound that he liked and take out his violin and play with us throughout the set. Everything was really shaky." He also enjoyed playing Bob Dylan's "Visions of Johanna" through the system before gigs, which led to Becker and Fagen penning the line, "All night long we would sing that stupid song," in "Doctor Wu."

As *Pretzel Logic*, and its first single "Rikki Don't Lose That Number," began to climb the charts, the tour gathered steam, and the band's fame began to grow at a rapid pace. They had a top ten album and a top five single, something that most bands would have been ecstatic about, but a growing number of people in the audience were interested not only in the music but in the members of Steely Dan as well. They were becoming bona fide "rock stars," and Becker and Fagen were very uncomfortable with their new status. Celebrities were now often at shows, and backstage the vibe was becoming increasingly tense. This put more pressure on Becker and especially Fagen, who had to sing the majority of the material every night, and they were both beginning to have serious reservations about continuing on the road. Fans were now trying to gain access backstage by any means necessary, including attempts through skylights, fire escapes, balconies, and other dubious entry points. The audiences had become so enthusiastic that the band was often given a standing ovation

Steely Dan in the spring of 1974.

A.S. CONCERTS BRINGS YOU

STEELY DAN

PLUS SPECIAL GUEST STARS
SUNDAY EVENING JUNE 23RD
ROBERTSON GYM UCSB 8 PM
TICKETS:$4.50 ASUCSB, $5.50 GENERAL, AT UCEN INFO BOOTH,
MORNINGLORY MUSIC, SALZER'S MERCANTILE, MUSIC ODYSSEY &
OPEN AIR BICYCLES PLUS ALL TICKETRON OUTLETS

A.S. CONCERTS
PACIFIC PRESENTATIONS

A flyer for one of Steely Dan's last live shows with the original band in June 1974. They would only play six more shows before they quit touring for nineteen years.

after their opening song, and some fans were crushed against the front of the stage at certain shows; this made Becker wary of continuing the tour. Both he and Fagen felt guilty about causing such a raucous scene, and as the band prepared for their first dates outside of the U.S. things began to unravel.

Steely Dan continued to tour the U.S. through mid-May and then the band, and the gear, headed to the U.K. After they were set up for the first gig at the Rainbow Theater in London, Becker approached Dawson after sound check and commented, "It's good that the room sounds great because Donald's going to need all the help he can get." Dawson inquired, "The cold?" Becker acknowledged that it was part of the problem, but there was much more.

There were issues with the band's management in the U.S., who was demanding a greater share of the money and royalties from the record label; and Fagen, who dealt with this part of the business, was bombarded with calls at all times of the day and night. They also weren't making any money touring. The only reason they were able to travel overseas was because the record company was footing the bill. It was apparent that if they continued at this pace, they would burn out completely. The reclusive duo were having a very hard time with the new problems that came with success and fame, and it was beginning to get the best of them. Although the reception in London was fantastic, they only played five of the twelve scheduled dates. The crew was notified while in Glasgow, Scotland, that the rest of the tour was cancelled due to Fagen's medical condition, which seemed to be equal parts physical and mental.

Many believed that it was the end of Steely Dan as a live act, but on June 21, 1974, one month after the group's last gig in London, they were performing in San Diego, California. It was, however, a short-lived reunion, and after only eight shows, Steely Dan played their last live show as a "band" on July 5, 1974, at the Santa Monica Civic Center. The tour had come full circle with driver Jerome Aniton's animated and somewhat inebriated introduction. Although he had worked with the band, he still thought that Steely, or at times Stevie, Dan was one person, Donald Fagen. His introduction heard before "Bodhisattva," the B-side of both the "Hey Nineteen" and "Time Out of Mind" singles, is priceless.

In April 1975, almost a year after Becker and Fagen disassembled the original Steely Dan, Becker told Richard Cromelin of the *New Musical Express* that the public could expect to see Steely Dan on the road again. "We have a situation where for a particular tour we select a band and then rehearse it and then go out and do it. You'll see two Steely Dan shows on different tours; it'll be different bands and a different kind of musical presentation. The nucleus of the band has always been the same." But drummer Jim Hodder had a different opinion of what happened. After the Santa Monica gig, the whole band took acid and Hodder ended up at Becker's house early the next morning. That's when he was told that the band was finished. After being sidelined during the *Pretzel Logic* sessions, he knew that it would happen eventually, but he didn't expect it so soon. They basically got rid of everybody that wanted to tour: Hodder, Baxter, and manager Joel Cohen. Hodder negotiated a deal for a piece of the next two albums, but he never fully recovered from his dismissal from the band.

So after three albums, three tours, and two years, Steely Dan as a conventional band was over. They would not tour to support any of their next four albums, and Denny Dias would be the only member of the original band to appear on any other Steely Dan LPs, contributing to *Katy Lied*, *The Royal Scam*, and *Aja*. As Fagen stated in their 1995 *MOJO* magazine interview, "The Beatles had not long before set the example of concentrating on records and not touring, and we were arrogant enough to follow their example . . . we split up shortly after too. We were following their example to the letter! And now we're back together, just like they are. We never make a move without consulting the Beatle Chronology." Becker expanded on that humorous notion a bit more seriously in an interview with Barney Hoskyns of *The Guardian* in 2000. "It didn't work beyond a certain point with that particular band for a lot of reasons. We found ourselves in an uncomfortable position with some of our early bandmates of constantly not wanting to do things that they wanted to do. You end up being this sort of un-generous collaborator who's constantly pissing on somebody's parade. In a way, it was very liberating not to have to deal with that afterwards. To be able to say, 'Let's not work for a while,' or 'Let's hire this guy to play the drums.'" Becker and Fagen would continue to use session musicians, and each successive album featured a larger cast of characters, culminating with the use of thirty-nine different players in addition to the songwriters on their last album before reuniting, *Gaucho*. Becker explained the reasoning behind dismantling the band in such a decisive fashion: their plan to prove that the band couldn't be reunited for a tour. As Becker commented, "What were they gonna do, send me and Donald with banjos?"

9

The Man Gave Me the News

Steely Dan's First Steps to Becoming a Studio Band

After the lackluster sales of *Countdown to Ecstasy* and the inability to release a suitable single, Steely Dan tightened up their arrangements, shortened their songs, and hired drummer Jim Gordon to play drums on eleven of the twelve songs. Although Steely Dan was still technically a band with four of five members contributing to the album, Gary Katz had convinced Becker and Fagen that using the studio as a workshop would benefit their songs and hopefully produce a successful album, so some of the best studio musicians in Los Angeles were brought in to augment, and in some instances replace, the "members" of the band. With the addition of more session musicians, Katz's role as producer changed significantly. In a 1993 interview with *The Independent*, Fagen spoke of Katz's new role in the studio. "We had a hard time talking to musicians. That's where our producer came in. He had an easy social manner and he could relax and talk to them about sports, which we didn't know about."

In addition to Jim Gordon, drummer Jeff Porcaro; bassists Chuck Rainey, Wilton Felder, and possibly Timothy B. Schmit; guitarists Ben Benay and Dean Parks; keyboard players Michael Omartian and David Paich; percussionist Victor Feldman; saxophonists Plas Johnson, Jerome Richardson, and Ernie Watts; trumpet player Ollie Mitchell; and trombonist Lew McCreary all contributed to tracks on the album; fifteen session musicians in all. That number would grow with every album until their breakup in 1981; even 2000's *Two Against Nature* credited over thirty musicians. Things wouldn't change until 2003's *Everything Must Go*, an attempt to return to the concept of a band playing live recorded on analog tape.

Their first two releases were true band albums, with all members playing significant roles interpreting Becker and Fagen's songs. Session musicians were primarily brought in to add horns, percussion, and background vocals. Additionally, Elliott Randall laid down two guitar solos on *Can't Buy a Thrill*, Ben Benay played acoustic guitar on two tracks on *Countdown to Ecstasy*, Rick Derringer played slide guitar on "Show Biz Kids" from *Countdown to Ecstasy*, and jazz legend Ray Brown played upright bass on "Razor Boy" from the same LP. But for their third album, things changed significantly.

Pretzel Logic

Pretzel Logic's new cast of characters left Jim Hodder sidelined, something that troubled him greatly. Although the photo on the inside of the gatefold sleeve showed all five members of Steely Dan, Hodder only contributed background vocals to one song, "Parker's Band." Becker and Fagen guaranteed him financial compensation as a band member, but the use of Jim Gordon and Jeff Porcaro still stung. Becker, Fagen, and Katz were careful to schedule sessions that included "the band" opposite those done with the session musicians.

Hodder would tour to support the album, but the band would be augmented by a second drummer, Porcaro; a second keyboard player and vocalist, Michael McDonald; and an additional male vocalist, Royce Jones (who had toured with them the year before and sang background vocals on the *Countdown to Ecstasy* LP). The inside cover photo was taken at photographer Ed Caraeff's house in the hills of Coldwater Canyon. He took a page from the Beatles playbook and tilted the photo paper while developing to create the elongated effect, similar to Robert Freeman's cover of the Beatles' 1965 LP *Rubber Soul*.

Critics and fans alike still believed that Steely Dan was a five-piece band, with *Rolling Stone*'s Bud Scoppa stating, "Steely Dan's five musicians seem to play single-mindedly, but each is actually contributing to a wonderfully fluid ensemble sound that has no obvious antecedent in pop. These five are so imaginative that their

The cover for Steely Dan's third album, *Pretzel Logic*, was conceived by Fagen and Gary Katz and was taken on Fifth Avenue and 79th Street at the Central Park entrance called Miners' Gate. Note that pretzel is spelled wrong on the vendor's sign.

mistakes generally result from too much clever detail. . . . In a short time, Steely Dan has turned into one of the best American bands, and surely one of the most original. Their only problem is the lack of a visual identity to go with their musical one. But with music as accessible and sophisticated as Steely Dan's, no one should care." Curiously, Scoppa mistakenly credits the two principal members as Fagen and Baxter. The liner notes on the album didn't make things any clearer with no specific credit given to the particular musicians that played on the album, only a generic "Special thanks" to the studio musicians listed in no particular order and ending facetiously with thanks to "Tubby, Bruce, Dee, etc."

Becker and Fagen initially wanted a title for the album that connotated the seedy, sexual side of life forming a trilogy with the first two albums. But they couldn't come up with anything that they deemed worthy, so they named it after a song from the album, something they would continue to do for every subsequent album except *Katy Lied*, which was named after a slightly altered lyric from the song "Doctor Wu." They also dropped the indecipherable comments that had followed each song in the liner notes.

While the majority of the songs from *Countdown to Ecstasy* were over five minutes long, five of the eleven songs on *Pretzel Logic* were under three minutes, three were under four minutes, one was under two minutes, and the two singles, "Rikki

Don't Lose That Number" and "Pretzel Logic," clocked in at four and a half minutes, the longest on the record. Becker and Fagen were, however, having trouble coming up with new songs, so they mined their past for material and recorded three songs from the Kenny Vance days: "Barrytown," "Parker's Band," and "Charlie Freak." They also recorded their first (and last) cover song, "East St. Louis Toodle-Oo," written by Duke Ellington and Bubber Miley.

The record cover was conceived by Fagen and Katz, who thought that a photo of a New York City pretzel vendor would make a witty cover for the album. The photo was taken on Fifth Avenue and 79th Street at the Central Park entrance called Miners' Gate. They had originally taken a photo with a younger vendor, but he refused to sign a release, so another photo was taken. This vendor also refused to

Although the photo used for the inside gatefold sleeve was of a five-piece band, drummer Jim Hodder didn't play a note on the record. His sole contribution was background vocals on one song.

sign the release, but after a bit of detective work on ABC's part, they realized that the vendor was working without a license, so they assumed that no legal action would be taken. Note that pretzel is spelled wrong on the vendor's sign.

Pretzel Logic was a departure for Steely Dan, and several musical styles were added to their already broad and varied palate. The funk of "Night by Night" and "Monkey in Your Soul" sat alongside their first shuffle, the title track, the country flavor of "With a Gun," and the hard to describe "Charlie Freak," comfortably creating a compact listening experience that travels through a multitude of genres cohesively. It is also the first album to significantly showcase the horns, both as a section and in a solo capacity, which are heard on five of the eleven tracks. Surprisingly, it would be the only Steely Dan album on which no female vocalists appear.

Their third album was released on February 20, 1974, and peaked at number eight on the *Billboard* 200. It was Steely Dan's third gold-certified album and would eventually be certified platinum by the Recording Industry Association of America on September 7, 1993. After the disappointing performance of *Countdown to Ecstasy*, the album restored their radio presence with the single "Rikki Don't Lose That Number," which became the biggest hit of their career, peaking at number four on the *Billboard* Hot 100.

The Songs

For *Pretzel Logic*, Becker and Fagen opted for concise compositions and introduced more diverse musical genres to their arsenal. In addition to the rock 'n' roll backbeats and jazz-infused chord changes they were famous for, the album showed shades of country and western, funk, Beatlesque pop, '60s soul, and even a clever cover of a Duke Ellington classic. The album is also the first instance where session musicians were used extensively, something that would become the norm with all future releases.

"Rikki Don't Lose That Number"

Besides "My Old School," another song was overtly inspired by Becker and Fagen's years at Bard, "Rikki Don't Lose That Number." In 2006, *Entertainment Weekly* ran a feature entitled *Back to Annandale*, which revealed who Rikki actually was, novelist Rikki Ducornet (born Erica DeGre). Ducornet recalled, "I was actually a young faculty wife, I was pregnant, and he thought I was cute. So he gave me his phone number, which I lost. But I thought they were brilliant. I didn't find out about it for ten years. I was living in France, and came back to Amherst, Massachusetts. I walked into a record store, and heard Fagen's voice. I recognized it at once. And I heard my name. Then a couple of days later, I ran into someone that I had just met, and he said, 'Hey, you know that song? Fagen wrote it for you.'"

The album version of the song begins with a somewhat avant-garde intro played by Victor Feldman on the musical cousin of the marimba, the flapamba. The twenty-five-second intro was cut from the single as well as the *Citizen Steely Dan* box set, but the flapamba also plays during the intro and after each chorus, adding a spooky vibe to the proceedings. Only three original Steely Dan members appear on the track: Fagen on vocals, Becker on bass, and Jeff Baxter on electric guitar. Many have

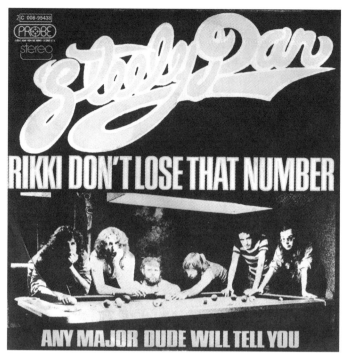

A picture sleeve for the French release of Steely Dan's highest-charting single, "Rikki Don't Lose That Number."

noticed the similarity of the intro to Horace Silver's 1965 composition "Song for My Father," but Fagen has denied this, explaining that it was a Brazilian bass line that was common to numerous songs. While at first glance the song seems harmonically simple, Becker and Fagen add various chords that don't fit in the key of the song, creating its subtle complexity.

The groove is incredibly tight due to Jim Gordon's drumming, Becker's Latin-flavored bass line, Dean Parks's acoustic guitar, and Michael Omartian's piano. The song builds from an easygoing, piano-heavy verse into a chorus that begins with a light Latin feel and two-part vocal harmony before effortlessly switching to a full-on rock groove with additional vocal harmonies provided by Poco and future Eagles bass player Timothy B. Schmit. Baxter's lead guitar during the chorus, plugged directly into the console, sets the stage for one of his finest moments on record. A more perfect guitar solo couldn't be imagined. Although the song isn't the first without a keyboard part ("Only a Fool Would Say That" didn't have keyboards, so it takes the honor), it is the first that would use a keyboard player other than Fagen. The song also contains one of Becker's coolest bass licks in Steely Dan history on the last chorus at 4:07.

"Night by Night"
Written for commercial purposes, "Night by Night" was the song that would prove to be the nail in Jim Hodder's coffin. After numerous unsuccessful attempts at recording the rhythm section, Becker and Fagen realized that they needed another

drummer to tackle the song, so in the middle of the night Denny Dias suggested nineteen-year-old drummer Jeff Porcaro. Porcaro showed up with his future Toto bandmate keyboardist David Paich, who played the extremely funky clavinet part. The horns round out the production with a blend of fluid unison lines, harmonized hits, and chordal pads, a sign of what was to come on future recordings.

"Night by Night" is arguably one of the funkiest songs that Steely Dan ever recorded, with Becker and guitarist Dean Parks laying down a unison line over the foundation of Porcaro's syncopated drum groove and Paich's Stevie Wonderish clavinet part. Once again Jeff Baxter steals the spotlight with his distorted rhythm guitar hits and lead licks before ripping into yet another fantastic solo. He returns for a second solo after the last chorus that builds the song to a frenzied fade out.

Fagen delivers this tale of despair as a solo vocal for the entire song with one exception: whenever the title is sung. During the chorus, the background vocals support the lead vocal and are relatively tame, but on the outro, the vocal harmonies become especially dissonant, creating an apocalyptic mood behind Baxter's frantic and furious guitar solo.

"Any Major Dude Will Tell You"
"Any Major Dude Will Tell You" is one of Steely Dan's smoothest-sounding songs and is a good example of the California vibe of the '70s, whether Becker and Fagen want to admit it or not. The thing that they could do so well was produce a record that could sonically fit into a certain style, yet was harmonically, melodically, and lyrically superior to its contemporaries. They could also put the word "dude" into a song without completely killing their credibility.

The song marks the first appearance of Chuck Rainey, who would play bass on more songs than any other player except Walter Becker. While Becker definitely had a natural feel for the instrument and contributed some superb lines and licks as the band's bassist, it's clear after hearing "Any Major Dude Will Tell You" why Rainey was hired. His flow and tone are impeccable and along with Jim Gordon's drums create the ultimate pocket for this mid-tempo ballad. This is the first occurrence of a Steely Dan song that Becker doesn't contribute to musically. The song's groove primarily relies on two acoustic guitars panned hard left and right and a Wurlitzer electric piano front and center.

The song also marked a new high for Steely Dan punch-ins. Denny Dias didn't play guitar with vibrato and didn't bend notes, and the guitar motif that occurs numerous times needed vibrato at the end. So for this occasion, Dias played the first part and Baxter played the last five notes. Curiously, when the song was played live, one note of the signature guitar lick was changed. Played by Fagen on piano, the more pleasing, diatonic F sharp was replaced by the harsher-sounding F natural. The short four-bar guitar solo, written by Becker and Baxter, is a perfect example of less is more starting as a single bluesy guitar part for the first half before morphing into a harmonized line.

The lyrics are truly beautiful and show a tender side that occasionally shines through on a Steely Dan song. Fagen explained in a 2009 interview with *Rolling Stone* that, "When we moved out to L.A., people called each other 'dude,' which we found funny. We were trying to speak their language." The song also contains a reference to the mythical woodland creature the Squonk from a book by Jorge Luis Borges. The creature has the ability to dissolve into its own tears and was the main character in the Genesis song "Squonk" from their 1976 album *A Trick of the Tail*.

"Any Major Dude Will Tell You" was released as the B-side to "Rikki Don't Lose That Number" and became a popular song in their live show. Fagen's solo vocals were handed over to Royce Jones, and Fagen's acoustic piano provided the rhythm that was originally performed on electric piano and acoustic guitars. Baxter's pedal steel guitar once again took center stage with a striking solo and tasty licks throughout.

"Barrytown"

One of the only Steely Dan songs written solely by Donald Fagen, "Barrytown" describes a pedestrian town close to Bard, and Fagen used the song to comment on the limits of the small-town mindset. Barrytown is also the home of the Unification Theological Seminary, founded by the controversial Reverend Sun Myung Moon in order to improve relations of his Unification Church with other churches. The religious organization had been accused of being anti-Semitic and heretical, as well as brainwashing its members.

The song's narration is told by two different people, someone from "Barrytown" defending his position and another outsider attacking the first narrator's views. The song was originally recorded as a piano/vocal demo with Kenny Vance and was revisited when Becker and Fagen were lacking new material for their third album. It's one of Steely Dan's simplest songs harmonically, lyrically, and musically and consists of a simple arrangement of drums, bass, piano, acoustic guitar, electric guitar, pedal steel guitar, and tambourine. Baxter's pedal steel doesn't appear until the last verse and in this instance adds a country twang to a song that has a definite West Coast flavor. Surprisingly, the band played the song live on their 1974 tour to support the *Pretzel Logic* LP in a slightly heavier, faster version.

East St. Louis Toodle-Oo

For *Pretzel Logic*, Becker and Fagen decided to do something that they had never done before, and would never do afterwards: record a cover song. But this was not your ordinary cover song; it was Duke Ellington's "East St. Louis Toodle-Oo," originally recorded in 1926. Written with trumpet player Bubber Miley, it was Ellington's first charting single, but it wasn't until his fourth recording of the song that it became a hit. Recorded in March 1927 for Columbia Records, the record was released under the name the Washingtonians and featured a trumpet solo played by Miley with a plunger mute, one of the first instances on record. People assumed they covered the song because it was mentioned in William Burroughs's novel *Naked Lunch* (from which Steely Dan took its name), but both Becker and Fagen denied this.

For Steely Dan's version they incorporated elements of four different recordings made by Ellington's band. Besides playing bass, the song gave Becker his first chance to play guitar on a Steely Dan song. Fagen revealed that Becker had been fooling around with the Ellington tune for years, so when it came time to record, Becker would play a guitar manipulated by a wah-wah pedal to recreate Miley's famous solo. Fagen's piano took over for what Becker described as "four bad clarinet solos" played by Rudy Jackson. He also played alto saxophone, the only Steely Dan track on which he would ever play the instrument, and a synthesizer part that takes the place of a saxophone/clarinet section. At this point, it seems that whenever Baxter gets behind a pedal steel guitar, magic happens. "East St. Louis Toodle-Oo" is no exception. His note-perfect transcription of Tricky Sam Nanton's trombone solo is as impeccable as his distorted tone. He also creates a faux horn ensemble with Fagen's sax and Becker's guitar after the piano solo. Round it out with Jim Gordon's drums, Dean Parks's banjo, and a gong played at the end by Roger Nichols, and you have an unexpected twist on a fifty-year-old classic.

While some fans and critics felt like it didn't fit in with the rest of the material on *Pretzel Logic*, it was apparent that they recorded the song strictly for their own amusement. As Fagen stated, "Walter and I are such jazz fans and this composition stood up so well, we wanted to hear it with all the expertise of modern hi-fi. Most of the great jazz compositions have been neglected." Fagen was quite proud of the recording and sent a copy to Ellington for his 75th birthday in April, but Ellington died less than a month later, so it still remains a mystery as to whether he ever heard the tribute.

"Parker's Band"

"Parker's Band" is another song resurrected from the Kenny Vance demos, and the second song in a row to pay homage to legendary jazz musicians. The demo shows just how developed Becker and Fagen's compositions could be before entering the studio. The bass line that anchors the song is already in place, as is the somewhat startling middle section that takes the tune in a completely different direction.

It's a known fact that Becker and Fagen were huge Charlie Parker fans, so it should come as no surprise that they would write a song that pays tribute not only to the legendary alto saxophone player, but to the entire jazz experience. The lyrics contain numerous Parker references including: the line "Savoy sides" (Savoy was one of the record labels for which Parker recorded), Kansas City (the city in Kansas where Parker was born and the city in Missouri where he was raised), "Groovin' High" (a song on which Parker played written by fellow bebopper, trumpet player John Birks "Dizzy" Gillespie, and considered by some to be the first famous bebop recording), "Relaxin' at Camarillo" (a Parker composition that refers to his six-month stay in the mental ward at the Camarillo State Hospital), the line "a bird in flight" (Parker's nickname was Bird), the line "We will spend a dizzy weekend smacked into a trance" (a name check for Dizzy Gillespie as well as a reference to Parker's heroin addiction), and the mention of 52nd Street (the hub of jazz and bebop in New York City from the '30s until the '50s). The last verse also alludes to a jam session where the musicians who "can't fly" are relegated to the rhythm section. A snapshot of a musical culture and a tribute to a legend.

The song is another first for Steely Dan: two drummers playing on the same song. For this occasion they had Jeff Porcaro, who had killed "Night by Night," play alongside one of his heroes, the drummer for every other song on *Pretzel Logic*, Jim Gordon. The bass line of the demo swings along with the drums, with piano and organ taking care of the chords on top. A dissonant chord played by the band starts the song before Denny Dias executes a brilliant blues and bebop solo on a distorted wah-wah guitar over the intro. At that point, the guitar doubles the bass before adding some other chordal flavor on top.

On the demo, Becker and Fagen harmonize throughout, but for *Pretzel Logic*, only the middle eight has harmony vocals, and what harmonies they are. The middle section feels as if it was flown in from another planet, in a good way, and adds a harmonic sophistication to an otherwise simple song. The background vocals are the only contribution on the album by drummer Jim Hodder. The song comes to a conclusion with dueling saxophone solos that continue to build until the song takes an abrupt left turn, and the band plays a rather odd four-and-a-half bar unison riff that ends the song abruptly.

"Through with Buzz"

Side two opens with Steely Dan's shortest song on record, with the fewest lyrics consisting of three one-line verses, a three-line chorus, and a four-line middle section. Clocking in at 1:33, "Through with Buzz" is also the only Steely Dan song, besides "FM (No Static at All)," to use a string section. Fagen described it as a "very saccharine sounding track with a very cynical lyric," something they often did. He stated that it was written about a platonic relationship that goes awry once one of the participants believes he's being taken advantage of, becomes paranoid, and ends the relationship. The lyrics are ambiguous, mentioning how Buzz stole the narrator's girlfriend, and in the last verse, the narrator wonders about Buzz's sexual orientation.

"Through with Buzz" is an oddity in the Steely Dan canon and sounds more like a Beatles song (in this case a double-time version of the Beatles' "For No One" from *Revolver*) than any of their other songs. The arrangement is sparse and classical-like during the majority of the song, with a close-miked, clever string arrangement; a quaint vibraphone part in the choruses; and a floaty drum, bass, and piano rhythm section. Fagen's double-tracked vocals are mellow during the verses and choruses, but take on a harsher tone for the middle section, which also grooves harder as the lyrics get darker. Somehow they're able to tell a compelling musical and lyrical tale in a minute and a half.

"Pretzel Logic"

This bluesy shuffle about time travel was a staple of their 1974 tour and gave Steely Dan the title for their third LP. Musically, Becker and Fagen would continue to write various songs with a shuffle groove over the years including "Black Friday," "Chain Lightning," "Home at Last," "Babylon Sisters," and others, but "Pretzel Logic" holds the distinction of being the first on record.

Becker and Fagen rarely explained their lyrics, but Fagen stated how each verse spoke of a time period to visit, including a minstrel show and the years of Napoleon's rule before he lost his mind. The bridge introduces "the platform," which he and Becker conceived as the teleportation device that would carry them to their selected time frame. The rhythm section defines the groove flawlessly yet simply with drums, bass, Wurlitzer electric piano, and rhythm guitar providing the foundation for a slick yet subtle horn arrangement and Becker's first appearance as a lead guitarist on an official Steely Dan record. Becker's skills shine, but his solos did not come without a bit of sonic manipulation. He was such a perfectionist that it became common to spend an entire session working on one of his solos, or as engineer Roger Nichols described it, "an hour per bar." Becker's lead guitar performance added another element to Steely Dan's sound, and it is fascinating to hear how a composer's take on the material could transform a track in such a way.

Solos on any instrument are very personal, and since so many are improvised, every player paints a new picture. It was ingenious that Becker, Fagen, and Katz understood this philosophy and were willing to implement it so early in the game. Becker would play several solos on Steely Dan, Donald Fagen, and his own albums in the future, and his moody, bluesy solos would surprise people who didn't expect his playing to be so lyrical and dexterous. When the Dan would eventually tour again in the '90s, Becker would play lead and rhythm guitar along with some of the finest guitarists of the time including Drew Zingg, Georg "Jojje" Wadenius, Wayne Krantz, Larry Carlton, and Jon Herington.

During Steely Dan's last tour in 1974, keyboard player and vocalist Michael McDonald, who would sing on countless Steely Dan records and eventually become the voice of the Doobie Brothers, would sing the middle break, "I stepped up on the platform/The man gave me the news." When McDonald toured with the New York Rock and Soul Revue, with Steely Dan, and with the Dukes of September (a touring ensemble comprised of himself, Fagen, and singer/songwriter/guitarist Boz Scaggs), he would reprise his role on the bridge.

"With a Gun"

"With a Gun" is another composition from *Pretzel Logic* that strikes a curious note. The lyrics tell a tale of a hapless loser and outlaw who solves all of his problems with murder. They even allude to the fact that the killer might be living his life as if he was in a western. Becker and Fagen have told similar stories in the past, and would tell many more in the future, so it isn't the lyrics that are novel for a Steely Dan song, it's the music.

Rather than juxtapose a cowboy lyric with a slick groove, rock 'n' roll feel, or R&B pocket, they create a musical backing that is the most country flavored of any Steely Dan song. "With a Gun" is one of the few Steely Dan songs that doesn't have any keyboard

On May 23, 1974, Steely Dan was featured on the cover of *Zoo World*, a biweekly music magazine that attempted to rival *Rolling Stone* as the premier music source in the United States.

parts choosing to create the mood with a double-time drum groove, bass, percussion, two acoustic guitars, and some down-home electric guitar provided by the "Skunk." Although the feel is somewhat different for the Dan, the song is harmonically advanced, moving through several different tonal centers throughout. The vocal harmonies on the chorus are exquisite, and those on the bridge take us into new territory, making it clear that this is Steely Dan's version of a country tune. An out-of-the-ordinary entry in the canon.

"Charlie Freak"

The song that follows the guitar-heavy, country-flavored "With a Gun" is the polar opposite; a sparse, piano-based song that's like nothing else Steely Dan has ever recorded. It is also one of the few songs that show the empathetic side of Becker and Fagen. The lyrics tell the story of a vagabond who sells his only thing of value, a gold ring, to an opportunist who pays him little for it, recognizing his desperation. Charlie Freak spends the money on his drug of choice and overdoses, an act that causes the narrator to go to the morgue and return the ring to the dead man to ease his guilt. The fact that Becker and Fagen would conclude a song with a sad yet hopeful sentiment that is neither sarcastic nor cynical shows a rare glimpse into another side of their writing.

"Charlie Freak" was the third, and final, song that was resurrected from the Kenny Vance demos for *Pretzel Logic*. The original demo was played in more of a bluesy shuffle style but contains all of the elements that would create the version for *Pretzel Logic*, including the haunting chordal descent that ends that song. The major change is Michael Omartian's piano treatment of the fast-moving chords that creates a spiraling sensation that echoes the lyrics. Baxter once again adds a sensational distorted pedal steel guitar part that builds throughout the song and adds a string-like quality that sonically creates a depth that one wouldn't expect from such an underproduced song. It would be the last time that a pedal steel guitar would be used on a Steely Dan song, the end of an era in more than one way.

"Monkey in Your Soul"

The album ends with another peek at the funky side of Steely Dan, a sound that would become more prevalent on their following albums. "Monkey in Your Soul" is possibly the purest example of '60s soul music that Steely Dan would ever record. They even add handclaps. The rhythm section is tight and grooving, with the bass being fed through a fuzz pedal, the Wurlitzer electric piano doubled in parts by Victor Feldman's marimba, and some appropriate rhythm guitar stabs. The saxophones play a simple yet effective swampy unison line during the breaks, followed by some sweet harmonized pads and hits. Jeff Baxter adds his signature sound with an eight-bar solo that packs a punch in a succinct manner.

The soulful mood of the song belies the darkness of the lyrics about a relationship in dire straits due to addiction. Although the couple apparently both enjoy getting deranged together, one is clearly in the midst of a downward spiral, and the narrator is unwilling to follow her down that destructive path. "Monkey in Your Soul" is an underrated gem from the Steely Dan songbook and in numerous ways points toward the future.

A Japanese picture sleeve for "Rikki Don't Lose That Number" used a photo from an early Steely Dan show with David Palmer.

Conclusion

Pretzel Logic marks a departure for Steely Dan. The decision by Becker, Fagen, and Gary Katz to incorporate session musicians to such an extent would mark a new era for the band. The music from their later albums would grow slicker, with more jazz and funk influence and less of a rock feel. *Pretzel Logic* would be the last time they would make an album as a "band," although in reality this wasn't the case; Hodder was already out of the picture (figuratively, not literally).

The most unfortunate result of going with session musicians from this point on is that it would be the last album to feature the unparalleled guitar skills of Jeff Baxter. His contributions on lead guitar and pedal steel guitar helped to create the early Steely Dan sound, and although there would be countless memorable guitar solos on albums to come, there is something truly unique about his approach to music that could not be duplicated. Also, we would never hear the sweet sound of his incomparable pedal steel guitar on a Steely Dan record. Luckily, we have numerous Doobie Brothers albums we can spin if we want to hear more of the "Skunk." In hindsight, Walter Becker denied that *Pretzel Logic* was a "Steely Dan" record, stating: "The list of names on the sleeve is really the truth of the matter. You can figure it out from there."

10

You've Been Telling Me You're a Genius

The Session Guitarists of Steely Dan

F rom their first album to their last, Steely Dan songs were known for a number of the most creative and flawlessly performed guitar solos. These solos were played by their two original guitarists (see chapters four and six for detailed biographies of Denny Dias and Jeff "Skunk" Baxter and chapters seven, nine, twelve, and fifteen for deeper analysis of their solos and rhythm guitar playing), Walter Becker, as well as several of the best session musicians of the past four decades. This chapter will discuss some of the top guitar moments on record as well as the guitarists who provided the outstanding rhythm guitar parts for some of the jazziest, funkiest, most soulful moments of the '70s.

Elliott Randall

One of the most famous guitar solos on a Steely Dan LP was not played by Denny Dias or Jeff Baxter, although the two were official band members at the time of the recording. This distinction goes to Elliott Randall. Becker, Fagen, and Katz all knew Randall from their early days in New York. Randall had played some gigs with Jay and the Americans and had contributed guitar parts for a few of their demos. Baxter had been struggling with the solo for "Reelin' in the Years" and could not come up with something that pleased Becker and Fagen. To remedy the situation, Baxter invited his childhood friend Randall to the Village Recorder, where the group was working on their debut LP. It was Baxter's idea to let Randall take a shot at the solo. The solo only took two takes, and many believe the first was best, but the assistant engineer didn't press record because it was supposed to be a run-through. Randall took a second pass, and the solo was complete without any editing.

Randall remembers the session for "Reelin' in the Years" well and spoke of it in the book *The 100 Greatest Solos of All Time*. "They were having trouble finding the right 'flavor solo for 'Reelin',' and asked me to give it a go. Most of the song was already complete, so I had the good fortune of having a very clear picture of what the solo was laying on top of. They played it for me without much dialogue about what I should play. It just wasn't necessary because we did it in one take and nothing was written. Jeff Baxter played the harmony parts, but my entire lead was one continuous take played through a very simple setup. The whole solo just came to me, and I feel very fortunate to have been given the opportunity to play it." Randall played a 1963 Fender Stratocaster with a PAF humbucker in the neck position plugged into an Ampeg SVT amplifier miked with an AKG 414 to create his signature tone. In the July 2007 issue of *Guitar Player* magazine, Randall added that "the SVT wouldn't have been my first choice for an amp—or even my fifth choice—but it worked a storm on that recording!"

Randall also laid down the blistering guitar solo on "Kings," which is a highlight of the album. Thankfully, he was able to have his amp of choice, a Fender Super Reverb, hired for the session. The dissonance and sheer energy reflected his personal struggles at the time. His first marriage had fallen apart earlier that year, and he used emotional recall to channel the disorder in his life into a stinging solo. The following day after he recorded these two fabulous solos, Becker and Fagen offered Randall a spot in Steely Dan. Randall turned down the offer because, based on the duo at the helm, he decided the group dynamic would never last.

Randall did, however, return as a session musician, and played the solo on "Throw Back the Little Ones" from *Katy Lied*, "Sign In Stranger" from *The Royal Scam*, and dueling guitar solos with Denny Dias on "The Fez" from the same album. Although Randall had been a professional musician for a number of years prior to working with Steely Dan, the chart success of "Reelin' in the Years" caused him to be in demand like never before. Soon, he was doing sessions for the Doobie Brothers, Carly Simon, Peter Wolf, Peter Frampton, Carl Wilson, and others. In addition to turning down Becker and Fagen's offer to join Steely Dan, Randall, a true individual, passed on offers to join the backing bands for Wilson Pickett, the Blues Brothers, and Toto. Instead, he released a number of solo albums for Polydor Records in the early '70s including one aptly named *Randall's Island*.

Rick Derringer

Born Ricky Dean Zehringer, guitarist Rick Derringer's first success as a musician was as a member of the 1960s band the McCoys with his brother Randy on the drums. The band had a number one hit with "Hang On Sloopy" in October 1965, followed by a number seven hit with their version of "Fever" the same year. After the group disbanded in 1969, the Derringer brothers and the McCoys' bassist Randy Jo Hobbs formed the group Johnny Winter And, the "And" referring to the McCoys. Derringer not only played guitar but also produced all of the gold and platinum Winter Brothers records. The first album, *And*, contained an early version of Derringer's "Rock and Roll Hoochie Koo," a song that would be rerecorded in 1973 for his debut solo album *All American Boy*. The song was released as a single and reached number twenty-three on the *Billboard* Hot 100, making it his highest showing on the charts.

Derringer first met Becker and Fagen when producer Gary Katz approached him to play on some demos they were working on. After they got a record deal, they called on Derringer to play the slinky slide guitar on "Showbiz Kids" from their second album, *Countdown to Ecstasy*. His part was played over a rhythm section loop, and not only are his licks throughout the song spot-on, his solo is

EVERYTHING HE HAS DONE FOR THE PAST DECADE HAS BEEN LEADING TO THIS MOMENT.
THE RICK DERRINGER ALBUM, "ALL AMERICAN BOY." ON BLUE SKY RECORDS AND TAPES

Rick Derringer's first Steely Dan session was playing slide guitar for "Show Biz Kids." His debut album as a leader, *All American Boy*, was released in 1973 and included his biggest hit, "Rock and Roll, Hoochie Koo."

in many ways the climax of the song. Derringer returned to play the solo on "Chain Lightning" from *Katy Lied*, rhythm guitar on "My Rival" from *Gaucho*, and rhythm guitar on "Green Flower Street" and "The Nightfly" from Fagen's debut solo album.

He has released over a dozen albums as a solo artist and has worked as a guitarist or producer for Cyndi Lauper, Todd Rundgren, Ringo Starr, Bette Midler, Richie Havens, Air Supply, Barbra Streisand, KISS, Alice Cooper, "Weird Al" Yankovic, as well as on projects that Becker and Fagen contributed to, including LPs by Thomas Jefferson Kaye, Eye to Eye, and Rosie Vela.

Ben Benay

Session guitarist Ben Benay was called in to play acoustic guitar on *Countdown to Ecstasy* and appeared on "The Boston Rag" and "Pearl of the Quarter." For their next album, *Pretzel Logic*, he was credited as one of two additional guitarists along with Dean Parks. Since Jeff Baxter and Denny Dias were still officially band members, Steely Dan's albums didn't yet feature the long list of guitarists that would become commonplace on their future albums.

Benay's illustrious career spanned over thirty years playing not only guitar but banjo, ukulele, and harmonica on records by Barbra Streisand, Tommy Roe, the Grass Roots, Neil Sedaka, Joe Cocker, Three Dog Night, Wayne Newton, Cass Elliot, Delaney and Bonnie, Jerry Garcia, Leo Sayer, John Mayall, Donna Summer, Duane Allman, the Four Tops, Bobby "Blue" Bland, Terence Boylan, and dozens of other artists.

Dean Parks

Session guitarist Dean Parks grew up in Fort Worth, Texas, but moved to Los Angeles in 1970 to play in Sonny and Cher's band, which future Steely Dan drummer Jeff Porcaro would join the following year. His first Steely Dan sessions were for the *Pretzel Logic* LP, contributing acoustic guitar to "Rikki Don't Lose That Number," rhythm guitar on "Night by Night," banjo on Duke Ellington's "East St. Louis Toodle-Oo," and rhythm guitar on other tracks as well. He returned the next year to play on *Katy Lied* and was given the task of playing a transcribed solo for "Rose Darling," a rarity on a Steely Dan record, as well as rhythm guitar on various other songs.

For *The Royal Scam*, Parks recorded a solo for "Haitian Divorce" that was also a first on a Steely Dan session. Although Parks played the solo, Walter Becker manipulated the sound with a talk box, a device that uses a tube connected to an amplifier on which the player makes different vowel sounds to create an extremely expressive sound. He also played guitar on an outtake from the sessions that would eventually end up on their 1978 *Greatest Hits* compilation, "Here at the Western World." His contributions to *Aja* include rhythm guitar on both "I Got the News" and "Josie," two of the funkiest tunes on the album.

After working on four Steely Dan albums in a row, Parks was surprisingly absent during the *Gaucho* sessions. He would, however, return to work on Fagen's debut LP, *The Nightfly*, playing rhythm guitar on "Green Flower Street" and "The Goodbye Look."

Becker used Parks on Rickie Lee Jones's 1989 album *Flying Cowboys* on more tracks than any other guitarist, seven of eleven. Becker and Parks not only worked together but became close friends, so when Becker began work on his first solo album, he wrote a number of songs with Parks, but only one, "Cringemaker," would make the cut. He did end up playing either acoustic or electric guitar on every song and played the first solo on the song "Lucky Henry." Fourteen years later, he played rhythm guitar on Becker's second solo album, *Circus Money*, on "Downtown Canon" and "Somebody's Saturday Night," and the guitar solo on "Upside Looking Down." In between those two albums, he would play on one more Steely Dan song, "Negative Girl" from 2000's *Two Against Nature*.

Parks has worked with some of the biggest names in music including Michael Jackson, Madonna, Stevie Wonder, Billy Joel, Elton John, Barbra Streisand, Celine Dion, the Monkees, Diana Ross, George Benson, Rod Stewart, Randy Travis, Bob Seger, Neil Diamond, Barry Manilow, David Lee Roth, Paul Simon, Dolly Parton, Kenny Loggins, B. B. King, Dusty Springfield, Randy Newman, Joe Cocker, Bread, and countless others. He also played along with Becker and Fagen on albums by Terence Boylan, Thomas Jefferson Kaye, and Eye to Eye.

Hugh McCracken

Session musician Hugh McCracken first met Becker and Fagen when he played acoustic guitar on their song "I Mean to Shine," recorded by Barbra Streisand for her 1971 eponymous album on which Fagen played organ. He had one of the longest relationships with Becker and Fagen, playing on albums from 1974's *Katy Lied* until Fagen's *Morph the Cat* LP thirty-two years later. For *Katy Lied*, he played rhythm guitar on "Bad Sneakers" and some other tracks but did not play on either of their next two albums, *The Royal Scam* and *Aja*. He returned for *Gaucho* playing the memorable guitar part on "Hey Nineteen" and rhythm guitar on "Time Out of Mind."

When Fagen began sessions for *The Nightfly*, he called on McCracken to not only play rhythm guitar on "I.G.Y. (What a Beautiful World)," "Ruby Baby," and "The Nightfly," but harmonica on "New Frontier" as well. Twelve years later when Steely Dan was working on *Two Against Nature*, they enlisted McCracken's services to play guitar on one track, "Almost Gothic." He played a much larger role on their next album, 2003's *Everything Must Go*, playing guitar alongside Steely Dan's regular guitarist Jon Herington on all nine songs on the album. His last Steely Dan-related work was on Fagen's third solo album, 2006's *Morph the Cat*, playing rhythm guitar on "Morph the Cat," "H Gang," "What I Do," and the reprise of the title track.

Over the course of his forty-plus years in the business, his guitar and harmonica work has been heard on records by John Lennon, Paul McCartney, Billy Joel, Roberta Flack, Hall and Oates, B. B. King, the Monkees, Aretha Franklin, Van Morrison, Paul Simon, Art Garfunkel, James Taylor, Phoebe Snow, Bob Dylan, Carly Simon, Yoko Ono, Lou Donaldson, Roland Kirk, the Four Seasons, Andy Gibb, and numerous others. In 1971, McCracken was so busy with session work that he turned down Paul McCartney's offer to join his newly formed band Wings after working on his *Ram* LP. He passed away at the age of seventy of leukemia in 2013.

Larry Carlton

When one thinks of Steely Dan guitar solos, Larry Carlton immediately comes to mind, but Carlton didn't play on a Steely Dan album until the sessions for their fourth LP, *Katy Lied*, were almost complete. In 1971, Carlton joined the Crusaders when original members Joe Sample (piano), Stix Hooper (drums), Wilton Felder (saxophone), and Wayne Henderson (trombone) decided to go in more of a jazz-funk direction. Felder was also a bass player and had played on both *Pretzel Logic* and *Katy Lied*, so when producer Gary Katz mentioned that they were looking for a new guitarist to add to their ever growing stable of session musicians, Felder recommended Carlton.

Carlton started playing guitar at six years old, taking lessons from Slim Edwards near his home in Torrance, California. In junior high school, he became interested in jazz after hearing the Gerald Wilson Big Band album *Moment of Truth* with guitarist Joe Pass. He then started to listen to albums featuring numerous guitarists such as Barney Kessel, Wes Montgomery, and B. B. King.

Carlton's career as a professional musician began in 1968 when he released the solo album *With a Little Help from My Friends*. The record was well received and garnered the attention of jingle singers the Going Thing. He began working with them recording radio commercials for Ford as well as appearing on camera. Mid-season in his second year, he became the Musical Director for the Emmy-nominated children's show, *Mrs. Alphabet*, which aired on the same network. It was here that he showcased his acting skills, performing as the show's co-star, "Larry Guitar."

Carlton's main axe at the time was a Gibson ES-335, which led to his nickname "Mr. 335." He also began using a volume pedal, and this progressive style of playing led to sessions with Barbra Streisand, Joni Mitchell, Billy Joel, Wayne Newton, Chuck Jackson, the Four Tops, Neil Diamond, Dusty Springfield, Linda Ronstadt, Minnie Ripperton, and the Crusaders. He would also release a second solo album entitled *Singing/Playing* and would join the Crusaders as a full member for 1974's *Southern Comfort* LP.

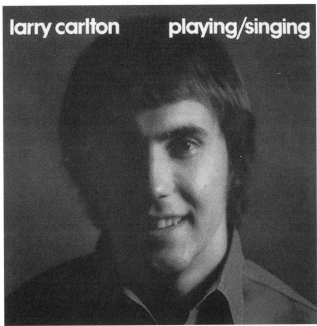

Larry Carlton first played with Steely Dan on *Katy Lied* and would appear on every album that followed. His second album as a solo artist, *Playing/Singing*, was released in 1973, five years after his debut LP.

The first Steely Dan song Carlton played on was "Daddy Don't Live in That New York City No More." His part was overdubbed on the already recorded rhythm section, and all involved were duly impressed by the effect that his playing had on the song. Carlton's involvement on their next LP, *The Royal Scam*, was much more pronounced, performing on "Don't Take Me Alive," "Everything You Did," "Green Earrings," "The Royal Scam," and "Kid Charlemagne." At the time of its release, his solo on "Kid Charlemagne" was listed as the third-greatest guitar solo in rock music history in *Billboard* magazine.

For *Aja*, Carlton not only wrote charts for the other musicians, but worked as the de facto musical director on the studio floor. He played on every song except "Peg," but only soloed on "I Got the News." The lead guitar part he played on "Third World Man" on the *Gaucho* LP was actually recorded during the *Aja* sessions, so Carlton was surprised when he picked up *Billboard* magazine and they mentioned "a wonderful guitar solo by Larry Carlton on the *Gaucho* album," given that he didn't actually contribute to those particular sessions. He returned for Fagen's *The Nightfly*, playing on every song except "I.G.Y. (What a Beautiful World)." He would also solo on a number of tracks including "Green Flower Street," "Ruby Baby," "New Frontier," "The Nightfly," and "The Goodbye Look."

Demand for Carlton as a session player continued throughout the '70s and '80s; he played on sessions for Sammy Davis Jr., Herb Alpert, Quincy Jones, Paul Anka,

Michael Jackson, John Lennon, Jerry Garcia, Christopher Cross, Dolly Parton, and countless others. At the same time, he played and contributed material to thirteen Crusaders albums and was performing more than fifty dates a year live with the group.

By the '80s, Carlton had performed on more than three thousand studio sessions, played on more than one hundred gold albums, and worked on soundtracks for television and film. He wrote the theme song for the television series *Who's the Boss*, co-wrote the score for *Against All Odds* with Michel Colombier, and played guitar for Mike Post's theme songs for *Magnum, P.I.* and *Hill Street Blues*. Over the years, Carlton would be nominated for nineteen Grammy Awards and win four. As a solo artist, he has released more than thirty records and owns his own studio, Room 335.

In 1989, while working on his next album for MCA Records, *On Solid Ground*, Carlton was the victim of random gun violence, and was shot in the throat outside his studio, Room 335. The bullet shattered his vocal cord and caused significant nerve trauma, but after intensive therapy he made a full recovery and continued to record and perform live.

Twenty-seven years after working on *The Nightfly*, Carlton joined Steely Dan as guest guitarist during their 2009 *Rent Party* tour. Overall he played seven shows in New York, Los Angeles, and Chicago: three special full-album shows that covered *The Royal Scam*, one *Gaucho* show, and three "Internet Request" shows. On September 23, 2011, Carlton joined the band at New York's Beacon Theatre for another special show entitled *21st Century Dan plus The Royal Scam*.

Jeff Mironov

During the sessions for *The Royal Scam*, Steely Dan recorded a song that wouldn't find its way onto either that album or the next, *Aja*. Instead, "Here at the Western World" would be saved for release on their *Greatest Hits* compilation in 1978. Guitarist Jeff Mironov played on his only Steely Dan song, alongside Steely Dan regular Dean Parks. He continued to be an in-demand session player working on albums by Ringo Starr, Carly Simon, Bonnie Raitt, Roberta Flack and Donny Hathaway, Ray Charles, James Taylor, Dionne Warwick, Ben E. King, Frankie Valli, the Spinners, Jimmy Buffett, Gloria Gaynor, Sister Sledge, Ashford and Simpson, the Blues Brothers, Diana Ross, Chaka Khan, Barry Manilow, Michael Franks, Maynard Ferguson, Laura Nyro, Nancy Wilson, Cissy Houston, Melissa Manchester, Lauren Hill, Mary J. Blige, George Michael, and dozens of others to the present day.

Jay Graydon

Jay Graydon started his musical career as a drummer, but soon realized that the guitar was his calling. But Graydon is not just a session guitarist. He is a successful producer and composer with twelve Grammy nominations and two wins. The first, in 1979, for Best R&B Song "After the Love Has Gone," which he co-wrote with David Foster and Bill Champlin, became a number one hit for Earth, Wind

& Fire; and the second, 1982's "Turn Your Love Around," which he co-wrote with Steve Lukather and Bill Champlin, reached number one on the soul singles charts, number five on the *Billboard* Hot 100, as well as the top ten on the jazz chart for George Benson.

As a session guitarist he's graced sides by Barbra Streisand, Hall and Oates, Dolly Parton, Diana Ross, the Jackson Five, Cheap Trick, Christopher Cross, Ray Charles, Joe Cocker, Marvin Gaye, Olivia Newton-John, and Albert King, to name a few. His production credits are just as impressive with albums by Al Jarreau, George Benson, the Manhattan Transfer, Air Supply, DeBarge, Sheena Easton, Art Garfunkel, Johnny Mathis, Patti LaBelle, Lou Rawls, Dionne Warwick, and Kenny Rogers.

Although he only worked on one song with Steely Dan, the story behind it is legendary. While recording "Peg" for the *Aja* LP, Becker and Fagen were having a hard time finding a guitar solo that worked for the song. Becker took several passes, as did Robben Ford, Elliott Randall, Rick Derringer, and three or four others, but nothing clicked. Engineer Roger Nichols recalled, "To me it was sort of like . . . we've got another day of this we've got to do . . . so some of it would go by like days of the week, 'here we go again another guitar solo.'" When Graydon came in, he nailed it quickly, playing a Hawaiian-style distorted solo that suited the track perfectly. Becker and Fagen played a few of the solos that didn't make the cut on the *Classic Albums: Steely Dan Aja* DVD, and it was apparent that they were wise to wait for Graydon's interpretation.

Steve Khan

Steve Khan was born in Los Angeles, California, on April 28, 1947, to Gloria Franks and one of the most famous lyricists of the twentieth century, Sammy Cahn. Cahn co-wrote a series of songs that would become hits with Frank Sinatra during the singer's tenure at Capitol Records, but his compositions were also interpreted with great success by Dean Martin, Doris Day, and countless others. His songs include "Let It Snow! Let It Snow! Let It Snow!," "Love and Marriage," "High Hopes," "(Love Is) The Tender Trap," "Ain't That a Kick in the Head," "Come Fly with Me," and innumerable others sung by some of the biggest stars of the day.

Steve Khan initially started his career using his birth name, but since it was misspelled so frequently, he began to go by Steve Khan rather than Steve Cahn. Ironically, he didn't realize until he was older that his father's birth name was Cohen, and he adopted Cahn as a pseudonym. His first instrument was drums, but Khan admits in his website bio, "I was a terrible drummer with no musical training. I had developed a love for the guitar, and when I was nineteen, I switched instruments. I decided that I would not make the same mistakes I had made with the drums, and studied hard in college along with private lessons from Ron Anthony." Khan graduated from UCLA in 1969 with a B.A. in music composition and theory and decided to move to New York City.

During the early '70s, he performed in a jazz guitar duo with Larry Coryell; joined the Brecker Bros. Band; and released his first albums as a leader, utilizing previous and future Steely Dan alumni: trumpet player Randy Brecker, keyboard player Don Grolnick, bassist Will Lee, and drummer Steve Gadd.

Engineer Elliot Scheiner recommended Khan to Becker and Fagen, and while he only played on one song from *Aja*, the rhythm guitar on "Peg," his work was featured heavily on *Gaucho*, playing on five of the seven songs. He played rhythm guitar on "Babylon Sisters," "Gaucho," and "Third World Man," and lead guitar on "Glamour Profession" and "My Rival." He would return to play electric and acoustic guitar on Fagen's "True Companion" from the *Heavy Metal* soundtrack; acoustic guitar on "The Goodbye Look" from *The Nightfly*; and would collaborate with Fagen on Thelonious Monk's "Reflections" for the tribute album *That's the Way I Feel Now*. Fagen would also pen some rather bizarre liner notes for Khan's 1979 solo album *Arrows*.

In the '80s, he worked steadily with his quartet Eyewitness, which included Anthony Jackson, Manolo Badrena, and Steve Jordan. He then joined Joe Zawinul's Weather Update for its one and only tour in 1986. Khan is known for his work with artists such as Billy Joel, Michael Franks, Miles Davis, James Brown, Aretha Franklin, Chaka Khan, Quincy Jones, Billy Cobham, Jack DeJohnette, Freddie Hubbard, Maynard Ferguson, Hubert Laws, and Weather Report, among others.

Lee Ritenour

Guitarist Lee Ritenour started his professional career at the tender age of sixteen playing on a session with the Mamas and the Papas and was given the nickname "Captain Fingers" due to his deftness as a player. Although he has contributed to over three thousand sessions with artists as diverse as Carly Simon, George Duke, Art Garfunkel, the Four Tops, Aretha Franklin, Sonny Rollins, Cher, Seals and Crofts, the Brothers Johnson, B. B. King, John Denver, George Benson, Barbra Streisand, Diana Ross, the Pointer Sisters, Roberta Flack, Sheena Easton, Olivia Newton-John, and too many to list here, he also has maintained a successful solo career. He has released over forty albums that have yielded thirty-five songs on the contemporary jazz charts since the mid-1970s.

His work with Steely Dan is limited to one song on *Aja*, "Deacon Blues," on which he played guitar along with Larry Carlton.

Cosmo Creek

Listed as the pedal steel guitar player on "FM (No Static at All)," Cosmo Creek is a mysterious player, with his only other credit being the debut LP of Root Boy Slim, *Root Boy Slim and the Sex Change Band with the Rootettes*, an album produced by Gary Katz after heavy persuasion by Becker and Fagen. He would be credited by his real name, Walter Andrews, for Root Boy Slim's sophomore album, *Zoom*.

Hiram Bullock

Hiram Bullock played piano, bass, and saxophone from a young age before picking up the guitar at age sixteen. After moving to New York in the mid-1970's, he immediately became an in-demand New York session player, appearing on albums by Billy Joel, James Brown, Paul Simon, the Brecker Brothers, David Sanborn, Gil Evans, Chaka Khan, Pete Townsend, Bob James, Sting, Miles Davis, Jaco Pastorius, Kenny Loggins, Barbra Streisand, Burt Bacharach, Roberta Flack, Spyro Gyra, Eric Clapton, Al Green, James Taylor and others. In the late '70s, he formed the 24th Street Band with bassist Will Lee, drummer Steve Jordan, and keyboard player Clifford Carter. The group recorded three albums, and when keyboard player/musical director Paul Schaffer was assembling the World's Most Dangerous Band for *Late Night with David Letterman*, he hired Bullock, Lee, and Jordan. Bullock was with the band from 1982 until 1984. He was also a singer, contributing vocals to albums by David Sanborn, Bob James, Jaco Pastorius, and others while releasing over a dozen albums as a solo artist, not only playing guitar but singing as well. Bullock only played on one Steely Dan song, "My Rival" from *Gaucho*, contributing rhythm guitar along with Rick Derringer and lead guitarist Steve Khan. Bullock died of cancer at age fifty-two in 2008.

Mark Knopfler

Gary Katz had gotten an advance copy of Dire Straits' eponymous debut LP in '78, and Katz, Becker, and Fagen were all impressed with Mark Knopfler's guitar work and thought that they might want to use him on a future date. They gave Knopfler a tape of *Time Out of Mind* in advance, which they didn't normally do, but he felt alienated during the session because he didn't know all the chords during the instrumental section, a part he didn't need to play. It was his first session outside of working with his band, and he wasn't used to having to play things repeatedly. He wasn't a session musician, he wasn't a jazz musician, and he wasn't a reader, so there was less musical common ground, which might explain why, as Becker put it, "he may have been a little wound up for it in advance."

Although Knopfler likened his experience with Steely Dan to "getting into a swimming pool with lead weights tied to your boots," he needn't have worried about his career. Dire Straits became one of the world's most commercially successful bands, with worldwide records sales of over 100 million. Over the years, they have won four Grammy Awards, three Brit Awards (including two for Best British Group), two MTV Video Music Awards, and countless others. The band split up twice, once from 1987 to 1990 and the second time in 1995. Since then, Knopfler has had a thriving career as a solo artist.

Georg "Jojje" Wadenius

Swedish guitarist Georg Wadenius began his musical career as a founding member of two Swedish supergroups in the late '60s/early '70s, Made in Sweden and Solar Plexus. In 1972, he relocated to the United States to become lead guitarist for Blood, Sweat & Tears for three years. From 1979 until 1985, he was a member of the Saturday Night Live Band and began working as a session player and/or touring musician with Aretha Franklin, Diana Ross, Dr. John, David Sanborn, James

Brown, Marianne Faithfull, Paul Simon, Dionne Warwick, Roberta Flack, Michael Franks, and Luther Vandross.

Wadenius first worked with Donald Fagen in 1988 on the song "Century's End" from the movie *Bright Lights, Big City*. He then worked on the Becker-produced Fagen album *Kamakiriad* in 1993, playing on all eight tracks. He followed his session work with the duo by going on the road with them in 1994 and appearing on 1995's *Alive in America* album, which was compiled from live shows from the 1993 and 1994 tours.

Adam Rogers

Walter Becker had produced the eponymous debut album for Brooklyn-based band Lost Tribe in 1993, so when he decided to begin work on his own debut album, *11 Tracks of Whack*, the next year, he enlisted drummer Ben Perowsky, bassist Fima Ephron, and guitarist Adam Rogers as the rhythm section. He initially recorded the entire album with the trio at his studio Hyperbolic Sound in Maui, Hawaii, but decided to only keep three tracks for the final running order, "Surf and/or Die," "Hat Too Flat," and "Lucky Henry," on which Rogers trades solos with Dean Parks.

Drew Zingg

Drew Zingg first worked with Donald Fagen in 1990 and 1991 for the New York Rock and Soul Revue shows at the Beacon Theatre on Manhattan's Upper West Side, and appeared on the resulting album *The New York Rock and Soul Revue: Live at the Beacon* and in the A&E television special *In Concert*. The next year, he continued with the band for a short thirteen-date summer tour that included Walter Becker on guitar. For this tour he not only performed lead guitar duties but served as musical director as well.

When Steely Dan staged their first tour in nineteen years in 1993, Zingg continued as guitarist and musical director. His work on the tour gave him his only credit on a Steely Dan record for 1995's *Alive in America*. For the 1994 tour, he was replaced by Georg Wadenius, a move that deeply upset him. He needn't have worried about his next gig. He was soon touring with New York Rock and Soul Revue alumnus Boz Scaggs.

Jon Herington

Like so many other guitarists, Jon Herington began his musical studies on piano and saxophone. He began playing guitar after various friends left their guitars at his house on the Jersey Shore in New Jersey. His first band, Highway, opened for Bruce Springsteen for a number of shows. Herington was a working musician in New York, juggling sessions, Broadway shows, and leading his own band when he got the call in 1999 to play on *Two Against Nature*. The album was almost completed, but Becker and Fagen were looking for another rhythm guitarist for some of the tracks. Ted Baker, a close friend of Herington's who was playing keyboards on the album, suggested the guitarist and gave the duo his 1992 album, *The Complete Rhyming Dictionary*. They were impressed and called Herington to play rhythm guitar on the title track, "Cousin Dupree," and "West of Hollywood" and acoustic guitar on "Almost Gothic." He embarked on the tour to support the album and has been the guitarist on every subsequent tour, eventually becoming musical director.

In 2003, he played alongside guitar legend Hugh McCracken on every song from *Everything Must Go*. He followed with Fagen's third solo album, *Morph the Cat*, performing on every song and contributing guitar solos to all but one song, "Security Joan." He also toured with Fagen to support the album. Becker was also fond of Herington's guitar work, enlisting him to play on his 2008 release, *Circus Money*. He returned to work on Fagen's fourth solo album, *Sunken Condos*, contributing guitar to

Guitarist Jon Herington first worked with Steely Dan on their comeback album, 2000's *Two Against Nature*, and has been with them ever since. The photo is from the tour program for the *2YK* tour.

every song except "Memorabilia." Herington also toured with Fagen, Michael McDonald, and Boz Scaggs on the 2010 and 2012 *Dukes of September Rhythm Revue* tours and has also toured with Boz Scaggs, Bette Midler, Phoebe Snow, Madeleine Peyroux, Bobby Caldwell, jazz/blues organ great Jack McDuff, and countless others.

Paul Jackson Jr.

Paul Jackson Jr. had been an extremely sought-after Los Angeles session guitarist, but his career took off just as Steely Dan's was winding down, so he never played on any of their first seven albums. He did, however, work with artists from various genres including Michael Jackson, Elton John, Aretha Franklin, Stevie Wonder, the Temptations, Whitney Houston, George Benson, Chicago, George Duke, B. B. King, Glenn Frey, Lionel Richie, Al Jarreau, Janet Jackson, Kenny Rogers, Rod Stewart, Roberta Flack, Celine Dion, Daft Punk, and hundreds of others over his nearly forty-year career. He has also worked as a producer and songwriter and has released seven albums as a solo artist. In 2000, he was finally called for a Steely Dan session to play alongside guitarist Dean Parks on the moody "Negative Girl" from *Two Against Nature*.

Wayne Krantz

Guitarist Wayne Krantz was primarily known as an artist in his own right, releasing a number of records with a trio that he fronts. For years he had a residency at the 55 Bar in Greenwich Village in New York City where Becker and Fagen first encountered him and future Steely Dan drummer Keith Carlock, who was a member of the trio. They hired Krantz for 1996's *Art Crimes* tour, but he wouldn't play on a Dan-related project for ten years. When Fagen began assembling the musicians for *Morph the Cat*, he decided to use Krantz on every song along with Steely Dan guitarist Jon Herington. Hugh McCracken also appeared on a number of tunes along with Krantz and Herington, and Fagen utilized some additional guitarists for particular tracks as well. Since the album had so many guitar parts intertwined, Fagen decided to bring both Krantz and Herington on the road for a short tour to support the album.

Frank Vignola

Guitarist Frank Vignola has an impressive résumé working with a diverse group of artists including Ringo Starr, Madonna, Wynton Marsalis, Leon Redbone, and Queen Latifah while solidifying his reputation as a successful solo artist with over a dozen albums to his name. In 2006, he played guitar along with Jon Herington, Wayne Krantz, and Hugh McCracken on both the title track of *Morph the Cat* and the reprise that ends the album, taking the solo on the outro.

Ken Emerson

Fagen used quite a few one-off guitarists on *Morph the Cat*, and Ken Emerson was one of them. Emerson was one of the most respected traditional Hawaiian steel guitar players, but his adaptability led to studio and touring work with Todd Rundgren, Taj Mahal, Jackson Brown, and Charlie Musselwhite, to name a few. For "What I Do," he played alongside Jon Herington, Wayne Krantz, and Hugh McCracken for a heavily layered guitar section.

Ken Wessel

Jazz guitarist Ken Wessel is probably most famous for the twelve years he played with avant-garde jazz saxophonist Ornette Coleman as a member of his revolutionary ensemble Prime Time. Fagen brought him in specifically to play the solo on "Security Joan," which he knocks out of the park.

Larry Campbell

Multi-instrumentalist Larry Campbell plays numerous stringed instruments including guitar, mandolin, pedal steel guitar, slide guitar, and violin in a variety of genres including country, folk, blues, and rock. He was a pioneer on the Country Music scene in New York City during the '70s and '80s, playing one of various instruments at numerous clubs around the city. It was this type of versatility that landed him the job that he is probably best known for: his place in Bob Dylan's Never Ending Tour band from 1997 to 2004.

Campbell also has extensive experience as a studio musician. Over the past years, he has recorded with artists including Paul Simon, B. B. King, Willie Nelson, Sheryl Crow, Little Feat, the Black Crowes, Leon Redbone, Cyndi Lauper, k. d. lang, Rosanne Cash, Edie Brickell, and others. Campbell toured regularly with Levon Helm, the ex-longtime partner of Fagen's wife, Libby Titus, in addition to producing his two Grammy-winning albums, *Dirt Farmer* and *Electric Dirt*. Campbell also served as the musical director for Helm's Midnight Ramble concerts held at his house/studio/live performance space where myriad artists, including Fagen, would gather to play concerts in an intimate setting in Woodstock, New York, in the Catskill Mountains. After playing live with Campbell at some of the Midnight Rambles, Fagen called him while recording 2012's *Sunken Condos* LP. Campbell played an understated, yet crucial distorted rhythm guitar part on "Weather in My Head."

Gary Sieger

Gary Sieger had worked as a vocalist, guitarist, composer, and arranger on numerous projects by artists as varied as Yoko Ono, Cornell Dupree, and Steely Dan saxophonist, the late Cornelius Bumpus, but he was incredibly excited to take part in the sessions for Fagen's *Sunken Condos*. Sieger played an Epiphone Joe Pass archtop through a Fender Champ amplifier for his two guitar parts on "Memorabilia," the only song on which Jon Herington doesn't play. Sieger stated in a 2013 interview for *Guitar Player* magazine that for him the session "was a dream come true. Donald said to me, 'I've heard you play,' and six months later, I get the call from Michael to do the session. It was like, 'You've got to be kidding me.'"

Kurt Rosenwinkel

While attending the Berklee College of Music, Rosenwinkel was approached by the dean of the college, vibraphonist Gary Burton, to leave school to tour with him. After his stint with Burton, he moved to Brooklyn and began playing with jazz legends Joe Henderson, Paul Motian, Larry Goldings, and even hip-hop pioneer Q-Tip from A Tribe Called Quest. He is also a successful solo artist with eleven albums.

Fagen called Rosenwinkel to play the solo on the album closer, "Planet D'Rhonda," which he did on an Italian-made Moffa archtop jazz guitar. Rosenwinkel was extremely pleased just to be called for the session, as he stated in an interview for *Guitar Player* magazine. "I've loved Steely Dan and Donald Fagen for my whole life, so I didn't care about making the record or not. The experience itself was something I just wanted to enjoy. I was doing a recording session with Donald Fagen, one of my musical heroes, and he was really cool."

The Soulful Secrets

Steely Dan Rarities

T here are many Steely Dan songs that even the most die-hard fans have never heard, from their first recordings with Kenny Vance to the soundtrack for "You've Got To Walk It Like You Talk It or You'll Lose That Beat" to their first single, "Dallas" b/w "Sail the Waterway," to lost songs from each of their albums. This chapter will cover some of these rare gems.

Guitarists Rick Derringer and Elliott Randall both played on some of these early demos, and Randall's comments prove that Becker and Fagen were perfectionists long before their first record contract. Randall commented in a 2012 interview with *Guitarist* magazine, "If I were to say we spent months in the studio making demos of Donald and Walter's early compositions I won't be exaggerating."

In 1983, Kenny Vance compiled an album that contained ten of the demos he produced for Becker and Fagen in the late '60s and early '70s entitled *Walter Becker/Donald Fagen—The Early Years* on Aero Records, a label that was created for the sole purpose of this release. This was the first of many unauthorized releases of these songs, and Donald Fagen referred to it as "part of a series of recordings dedicated to financing the college education of a former manager's children." An additional nineteen songs have come to light on various bootlegs, giving a glimpse at some of the earliest compositions by the duo, a handful of which would be revisited on future Steely Dan albums.

The bootleg *Calling from Rikki* captured a radio station show from the University of California in Irvine on March 10, 1974, and the back cover used a photo of the band with Michael McDonald and Royce Jones.

Gary Katz, who in essence stole Becker and Fagen from his friend Kenny Vance, reminisced about the early days in a 1973 interview with Judith Sims for *Rolling Stone* after the release of their debut album *Can't Buy a Thrill.* "In those days the songs were weirder than what's on the album, but there was still no denying the lyrics. We played those songs for every record company in New York. Nothing. We believed we didn't have a shot. The one guy who knew was Jerry Leiber. He knew. He just wasn't doing anything then, but he understood and loved it. He was the one reason we never gave up; he was the only encouragement."

"Brain Tap Shuffle"

Vocals, Keyboards: Donald Fagen
Vocals, Bass, Guitar: Walter Becker
Drums: John Discepolo
Guitar, Percussion: Denny Dias
Background Vocals: Donald Fagen, Walter Becker, Keith Thomas

"Brain Tap Shuffle" has a definite '60s feel to it with acid-influenced lyrics and pseudo-soul background vocals. The song also gives us an opportunity to hear Becker and Fagen sing a true vocal duet, with Fagen singing the higher harmony to Becker's lower melody. They even trade lines on the bridge section. Dias was credited on *The Early Years*, released by Kenny Vance, as the sole guitarist, but the lead guitar is actually played by Becker.

"Come Back Baby"

Vocals, Keyboards: Donald Fagen
Vocals, Bass, Guitar: Walter Becker
Drums: John Mazzi
Guitar: Denny Dias

"Come Back Baby" is another R&B-inspired number whose melody is strikingly similar to that of "Pearl of the Quarter" from *Countdown to Ecstasy*, although the essence of the song is completely dissimilar. It's surprising that nobody saw the commercial potential of this relatively straightforward tune, its only dissonance coming from the quirky yet effective melody at the end of the chorus. It's one of the best of their unreleased songs from this period and could easily have worked on *Pretzel Logic*.

"Don't Let Me In"

Vocals, Piano: Donald Fagen
Bass, Guitar: Walter Becker
Drums: John Mazzi
Guitar: Denny Dias
Background Vocals: Walter Becker, Kenny Vance

This is one of Becker and Fagen's earliest compositions, but it sounds as if it could have been played by mid-era Steely Dan. With its shuffle groove, unexpected harmonic movement, catchy chorus, and biting guitar solo by Becker, "Don't Let Me In" is another song that would have fit perfectly on *Pretzel Logic*. The juxtaposition of the bluesy intro and the sweet major seventh sound of the verse is also quite similar to the harmonic change between the same two sections in "Home at Last." The song was covered by the band Sneaker for their eponymous debut LP in 1981, produced by none other than Jeff "Skunk" Baxter.

"Old Regime"

Keyboards: Donald Fagen
Bass, Guitar: Walter Becker
Vocals: Keith Thomas
Drums: John Discepolo
Guitar, Percussion: Denny Dias
Background Vocals: Donald Fagen, Walter Becker, Keith Thomas

"Old Regime" is a curious song because it has a strangely progressive rock sound to it, with various seemingly unrelated sections melded together. There are harmonic elements that are Steely Danesque, and the Latin feel of the middle section is something that they would return to on their first two albums. Also, the use of multiple sections is quite a bit like the closing number of their debut album, "Turn That Heartbeat Over Again," but for some reason the song feels forced. It's interesting to note how Keith Thomas and early Steely Dan vocalist David Palmer have similar qualities to their voices; traits that make their interpretations seem disingenuous compared to Fagen's.

"Brooklyn (Owes the Charmer Under Me)"

Vocals, Keyboards: Donald Fagen
Vocals, Bass: Walter Becker
Drums: John Discepolo
Guitar: Elliott Randall

Becker and Fagen's demo of "Brooklyn," with the duo sharing lead vocals, shows how their arrangements were often conceived before entering the studio. The signature intro melody is in place, but is played by Fagen on organ rather than the guitar heard on the version released on *Can't Buy a Thrill*. The demo is also unique for three reasons: the third verse is sung by Walter Becker, there is an additional verse not heard on the released recording, and Elliott Randall plays a guitar solo rather than the pedal steel guitar solo played by Baxter on the final version.

"Mock Turtle Song"

Piano, Marimba: Donald Fagen
Vocals, Bass: Walter Becker
Drums: John Discepolo
Guitar, Percussion: Denny Dias
Background Vocals: Donald Fagen, Walter Becker, Keith Thomas

"Mock Turtle Song" is one of the few Becker and Fagen compositions on which they didn't write the lyrics. That task fell to Charles Dodgson, better known by his pseudonym Lewis Carroll. The lyrics come from the song "The Lobster Quadrille," a parody of "The Spider and the Fly," sung by the Mock Turtle in chapter ten of Carroll's *Alice's Adventures in Wonderland*. Becker takes the lead vocals, singing in a surprisingly confident manner, with himself, Fagen, and Thomas providing some effective background vocals. The relaxed feel of the tune along with marimba and tambourine create the perfect backdrop for Dias's flawless bebop-influenced guitar solo.

"Soul Ram"

RMI Electra-Piano: Donald Fagen
Bass: Walter Becker
Vocals: Keith Thomas
Drums: John Discepolo

"Soul Ram" is an ideal example of sexually perverted lyrics set to an extremely lightweight groove, a precursor to "Everyone's Gone to the Movies." Keith Thomas sings the song without a hint of irony, almost as if it's a children's lullaby. Musically, the darkest part comes toward the end of the chorus, but it's fleeting, and we soon find ourselves back in la-la land. The song also contains the first reference to the name of their future band in the following lyrics: "Never knew she dug the heavy stuff, Steely Dan/Play it rough, back door man."

"I Can't Function"

Vocals, Keyboards, Saxophone: Donald Fagen
Vocals, Bass, Guitar: Walter Becker
Drums: John Mazzi
Guitar: Denny Dias

"I Can't Function" is an R&B song with some interesting chord changes and a melody that is very similar to a Steely Dan song from an album released thirty-one years later, "What a Shame About Me" from the Grammy-winning 2000 release *Two Against Nature*. It is also peculiar for two reasons; first, Fagen plays saxophone on the track, something he would only do once during Steely Dan's career, on the

CHARLIE FREAK/THE ROARING OF THE LAMB
SOUL RAM/BROOKLYN/A LITTLE WITH SUGAR
YOU GO WHERE I GO/IDA LEE/ANY WORLD
THIS SEAT'S BEEN TAKEN/BERRYTOWN
SUN MOUNTAIN

Another bootleg of Becker and Fagen's early demos titled *Becker and Fagen: Founders of Steely Dan*.

Duke Ellington composition "East St. Louis Toodle-Oo" from *Pretzel Logic*; and second, Becker and Fagen do a spoken-word part on the outro, something they would only do live on "Hey Nineteen" starting on their 1994 tour of Japan.

"Yellow Peril"

Vocals, Piano: Donald Fagen
Guitar, Vocals: Walter Becker
Hi-Hat: Kenny Vance

"Yellow Peril" is rather sophisticated harmonically, with chord changes and a melody that have more in common with *Aja* than *Can't Buy a Thrill*. The song was originally titled "Finah Minah from China" and demonstrates Fagen's early obsession with the Far East. It also name checks a character named Josie. These elements would find their way onto the band's sixth album, *Aja*. Unfortunately, Becker turns in an inept solo, proving that the song unquestionably would have benefited from a full band recording with Dias on guitar.

"Let George Do It"

Piano: Donald Fagen
Bass: Walter Becker
Vocals: Keith Thomas
Drums: John Discepolo
Guitar: Denny Dias
Background Vocals: Donald Fagen, Walter Becker, Keith Thomas

"Let George Do It" is another slow altered blues shuffle that is a bit like "Chain Lightning." It effortlessly switches from a somewhat dissonant verse to an unexpected set of chords, incorporating effective breaks that lead us back to the dark-sounding verse the first time and then into a straight-ahead blues chorus. It's Thomas's best vocal by far, but screams for a guitar solo in the middle.

"A Little with Sugar"

Vocals, Piano: Donald Fagen
Background Vocals: Walter Becker, Keith Thomas

An interesting spin on how a child perceives the fact that his mother has left the family. The song could not be considered autobiographical if the lyrics were written by Fagen due to his close relationship to his parents. However, Becker's parents separated when he was a young boy, and his mother, who is British, moved to England, so it can be assumed that Becker channeled his feelings as a child into the song. Musically, the verse and pre-chorus are somewhat wistful sounding before turning to a darker, more melancholy chorus. The cyclical movement of the chords on the outro conveys the confusion the narrator is expressing as Fagen bares his soul with some expressive belting, not really his comfort zone.

"Sun Mountain" (versions one and two)

Vocals (version one), Piano: Donald Fagen
Bass (version two): Walter Becker
Drums: John Discepolo
Vocals (version two): Kenny Vance

"Sun Mountain" was recorded on two separate occasions, initially as a piano and vocal demo with Fagen singing, and later as a band recording with Kenny Vance handling the vocals. The waltz-style song is an oddity for Steely Dan. They only used the 3/4 time signature for one song in their canon, the swinging "Your Gold Teeth II" from *Katy Lied*. The original demo doesn't have the gospel flavor of the band recording and comes off as more of a ballad. The band arrangement swings with some appropriate piano work by Fagen and a vocal by Vance, the singer for Jay and the Americans who was wise enough to see the talent of Becker and Fagen, sign them to a publishing deal with JATA Enterprises, and record these early demos that we are so lucky to hear today. "Sun Mountain" is another example of a song that could have been resurrected for *Pretzel Logic* when Becker and Fagen were short on material, rather than the three that they eventually chose.

"More to Come"

Vocals, Piano: Donald Fagen
Handclaps: Walter Becker
Background Vocals: Walter Becker, Keith Thomas

Another simple up-tempo piano/vocal demo, but this one has an element that is extremely rare, a falsetto vocal singing an octave above Fagen's lead vocal, sung by Keith Thomas. Becker adds a low harmony on the chorus, and Fagen's piano playing is strident, with a '70s-style rhythm part embellished with blues licks.

"Parker's Band"

Vocals, Piano: Donald Fagen
Vocals: Walter Becker
Hi-hat: Kenny Vance

"Parker's Band" was fully realized when they recorded the demo including the bass part, played by Fagen on piano. The one change is the chord change at the end of the chorus, something that adds a dramatic touch. It's sung as a duet, with incredibly sloppy vocals by Becker, which thankfully they dropped. It was one of three songs from the early demos to be resurrected for their third album, *Pretzel Logic*.

"Stone Piano" (versions one and two)

Vocals, Piano (both versions): Donald Fagen
Background Vocals (version one), Bass (version two): Walter Becker
Drums (version two): John Discepolo
Background Vocals (version two): Keith Thomas
Hi-Hat (version one): Kenny Vance

"Stone Piano" was another song that was recorded twice. The first is a piano-and-vocal demo version with harmony vocals by Becker and hi-hat presumably played by Kenny Vance. The second, full-band version has double-tracked vocals by Fagen and is unlike anything Steely Dan would release during their recording career. Its happy-go-lucky vibe is apparent from the first bar, and it has a California-style, Beach Boys meets the Turtles type of sound, but with a somewhat sinister twist. It's ironic that it was written years before the duo actually landed in Los Angeles.

"Take It Out on Me"

Vocals, Piano: Donald Fagen

Besides the dissonant intro, "Take It Out On Me" sounds more like a song that was written in hopes that another artist would cover it rather than one that Becker and Fagen had any interest in for themselves. The lyrics can be interpreted as a bit sadomasochistic, but the music is relatively tame, besides the Steely Danesque pre-chorus.

"You Go Where I Go"

Vocals, RMI Electra-Piano: Donald Fagen
Bass: Walter Becker

It's amusing that Becker and Fagen would write so many early tunes in 3/4 waltz time, but would only record one official song with that time signature and feel on record, "Your Gold Teeth II." "You Go Where I Go" doesn't break any new ground, but is a well-written number with enough harmonic twists and turns to sound like a Steely Dan song along with a lyric about somebody going insane, yet depending on his/her partner to shield them from the world and therefore their lunacy.

"Barrytown"

Vocals, Piano: Donald Fagen

The piano/vocal demo of "Barrytown," a song written solely by Fagen, is almost identical in every way to the released version on *Pretzel Logic*. One word is changed, "feel" to "think" in the second pre-chorus, and Fagen switches to the high harmony for part of the bridge. Other than that, nothing was changed when they brought it into the

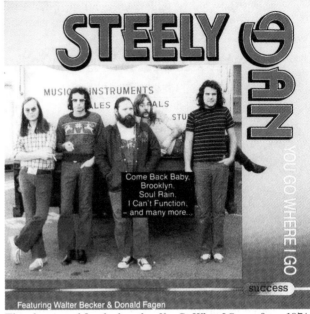

The photo used for the bootleg *You Go Where I Go* was from 1974, although the music was recorded during the Kenny Vance years in the late '60s.

studio to record in 1974, the second of two songs from these sessions.

"Android Warehouse"

Vocals, Piano: Donald Fagen
Vocals: Walter Becker

The composition that would eventually become the second number on *The Royal Scam*, "The Caves of Altamira," possessed the essential vibe of the finished track at this early juncture, but much would change from this piano demo. The entire second verse would be excised from the song, but the third would be kept intact. They also dropped the odd major sounding, choppy instrumental that was heard after each chorus and of course had some of the most renowned session musicians on the record and a killer horn section.

"Charlie Freak"

Vocals, Piano: Donald Fagen
Vocals: Walter Becker

"Charlie Freak" is a song that didn't change much from the initial demo, besides the bluesy intro, and was the third, and final, song from these early demos to find a place on *Pretzel Logic*. The lyrics, chords, and arrangement were already in place down to the melancholy ending, but the fully realized version is a beautiful example of how certain choices in instrumentation could bring a song to fruition.

"Any World (That I'm Welcome To)"

Vocals, RMI Electra-Piano: Donald Fagen
Bass: Walter Becker
Background Vocals: Walter Becker, Keith Thomas

"Any World (That I'm Welcome To)" kept its feel and lyrical significance when it was resuscitated for Steely Dan's fourth album, *Katy Lied*. Some lyrics were changed, for the better, as well as the melody at the beginning of the pre-chorus, but it was a completely developed song, including its bridge. The worst part of this demo: Becker's glaring bass missteps.

"Oh Wow It's You Again"

Vocals, Piano: Donald Fagen
Background Vocals: Keith Thomas

An odd pop/rock piano demo that seems like another "work job." The song does, however, have some unexpected chord changes and a lyric that might not work for a typical artist from the '70s. It's hard to see the song's potential in this early demo, the most incongruous section being the bridge that connects the verse and chorus, the two sections that actually work in the song.

"Roaring of the Lamb"

Vocals, Piano: Donald Fagen
Percussion, Background Vocals: Walter Becker

The verse of "Roaring of the Lamb" has a number of similarities to "Android Warehouse," written around the same time, but the chorus has its own particular chord sequence and melody, creating a completely different atmosphere. Fagen's vocals are full of energy, and they did attempt to record it during their early sessions with Steely Dan, but decided to leave it on the cutting-room floor.

"This Seat's Been Taken"

Vocals, Piano: Donald Fagen
Guitar: Walter Becker
Hi-hat: Kenny Vance

One of Becker and Fagen's simplest early songs both lyrically and musically, "This Seat's Been Taken" was an apparent attempt to attract an artist with a track record to record the song. Becker adds a bit of bluesy guitar, but "This Seat's Been Taken" is an easily forgotten moment in Steely Dan's history.

"Ida Lee"

Vocals, Piano: Donald Fagen
Bass, Guitar: Walter Becker
Drums: Kenny Vance

"Ida Lee" is an interesting song because musically and lyrically it contains elements that would be heard in later songs. First of all, the story of the main character is strikingly similar to "Josie." It even includes the lyrics "we threw out the favors, the hooters and the hats," a line that would be reworked for "Josie." The musical similarity, however, is to a song from Fagen's 1994 solo album *Kamakiriad*. Although the verse melody is relatively simple, it is strikingly similar to the verse of "Tomorrow's Girls." Kenny Vance provides the drums for the track.

"Undecided"

Piano: Donald Fagen
Bass, Guitar: Walter Becker
Drums: John Discepolo
Vocals: Keith Thomas
Guitar: Denny Dias
Background Vocals: Donald Fagen, Walter Becker, Keith Thomas

"Undecided" sounds quite a bit like an early Doobie Brothers song, with big harmonies on the chorus and a mix of strumming acoustic guitar and blues licks. One would think that this song could have worked for any number of artists at ABC Dunhill Records once Becker and Fagen went to work for them as staff songwriters with its straightforward lyrics and '70s-style, easygoing groove. It sounds as if the duo had already relocated to Los Angeles.

"A Horse in Town"

Piano: Donald Fagen
Bass: Walter Becker
Drums: John Discepolo
Vocals: Keith Thomas
Guitar: Denny Dias
Background Vocals: Donald Fagen, Walter Becker, Keith Thomas

One of the more interesting songs from these early demos, "A Horse in Town" is another slice of '60s soul with interesting background vocals, a well-developed guitar part, some harmonic surprises, and lyrics that are worthy of a Steely Dan song. When they mined their early catalog for material for *Pretzel Logic*, they passed on the songs that had more of an R&B influence, possibly thinking they were too derivative, and instead chose three that could be considered more esoteric: "Parker's Band," "Barrytown," and "Charlie Freak."

"You Gotta Walk It Like You Talk It (Or You'll Lose That Beat)"

In 1970, Kenny Vance, who was managing and producing Becker and Fagen at the time, secured a deal for them to write and record the soundtrack for the low-budget film *You've Got to Walk It Like You Talk It or You'll Lose That Beat*. The soundtrack album was for some reason entitled *You Gotta Walk It Like You Talk It (Or You'll Lose That Beat)*. Although the movie only ran for a few weeks, its importance lies in the fact that it is the first officially released music of Becker and Fagen. In addition to Fagen's keyboards and vocals and Becker's bass, future Steely Dan member Denny Dias (incorrectly credited as Denny Diaz) took part in the sessions playing guitar and percussion along with Jay and the Americans' drummer John Discepolo.

For the soundtrack, Becker and Fagen did something that was quite foreign to them; they collaborated on the lyrics. Of the seven songs on the soundtrack (not counting the reprise of the title track), Becker and Fagen only wrote two as a duo. The title track's lyrics were written by the writer/director of the movie, Peter Locke, and sung by Jay and the Americans' guitarist/vocalist Marty Kupersmith, and has some very Steely Danesque moments, but Fagen would have delivered the vocals in a much stronger manner.

The instrumental "Flotsam and Jetsam," written by Becker, Fagen, and Vance is based around a dirge-like organ part along with a distorted, envelope-filtered psychedelic clavinet. "War and Peace" is the only song not credited to Becker and Fagen, given that it's essentially a drum solo by Discepolo, who gets the songwriting credit, along with some avant-garde piano playing by Fagen. "Roll Back the Meaning" is very Crosby, Stills & Nash-like with its three-part harmony and sweet-sounding lead vocal spots by Kenny Vance and was co-written with Fagen's girlfriend at the time, Dorothy White. The song would be covered by Linda Hoover for an unreleased album on which Becker, Fagen, Dias, and producer Gary Katz would play a significant role (see chapter twenty).

"Dog Eat Dog," one of the two Becker and Fagen compositions, is by far the standout song of the soundtrack and the only song with a lead vocal by Fagen. It's the most rocking of the entire album, and Fagen's vocals are so good that you wonder why he ever doubted himself as a lead vocalist. The instrumental "Red Giant/White Dwarf," credited to Becker, Fagen, and Vance, is the longest track on the LP, clocking in at just over eight minutes, and is basically a long guitar solo over a fistful of chords. "If It Rains" is the second song written by Becker and Fagen, yet the lead vocals are again handled by Vance. This gospel-influenced tune begins with piano and vocal and builds throughout, initially adding organ and acoustic guitar followed by drums, bass, and background vocals. Once again it's a question of someone other than Fagen interpreting their material poorly, and the song would have been far more interesting had Fagen sung it himself.

The Debut Single—"Dallas" b/w "Sail the Waterway"

Steely Dan's first single disappeared almost immediately after its release. In actuality, many sources claim that it was never officially released and was only pressed for promotional purposes. The songs were recorded before Dias arrived in Los

Angeles, with the A-side sung by drummer Jim Hodder and the B-side handled by Fagen. Fagen's Wurlitzer electric piano and Baxter's pedal steel guitar are the main attractions, and while Hodder's vocals are acceptable, they are certainly nothing to write home about.

The B-side, "Sail the Waterway," is a ballad with Fagen on lead vocals and piano and does have some Steely Danish chord changes and melodic content. Baxter turns in a short double-tracked solo, and the background vocals in the chorus help to strengthen the hook. Becker and Fagen were never fond of either song and have not allowed their release on CD.

Can't Buy a Thrill Sessions

During the sessions for *Can't Buy a Thrill*, a number of songs were recorded that didn't make the final running order. "Running Child" has a groove similar to "Barrytown," and although it has its moments, it's not surprising that the song wasn't considered for their debut album. It did, however, find an official release on Canadian Christopher Kearney's 1975 *Sweet Water* album. One of the other songs that didn't make the final cut was "Sacajawea," a bouncy tune that would have fit perfectly on their debut LP. There is even some pre-song studio chatter, with Dias saying, "Hey, man, just remember it's just that I like to do it at the beginning of the day."

One curious outtake is an early version of "Megashine City (Talkin' About My Home)." The song was written for David Palmer to sing live, but the band recorded a version during the *Can't Buy a Thrill* sessions with Fagen singing lead. Played as a fast shuffle, the song is catchy, with an unexpected harmonic twist at the end of the chorus. They would return to the song during the *Gaucho* sessions.

One other song would also be recorded during the sessions for their debut album. "Gullywater" is an odd number with strange lyrics, weird sound effects, and a blistering guitar solo by Jeff Baxter.

Countdown to Ecstasy Sessions

During the *Countdown to Ecstasy* sessions, the band was under such pressure to record a new album while on the road, there weren't many outtakes. There is one song that they attempted during the sessions, "This All Too Mobile Home." Becker spoke of it when discussing their early '70s live shows in an interview with *Melody Maker* in 1974. "Incidentally, we record every show we play live on tape—I'm not kidding. If we wanted to we could put out a live LP, but there is only one song that we play on the road that hasn't been recorded before, and that's 'This Mobile Home,' which is a song about a trailer. We tried to record it for *Countdown to Ecstasy* and *Pretzel Logic* and if it was like it is now we might have succeeded." The song has a similar groove to "Show Biz Kids" but with a more developed chord progression and closed many of their shows on the 1974 tour. For the "Rarities" night of their 2011 *Shuffle Diplomacy* tour, they played the song as an encore with added horns and background vocals.

Katy Lied Sessions

The sessions for *Katy Lied* provided not only two unreleased tracks but also numerous early mixes and alternate takes of every song except "Any World (That I'm Welcome To)." The first song, "Mr. Sam," would have sounded right at home on *Katy Lied* with its Motown-like drum groove, unexpected harmonic twists, sparkling combination of piano and acoustic guitar, and lyrics that vividly paint a picture of a failed relationship.

The other unreleased composition, "Funky Driver," is often credited incorrectly as "Gullywater." The song is an instrumental with Jeff Porcaro on drums, Chuck Rainey on bass, and Michael Omartian on piano, and they groove like a well-oiled machine with a bevy of chord changes that suit the vibe of *Katy Lied* to a tee. One can only imagine what the song could have been had Becker and Fagen finished it. The various alternate takes and early mixes of the songs from the final release give insight into the creation of an album that unquestionably was leading Steely Dan in a new direction.

The Royal Scam Sessions

"I Got the News" was originally written during the sessions for *The Royal Scam* and in essence was a completely different song than the version that would appear on *Aja*. Other than the title and some of the lyrics, the first attempt of the song had a different melody, chord changes, and an entirely different groove. While this arrangement is energetic, Becker and Fagen were wise to go back to the drawing board and rewrite this one from scratch.

There are also some outtakes of songs that ended up on the album, including an early instrumental take of "Sign In Stranger"; an instrumental of "Kid Charlemagne" without the lead guitar; a drums, bass, and piano mix of "Everything You Did"; a rhythm section mix of "Green Earrings"; and an alternate take with vocals of "Don't Take Me Alive."

Aja Sessions

The sessions for *Aja* produced several outtakes, including "You Got the Bear." The song is one of the Dan's funkiest with a deep pocket, Fender Rhodes electric piano, clavinet, and a double-tracked vocal by Fagen. The line "If I/ you got the bear or if the bear got me/you" resurfaced in "Down in the Bottom" from Becker's *11 Tracks of Whack* in 1994. Although the song was never officially released, it would be played live on the "Rarities" night of their 2011 *Shuffle Diplomacy* tour, as well as on a few select dates early in the tour.

"Stand by the Seawall" is an instrumental recorded with some of Steely Dan's favorite musicians: Steve Gadd on drums, Chuck Rainey on bass, Michael Omartian on piano, and Larry Carlton on guitar. The song has some "Aja"-like elements and would become one of the sections, with alterations, for the title track of their sixth album.

"Were You Blind That Day" is the original recording of what would become "Third World Man." It's odd that it was left off of *Aja* because it was one of the songs that Fagen spoke of when Susan Shapiro interviewed him in the studio in 1976, nine months before the album's release. The lyrics were rewritten, and female background vocals were added for its eventual release four years later.

Two piano demos of "Black Cow" have also surfaced and prove how developed the arrangement of the song was before it was introduced to the session musicians that would create the ultimate backing for this classic slice of Steely Dan.

The Lost *Gaucho*

The sessions for the *Gaucho* LP spanned nearly two years and provided a number of unreleased tracks. "The Second Arrangement" is possibly the best-known Steely Dan outtake due to the circumstances that led to it being dropped from the final running order. The song was the first to be completed for the album in December 1979, and at the time it was everybody's favorite track. One night when an engineer was preparing the 24-track tape for playback, he inadvertently erased three-quarters of the song. When engineer Roger Nichols advised Fagen of the situation. he had nothing to say; he just left the studio.

They attempted to record it again, but for some reason, they only used three of the four musicians from the original recording. Bassist Will Lee, keyboard player Don Grolnick, and guitarist Hiram Bullock returned, but rather than use Ed Greene on drums, they brought in Steve Gadd. The two drummers had a completely different feel and approach to the music, so they weren't satisfied with the results, and the song was shelved.

It is a beautiful song and would have been a welcome addition to *Gaucho*. Three versions currently circulate. The first is a demo with bass, Fender Rhodes electric piano, and a reggaeish piano part along with Fagen's vocals; and even with this simple, sparse arrangement, it shows why everybody was enamored with the tune. The second is a two-and-a-half-minute instrumental fragment of the original full-band take that still utilizes the piano and Fender Rhodes electric piano. The third has a similar feel to "Glamour Profession" with shades of "Deacon Blues" on the breakdown. Guitarist Hiram Bullock plays the instrumental hook, and this version also contains some fantastic background vocals. It still has a reggae-like groove, but it's more subdued, with the Fender Rhodes electric piano incorporating the original piano part with jazz-inflected fills, and what sounds like Wendel the drum machine (discussed in further detail in chapters six and sixteen). The song was played live once, on September 17, 2011, on the "Rarities" night at the Beacon Theatre in New York City.

Another song that was shelved was "I Can't Write Home About You." It was only recorded in demo form, with Becker on bass and Fagen on piano, Fender Rhodes electric piano, and vocals, just like the Brill Building days. It's another song that most songwriters would have been happy to write. It's one of their most harmonically complex and Fagen contributes a cool electric piano solo.

"Kulee Baba" is another song from the sessions that produced two versions. The first, a piano/vocal demo by Fagen, contains all the elements of a *Gaucho*-era

The *Gaucho Outtakes* includes not only early versions of certain songs, but a number of unreleased tracks, demos, and outtakes.

Steely Dan song: jazzy chord changes over a funk-disco-influenced groove, with difficult melodies that somehow are extraordinarily catchy, and lyrics that paint mental pictures. The second is a full-band recording with drums, bass, Fender Rhodes electric piano, guitar, and Fagen's vocals. The lyrics are quite forward thinking, with the topic being Reality TV, something that would eventually dominate the airwaves.

"Kind Spirit" begins with a piano part that sounds strikingly similar to both "The Caves of Altamira" and "Home at Last," but it has a bit of a different groove than the songs that would end up on *Gaucho*. Although Fagen has no lyrics for the verse or the pre-chorus, his chorus seems to be in place. It would have been insightful to see where they could have gone with this shell of a song had they deemed it worthy.

The *Can't Buy a Thrill*-era tune "Megashine City (Talkin' About My Home)" was resurrected during the *Gaucho* sessions, dropping "Megashine City" from the lyric in favor of "The City in the Sky" and rearranging the song with a different, more developed chord progression. Ex-Steely Dan guitarist Drew Zingg recorded an instrumental of this new version of the song for his eponymous debut release in 2012. Early stripped-down mixes and alternate takes of songs from the final running order of *Gaucho* have also become available. These recordings give the listener an "in the studio" glimpse into the working process of Becker and Fagen.

Other Steely Dan Rarities

During their 1996 tour, Becker and Fagen premiered three new songs that they were working on, "Wet Side Story," "Cash Only Island," and "Jack of Speed." The first sounds a lot like an early version of "Cousin Dupree," with a chorus that is somewhat uninspired. The second, "Cash Only Island," is better, and focuses on the dueling guitars of Becker and Jon Herington. The problem with both of these songs is that the melodies are unimaginative, something that began with Fagen's *Kamakiriad*, and like so many other songs from this time period, this one is based on a one-chord groove. The only one to make the final cut for the next album, *Two Against Nature*, was "Jack of Speed," but at this point Becker was handling the lead vocals. He would return as lead vocalist for their performance of the song on "Rarities" night in 2011 at the Beacon Theatre in New York City.

Marian McPartland Piano Jazz

In 2002, Becker and Fagen were guests on eighty-four-year-old jazz pianist Marian McPartland's *Piano Jazz* show on National Public Radio. McPartland and Fagen both played piano, Becker was on guitar, Jay Leonhart (father of Steely Dan trumpet player Michael Leonhart) played acoustic bass, and Keith Carlock was on drums. The band opened the show with Duke Ellington's "Limbo Jazz" and did stripped-down versions of the Steely Dan songs "Josie," "Chain Lightning," and "Black Friday," a fascinating listen. Carlock did a wonderful job of changing up the grooves just enough to work with acoustic bass and two pianos extremely well. Fagen and McPartland played piano duets of Duke Ellington's "Mood Indigo" and his son Mercer's "Things Ain't What They Used to Be." The band also did a swinging rendition of W. C. Handy's "Hesitation Blues" featuring a soulful vocal delivery from Fagen.

12

You Won't Believe What the Boys Are Blowing

The Next Two Steely Dan Albums

After Steely Dan's third LP, *Pretzel Logic*, Becker and Fagen refused to return to the road and broke up the band. They would rely solely on session musicians for all future records, although Denny Dias was still involved as a hired player and would continue to help with mixing duties on their fourth LP. Jeff Baxter had already joined the Doobie Brothers, but unfortunately, drummer Jim Hodder refused the gig before he knew that Becker and Fagen had no intention of keeping the band together, so drummer Keith Knudsen got the job. Baxter was playing at the Knebworth Festival in England with the Doobie Brothers when Fagen called him with the news that he and Becker wanted to continue without him and Hodder.

For their next two albums, *Katy Lied* and *The Royal Scam*, the duo enlisted some of the finest musicians in the world, and their compositions took on a more refined, jazzier feel than their previous LPs. The pair of albums would also showcase the funkier side of the Dan heard on a few tracks on *Pretzel Logic* and laid the groundwork for what many consider Steely Dan's masterpiece, *Aja*.

Katy Lied

With Becker and Fagen permanently off the road, they were able to bunker down in the studio and fully concentrate on the task at hand, the recording of their fourth album. They once again opted for shorter songs, although not as short as *Pretzel Logic*, with all except "Your Gold Teeth II" clocking in between three and four minutes. They also followed another trend set with *Pretzel Logic*, using only one drummer for 90 percent of the tracks. Becker and Fagen were so impressed with drummer Jeff Porcaro and vocalist/keyboard player Michael McDonald on the final Steely Dan tour that they hired them for extensive work on the album. Porcaro would play drums on every song on the album bar one, "Any World (That I'm Welcome To)," on which drum legend Hal Blaine plays. McDonald's rich, soulful baritone voice, which would soon become a staple of pop and rock records in the '70s and '80s, was utilized on numerous tracks and played a significant role in creating the sound of songs such as "Black Friday," "Bad Sneakers," "Rose Darling," and "Any World (That I'm Welcome To)." It's important to note that the sessions for *Katy Lied* were McDonald's first in a recording studio, and he handled them with aplomb.

Counting Denny Dias, nineteen session musicians and singers were used on *Katy Lied* in addition to Becker and Fagen, up from the fifteen utilized on *Pretzel Logic*. Pianist Michael Omartian, who had first worked with Steely Dan on *Pretzel Logic*, was instructed to choose a piano for the sessions, so he went to Dave Abell Music, which was across the street from the ABC recording studio in North Hollywood, and chose a seven-foot-six Bösendorfer that cost $13,000. Needless to say, the executives at ABC Dunhill weren't pleased when they received the bill.

An advertisement for *Katy Lied* as well as the rest of Steely Dan's back catalog.

Although the musicians were the cream of the crop and the songs were exceptional, things didn't proceed so smoothly once it was time to mix the album. The problems actually began during tracking when a steam generator that was supposed to keep the air at 50 percent humidity failed, causing the air in the studio to become thick and wet. Although it was fixed within a day, some, including Denny Dias, believe that some oxidation had occurred that in his words "caused the studio and even the tapes themselves to fester."

The whole album was mixed before they realized that there was a serious problem with the new, supposedly superior, dbx noise reduction system they were using. The mixes lost clarity and were dull in comparison to what was recorded. After aligning the systems several times with no improvement, Becker, Fagen, producer Gary Katz, and engineer Roger Nichols flew to the dbx headquarters on the East Coast to see if they had any explanation. They didn't. Although they were given a special unit that allowed them to calibrate certain settings that were normally fixed, they still had no luck.

Denny Dias has stated that the original twenty-four-track masters were still in good shape, so they remixed the album using the older Dolby noise reduction system. But Becker has contradicted Dias's recollection, saying that what was on the original master tapes was definitely affected by the faulty dbx system.

They came close to scrapping the entire album, and to this day Katz has a hard time listening to it. Dias, however, recently compared the original mixes and the finished mixes, wondering whether they made different choices the second time around. He professed that the new ones were better in every way. Some changes that occurred:

1. On the original mix of "Doctor Wu," the entire band faded at the end while Phil Woods's saxophone solo soldiered on alone.
2. The original vocals on "Daddy Don't Live in That New York City No More" didn't utilize the manual phasing technique as heard on the final mix.
3. A drum figure heard during the guitar solo of "Bad Sneakers" was compressed in a way that made it sound quite different than the original.

More problems arose when it came time to master the recording. The way certain instruments were recorded made it next to impossible to duplicate on vinyl without making the needle jump. They used two different mastering facilities and were still unhappy, so Dias attempted to master the album himself. Although it was better than the first two attempts, it still wasn't up to their standards, so Becker mastered the recording released in 1975; a version that in their opinion wasn't up to par either but sounded better on more sound systems. To date, the best-sounding version of the album is the one heard on 1993's *Citizen Steely Dan* box set or the stand-alone CD released in 1998.

The Songs

Katy Lied was Steely Dan's jazziest album to date, and without the hassle of touring, Becker, Fagen, and Katz were able to use the studio in increasingly cutting-edge ways. The songs run the gamut, with bluesy shuffles, straight ahead jazz, cha-cha rhythms, and R&B pockets all sharing space within the grooves. With *Katy Lied*, Becker and Fagen had found a perfect blend of rock and jazz, but they would continue to alter their sound with each successive album.

"Black Friday"
The album's first track creeps in with an extended fade before kicking in with a sinister groove about the aftermath of a stock market crash. Fagen has stated that it was about the crash of 1929, which occurred on a Tuesday, but it is more likely about the crash that occurred on Friday, September 24, 1869, known as "Black Friday," when two wealthy investors attempted to corner the market on gold, but their plans were thwarted when President Ulysses S. Grant ordered the U.S. government to release $4 million in gold into the market. The premium plummeted, and many investors were financially ruined, but ironically the two men who began hoarding gold in the first place escaped unscathed. In Steely Dan's "Black Friday," the main character also escapes with his finances intact, but in the song he disappears to Muswellbrook in New South Wales, Australia, a town where many wealthy investors traveled to fund the profitable mines in the area. Fagen stated that they picked the town randomly out of an atlas looking for the farthest place from New York, but that seems highly unlikely.

While the backing track sounds like a typical shuffle groove, it took quite a bit of time to work out the way the two keyboard parts and the guitar play against each other. They originally utilized an acoustic piano along with the Wurlitzer electric piano, and a much busier bass line, but decided to use a phased Hohner pianet and a Wurlitzer electric piano played by Michael Omartian and David Paich panned hard left and right in the stereo spectrum to great effect. Porcaro and Becker lay down the ideal groove, and Becker proves just how good a bass player he is with perfectly executed runs in all of the right spots. Porcaro was initially having a hard time finding the perfect pocket for the

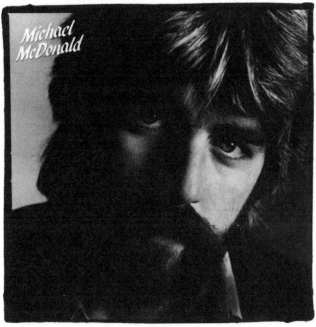

Michael McDonald's first professional recording session was for *Katy Lied*. McDonald had toured with the band in 1974 to promote *Pretzel Logic* playing keyboards as well as singing, and his signature vocal style would be heard on a number of tracks on their fourth album. His debut solo LP, *If That's What It Takes*, was released in 1982 and spawned the hit "I Keep Forgettin' (Every Time You're Near)."

song and was extremely frustrated, telling them they should have gotten Jim Gordon. Becker also shows his prowess as a guitar player, laying down two superbly performed, heavily distorted solos played on a Fender Mustang with rusty strings, as well as some tasteful rhythm guitar playing. Fagen's impassioned lead vocal is bolstered on the choruses by Michael McDonald, a sound that would become synonymous with Steely Dan over the next few albums. "Black Friday" would be released as the lead-off single, but would only reach number thirty-seven on the charts.

"Bad Sneakers"
"Bad Sneakers" is arguably the "smoothest" song recorded by Steely Dan to date and is a true sign of what we were in store for. In some ways it's almost like a mini "Aja" with the crack rhythm section of Porcaro, Rainey, Omartian, and Steely Dan newbie, guitarist Hugh McCracken, deftly moving from one disparate section to the next. The melancholy verse and bridge lead into an optimistic chorus that then transforms into a reggae-like, funk feel for the solo, but they all fit together seamlessly.

Although the rhythm section laid down the foundation for the tune, the addition of Victor Feldman's vibraphone and Denny Dias's Coral electric sitar, the first time heard on a Dan song since "Do It Again," adds another musical layer that makes the song that much more interesting. Becker again turns in a fabulous solo, his second and final one on the album, ripping from the start while demonstrating his jazz and blues phrasing in spades. One of the highlights of the song, however, is the second bridge that introduces Michael McDonald's background vocals. For many, the "going insane" line is the most memorable part of the song.

Lyrically, the song is told from a New Yorker's perspective of living in Los Angeles and the simple things he misses about New York City. Many believe that the "Five names that I can hardly stand to hear" are the original members of Steely Dan, which is quite possible. If so, Becker and Fagen include themselves in the next line, and it's probable that the "one more chimp who isn't here" is Jeff "Baxter. It was released as a single, but peaked at a disappointing 103 on the charts.

"Rose Darling"

Becker and Fagen were huge fans of the writer Vladimir Nabokov, so it is entirely possible that the title of the third tune from the *Katy Lied* LP came from the line "My lovely young girls, my darling rose-flushed young girls" from his novel *Lolita*. The groove is more of a straight rock feel, reminiscent of their first two albums, but with harmonic twists at every corner.

The song's guitar-laden yet concise intro leads us into another song of infidelity delivered by Fagen in a Dylanesque voice that somehow convinces the listener that one should be sympathetic to his unfaithful tendencies, although they seem slightly skewed. Guitarist Dean Parks, who had played acoustic and electric guitar on the *Pretzel Logic* LP, performs his first solo on "Rose Darling," a rousing blend of melodic motifs and bluesy riffs that actually bring the song to a halt for a moment before the last chorus. "Rose Darling" is a rare case of a musician playing a transcribed solo for a Steely Dan record, and Parks rises to the challenge. Michael McDonald's background vocals are a significant part of the hook and add weight in a way that Becker and Fagen never expected.

One aspect of the song that is felt more than heard is the tambourine that plays throughout the song. There was, however, a rare moment when engineer Roger Nichols made a mistake and erased part of Victor Feldman's tambourine part. Luckily, it wasn't too difficult to remedy the situation.

"Daddy Don't Live in That New York City No More"

"Daddy Don't Live in That New York City No More" tells the tale of a gangster who is run out of town by his rivals and can no longer live the high life he was enjoying in the city. It is another throwback to '60s soul music (think of it as a more advanced "Monkey in Your Soul"). The song originally was more piano based, but they wisely rethought what the song needed and dropped the piano altogether. The track slinks along with a strong R&B-flavored backbeat provided by the drums, bass, swirling organ, handclaps, and two rhythm guitar parts: Becker playing a chicken-pickin' single-note line and Dean Parks focusing on the chordal elements by accenting the two and four with the snare drum. Interestingly both rhythm guitar players get short four-bar spotlights; Becker takes two, one before the second verse and one before the third verse, and Parks handles the one before the outro. The rhythm section lays the foundation for guitarist Larry Carlton's first appearance on a Steely Dan record.

Carlton recalled how he first got the call to work with Steely Dan in a 1991 article from the fanzine *Metal Leg*. "They had everything cut except for one song, and they'd tried virtually every guitar player in town except me. I think they thought I was a jazzer, because of my Crusaders work . . . prior to this I had arranged an album for Joan Baez, called *Diamonds and Rust*. . . . I got this call to do an overdubbed rhythm part for Steely Dan . . . So we started running it and what I played was exactly what they wanted. So we did the take and I was out of there in an hour. . . . I asked them later how come they never called me before that . . . Walter Becker said 'I'm not a Joan Baez fan at all, but when I heard what you could do with the music of somebody I don't like, I thought this guy's got something, we should check him out.'" Like the other guitar parts, Carlton's straddles the fine line between rhythm and lead guitar, although he takes more of the lead role and provides the perfect counterpoint to Becker and Parks's parts, adding the stinging guitar part that was missing.

"Doctor Wu"

Fagen explained in a 1977 interview with *New Times* magazine that "Doctor Wu" was about "kind of a love-dope triangle. I think usually when we do write songs of a romantic nature, one or more of the participants in the alliance will come under the influence of someone else or some other way of life, and that will usually end up in either some sort of compromise or a split. In this song the girl meets somebody who leads another kind of life and she's attracted to it. Then she comes under the domination of someone else and that results in the ending of the relationship, or some amending of the relationship. In 'Doctor Wu' that someone else is a dope habit, personified as Doctor Wu."

Harmonically, "Doctor Wu" is a sophisticated piece of music, but production-wise it's relatively simple: drums, bass, piano, tone-pedal guitar, vocals, and alto saxophone. But it is the first take saxophone solo of jazz legend Phil Woods, who would also contribute an unforgettable solo to Billy Joel's "Just the Way You Are" two years later, that makes the song the hidden gem that it is. There was, however, one problem. The tape head developed an irregularity on track seventeen, which contained Woods's saxophone, and each time it was played bits of oxide were scraped off, making it sound dull. The solution was to avoid any part of the song with saxophone while they were working until they were ready for the final mix. The solo is one of the most intoxicating moments in the entire Steely Dan catalog.

Woods released over fifty albums as a leader and played with everybody from Dizzy Gillespie to Thelonious Monk to Clark Terry. He died of emphysema in 2015 at age eighty-three.

"Everyone's Gone to the Movies"

"Everyone's Gone to the Movies" is one of two songs from *Katy Lied* that was resurrected from the *Can't Buy a Thrill* and pre-record-deal days. It was originally recorded during the sessions for their debut album with background vocals by Mark Volman and Howard Kaylan, better known as Flo and Eddie from the

Turtles, and in myriad ways is the most perverse of all Dan tunes. It tells the story of a neighborhood lecher who is somehow able to persuade underage teens to "Mr. LaPage's den" to show them pornographic material.

The new version recorded for *Katy Lied* originally incorporated a heavy piano part and a somewhat out-of-control clavinet. Luckily, they rethought the process, slowed the song down, and went with a Latin-flavored feel highlighting Porcaro's rock-steady groove, Rainey's double-time funk bass, myriad layers of Victor Feldman's percussion and vibraphone, and Michael Omartian's funky Wurlitzer electric piano. The electric piano solo alone is worth the price of admission.

While female background vocals would become more prominent on their later albums, Steely Dan had only used them on two songs on *Can't Buy a Thrill* and one song on *Countdown to Ecstasy*. *Pretzel Logic* featured no female background vocals, but *Katy Lied* utilized them for one song, "Everyone's Gone to the Movies," and it somehow softened the depraved, perverse sentiment of the lyric.

"Your Gold Teeth II"

Many critics and fans often use the term "jazz" when describing Steely Dan, but "Your Gold Teeth II," the so-called sequel to "Your Gold Teeth" from *Countdown to Ecstasy*, is arguably the most "jazz-like" song Steely Dan ever recorded. It begins with an intricate prelude that incorporates a completely different feel from the rest of the song. This prelude had been played during live shows in 1974 as a five-minute-plus intro to "Reelin' in the Years" with solos by both Dias and Baxter, but at this point it was shortened in order to serve as an introduction to the second song on side two of *Katy Lied*.

After the synthesizer-laden, vibraphone-heavy intro, the groove settles in with a swinging waltz that flows freely, but that wasn't always the case. The mixed-meter, Coltrane-like waltz initially caused drummer Jeff Porcaro quite a lot of grief. After spending a full day working on the song, his swing groove still wasn't quite right, and he was feeling the pressure. Rather than bring in another drummer, Fagen had another idea. Porcaro recalled in an interview for *Modern Drummer* magazine, "'Your Gold Teeth II' is a song with lots of bars of 3/8, 6/8, and 9/8. And it's bebop! I could swing the cymbal beat and fake it, but that always bothered me. After recording it, Fagen gave me a Charles Mingus record with Dannie Richmond on drums. It had a tune that was full of 6/8 and 9/8 bars. I listened to that for a couple of days, and we tried it again and it worked."

The highlight of the song, however, is Denny Dias's flawless solo. His guitar prowess is on full display with bebop licks that flow effortlessly and an intensity that is hard to match. His playing on "Your Gold Teeth II" is a precursor to the stellar solo he would lay down for the title track of their 1977 LP, *Aja*. Dias's solo was so ridiculous that on a bootleg of early mixes and alternate takes Fagen exclaims, "Holy fuck, that's great!" and it is.

"Chain Lightning"

When Becker and Fagen were initially asked to divulge the meaning of "Chain Lightning" in an interview with *Sounds* magazine in 1976, the duo didn't divulge too much.

Becker: No one will ever come close to "Chain Lightning." No one will ever touch "Chain Lightning."

Fagen: Even the clue wouldn't have helped. I'll tell you what the clue was. In the guitar break just before the second verse I was going to say "40 years later," but we decided it wasn't a good musical idea.

Since then, they have been a bit more forthcoming, and Fagen eventually gave the listeners some insight into the song's origin. "Chain Lightning" is about two men attending a fascist rally during Hitler's reign and revisiting the site decades later, albeit quietly, to reminisce.

The song gets off to a rollicking start with a gorgeous Wurlitzer electric piano intro played by Michael Omartian that leads into the second shuffle on the album. The rhythm section of Porcaro, Rainey, and Omartian lays down a swampy groove that leaves room for Rick Derringer's slide guitar, in many ways the focal point of the track. Note that during the first half of the solo he plays a hammer-on guitar figure in the background that cuts out abruptly, revealing the punch-in. Omartian adds a Wurlitzer solo on the outro as Fagen harmonizes with himself and makes fascism sound slick and subdued.

"Any World (That I'm Welcome To)"
"Any World (That I'm Welcome To)" is the earliest song written by Becker and Fagen that was recorded for the album. The song was originally demoed during the Kenny Vance days and offered to both Linda Hoover and Dusty Springfield, but since it wasn't recorded by either artist, Becker and Fagen dusted it off for *Katy Lied*. The song hardly changed from the original demo, with only the melody of the pre-chorus getting a slight overhaul and the lyrics of the last pre-chorus being reworked. The instrumentation, however, is what completely transformed the song from its humble beginnings.

The understated yet commanding piano part is one of the major changes, with Michael Omartian's reharmonization of the chords significantly altering the overall mood, adding an air of mystery not heard on the original demo. The use of the Hammond organ is also clever, entering during the second verse and creating another texture. The song isn't very guitar heavy, with a phased rhythm guitar part on the chorus and a simple, melodic lead that pops in and out throughout the song. "Any World (That I'm Welcome To)" is the only song on *Katy Lied* on which drummer Jeff Porcaro didn't play, but his shoes were filled by legendary L.A. session musician Hal Blaine. While Fagen's vocals perfectly tell the tale of a man who is at odds with his surroundings, Michael McDonald's background vocal is what takes the song to the stratosphere and makes "Any World" one of the standout tracks from *Katy Lied*, although it is often overlooked.

"Throw Back the Little Ones"
Another piano-based song, "Throw Back the Little Ones" is a perfect album closer, a tune with a backbeat, a harmonically challenging chord progression and arrangement, and lyrics that evoke the image of a con man working his way

through the city. Porcaro weaves through the stylistic modulations with ease, making the feel and time changes sound effortless. It's the only song on *Katy Lied* with horns, and it's the most challenging horn chart written to date. It's also the second song on the album to rely on Denny Dias's Coral electric sitar, an instrument they hadn't used since "Do It Again" from *Can't Buy a Thrill*.

Elliott Randall returns to perform on his first song since "Reelin' in the Years" and "Kings" from *Can't Buy a Thrill*. His extended solo twists through myriad key changes and floats atop the horn arrangement impeccably. The song's coda is a completely new section showcasing the tasteful and urbane piano playing of Michael Omartian. The superimposed triads that close the song, and therefore the album, were Omartian's idea and end *Katy Lied* with a gentle touch.

Conclusion

Katy Lied was most definitely a step in a new direction for Steely Dan. While the band kept the songs short, as they had done on *Pretzel Logic*, these compositions were jazzier both harmonically and stylistically. They still included ferocious guitar solos, but for their fourth album, they used seven different guitarists for ten songs. Fagen hardly played any keyboards on the album, relying heavily on Michael Omartian to handle the majority of the parts, with David Paich helping out on a few songs.

Jeff Porcaro tackled the drumming duties with aplomb and a sense of style not typical for a twenty-one-year-old. Larry Carlton also made his debut on *Katy Lied* and would play a significant role on both *The Royal Scam* and *Aja* as well as *The Nightfly*. *Katy Lied* is also noteworthy for the recording debut of Michael McDonald. His soul-stirring baritone transformed every song he performed on and made each chorus he sang a moment that was not easily forgotten.

The album got mixed reviews but still reached number thirteen in both the U.S. and the U.K., their highest chart position to date overseas and second highest in the states. John Mendelsohn's review of the album for *Rolling Stone* was odd, with the critic heaping praise on the band before doing an about face and stating that he doesn't care if he ever again hears "any of Steely Dan's music up to and including *Katy Lied*." Although he thought they were "immaculately tasteful and intelligent," he felt they lacked passion. Mike Flood of *Sounds* was more complimentary, recognizing that "they've never made a bad record" and concluding that "All the familiar hallmarks of Steely Dan are here: the progressive chord changes with guitar, piano and voices in harness, the ethereal voices, the deft instrumental work, the smoothness that never degenerates into blandness; even the occasional dash of real punchy rock and roll. Hell, it's the superfine mixture as before, what more could you ask for?" Becker and Fagen would continue to develop, and their productions would become even slicker over the next three albums, leaving some fans dismayed and others ecstatic.

The Royal Scam

The sessions for *The Royal Scam* took the idea of the workshop environment to new levels. They began working on the album in Los Angeles with engineer

Elliot Scheiner manning the desk during the tracking sessions. They had first met Scheiner in 1970 when working on the *Capture the Moment* LP with Jay and the Americans; and since they were looking for a different sound for the album, it made sense to start with the engineer. They spent two weeks at Davlen Sound Studios in North Hollywood but weren't happy with anything they tracked there, so they flew to New York, Scheiner's home turf, and began recording at A&R Studios. They had already attempted the songs with six or seven different rhythm sections, so when they arrived in New York, they only brought one musician, guitarist Larry Carlton.

The New York sessions were infinitely more successful with half of the backing tracks cut in two weeks. Becker and Fagen once again were looking to use the most cutting-edge technology, but as had happened on *Katy Lied*, they had technological problems. Scheiner told them of a system where they could link two 16-track recorders, thus giving them eight more tracks than the 24-track machines they were used to using. Unfortunately, the manufacturers didn't advise them that the tape couldn't be edited once linked together, so they transferred the material to 24-track tape and headed back to Los Angeles. Becker, Fagen, and Katz all blamed Scheiner for the trouble, and he did not participate in the rest of the sessions. Scheiner was upset by their decision, especially because in a two-week period he successfully recorded the backing tracks for more than half of the album. They would eventually forgive him, and he would return to mix *Aja*.

After experimenting with so many drummers and rhythm sections in Los Angeles, Becker and Fagen found who they were looking for in New York: drummer Bernard "Pretty" Purdie. Purdie played on six of the nine tracks with another Steely Dan newcomer, Rick Marotta, providing drums for the remaining three songs. Bassist Chuck Rainey was back, as were percussionist/keyboard player Victor Feldman; guitarists Larry Carlton, Dean Parks, Denny Dias, and Elliott Randall; saxophonist Plas Johnson; and background vocalists Venetta Fields, Clydie King, Shirley Matthews (listed as Sherlie Matthews), Michael McDonald, and Timothy B. Schmit. One of the major changes was in the keyboard section. Paul Griffin and Don Grolnick played on their first Steely Dan sessions for *The Royal Scam* and added a funkiness that is prevalent throughout most of the tracks. In many ways, *The Royal Scam* is the album where Becker and Fagen truly embraced their love of a good groove, and it makes for an exceptional album that blends elements of funk, reggae, and soul to perfection.

The Songs

The Royal Scam is arguably the funkiest album that Steely Dan ever recorded due to the addition of some New York members to the rhythm section. In addition to the myriad genres that Becker and Fagen had already mined, they added reggae, Stevie Wonderesque funk, disco, and the dark, haunting film score quality of the title track to their ever-growing stockpile of musical styles. Their next album would be an amalgamation of everything they had learned so far.

"Kid Charlemagne"
There had always been references to drug dealers, addicts, alcoholics, prostitutes, and other members from the underworld in their work, but "Kid Charlemagne"

was a bit different. Becker and Fagen admitted that the song was loosely based on Augustus Owsley Stanley, the infamous LSD manufacturer who was also the audio engineer for the San Francisco band the Grateful Dead. He was the first private individual to manufacture mass quantities of LSD, and between 1965 and 1967, it is estimated that he produced more than ten million doses of the drug.

The rhythm section of Purdie, Rainey, Carlton, Grolnick, and Griffin recorded the song in one take, something that is a bit of a miracle for a Steely Dan song. The Fender Rhodes electric piano, clavinet, and rhythm guitar dance around each other as the drums and bass lay down the foundation for one of the funkiest Steely Dan tracks ever recorded. Although Rainey was often given a specific bass line to give him an idea of what they were looking for, *Kid Charlemagne* was his own invention, using Motown bassist James Jamerson for inspiration.

Although Larry Carlton's famous guitar solo was a composite of only two takes, he had already spent close to two hours playing solos that they didn't keep. When asked if it was a high point of his career as a session musician Carlton replied, "Probably so. I can't think of anything else that I still like to listen to as strongly as that." It was released as a single with "Green Earrings" as the B-side, but for some unknown reason it only reached number eighty-two on the charts, their lowest-charting single ever.

"Caves of Altamira"

"The Caves of Altamira" is based on an early composition entitled "Android Warehouse." The song retained the majority of the original lyrics, although the second verse was dropped entirely. The melody arrived intact, as did most of the chord changes, but the song was streamlined, with some awkward breaks cut to keep the groove steady. And what a groove it is. Rick Marotta lays down the slow-burning funk reminiscent of Earth, Wind & Fire, and the rest of the rhythm section simply lets the drums breathe while hitting all the accents tightly. The horn section is also an integral part of the sound of the track, arranged by Becker and Fagen along with trumpet player Chuck Findley. They also hired Garry Sherman, a veteran in the business, to write the charts, but he only got a thank you in the liner notes, possibly because of his patronizing attitude that had led the duo to contemplate locking him in the studio overnight.

Becker and Fagen's inspiration for the lyrics for "Caves of Altamira" came from an odd place. German Nationalist Hans Baumann, who was recruited by the Nazi Youth party as a songwriter, author, and journalist and served in the SS, wrote a book entitled *The Caves of Great Hunters* in 1955 that tells the tale of a visitor to the Caves of Altamira in Spain who is astonished by the Upper Paleolithic paintings on the walls. The song's fabulous saxophone solo was played by John Klemmer, only the fourth on a Steely Dan album to date.

"Don't Take Me Alive"

"Don't Take Me Alive" was inspired by a series of news articles in Los Angeles about people who would barricade themselves with an extensive arsenal of weapons. It's astonishing that Becker and Fagen could tell such a compelling tale in two verses and a chorus. The lyrics perfectly encapsulate the sense of fear and madness that the narrator feels and paints the picture with astounding clarity. Fagen believed that the most important qualities were apparent in the lyrics, but he understood that certain parts of a story had to be condensed within the confines of a song. The fact that the duo were so well read led them to use more literary techniques than most other writers, which is demonstrated in "Don't Take Me Alive."

"Don't Take Me Alive" was originally recorded by drummer Herb Lovelle, but his take didn't make the final recording. They loved his snare sound so much that they looped it and sampled it for use on the *Gaucho* LP. Drummer Rick Marotta ended up playing on the track, his first Steely Dan session, and he was so taken by the song that he almost stopped playing. Marotta claims that he hadn't heard of Steely Dan when he arrived at the session, but this seems highly unlikely. He was incredibly impressed by Becker and Fagen's level of focus and their attention to detail and discussed it in a 1992 interview with *Modern Drummer* magazine. "On 'Don't Take Me Alive' there's one backbeat in the sixteenth or seventeenth bar that was a little softer than the others. I'd say, 'Donald, show me where.' He'd wait for the tape to come around and he'd point it out. 'Right here.' He'd pick the same spot each time."

The song is haunting from the first heavily distorted six-note arpeggiated chord played by Carlton. It leads directly into a striking guitar solo before settling into the pocket for the verse. The production is sparse, with drums, bass, Fender Rhodes electric piano, and guitar creating the backdrop for this tale of terror.

"Sign In Stranger"

Becker and Fagen rely on their love of science fiction novels for this reggaeish tale of an imaginary planet where all types of criminals are banished. Given that it is a planet full of underworld characters, some have found a way to erase a criminal's past, for a price. The images are tangible, and one can feel the seediness and danger apparent at every turn.

Purdie and Rainey lay down a reggae-funk groove, and Elliott Randall plays some stinging lead guitar over their pocket, harmonizing with himself at the end of the chorus. But the highlight is Paul Griffin's rollicking piano part. He starts off with the main riff of the song and trades licks with Randall throughout until he takes off into the stratosphere after the middle. There is not a misplaced note in his entire sixteen-bar, New Orleans–style solo, and his feel is impeccable. Randall rips another magnificent solo on the outro as the horn section enters to take us home.

"The Fez"

"The Fez" is one of only three songs on any Steely Dan record that is not strictly a Becker and Fagen composition. The others: Duke Ellington and Bubber Miley's "East St. Louis Toodle-Oo" and "Gaucho," the song that Becker and Fagen had to add Keith Jarrett's name to after they lost a plagiarism lawsuit citing the similarity between "Gaucho" and Jarrett's "Long as You Know You're Living Yours." Becker, Fagen, and Griffin have never agreed on the origins of the song, with Becker and Fagen claiming that Griffin came up with the keyboard melody for the song during the session. Becker stated, somewhat facetiously in an article in the fanzine *Metal Leg*, "we had some suspicion that perhaps this melody wasn't entirely Paul's invention, [so] we decided to give him composer credit in case later some sort of scandal developed, he would take the brunt of the impact." Griffin tells the opposite story, saying that they had a melody in place that was extremely similar to a classical composition so he altered it to avoid a plagiarism suit.

Either way, this ode to safe sex is downright funky and highly rhythmic, with the piano and rhythm guitar playing off each other while the drums and bass lay down the pocket dead center. Add a layer of Fender Rhodes electric piano and the synthesizer melody, and you have one catchy track. Becker plays two guitar solos on "The Fez," his only ones on the album. Playing through a phaser, he navigates around myriad chord changes with ease and builds his first solo to an arresting conclusion. His solo on the outro is equally deft and demonstrates his imaginative approach to playing the guitar. The second single from *The Royal Scam* did better than "Kid Charlemagne" but still stalled at number fifty-nine.

"Green Earrings"

Side two opens in a similar manner to how side one closed, with another groove-fueled track, "Green Earrings." The rhythm section carries the song, with a spectacular drum part by Purdie along with a bubbling bass line by Rainey finished off by Carlton's chicken-pickin' guitar and Griffin's Stevie Wonderish clavinet part, all played live on the basic tracks. Originally, the tune was over seven minutes long, but once Don Grolnick overdubbed a Fender Rhodes electric piano, additional guitar work was added, and Fagen topped it off with a synthesizer line played during the middle section, the song was trimmed to a more manageable 4:09. It is fascinating to hear the last three minutes, as the rhythm section players come up with various ways to embellish the groove.

Denny Dias plays the first solo, his only one on the album, over some beautiful chord changes, adding the right touch of bebop phrasing, his specialty. Elliott Randall takes over once the band kicks back into the song's main groove, and the disparity between the solos is remarkable, demonstrating Becker and Fagen's eye for detail. Randall picks up where he left off for the outro solo as it dissolves into a spacey conclusion as effects are added to his guitar just before the fade.

"Haitian Divorce"

During the sessions for *The Royal Scam*, engineer Elliot Scheiner had separated from his wife and for tax reasons needed to get divorced before the end of the year. He flew to Haiti with his lawyer, and within five minutes of entering the court, he was divorced. Becker and Fagen pressed him for details and used his experience as the basis for "Haitian Divorce." The twist, of course, was the baby born out of wedlock in the last verse.

Although many tracks on *The Royal Scam* showed a reggae influence, "Haitian Divorce" is for all intents and purposes a true reggae track. From the drum pattern to the bass line to the piano and guitar skank, the tune drips with the flavor of the islands. Unlike most reggae songs, "Haitian Divorce" is full of chord changes that would be more at home in a jazz tune and a tasteful vibraphone part by Victor Feldman. Dean Parks played the prodigious lead guitar and solo, but with the aid of Becker. To achieve the effect they were going for, Becker manipulated Parks's solo after the fact by running it through a talk box, a guitar effect that uses a surgical tube fed to a small overdriven amplifier that allows you to sing vowels into it to attain a "talking guitar" sound. The song wasn't released in the U.S. as a single due to the fact that reggae music wasn't that popular at the time, but it was released in the U.K., where it peaked at number seventeen, their highest-charting single overseas.

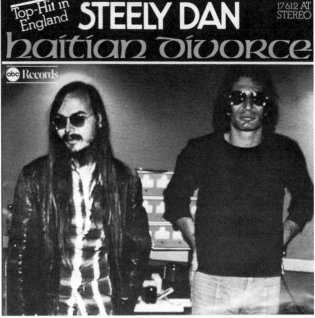

"Everything You Did"

"Everything You Did" is the most straightforward song on the album, but even these lyrics have a twist. After catching his lover with another man, the narrator spends the entire song chastising her for her infidelities, but by the end he's actually turned on, hence the change from "tell me everything" to "do me everything," expressing his desire to experience everything she did. The song also name checks the Eagles, who shared the same manager, Irving Azoff, with Steely Dan. The line "Turn up the Eagles the neighbors are listening" allegedly came from a real argument that Becker was having with his girlfriend, who was a big Eagles fan. Whether or not it was meant as a dig, the Eagles responded with the line "They stab them with their steely knives but they just can't kill the beast" from "Hotel California" a few months later. Eagles bass player Timothy B. Schmit had contributed to a number of Steely Dan sessions, and Don Henley and Glenn Frey would sing background vocals, along with Schmit, on "FM (No Static at All)."

The picture sleeve for the U.K.-only single "Haitian Divorce," which reached number seventeen on the charts.

The arrangement is sparse and sinewy, with drums (Marotta's third and final appearance), bass, piano, Hammond B3 organ, and rhythm guitar creating an atmospheric backdrop for Larry Carlton's guitar swells and crunchy lead guitar. He performs yet another outstandingly slinky solo that slithers around the changes with guitar bends galore.

"The Royal Scam"

The title track is a moody piece about immigrants coming to the U.S. to seek out a new, and hopefully better, life for themselves and their families. Becker and Fagen, trying to keep journalists in the dark, often rejected the claim that it was about Puerto Rican immigrants, which isn't necessarily untrue considering the opening line, "And they wandered in from the city of St. John without a dime."

An advertisement for Steely Dan's fifth album, *The Royal Scam*.

St. John could be referring to one of the U.S. Virgin Islands, or the English translation of San Juan, Puerto Rico, which is the more likely of the two.

The feel is somewhat schizophrenic as it continuously switches from a half-time vibe that leaves space to a more groove-based section. This constant movement effectively mimics the sense of awe, and fear, that the new U.S. residents feel since they've arrived. The foundation of the song is the drums, bass, and Fender Rhodes electric piano, but the overdubs make it shine. From the swirling Hammond B3 organ to the plunger-muted trumpet swells and lead guitar licks to the female background vocals and horn section, the song has a multitude of layers that help to achieve the dark atmosphere that is so prevalent. The song builds to a frenzy before returning to the eerie groove, with additional dissonant piano, for the fade-out.

"Here at the Western World"

"Here at the Western World" is usually credited as an outtake from *The Royal Scam* sessions that was deemed inappropriate for the album, but some claim that it was recorded earlier, possibly as early as *Pretzel Logic*, with Jim Gordon on drums rather than Bernard Purdie as credited. It features some beautiful piano playing by Michael Omartian and a blend of electric and acoustic guitars played by Dean Parks and Jeff Mironov, his only Steely Dan session. A tender ballad about a brothel, with definite drug allusions, the song was also passed over for the *Aja* LP.

The female background vocals were added when they decided to include it on 1978's double album *Greatest Hits*. Once ABC Records realized they would have no new product from Steely Dan that year, the first time that had happened since their debut in 1972, the double album was released and was incredibly successful. The songs were chosen by Becker and Fagen, and the release reached number thirty in the U.S. and number forty-one in the U.K. The album was arranged chronologically, and although Purdie is credited as the drummer, "Here at the Western World" appears between the *Pretzel Logic* and *Katy Lied* material. Also, the fact that Michael Omartian plays piano on the track gives another possible clue to the date, given that he didn't play on any songs from *The Royal Scam*. Whenever it was recorded, it is a sublime piece that many Dan fans forget about.

Conclusion

Overall, *The Royal Scam* was a sparsely produced affair with few overdubs needed to convey what Becker and Fagen were after. The duo hardly play on the album, with Chuck Rainey handling the majority of the bass lines; Larry Carlton playing guitar on most of the songs with help from Elliott Randall, Dean Parks, Denny Dias, and Becker; and Paul Griffin and Don Grolnick laying down the keyboards for many of the tracks. The album is without a doubt steeped in the funk and reflects the trends in music more than any other Steely Dan album.

They embraced disco and reggae grooves and put together yet another fabulous rhythm section that handled most of the basic tracks. Fagen had stated that they were looking to produce an album with heavier bass and drums, and with *The Royal Scam*, that is exactly what they got. Bernard Purdie and Rick Marotta split the drumming duties, and along with Chuck Rainey's distinctive bass playing lay the foundation for the Dan's most funk-infused album. While Michael Omartian and David Paich had provided extraordinary piano and keyboard parts for both *Pretzel Logic* and *Katy Lied*, Becker and Fagen knew that they wanted something different for *The Royal Scam*. With Paul Griffin and Don Grolnick, that aspiration became reality. The piano took a back seat on *The Royal Scam* to the funkier sounds of the clavinet and Fender Rhodes electric piano, and both players brought their special touch to the sessions.

The Royal Scam is also the first album that guitarist Larry Carlton significantly contributed to. He played on the majority of the album, wrote charts, acted as the liaison with studio musicians, and contributed memorable solos to four out of nine songs. It was the beginning of a beautiful friendship.

A Japanese advertisement for *The Royal Scam* featuring Becker; Fagen; drummer Jeff Porcaro, who played on Steely Dan's previous album *Katy Lied*; and Denny Dias, who was contributing less and less to the recordings.

The lyrics were more topical as well and told stories that were from the time period in which they were living. They still featured many characters that listeners had gotten to know including drug dealers, prostitutes, infidels, and criminals, but this time added immigrants, terrorists, and somebody who just enjoyed prehistoric cave paintings.

Interestingly, *The Royal Scam* charted higher in the U.K., reaching number eleven, than it did in the U.S., peaking at number fifteen. The reviews were favorable, with *Rolling Stone*'s Kenneth Tucker stating, "In any event, I doubt that Steely Dan will ever become merely precious or insular; through five albums they have consistently circumvented their complexity with passionate snazziness and fluky, cynical wit. If *The Royal Scam* lacks ready-made Top 40 fodder, it also widens Steely Dan's already considerable parameters." *Newsweek* called them "perhaps the best and certainly the most imaginative American rock group of the '70s." Bud Scoppa from *Circus* magazine stated, "There's more wit, imagination, and musical sophistication in the songs and structures of *The Royal Scam* than on any LP I've heard in ages . . . They're utterly calculated, perverse, and—like the 'Show Biz Kids' they described a couple years back—'They don't give a fuck about anybody else.' But somehow these elitist oddballs continue to make remarkably human records—records I can't help falling in love with. Let 'em do it their way."

While many journalists praised the album, an equal number concluded that it was a notch below their previous album, *Katy Lied*. Max Bell of *New Musical Express* had mixed feelings about it. "*The Royal Scam* has confused me even more than its predecessor. The common reaction on first hearing is one of total indifference, which changes gradually to a recognition that this album is different again and that, while this doesn't always reach the imaginative heights of old, it is getting there. Every play leads me to think that this isn't the absolute let-down I first thought . . . Only time will tell whether it matches the best of Steely Dan although whether it does is irrelevant in a sense. After a while it stands on its own, just like the band." *The Royal Scam* has held up incredibly well over the years and is considered with almost the same reverence as *Aja*, the follow-up album that would take nearly a year and a half to complete. Steely Dan was already considered one of the preeminent acts of the '70s, but their next album would solidify their place as rock icons.

13

What Made the Preacher Dance

The Drummers of Steely Dan

W hen Steely Dan was formed in 1972, it was initially a five-piece band designed as a vehicle for Walter Becker and Donald Fagen's original compositions. Reflecting on this time in their history, Becker once said that they saw their staff songwriter positions as a ruse. The plan all along was to organize a band to perform their songs, since most of their compositions were pretty unusual. While Steely Dan would go on to heavily incorporate session musicians from their third album on, the sessions for their debut LP, *Can't Buy a Thrill*, marked the first instance of this and foreshadowed what would become Becker and Fagen's modus operandi. By their third album, *Pretzel Logic*, Jim Hodder's drumming wasn't working for the compositions that Becker and Fagen were bringing to the band, so they recruited drummer Jim Gordon to play on the majority of the album, with Jeff Porcaro contributing to two tracks. They would use multiple session drummers on every subsequent album until 2003's *Everything Must Go*, the first LP to use only one drummer, Keith Carlock, since 1973's sophomore LP, *Countdown to Ecstasy*. We begin this chapter with the only musician to play on every Steely Dan album from *Can't Buy a Thrill* to *Gaucho*, multi-instrumentalist Victor Feldman.

Victor Feldman

Victor Feldman began his career with Steely Dan as a percussionist on their debut LP, *Can't Buy a Thrill*. Becker recalled in a 2003 interview for *Downbeat* how they initially met him. "We used to see cases in the hall and saw Victor Feldman's name. I said, 'Wow, Victor Feldman's in there from Miles Davis and Cannonball Adderley.'" He would go on to become an integral part of the band's later work. Feldman started in the music industry in England at the age of six when he appeared on stage with Glenn Miller. Feldman was the only British musician to ever perform with the Glenn Miller Orchestra. Following performances in several BBC motion pictures, the young Feldman was dubbed "The Kid Krupa of the Sticks." At the age of seven, Victor and his brothers Bob and Monty formed the Feldman Trio with Victor on drums. Feldman soon grew bored only playing drums, so he added vibraphone to his arsenal. He went on to record twenty albums with British jazz saxophonist Ronnie Scott's band before moving to New York in

Victor Feldman's 1961 release *Merry Olde Soul*. Feldman played on every Steely Dan record from *Can't Buy a Thrill* to *Gaucho*.

1955 at the age of twenty-one. While in New York, Feldman played with Woody Herman's band for a year and a half. He went on to study arranging with Marty Paich, father of David Paich, who played keyboards on a number of Steely Dan recordings and later formed Toto, the supergroup of session musicians.

When Cannonball Adderley heard Feldman's playing on a Shelley Manne album, he called him to play on what became an all-star LP. The record, *Cannonball Adderley and the Poll-Winners*, featured Wes Montgomery; Ray Brown, who would play on "Razor Boy"; and Louis Hayes. Adderley asked Feldman to join his band as the pianist, replacing Wynton Kelly, and he accepted. At the time, it was rare to have a white musician, especially an Englishman, in an all-black band, but Feldman's talent was enough to break racial barriers. He would go on to play with Miles Davis and write the title track for Davis's *Seven Steps to Heaven* LP as well as the song, "Joshua."

Victor Feldman is rare in the world of Steely Dan in that he played on every Steely Dan LP from *Can't Buy a Thrill* to *Gaucho*. He played percussion on "Do It Again," "Only a Fool Would Say That," and "Turn That Heartbeat Over Again" from *Can't Buy a Thrill*; vibes on "Razor Boy," "Home at Last" and "I Got the News"; marimba on "Everyone's Gone to the Movies"; Fender Rhodes on "Kid Charlemagne," "Black Cow," "Deacon Blues," and "Josie"; piano on "Home at Last" and "I Got the News"; the creative flapamba intro to "Rikki Don't Lose That Number"; and percussion on multiple songs on every Steely Dan album.

Feldman was also an accomplished arranger, so when big band leader Woody Herman decided to do an album featuring an extended piece by Chick Corea and the songs of Steely Dan, he approached Victor to arrange and play on one of the tunes. The album, *Chick, Donald, Walter and Woodrow*, was released in 1978 and included Feldman's arrangement of "I Got the News," with Steely Dan alumnus Tom Scott on tenor saxophone. Ten years later, he would be a member of the Hoops McCann band, a jazz group that performed Steely Dan compositions. For their one and only album, *The Hoops McCann Band Plays the Music of Steely Dan*, Feldman wrote an arrangement for "Babylon Sisters." The band was comprised of a number of musicians who had played on Steely Dan's albums including drummer Paul Humphrey, saxophonist/flutist Jerome Richardson, trumpeter Chuck Findley, and trombonist Slyde Hyde. Fagen even mixed a song with Daniel Lazerus that he and Becker had written for tenor saxophonists Warne Marsh and Pete Christlieb entitled "Rapunzel," from their album *Apogee*, produced by Becker and Fagen.

In addition to playing with Steely Dan, Feldman toured, recorded, and played with some of the biggest names in popular music. These include Elton John, Frank Sinatra, Barbra Streisand, the Doobie Brothers, the Beach Boys, Marvin Gaye, Joni Mitchell, Seals and Crofts, Boz Scaggs, Kenny Loggins, Joe Walsh, Tom Waits, Frank Zappa, Freddie Hubbard, Sonny Rollins, Johnny Cash, James Taylor, Stan Getz, and Elvis Presley. Ironically, he also played on Poco's 1975 version of Steely Dan's first single, "Dallas," from their *Head Over Heels* LP. Feldman died of a heart attack at fifty-three in 1987.

The Twenty-Three Drummers

Jim Gordon

At age seventeen, Jim Gordon passed up a music scholarship to UCLA to go on the road backing the Everly Brothers. A protégé of session giant Hal Blaine, Gordon would soon be one of the most in-demand session drummers in L.A., commanding as much as triple the usual scale rate paid to musicians at the time. In the 1960s, he played on the Beach Boys' *Pet Sounds*, the Byrds' *The Notorious Byrd Brothers*, and the hit record "Classical Gas" by Mason Williams. In 1969 and 1970, Gordon toured with Delaney & Bonnie, whose guitarist at the time was Eric Clapton. Soon after, Clapton took over the band's rhythm section to form Derek and the Dominos. The

band's first work as a unit was on George Harrison's three-LP masterpiece *All Things Must Pass* in 1970. After that, they hit the studio to record the double album *Layla and Other Assorted Love Songs*, where he supposedly wrote the outro piano section for the title track and received credit. In recent years, however, keyboardist Bobby Whitlock claimed that Gordon didn't write that section. In a 2011 interview with the Eric Clapton fanzine *Where's Eric*, Whitlock explained, "Jim took that piano melody from his ex-girlfriend Rita Coolidge. I know because in the Delaney & Bonnie days I lived in John Garfield's old house in the Hollywood Hills and there was a guesthouse with an upright

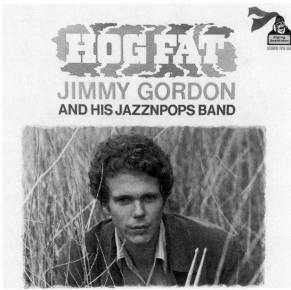

Although original drummer Jim Hodder was still technically a member of the band when they recorded *Pretzel Logic*, he was replaced by studio drummer Jim Gordon (along with Jeff Porcaro) and did not play on the album. He released one album, *Hogfat*, as Jimmy Gordon and His Jazznpops Band.

piano in it. Rita and Jim were up there in the guesthouse and invited me to join in on writing this song with them called 'Time.' . . . Her sister Priscilla wound up recording it with Booker T. Jones. . . . Jim took the melody from Rita's song and didn't give her credit for writing it. Her boyfriend ripped her off." Graham Nash also made the same claim in his book *Wild Tales: A Rock and Roll Life.*

Gordon was called into the studio in 1973 to play drums on *Pretzel Logic*, even though drummer Jim Hodder was officially still a member of the group. Gordon laid down the drums for nearly every song, from the bossa nova groove of "Rikki Don't Lose That Number" to the R&B-flavored pocket of "Monkey in Your Soul," which showcased his diversity as a player. *Pretzel Logic* was a turning point for Steely Dan. There is a certain sophistication to the album, much of which can be attributed to Jim Gordon's drumming.

Gordon would also play with John Lennon; Carly Simon; Barbra Streisand; Carole King; Joe Cocker; Crosby, Stills & Nash; Neil Diamond; Hall and Oates; Jackson Browne; Glen Campbell; the Carpenters; Dr. John; Gordon Lightfoot; the Monkees; Randy Newman; Harry Nilsson; Tom Petty; Leon Russell; Seals and Crofts; Mel Tormé; Traffic; Tom Waits; Frank Zappa; and others. Unfortunately, in the late '70s, Gordon's undiagnosed schizophrenia began to escalate, and he started to hear voices. The most prominent voice was that of his mother, who reportedly forced him to starve himself and prevented him from sleeping, relaxing, or playing drums. In 1983, Gordon attacked his mother with a hammer before fatally stabbing her and, as a result, received a sentence of sixteen years to life. Although the court accepted that he had schizophrenia, changes in the California laws prevented him from using insanity as a defense. Gordon has been denied parole a number of times and currently resides at the California Medical Facility in Vacaville, California.

Jeff Porcaro

If Jim Gordon had been influenced by Hal Blaine, Jeff Porcaro was most definitely influenced by Jim Gordon. Porcaro came from a musical family and was the eldest son of percussionist Joe Porcaro and his wife Eileen. At seventeen, Porcaro started his professional career as the drummer for the Sonny and Cher touring band, and in 1973, he began doing session work for Seals and Crofts and Joe Cocker.

Porcaro first worked with Steely Dan on the track "Night by Night" on *Pretzel Logic.* Jim Hodder originally attempted to record the song, but Becker and Fagen's need for perfection led to Hodder playing no drums on the album. Porcaro would go on to be the most frequently used drummer on Steely Dan-related sessions until current drummer Keith Carlock entered the picture in 2000 for *Two Against Nature.* Denny Dias recommended Porcaro, and forty-five minutes after the call, he was in the studio. In addition to "Night by Night," Porcaro played with Gordon, who was one of his heroes, on the dual drummer cut "Parker's Band." Porcaro also played alongside Hodder on Steely Dan's final tour of their early years, which was in the spring of 1974.

For their next album, *Katy Lied,* Porcaro played on all but one song. The groove was a major shift from Jim Gordon's drumming on *Pretzel Logic. Katy Lied* was a jazzier record and showcased more bluesy shuffle grooves, but Porcaro states that he was constantly thinking of Gordon's playing as well as Jim Keltner's. He explained this in a 1992 interview with *Modern Drummer.* "On *Katy Lied,* all that went through my mind was Keltner and Gordon. It was do or die for me. All my stuff was copying them. For instance, on 'Chain Lightning,' all I thought about was the song 'Pretzel Logic,' which is Gordon playing a slow shuffle. On 'Doctor Wu,' I was thinking of John Guerin, especially those fills going out between the bass drum and toms. He'd do it in a bebop style. Guerin was on Joni Mitchell's *Court & Spark,* which was in that same Steely style. Things were getting cool and bent." This album was indicative of the direction the band would take on future albums. Porcaro would join Becker and Fagen two additional times, on the non-album track "FM (No Static at All)" and on the title track of their seventh LP, *Gaucho.* After Steely Dan broke up, Porcaro would play on several songs on Fagen's *The Nightfly* album: "I.G.Y. (What a Beautiful World)," "Green Flower Street," "Ruby Baby," "The Nightfly," and "The Goodbye Look." Porcaro also

Jeff Porcaro made his Steely Dan debut on *Pretzel Logic* playing "Night by Night" and dual drums with Jim Gordon on "Parker's Band." He returned to play all but one song on *Katy Lied.* After the success of his band Toto, he appeared in this 1982 advertisement for Pearl drums.

enjoys the distinction of being the only drummer that Steely Dan used whose tracks were never redone by another player. Porcaro's versions of the songs were always keepers, and every song he played on made it to the albums.

In 1977, while touring with Seals and Crofts and Boz Scaggs, Porcaro worked as a session musician with keyboardist David Paich, who had played on both *Pretzel Logic* and *Katy Lied.* Later, having found they made for excellent partners, Porcaro and Paich formed the band Toto. To complete their vision of the ultimate session musician supergroup, they brought in bassist and fellow session vet David Hungate, who had played in Scaggs's backing band. To round out the group, they added guitarist Steve Lukather, who had filled in for Les Dudek in Scaggs's band; Porcaro's brother Steve as an additional keyboard player; and lead singer Bobby Kimball. With this lineup, Toto was complete. Toto recorded fourteen albums, the most famous of which was 1982's triple-platinum *Toto IV,* which spawned the hits "Rosanna," "Africa," and "I Won't Hold You Back," and beat Fagen's *The Nightfly* LP for a number of Grammy Awards they were both nominated for.

In addition to his work with Steely Dan and his successful career as a member of Toto, Porcaro would go on to play on some of the most popular cuts from the

'70s and '80s. He contributed to hits by artists including Paul McCartney, Dire Straits, Rickie Lee Jones, George Benson, Stan Getz, Sérgio Mendes, Christopher Cross, Diana Ross, Eric Clapton, Miles Davis, Bruce Springsteen, Elton John, Larry Carlton, David Gilmour, and others. He also played on four tracks on Michael's Jackson's multi-platinum LP *Thriller.*

While Becker and Fagen were rehearsing for the 1992 *New York Rock and Soul Revue* tour, Porcaro passed away on August 5th of a heart attack caused by inhaling the pesticide he was using on his rose bushes. Although the coroner's report stated that he died of hardening of the arteries due to cocaine use, friends and family deny that this was the case, saying that he had an undiagnosed heart disease that had caused his death along with an allergic reaction to the pesticide.

Producer Gary Katz was a pallbearer at Porcaro's funeral and gave a eulogy along with fellow drummer Jim Keltner. Four songs by two of his favorite artists were played at his funeral: "The Wind Cries Mary" by Jimi Hendrix, and "Home at Last," "Deacon Blues," and "Third World Man," by Steely Dan, none of which Porcaro played on. On December 14, 1992, a concert was put on at the Universal Amphitheatre in Los Angeles to pay tribute to the late drummer and raise money for a trust fund for his children. Toto was the backing band (with Simon Phillips on drums) for myriad artists including Donald Fagen, Michael McDonald, David Crosby, Boz Scaggs, Don Henley, and Eddie Van Halen. Fagen performed "Chain Lightning" and "Josie," with Denny Dias playing guitar. Toto guitarist Steve Lukather played Jimi Hendrix's "Little Wing" after announcing to the audience that he and Jeffrey had two favorite artists, Steely Dan and Jimi Hendrix. To close the tribute, ex-Beatle George Harrison joined all of the performers for a rousing rendition of "With a Little Help from My Friends." A fitting tribute to a phenomenal musician and a great friend to many.

Hal Blaine

Hal Blaine was *the* session drummer of the '60s and '70s as part of the world-famous Wrecking Crew. Blaine played on hits by popular artists including Elvis Presley, the Beach Boys, Diana Ross, the Supremes, Frank Sinatra, Dean Martin, Sammy Davis Jr., Paul Simon, Ike and Tina Turner, Neil Diamond, Barbra Streisand, Ray Charles, Nat King Cole, John Denver, the Mamas and the Papas, the Ronettes, Simon and Garfunkel, the Carpenters, the Monkees, Nancy Sinatra, and for one song, Steely Dan. "Any World (That I'm Welcome To)," the penultimate track on the *Katy Lied* LP, was the only song on which Blaine played as opposed to Jeff Porcaro. Although Blaine played on one of Steely Dan's often forgotten tracks, this was not indicative of his past or future as a session musician. He has played on fifty number-one hits, more than 150 top ten hits, and has recorded on more than 35,000 pieces of music over the past four decades.

Bernard "Pretty" Purdie

After recording the majority of *Katy Lied* with Jeff Porcaro in the drum chair, Becker and Fagen decided that they wanted a different sound for their next LP, *The Royal*

Scam. The previous two albums had relatively short songs with only three of twenty-one clocking in at over four minutes. For *The Royal Scam,* they desired more extended compositions together with a bigger drum and bass sound. Becker and Fagen brought in three different drummers for the sessions, but only two would end up on the album—Bernard "Pretty" Purdie and Rick Marotta. Interestingly, while Herb Lovelle's performance on "Sign In Stranger" didn't make the final cut, Becker and Fagen loved his snare sound so much that they preserved it on a two-bar loop. That loop was later loaded into engineer Roger Nichols's self-built drum machine, which he called Wendel, and the snare sound was used on the band's 1980 LP, *Gaucho.*

One drummer whose performances did end up on wax was the legendary Bernard "Pretty" Purdie. Purdie had a reputation in the business as not only a phenomenal drummer, but also as quite a character. Infamously, he would bring three signs to recording sessions; they read "Bernard 'Pretty' Purdie," "The World's Greatest Drummer," and "The Hitmaker." He would display these signs around his kit during sessions along with a neon sign that declared "Another Hit Being Made," accompanied by the albums on which he had played laid on the floor. While some of Purdie's claims have come to be disputed, he did play on more than three thousand albums by artists as diverse as Aretha Franklin, Miles Davis, Hall and Oates, Isaac Hayes, Donny Hathaway, Frank Sinatra, Joe Cocker, Robert Palmer, Roy Ayers, Gil Scott-Heron, Roberta Flack, the Rolling Stones, James Brown, Tom Jones, Lou Donaldson, Jimmy McGriff, Michael Bolton, B. B. King, Cat Stevens, and King Curtis.

For Steely Dan, Purdie laid down some of the most unique grooves in popular music on the last three LPs of the first phase of the band's career. He played on six of the nine songs on *The Royal Scam:* "Kid Charlemagne," "Sign In Stranger," "The Fez," "Green Earrings," "Haitian Divorce," and "The Royal Scam." Working with perfectionists Becker and Fagen was initially challenging for Purdie, a session musician who had strong opinions. Purdie stated in a 1992 interview with *Modern Drummer* magazine, "They were very strict to the point of super precision . . . They wouldn't take no for an answer and they wouldn't accept mistakes. It was truly frustrating in the beginning. I come from the school that when you feel good about what you've done, it's hard to do better." On their next album, *Aja,* Purdie would be the only

Bernard "Pretty" Purdie not only played on all but three songs on *The Royal Scam,* he contributed to *Aja* and *Gaucho* as well. In 1968, he released his debut album as a leader, *Soul Drums,* credited simply as Pretty Purdie.

drummer to play on more than one track, laying down his famous "Purdie Shuffle" on "Home at Last" as well as providing the easygoing groove to "Deacon Blues." Purdie would work with Steely Dan one more time on record, adding his magical "Purdie Shuffle" to "Babylon Sisters" on the *Gaucho* LP. He would also appear on the *Classic Albums Steely Dan Aja* DVD playing instrumental remakes of songs from the LP.

Rick Marotta

Drummer Rick Marotta entered the world of Steely Dan at the same time as Bernard Purdie. Marotta would bring his own style to the ever-changing sound of the band starting with their fifth LP, *The Royal Scam*. Although he was a new face at a Steely Dan session, Marotta was already a seasoned veteran who had contributed to sessions for John Lennon, Donny Hathaway, LaBelle, Paul Williams, Jim Croce, James Taylor, Don McLean, Aretha Franklin, Carly Simon, Todd Rundgren, and countless others. He even shared drum duties with Bernard Purdie on the 1973 Hall and Oates breakout LP, *Abandoned Luncheonette*. Interestingly, Marotta didn't start playing drums until the age of nineteen when a drummer friend enlisted in the army and left him his kit. After recording with guitarist David Spinozza's group Giant and the band Riverboat Soul and the Vagrants, the Vagrants asked him to join their new band Brethren, based out of Los Angeles. Marotta made the move west and recorded two albums with the band. Now that he was in Los Angeles, he was called in to play on "Don't Take Me Alive." At the time, he claims he didn't even know who Steely Dan was. In a 1992 interview with *Modern Drummer*, Marotta recalled his first Steely Dan session. "I remember I wanted to get in and out as soon as possible . . . Then they counted off this tune . . . the first thing I heard was the lyrics 'Agents of the law/Luckless pedestrians' and I almost stopped playing . . . After that I had to stop and collect myself . . . Every time I went in with them, I knew it was going to be something really historic."

While Marotta generally enjoyed the sessions with Becker and Fagen, he has said that they were the most demanding musicians for whom he had ever played. For example, he played one snare hit on "Don't Take Me Alive" that was slightly softer than the others. At any given time, Fagen was able to rewind the tape and point it out, illustrating just how meticulous he was about his compositions. This didn't bother Marotta, and he would go on to play on two additional *Royal Scam* cuts, "The Caves of Altamira" and "Everything You Did." He would return to play on "Peg" from *Aja*, and on both "Hey Nineteen" and "Time Out of Mind," on the *Gaucho* LP, although his parts were somewhat manipulated by engineer Roger Nichols's groundbreaking invention, the drum machine he called Wendel.

Rick Marotta would continue to be a first-call session player who would lend his talents to albums by Michael Jackson, Linda Ronstadt, Randy Newman, Paul Simon, Chaka Khan, Phoebe Snow, Michael Franks, Bonnie Raitt, the Pointer Sisters, Boz Scaggs, Jackson Browne, Joe Walsh, and Donald Fagen's future wife, Libby Titus. Later, he would embark on a career as a television and film composer; his most famous work to date is the theme song and score for the television series "Everybody Loves Raymond." Marotta's brother Jerry is also a highly accomplished drummer who was a member of Hall and Oates, the Indigo Girls, Peter Gabriel's band, and Orleans. Jerry also played on albums by Paul McCartney, Elvis Costello, Tears for Fears, Iggy Pop, Carly Simon, Cher, Marshall Crenshaw, John Mayer, Suzanne Vega, Ani DiFranco, and Sarah McLachlan.

Jim Keltner

When most people think of session drummer Jim Keltner, they think of the count-less pop and rock albums that he played on, but Keltner started his career as a jazz drummer in Tulsa, Oklahoma. Keltner moved to Los Angeles with his family in 1955 when he was thirteen years old. The popularity of jazz was waning in the late '50s and early '60s, and Los Angeles was a hotbed of pop and rock recording, so session work for musicians was plentiful. Keltner's first session was for the pop group Gary Lewis and the Playboys' 1966 number three hit, "She's Just My Style." Many fans assumed that Gary Lewis played the drums on his records, but the arranger and leader on these sessions, Oklahoma-born multi-instrumentalist Leon Russell, did what was common in recording studios at the time; he brought in ses-sion musicians to augment, and often supplant, the work of the artists credited on the album. Although Keltner was somewhat busy with session work in the late '60s flexing his jazz chops on records by Gabor Szabo, Cal Tjader, and Clare Fischer, he was barely making a living.

That would all change in 1969 when he appeared on Delaney and Bonnie's second album, *The Original Delaney and Bonnie and Friends (Accept No Substitute)* after Russell recommended his fellow Oklahoman. British singer Joe Cocker was so impressed by the band on that album that he hired Russell, Keltner, bassist Carl Radle, saxophonist Bobby Keys, brass player Jim Price, and background vocalist Rita Coolidge for his tour that was starting in a week. The tour was filmed, and the live album that was released, *Mad Dogs and Englishmen*, reached number two on the *Billboard* album charts. Keltner played alongside fellow session drummers Jim Gordon and Chuck Blackwell for the tour.

After playing with Cocker, Keltner was one of the most sought-after session drummers in Los Angeles, splitting the bulk of the work with Gordon and Hal Blaine. In 1970 and 1971, he recorded with Carly Simon, Barbra Streisand, Booker T. Jones, Bill Withers, B. B. King, Harry Nilsson, and others. He is probably best known for his session work with three ex-members of the Beatles, playing on John Lennon's *Imagine, Sometime in New York City, Mind Games*, and *Walls and Bridges*; George Harrison's *Living in the Material World, Dark Horse, Extra Texture (Read All About It), Somewhere in England, Gone Troppo, Cloud Nine*, and *Brainwashed*; and Ringo Starr's *Ringo, Goodnight Vienna, Ringo's Rotogravure*, and *Stop and Smell the Roses*. Keltner was Harrison's first choice for his epic *All Things Must Pass* album, but since he was touring with Gabor Szabo at the time, Steely Dan alumnus Jim Gordon ended up sharing the drumming chores with Ringo Starr.

He played live with all three ex-Beatles as well, playing alongside Starr for Harrison's *Concert for Bangladesh* and the 1974 *Dark Horse* tour; with Elephant's Memory for Lennon's One to One concerts at Madison Square Garden in 1972; and in Ringo Starr's first All-Star Band in 1989. In 1988, George Harrison,

Roy Orbison, Bob Dylan, Jeff Lynne, and Tom Petty formed the supergroup the Traveling Wilburys, and Keltner played on both of their albums; and although he wasn't credited on either, the DVD released in 1997 listed him as Buster Sidebury.

Although Keltner only played on one Steely Dan song, it was an extraordinary performance. The groove for "Josie" works perfectly with Chuck Rainey's bass and the rhythm section of Victor Feldman on Fender Rhodes and Larry Carlton and Dean Parks on guitars. The week before the session, Keltner had traded in a vintage Ludwig Black Beauty snare drum, worth approximately $7,500 today, for a $90 Ludwig Vistalite snare drum that he never tuned. Although the Black Beauty was a superior instrument, Keltner could never get it to sound or feel right. He used the new super-sensitive Vistalite for the first time on "Josie," the only time he used it on a session. Initially, he didn't like his playing on "Josie," feeling that it was a "funny groove" on an "odd song." Becker and Fagen had been through several drummers for the tune, and in retrospect Keltner grew to love the feel of the song. He felt that Fagen was a commanding musician, and if he told you to play something, you needed to play exactly what he wanted.

By 1977, Keltner was a studio pro, yet he still felt the pressure of laying down this five-page chart with no repeats. He might have worried that the groove wasn't the right fit, but Becker and Fagen loved it and were relieved that they had finally found the right drummer for the song. Besides drums, Keltner added an overdub for the instrumental break before Becker's guitar solo. Keltner elaborated on this mysterious overdub in a 1992 interview with *Modern Drummer*. "Later, they wanted me to overdub something over the breakdown, but they didn't know what. The beauty of those guys is that they truly wanted something weird. So I played this garbage can lid with rivets in it that I'd been given for Christmas. They liked the way it sounded, so it became a part of the song." Many people have also wondered about the strange fill that brings the song back in for the instrumental coda. "As for that fill near the end, it was a bar of 7/8. That's definitely not something that I would've played. That figure was written on the paper, it was totally Fagen's thing: I wish I could get a copy of that chart." Keltner also cut "Peg," but his version didn't make the cut and drummer Rick Marotta's take would be the keeper.

Keltner continued to play on countless sessions for the Rolling Stones, Eric Clapton, the Steve Miller Band, Bob Dylan, Bruce Springsteen, Ray Charles, Roy Orbison, Brian Wilson, Elvis Costello, Tom Petty, Joni Mitchell, Neil Young, James Taylor, Bobby Womack, José Feliciano, Harry Chapin, Alice Cooper, Sheryl Crow, the Bee Gees, Don Henley, Toto, Pink Floyd, Roberta Flack, Aimee Mann, Fiona Apple, John Mayer, and numerous others.

Paul Humphrey

Like Jim Keltner, Paul Nelson Humphrey only played on one song on *Aja*, the LP opener, "Black Cow." Humphrey was a session drummer who primarily played on jazz sessions in the 1960s for artists such as Wes Montgomery, Les McCann, Kai Winding, Jimmy Smith, Charles Mingus, Lee Konitz, Monty Alexander, Blue Mitchell, and Gene Ammons. In 1969, he crossed over into the rock and pop world playing on Joe Cocker's hit "Feeling Alright." He continued in both the jazz and rock world, recording with Richard "Groove" Holmes, Jimmy Smith, Kenny Burrell, Etta James, Al Kooper, the Four Tops, Quincy Jones, Jean-Luc Ponty, Frank Zappa, Jerry Garcia, Jackie DeShannon, Natalie Cole, Albert King, Dusty Springfield, and on Marvin Gaye's 1973 classic *Let's Get It On*.

As a bandleader, he recorded under the name Paul Humphrey and the Cool Aid Chemists, with keyboardist Clarence MacDonald, guitarist David T. Walker, and bassist Bill Upchurch. In 1971, this ensemble had two hits, "Cool Aid" (U.S. number twenty-nine, U.S. Black Singles number fourteen), and "Funky L.A." (U.S. Black Singles number forty-five). He was the drummer for both the Lawrence Welk orchestra and television show from 1976 to 1982, and he was also the drummer for the Hoops McCann Band, a big band first assembled to perform Steely Dan songs in the summer of '82 at the First Annual Mt. Hood Festival of Jazz in Gresham, Oregon. The audience response was so positive that in 1988 they released an eight-song album entitled *The Hoops McCann Band Plays the Music of Steely Dan*.

Steve Gadd

Steve Gadd was yet another drummer who only played on one song on *Aja*, the extremely challenging title track. Gadd got his first drum set at age seven from his grandfather, and at age eleven he performed with bebop legend, trumpeter Dizzy Gillespie, who let him sit in during a Sunday matinee. At this time, he also met trumpeter Chuck Mangione, whose quintet he would later join with an unknown pianist, Chick Corea. Mangione realized the incredible talent of Gadd, stating in a 2014 article on Gadd for *The Dishmaster*, "Steve was amazing at the age of eight. He was fundamentally sound in every area of the drums." His first session was on Chuck's brother keyboardist Gap Mangione's 1968 debut solo album, *Diana in the Autumn Wind*, which also featured woodwind player Jerome Richardson and trumpet player Snooky Young, who both played on "Dirty Work," and trumpet player Marvin Stamm, who played on Fagen's *Morph the Cat* LP. Shortly after, Gadd enlisted in the U.S. Army and played in their big band for the next three years before returning to the New York studio scene.

In the early '70s, he played on albums by Jim Croce, Frank Sinatra, Chet Baker, Bonnie Raitt, George Benson, James Brown, Aretha Franklin, Weather Report, Gladys Knight and the Pips, Leon Redbone, Grover Washington Jr., and on Van McCoy's disco anthem, "The Hustle." The record that solidified his status as session drummer extraordinaire was Paul Simon's "50 Ways to Leave Your Lover," his biggest solo hit that reached number one on the *Billboard* Hot 100 on February 7, 1976. The same year, Gadd and New York City session musicians Gordon Edwards, Richard Tee, Eric Gale, Cornell Dupree, and Chris Parker formed the group Stuff. Their work included appearances on NBC's *Saturday Night Live*, both performing as a band and also backing up singer Joe Cocker.

Becker, Fagen, and Gary Katz were always looking for new musicians to work with, and Gadd was one of the hottest session musicians on the New York City scene in 1977. Whenever they asked other producers about who was being hired, Gadd's name kept coming up, so he was invited into the studio to play the nearly eight-minute epic title track for Steely Dan's sixth LP, *Aja*. They had already tried the song with other drummers, but nobody had played it to their satisfaction. Gadd shocked them with his performance as he sight-read the seven-page chart and perfected it on the first take. Fagen didn't expect such a quick session. The song was done in an hour and a half, the only time that ever happened on a Steely Dan session. As Becker stated, "Steve Gadd had pretty much everything that you'd want a drummer to have."

Gadd's technical skill, sound, and ability to read a chart and immediately make it sound as if he had been playing it for years astonished Becker, Fagen, and Katz so much that he would return to play on three songs for their next album, *Gaucho*, more than any other drummer. He showed his flexibility with the funk groove of "Glamour Profession," the slow burner "My Rival," and the ballad "Third World Man." He also added percussion to "Hey Nineteen." Gadd would continue to be in demand playing with Paul McCartney, Al Jarreau, Rickie Lee Jones, James Taylor, Eric Clapton, Edie Brickell, and countless others to this day.

Ed Greene

Although his name might not be as familiar as others, Ed Greene is one of the most versatile session drummers and has contributed some of the deepest pockets on numerous albums by a variety of stylistically different artists. He got his start in the early '70s playing with the Friends of Distinction, the Mamas and the Papas, Tim Buckley, Donald Byrd (with Steely Dan alumnus Wilton Felder on bass), the Temptations, the Four Tops, Bobby "Blue" Bland, as well as an uncredited role as the drummer on almost every Barry White production from the 1970s. He played violin as a child and credited his steady time and his skills as a sight reader to his years playing in an orchestra. The first number one song he played on was Sammy Davis Jr.'s 1972 hit, "The Candy Man." You can hear him on Hall and Oates' "Sara Smile," the Captain and Tennille's "Love Will Keep Us Together," the Jacksons' "Shake Your Body (Down to the Ground)," and Marvin Gaye's 1974 *Live!* LP with Motown legend James Jamerson on bass.

Greene was the perfect player for one of the funkiest numbers on *Aja*, "I Got the News." He knew just when to change his groove for certain bars to elevate the song, and his laid-back, intuitive style was just what they needed for the song. He and bassist Chuck Rainey showcased some truly inspired playing on this track, and Greene's Benny Benjamin-like fills pepper the tune in all the right spots. He returned to play on the *Gaucho* album, but unfortunately for everybody involved, an engineer while aligning the 24-track tape machine erased the song he played on, "The Second Arrangement," considered to be the best on the album by Becker and Fagen. Although they attempted to rerecord the song, for some reason they replaced Greene with Steve Gadd, two completely different kinds of drummers, so it was no surprise that it fell short of their initial recording.

He was called upon to lay down grooves for two songs that couldn't be more different from Fagen's 1982 solo album *The Nightfly*, "New Frontier" and "Maxine." While "New Frontier" had a similar funk groove to "I Got the News," the shuffle of "Maxine" was a whole different bag. The slinky groove beneath the transcendent chord changes and close harmonies was simple but perfect. The way these tracks were constructed was different in that they were built layer by layer rather than with the full band, which Steely Dan began doing during the *Gaucho* sessions, a sign of the times and unfortunately not always as successful.

Greene would also play alongside Steely Dan session musicians bassist Chuck Rainey, keyboardist Michael Omartian (on whose album he would play), and guitarist Steve Khan for saxophonist David Sanborn's recording of Donald Fagen's composition "The Finer Things." The song was part of the soundtrack for Martin Scorsese's 1982 dark comedy *The King of Comedy*, starring Robert De Niro and Jerry Lewis.

He continued to record through the 2000s with Chuck Jackson, Boz Scaggs, Dionne Warwick, Eddie Hendricks, Freddie Hubbard, Marvin Gaye, Aretha Franklin, Robert Palmer, Jeff Beck, Phoebe Snow, Smokey Robinson, Allen Toussaint, the Carpenters, the Pointer Sisters, Three Dog Night, Tina Turner, Paul Anka, Glenn Campbell, Michael Franks, Bobby Caldwell, Clint Black, Leo Sayer, and many more.

James Gadson

It's surprising that Becker and Fagen never hired James Gadson during their run as Steely Dan with such an impressive résumé. Gadson began his career not as a drummer, but as a singer and songwriter for the doo-wop group the Carpets, which he started with his brother Tom while they were still teenagers in Kansas City, Missouri. After a stint in the Air Force, he returned to Kansas City and began to learn jazz drumming while sitting in with local organ trios. He moved to Los Angeles in 1966 for a band opportunity that didn't pan out, but his friend and fellow drummer John Boudreaux knew of a new bandleader who was looking for musicians, Charles Wright.

Gadson's career as a drummer started with the first lineup of Charles Wright's Watts 103rd Street Rhythm Band in 1967, and he would go on to record four albums with them, but there were definitely some bumps in the road. Gadson recalled in a 2012 interview with television station KCET, "I had become a jazz drummer. I was playing a lot of outside stuff in Kansas City . . . we could get away with certain things. I couldn't play the R&B stuff . . . because I couldn't play in the pocket. I didn't know nothing about none of this, so Charles fired me about five times." The B-side of their first single, "Do Your Thing," was a song written and sung by Gadson entitled "A Dance, A Kiss and A Song."

His groove playing developed quickly, and after the release of Bill Withers's *Still Bill* album in 1972, Gadson's star began to shine. He played with the Temptations, David Ruffin, Eddie Kendricks, Freddie King, Quincy Jones, Willie Hutch, Bobby Womack, Herbie Hancock, Phoebe Snow, Nancy Wilson, Patti LaBelle, Boz Scaggs, the Four Tops, Ben E. King, Jimmy Smith, Gladys Knight, Smokey Robinson, Albert King, B. B. King, Booker T. Jones, Herbie Hancock, Gloria Gaynor, Billy Preston, Marvin Gaye, Ray Charles, and shared the drum chair with fellow Steely Dan drummer Jeff Porcaro on the theme song for the television show *Kojak*. He also released two singles as a solo artist in 1972, playing drums and singing, but neither one was a hit, and Gadson continued as a session drummer.

While Gadson never played on a Steely Dan album, he was employed by Fagen for *The Nightfly* LP, playing on both the first single, "I.G.Y. (What a Beautiful World)," and Leiber and Stoller's "Ruby Baby." It's interesting to note that he is credited as the main drummer for the former, with Jeff Porcaro adding "additional drums," but on the latter he is playing the "additional drums" to Porcaro's main groove. The shuffle bounces along easily on "I.G.Y." with few drum fills, just a few well-placed cymbal splashes. Gadson shows incredible restraint and only plays sparse fills to lead into each chorus. For "Ruby Baby," it's apparent that the main groove isn't Gadson. It isn't as laid-back, with constant triplet eighth notes on the hi-hat moving the song forward with perpetual motion. Gadson did play drums for a cover of a Steely Dan song: jazz violinist Michael White's version of "Rikki Don't Lose That Number" from his 1979 album *White Night*.

Gadson was also credited as a producer on Bill Withers's albums as well as releases by Bobby Womack, Gwen McCrae, Steely Dan alumnus Wilton Felder, Thelma Houston, and others. Gadson is still on the scene and in recent years has played on records by Paul McCartney, Norah Jones, Justin Timberlake, Beck, D'Angelo, Amos Lee, Lana Del Rey, Elle King, Joe Cocker, and Jamie Cullem; and at age seventy-seven, he doesn't seem to have any intention of slowing down.

Steve Jordan

While New Yorker Steve Jordan is known primarily as a drummer, he is actually a multi-instrumentalist, composer, musical director, and producer as well. The first drummer that impressed him was Ringo Starr. Al Jackson Jr. and Benny Benjamin followed, due to his love of R&B and soul music. Jordan began playing drums at the age of eight when his grandmother gave him a snare drum. He attended the prestigious Fiorello H. LaGuardia High School of Music and Performing Arts in New York City, where he studied as a classical percussionist before switching to drum set.

After graduating from high school, Jordan played a gig at the Bottom Line with guitarist John Tropea; that night he played alongside Steve Gadd. Although he was extremely nervous, his playing was impressive, and he landed the gig as the drummer for the Saturday Night Live Band. While the SNL gig was an incredible opportunity, Jordan was not one of the A-list drummers on the session circuit. With Steve Gadd, Rick Marotta, and Chris Parker, who would ironically become the drummer for SNL in 1986, playing on the majority of the sessions at the time, Jordan wasn't working as much outside of the SNL band. Many of the top session drummers lived outside of the city, so when a massive snowstorm hit in 1977, Jordan, who lived in the city, played on several sessions over a three-week period. His performance on these sessions led to a number of others, and his career as a session drummer began.

SNL launched the career of many actors, but it was also the launching pad of a fictitious band created by two of the comedians. One of the sketches from SNL was the Blues Brothers, a soul-revival band created by John Belushi and Dan Aykroyd. When they became a musical act outside of SNL, they asked Jordan to tour with them, and he played on their first three albums: *Briefcase Full of Blues* in 1978, which reached number one on the *Billboard* 200; *The Blues Brothers: Music from the Soundtrack* in 1980; and *Made in America*, also from 1980. Although he played on the majority of their material, he did not appear in the movie. Jordan was also the drummer for another late-night television program. From 1982 to 1986, he was a member of Paul Shaffer's World's Most Dangerous Band for the *Late Night with David Letterman* show until Anton Fig replaced him.

In 1981, Jordan was recruited to play on Donald Fagen's "True Companion," a song recorded for the soundtrack to the movie *Heavy Metal*. While working on *The Nightfly*, Fagen called upon Jordan once again to play on one cut, "Walk Between the Raindrops," with fellow David Letterman musician, bassist Will Lee. The song is a perfect example of a perfectly executed swing-like shuffle beat. The shuffle groove is used on half of the songs on *The Nightfly*, four songs with four different drummers. The record is an ideal example of how different drummers interpret a similar feel.

Jordan has recorded and played live with artists such as the Rolling Stones, Aretha Franklin, Chuck Berry, Bruce Springsteen, Don Henley, John Mellencamp, Eric Clapton, Bob Dylan, James Taylor, Sonny Rollins, B. B. King, Alicia Keys, and many others. After working with Keith Richards on the Rolling Stones' *Dirty Work* LP due to drummer Charlie Watts's substance abuse problem, he played with Richards and Chuck Berry for the documentary *Hail! Hail! Rock 'n' Roll*. Both projects were so successful that Richards invited him to join his band the X-pensive Winos. Besides touring, they recorded two albums, *Talk Is Cheap* in 1988 and *Main Offender* in 1992. Jordan co-produced both albums and is credited with songwriting along with Richards. One of these collaborations made it onto the *Billboard* Hot 100 via a version the Rolling Stones recorded for their 1989 album *Steel Wheels*. "Almost Hear You Sigh" peaked at number fifty in the U.S. and number thirty-one in the U.K.

Jordan won a Grammy Award for producing Robert Cray's 1999 album *Take Your Shoes Off*, was nominated for Buddy Guy's *Bring 'Em In* from 2005, won a Grammy for producing John Mayer's *Continuum* in 2006, and received another Grammy Award nomination in 2010 for Best Compilation Soundtrack Album for a Motion Picture, Television or Other Visual Media for his work on the soundtrack for the movie *Cadillac Records*. Mayer is one of the musicians that Jordan has worked with for the longest periods, playing drums for 2003's *Heavier Things* and working as a producer and drummer for 2006's Grammy-winning *Continuum*, 2009's *Battle Studies*, and for the John Mayer Trio's debut album *Try!*

Leroy Clouden

Leroy Clouden first entered Steely Dan's orbit in 1984 when he played drums on the original cast recording for the musical *The Gospel at Colonus*, produced by Gary Katz and Donald Fagen. In 1988, Fagen enlisted him to play on another song that had a theatrical bent, "Century's End" for the film *Bright Lights, Big City*.

Clouden didn't work with Fagen again until 1992, when he replaced drummer Dennis McDermott for the *New York Rock and Soul Revue* summer tour, the first time that Becker and Fagen had toured together since 1974. Over the course of the tour, he not only played Steely Dan classics "Chain Lightning," "Pretzel Logic," "Green Earrings," "Black Friday," "Deacon Blues," "Josie," and "My Old School" but soul and R&B covers and hits by Michael McDonald, Boz Scaggs, and Phoebe Snow including "Minute by Minute," "Lowdown," and "Poetry Man."

Becker and Fagen had been working on Fagen's sophomore release *Kamakiriad* at the time, and along with session giant Chris Parker and Dennis McDermott, who played drums on the *New York Rock and Soul Revue: Live at the Beacon* LP, brought Clouden into the sessions for the album. He played on the second single released, "Tomorrow's Girls," as well as the album tracks "Springtime" and "Teahouse on the Tracks." His pocket is deep, but I've always felt that the drum sounds on *Kamakiriad* are too synthetic and lack the organic vibe of the records that Steely Dan made before their breakup.

In 2000, they hired Clouden again to play on "Almost Gothic, "Cousin Dupree," and "Janie Runaway" from their Grammy-winning album *Two Against Nature*. Clouden once again laid down some seriously tight grooves, and with a more natural drum production his playing can be appreciated much more.

Clouden continues to be one of the busiest drummers in New York City and in addition to Donald Fagen and Steely Dan has recorded with such artists as Herbie Mann, Marc Anthony, Joan Osborne, Lenny Pickett, and on the B-52's top ten record, 1989's *Cosmic Thing*, produced by Nile Rogers. He also played on the Walter Becker–produced band Fra Lippo Lippi's 1987 album *Light and Shade* and for the hit Broadway show *Bring in Da Funk, Bring in Da Noise*.

Chris Parker

Chris Parker grew up in a musical environment due to the fact that his father was a jazz drummer. He listened to Monk and Mingus as a child, playing along on wooden blocks attached to the hi-hat and kick drum pedals of his father's kit at age three. His first professional gig was at age eleven, and by the time he was in his teens, he was bit by the rock 'n' roll bug and was influenced by some of the rock and soul greats such as Roger Hawkins, D. J. Fontana, and Al Jackson Jr., to name a few. He also began to take jobs backing up strippers and exotic dancers in nightclubs.

After graduating from high school, he attended the School of Visual Arts in New York City on scholarship to study painting. While there, he answered an ad for a drummer in *Rolling Stone* magazine. He joined the band Holy Moses and moved to Woodstock, New York, in the Catskill Mountains. Although they released one album for RCA Victor in 1971, *Holy Moses!!*, the group folded shortly after its release. Parker had, however, met numerous high-profile musicians in Woodstock including Paul Butterfield, Bonnie Raitt, Tim Hardin, Rick Danko, Mike Bloomfield, and Merl Saunders. His other early sessions included records with Don McLean, Barry Manilow, Todd Rundgren, and Maria Muldaur, whose album included fellow Steely Dan drummers Jim Gordon and Jim Keltner.

Parker moved back to Manhattan after four years in Woodstock and began to play in a band called the Encyclopedia of Soul, later to become Stuff, with bassist and bandleader Gordon Edwards, guitarist Cornell Dupree, keyboardist Richard Tee, Charlie Brown on tenor saxophone, and sometime vocalist Esther Marrow. Brown and Marrow eventually left, but the group added a second guitarist, Eric Gale. The band gained a loyal following at their Monday and Tuesday night residency at Mikell's on 97th Street and Columbus Avenue in New York City, and after two years, Parker was in the jazz club the Village Vanguard watching saxophonist

Joe Farell and met drummer Steve Gadd. Gadd had told Parker of his desire to play R&B, as his background had been in jazz. Parker knew that Gadd would fit in with the Encyclopedia of Soul, so he asked Gadd to sub for him while he was working for the Brecker Brothers Band. Eventually, Edwards told him he needed them both, and they became a two-drummer band. Michael Lang, the producer of Woodstock, approached Edwards and told him he could get the band a record deal, so a representative of Warner Bros. flew in from California to hear them live and signed them on the spot. The one change they wanted to make was to their name. They felt the Encyclopedia of Soul was too long, so the band became Stuff.

Their funky, jazz- and R&B-infused, New York sound not only gained them a following amongst other musicians, but attracted singer-songwriters and producers as well. They were all in-demand session players, and Parker worked on albums by many artists, including Aretha Franklin, James Brown, John Lennon, Joe Cocker, Paul Simon, Miles Davis, Ashford and Simpson, Robert Palmer, the Spinners, Gladys Knight and the Pips, Michael Franks, Patti LaBelle, Chaka Khan, Salt n' Pepa, Lou Rawls, Lionel Hampton, Laura Nyro, Phoebe Snow, and Peter, Paul and Mary. He also spent three and a half years touring with Bob Dylan with various musical guests including George Harrison, Ringo Starr, Van Morrison, Neil Young, Joe Walsh, and Jerry Garcia.

In the '70s, Parker co-founded the Brecker Brothers band with Michael and Randy Brecker, David Sanborn, Buzzy Feiten, Steve Khan, Will Lee, and Don Grolnick. He also played on the 1977 album of Fagen's future wife, Libby Titus, contributing drums to the song "Can This Be My Love Affair" with Steely Dan alumni, keyboard player Don Grolnick and guitarist Hugh McCracken.

Parker's first experience with Becker and Fagen was not very successful. He was called in to work on "Time Out of Mind" from the *Gaucho* album, but a number of issues plagued the sessions. First of all, the bass player on the date was extremely late, so this gave Becker, Fagen, and Katz quite a bit of time getting a drum sound; so much time that Parker's focus was shot by the time they began recording. He was also receiving various directions from the composers as well as producer Katz and engineer Elliot Scheiner. His work was never used on the finished album. From 1986 to 1992, Parker was the house drummer for the NBC television show *Saturday Night Live*, a position that drummer Steve Jordon, who worked with Fagen on "True Companion" and *The Nightfly* and shared the stage with Steve Gadd in the double drummer role, had previously held.

Ten years after the unsuccessful session for *Gaucho*, Parker was enlisted as a drummer for the Becker-produced Fagen album *Kamakiriad*. In May 1990, he entered the Hit Factory on West 54th Street in New York City to begin sessions for the record. Fagen and engineer Roger Nichols spent days editing together the perfect drum tracks from Parker's performances.

In November 1990, Parker was flown out to Maui, Hawaii, to record more drum tracks for *Kamakiriad*. He had just finished a Bob Dylan tour the day before, and Becker wanted him straight off the road "with the blood, and the beer and the sweat." When Parker told him he didn't drink, Becker replied, "Well, the blood and sweat, then." Every morning he would be transported to the studio by Becker while listening to Sonny Rollins. They still spent ten days working only on drum sounds and parts, but it was a more relaxed atmosphere than the sessions in New York. During the Hit Factory sessions, Parker played his own drums, but in Maui he played on a Gretsch kit that had been set up for the sessions. They were specific about the sound they were interested in achieving and instructed Parker to tune his drums as high and tight as possible.

Parker stated in a 1993 interview with the fanzine *Metal Leg* that Becker, Fagen, and engineer Roger Nichols are "inseparable . . . like one person. They have worked together so long they have this communication . . . you really have to be on your toes to keep up with it. There're so many double entendres and word plays and you're lucky if you catch half of it—at least I was." Although they are all hard to please in the studio, he felt that Becker was the toughest. Parker's playing style often included ghost notes on the snare drum (notes played softly in between the big hits), and while Fagen loved it, Becker would at times think there was too much going on. The sessions were far more successful, and enjoyable, than the one he did ten years earlier for *Gaucho*. With just Becker, Fagen, and Nichols guiding the way, Parker was able to focus and take their directions more easily. They weren't necessarily specific about particular patterns. Their suggestions were more about "attitude and inflection," as Parker put it.

His drum solo on the song "On the Dunes" is in many ways the modern version of Steve Gadd's "Aja" outro. The drum track was recorded live, with Fagen playing the Fender Rhodes electric piano, and the drum outro was completely spontaneous. Parker was in the groove and just continued playing, and wasn't stopped by Becker or Fagen. He played on four of the eight songs, the most of any drummer: "Trans Island Skyway," "Countermoon," "Florida Room," and "On the Dunes." He has stated that he would have approached the songs differently had he known that Becker was slated to be the bass player, but during the five years of spread-out recording, Becker and Fagen didn't know who the bass player was going to be. They continuously joked that whoever played bass on the album had to have an odd name like Lincoln Schleifer, Zev Katz, or Teaker Barfield.

Dennis McDermott

Dennis McDermott first worked with Donald Fagen as the drummer for keyboard player Jeff Young's band Curious George, later known as Jeff Young and the Youngsters, the band that backed up the New York Rock and Soul Revue from 1990 to 1992. He was the drummer for the 1991 release of the LP *The New York Rock and Soul Revue: Live at the Beacon*, played on one song from Fagen's *Kamakiriad* LP in 1993, the Steely Danish "Snowbound," as well as the B-side of "Tomorrow's Girls," "Confide in Me."

Speaking about his work on *Kamakiriad*, McDermott gave a clue about Becker and Fagen's process when recording drums for the album in a 1991 interview for *Metal Leg*. "I did quite a number of passes playing different things to a sequencer and a drum machine pattern with pretty much everything on there. At first I played everything, then they left off the kick drum. They added up the kick drum so I could actually feel like I was playing, but left it off because they liked the sound of the kick drum on the sequencer. On one track, there was a guitar part and a bass part. Donald's real good at relating what he wants. He's a physical player and I am that way on drums." McDermott has recorded and performed with Roseanne Cash, Johnny Cash, David Johansen, Shawn Colvin, Marc Cohn, Graham Parker, Leni Stern, and numerous other artists.

Ben Perowsky

Drummer Ben Perowsky is yet another musician in the Steely Dan story who came from a family with an arts background. His father, Frank, was a clarinetist, saxophonist, and arranger, and his mother worked as a choreographer. He attended the High School of Music and Art in Harlem, now LaGuardia Arts, and while in the high school jazz band played with Dizzy Gillespie and Jimmy Heath. Perowsky studied at both the Berklee College of Music and the Manhattan School of Music before going on the road with the legendary saxophonist James Moody. He continued to tour and record with Rickie Lee Jones on a double bill with Ray Charles, vibraphonist Roy Ayers, guitarist Mike Stern, John Zorn, John Cale, and numerous others. He also recorded with pianist/producer Jim Beard and baritone saxophonist Ronnie Cuber, two musicians who would work with Steely Dan.

Becker met Perowsky while working on pianist Dave Kikowski's album *Persistent Dreams*. He heard him playing a speed-metal type of groove, and when asked if he knew of any bands that played a fusion of punk, jazz, and metal, Perowsky handed him the demo tape of his band Lost Tribe. Becker offered to produce them that night. The band flew out to Becker's studio in Maui, Hawaii, Hyperbolic Sound, and recorded their debut album in thirteen days.

While they were recording their album, Becker expressed interest in having the rhythm section play on a few of his songs for his upcoming debut solo LP. They didn't have enough time, but Perowsky, bassist Fima Ephron, and guitarist Adam Rogers returned in February 1993 for a month to cut tracks along with keyboard player John Beasley and guitarist Dean Parks, who had worked on countless Steely Dan albums.

While Becker was in New York working on *Kamakiriad* with Fagen, he would play them demos of the songs. Before leaving for Maui, he gave them a tape so that they could become familiar with the material. Once in Maui they cut the songs as a band, with Becker singing live. Although they initially played on all the tracks for the album, they only ended up on three, "Surf and/or Die," "Lucky Henry," and "Hat Too Flat."

Peter Erskine

Peter Erskine started playing drums when he was four years old and graduated from the Interlochen Arts Academy in Michigan. His professional career began at age eighteen in 1972 when he joined the Stan Kenton Orchestra. After four years with Kenton, he joined Maynard Ferguson's band for two years, but 1978 would prove to be the turning point for Erskine's career. That year he joined Weather Report and recorded five albums with them, winning his first Grammy Award for their album *8:30*. Erskine moved to Los Angeles and worked with jazz greats Freddie Hubbard, Joe Henderson, Chick Corea, Bobby Hutcherson, Joe Farrell, and numerous other jazz musicians before moving to New York City, where he collaborated with Michael Brecker, Randy Brecker, Steps Ahead, John Scofield, Linda Ronstadt, Rod Stewart, Bill Frisell, Marc Johnson, Joe Henderson, Bobby Hutcherson, Mike Stern, Diana Krall, the John Abercrombie Trio, and Bob Mintzer's Big Band.

Becker first met Erskine when he played on Rickie Lee Jones 1989 album *Flying Cowboys*, which Becker produced. Becker later called him to play on albums by Michael Franks, saxophonist Bob Sheppard, and pianist John Beasley (both of whom would work with Steely Dan shortly after). In 1993, Erskine got a call from Becker asking him to play drums on the first Steely Dan tour in nineteen years. Erskine was in Europe touring with his trio when his wife informed him of the upcoming opportunity. Although he hesitated slightly, he accepted the offer and prepared for three and a half weeks of rehearsal followed by a one-month tour that was extended to six weeks.

Although he was used to playing jazz gigs, he enjoyed the opportunity to groove and enjoyed interpreting the recordings that drum legends Jim Gordon, Jeff Porcaro, Bernard Purdie, Steve Gadd, Jim Keltner, and others had played on. In addition to the playing, he was a big fan of Becker and Fagen's songwriting. Erskine commented on his preparation for the tour in a 1993 interview with the *Rhythm Tech* newsletter. "I realized that it's so great playing just real simple. And it's the open spaces that really count . . . The more we rehearsed the music with Steely Dan I realized it's just not when you play the notes; but it's when you don't play the notes. It's the whole release in the space between things. And Donald's very specific about that kind of phrasing . . . It says an awful lot about the musician that's doing it. It leaves a very strong mark on the music." Along with Dennis Chambers, Erskine's work from the tour would be heard on a number of songs from Steely Dan's only official live album, 1995's *Alive in America*. Erskine continues to be a first-call jazz drummer and has released over fifty albums as a leader or co-leader.

Dennis Chambers

Like Peter Erskine, Dennis Chambers began drumming at age four, and by six he was playing gigs in nightclubs in Baltimore, Maryland. He joined Parliament-Funkadelic in 1978 when he was eighteen and worked with the band until 1985. During his tenure with Parliament-Funkadelic, he worked for the Sugar Hill record label as their house drummer and played on the iconic hit "Rapper's Delight," recorded in one fifteen-minute take, as well as numerous other releases by the label.

In the mid-'80s, he began a long relationship with guitarist John Scofield, appearing on his acclaimed albums *Loud Jazz*, *Blue Matter*, and *Pick Hits: Live*, and became one of the most requested session musicians in New York. He appeared on over two hundred records including those of John McLaughlin, George Duke, and Stanley Clarke, plus the release of four albums as a leader. Chambers has also been an integral part of two organ trios—the Free Spirits with guitarist John McLaughlin and organist Joey DeFrancesco, and Niacin, a rock/jazz project featuring bassist Billy Sheehan and organist John Novello.

On August 19, 1994, Steely Dan hit the road, with Chambers taking over for fellow jazz drummer Peter Erskine. Chambers had been approached the year before for their first tour as Steely Dan, but because of other commitments, Peter Erskine was hired instead. His deep pocket and relentless groove worked perfectly for the band, and along with Erskine, Chambers would appear on *Alive in America*. From 2005 until 2014, he spent most of his time on the road as the drummer for Santana.

Ricky Lawson

Ricky Lawson didn't begin playing drums until he was sixteen, but it didn't take long for him to master the instrument. As a teenager, he would borrow his uncle's kit and take it cross-town on a Detroit bus to practice. His band at the time, the Sons of Soul, was one of the opening acts for the Jackson 5 at the 1969 Michigan State Fair. After graduation, he earned a swimming scholarship to college, but he left after only one year when Stevie Wonder approached him to play drums for him.

In the '70s, he began playing sessions for Roy Ayers, Tom Waits, the Jacksons, George Duke, the Emotions, and Robben Ford. The group Ford assembled for his 1979 solo album *The Inside Story* would become the Yellowjackets. Lawson would record four albums with the band and win a Grammy Award in 1987 for Best R&B Instrumental Performance for the song "And You Know That" from the album *Shades*, the title track written by none other than Donald Fagen. He left the band after its release to play with Lionel Richie.

Throughout the '80s, '90s, and '00s, Lawson stayed busy with session work and touring with Michael Jackson, Eric Clapton, Phil Collins, Beyoncé, Babyface, Whitney Houston, Paul McCartney, Rod Stewart, Anita Baker, Aretha Franklin, Smokey Robinson, John Mellencamp, Michael McDonald, Kenny Loggins, Mariah Carey, Kenny G, Gladys Knight, Quincy Jones, Bette Midler, Toto, George Benson, Bobby Brown, DeBarge, Sister Sledge, Teena Marie, Philip Bailey, and countless others.

Fagen had already worked with Lawson, having written a song for his band, the Yellowjackets, but in 1992, while producing pianist John Beasley's album *Cauldron*, Becker would actually work with the drummer in the studio. Becker was suitably impressed, as was Fagen, by his skills, and they would hire Lawson four years later to tour with Steely Dan on the 1996 *Art Crimes* tour. He would also play with the duo on 2000's *Walking Distance* and *Two Against Nature* tours, on "Gaslighting Abbey" from the *Two Against Nature* album, as well as the VH1 *Storytellers* show and the *Plush TV Jazz-Rock Party* DVD. Fagen would play acoustic piano on the Phil Collins/Nathan East–composed track "Sweet Love" from Lawson's debut solo album, *First Things 1st*.

Lawson would record one other solo album in 2008, a Christmas album entitled *Christmas with Friends* with Ron Reinhardt and Philippe Saisse on acoustic piano; Rick Braun on trumpet; Richard Elliot, Michael Paulo, and Steve Alaniz on saxophone; Paul Brown, Adam Hawley, and Ian Keene on guitar; Lenny Castro on percussion; and Roberto Vally and Sekou Bunch on bass.

On December 13, 2013, Lawson was playing a gig at the Spaghettini jazz club in Seal Beach, California. He felt disoriented and was brought to the Long Beach Memorial Medical Center, where he was diagnosed with a brain aneurysm. He passed away ten days later on December 23, 2013, when he was removed from life support.

Keith Carlock

In 2000, Becker and Fagen met one of the most important musicians who would eventually become a somewhat permanent member of Steely Dan 2.0, drummer Keith Carlock. Carlock was born in Clinton, Mississippi, and began playing drums at age five. As a teenager, he primarily played rock, R&B, and soul music, but after graduation, he attended the University of North Texas to study jazz. He continued to play professionally in the Dallas/Fort Worth area for a number of years before moving to New York City. Soon after arriving, he began playing on the club circuit with guitarist Wayne Krantz, singer Leni Stern, bassist Oz Noy, and other jazz musicians around town. Krantz had toured with Steely Dan during their 1996 *Arts Crimes* tour, and one night Becker and Fagen entered the 55 Bar on Christopher Street in New York City where Krantz's trio had a regular Thursday night gig and heard Carlock behind the kit. They came back a few more times and even sat in with the trio. They were incredibly impressed with his ability to play not only jazz, but other styles as well with the same confidence.

Carlock was hired to play on the *Two Against Nature* LP and recorded three songs, the title track, "West of Hollywood," and "Negative Girl," but only the title track made the final cut. He played along to a stark drum machine and bass line demo by himself, not realizing that the drum machine was going to be on the final recording as well as his live drums. Since only one of three songs was chosen for the album, he thought he had blown his opportunity. But in 2001, he got the call to play on a track that Becker and Fagen were doing for a Joni Mitchell tribute album. The track, "Carey," from her *Blue* album, was never released, but Carlock kept getting called for sessions for their 2003 follow-up to the Grammy Award-winning *Two Against Nature* album, *Everything Must Go.* Carlock would play on every track on the album, something no other drummer had done since Jim Hodder's performances on the first two albums. He would go on to play on every song on both Fagen's *Morph the Cat* album and Becker's *Circus Money.* The 2003 *Everything Must Go* tour would be his first, and he would continue to play on every subsequent Steely Dan tour as

Keith Carlock was first called in to play on the *Two Against Nature* album in 2000. He followed with *Everything Must Go* and has been their drummer ever since. He plays Gretsch drums and was featured in this ad to "Earn Your Badge."

well as Fagen's short tour in 2006 to promote *Morph the Cat*. After over thirty years, Steely Dan had finally found a drummer they could always count on.

Besides his busy touring schedule with Steely Dan, Carlock has recorded and/ or toured with Sting, John Mayer, James Taylor, Diana Ross, Faith Hill, Bette Midler, the Blues Brothers Band, David Johansen and the Harry Smiths, Richard Bona, Chris Botti, Harry Belafonte, Clay Aiken, Rascal Flatts, Paula Abdul, and Grover Washington Jr., to name a few. In January 2014, Carlock replaced longtime Toto drummer Simon Phillips for a Japanese tour. When they returned, work began on *Toto XIV*, and he began tracking a few tunes for the album. Things went so well that he kept getting called back and eventually played on every track.

Michael White

Michael White was born in Chicago, Illinois, and worked with Curtis Mayfield and Lou Rawls in the early part of his career. In 1982, he moved to Los Angeles to work as a session musician and contributed his signature style to albums by Luther Vandross, David Sanborn, the Emotions, the Four Tops, Teena Marie, Marcus Miller, Najee, George Benson, Al Jarreau, Lalah Hathaway, Vanessa Williams, Will Downing, Ledisi, and others over the course of a thirty-plus-year career. One of his main gigs, however, was as the drummer for Maze, featuring Frankie Beverly, of which he has been an on and off member since the mid-1980s. He also recorded three albums as a solo artist in the '90s.

When Becker and Fagen were beginning to put musicians together for their first album in nineteen years, drummer Ricky Lawson, who had played on their 1996 *Art Crimes* tour, wasn't available for the majority of the sessions and would only play on the first track, "Gaslighting Abbey." They asked bassist Tom Barney whom he could recommend, and Michael White came to mind. Although Becker and Fagen would revert to the tendency to use a multitude of drummers for a single album (*Two Against Nature* used six drummers for nine songs), White ended up playing on two tracks, "What a Shame About Me" and "Jack of Speed." Although he wouldn't record with Steely Dan again, he would tour with Fagen, Michael McDonald, and Boz Scaggs for their 2010 *Dukes of September Rhythm Revue* tour.

Vinnie Colaiuta

Vinnie Colaiuta was born in Republic, Pennsylvania, and began playing drums as a child. He attended the Berklee College of Music in Boston for a year before dropping out to join the Christopher Morris Band in 1976. The next year, he relocated to Los Angeles with the band, but left soon after. He played around town with some less than stellar acts before his next break came in April 1978. He auditioned for Frank Zappa and went on to work with him as his principal drummer for studio and live performances, playing on *Tinsel Town Rebellion, Joe's Garage*, and *Shut Up 'n Play Yer Guitar*. After working with Zappa, Colaiuta's session work increased, and he has played on over six hundred albums with artists such as Paul McCartney, Billy Joel, Eric Clapton, Jeff Beck, Herbie Hancock, Joni Mitchell, Smokey Robinson, Duran Duran, Don Henley, Barry Manilow, Glen Campbell, Bette Midler, Gino

Vannelli, Al Kooper, Olivia Newton-John, Frankie Valli and the Four Seasons, Juice Newton, Paul Anka, Poco, the Commodores, Steely Dan stalwarts Michael McDonald, Victor Feldman, Tom Scott, and Drew Zingg, and far too many others to list here. In 1990, Colaiuta joined Sting's touring band and contributed to *The Soul Cages*, *Ten Summoner's Tales*, *Mercury Falling*, *Brand New Day*, and *Sacred Love*.

He played on one song for *Two Against Nature*, "Negative Girl," which drummer Keith Carlock had already attempted to record. Colaiuta also played drums for the 2006 Steely Dan tribute album, *The Royal Dan*, which featured different guitarists interpreting Becker and Fagen's compositions.

Sonny Emory

Sonny Emory was born in Atlanta, Georgia, and received his first drum set at the age of four. During his childhood, he was surrounded by music, playing with his father, a saxophonist, and his grandfather, a keyboardist, from a young age. He graduated from Georgia State University with a bachelor's degree in jazz performance, but when he turned twenty-four in 1986, he moved to Los Angeles and began his professional career playing with the Crusaders, a band that had at different times included Steely Dan session musicians, guitarist Larry Carlton, bassist Wilton Felder, and keyboard player Joe Sample, who was still leading the group when Emory joined.

From 1987 to 1999, he held down the drum chair for one of the most coveted, and difficult, positions in music as the drummer for legendary R&B group Earth, Wind & Fire. His various credits include records with Bruce Hornsby, Bette Midler, Phyllis Hyman, Chic, the B-52's, and Steely Dan session player, guitarist Lee Ritenour. Emory only played on one Steely Dan song, *Two Against Nature*'s closer, "West of Hollywood," the longest song on any Steely Dan record, clocking in at 8:22 due to the nearly four-minute tenor saxophone solo of Chris Potter.

Earl Cooke, Jr.

The last drummer associated with Steely Dan, Earl Cooke Jr., isn't actually a full-time session drummer at all. It is a pseudonym for trumpet player Michael Leonhart, who has toured with Steely Dan since their 1996 *Art Crimes* tour. The son of noted jazz bassist Jay Leonhart, he would play on all but one (the short *Left Bank Holiday Tour* of Europe in 2009) of Steely Dan's subsequent tours and would co-produce and play drums, keyboards, percussion, trumpet, flügelhorn, mellophone, and add background vocals to Fagen's fourth solo album, 2012's *Sunken Condos*.

It's odd that Donald Fagen, a man who used to worry about a snare drum beat being a millisecond off, would use someone on drums who wasn't really a drummer. Fagen recalled that during sound checks Leonhart would get behind the drums, and Fagen was impressed and thought he could play funk grooves exceptionally well. When they began work on *Sunken Condos*, he was initially going to play on a few demos, but since the album was more groove based and didn't require flawless technique on the drums, he ended up played on all nine songs. As Fagen remarked in a 2013 interview with *Keyboard* magazine, "He had an old-school groove, maybe from being a jazz player. It was just a really comfortable groove that was exactly what the music needed."

14

If You Can't Fly, You'll Have to Move In with the Rhythm Section

The Bass and the Keys

A lthough Becker and Fagen were known to be quite hard on drummers, they seemed to be a bit more flexible with the bass players and keyboard players. After all, they were hiring them because they thought that they could do the job better than either of them could do themselves. While Fagen's role as keyboard player was relegated to mostly synthesizer parts from *Pretzel Logic* to *Aja*, he played the main keyboard parts on four of the seven songs from their 1980 release, *Gaucho*. Becker continued to play bass and guitar to varying degrees on all of their records, and during Steely Dan's initial run, they only used three (or four if you count the questionable contributions of Timothy B. Schmit) electric bass players besides Becker.

The Fourteen Bass Players

Although Walter Becker played bass on more songs than any other musician, fourteen different bass players contributed to Dan-related projects over the years. This number is a bit misleading because only three session bassists performed on the original seven Steely Dan records (four if you count Timothy B. Schmit's involvement, which is dubious at best). The only other bass player to appear on an early Steely Dan record is the first one we will discuss.

Ray Brown

The first Steely Dan song that Walter Becker didn't perform on was "Razor Boy" from their sophomore LP *Countdown to Ecstasy*. They decided they wanted an acoustic bass on the Latin jazz–flavored tune, and who better to call than jazz legend Ray Brown. Brown's résumé is truly remarkable; he played with some of the most important musicians in the history of jazz including Ella Fitzgerald, Count Basie, Dizzy Gillespie, Frank Sinatra, Billie Holiday, Sonny Rollins, Quincy Jones, Buddy Rich, Gene Krupa, Benny Carter, Roy Eldridge, Milt Jackson, Ben Webster, and too many more to list. He was part of the Oscar Peterson Trio for forty years, recording over seventy albums with the group. Elvis Costello handpicked Brown to play on "Eisenhower Blues" from his 1986 album *King of America*. During his illustrious career, Brown has also released dozens of albums as a leader or co-leader from 1946 until his death in 2002 at seventy-five.

Chuck Rainey

For the first two albums, co-founder Walter Becker handled all of the bass duties, with the exception of the acoustic bass on "Razor Boy," which was played by Ray Brown. On their third LP, *Pretzel Logic*, Becker continued to be a contributor in the bass department, but two session players were used for specific tunes, Wilton Felder and Chuck Rainey. For "Any Major Dude Will Tell You," session ace Rainey was brought in, which would mark the beginning of a long and fruitful working relationship with Steely Dan. His choice of bass for many Dan sessions was his original Fender '57 Precision Bass going through a direct box. From then on, Rainey would appear on every Steely Dan album from the band's first phase, which ranged from 1972 to 1980. Like Rick Marotta, Rainey had never heard of Steely Dan before his first session. Rainey recalled in a 2004 interview with Mike Connolly, "I was not familiar with them at all—had no idea who they were. At the time of doing the dates for the first time, I basically had no specific opinion of the music other than that it was a job that was easy and I understood the concept. Actually it was a pleasant experience, because I love to play all kinds of music and this was a rare occasion to perform on a recording of what I call a 'hard rock' style of music."

After playing violin, piano, trumpet, and baritone horn in his youth, Rainey began playing rhythm guitar while on active military duty. Due to his lack of improvisational skills, he switched to the bass and soon began a career as a highly regarded session musician in New York. Throughout the 1960s, the majority of his sessions were with jazz musicians such as Dizzy Gillespie, Louis Armstrong, Jimmy McGriff, Gary Burton, Lena Horne, Hubert Laws, Cal Tjader, Eddie Harris, and Yusef Lateef. He did, however, play on some pop sessions for Laura Nyro, the Rascals, and Al Kooper, and as a member of the King Curtis All-Stars, who toured with the Beatles during their 1965 tour of America. Rainey was also a member of

Chuck Rainey played bass on more Steely Dan tracks than anybody other than Walter Becker. In 1972, he released his debut album as a leader entitled *The Chuck Rainey Coalition*.

Quincy Jones's big band. In 1972, he moved to Los Angeles, where his first-call status as a session musician followed him.

The '70s and '80s found Rainey playing on albums from some of the biggest names in the music business including Roberta Flack, Donny Hathaway, Aretha Franklin, Robert Palmer, Jackson Browne, Marvin Gaye, Joe Cocker, Minnie Ripperton, Leo Sayer, Rickie Lee Jones, Bette Midler, the Crusaders, Dave Mason, Joe Walsh, Cheryl Lynn, Tavares, Lowell George, and after a chance meeting with Gary Katz on the freeway in 1974, Steely Dan. He also played the signature bass part on the theme for the television series *Sanford and Son* written by Quincy Jones. Over the course of five albums, he played on more Steely Dan songs than any other bassist with the exception of Walter Becker.

On their fourth LP, *Katy Lied,* Rainey played a slightly bigger role, laying down his signature groove for "Bad Sneakers," "Doctor Wu," and "Your Gold Teeth II." On 1976's *The Royal Scam,* however, Rainey played bass on nearly every song including "Kid Charlemagne," "Don't Take Me Alive," "Green Earrings," "The Fez," and "The Royal Scam." On *Aja,* he laid down the groove for every song except "Deacon Blues," on which Becker plays. Rainey returned for *Gaucho,* playing on "Babylon Sisters" and "Third World Man." However, after a stressful session with Donald Fagen for "Green Flower Street" on *The Nightfly,* they parted ways. With the exception of an on-camera reunion for the filming of the *Classic Albums: Steely Dan Aja* DVD, they never worked together again.

Wilton Felder

Multi-instrumentalist Wilton Felder is known for two things; playing the tenor saxophone with the Crusaders and being one of the most sought-after session bass players in the '60s and '70s. Born in Houston, Texas, on August 31, 1940, Felder was the youngest of thirteen children, three of whom had passed away before he was born. As a child, Felder contracted pneumonia, and his brother promised him that he would get him a saxophone if he got better. Once he recovered, his brother was true to his word and gave Felder his first horn. He played in the junior high school band and was formally trained on the instrument.

Once Felder entered high school, he began playing saxophone and bassoon with high school friends, keyboardist Joe Sample, drummer Nesbert "Stix" Hooper, trombonist Wayne Henderson, flutist and alto saxophonist Hubert Laws, and bassist Henry Wilson in two short-lived bands called the Swingsters and the Nite Hawks. They were also known as the Modern Jazz Sextet. In 1960, they moved to Los Angeles, changed their name to the Jazz Crusaders, and signed a deal with Pacific Jazz Records. Shortly after arriving in Los Angeles, Hubert Laws won a scholarship to Juilliard and left for New York City. Wilson also departed, making the group a quartet. Laws would only play on one Jazz Crusaders album, 1965's *Chili Con Soul,* the group's sixth LP.

During the '60s, the Jazz Crusaders utilized session bass players and guitarists to augment their sound in the studio and on stage, but an interesting turn of events would change Felder's career path significantly. Joe Sample was playing organ at the time, but when he grew tired of playing bass pedals, club owner

Harry Lieberman gave Felder a bass, and he taught himself how to play. His first big break as a session musician came when he subbed for bassist Ron Brown on a Motown session for Barrett Strong. Strong liked what he heard and began calling Felder for more sessions.

The Jazz Crusaders released seventeen albums between 1961 and 1970, including one with pianist Les McCann and three live albums, before shortening their name to the Crusaders and moving into more of a jazz-funk direction. On their second album with this new moniker, 1972's *Hollywood*, Felder contributed bass to a number of songs. Their next LP, *Crusaders 1*, was the first with guitarist Larry Carlton. He would play on their next three albums before joining as a full member for 1974's *Southern Comfort*. Bassist Robert "Pops" Popwell also played on a number of their albums from the '70s. With this new musical direction, the band began to have crossover hits, peaking in 1979 with *Street Life*, which featured Randy Crawford on vocals. By this time, founding member Wayne Henderson had left to pursue a career as a producer, and Carlton and Popwell were no longer in the band. The album peaked at number eighteen on the pop album charts, and the title track from the album made the top ten on the R&B chart and number thirty-six on *Billboard*'s Hot 100 chart.

Throughout the '70s, Felder continued to book more sessions as a bass player than as a saxophonist. He performed on the Jackson 5's first number one single, "I Want You Back," as well as their 1970 hit "The Love You Save." He has graced the albums of Marvin Gaye, Grant Green, Billy Joel, Joni Mitchell, Seals and Crofts, the Four Tops, Ringo Starr, Randy Newman, Anne Murray, Joan Baez, Richard "Groove" Holmes, Jimmy Smith, Stanley Turrentine, Shuggie Otis, Donald Byrd, Nancy Wilson, B. B. King, Harry Nilsson, Al Jarreau, Joe Cocker, Bobby Womack, and countless others. Along with bandmates Joe Sample and Larry Carlton, Felder would play on Michael Franks's 1975 breakthrough album *The Art of Tea*. Also, his bass groove from Jimmy Smith's "Root Down (and Get It)" was sampled to great effect for the Beastie Boys 1994 track "Root Down" from their *Ill Communication* LP.

In 1974, Felder was called into the studio to play bass on Steely Dan's *Pretzel Logic* LP. He returned for 1975's *Katy Lied*, laying down his signature shuffle on "Chain Lightning." His performance was not the only significant role he played on Steely Dan's fourth album. He also introduced Larry Carlton to Becker and Fagen, a relationship that continues to this day. Felder also released nine solo albums during his career, his last being 2006's *Let's Spend Some Time*. He passed away in 2015 at the age of seventy-five.

Timothy B. Schmit

Bass player and vocalist Timothy B. Schmit of Poco and the Eagles was listed in the credits for *Pretzel Logic*, and it has been stated that he not only sang background vocals but contributed bass as well. This seems a little far-fetched. While Schmit is a fine bassist, he is a pop/rock player, and it would seem odd that Becker and Fagen would bring in that type of player rather than Becker himself, who played on numerous tracks on the record. Rather than leave Schmit out, we'll list him with a question mark.

Anthony Jackson

From their third album, Steely Dan added bassists Chuck Rainey and Wilton Felder to take over some bass duties from Walter Becker. By *The Royal Scam*, Rainey and Backer handled all of the bass parts, and on *Aja* Rainey played on all but one song, "Deacon Blues," which Becker handled beautifully. It wasn't until Steely Dan's last album before their nineteen-year hiatus, that they would introduce a new bass player to the fold, Anthony Jackson.

Jackson was the first bassist to play a six-string bass, approaching several luthiers in 1974 to see who would be willing to bring his trailblazing idea to fruition. A year later, Carl Thompson built the first six-string bass for Jackson, changing the face of bass playing forever. He laid down the grooves for "Glamour Profession" and "My Rival" from *Gaucho* and worked with Fagen on *The Nightfly* adding his signature groove to "I.G.Y. (What a Beautiful World)" and "Ruby Baby." Although his work has been primarily on jazz albums by artists such as Dizzy Gillespie, Pat Metheny, Buddy Rich, Mike Stern, Michel Petrucciani, and others, his work with rock, pop, and soul artists is quite impressive, including Paul Simon, Roberta Flack, Chaka Khan, the O'Jays, and Madonna.

Will Lee

Lee began his musical career as a drummer in San Antonio, Texas, at age twelve after seeing the Beatles on *The Ed Sullivan Show*. While at the University of Miami, he studied French horn before switching to bass. When he moved to New York City, he became a first-call session musician as both a bass player and vocalist, and over his forty-five year career he has worked with Ringo Starr, Billy Joel, Carly Simon, Miles Davis, B. B. King, Bob Dylan, Cher, Dionne Warwick, Bette Midler, Al Green, Barry Manilow, Cat Stevens, Dr. John, D'Angelo, Chaka Khan, George Benson, Cyndi Lauper, Nina Simone, Carl Perkins, Michael Franks, Jimmy Cliff, Dusty Springfield, Patti Austin, Gloria Estefan, Nancy Wilson, Liza Minnelli, Leo Sayer, the Brecker Brothers, Bob James, Grant Green, Roberta Flack, Pat Metheny, Tom Scott, Elliott Randall, Melissa Manchester, Buddy Rich, and countless others. Lee also played on the eponymous solo LP from Libby Titus in 1977, two years before he worked with Steely Dan.

That work, however, was never released. Not only did he play on the original, and rerecorded, versions of "The Second Arrangement" (the song accidentally erased by an engineer during the *Gaucho* sessions), he also attempted other songs. But Lee didn't hesitate to tell Becker and Fagen when he thought he had recorded the best take, and therefore his work was never used. He wouldn't actually record a released Dan-related take until 1981's "True Companion" from the *Heavy Metal* movie and accompanying soundtrack album.

He next worked with Fagen on "Walk Between the Raindrops," his walking bass line doubling Greg Phillinganes's synth bass, from *The Nightfly*. The year 1982 was an important one for Will Lee; not only did he play on "Raindrops," he became one of the original members of the World's Most Dangerous Band, the house band on NBC's *Late Night with David Letterman*. He holds the distinction of playing with Paul

Shaffer longer than any other member working on both *Late Night* and the *Late Show*. In 1998, he co-founded the Fab Faux, one of the most critically acclaimed Beatles cover bands in the world.

Marcus Miller

Multi-instrumentalist Marcus Miller, who is a classically trained clarinetist, is primarily known as a bass player. He grew up in Brooklyn in a musical family. His father was a church organist and choir director, and his cousin was jazz pianist Wynton Kelly. By age fifteen, he was working professionally in New York City. In 1982, he worked with Donald Fagen on *The Nightfly* LP, playing on three tracks, "Maxine," "The Goodbye Look," and the title track. In 1988, he returned to play his signature slap bass on the B-side to "Century's End," the instrumental "Shanghai Confidential."

He's recorded over twenty albums as a leader and has won numerous Grammy Awards as a producer for Miles Davis, Luther Vandross, David Sanborn, Bob James, Chaka Khan, and Wayne Shorter. As a session musician, his versatile skills have graced albums by Michael Jackson, Aretha Franklin, Elton John, Frank Sinatra, Carly Simon, Roberta Flack, Herbie Hancock, Mariah Carey, Wayne Shorter, McCoy Tyner, George Benson, Dr. John, Grover Washington Jr., Bill Withers, LL Cool J, and numerous others in nearly every musical style.

Abraham Laboriel

Guitar Player magazine listed bassist Abraham Laboriel as the most widely used session bassist, with over three thousand recordings and soundtracks to his credit. Laboriel was born in Mexico City and was originally trained as a classical guitarist. While studying at the Berklee College of Music in Boston, Massachusetts, he switched to bass and began to work with faculty member vibraphonist Gary Burton. While on the East Coast, he toured with singer Johnny Mathis, pianist Michel Legrand, and one of Donald Fagen's musical heroes, composer Henry Mancini. It was Mancini who convinced Laboriel to move to Los Angeles to seek work as a session musician, so in 1976 he arrived and began an astonishing career.

Laboriel's feel and innovative style quickly found him an enormous amount of work. Over his forty-plus-year career as a session bassist, he has worked with Stevie Wonder, Ray Charles, Michael Jackson, Elton John, Lionel Richie, Madonna, Paul Simon, Quincy Jones, George Benson, Barbra Streisand, Ella Fitzgerald, Larry Carlton, Herbie Hancock, Herb Alpert, Chris Isaak, Christopher Cross, Jeffrey Osborne, Chaka Khan, Robbie Robertson, Kenny Rogers, Kenny Loggins, Ruben Blades, Freddie Hubbard, Al Jarreau, the Crusaders, the Manhattan Transfer, Leo Sayer, Lisa Loeb, Dave Grusin, Joe Pass, Joe Sample, Lalo Schifrin, Diane Schuur, Sarah Vaughan, Joe Zawinul, and literally too many to list.

It's surprising that he was never called to play on any of the Steely Dan sessions, but in 1982, he played on the second single from *The Nightfly* album, "New Frontier." His funk-infused, sliding bass line is imaginative and graceful and makes one wonder what he would have sounded like on a Steely Dan track. Laboriel's son, Abe Laboriel Jr., is a successful musician in his own right with countless sessions under his belt. He has also been Paul McCartney's drummer for the past fifteen years.

Jimmy Haslip

Bassist Jimmy Haslip was one of the founding members of jazz-fusion group the Yellowjackets. His playing has been heard on albums by artists as varied as Crosby, Stills & Nash; Cher; Bobby McFerrin; Kenny G; Bobby Caldwell; Kiss; Randy Crawford; Anita Baker; Gino Vannelli; Lee Ritenour; Gary Wright; Jon Anderson; Take 6; and others. He worked with Fagen on two songs, 1988's "Century's End" from the movie *Bright Lights, Big City* and its accompanying soundtrack as well as the short music cue of the Jimmy Reed song that provided the movie with its title. He also took part in sessions that either Becker or Fagen contributed to including dates by Diana Ross, Eye to Eye, and Fra Lippo Lippi. In addition, he was also part of the rhythm section for the album *A Tribute* by the "band" the Royal Dan. The LP was actually a guitar tribute to Steely Dan with ten different world-renowned guitarists tackling their songs (see chapter twenty-four).

Fima Ephron

Bassist Fima Ephron first worked with Walter Becker in 1993 when he produced the Brooklyn-based band Lost Tribe, of which he was a member. The band flew out to his studio, Hyperbolic Sound, in Maui, and cut their debut album in thirteen days. While working on their album, Becker expressed interest in having them record tracks for his debut solo LP, *11 Tracks of Whack*. The initial plan was to have a functioning rhythm section for tracking consisting of Ephron; bandmates drummer Ben Perowsky and guitarist Adam Rogers; keyboard player John Beasley; and guitarist Dean Parks, who had worked on countless Steely Dan albums. Although they expected to be on the entire album, they only appeared on three tracks, "Surf and/or Die," "Lucky Henry," and "Hat Too Flat."

Tom Barney

Bassist Tom Barney's professional career began in the '70s playing on jazz records by Turk Mauro and Walter Davis Jr. Soon after, his session work multiplied working with artists such as Aretha Franklin, Eric Clapton, Miles Davis, Dizzy Gillespie, Rod Stewart, Herbie Hancock, George Duke, Chaka Khan, David Sanborn, Jeffrey Osborne, Stevie Ray Vaughn, Burt Bacharach, Mary J. Blige, Carlos Santana, Lauryn Hill, Lonnie Liston Smith, Bob Mintzer, Judy Collins, Jane Fonda, Joss Stone, Mike Stern, Tania Maria, Grover Washington Jr., Teddy Pendergrass, Ice T., Al B. Sure, Regina Belle, and others. He was also a member of the Saturday Night Live Band in the '80s and '90s.

Tom Barney had first worked with Donald Fagen when he filled in for Harvey Brooks at some of the New York Nights shows at the Lone Star. In 1993, when Becker and Fagen were putting together the band that would accompany them on their first tour as Steely Dan in nineteen years, the New York Rock and Soul

Revue band that had played with them the previous summer was completely reconfigured with only guitarist Drew Zingg (who was now musical director), saxophonist Cornelius Bumpus, and background vocalists Catherine Russell and Brenda White-King returning. Barney was hired as the bassist and played three tours in 1993, 1994, and 1996 before Becker and Fagen took a four-year hiatus to work on songs for their first album in twenty years. In 1995, the album *Alive in America* was compiled from live shows from the 1993 and 1994 tours, marking the first time Barney would appear on a Steely Dan album.

When work began on *Two Against Nature*, Becker ended up playing bass on the majority of the tunes, but Barney was called to play on three: "Gaslighting Abbey," "Negative Girl," and "West of Hollywood." To promote the album, Steely Dan did two television shows, VH-1's *Storytellers* and PBS's *In the Spotlight*, which would eventually become the DVD release *Plush TV Jazz-Rock Party*. Barney was onboard for both and would tour with the band until the conclusion of 2003's *Everything Must Go* tour.

Freddie Washington

While working on his 2006 album *Morph the Cat*, Fagen called "Ready Freddie" Washington to lay down his signature groove for every song on the album and for the short tour to promote it. Washington grew up in Oakland, California, and began studying the bass at fourteen. Five years later, he became Herbie Hancock's bassist, touring and recording with him for several years. His credits are a who's who of funk, pop, jazz, and rock artists including Michael Jackson, Stevie Wonder, Smokey Robinson, Whitney Houston, Boz Scaggs, Gladys Knight and the Pips, Al Jarreau, the Commodores, Diana Ross, Christopher Cross, George Duke, B. B. King, the Temptations, Billy Preston, Aaron Neville, Elton John, George Benson, Lionel Richie, Keb' Mo', and dozens of others. Washington is also a composer and producer, co-writing Patrice Rushen's hit "Forget Me Nots," later sampled by Will Smith for his multi-platinum smash "Men in Black," and her song "Haven't You Heard," sampled for Kirk Franklin's hit "Lookin' for You."

After Tom Barney left the band in 2003, Freddie Washington took over bass duties for the 2006 *Steelyard Sugartooth McDan* tour and every other Dan tour to the present day. He also partook in *The Dukes of September Rhythm Revue* tours in both 2010 and 2012 and played on one song on Fagen's *Sunken Condos*.

Joe Martin

The last time an acoustic bass was used on a Steely Dan-related project was 1973's "Razor Boy," from their second album *Countdown to Ecstasy*, played by jazz heavyweight Ray Brown. For Fagen's "Slinky Thing" from *Sunken Condos*, he enlisted Joe Martin, one of the most sought-after jazz bassists in New York, for the honor. Martin was a vital member of guitarist Kurt Rosenwinkel's group for several years and has performed with the Mingus Big Band, Andy Bey, Bill Charlap, Art Farmer, Larry Goldings, Brad Mehldau, Chris Potter, Grady Tate, and countless other jazz artists.

Lincoln Schleifer

Although bassist Lincoln Schleifer had been a part of the original New York Rock and Soul Revue band in 1990, he wouldn't record with Fagen until the sessions for *Kamakiriad*. Walter Becker ended up replaying all the bass parts that session musicians, including Schleifer, had laid down, but Schleifer's playing remained on the B-side to "Tomorrow's Girls," "Confide in Me." He would return to contribute bass to three songs on Fagen's *Sunken Condos*. His performances on "Memorabilia," "Weather in My Head," and "Planet D'Rhonda" make one wonder why it took Fagen almost nineteen years to use him on a session.

The Fifteen Keyboardists

Although Donald Fagen was a proficient keyboard player with a fantastic feel, by *Pretzel Logic* the songwriting team decided that they wanted to augment their sound and use players that were steeped in jazz. They used some of the best in the world, and their fluid, imaginative styles added another level of musicianship to the recordings. Fagen would contribute more as a keyboard player to *Gaucho*, *Two Against Nature*, *Everything Must Go*, and his solo albums, but there were always serious jazz players involved as well.

Michael Omartian

Michael Omartian is a bit of a singular character in the world of Steely Dan session musicians. Not only has he played on countless sessions for albums by John Lennon, Billy Joel, Bobby "Blue" Bland, the Four Tops, Jerry Garcia, Johnny Rivers, Boz Scaggs, Al Jarreau, George Benson, the Manhattan Transfer, Michael McDonald, and Loggins and Messina, he has also produced chart-topping albums for myriad artists.

During the *Pretzel Logic* sessions, Becker and Fagen began to replace original members—including themselves—with session musicians. Michael Omartian was the first musician aside from Donald Fagen to play keyboards on a Steely Dan song. The duo were looking for a sophistication that they believed was not possible with Fagen on keys. Omartian's contributions to both *Pretzel Logic* and *Katy Lied* were immense. He served as the primary piano player, wrote charts and chose the Bösendorfer piano the band would use during the *Katy Lied* sessions. The seven-foot-six piano was delivered to ABC recording studios as well as the $13,000 bill, which went directly to the ABC record label. Omartian's contributions to "Rikki Don't Lose That Number," "Your Gold Teeth II," "Chain Lightning," "Black Friday," "Bad Sneakers," "Throw Back the Little Ones," and "Here at the Western World" are superb examples of his taste and sophistication. Additionally, his piano playing on "Aja" is nothing short of game changing. He would often offer ideas for particular sections of songs and, based on his track record, was given a freedom that the majority of musicians were not afforded during Steely Dan sessions. Becker even admitted that the superimposed triads that close "Throw Back the Little Ones," and therefore the *Katy Lied* LP, were Omartian's idea. Although he wouldn't play on the *Gaucho* LP, Omartian would return for *The Nightfly*, contributing piano to "Ruby Baby," piano and electric piano to "New Frontier," and electric piano to the title track.

Like Steely Dan producer Gary Katz, Omartian was a part of the A&R staff at ABC Dunhill Records as a producer as well as an artist and arranger. He released a number of contemporary Christian albums as a solo artist and with his wife Stormie. This notwithstanding, his best-selling record as a producer was Christopher Cross's 1979 eponymous debut album. Cross hired Omartian based on his work with Steely Dan in general and his work on *Katy Lied* in particular. Cross's album was nominated for ten Grammys, of which Omartian won three. He also produced albums for Dionne Warwick, Rod Stewart, Donna Summer, the Jacksons, Peter Cetera, Debbie Boone, Michael Bolton, Cliff Richard, Amy Grant, and Vince Gill, and his work has resulted in number-one records in three consecutive decades. He has also continued to be active as a television and film music producer, with credits including "Theme from S.W.A.T.," "Baretta," "Theme from Rocky (Gonna Fly Now)," "Arthur's Theme (Best That You Can Do)," "Theme from Starsky & Hutch," and the original soundtrack for the Mel Brooks film *Young Frankenstein*.

David Paich

The son of jazz composer and arranger Marty Paich, David Paich is best known for being a member of the group Toto along with Jeff Porcaro, a frequent collaborator with the Dan. As a songwriter, he has co-written the hits "Hold the Line," "99," and "Rosanna" for Toto; "Lowdown" and "Lido Shuffle" for Boz Scaggs; and countless others. As a session musician, songwriter, and arranger he worked with Chicago, the Doobie Brothers, Aretha Franklin, Diana Ross, Rod Stewart, Cher, and too many to count. He was also part of the session band that recorded Michael Jackson's multi-platinum album *Thriller*.

In 1974, drummer Jeff Porcaro brought Paich to his first session for Steely Dan, the recording of the track "Night by Night." He laid down the Stevie Wonderesque clavinet part for the tune and played keys alongside Michael Omartian on *Pretzel Logic* and the next album, *Katy Lied*. His dueling electric piano part with Omartian on "Black Friday," the opening track of *Katy Lied*, is worth a detailed listening.

Paul Griffin

After *Katy Lied*, Becker and Fagen decided that they needed some new blood in the keyboard department. They found the perfect player for their funkiest record to date, *The Royal Scam*, a musician who had played with everybody from the Shirelles to Bob Dylan, Paul Griffin. Griffin was born in Harlem, New York, and began his career as King Curtis's pianist.

He worked extensively on *The Royal Scam* and *Aja* playing Fender Rhodes electric piano on "Kid Charlemagne" and "Peg," clavinet on "Green Earrings," piano on "Sign In Stranger," and various keyboards on countless others. He returned in the '90s to contribute Hammond B3 organ to the *Kamakiriad* LP. He even added background vocals, along with Michael McDonald, on "Peg" after Becker, Fagen, and producer Gary Katz heard him singing along while laying down his electric piano part and thought that his vocals blended well with McDonald's. He is also the only person—other than Keith Jarrett, who won a plagiarism suit against the duo for "Gaucho"—who would receive a co-writing credit on a Steely Dan album. There have been many stories about how "The Fez" came to be, with Becker and Fagen claiming that Griffin came up with the keyboard melody for the song during the session. But Griffin has stated that they already had the melody in place, but it was so similar to a classical composition that he changed it to avoid a plagiarism suit.

Paul Griffin laid down funky keyboards for *The Royal Scam*, *Aja*, and Fagen's *Kamakiriad*. He released a number of albums for Audio Spectrum Records including *Paul Griffin Swings with 101 Strings, Paul Griffin Salutes the Swingin' Bands, Paul Griffin Swings in Nashville,* and *Paul Griffin the Swingin' Sound of Soul.*

Griffin served as musical director, arranger, and keyboard player for Fagen's first "New York Soul" show in 1989 and performed in the reunion of some of the session players from *Aja*, including drummer Bernard Purdie and bassist Chuck Rainey, for the *Classic Albums: Steely Dan Aja* DVD. His playing can be heard on records by Van Morrison, Aretha Franklin, Herbie Hancock, Dizzy Gillespie, Al Kooper, Quincy Jones, Don McLean, Carly Simon, Roberta Flack, Donny Hathaway, Yoko Ono, Michael Franks, Wilson Pickett, Nina Simone, Harry Belafonte, Grover Washington Jr., George Benson, the Manhattan Transfer, Neil Diamond, John Denver, Bonnie Raitt, Lena Horne, David Ruffin, Blues Traveler, and dozens of others. Griffin died of a heart attack in 2002 at the age of sixty-two.

Don Grolnick

New Yorker Don Grolnick began his musical tuition as an accordionist, but later switched to piano. He worked with jazz, rock, and pop artists including Linda Ronstadt, James Taylor, Roberta Flack, Carly Simon, Ringo Starr, George Benson, Bette Midler, Bonnie Raitt, David Sanborn, Michael Franks, the Manhattan Transfer, Billy Cobham, JD Souther, Marcus Miller, the Brecker Brothers, Bob Mintzer, Dave Holland, and was also member of the groups Steps Ahead and Dreams, both with Michael Brecker. Grolnick was also a producer, sitting on the other side of the glass for albums by James Taylor, Michael Brecker, John Scofield, Bob Berg, and Peter Erskine.

When Becker and Fagen were looking for some new players for *The Royal Scam*, they hired Grolnick, who shared the keyboard responsibilities with Paul Griffin, Victor Feldman, and Fagen himself. He not only played the memorable clavinet part on "Kid Charlemagne," Fender Rhodes electric piano on "Green Earrings," and others from *The Royal Scam*, but also worked on Steely Dan's next two albums, laying down clavinet on "Peg" and Fender Rhodes electric piano and clavinet on "Babylon Sisters." He returned to work with Fagen one more time in an uncredited Fender Rhodes electric piano role on 1981's "True Companion" from the *Heavy Metal* movie and soundtrack. Grolnick died in 1996 from non-Hodgkin's lymphoma at the age of forty-eight.

Joe Sample

Although keyboard player Joe Sample wouldn't record with Steely Dan until 1978's *Aja* LP, his bandmates from the Jazz Crusaders, Wilton Felder and Larry Carlton, had worked with the Dan on numerous occasions starting with *Pretzel Logic* (Felder) and *Katy Lied* (Carlton). Sample doubled Chuck Rainey's funk bass line on clavinet for "Black Cow," played the sparkling Fender Rhodes electric piano part on "Aja," and the subdued Fender Rhodes electric piano on the closing track from *Gaucho*, "Third World Man."

Sample was one of the founding members of the Crusaders along with Felder and drummer Nesbert "Stix" Hooper. They started the band in high school, and while studying piano at Texas Southern University, Sample met trombonist Wayne Henderson, who was added to the fold. Once they moved to Los Angeles, the Jazz Crusaders released as many as four albums a year in the '60s before changing their name to the Crusaders and adopting more of a funk-jazz groove for their records.

Sample also became a first-call session musician on the pop, rock, soul, and jazz scenes, recording with artists such as Joni Mitchell, Marvin Gaye, Ella Fitzgerald, Eric Clapton, Miles Davis, Al Jarreau, Tina Turner, B. B. King, Boz Scaggs, Michael Franks, Joe Cocker, Minnie Ripperton, George Benson, Gladys Knight, the Mamas and the Papas, Cher, Lou Rawls, Joan Baez, Seals and Crofts, Anita Baker, and numerous others. He has also released nearly two dozen albums as a leader or co-leader during his career. Sample died of mesothelioma in 2014 at age seventy-five.

Rob Mounsey

Berklee College of Music graduate Rob Mounsey was one of only four new rhythm section members to perform on *Gaucho*; the others being bassist Anthony Jackson, guitarist Hiram Bullock, and keyboard player Patrick Rebillot. Not only did he play piano on "Glamour Profession" and "Gaucho"; synthesizer on "Third World Man" and piano, Fender Rhodes electric piano, and synthesizer on the solo section of "Time Out of Mind," he also arranged the horns, along with an uncredited Fagen, for "Babylon Sisters" and "Time Out of Mind."

After Steely Dan, Mounsey continued to work with Fagen on *The Nightfly*. He played synthesizer on "I.G.Y. (What a Beautiful World)," "Green Flower Street," and the title track. He also arranged the horns with Fagen for "Century's End," co-wrote the score with him for the film *Bright Lights, Big City*, and played keyboards on the song of the same name heard briefly in the film.

His work as a studio musician, arranger, and producer has touched a variety of genres including work with artists such as Paul Simon, James Taylor, Phil Collins, Chaka Khan, Eric Clapton, Billy Joel, Aretha Franklin, Madonna, Diana Ross, Aaron Neville, Michael Franks, Carly Simon, Natalie Cole, Diana Krall, George Benson, Brian Wilson, Aztec Camera, Karen Carpenter, Usher, Mary J. Blige, Rihanna, and countless others.

Patrick Rebillot

Keyboard player Patrick Rebillot is a rarity as a session musician in Steely Dan's world: he only played on one song. He was an integral part of flutist Herbie Mann's various groups and played on eleven of his albums including 1973's *Turtle Bay*, which included Mann's version of "Do It Again." Six years later, he would work with Becker and Fagen for the first and last time, contributing Fender Rhodes electric piano to the slinky groove of "My Rival" from *Gaucho*.

Over his fifty-year career, he has worked with James Brown, Aretha Franklin, Hall and Oates, Barbra Streisand, Patti Austin, Jimmy McGriff, the Average White Band, Bette Midler, Michael Franks, Chico O'Farrill, Gladys Knight and the Pips, Doc Severinsen, Frank Foster, Eddie Kendricks, Diana Ross, the Spinners, Gloria Gaynor, Sister Sledge, Judy Collins, and a varied number of other artists.

Greg Phillinganes

Although Greg Phillinganes was a first-call session musician in the '70s, playing on records by Stevie Wonder, Michael Jackson, George Benson, the Pointer Sisters, Eddie Money, Lionel Richie, Leo Sayer, Donna Summer, Michael McDonald, and countless others, he never played on a Steely Dan record. He wouldn't work on a Dan-related project until Fagen's album *The Nightfly* in 1982 playing Fender Rhodes electric piano on "I.G.Y. (What a Beautiful World)," Fender Rhodes electric piano and clavinet on "Green Flower Street," the piano solo on "Ruby Baby," piano on "Maxine," and synth bass on "Walk Between the Raindrops."

Phillinganes's résumé would continue to grow as he played countless sessions with Paul Simon, Joe Cocker, Rickie Lee Jones, Eric Clapton, Diana Ross, Stevie Nicks, Whitney Houston, Kenny Loggins, Neil Diamond, Patti LaBelle, Mick Jagger, the Bee Gees, Roberta Flack, Quincy Jones, the Manhattan Transfer, George Harrison, Elton John, Richard Marx, Barbra Streisand, Anita Baker, Babyface, Boyz II Men, Elvis Costello, Burt Bacharach, Phil Collins, Mariah Carey, Randy Newman, Luther Vandross, James Taylor, Christina Aguilera, Willie Nelson, Steve Vai, Aretha Franklin, Boz Scaggs, Herbie Hancock, Michael Bublé, Toto, Kanye West, Adele, and many others until the present day.

John Beasley

Pianist John Beasley came from an extremely musical background. His mother, Linda Beasley, is a brass instrumentalist and taught music at various public schools and colleges, leading to him mastering trumpet, oboe, drums, saxophone, and flute as a child. After high school, he declined an oboe scholarship to the Juilliard School of Music and opted to begin his professional music career. Within a few years, he was touring with bandleader Sérgio Mendes and trumpet player Freddie Hubbard. He's worked with a variety of artists including Miles Davis, Carly Simon, Barbra Streisand, Queen Latifah, Chaka Khan, James Brown, and John Patitucci, to name but a few.

Beasley first met Walter Becker when he was hired to play on the three Becker-produced tracks from Michael Franks's 1990 LP *Blue Pacific*. The next year, Becker produced future Steely Dan saxophonist Bob Sheppard's debut album for Windham Hill Jazz entitled *Tell Tale Sings*. The pianist: John Beasley. In 1992, Becker would become more familiar with Beasley's style when he produced Beasley's debut album for a major label, *Cauldron*. In 1993, Becker and Beasley would record the music for a children's short film, *Mose the Fireman*, narrated by Michael Keaton and illustrated by Everett Peck; and Becker would return in the producer's chair for Beasley's *A Change of Heart* LP.

Becker would enlist Beasley's talents in 1994 for his debut solo album *11 Tracks of Whack*, where Beasley spilt keyboard duties with Donald Fagen. Two years later, he would tour with Steely Dan for his first and last time, on the *Art Crimes* tour of 1996. In addition to his session work, Beasley has from the age of twenty-four written music for television shows including *Cheers*, *Family Ties*, *Star Trek*, and *Fame*, and he wrote the Touchstone TV logo, which is still in use today. Besides projects as a leader, touring as a sideman, and television and film work, he's performed on numerous hit reality and game shows including *American Idol*, *Pussycat Dolls Present*, *America's Got Talent*, and *Singing Bee*. In 2013, he formed a seventeen-piece big band called MONK'estra to showcase the songwriting of piano genius Thelonious Monk with new arrangements of his classic compositions.

Ted Baker

When Ted Baker first moved to New York after graduating from Oberlin College, he spent quite a bit of time working as a keyboard player for various theater and musical productions such as the Who's *Tommy*, Randy Newman's *Faust*, Pete Townshend's *The Boy Who Heard* and *Music Psychoderelict*, Disney's *The Lion King*, and *Smokey Joe's Café*. He first worked with Steely Dan during the sessions for *Two Against Nature* when bassist Tom Barney recommended him. He played Fender Rhodes electric piano on "Janie Runaway," "Almost Gothic," "Cousin Dupree," "Negative Girl," and "West of Hollywood," toured to support the album, and took part in two television shows, VH-1's *Storytellers* and PBS's *In the Spotlight*, which would eventually become the DVD release *Plush TV Jazz-Rock Party*.

In 2003, Baker returned to the studio with Becker and Fagen for the album *Everything Must Go*. The rhythm section recorded the majority of the material in the studio live, and Baker contributed piano to "The Last Mall," "Things I Miss the Most," "Blues Beach," "Green Book," and the title track; played Wurlitzer electric piano on "Slang of Ages"; and played Fender Rhodes electric piano on "Lunch with Gina." He would tour to support this album as well, but it would be his last.

He continued to work with both Fagen and Becker, playing major roles on Fagen's 2006 release *Morph the Cat* and Becker's *Circus Money* in 2008. For Fagen's album he played piano on "H Gang," "Brite Nightgown," and "The Great Pagoda of Funn" Wurlitzer electric piano on "What I Do" and "Security Jones"; and Fender Rhodes electric piano on "The Night Belongs to Mona" and "Mary Shuts the Garden Door." On Becker's album he played keyboards, electric piano, or piano on ten out of eleven tracks alongside keyboard player Jim Beard, who replaced Baker on tour and has continued to tour with Steely Dan to this day.

Bill Charlap

New Yorker jazz pianist Bill Charlap comes from a musical background on both sides. His mother, Sandy Stewart, is a singer who had a top-twenty hit in 1963 with "My Coloring Book," and his father was Broadway composer Moose Charlap, best known for the *Peter Pan* musical. He's recorded nearly twenty albums as a leader or co-leader, including one with his mother and one with singer Tony Bennett released in 2015 entitled *The Silver Lining: The Songs of Jerome Kern*. He has also worked with jazz masters Gerry Mulligan, Phil Woods, Benny Carter, and others. Although Fagen played most of the electric piano parts and Ted Baker played the majority of the piano parts on 2003's *Everything Must Go*, Charlap was enlisted to play Fender Rhodes electric piano on "Godwhacker" and piano on "Pixeleen."

Jim Beard

Jazz pianist Jim Beard established himself in the contemporary jazz community in New York City in the mid-1980s. Within a year of moving to Manhattan from Philadelphia, he became a touring member of John McLaughlin's Mahavishnu Orchestra. Soon after, he began working with Wayne Shorter, Dizzy Gillespie, Pat Metheny, John Scofield, Dennis Chambers, Dave Liebman, and countless other jazz musicians. He also began a successful career as a producer, working on projects for artists such as guitarist Mike Stern, saxophonist Bob Berg, and saxophonist Bill Evans.

In 2008, Beard played on eight of eleven tracks on Becker's second solo album *Circus Money*; seven of them alongside former Steely Dan keyboard player Ted Baker. In November of the same year, Steely Dan added four dates to their *Think Fast* tour and their keyboard player Jeff Young, who had worked on and off with Fagen and Steely Dan since 1990, had left. Becker was so impressed with Beard's performance on his album that he suggested that he play on those dates. He returned for the entire 2009 tour season and would play on every subsequent Steely Dan tour, as well as both *Dukes of September Rhythm Revue* tours.

Henry Hey

Henry Hey had played with artists as disparate as Rod Stewart, Taylor Dane, Bill Bruford, Bill Evans, and Roger Waters before contributing to Becker's 2008 release *Circus Money*. He played keyboards on "Upside Looking Down" along with Ted Baker (piano) and keyboards along with Jim Beard on "Do You Remember the Name." Hey has continued to work with popular artists including David Bowie, Dionne Warwick, George Michael, Wayne Krantz, and the Tedeschi Trucks Band.

Larry Goldings

Steely Dan always knew which jazz musicians they wanted to call for specific parts, so it's no surprise that when Walter Becker wanted a phenomenal Hammond B3 organist for two songs on his second album, *Circus Money*, he would call one of the hottest young jazz organists, Larry Goldings. Goldings was originally a pianist attending the New School for its new jazz studies program, but while playing a steady gig at a pianoless bar in New York City called Augie's Jazz Bar, he began to develop an organ trio and play with various musicians at the venue. He developed such an original style that artists from every genre sought out his talents, including James Taylor, John Mayer, Rickie Lee Jones, Tracy Chapman, De La Soul, India. Arie, Madeleine Peyroux, Robben Ford, Steve Gadd, Leon Russell, and Norah Jones. He has also collaborated with jazz musicians such as John Scofield, Carla Bley, Michael Brecker, Pat Metheny, John Pizzarelli, Jack DeJohnette, Maceo Parker, and countless others. In 2003 Goldings formed the Trio Beyond with drummer Jack DeJohnette and guitarist John Scofield. In 2007 they received a Grammy nomination in the category of Best Jazz Instrumental Album, Individual or Group for their live album, *Saudades*. Becker had him lay down his incomparable Hammond B3 organ on the reggae-flavored tunes "Downtown Canon" and "Darkling Down." It's a shame that he didn't get any solo time.

Michael Leonhart

Michael Leonhart has the distinction of being the only musician to play three completely different instruments, as well as contribute background vocals, on Steely Dan-related material. He is known primarily as a trumpet/brass player touring with the band since 1996's *Art Crimes* tour and performing on *Two Against Nature* and *Everything Must Go*, but he also made his keyboard debut on a Dan album playing Wurlitzer electric piano on the title track of *Two Against Nature*. In 2012, he co-produced Fagen's *Sunken Condos* album and not only played trumpet, flügelhorn, mellophone, mellophonium, trombonium, drums, percussion, vibraphone, glockenspiel, and added background vocals, he also played a variety of keyboards including the Fender Rhodes electric piano, Wurlitzer electric piano, Mellotron, Minimoog synthesizer, Prophet 5 synthesizer, Juno 6 synthesizer, Hammond B3 organ, L100 organ, M100 organ, and accordion.

15

They Got the Steely Dan T-Shirt

Steely Dan's Masterpiece: *Aja*

W hile *The Royal Scam* garnered rave reviews from myriad journalists and was their highest-charting album to date, it was their sixth album, *Aja*, that catapulted them to the upper echelons of rock royalty. Unlike *The Royal Scam*, the basic tracks for *Aja* were cut in Los Angeles except for "Peg," the last tune tracked for the album. They cut it in New York with Elliot Scheiner, who was back from exile after *The Royal Scam* recording debacle, while the rest of the album was being mixed.

Aja expanded on the foundation that was laid during the recording of *The Royal Scam*, melding funk and R&B grooves with intricate chord changes and melodies atop. The songs were longer and more complicated, the arrangements more elaborate, and the musician count had once again grown. For seven songs they used six drummers, one bass player, five keyboard players, seven guitarists, three percussionists (two of whom doubled on other instruments), ten horn players, and seven background vocalists in addition to Becker and Fagen. Fagen spoke of their use of session musicians in a 2011 interview with Marc Myers for *JazzWax*. "In the mid '70s there was a style change, a paradigm shift, in the way session musicians were playing. Younger players had started to add more jazz flavored stuff in their playing. In the early days, it was hard to find a player who was familiar with R&B's backbeat and could negotiate jazz harmony with ease. And a jazz player tended to play much looser than we required. But by the mid '70s, there were players like Steve Gadd and Larry Carlton who could do both. They had no trouble playing jazz chords and also had a very rhythmic sense."

Becker and Fagen were, however, somewhat frustrated during the sessions, and Fagen, who rarely complained about the musicians they used for their albums, vented when he and Becker were guests on radio station KPFK in Los Angeles. "I can't mention any names, but we've been greatly disappointed by a lot of people who we thought were more versatile. They're all good musicians, but we have them in mind for ten tracks and it'll turn out they were only good for two." This wasn't the case regarding Victor Feldman, who had contributed to every Steely Dan album thus far. He added his most significant contributions to *Aja*, playing on every track; keyboards on five songs, percussion on three, and vibraphone on two.

Aja marked a new direction for Steely Dan in the use of horns. Five of the seven songs employed a horn section, two had saxophone solos, and one featured the Lyricon, an electronic wind instrument. Becker and Fagen were always fond of horns, but they were never used to this extent before. The arrangements by Tom Scott were dense yet memorable, Becker and Fagen giving him more latitude than they had ever given an arranger before. Horns would play an ever-growing role on all of Steely Dan's subsequent albums and on their tours once they re-formed in the mid-'90s, adding horns to numerous songs that didn't originally have them.

The Songs

Many consider *Aja* to be Steely Dan's high-water mark; a piece of work that could not be matched. Overall the songs were longer and more challenging (the title track was the longest to date) and were fueled by Becker and Fagen's love of R&B and jazz. They also used more studio musicians than ever before (thirty-seven in all) and often tried the songs with numerous different configurations of players. The hard work paid off, and to this day it is Steely Dan's best-selling album.

"Black Cow"

The opening song sets the mood for the entire album within seconds. The electrifying funk of "Black Cow" takes the listener on a journey from the first bar, with Joe Sample's clavinet doubling Chuck Rainey's bass line and Paul Humphrey's drum groove underpinning this R&B song that name checks Rudy's Bar and Grill in Manhattan. The song contains not one, but two fantastic solos. The first, played by longtime Steely Dan cohort Victor Feldman on Fender Rhodes electric piano, was actually recorded along with the basic tracks. The second, played by tenor saxophonist Tom Scott, plays over the outro and is his first appearance on a Steely Dan album. He would also write the horn arrangements for the album with some guidance from Becker and Fagen.

While one might think Black Cow is some sort of alcoholic concoction, it is actually a type of ice cream float. An alcoholic drink, sometimes referred to as a Black Cow #2, does exist and is made with Kahlúa, half-and-half, and Coca-Cola, but the composers have stated that they were thinking of the non-alcoholic drink when writing the song. Fagen elaborated on the song's origins in a 1989 article for the fanzine *Metal Leg*. "A lot of time when a relationship ends or there's some sort of a crisis in a relationship one particular incident will stand out in your mind as you remember it; in this case, we thought that particular scene of this woman downing a black cow in a small luncheonette—the place where the shit hit the fan, so to speak—is what stood out in the narrator's mind. It was probably in Brooklyn, I would imagine."

"Aja"

It took quite a while to get Wayne Shorter to perform on a Steely Dan album, most probably because he doubted whether it would be musically challenging. They initially had producer Gary Katz reach out to see if he was interested in playing on the title track. His initial response: a resounding "no." They then approached the manager of the studio that they had worked in from their debut album, Dick LaPalm, who knew Shorter personally. He vouched for them, telling Shorter, "These are nice guys, they record here a lot, they seem to like a lot of old jazz records, they talk about Jackie McLean!" Shorter decided to do the date.

He approached the session like a pro, and after a few takes, he spent half an hour at the piano with the chart in order to write out the scales over the chords because he didn't want to play a typical bebop solo. He preferred to handle it in an innovative way and create something different. He realized immediately that this piece of music was something original and imaginative and played an outstanding solo behind a fierce drum track by Steve Gadd.

An advertisement for Steely Dan's sixth album, *Aja*.

Gadd was a new face in the revolving characters that were assembled to create a Steely Dan album, and his presence was felt after the first take of "Aja." They expected to rehearse it for a day because it was the most complicated composition they had recorded to date, with a seven-page chart, multiple sections, changes in feel, and numerous solos. When they arrived at the studio, they decided to play through the song as a rehearsal. They were aware of the fact that Gadd was a phenomenal drummer, but they had never worked with him in the studio, so they had no idea that he was as adept at sight-reading as he was at playing. They had marked a spot in the chart where they wanted Gadd to ad-lib and assumed that they would have to talk through it before the take, but the band nailed it on the first take, leaving those in the control room flabbergasted. Over their five-year career in the studio, nobody had ever done that before. As Gary Katz succinctly put it, "it freaked us out." Some of the other musicians on the date were so taken with his playing, especially during the solo, that they lost track of their own parts and had to fix them after the fact. Although they originally had jazz drummer

Tony Williams in mind for the song, Gadd made it apparent that he was the man for the job.

The song was more of a suite and was composed of a number of different sections strung together to create Steely Dan's longest song to date, clocking in at eight minutes. One part of the song came from an unfinished instrumental entitled "Stand by the Seawall" that utilized the same rhythm section as *Aja*. Wayne Shorter and Steve Gadd were not the only musicians to contribute astounding solos. Becker and Denny Dias both take solos, with Becker playing over the section when the band plays a full groove and Dias taking over whenever the band breaks down for a softer section. Dias's solo is arguably his finest moment on a Steely Dan record. His opinions of the song make clear how difficult he thought it was. He recalled recording the song in the *Classic Albums: Steely Dan Aja* DVD. "Its very existence is a contradiction . . . When have you ever heard a song on a rock and roll record that absolutely cannot be played on a guitar? There's clusters where the notes are so close together that you can't stretch your fingers far enough to get all the notes out at the same time."

"Deacon Blues"

Becker and Fagen always wrote about outsiders, characters at the end of their rope that can't seem to get a break. "Deacon Blues" encapsulates that sentiment perfectly. The fact that the narrator would rather be a part of a culture of losers than follow the typical American mores mirrors their own choices to a tee. The character believes that since society has bestowed names upon the winners in the world, they should also follow suit for the losers as well.

The song is one of the relatively rare occasions where the music and lyrics fit together like hand in glove. The despondent subject matter is reflected in the laid-back, melancholy groove provided by Bernard Purdie and Walter Becker, his only appearance as bassist on the album. The sparkling Fender Rhodes electric piano, constant movement of the rhythm guitar, lead guitar licks sprinkled throughout, and dense horn chart prepared by Tom Scott do, however, give the song a sense of hopefulness.

The picture sleeve for the "Deacon Blues" single.

One of the highlights of the song is the tenor saxophone solo played by *Tonight Show* band member Pete Christlieb. After hearing his playing before the commercial breaks for Johnny Carson's show, they brought in one saxophone player after another who was part of the band until they found the man they were looking for. He takes two solos on the track, one during the instrumental break and another during the fade-out. He took two passes, and they chose the second one. As Christlieb recalls, "I was gone in a half hour."

The seven-and-a-half-minute track was edited to six and a half minutes by cutting out the first ten measures of Christlieb's solo and shortening the outro. This edited version was released as the second single from the album with "Home at Last" as the B-side. It was their fifth top twenty hit, peaking at number nineteen.

"Peg"

"Peg," the last song recorded for *Aja*, was an obvious choice for the first single. The groove that drummer Rick Marotta and Chucky Rainey laid down is perfect for the song and its execution flawless. Drummer Jim Keltner had attempted the song before Marotta, but the part wasn't exactly what they had in mind. Becker had written the bass part for the verse, and the duo were rather explicit when they told Rainey that they didn't want any slap bass on the song due to the fact that it was extremely popular at the time. Rainey felt that he knew what the song needed, and when tracking, he moved into position so that they couldn't see what he was doing and slapped on the chorus. He believed he pulled a fast one on the composers, but they apparently were aware of the change and agreed that it was right for the song, although it was never discussed. Keyboard players Paul Griffin and Don Grolnick, who had played such significant roles on *The Royal Scam*, return for their only appearance on *Aja*, playing Fender Rhodes electric piano and clavinet respectively to great effect. Guitarist Steve Khan rounds out the rhythm section, making his debut on a Steely Dan record with a single-note line that bounces around the rhythm section with jubilance.

Like so many other Steely Dan songs, "Peg" is an altered blues that doesn't sound like a blues. The juxtaposition of a major seventh chord with added nine and a minor seventh chord with a sharp five creates a joyous, yet ambiguous, sound. The extensive use of the second chord led numerous musicians to dub it the "Steely Dan chord" rather than refer to it with its proper terminology. Tom Scott's Lyricon also plays a significant role, adding the perfect punch to the liquid groove beneath it. The Lyricon was the first electronic wind instrument and gave wind players the opportunity to control a synthesizer from a soprano sax-like controller.

The idea behind the background vocals was to create the feeling of a big band horn section with voices. They initially tried to track it with a particular session singer, who the duo refused to name, but weren't happy with the results. So they called Michael McDonald, who took to the challenge of singing such close harmonies. While tracking the song, keyboard player Paul Griffin was singing along, and Katz, Becker, and Fagen liked the sound of his voice, so they decided to keep his vocals on the final track as well. They can be heard most prominently improvising on the last chorus and outro along with McDonald's memorable background vocal part for this ode to a pornographic actress.

The largest obstacle they faced when recording "Peg" was when it came time to record the guitar solo. Becker attempted the solo several times, as did Larry Carlton, Elliott Randall, Rick Derringer, Robben Ford, a friend of Victor Feldman's, and three or four others before they found what they were looking for when Jay Graydon laid down his Hawaiian-influenced solo with a slide at the top. He allegedly worked on the solo for six hours before they were satisfied. The single, backed with "I Got the News," peaked at number eleven on the *Billboard* Hot 100 and number eight on the *Cashbox* Top 100. Clocking in at four minutes, it's the shortest song on the album.

"Home at Last"

"Home at Last" is notable for the presence of the "Purdie Shuffle." Although Steely Dan had recorded a number of shuffles in the past including "Pretzel Logic," "Black Friday," and "Chain Lightning," they were looking for a new approach for "Home at Last" and depended on Bernard Purdie, the only drummer to play two songs on *Aja*. His approach to playing a shuffle was completely different than that of Jim Gordon and Jeff Porcaro. They expressed the fact they didn't want a typical Motown or Chicago type of shuffle, so the drummer suggested the "Purdie Shuffle." The drummer explained that it would achieve their goals: a half-time feel that was funky and laid back, but not an ordinary shuffle. It would reappear on "Babylon Sisters" from their next album, *Gaucho*.

Victor Feldman played not only the highly infectious piano part, but the vibraphone as well, and Larry Carlton's Chicago blues licks add grittiness to the song and transform it into a harder-hitting track. Another stellar horn arrangement graces the song and provides the hook of the intro. Both Becker and Fagen contribute solos. Fagen's, on synthesizer using the pseudo-harmonica patch that he would become famous for, occurs during the instrumental break. Becker's solo that follows is extremely melodic and shows his penchant for jazz phrasing that would become a trademark of their albums as a group and as solo artists in years to come. He returns on the outro, adding another equally deft solo for the fadeout.

"I Got the News"

"I Got the News" was originally written during the sessions for *The Royal Scam*, but was completely rewritten for *Aja*, retaining only the title and some of the lyrics. The song's drummer, Ed Greene, on his only Steely Dan date, lays down a pocket with Rainey that is hard to beat. Victor Feldman provides the piano and vibraphone, punctuating the disco-infused groove with Thelonious Monk-like dissonant accents and a memorable solo during the intro. The subtlety of Fagen's synthesizer along with the close horn chart add a sonic depth to the song that grows as it progresses. It's also notable that such a funk-inspired song doesn't have much rhythm guitar; it does, however, contain an uncredited clavinet part on the middle section.

A Japanese advertisement for *Aja* using an alternate photo of model Sayoko Yamaguchi.

The background vocals during the bridge feature Michael McDonald in more of a lead vocal role, the prominent voice in the five-part vocal harmony. He would play the role of the background vocalist who steals the show on numerous hits in the '70s and '80s by artists such as Kenny Loggins, Christopher Cross, Robbie Dupree, and countless others. Walter Becker turns in another splendid solo, his second of three for the album. Besides the main solo, he returns for a second short jaunt before the last chorus. Larry Carlton solos over the outro, but this is more of a rhythmic, bubbling single-note line rather than a full-blown solo.

"Josie"

The story of the album's closing track, "Josie," had been told before in an early Becker and Fagen composition, "Ida Lee." They even used the line "The hooters and the hats" rearranged for "Josie," but the sentiment is the same: a celebration of a hard woman returning to her old neighborhood with a number of nefarious characters on hand.

Session drummer extraordinaire Jim Keltner played on the track, surprisingly the only time he would perform on a Steely Dan song. Besides his magnificent drum groove, he also played a garbage can lid on the middle section, another unusual sound on a Dan record that would elevate the funk. The odd drum break in the 7/8 time signature that occurs before the outro was a specific part written by Becker and Fagen. Chuck Rainey laid down the bass part, which was primarily written by Becker. While his interpretation included many of his own devices, the majority of the part was conceived before the tracking date.

The rhythm guitars played by Larry Carlton and Dean Parks give the song its signature sound from the first note, played in harmony with a sinister edge. As the verse begins, they split duties, with one part covering the rhythm along with Victor Feldman's luminous Fender Rhodes electric piano part and the other doubling the bass line in true Henry Mancini "detective style." Tom Scott prepared another radiant horn arrangement that melds with the electric piano and Fagen's synthesizer to create a sparkle on top of the foundation. The harmonized slide guitar line before the solo is arresting and played over a section that only occurs once, giving it that much more weight.

Becker once again provides the guitar solo, his third on the album. His bluesy approach to soloing is extremely unique, and as one of the songwriters, his style was often exactly what the song needed. He was, however, notorious for spending "an hour per bar" when tracking a solo. Chosen as the third single, with "Black Cow" on the B-side, it reached number twenty-six on the charts nearly a year after the album's release.

"FM (No Static at All)"

In 1978, Becker and Fagen were asked by their manager, Irving Azoff, to write the title song for a film entitled *FM*. They accepted, and looking to produce a song that would sound grandiose in a movie theater, they hired arranger Johnny Mandel to score the song for strings. They had used strings once before, on "Through with Buzz," but it was a small section, not the lush arrangement that Mandel devised.

Drummer Jeff Porcaro, who was missing from both *The Royal Scam* and *Aja* albums, laid down the rock-solid groove, with Becker and Fagen taking a more active role in the tracking of the song. Fagen played piano and sang lead vocals and Becker played bass, rhythm guitar, and provided the brilliant guitar solos. Pete Christlieb, who had contributed the hard-bop solo to "Deacon Blues," returned to add an equally fiery solo that appeared in various forms.

The full-length version, which appeared on the soundtrack for the film, had Becker's guitar solo on the outro, but the song was shortened for the single release. The flip side was "FM (reprise)" and featured an extended saxophone solo by Christlieb. The fourth version was created by removing the guitar solo from the end of the original track and using the "FM (reprise)" saxophone solo for a new ending, yielding a running time of 5:06. This hybrid version appears on the 1991 compilation *Gold (Expanded Edition)* as well as the *Citizen Steely Dan* box set. AM radio refused to play a song entitled "FM," so they used the "A" syllable from "Aja," which happened to be the correct note, and edited it in place of the "F" of the title, creating a fifth version of the song. Timothy B. Schmit, Don Henley, and Glenn Frey of the Eagles sang background vocals on the tune, which reached number twenty-two on the *Billboard* Hot 100 chart.

"FM (No Static at All)" won a Grammy for Best Engineered Recording, Non Classical, in 1979, an award that they had won for *Aja* the year before, the only occasion on which this particular Grammy has been awarded for a single song. Becker and Fagen both thought that the song would have been more successful had the movie been better, but regardless of the film's popularity, "FM (No Static at All)" has become one of Steely Dan's most revered songs, one that didn't appear on any album.

On October 29, 2015, thirty-eight years after its release, the song was used for a synchronized light show at the Empire State Building to celebrate the fiftieth anniversary of the installation of its master FM antenna. It was a first for the Empire State Building and another example of Steely Dan finding themselves at the forefront of technology.

Conclusion

Aja was the most successful Steely Dan record, selling over five million copies with more than $1 million in advance orders. It peaked at number three on the U.S. chart and number five in the U.K., where no singles were issued from the album. In 1978, it was nominated for three Grammy Awards: Album of the Year, Best Pop Vocal Group, and Best Engineered Recording, Non Classical. While the Album of the Year award went to Fleetwood Mac for *Rumours* and the Best Pop Vocal Group award went to the Bee Gees for "How Deep Is Your Love," they won the Grammy for Best Engineered Recording, Non Classical, thanks to engineers Roger Nichols, Elliot Scheiner, Bill Schnee, and Al Schmitt. In 1979, Roger Nichols and Al Schmitt won the award for a second time for "FM (No Static at All)," although Steely Dan lost the Best Pop Vocal Group award to the Bee Gees' *Saturday Night Fever* soundtrack album.

The album received rave reviews across the board and was popular with critics and fans alike. Even Michael Duffy's review for *Rolling Stone*, which accuses them of possibly being too slick and isolating themselves from their audience with oblique lyrics and indecipherable jazz harmonies, ends on a high note. "What underlies Steely Dan's music . . . is its extreme intellectual self-consciousness, both in music and lyrics. Given the nature of these times, this may be precisely the quality that makes Walter Becker and Donald Fagen the perfect musical antiheroes for the Seventies."

Although the album was doing infinitely better than any other Dan album, Becker didn't believe that they purposely set out to make a hit record and stated his feelings in a 1977 interview with *Rolling Stone*. "I certainly don't think it's any more commercial than any of our other albums. I haven't heard it on the radio yet . . . but I read how well we're doing. I guess we're achieving the success we so richly deserve. On the whole, I think this is a very rewarding thing."

16

We'll Move Up to Manhattan and Fill the Place with Friends

Becker and Fagen Return to New York City and Record Their Swan Song: *Gaucho*

After the huge success of *Aja*, Becker and Fagen decided to take a year off from Steely Dan and work on some pet projects. They produced their first jazz album for tenor saxophonists Pete Christlieb, who played the solos on "Deacon Blues" and "FM (No Static at All)," and Warne Marsh, entitled *Apogee*. The same year, 1978, also saw the release of *Chick, Donald, Walter and Woodrow*, an album by jazz woodwind player Woody Herman's big band that consisted of a suite by jazz pianist Chick Corea on side one, and big band arrangements of five Steely Dan songs on side two. Becker and Fagen attended the sessions, which Becker described as the happiest two days of his life. The only Steely Dan-related work they embarked on that year was choosing the songs for the double album *Greatest Hits*, which included one unreleased track, "Here at the Western World."

The biggest change that occurred after *Aja* was location. After over six years of living on the West Coast, Becker and Fagen had had enough of the California lifestyle and decided to move back to New York. Fagen originally lived at the Stanhope Hotel on Fifth Avenue and East 81st St., but soon after, he and Becker were living in the same luxury building on Central Park West.

In 1979, they began recording their next album, which proved to be the most difficult of their career. They used four different studios in Manhattan: Soundworks, A&R Studios, Sigma Sound, and Automated Sound, and occasionally worked in Los Angeles at their regular spots the Village Recorder and Producer's Workshop. Sessions were arduous, with different sets of musicians working for a few days at a time before Becker and Fagen decided they had recorded nothing of use. It took nearly two years to complete the album, which would be the most expensive non-soundtrack album recorded to date.

While the duo blamed the failed sessions on new musicians, a lack of material, legal problems with their record company, and technical difficulties including the erasure of one of the best tracks on the album, personal problems were actually causing much of the stress felt during the recording. Becker had a serious narcotics problem and had disappeared for weeks during the *Aja* sessions. Fagen didn't blame his partner for the issues they were having in the studio but was aware of the problem. He elaborated in a 1991 interview with Richard Cromelin of the *Los Angeles Times*. (Although he had covered Steely Dan for years, the resulting article made him temporarily persona non grata in the Steely Dan camp.) "Music wasn't his first love at that point . . . He was kinda leaping towards destruction." The situation culminated in January 1980 when Becker's girlfriend, Karen Stanley, who he met in 1976 and left his first wife, Juanna Fatouros, for, died of an overdose that was believed to be a suicide in their Upper West Side apartment. Becker rarely spoke of this devastating event but opened up about it in a 1995 interview for *MOJO* magazine, "I could barely understand what was going with her. If you've never known anyone that's chronically depressed like that, it's hard to appreciate what's going on: you're looking straight at it and you still don't get it because you've never gone through that." In 1981, her mother, Lillian Wyshak, who was a lawyer from Beverly Hills, sued Becker for $17 million, claiming that he had introduced her to heroin and cocaine, but the case was settled out of court in Becker's favor.

Becker's misfortune continued, and in April 1980, he was hit by a speeding yellow taxi, fracturing his leg in several places, and was in a cast for seven months. Although the basic tracks were completed, they still had overdubs to complete as well as performing the final mixdown, two elements that always had Becker's indelible stamp. He attempted to attend a mixing session, but wheelchair-bound, he was in too much pain to contribute much.

Gaucho also had a different sound in comparison to *Aja*. Acoustic piano played a less significant role than it had on their past albums because allegedly Fagen was unhappy with the sound of the pianos in the studios they were working in. It does seem like an odd reason, considering that they had worked in a number of these studios before. Instead, the Fender Rhodes electric piano was the main keyboard used, along with more synthesizer than on any other album. Although the sessions were fraught with problems, both Becker and Fagen contributed more as musicians than they had in quite some time, with Fagen performing on five of the seven songs and Becker playing bass on three songs and guitar on three songs as well. Becker has claimed that he would have played more had he not been

An advertisement in the *New Musical Express* for the 1978 U.K. *Greatest Hits* LP on Anchor Records.

An interesting accolade for Steely Dan: 1979's *Playboy* Poll Winners best group.

laid up after his taxi accident. They used an astounding number of session musicians, thirty-nine in all, to create the album, more than they had ever used before or since. Keyboard players Rob Mounsey and Patrick Rebillot, bassist Anthony Jackson, and guitarist Hiram Bullock, however, were the only rhythm section newcomers.

They also had another new "member" of the band that contributed greatly to the *Gaucho* sessions thanks to Roger Nichols. Its name: Wendel. Nichols was working on Wendel, a drum machine that used digital samples, around the same time that Roger Linn was inventing the Linn LM-1 Drum Computer, the first commercially available drum machine to use digital samples at a cost of $4,995. Nichols created a machine that could mimic the feel of a real drummer, but in a steadier fashion, and used multiple samples of each instrument in order to create a more realistic, yet machine-like, drum track.

By the time Becker and Fagen were working on their swan song, Fagen expressed his longing for the perfect band for Steely Dan due to their issues working with session musicians during the recording of *Gaucho*, although they had worked with the majority of them before. He explained that when choosing musicians they would decide who would work best on each track stylistically, but problems could arise if said musician didn't interpret the material to their liking. Although Steely Dan was originally a real "band," they were assembled haphazardly to make a record of Becker and Fagen's compositions. They would never be like the Beatles or the Band because they didn't have the history, or in many ways, the chemistry. Steely Dan was always destined to be a studio band, and although Fagen might have liked the idea of a band, it was apparent that the only way Steely Dan could succeed was with Becker and Fagen at the helm.

The Songs

Gaucho was a trying album to make, but it does show Becker and Fagen's desire to not repeat themselves. They embraced the sound of the times, using more synthesizers and taking advantage of Roger Nichols's drum machine Wendel to create incredibly accurate drum tracks for four of the seven songs. The problem with Wendel was that although it was cutting-edge technology, its use added months to the process due to the primitive nature of computers at the time. Although they used the most session musicians they would ever use on an album (thirty-nine), Becker and Fagen played more on record than they had in years. Some critics and fans think that *Gaucho* is overly slick, but it is merely the next step in the progression of Steely Dan and is an album full of unforgettable compositions and electrifying performances.

"Babylon Sisters"

Gaucho's opening track brings back the rhythmic duo of drummer Bernard "Pretty" Purdie and bassist Chuck Rainey grooving on the "Purdie Shuffle," heard on "Home at Last" from the *Aja* LP. While the backbeat might be similar, "Babylon Sisters" is harmonically more advanced, with Don Grolnick's Fender Rhodes electric piano and clavinet taking center stage as guitarist Steve Khan accentuates the rapidly changing chord progression before switching to a reggae-like skank. For *Gaucho*, Fagen brought in keyboard player/arranger Rob Mounsey to arrange the horns for two songs, "Babylon Sisters" being one of these. The initial ideas came from Fagen, but Mounsey created an intense horn arrangement for the song that included not only trumpet, alto, and tenor saxophones but flügelhorn, clarinet, and bass clarinet because Fagen wanted a distinctive sound for the section. Trumpet player Randy Brecker contributes some fine plunger-mute-style fills as well as a full-blown solo, reminiscent of Chuck Findley's work on "The Royal Scam," only a bit mellower.

The basic track that they used was the second take, proving that it didn't always take a long time to record a proper backing track. Mixing wasn't quite as easy, with Fagen, Katz, and Nichols mixing the fade-out to the song over sixty times before Fagen was content. The song took three weeks to mix with over 250 mixes done, and that was with a new computerized Neve console with automation.

The six-piece background vocal section not only sings the hook on the chorus but adds some sultry, off-kilter "You've got to shake it baby" vocal lines on the outro, one of the song's crowning moments and a hook in itself. The lyrics about a man trying to regain a feeling of youth by engaging in a threesome with two prostitutes are exquisite rather than seedy and paint a picture where you can not only feel the Santa Ana winds, but actually "experience" the road trip itself.

"Hey Nineteen"

The first single released from the album, "Hey Nineteen" would be Steely Dan's first top ten single in six and a half years, their last being "Rikki Don't Lose That Number." The song's lyrics about an older man dating a nineteen-year-old woman

VIMX-1514

ヘイ・ナインティーン

HEY NINETEEN

B/w: 菩薩 BODHISATTVA

未発表ライヴ・ヴァージョン！
(1974年7月4日 サンタ・モニカ・シビックにて収録)

steely dan
スティーリー・ダン

MCA RECORDS

¥700

A Japanese picture sleeve for the first single released from *Gaucho*, "Hey Nineteen."

would take on a new, slightly sleazier, significance when the duo began performing it in the '90s when they were middle-aged. Becker and Fagen were in their early thirties when they wrote the song, so a generation gap, although not as wide, could still be felt with a partner more than a decade younger. The lyrics of the bridge alluding to the use of Cuervo Gold tequila and Colombian cocaine to ease the mood have become legendary in classic rock circles.

While Rick Marotta is credited as the drummer, "Hey Nineteen" marks the first use of Roger Nichols's drum machine Wendel. Unable to get a backing track with live musicians, they fed Marotta's performance into Wendel, which then created a rock-steady, mechanical R&B groove. Becker and Fagen both played on the track, with Becker handling bass and rhythm guitar duties and Fagen playing Fender Rhodes electric piano and his signature harmonica-like synthesizer patch. He even plays solos on both the synthesizer and electric piano on the fade-out. Victor Feldman and Steve Gadd overdubbed percussion; Frank Floyd and Zack Sanders contributed background vocals; and Hugh McCracken played the memorable lead guitar part that starts the song with an unforgettable bend and punctuates key moments with tasty licks.

"Glamour Profession"

The hook to "Glamour Profession" was written while Becker and Fagen were still at Bard College but rewritten with new lyrics that capture the vibe of the Hollywood lifestyle flawlessly, and tragically. The sense of entitlement that the main character of the song experiences is described through a number of vignettes, taking the famous basketball player from the court to a number of places frequented by the jet set.

"Glamour Profession" proved to be another track that was difficult to record, with the duo spending an inordinate amount of time recording what were basically demos. Wendel was once again utilized to "reinterpret" Steve Gadd's drum part, creating a perfect dance beat that grooves alongside Anthony Jackson's bouncy bass line, his debut appearance on a Steely Dan record. Fagen again played Fender

Rhodes electric piano and synthesizer, and guitarist Steve Khan provided rhythm and lead guitar, including an incredible harmonized solo before Rob Mounsey takes over with a piano solo that was surprisingly recorded in only an hour and a half. Mounsey also adds fills throughout the song that add a live feel to the mechanized drum groove. Tom Scott arranged a simple horn chart for two tenor saxophones and the Lyricon first heard on "Peg," and Leslie Miller and Valerie Simpson, of Ashford and Simpson, contribute some soulful background vocals.

The song is the longest on the album, clocking in at over seven and a half minutes, and includes a fade-out that is over two minutes long. This gives guitarist Steve Khan the opportunity to play an extended solo that is quite captivating, building from a sparse smattering of licks into a fully realized, melodic set of lines.

"Gaucho"

As was par for the course during the recording of *Gaucho*, the title track, about a gay couple that faces a crisis when a "bodacious cowboy" enters their lives, was another song that took what seemed like forever to capture. Guitarist Steve Khan had tried the song with a few different rhythm sections, but Becker and Fagen weren't happy with the results. Khan returned with the rhythm section of Jeff Porcaro on drums, Anthony Jackson on bass, Rob Mounsey on piano, and Victor Feldman on percussion. They recorded the song for four hours before taking a

well-deserved break. They felt that they had the take, but the songwriters didn't, so they continued for another four hours until Becker and Fagen gave up and went home for the night along with percussionist Feldman. The rest of the musicians recorded eight more full takes with Gary Katz leaving the studio at five o'clock in the morning. The next day, the duo thanked the band for their extra effort and edited together a drum track they were happy with. They discarded the tracks that were already recorded and built the song around Porcaro's slinky groove, with Fagen playing Fender Rhodes electric piano and synthesizer, Becker on bass and lead guitar, Steve Khan on guitar, Rob Mounsey on piano, and Crusher Bennett on percussion. Tom Scott played the tenor saxophone solo and wrote a horn chart for sax and trumpet, and Leslie Miller, Valerie Simpson, and Patti Austin added the sublime background vocals.

An advertisement for Steely Dan's seventh album, *Gaucho*.

When Becker and Fagen were interviewed by *Musician Player and Listener* magazine's David Breskin in 1981, he mentioned that the title track resembled pianist Keith Jarrett's song "Long as You Know You're Living Yours" from his album *Belonging*. Fagen responded, "We were heavily influenced by that particular piece of music . . . Hell, we steal. We're the robber barons of rock and roll." Jarrett sued for copyright infringement, and due to the similarity between the two songs, and Becker and Fagen's comments in the interview, he was added as a co-author on future pressings of the album. Although it's apparent that the duo used the groove of Jarrett's song, as well as the saxophone phrasing as a starting point, Becker stated that they tried many other instruments before settling on the saxophone, which seems odd given that Jan Garbarek's sax part was such an integral part of the tune. The truth is that the first few bars were what the duo copped, and the rest of the song is nothing like *Gaucho*, Becker and Fagen developing the idea into so much more.

"Time Out of Mind"

An ode to smoking heroin written at Fagen's Malibu home before the duo returned to New York, "Time Out of Mind" is another Wendel-manipulated drum track credited to Rick Marotta. Becker once again laid down both bass and rhythm guitar along with Hugh McCracken, and Fagen played piano, Fender Rhodes electric piano, and synthesizer for the majority of the song, but there was a catch that wasn't exposed in the original liner notes. During the solo, keyboard player Rob Mounsey, who also arranged the five-piece horn section, played the same three instruments for the elaborate instrumental section, but since it was difficult to credit it in such a way, Fagen was credited with electric piano and synthesizer and Mounsey with piano. The three female background vocalists from "Gaucho" were back, but with a secret weapon: Michael McDonald in his only appearance on the album. His ad-libs on the last pre-chorus are emotionally charged and add a sense of urgency to the lyrics.

Something that was different about the guitar solo for "Time Out of Mind" was the fact that they brought in a guitarist who wasn't a session musician for the track. After hearing Dire Straits' debut LP, Becker, Fagen, and Katz decided to bring Mark

The picture sleeve for the second single released from *Gaucho*, "Time Out of Mind."

Knopfler in to play guitar on "Time Out of Mind." Because Knopfler had never worked as a session musician before he was uncomfortable with the process and was extremely tense during the session. Some have complained that his playing wasn't prominent enough, but it is all over the song from start to finish, and Becker and Fagen were quite pleased with Knopfler's work, regardless of what the guitarist thought of them or the session.

The song was released as the album's second single in March 1981, but not without more drama created by their default record label MCA. Becker, Fagen, and Katz had already chosen "Third World Man" as the B-side, but MCA decided to release the single with the same B-side as the first single, "Hey Nineteen," the live 1974 version of "Bodhisattva." Their manager, Irving Azoff, was furious, believing that their decision was not only greedy but malicious. MCA claimed that since the album only had seven cuts, sales would suffer if they used another track as the next B-side. Azoff facetiously stated that he believed the label was foolish enough to release seven singles from the LP. Sales weren't really affected with the single reaching number twenty-two in the U.S.

Becker and Fagen spent so much time working on "Time Out of Mind" that the oxide was shredding off the tape to the point that they had to limit playback during the mixing process. For all their meticulousness, and playbacks, from time to time mistakes crept in. After the line "Put a dollar in the kitty," there is an obvious edit; the abrupt cutoff of the reverb on the vocals gives it away.

"My Rival"

"My Rival" was the fourth, out of seven, songs that used Wendel to create the perfect drum track, with credit given to Steve Gadd. Anthony Jackson provided the bottom, his second and final appearance on the album; Patrick Rebillot provided the Fender Rhodes electric piano (his only Steely Dan appearance); and Fagen played the haunting Hammond B3 organ that leads us into the song as well as the synthesizer part. The song's percussionist, Ralph McDonald, and timbale player Nicholas Marrero add appropriate flavor, while the guitar section of Rick Derringer, Steve Khan, and Hiram Bullock creates a perfectly balanced blend of six-stringed bliss.

Derringer originally recorded not only the fiery intro and licks, but attempted a guitar solo as well. They kept his licks, but had Steve Khan record the solo along with Hiram Bullock's subtle single-note guitar part. Tom Scott's horn arrangement for flügelhorn, tenor saxophone, and trombone is the focal point of the instrumental section and adds depth to every section in which it appears. The lyrics create a film-noir atmosphere that is hard to mistake, and the mixed male and female background vocals provide the ideal backdrop without question.

"Third World Man"

One of the first songs completed for the album, "The Second Arrangement," was a favorite of everybody involved in the session. Unfortunately, an engineer who was preparing the 24-track tape for playback accidentally erased nearly the entire song. They attempted to rerecord it, but when the results proved unfruitful, Becker and Fagen resurrected a rejected song from the *Aja* sessions originally entitled, "Were You Blind That Day." The rhythm section of drummer Steve Gadd, bassist Chuck Rainey, Joe Sample on Fender Rhodes electric piano, and Steve Khan covering both electric and acoustic guitars laid down the haunting groove as Larry Carlton contributed a fitting guitar solo. Carlton hadn't worked on *Gaucho* and was shocked when he read a review complimenting him on his solo, but it deserved the praise as one of the most creative solos on the album, blending harmonic lines, double-stops, and soaring lead licks to create a memorable moment that might never have been heard.

The lyrics were rewritten, Rob Mounsey added a synthesizer part to the nearly three-year old song, and Fagen recorded not only the lead vocals but the dense harmonies as well; proof that a song that Becker and Fagen deemed unworthy for release could actually become a classic. It's the perfect closer, bookending the album with "Babylon Sisters," only two of three songs, along with the title track, that escaped the manipulation of Wendel. There is, however, a slight mistake that ended up on the final recording. At 4:17, Chuck Rainey makes a rare, and fleeting, mistake, hitting the wrong note for a split second.

Conclusion

Gaucho took almost two years to complete, cost over $1 million to make, took three months to mix, incorporated thirty-nine different musicians in addition to Becker and Fagen and a $20,000 drum machine, and used 360 two-inch 24-track tapes. The legal issues Becker and Fagen were facing were also a major source of stress. Their label, ABC, was about to be absorbed by MCA Records, and the duo wanted to follow producer Gary Katz to Warner Bros. Records. After auditing the label's books, manager Irving Azoff determined that the Dan were owed several million dollars in unpaid royalties, but MCA claimed that they were not responsible for payment. Before MCA took over ABC, Becker and Fagen had signed a contract for one additional album, so MCA insisted that they release it on their label. After a court case, MCA paid partial royalties, and the record was in stores on November 21, 1980. MCA raised the price from $8.98 to $9.98, the first non-soundtrack album to carry that price tag, which incensed Becker, Fagen, Katz, and Azoff. They believed the higher price caused the album to not follow the extreme success of *Aja*.

Another issue was Becker's growing dependence on narcotics. His drug problem had made him unreliable, showing up late for sessions or not showing up at all and at times being very difficult to work with. Without the usual support of his partner, Fagen was at his wit's end. They were both suffering from depression, something that Fagen realized years later had come through in some of the songs. They also were trying to surpass what they had achieved with *Aja*, and as Fagen said in retrospect, with *Gaucho* they had gone overboard "trying to realize a technical perfection that started to deaden the material."

Regardless of all of the problems they encountered while making *Gaucho*, it was voted Rock/Blues album of the year in *Downbeat* magazine's 46th annual readers poll, reached number nine on the charts in the U.S., and peaked at number twenty-seven in the U.K. It also spawned two hit singles, one top ten and one top thirty. The third single, however, "Babylon Sisters" b/w "Gaucho," failed to chart in either country. Although the album had been a success, both Becker and Fagen knew that they needed a break from each other, so on June 21, 1981, they announced that they were going on an indefinite hiatus. They wouldn't work together in the studio for over five years. Fagen explained the making of *Gaucho* succinctly in his 1991 interview with Richard Cromelin for the *Los Angeles Times*. "That album is almost a document of despair. We were running out of steam as far as our youthful energy was concerned and we hadn't matured enough to deal with it. We were still adolescents."

17

I Think the People Down the Hall Know Who You Are

Donald Fagen's Solo Career

While Walter Becker would not record a solo album until 2008, Donald Fagen jumped right back into the studio soon after *Gaucho* was released to work on his first post-Steely Dan recording, 1981's "True Companion," for the movie *Heavy Metal*, a series of animated vignettes. Although it was a somewhat discouraging solo debut from an ex-Steely Dan member, Fagen needn't have worried. In 1982, he released his critically acclaimed debut solo LP, *The Nightfly*. Fagen would go on to release three additional solo LPs, *Kamakiriad*, produced by Becker; *Morph the Cat*; and *Sunken Condos*. His first three albums formed *The Nightfly Trilogy*, which would be released as a box set with multi-channel mixes and an additional disc of bonus material in 2007.

Overall Fagen kept much busier after he and Becker parted ways, writing songs for films, scoring a movie, producing a soundtrack for a play, conceiving the New York Rock and Soul Revue, and taking part in a comedy album. He would also tour with Michael McDonald and Boz Scaggs as the Dukes of September, of which a live Blu-ray/DVD of the tour would be released.

Heavy Metal Soundtrack

"True Companion" is mainly an atmospheric instrumental with layered harmony vocals by Fagen and Zack Sanders, who contributed background vocals to *Gaucho* and would do the same for Fagen's *Nightfly* album, not entering until three and a half minutes into the five-minute song.

Along with Fagen's vocals and keyboards, drummer Steve Jordan, bassist Will Lee, guitarist Steve Khan, and Don Grolnick in an uncredited Fender Rhodes electric piano role, filled out the rhythm section. Khan had already worked with Steely Dan playing rhythm guitar on "Peg," "Babylon Sisters," "Gaucho," and "Third World Man"; lead guitar on "Glamour Profession" and "My Rival"; and would return to play acoustic guitar on "The Goodbye Look" from *The Nightfly*. His guitar work on "True Companion" steals the show going from mellow-tone pedal work and acoustic guitar fills into a full-blown electric guitar solo that leads the song through a series of interesting changes before returning to the original theme with vocals.

Will Lee had worked with Steely Dan on "The Second Arrangement," one of their favorite songs from *Gaucho* until it was erased, as well as some other songs from the album, but his takes were not chosen for the final running order. For Steve Jordan, this was his first Steely Dan related session, but he would return, along with Lee, to play on "Walk Between the Raindrops" from *The Nightfly*.

Poster for the film *Heavy Metal*, whose soundtrack included Fagen's first post-Steely Dan production, "True Companion."

The accompanying soundtrack included songs by Sammy Hagar, Journey, Cheap Trick, Black Sabbath, Stevie Nicks, Devo, and others and peaked at number twelve on the *Billboard* 200 chart, but did not produce any hit singles. "True Companion" gained more widespread attention when it was included on the expanded version of the Steely Dan greatest hits album *Gold* in 1991. It was also used as an opening song during their 1994 tour.

The Nightfly

The Nightfly was the most autobiographical album that Fagen would ever release. It if wasn't apparent after listening to the eight tracks that make up the album, Fagen's wry liner notes tell all: "The songs on this album represent certain fantasies that might have been entertained by a young man growing up in the remote suburbs of a northeastern city during the late fifties and early sixties, i.e., one of my general height, weight and build."

Gary Katz was back in the producer's chair as were engineers Roger Nichols and Elliot Scheiner. Engineer Daniel Lazerus was added to the team while Nichols was producing a newer, higher-fidelity version of his drum machine Wendel named Wendel II, which was used on "Ruby Baby," "I.G.Y. (What a Beautiful World)," and "Walk Between Raindrops," as well as other tracks in a less defined manner.

Although Becker was absent, a number of Steely Dan alumni performed on *The Nightfly* including drummers Jeff Porcaro and Ed Greene; bassists Chuck Rainey, Anthony Jackson, and Will Lee (although Lee's work on *Gaucho* didn't make the final cut); guitarists Larry Carlton, Rick Derringer, Dean Parks, Steve Khan, and Hugh McCracken; keyboard players Michael Omartian and Rob Mounsey; horn players Michael Brecker, Randy Brecker, Ronnie Cuber, and Dave

The record cover for Fagen's most autobiographical project, *The Nightfly*.

Tofani; and background vocalists Frank Floyd, Gordon Grody, Leslie Miller, Zachary Sanders, and Valerie Simpson. There were also some new musicians on board including drummers Steve Jordan and James Gadson; bassists Marcus Miller and Abraham Laboriel Jr.; keyboard player Greg Phillinganes; horn player Dave Bargeron; and percussionist Starz Vanderlocket. *The Nightfly* reached number eleven on the U.S. *Billboard* 200 and number twenty-four on the U.S. *Billboard* R&B charts.

Overall, the feel of the album is upbeat and joyful sounding, with plenty of Fender Rhodes electric piano, velvety background vocals, and countless top-shelf solos. The horn arrangements were written by Fagen on his own, a first for a Steely Dan-related project. As he had done on *Gaucho*, Fagen plays various keyboards on all but two songs, "New Frontier" and "The Goodbye Look." One of the main differences between *The Nightfly* and Steely Dan is the straightforward nature of the lyrics. They are far less impenetrable and tell full stories with little left out in the middle.

The Songs

The album begins with the bouncy shuffle "I.G.Y. (What a Beautiful World)," written about the International Geophysical Year, which ran from July 1957 to December 1958 when Fagen was ten years old. It was an international scientific project that sixty-seven countries participated in after the Cold War had stifled an exchange of ideas between the East and West. Although the song has an optimistic bent, it is told through the eyes of someone living at that time before reality sets in and he realizes that his optimism was naive. The song was released as a single and peaked at twenty-six on the *Billboard* Hot 100.

"Green Flower Street" tells a Steely Danish story of murder and mayhem in New York City set to a funk groove laid down by Steely Dan stalwarts Jeff Porcaro and Chuck Rainey and the three-guitar team of Dean Parks and Rick Derringer on rhythm and Larry Carlton on lead. It is arguably the funkiest tune on the album, and Fagen would perform it live during his comeback shows in 1990 as well as the early Steely Dan tours in the '90s, his *Morph the Cat* tour in 2006, and with the Dukes of September.

Fagen performed a rare cover on *The Nightfly*: "Ruby Baby" written by Jerry Leiber and Mike Stoller and originally recorded by the Drifters in 1956. Although the resulting track seems simple enough, piano player Michael Omartian was asked to do the impossible; play his left hand part separate from his right hand part so they would fall in different places of the beat. In order to accomplish this feat, Fagen had Omartian and keyboard player Greg Phillinganes sit at the piano together, with Omartian playing the left hand and Phillinganes taking care of the right, which also included a solo whose opening line was based on the Kinks' "You Really Got Me."

"Maxine" is one of the most beautiful songs Fagen ever wrote, with a laid-back jazz-waltz groove played by Ed Greene and uplifting vocal harmonies performed by Fagen alone. The close harmonies are executed flawlessly and tell the story of a teenager's aspiration to move to the city from the suburbs with his dream girl. The drum groove was originally from a song that was discarded, but Fagen was so pleased with what Greene, who had played on "I Got the News," laid down that he wrote a new song based on the drum track. It features a raspy tenor saxophone solo by Michael Brecker and a stunning piano part by Greg Phillinganes, who played on five of the eight songs. If you listen closely to the fade-out, you can hear the click track in the background.

Side two begins with the second single from the album, "New Frontier," a whimsical look at a teenager trying to entice a girl into his dad's bomb shelter for some canoodling. With its syncopated groove provided by Ed Greene, Abraham Laboriel, and Michael Omartian; Larry Carlton's lead guitar; Hugh McCracken's harmonica; an emotional vocal delivery by Fagen; and a video, one would think it would have reached a higher chart position than number seventy.

The title track follows, a story inspired by the late-night New York DJs that Fagen listened to as a child. The song bounces along with a four-on-the-floor cowbell that underpins a sophisticated series of syncopated chords along with a bass line played by Marcus Miller that takes center stage at times. The background vocals are dazzling, and Larry Carlton contributes yet another bluesy solo that fits well among the numerous synthesizer lines that play around it.

Fagen's first foray into bossa nova, "The Goodbye Look" tells the tale of a man's experience as an ex-pat on a Caribbean Island and his need to leave before things get ugly. The groove is one of the most natural sounding on the album and adds a musical depth to *The Nightfly*. The song has become a favorite of jazz musicians, securing its inclusion in the second *Real Book*, a bible of jazz standards.

The album closes with the swinging "Walk Between the Raindrops," a song based on a Jewish folk tale of a rabbi who could actually perform the miracle of walking between the raindrops. While the song swings like a jazz song, it is a bit overproduced and would have benefited from a more organic approach, although Fagen does turn in an impressive organ solo.

That's the Way I Feel Now: A Tribute to Thelonious Monk

Two years after jazz composer and pianist Thelonious Monk passed away, a two-LP tribute to the groundbreaking musician was released. The twenty-three tracks were interpretations of Monk's compositions by varied artists from the jazz world and beyond. Bobby McFerrin did "Friday the 13th" with Bob Dorough, Joe Jackson covered "'Round Midnight," Gil Evans and Steve Lacy offered "Bemsha Swing," Todd Rundgren played an inventive version of "Four in One," John Zorn contributed an extremely different version of "Shuffle Boil," and guitarist Steve Khan collaborated with Donald Fagen for their take on "Reflections."

Monk was an influence on Fagen from an early age, and he tried to emulate his style of playing at times. He elaborated in an interview with Marc Meyers for *Jazzwax*: "I've always thought of my style as quirky. I always thought I could do something the way Thelonious Monk does, where he has his own eccentric way of improvising that wouldn't require great speed. But it seems the more I practice, the worse I get." Khan's acoustic guitar work is simply beautiful, and Fagen adds understated, yet expressive, synthesizer pads to fill out the track. Although Khan is the featured performer, Fagen plays a dazzling solo full of pitch bends and harmonica-like phrasing. In 1988, "Reflections" would appear in the movie *Arthur 2: on the Rocks* as well as on the soundtrack LP.

Bright Lights, Big City Score with Rob Mounsey and "Century's End"

In 1988, director James Bridges, whose career was launched as a writer on the *Alfred Hitchcock Hour* television series, was chosen to direct *Bright Lights, Big City*, the big screen adaptation of Jay McInerney's novel. The film starred Michael J. Fox, Kiefer Sutherland, Phoebe Cates, Dianne Wiest, and Jason Robards and was Bridges's last project before his death in 1993. The film was co-produced by Fagen's cousin Mark Rosenberg, and although Fagen had complained in the past about how the director of a movie has the final say about the music, he had enjoyed McInerney's novel and decided to take on the challenge of scoring the film. He worked with keyboard player Rob Mounsey, who had played on *Gaucho* and *The Nightfly* and had arranged horns for both albums along with Fagen.

Executive music producer Joel Sill remarked that once Fagen did a few cues, he was immediately at home with scoring the film. Not only did he score the film, he contributed "Century's End," a song whose lyrics were co-written by Timothy Meher. The infectious shuffle was Fagen's sole original release between *The Nightfly* and *Kamakiriad* and utilized the tight rhythm section of drummer Leroy Clouden, bassist Jimmy Haslip, guitarist Georg "Jojje" Wadenius, and Fagen on keyboards. Although the keyboard sounds are a bit dated, the song swings nicely with a punchy horn arrangement, dulcet background vocals, and a harmonically clever middle section that's so good it appears twice. Fagen turns in a jazzy synth harmonica solo over a unique musical interlude that leads back to a verse as well as over the outro. The song peaked at number eighty-three on the *Billboard* Hot 100 chart. Fagen also recorded a one-verse, one-chorus version of Jimmy Reed's "Bright Lights, Big City," but since it was more of a cue than a full song, it was left off of the soundtrack LP. Songs by Prince, Bryan Ferry, New Order, Depeche Mode, and Narada Michael Walden. Walden also appeared on the album. Fagen also produced "BNT Blues" for Bobby Forester, but the song wasn't on the soundtrack, only in the film. Fagen didn't fully enjoy the experience and told friends at the time that he probably wouldn't do it again. As of 2016, he hadn't.

Kamakiriad

The '80s were not the most productive decade for Donald Fagen, but he was consistently working. As he recalled in a 1991 interview with the *Los Angeles Times*, "I went through a lot of personal metamorphoses during the '80s. I had come to the end of whatever kind of energy was behind the writing I had been doing in the '70s, and *The Nightfly* sort of summed it up for me in a way." Although Fagen wrote every day, he was experiencing writer's block and wasn't pleased with the end result. No matter how many songs he wrote, when he listened back to them he felt that he was repeating himself or they simply bored him. He went into therapy after finishing *The Nightfly*, and by the end of the decade he was ready to get serious about writing and recording the follow-up.

Kamakiriad, named after the Japanese word for praying mantis, *kamakiri*, was the science-fiction tale of a man, in his mid-forties, on a journey in a modern car that provided everything one could need. Fagen had demoed the majority of the songs on his own and originally planned on producing the album himself, but he decided that he needed a producer to assess his vocal tracks and help him refine them. The album's expenses over three years of studio time had added up, coming close to $1 million. Fagen felt that his old partner was perfectly suited for the task at hand, so Walter Becker became the producer for Fagen's sophomore album. Fagen was ecstatic to be working with his former Steely Dan partner again and felt that after a twenty-five-year relationship, they were able to read each other's minds in the studio. He was also fond of Becker's laid-back, swinging style of playing and liked the chances he took as a musician. He knew that Becker would be more than a producer if he got involved. Fagen needed a collaborator, and that's what he got.

Becker did contribute significantly as a musician, playing bass and lead guitar on every song on the album, although myriad musicians had already attempted the tracks. The final album enlisted the talents of three drummers (Christopher Parker, Leroy Clouden, and Dennis McDermott), guitarist Georg Wadenius, Paul Griffin on Hammond B3 organ, an

Fagen's 1993 LP *Kamakiriad*, produced by Walter Becker.

extensive horn section, and eleven background vocalists. Fagen of course handled keys and provided the lead vocals for every track.

Sessions for the album were started in the spring of 1990 at the Hit Factory in New York City. Soon after, Fagen and Gary Katz opened their own studio, River Sound, so the album was recorded there, at Becker's studio, Hyperbolic Sound, in Maui, Hawaii, and at Clinton Recording in Manhattan. The fact that Fagen had demoed the tracks so extensively, with exact drum, bass, and rhythm parts played on drum machines and synthesizers, affected the final result, giving the album a somewhat cold and mechanical feel and sound. Becker and Fagen made no effort to keep the songs succinct. The majority of them run over six minutes long, and one clocks in at over eight minutes. The album did well on the charts peaking at number ten on the *Billboard* 200 and number three on the U.K. Albums Chart.

The Songs

The album's journey begins with "Trans Island Skyway." The song, originally titled "The Trip," tells of the delivery of the super car to its owner and his initial experience on the road. Fagen introduces a sexy female companion in a novel and witty manner, picking her up from the scene of an automobile accident. The song's bouncy groove sets the foundation for fiery background vocals and an elaborate horn arrangement written by Fagen. Fagen would write all the horn charts on the album by himself as he did for *The Nightfly*. The song was released as the album's second single, but failed to chart.

The next song, "Counter-moon," has a similar feel to the opener, but is taken a bit slower. Fagen takes a different approach than most songwriters when speaking of the moon. While the moon is often used in a romantic way lyrically, Fagen tells

the story of a moon that makes people fall out of love. He plays a synthesized saxophone solo under the pseudonym Illinois Elohainu. He actually had a few names that he used when playing a sample on a synthesizer trying to replicate the actual instrument. His stepdaughter, Amy Helm, the daughter of The Band's Levon Helm and Fagen's wife Libby Titus, sang the memorable line "You're not my Jackie." Six months after the release of the album, Fagen realized that some drum fills were inaudible, so he had Roger Nichols insert them into the mix, and all subsequent releases of the album included this new version.

The picture sleeve for the U.K. 12" "New Frontier" single that also included "Maxine" and "The Goodbye Look."

After a somber introduction, we're off with "Springtime" a straight-ahead funk tune with longtime Steely Dan session musician Paul Griffin on Hammond B3 organ and a '60s soul-infused horn section. This stop on the journey is an amusement park named Springtime where you can scan your brain for memories of old lovers and relive them in a virtual reality setting. Fagen elaborated on the song and the Steely Dan method of using contrasting music and lyrics in a 1993 interview for the radio show *Words and Music*. "At that point, the music becomes manic rather than nostalgic. Because nostalgia is really a sort of a trap we fall into sometimes that prevents us from moving forwards. I feel by putting the wrong music under the lyric, it basically sabotages the sentimentality."

"Snowbound" is the only Becker and Fagen composition on the album and was written in 1985, long before Fagen's idea for a concept album. Another stop on the journey, the song tells of a frozen city where its residents continue to celebrate the good times regardless of the inclement weather. The narrator gets stuck in the city, but rather than focus on the negative gets caught up in the decadent lifestyle. At over seven minutes, it's the second-longest song on the album and again features Paul Griffin's Hammond B3 organ as well as an extended guitar solo by Becker. It was edited to just under five minutes and released as the album's third single, but even with an accompanying music video in which Fagen appears, didn't fare well in the charts.

Fagen has stated that the album is about loss, and "Tomorrow's Girls" conveys the feeling that one can have after being with a partner for so long and realizing that they've drifted apart. An extreme example is that it can seem like your mate is an alien. Although "Tomorrow's Girls" is in essence about aliens coming to Earth and taking over the bodies of the women on the planet, it's apparent that it's also a metaphor for this feeling of loss. The song was edited to 4:41 and released as the first single from the album along with a campy video with Rick Moranis and Fagen but failed to chart.

"Florida Room" was co-written by Libby Titus and projects the opposite sentiment of "Snowbound." Rather than getting caught up in the decadent lifestyle of the frozen city in "Snowbound," the narrator is in his element soaking up the sun and enjoying the time spent with his partner. He still has doubts as to long-term happiness and wonders if he can be brought back to life by this woman in

The picture sleeve for the CD single "Snowbound."

paradise. The horn arrangement is truly the focal point of this slice of upbeat soul music.

"On the Dunes" was the oldest song on the album, having been written in 1983, and is the most downbeat on the album both lyrically and musically. The narrator's traveling companion has left him and he's now on his own, lonely and depressed, reminiscing about the breakup. The longest song on the album not only features a brash tenor saxophone solo by Cornelius Bumpus, but some ridiculous improvisation by drummer Christopher Parker on the outro.

The last song on the album, "Teahouse on the Tracks," was actually the last song written. Throughout the recording process, Fagen wasn't sure of where the narrator would end up, so there was a bit of anxiety as to whether he would find a suitable conclusion to the story. The driver arrives in Flytown and is about to give up when he hears music coming from a place called Teahouse on the Tracks. He enters and finds characters from his past on the bandstand, and their joyous attitude brings him back to life. Birch "Crimson Slide" Johnson's trombone solo perfectly demonstrates this enthusiastic rebirth. With his newfound exuberance, he decides to continue his journey into the unknown.

Morph the Cat

Morph the Cat was the final installment in the trilogy Fagen started in 1982 with *The Nightfly*. Eleven years after his debut solo album about youthful naiveté, he released *Kamakiriad*, which follows our forty-something-year-old narrator on a trip where he faces obstacles that eventually help him find himself. Fast-forward to 2006. It's now thirteen years later, and the narrator is pushing sixty and contemplating his own mortality. Fagen discussed this in detail in a 2006 *New York Times* article." "This is my death album. It's about the death of culture, the death of politics, the beginning of the end of my life." Having lived through the terrorist attacks of 9/11, he created an album about fellow New Yorkers and their reaction to the way the city has changed since that fateful day. The album, however, still has humorous elements, as one would expect. As Fagen put it when speaking of his own mortality, "You can either approach it with fear or just make a lot of jokes about it. I prefer the jokes strategy. With things that you have no control over, humor is usually the best way to go."

The majority of the album was recorded at Avatar Studios on West 53rd Street in New York, but while on vacation in Kauai, Fagen got bored and recorded some vocals. Additional work was also carried out at Clinton Recording Studios and Sear Sound, both in Manhattan. Like *Kamakiriad*, the songs are lengthy, with the majority of them running over six and seven minutes long with numerous solos. Fagen plays on all but two of the tracks and even takes a melodica solo, his only solo on the album.

The album has a more organic sound than his previous albums due to the use of a band backing him. Drummer Keith Carlock, bassist Freddie Washington Jr., and guitarists Jon Herington and Wayne Krantz play on every song; and keyboard player Ted Baker appears on every song except the title track, its reprise, and "Brite Nightgown." Guitarists Hugh McCracken, Frank Vignola, Ken Emerson, and Ken

Wessel make special appearances; a crack horn section comprised of Marvin Stamm, Mark Patterson, Walt Weiskopf, Lawrence Feldman, and Roger Rosenberg is used to great effect on a number of tracks; and percussionists Gordon Gottlieb, Bashiri Johnson, and Joe Pasaro round out the rhythm section. Jerry Barnes, Michael Harvey, Amy Helm, Carolyn Leonhart, and Cindy Mizelle provide background vocals, but on *Morph the Cat*, female background vocals are only heard on two songs. Phonus Quaver, another pseudonym for Fagen, makes an appearance on synthesized vibes and marimba. The album reached number twenty-six on the *Billboard* 200

The cover for Fagen's *Morph the Cat* album released in 2006.

chart and number thirty-five on the U.K. Albums Chart.

The Songs

The title track initially seems like a playful song about a giant feline that hovers over New York, enters people's apartments, and generally makes the public feel good, but as Fagen explained, it's actually narcotizing the citizens, or in other words, brainwashing them. Fagen stated in an article for Newhouse News Service, "The mass-media, advertising-saturated brain death in our country can be alarming." The tension of the song builds, and by the bridge, the music begins to sound more ominous, shedding new light on the lyrical content and making Morph seem less benevolent. After the other seven songs that deal with death, paranoia, and destruction play out, the reprise makes Morph seem more menacing than he did at the outset. The tight funk groove lays the basis for dense vocal harmonies, a bluesy horn arrangement, and solos by Jon Herington and tenor saxophonist Walt Weiskopf. Although "Morph the Cat" was the title of the album, it was the last song written.

"H-Gang" is an amusing tale of a woman who is released from prison, starts a successful rock band, leaves the band, and gets married and moves to the Midwest. The song's conclusion: a movie is made of her rather strange life. Weiskopf plays another soaring solo over the middle section, and Herington turns in two magnificent solos, with a wah-wah pedal adding a growl that juxtaposes the silky vocal harmonies and jazz combo-style horn arrangement. The song was edited from

"Morph is brilliant and beautiful... Fagen is the real deal." –Rolling Stone

"As lush as ever   don't miss." –GQ

MORPH THE CAT

The new solo album from Donald Fagen

FEATURING "H GANG"

Also available as a Special Edition CD + DVD-A with audio mixes in 5.1 Surround Sound.
donaldfagen.com

A promotional poster for *Morph the Cat* and the single "H Gang."

5:14 to 3:59 and released as the first single two weeks before the release of the album, but failed to chart.

"What I Do" is an imagined conversation between a younger version of Fagen and the ghost of Ray Charles, who gives him advice on everything from music to women. A version of the song was written before the sessions for *Morph the Cat*, but after Charles's death in June of 2004, Fagen rewrote it and it found a spot on the album. Howard Levy contributes an exceptional harmonica solo that sits on top of a mellow R&B groove layered with four guitar parts and Wurlitzer electric piano. Fagen had originally heard him on the radio show *A Prairie Home Companion* and made a mental note to call him for a session in the future. "What I Do" is the only song on the album with a female background vocal section. The song was released as the second single from *Morph the Cat.*

The first song on *Morph the Cat* that deals overtly with death is "Brite Nightgown." Based on a quote by W. C. Fields referring to the grim reaper as "the fellow in the bright nightgown," the song bounces along with a joyful exuberance that belies the heaviness of the lyrics. Each verse deals with a different near-death experience: the first as a child with a high fever, the second as a mugging victim (something that happened to Fagen while recording the album), and the third during a hallucinogenic drug trip. Phonus Quaver's back on marimba, and the horn section provides an off-kilter vibe that demonstrates the paranoia felt by the narrator when discussing his own mortality. Wayne Krantz's envelope-filtered guitar solo is striking and adds a discordant element to the song along with Fagen's haunting organ.

The longest track on the album, at seven and a half minutes, "The Great Pagoda of Funn" was written after Fagen had witnessed several beheadings in Iraq on the news and decided to write a song about a couple living through it and how they cope. The downtrodden lyrics are not sung over a jaunty beat, but live alongside a moody, atmospheric track that is the most poignant-sounding tune on the album. Phonus Quaver's marimba adds flavor to a simply produced tune and compliments the superb muted trumpet solo by Marvin Stamm. Wayne Krantz's deft solo on the outro is over two minutes long and is worth every second.

Fagen's sense of humor is apparent on "Security Joan," where he turns a mundane event like a security check at the airport into a sexual fantasy. Fagen stated that he was often chosen for the deep security check, and it was at the same time boring and anxiety-provoking. He elaborated on one such incident in a 2006 interview with the *Toronto Sun.* "The last time, while all that was happening to me, the security guy was saying to me how much he liked my work, so he obviously knew who I was, and yet it was the most severe security check I'd ever had." Fagen changes the security guard's sex for the lyric and over a slinky groove tells the tale of his infatuation with the guard after his pat down with a verse melody similar to *Two Against Nature*'s "What a Shame About Me." Within this comical story, he manages to subtly put down Homeland Security while providing some stylish piano and smoking organ. Guitarist Ken Wessel adds a short, but rocking, solo on his only Steely Dan-related outing.

Although the events of 9/11 permeate the entire album, only one song explicitly mentions "the fire downtown," "The Night Belongs to Mona." It's one of the most harmonically intricate yet melancholy songs on the album, but it still grooves. The song about a depressed recluse living alone in her Chelsea apartment is actually written in an empathetic manner, with the narrator hoping that she'll make it. Another Fagen pseudonym, Harlan Post Jr., makes an appearance on synthesized acoustic bass, and Howard Levy returns to add some tender harmonica licks.

"Mary Shut the Garden Door" was inspired by the 2004 Republican convention held in the predominantly Democratic city of New York. Fagen, along with many other New Yorkers, left town for the weekend, feeling that the city was overrun with tourists that had a fundamentally different political view. The song was written with George Orwell's *1984* in mind and was overtly political, commenting on what it would feel like to have an authoritarian government in power, taking potshots at the Bush administration in the process with the statement under the title, "Paranoia blooms when a thuggish cult gains control of the government." Phonus Quaver returns on vibes as does another Fagen pseudonym, Illinois Elohainu, on flutes. He also plays two swinging melodica solos that sit perfectly on top of this dark funk groove.

The album closes with the reprise of "Morph the Cat," but this version is darker sounding with a focus on a more discordant take of the portentous bass and guitar line along with a more threatening sounding horn section. Jon Herington and Frank Vignola both add solos that are at times dissonant yet lively. The album ends with an extremely jarring horn part that brings us to a haunting conclusion. As Fagen said, "There's nothing sexier than the Apocalypse. I suppose you could call this album *Apocalypse Wow*."

A bonus track was available on iTunes, a cover of Al Green's 1975 song "Rhymes." Co-produced by Todd Rundgren and Fagen, the song sounded more like a Rundgren production, with the multi-instrumentalist sequencing the drums and bass. The song still has some Steely Dan elements such as R&B style horns, soulful female background vocals, a fiery guitar solo by Wayne Krantz, and a somewhat brashly delivered vocal by Fagen.

Sunken Condos

Steely Dan's trumpet player Michael Leonhart had often offered his assistance to Fagen when he was ready to work on a new solo album. In February 2010, Fagen took him up on his offer, and the next month they gathered at Leonhart's apartment cum studio, Candyland, to listen to the demos Fagen had made on

The cover for Fagen's 2012 album *Sunken Condos*.

GarageBand and discuss the project. They did a bit of recording in April 2010, but the sessions were halted due to the *Dukes of September Rhythm Revue* tour with Michael McDonald and Boz Scaggs, and by the *Shuffle Diplomacy* world tour Steely Dan embarked on in 2011. Leonhart would be the only person to date to co-produce a Steely Dan-related album besides Becker, Fagen, or Katz, a chore he was up for and an achievement that would make any musician proud.

Fagen and Leonhart approached the recording of *Sunken Condos* quite differently than Fagen's past solo albums. Leonhart was not just a trumpet player, but also a multi-instrumentalist, and Fagen was impressed with his laid-back, simple funk approach to playing drums, something he had heard during countless Steely Dan sound checks. Initially, Fagen encouraged him to play drums on the demos, planning on bringing in Keith Carlock to play on the final tracks, but Leonhart's straightforward grooves worked well, and he ended up playing on every track under the pseudonym Earl Cooke Jr., quite an old-school-sounding moniker.

Leonhart also had a huge arsenal of vintage keyboards, struck idiophone percussion instruments, and odd brass instruments, and somehow found appropriate moments for not only Steely Dan and Fagen staples such as the Fender Rhodes and Wurlitzer electric pianos, acoustic piano, clavinet, Hammond B3 organ, and vibraphone, but also the Prophet 5, Minimoog, and Roland Juno 6 synthesizers; the tape-based '60s sampler the Mellotron; accordion; Hammond M100 organ; and brass instruments the mellophonium, trombonium, and mellophone. The album also employed fewer musicians than had been used in the past. Between Fagen and Leonhart, all of the keyboard parts were covered; Leonhart played drums on every track; and Fagen played keyboard bass, credited as Harlan Post Jr. on five of the nine songs. Female background vocals also played a more important role than on his previous release, gracing six of the nine tunes, and were provided by Carolyn Leonhart, Catherine Russell, Cindy Mizelle, and Jamie Leonhart.

Acoustic bass was provided by Joe Martin and Michael Leonhart's father, Jay, on two songs; Lincoln Schleifer contributed electric bass to three songs; and Freddie Washington played on one. While guitarist Jon Herington played on eight of the nine songs, three additional guitarists were brought in for specific tasks.

Since Fagen didn't think any song should have the burden of carrying an album title, he distorted the name of Claude Debussy's *The Sunken Cathedral* and named the album *Sunken Condos*, a metaphor for the economic and sociological problems in the world, as well as his own personal situation, the fact that he was growing older. The songs are more compact than Fagen's past few outings, with the majority of them running under five minutes.

The Songs

The opening track, "Slinky Thing," tackles one of his and Becker's favorite subjects, a May-December romance. But as Fagen was writing the song as a fifty-something rather than the thirty-something of the "Hey Nineteen" days, it includes the comments of the general public about how to "Hold onto that slinky thing." The use of acoustic bass and Leonhart's simple drum track sets the vibe for the record.

The disco groove of "I'm Not the Same Without You" is the perfect backdrop for a breakup song where the narrator conveys to his ex how much better he's doing since they split. Since it is a Fagen lyric, it's not quite so straightforward. He elaborated in a 2013 interview with Jon Regan for *Keyboard* magazine. "I thought it'd be funny if you extrapolated from that idea, so that the person actually starts to mutate into something that's not quite human. Although it's supposed to make the listener wonder if in fact the guy *was* so devastated that he's become somewhat psychotic. It's the 'unreliable narrator' device." Fagen plays piano as well as a grooving keyboard bass part credited as Harlan Post Jr. Jon Herington not only contributes guitar but 12-string guitar as well, a first on a Steely Dan-related project. Fagen has often stated how fond he was of harmonica players like Toots Thielemans and Stevie Wonder and how he wished he could play like them, hence his many synth harmonica solos over the years. For "I'm Not the Same Without You," he brought in jazz harmonica player William Galison, who has played with countless artists including Carly Simon, Sting, Barbra Streisand, Peggy Lee, Chaka Khan, and Astrud Gilberto. It was released as the album's first single.

"Memorabilia" is a song with a breezy, hip-hop-style groove whose subject matter is remarkably strange and quite out of the ordinary. Fagen's wife had a friend, Tony Price, who moved to Los Alamos, New Mexico, in the late '60s and began creating sculptures from atomic trash from the Los Alamos National Laboratory salvage yard. Fagen used Price as the basis for the Louis Dakine character and added a woman, Ivy King (named after a nuclear bomb tested by the Truman administration), who collects memorabilia from nuclear test sites. When she meets Dakine, she is in awe of his collection of artifacts. Leonhart's burning trumpet solo, as well as his licks throughout, are stunning and work well with Gary Sieger's subdued layer of guitar tracks. Fagen makes another appearance on keyboard bass along with Lincoln Schleifer's electric.

"Weather in My Head" is musically similar to "What I Do" from *Morph the Cat* but with a heavier guitar sound due to Larry Campbell's distorted rhythm guitar and Herington's scorching lead. The song uses the apparent weather problems happening in the world due to global warming as a metaphor for the narrator's depression and the feeling that he's losing his mind. Fagen, who has suffered from depression and takes, as he puts it, "an interesting anti-depressant that's helped a little bit" is writing from experience, and the metaphor is magnificent.

"The New Breed" updates the lyrical content of a young woman with an older man by introducing a new character, a young computer nerd hipster who sweeps the woman off of her feet. Fagen has often complained about how technology has permeated our lives, stating in a 2013 interview with *Keyboard* magazine, "I really feel isolated when I'm out in the world. I mean when everyone is just staring at the devices in their hands . . . They just look at their palm. They're *palm people*. It's like *Invasion of the Body Snatchers*. They've been snatched and there's nothing I can do about it." The story of heartbreak is sung over a hip-hop groove, with Michael Leonhart's father, Jay Leonhart, laying down an acoustic bass part filled with slides under a swirling Hammond B3 organ played by Fagen. William Galison returns to turn in an incredible harmonica solo as well as a bass harmonica part. The close harmonies on the chorus sung by Fagen and Leonhart are the darkest and most dissonant part of the song and clue the listener in to the dejected attitude of the narrator.

For *Sunken Condos*, Fagen decided to do a cover song, his first since "Ruby Baby" from *The Nightfly*, Isaac Hayes's 1977 single "Out of the Ghetto." While researching material for the *Dukes of September Rhythm Revue* tour, he came across Hayes's tune and realized that most people associate the word "ghetto" with the inner city, but the meaning is much older, so Fagen decided to "reclaim it for the Jews . . . so we added a Klezmer horn chart, and now the ghetto is back in Warsaw." The song is a funktastic take on Hayes's original with Freddie Washington providing a grooving bass track, his only on the album, and violin played by Antoine Silverman adding to the Klezmer feel.

What would a Fagen or Steely Dan album be without a shuffle? "Miss Marlene" grooves like "Babylon Sisters" with its smooth, tranquil vibe; sophisticated chord changes; exquisite horn arrangement; and sultry female background vocals. The song's story is one of the oddest that Fagen ever wrote. The topic: a young bowling queen whose prowess on the lanes was unparalleled, but was struck by a taxi in New York City's Greenwich Village, like his partner Walter Becker, but didn't survive her injuries. Jon Herington contributes a remarkable guitar solo over a chord progression that he claimed was one of the most difficult he had ever played over.

"Good Stuff" is a simple funk groove with a discordant, repetitive piano figure over the verse and expanded harmonic content for the chorus. The lyrics deal with familiar characters, gangsters, but with a spin: the song is specifically about the Jewish mafia of New York City. It's graphic and has a cinematic effect that puts the listener in the middle of every chilling situation. Leonhart spices up the middle section with lush vibraphone before Fagen takes over with a perfectly executed melodica solo. The layers of keyboards fit into all of the spaces perfectly over Leonhart's drums and Fagen's keyboard bass.

The album closes with a song about a female character that has been written about from Becker and Fagen's late '60s demo of "Ida Lee" to *Aja*'s "Josie." The wild child of "Planet D'Rhonda" has been updated, but at heart she's still the same. The groove is a slow burner, with Fagen playing Wurlitzer electric piano and clavinet over a series of interesting chord changes, with Leonhart's vibraphone floating on top. Jazz guitarist Kurt Rosenwinkel not only contributes two extraordinary solos but punctuates the song with some impeccable licks throughout.

Tom Schiller and Donald Fagen

Tom Schiller's father, Bob Schiller, was a writer on *I Love Lucy*, and Tom grew up on the set. A fond memory was the day when he was six when they filmed the famous grape-stomping scene. At the young age of seventeen, he was working for a documentary filmmaker in the Pacific Palisades, where he directed his first film, about Henry Miller, in 1973. Soon after, his father told him of a Canadian writer he had met who knew the best restaurants in Los Angeles. Schiller wasn't very interested, but he went along and met future creator and producer of *Saturday Night Live* Lorne Michaels. Schiller remembered that when he first met him, he lit a joint in his room, something Schiller would never do under his father's roof. They became fast friends and began to socialize at the Chateau Marmont, a popular spot for the more adventurous actors, musicians, and entertainers at the time.

Michaels was extremely excited about his idea for a new late-night show and would constantly ask Schiller to come write for it. Schiller reminisced about his early days on *Saturday Night Live* in the book *Nothing Lost Forever: The Films of Tom Schiller*. "He kept asking me if I'd like to come work on it, and I was conflicted, because my then-pal Henry Miller said, 'Don't go work on TV, it'll kill your soul.' But Lorne kept painting this picture of New York . . . and working on a late-night show . . . sounded kind of interesting. Since I wanted to be a foreign-film director, L.A. didn't seem like the place to be, and I finally succumbed and took his invitation. I was sitting there with him as he started hiring all the writers and cast." Schiller began his eleven-year stint with *SNL* as a writer, but eventually directed his own shorts after original short filmmakers Albert Brooks and Gary Weis left.

Schiller was producing music shows with Fagen's then girlfriend, and future wife, Libby Titus at a small Italian restaurant on Thirty-ninth Street in Manhattan that seated approximately thirty people. Due to the intimate setting of the venue, these invitation-only events were extremely popular, with artists such as Dr. John and Carly Simon playing sets for an exclusive audience. Fagen attended the night Duke Ellington's bass player, Aaron Bell, was playing and had a wonderful time. Soon after, he played a Titus-produced show with Dr. John at Elaine's, the first time he had performed live in fifteen years.

In 2013, Tom Schiller and Donald Fagen released *The Tom and Don Tapes: Vol. 1*, a comedy compilation of improvisational interviews between Schiller and Fagen. A few of the skits had been on the Donald Fagen website, but until their release as part of a full album, few people were aware of the existence of these comic nuggets. Hearing Schiller crack up Fagen is worth the price of admission.

18

Tearful Reunion in the U.S.A.

The Return of Steely Dan

The reality of seeing Steely Dan live after their long, and vocal, sabbatical from touring didn't come quickly. After their last show at the Santa Monica Civic Center on July 5, 1974, Becker and Fagen toyed with the idea of touring again in support of 1977's *Aja*. After releasing five albums in quick succession, it had been fourteen months between the release of *The Royal Scam* and *Aja*, and surprisingly, the duo spoke of the possibility of a tour in the interviews that followed. Fagen may have jumped the gun when he claimed that they would go out on tour once they handled their business matters. He admitted that he didn't like to travel, but was willing to do twenty dates to test the waters and see how much he could withstand. But when asked point blank if they were planning on touring by Sylvie Simmons for the October 22, 1977, issue of *Sounds* magazine, they answered quite differently.

Rumour has it that you'll be touring the States before long.

Becker: Not that I know of! We had intended to tour, but the album release was delayed, so we put it off. Now we've no plans to tour.

Fagen: Making these records pretty well takes up our time. Once we've finished one we start the next. That's the reason we haven't been touring.

Becker: Touring is an expensive hobby.

Fagen: We spend money on a tour. We have an expensive set-up. We don't like playing big halls—the sound is bad. So we have 4,000 people coming in, and it's not enough money to meet the expenses of putting on a show.

Becker: And we spend a longer time preparing our albums, I guess, than other people do.

Fagen: Stevie Wonder spent 2½ years on his record.

Becker: But we found from past efforts that being on the road wasn't enhancing what we were doing in the studio. So we decided that we'd do either one thing or the other.

They realized that they had spoken out of turn when they initially announced plans to tour, but at the time they actually thought that it was a good idea. The problem was they hadn't taken into account that it would be extremely difficult, and time consuming, to start a live band from scratch. To present their music effectively to an audience in 1977, they would need a bigger ensemble with more experienced players, a dilemma that proved to be impossible to resolve. Gary Katz also took part of the blame because he thought that they owed it to themselves to go on the road and present this exceptional material. He also admitted that selfishly, he wanted to see it himself.

They had actually bought a seven-foot Yamaha piano and set up shop at Denny Dias's house with genuine intentions of rehearsing there. Fagen had allegedly even put together a forty-five-minute medley of their early material so that they could concentrate on the newer songs for the show. They planned on treating the tour as they had their albums, using the best session musicians available, but this comes at a price. Since the musicians they intended to use were all extremely busy session players, they had to come up with a sliding pay scale based on the amount of money a player would lose by not being available for record dates. When some of the members became aware that they were on the lower end of the spectrum, they were understandably upset, and Becker and Fagen began to feel like capitalists that were manipulating the musicians. After the first rehearsal, which was for the keyboard players, the tour was cancelled. Allegedly tickets were already on sale, but when they told manager Irving Azoff that they would not be touring after all, he was unfazed. The tickets had sold out so quickly that he was convinced there was no need to tour.

In 1995, Fagen made a rather candid statement about the reason they wanted to stop touring. "It was possible that we took the Beatles example. They stopped touring and just started . . . concentrating on making records and their records . . . certainly didn't go down terribly in quality." Becker agreed with the fact that touring interfered with recording because not only was Fagen's voice strained after a number of dates playing live, but the gear would come back in less than optimal condition. They also couldn't concentrate on writing while on the road, so the pressure was on every time they returned to Los Angeles. The rest of the band didn't understand how their leaders couldn't enjoy the fringe benefits of touring life. Becker understood that in a band every member sees a different version of the situation depending on their position, but they were still young and hadn't developed the tools to realize what the other members were going through, which to some seemed selfish.

After the release of their final studio album, *Gaucho*, on November 21, 1980, Becker and Fagen parted ways, and Steely Dan was apparently finished. Fagen went as far as saying in a 1989 interview with New York City radio station KROQ, "There is no more Steely Dan. They're gone." But during the fall of 1989, Fagen began to perform around Manhattan at various clubs, and he began to actually enjoy playing live with other musicians. It took almost four years before a full-blown Steely Dan tour would happen, and a new album would take eleven, but this was a beginning; a moment that most Steely Dan fans never thought would happen.

As is often the case, a good woman was responsible for these events from behind the scenes.

Phase One: 1989–1992

In 1989, Donald Fagen's future wife, Libby Titus, produced a series of concerts around New York entitled New York Nights. Titus had attended Bard College the year before Fagen began, but at age nineteen she got pregnant and left school to get married. Fagen recalls seeing her "from a distance" when she returned to see friends and described her as "bohemian royalty" with an ultra-short mini-skirt and fur coat. She married novelist Barry Titus, grandson of Helena Rubinstein, and had a son, novelist Ezra Titus. The couple divorced in 1968, the year that Titus released her eponymous debut LP.

Her partner from 1969 throughout the '70s was the drummer/singer for the Band, Levon Helm. The couple had a daughter, Amy, in 1970. Titus continued to sing with various artists as she began to develop her songwriting chops. She has co-written songs with Burt Bacharach, Carly Simon, Al Cooper, Eric Kaz, and Dr. John. After splitting up with Helm, Titus would be not only a musical partner of Dr. John but a personal one as well.

In 1987, she met Fagen backstage at a Dr. John concert, and they began dating. At the time she was producing invitation-only shows hosted by former *Saturday Night Live* writer/filmmaker/comedian Tom Schiller in Manhattan. Fagen attended the night that Duke Ellington's bass player Aaron Bell was the featured artist, which excited the reclusive ex-Steely Dan singer and keyboardist. In May 1989, Fagen returned to the stage for the first time in many years for a show with Dr. John and Carly Simon at Elaine's on the Upper East Side and enjoyed the experience so much that he and Titus came up with an idea to perform '60s soul songs for a show entitled New York Soul. Fagen and Paul Griffin, who had played on countless Steely Dan sessions, wrote charts for between thirty and forty soul songs. He also recruited some of the best session musicians for the sold-out show on September 20, 1989, at the Lone Star Roadhouse in New York City.

The band consisted of Jerry Jemmott on bass, George Naha on guitar, Joe Ascione on drums, and musical director Paul Griffin and Dr. John on keyboards. The horn section of trumpet player Alan Rubin and saxophonists David "Fathead" Newman and Lou Marini were tight, and the vocals were shared between Phoebe Snow; Jeff Young; Jevetta Steele; singer, harmonica, and violin player Mindy Jostyn; and Griffin. The musicians assembled for this event had played with some of the biggest artists of the past three decades including Ray Charles, Aretha Franklin, Wilson Pickett, Rufus Thomas, Willie Dixon, the Rascals, Roberta Flack, and the Blues Brothers.

The band played a number of songs written by the Brill Building songwriting/production team of Bert Berns and Jerry Ragavoy, both together and separately, including "Time Is on My Side," "Twist and Shout," "Piece of My Heart," "Everybody Needs Somebody to Love," "Stay with Me," "It's Your Move," "Cry to Me," "Cry Baby," "Stop!," "That's When It Hurts," and "Look at Granny Run Run." The shows were a success, but people were hoping to hear some Steely Dan numbers, something that irritated Fagen immensely. Fagen played synthesizer and melodica, but refused to sing any songs, whether they were by Steely Dan or Bert Berns and Jerry Ragavoy. He even had to tell the audience after numerous shouted requests for Steely Dan songs, "Please don't be rude to these other great performers." As the show came to a close, the band left the stage, and it was obvious that the crowd hoped for a Steely Dan encore. Paul Griffin had even confided in a member of the audience between shows that he was trying to convince Fagen to do "Green Earrings" as the encore. Instead, Fagen invited the Brigati Brothers from the Rascals up to the stage, and they performed "Good Lovin'" with the other performers to close the show.

Although Fagen had decided to stay away from his past for this show, it wouldn't be long before the Steely Dan songs people were clamoring for would be heard live. The New York Soul show was so popular the group returned to the Lone Star in November for a "Thanksgiving Soul Party." The band had changed a bit, including the disappearance of Musical Director Paul Griffin, but vocalist Jeff Young proved to be an accomplished keyboard player, and his talents as such were evident along with his signature vocals. The major difference was that this time Fagen did sing, but not a Steely Dan song. He opted for Kenny Gamble and Leon Huff's "Drowning in the Sea of Love," a 1972 top twenty hit for Joe Simon. Fagen was becoming more comfortable on stage and explained his thoughts on singing live in an interview with KROQ in New York to publicize the November shows. "I think for my psychological profile it's a good idea that I sing. I owe it to people who want to hear me sing. On the other hand, I'd like to hear what I sound like." The shows were again incredibly successful, so a larger venue was needed if they were to expand on their current setup.

On April 4, 1990, the New York Soul show, rechristened the New York Rock and Soul Revue, moved to bigger digs, the twenty-nine-hundred-seat Beacon Theatre on Manhattan's Upper West Side. The show was expanded, with Fagen, Patti Austin, Michael McDonald, and Phoebe Snow taking care of the lead vocals and Musical Director Jeff Young's R&B outfit Curious George backing the band. Young handled keyboard duties and provided lead and background vocals, Drew Zingg played lead guitar; Sam Butler was on rhythm guitar; Lincoln Schleifer on bass; Dennis McDermott on drums; Cornelius Bumpus and John Hagen on tenor saxophones; Chris Anderson on trumpet; Philip Hamilton on percussion and background vocals; Mindy Jostyn on harmonica, violin, and background vocals; and additional background vocals by Diane Sorel and Ula Hedwig.

The music was once again predominantly classic soul of the '60s and '70s, with Patti Austin performing "I'm Sorry," "Everyday People," and "Smoke Gets in Your Eyes"; Phoebe Snow singing "Standing on Shaky Ground," "At Last," and "Poetry Man"; and Michael McDonald playing some of his most famous songs from his Doobie Brothers tenure including "Minute by Minute," "You Belong to Me," and "Little Darling." The show also hearkened back to the Lone Star days, with background vocalist Mindy Jostyn singing Ben E. King's "That's When It Hurts" written by Bert Berns and Jerry Wexler, Jeff Young delivering Harry Belafonte's "Man Smart (Woman Smarter)," and guitarist Sam Butler and percussionist/background vocalist Philip Hamilton taking on the 1966 Sam Cooke song "Soothe Me," which was covered in '67 by Sam and Dave. The Brigati brothers of Rascals fame joined everybody on stage for a joyous version of their 1968 hit "People Got to Be Free."

The show was fantastic, but a major reason it was such a success was the fact that Fagen was finally playing some Steely Dan songs. Even Fagen, who at this point still didn't think fans were as interested in his former band as they were, understood that some people thought he owed it to the audience to play Steely Dan songs. But he wasn't interested in doing a nostalgia show, caring more about honestly project-ing where he was at the time and to show some evolution as a musician. He did, however, recognize that the constant calls for Dan songs during the more recent shows were a distraction that could easily be remedied, so he added a few Steely Dan songs, and they sat well within a set of soul and R&B covers.

Fagen opened at the piano with "Black Friday," followed by "I.G.Y (What a Beautiful World)," which he not only sang but played some inspired melodica on as well. The band closed the show with his third performance of the night, "Pretzel Logic," which took us back to the Steely Dan 1974 tour with Michael McDonald reprising his role on lead vocals for the "I stepped up on the platform . . ." break. It had finally happened. Steely Dan songs were being performed live by one of the writers; luckily, he was also the lead vocalist.

Fagen continued to perform around Manhattan and found one particular live music venue in his neighborhood where he felt comfortable. Keyboardist/vocalist Jeff Young had a Tuesday night residency with future musical director of the Conan O'Brien Show, guitarist Jimmy Vivino and his Little Big Band at a club called Hades on 94th St and Second Avenue in Manhattan, and he thought that Fagen would enjoy it. The Little Big Band consisted of Jimmy Vivino on guitar, drummer Gary Gold, Harvey Brooks on bass, Jerry Vivino on tenor saxophone, trombonist Bob Smith, Mike Spengler on trumpet, Kevin Bents on keyboards, and Jeff Young on keyboards and vocals. Eventually, Fagen began to sit in on keyboards. On May 15, 1990, while working on Fagen's new solo album at the Hit Factory, Becker and Fagen took a break and joined the Little Big Band background vocalist Phoebe Snow on stage. Fagen shared background vocals and played melodica, and Becker played guitar alongside Vivino. The set list was once again heavy on old rock and soul classics and included "Shaky Ground, " "Blue Monday," "I Saw Her Standing There," "Just to Be With You," "Woolly Bully," "Mustang Sally," "Come On in My Kitchen," "Iko Iko," "Man Smart (Woman Smarter)," "I Feel Good," "Papa's Got a Brand New Bag," "Love Machine," "634-5789" (a duet between Fagen and Snow), "You Send Me," and the closer, a duet by Fagen and Snow on Wilson Pickett's "In the Midnight Hour."

By this time, Fagen was more at ease on stage and began singing more as well. He originally stuck to classic soul numbers, but soon after, he began to perform Steely Dan songs at these impromptu gigs as he had done during the New York Rock and Soul Revue shows. When they debuted "Black Friday" at Hades, Vivino had been rehearsing it with the band for a few weeks and even wrote a horn chart for the song. "Pretzel Logic" was a popular choice, with Jeff Young singing the middle section that Michael McDonald sang in 1974 and 1990. Fagen continued with the bluesy shuffle tunes by adding "Chain Lightning" from *Katy Lied* as well and even rehearsed a bit with Vivino's band before shows. Special guests such as keyboardist and musical director of the *Late Show with David Letterman*, Paul Schaeffer, and Jimi Hendrix's bassist Noel Redding sat in with the band, and Tuesday nights at Hades became increasingly popular. Fagen was enjoying performing live so much that he began to show up on Wednesday nights as well for singer Mindy Jostyn's gig.

Fagen was busy in the spring and summer of 1990 performing at the Lone Star Roadhouse with Dr. John, Elaine's with Phoebe Snow, Spodeeodee's with Rickie Lee Jones, and as a surprise guest at Michael McDonald's show at the Westbury Music Fair on Long Island, a venue Steely Dan played on March 16 and 17, 1973 with Cheech and Chong. He played the current staples "Black Friday" and "Pretzel Logic" and added melodica to McDonald's encore of "When a Man Loves a Woman." He even jumped on stage at the Dancing Crab Bar in Montauk, Long Island, with the Big Blue Squid, a band whose lead singer was the daughter of a friend.

Fagen finished off his summer of Long Island gigs at the Evian Music Festival on August 24, 1990, in South Hampton, the brainchild of Paul Simon's brother Eddie. Fagen originally wanted to double bill with Michael McDonald, but McDonald was already on tour, so singer-songwriter Bill Withers was recruited, and the show was billed as "Donald Fagen & Bill Withers: New York Rock & Soul Revue." The band was primarily the same as the April 4th gig at the Beacon Theatre except for a new background vocalist, Catherine Russell. The show followed the same template as the other Rock and Soul shows, but besides the three Steely Dan songs that Fagen had been performing during the spring and summer, another shuffle was added, "Home at Last" from the *Aja* LP. Although Bill Withers cancelled at the last minute, hearing a Steely Dan song that had never been performed live before was enough to satiate the fans' thirst for a true Steely Dan reunion, for the time being.

Ironically, back in New York City Fagen's favorite new venue Hades was closed down in October due to the growing crowds that were coming there to see him. The venue only had a license for three people to perform on the stage at once, and it was decided that there were insufficient fire exits. Jimmy Vivino's Little Big Band needed a new residency, and so did Fagen. Vivino temporarily relocated to the comedy club Catch a Rising Star, but it wasn't the right fit, and he quickly moved the Little Big Band to the China Club on 75th St. and Broadway. Fagen debuted "Green Flower Street" during one of the shows, and the song would become a staple of future performances. The crowds grew bigger and bigger, and there were even more guest appearances, including some Steely Dan session musicians. Guitarist Hiram Bullock, who had played on "My Rival," and drummer Steve Jordan, who played on Fagen's "Walk Between the Raindrops," sat in, as did Walter Becker's guitar mentor from his Bard College days, Randy California from the band Spirit, and drummer Max Weinberg from Bruce Springsteen's E Street Band.

The New York Rock and Soul Revue, which now featured Fagen alongside Phoebe Snow, Michael McDonald, Boz Scaggs, Charles Brown, and the Brigati Brothers from the Rascals, returned to the Beacon Theatre backed by Jeff Young and the Youngsters, the new name of the Curious George band, on March 1 and 2, 1991, to record a live album and film the show for future release. Certain songs were interspersed with interviews for a special entitled *In Concert* that aired on the A&E network, with Scott Muni, DJ at New York City's WNEW-FM, and Dr. John providing introductions before specific songs.

The show began with Jeff Young and the Youngsters' original song "Working My Way Downtown," which was a showcase for the rhythm section along with the three background vocalists: Mindy Jostyn, Diane Sorel, and Ula Hedwig. Fagen then took the stage for jazz pianist Ray Bryant's only top forty hit, "Madison Time." The Madison became a '60s dance sensation, and the song would be heard in the John Waters movie *Hairspray*. Phoebe Snow and Michael McDonald followed with Eddie Floyd's 1966 number one soul single that also peaked at number twenty-eight on the *Billboard* Hot 100, "Knock On Wood." Fagen followed with *Aja*'s "Home at Last" before Boz Scaggs hit the stage for his 1976 number three hit "Lowdown." The song was co-written with future Toto keyboardist/vocalist David Paich, who had contributed keyboards to both *Pretzel Logic* and *Katy Lied*. In addition to Paich's songwriting and keyboard playing, Steely Dan alumni Jeff Porcaro played drums on the original recording. Scaggs followed with Gamble and Huff's "Drowning in the Sea of Love," which Fagen had covered at the Lone Star Cafe shows. McDonald then wowed the audience with the Doobie Brothers' 1978 hit "Minute by Minute" before Snow returned for two songs, the Temptations' "Shakey Ground" from 1975 and a fabulous version of Etta James's signature song, "At Last." Jeff Young and percussionist/background vocalist Philip Hamilton took center stage for Sam Cooke's "Soothe Me," with Young taking over vocals for rhythm guitarist/vocalist Sam Butler, who was no longer in the band. Fagen closed the first half of the show with the staple "Black Friday."

After intermission, blues pianist Charles Brown took the stage and played "Quick Sand," "Driftin' Blues," and, from his new album *All My Life*, "Joyce's Boogie." Then the Brigati Brothers from the Rascals made a surprise appearance singing "Good Lovin'," "Groovin'," and "How Can I Be Sure" with Jimmy Vivino, who served as the Brigatis' musical director, on guitar. McDonald's next song was one of the most memorable of the evening, Jackie Wilson's "Lonely Teardrops." Fagen was very impressed with this version and spoke of it in an interview about the show. "Michael's version is particularly interesting because you need an incredible voice to even try to sing it and he does a lot more than that."

Steely Dan fans were next treated to "Chain Lightning" before background vocalist Mindy Jostyn stepped up for her take on Ben E. King's "That's When It Hurts." Boz Scaggs then sang a duet with background vocalist Diane Sorel of Mickey and Sylvia's 1956 crossover hit "Love Is Strange." McDonald followed with Holland/Dozier/Holland's "Little Darling," which he had recorded for the Doobie Brothers' 1977 album *Livin' on the Fault Line*. The band switched gears for "Pretzel Logic," with Michael McDonald once again singing the bridge. Phoebe Snow then turned in an impassioned performance of Jerry Ragavoy and Bert Bern's "Piece of My Heart," one of the songs performed at the first New York Soul show in the fall of '89. The last song of the show was a surprise for anybody who had missed Fagen's recent shows at the China Club, "Green Flower Street" from *The Nightfly*. The crowd went wild, and the entire company returned to the stage for an encore of the Rascals' 1968 hit "People Got to Be Free." The show was edited and resequenced for release on October 29, 1991, on Giant Records and briefly entered the *Billboard 200*. A few overdubs were necessary, but for the most part the show was live.

On May 9, 1991, Donald Fagen took part in a show that was part of the series entitled *In Their Own Words: A Bunch of Songwriters Sittin' Around Singing*, hosted by radio personality Vin Scelsa of WXRK-FM at the Bottom Line on West 4th St. in Greenwich Village. He was joined on stage by songwriters Al Kooper and Spooner Oldham, both playing keyboards, and Dan Penn and Gary Nicholson, who both played acoustic guitar. Fagen performed "Black Friday" and "Green Flower Street" before he was joined by Jimmy Vivino on acoustic guitar for "Home at Last." He was then asked to play a song that he wished he had written, and he chose Burt Bacharach and Hal David's "(In the) Land of Make Believe," first recorded by Dionne Warwick in 1964 and again by Dusty Springfield for her classic LP from 1969, *Dusty in Memphis*.

Fagen headed to upstate New York in July 1991 to play a show with Vivino's Little Big Band at the Bearsville Theater in Woodstock. More Steely Dan songs were added to the set after playing them a week earlier at the China Club. Fans were now treated to renditions of both "Josie" and "Green Earrings," the first songs added from Steely Dan's back catalogue that weren't shuffles. They had also rehearsed "Sign In Stranger" and "Deacon Blues" before the China Club show, but they weren't performed that night. "Deacon Blues" would, however, be debuted at the show at the Bearsville Theater.

In addition to producing the New York Rock and Soul Revue, Libby Titus continued to produce a similar show called New York Nights at the Lone Star Roadhouse with artists as varied as saxophonist/vocalist Curtis Stigers; Dion DiMucci of Dion and the Belmonts; Annie Ross of Lambert, Hendricks and Ross fame; and actor Gary Busey. On October 23, 1991, Fagen and the Little Big Band with Rick Danko from the Band playing bass, Cyndi Lauper on vocals, and Rob Hyman and Eric Bazilian from the Hooters had a few extra special guests in the audience, engineer Roger Nichols and Walter Becker. Although Becker was reluctant to come on stage when Vivino initially invited him, he eventually joined the band and his partner on stage to play Steely Dan songs for the first time since July 5, 1974—more than seventeen years. The duo treated the crowd to "Josie," "Chain Lightning," and "Black Friday." Their prior reunion on the stage on May 15, 1990, had been a surprise to all, but they hadn't played anything from the Steely Dan catalog. This was definitely a step in the right direction and foreshadowed what was to come.

The *New York Rock and Soul Revue* Tour—1992

In August 1992, the New York Rock and Soul Revue took to the road with both Becker and Fagen. The tour was a short thirteen-show jaunt and was a '90s take on Dylan's freewheeling *Rolling Thunder Revue* of the '70s. Although it was brief, it was becoming apparent that there was a chance for a full-blown Steely Dan tour in the not-too-distant future. In addition to Becker and Fagen, Michael McDonald, Phoebe Snow, Boz Scaggs, and Chuck Jackson, who replaced Charles Brown, took the stage each night to deliver a sensational show. In the 1970s, Becker and Fagen had toyed with the idea of putting together an orchestra, and nineteen years later they finally were able to do it. The twelve-piece band (including Becker and Fagen) that went on the road was a bit different from the band that had played the Beacon Theatre shows in 1991, before Becker joined. Leroy Clouden replaced Dennis McDermott on drums, Harvey Brooks replaced Lincoln Schleifer on bass, Kevin Bents replaced Jeff Young on keyboards, and Brenda White-King took over the background vocals from Ula Hedwig.

Percussionist/background vocalist Philip Hamilton had left as well, but Catherine Russell returned as a background vocalist, Mindy Jostyn continued singing background vocals and adding harmonica and violin, Drew Zingg shared lead guitar duties with Becker, and the horn section returned with trumpet player Chris Anderson and saxophonists Cornelius Bumpus and John Hagen.

For Steely Dan fans, this was the moment they had been waiting for: Walter Becker and Donald Fagen on tour playing Steely Dan numbers. In addition to the songs that had become familiar at recent performances such as "Chain Lightning," "Pretzel Logic," "Green Earrings," "Black Friday," "Deacon Blues," and "Josie," they added "My Old School," which was the oldest Steely Dan song they had played to date.

Terry Perkins of the St. Louis *Riverfront Times* interviewed Michael McDonald, who was a native of St. Louis, for his preview of the opening date of the tour at the Riverport Amphitheatre. When asked about how he began working with Becker and Fagen after eleven years, McDonald stated, "Donald called me in California and explained what he was trying to do with the Revue, and asked me if I'd be interested in being part of a performance at the Beacon Theatre in New York City in early 1991 to benefit the R&B Foundation. I told him that I definitely was, and it turned out to be something that continued . . . that seemed to have a life of its own. When I'm not singing upfront, I'll be playing keyboards along with Donald. Doing the old songs and hearing the diversity that everyone brings to the show is great, but for me the old Steely Dan stuff is the real show. Hearing Donald sing those songs live, and having Walter up there to play, too . . . that's the ticket for me."

Becker even had a vocal spot, singing "Mary, Mary," a song written by Michael Nesmith of the Monkees and first recorded by Paul Butterfield in 1966. The Monkees would record their own version on July 25, 1966, with Nesmith on board as producer. Nesmith used some of Los Angeles' top session musicians known as the Wrecking Crew for the song including James Burton, Glen Campbell, Michael Deasy, and Al Casey on guitars; Michael Cohen on piano; Larry Knechtel on organ; Bob West on bass; Hal Blaine on drums; and Jim Gordon and Gary Coleman on percussion. Gordon would play drums on all but one song on *Pretzel Logic*, Blaine would play drums on "Any World (That I'm Welcome To)" from *Katy Lied*, and Coleman would add percussion to "Peg" from *Aja*. The Monkees' version was released on their sophomore LP *More of the Monkees* in 1967 and became a number five hit in Australia in 1968.

Most of the East Coast dates of the tour were sold out, but some of the Midwest shows were not. It was still considered a success and gave fans an opportunity to finally hear the duo behind Steely Dan playing seven of their songs live, five of them for the first time. The stage was set for a Steely Dan tour, and in 1993, Becker and Fagen put together the Steely Dan orchestra, and the first Steely Dan tour in nineteen years commenced in support of Fagen's second solo album, the Becker-produced *Kamakiriad.*

Phase Two: 1993–1994

On Friday August 13, 1993, Steely Dan kicked off their first tour since 1974 at the Palace of Auburn Hills in the Detroit, Michigan, suburb of the same name. The thirty-four date tour kept them on the road until September 26th and introduced an almost entirely new band from the *New York Rock and Soul Revue* tour in 1992, with guitarist Drew Zingg (who was now musical director), saxophonist Cornelius Bumpus, and background vocalists Catherine Russell and Brenda White-King being the only musicians returning. The band included a number of jazz heavy-weights, with former Weather Report drummer Peter Erskine; bassist Tom Barney, who had filled in for Harvey Brooks at some of the New York Nights shows at the Lone Star; keyboardist Warren Bernhardt; Bill Ware III on vibraphone; Diane Garisto on background vocals; and Chris Potter and Bob Sheppard filling out the three saxophone horn section.

The tour almost had three guitarists as well. Jazz virtuoso Pat Metheny had seen one of the New York Nights shows at the Lone Star in the fall of 1991 and was very impressed, so much so that he returned the next week and sat in for "Chain Lightning" even though he was hesitant to play a guitar that wasn't his own. Although he was busy at the Power Station recording studio finishing up his solo album that was due months earlier, on December 2 he returned for a full set, which included "Sign In Stranger," a highlight of the show. When Becker and Fagen were putting together the band for the first Steely Dan tour since 1974, they were very interested in having Metheny join them on the road. Soon after, he heard a radio DJ announce that Steely Dan would be reuniting for an upcoming tour and that he was one of the guitarists.

Metheny elaborated on the situation in a Q&A on his website in 1999. "Well, I was shocked, a little bit pissed, but mostly flattered, but I was touring with Joshua Redman and my own band. Becker called me about doing it. . . . But I realized that if I did it, there would be three guitar players in the band. I would not really have been that comfortable doing it for more than a few nights anyway, it was like a greatest hits of the '70's kind of thing—they wanted it to sound as much as possible like the record versions which would have been difficult for me to feel good about doing."

When interviewed by DJ Mark Drucker on Philadelphia's WMMR, Becker shared his excitement about the tour: "[It] is very flattering to hear there is that faithful group of Dan fans out there and that the music has stood up on its own so well after all these years. We must show our appreciation, and we're looking forward to going out and performing live for our fans." They continued to play "Chain Lightning," "Green Earrings," "Black Friday," "Deacon Blues," "Josie" and "My Old School"; and "Home at Last" was back after its disappearance from the 1992 *Rock and Soul* tour, but for some reason "Pretzel Logic" was dropped from the set. This was, however, a legitimate Steely Dan tour. The tour was comprised of thirty-one classic Steely Dan songs, with the addition of a number of new songs from Fagen's two solo albums and Becker's yet to be released LP *11 Tracks of Whack*, which he would produce together with Fagen. The three-and-a-half hour set list breaks down by album as follows:

Can't Buy a Thrill: "Reelin' in the Years"

Countdown to Ecstasy: "Bodhisattva," "My Old School"

Katy Lied: "Black Friday," "Bad Sneakers" (part of opening instrumental medley), "Chain Lightning"

The Royal Scam: "Green Earrings," "The Royal Scam" (part of opening instrumental medley)

Aja: "Aja" (part of opening instrumental medley), "Deacon Blues," "Home at Last," "Josie," "Peg" (part of opening instrumental medley)

Gaucho: "Babylon Sisters," "Hey Nineteen," "Third World Man"

The Nightfly: "Green Flower Street," "I.G.Y. (What a Beautiful World)"

Kamakiriad: "Countermoon," "Springtime," "Teahouse on the Tracks," "Tomorrow's Girls," "Trans-Island Skyway"

11 Tracks of Whack: "Book of Liars," "Cringemaker," "Girlfriend"

Miscellaneous: "Fall of '92" "FM (No Static at All)," "Our Lawn," "Tuzz's Shadow" (second set instrumental overture)

Each show began with an instrumental medley of three Steely Dan songs. Originally they were "The Royal Scam," "Peg," and "Aja" but after three shows, Fagen thought that the vibe of "Peg" stuck out, so it was replaced by "Bad Sneakers." Becker and Fagen had always wanted an orchestra, and now they had one, and although the intro might have been a bit theatrical, it set the stage for an evening of unparalleled music. They had also wanted to begin the show with an overture since 1977 when Fagen prepared one for the quickly aborted tour to support *Aja*. They had actually attempted one during an earlier show to lead into "Do It Again," but it received such a lackluster response from the audience that it was quickly dropped. After the nearly nine-minute opening that highlighted their eight-piece backing band, Becker and Fagen hit the stage with "Green Earrings." Although there was a bit of a high-gloss sheen on it, it was still as funky as it had been seventeen years earlier.

It was apparent that although it was a Steely Dan tour, it was also an opportunity to promote Fagen's new album, the first recordings that Becker and Fagen had collaborated on since 1980's *Gaucho*, as well as Becker's forthcoming release. Of the eight songs on *Kamakiriad*, five were played during the tour as well as three songs from Becker's *11 Tracks of Whack*, which would be released in September 1994, and two unreleased songs from those sessions entitled "Our Lawn" and "Fall of '92," written by Becker and Fagen. They would also play two songs from 1982's *The Nightfly*, "Green Flower Street" and "I.G.Y. (What a Beautiful World)" The show was constantly evolving, and within the first week, Fagen's "Springtime" and three of Becker's vocal spotlights ("Girlfriend," "Our Lawn," and "Cringemaker") were dropped from the set.

The shows were definitely geared toward their later material, with songs from *Aja* heavily represented with five of its seven songs finding space in the set list. Three from *Gaucho* were also played, as well as the title track from the 1978 film *FM*, a song that Fagen had debuted at a New York Nights show at the Lone Star Roadhouse on January 8, 1993. The Lone Star backup band consisted of Dr. John's guitarist Joe Caro, bassist from *Late Night with David Letterman* and *The Nightfly* Will Lee, Steve Ferrone on drums from Eric Clapton's band, and Leon Pendarvis from the *Saturday Night Live Band* on keyboards.

The second half of the show began with the instrumental "Tuzz's Shadow," from musical director/keyboard player Warren Bernhardt's solo album, *Reflections.* Although the shows were heavily weighted toward later material, they didn't deprive fans of their earlier work. They played one song from their debut LP, two from their sophomore release, three from their fourth album ("Bad Sneakers" was part of the instrumental overture), and two from their fifth ("Royal Scam" was also an instrumental used for the overture). Surprisingly, no songs were played from their third album, *Pretzel Logic*, even though the title track was one of the first Steely Dan songs Fagen chose to play live with the New York Rock and Soul Revue after such a long hiatus. This was likely because Fagen had gotten used to somebody else singing the middle section, and without Michael McDonald or Jeff Young to handle the vocals, he decided to drop the song from the set.

While the *New York Rock and Soul Revue* tour the previous year had been successful, even Becker and Fagen couldn't fathom how popular their first official Steely Dan tour in nineteen years would be. Most of the thirty-four shows sold out within hours, and in some markets, minutes. The Madison Square Garden Shows allegedly were sold out in ten minutes, with a number of ticket scalpers reaping the rewards by reselling tickets for upwards of $250 each. They also sold out the Greek Theatre in record time (seventy-five minutes), the fastest Los Angeles sellout since Paul McCartney's 1989 Forum show. Over the course of the tour, they played to more than 415,000 people and grossed approximately $12 million in ticket sales.

Fagen put it very simply to Chris Whitten when interviewed for a *Los Angeles Times* article about the tour. "I just got comfortable being on stage again. Now we have an opportunity to go out with musicians of our own choosing and we're touring under conditions which can't even be compared with what we were doing then, which was opening for a lot of heavy metal groups. And the technology of touring has become refined and much more comfortable, much more human." Becker was also feeling a thrill from the adulation they were receiving on the road and joked, "it made up for some of the love we never got as kids."

After a break of nearly seven months, the band headed to Japan for eight shows in Osaka, Nagoya, Tokyo, and Fukuoka on April 15, 1994. The band was still the same, as was the set list. The only differences were that "Tomorrow's Girls," "Countermoon," and "Trans-Island Skyway" were dropped from the shows due to time constraints, and "Parker's Band" replaced "Bad Sneakers" in the overture. This was also the tour when Fagen began to do his spoken-word section during the instrumental of "Hey Nineteen," something he, and eventually Becker, would continue to replicate to this day. The tour booklet included a brief "poem" to their Japanese fans that, needless to say, contained the humor of Becker and Fagen. stating "the Japanese people have long admired, the icy and sophisticated rhythmic stylings identified with the group Steely Dan, consisting at various times of whoever was so great as to make the particular session that day. Similarly, we have long ago learned to apprehend the strength and wisdom of the heroic Japanese people, with their land of mountain splendor and gracious temples, mixed in with their awesome balance of trade and majestic currency, the almighty Yen. So it is hoped that tonight may someday be remembered as having been an epic exchange between the cultures of Japan and of Steely Dan, featuring the massive swap of icy rhythmic stylings for ancient wisdom and almighty Yen, in the greatest amounts imaginable."

Steely Dan was on a roll, so on August 19, 1994, they hit the road yet again for twenty-two dates beginning with a show at the Thunderdome in St. Petersburg, Florida with the newly christened Citizen Steely Dan Orchestra, named after the *Citizen Steely Dan* box set released on December 14, 1993. The band was almost identical to the '93 tour of the states and the '94 tour of Japan with two significant changes. Peter Erskine was replaced by ex-Parliament-Funkadelic drummer

A Japanese advertisement for 1993's *Citizen Steely Dan* box set, their newest greatest hits collection, as well as their entire back catalog.

Dennis Chambers, and Drew Zingg was replaced by ex-Blood, Sweat & Tears guitarist Georg "Jojje" Wadenius. Zingg was allegedly quite upset that he was replaced, but his work with Becker and Fagen would be instrumental in securing his next gig as guitarist for Rock and Soul alumnus Boz Scaggs. With Zingg's departure, keyboardist Warren Bernhardt took over as musical director. Chambers had been asked to participate the year before, but since he had other commitments, Erskine was hired. Wadenius had contributed guitar to Fagen's 1988 song "Century's End" for the *Bright Lights Big City* soundtrack and had recently played on every song on *Kamakiriad*, so he was a familiar player and fit into the band easily.

Many critics complained that launching a tour so soon after the last one was a bad idea, but there were quite a few changes in the set list. Fagen's 1981 composition "True Companion" from the film *Heavy Metal* often opened the show, and the opening instrumental medley from the previous year had been reinvented yet again with "The Royal Scam" and "Parker's Band" remaining and "Aja" being dropped to be replaced by "The Fez." The placement of the medley was also changed for certain shows and would be played to open the second half of the show. When they didn't play the overture to open the second set, they began with an instrumental version of "Chain Lightning" that featured a George Bensonish scat solo by Wadenius.

They also dropped Becker's "Book of Liars" and "Fall of '92" and replaced them with "Down in the Bottom" and "Hard Up Case" from his *11 Tracks of Whack* LP. During the first reunited Dan tour in 1993, Fagen's *Kamakiriad* had just come out, and the group initially played five songs from the album. "Springtime" was the first to go, followed by "Tomorrow's Girls," "Countermoon," and "Trans-Island Skyway" during '94's tour of Japan, leaving only "Teahouse on the Tracks." For the *Citizen Steely Dan* tour, they scratched this as well, but added "Tomorrow's Girls" back to the show. They did, however, drop two audience favorites, Fagen's "I.G.Y. (What a Beautiful World)" and Steely Dan's own "Home at Last." The songs that were added were sensational. With "Aja" and "Peg" no longer a part of the instrumental medley, they were fair game for being included in the show in full, which was a significant addition to an already stellar show. Besides these two classics from the *Aja* LP, Becker and Fagen supplemented the set with two songs from *The Royal Scam*, "Sign In Stranger" and "Kid Charlemagne." It had become apparent that if the duo were to continue to perform live, the show would need to evolve each time they set out on the road. The set list breaks down by album as follows:

Can't Buy a Thrill: "Reelin' In the Years"

Countdown to Ecstasy: "Bodhisattva," "My Old School"

Katy Lied: "Black Friday," "Parker's Band" (part of opening instrumental medley), "Chain Lightning" (second set instrumental overture)

The Royal Scam: "Green Earrings," "Kid Charlemagne," "The Royal Scam" (part of opening instrumental medley), "Sign In Stranger," "The Fez" (part of opening instrumental medley)

Aja: "Aja," "Deacon Blues," "Josie," "Peg"

Gaucho: "Babylon Sisters," "Hey Nineteen," "Third World Man"

The Nightfly: "Green Flower Street"

Kamakiriad: "Tomorrow's Girls"

11 Tracks of Whack: "Down in the Bottom," "Hard Up Case"

Miscellaneous: "Fall of '92," "FM (No Static at All)," "Our Lawn," "True Companion" (instrumental overture)

On October 17, 1995, Steely Dan released their first live album, *Alive in America*, culled from numerous shows during the 1993 and 1994 tours. Reviews were mixed, with Greg Kot of *Rolling Stone* giving it one of the worst. His two- out of five-star review stated, "While their 1993-94 reunion tour was well received, *Alive in America* is a pristine-sounding and pointless document of it. The immaculate versions of

The only live Steely Dan album ever officially released was 1995's *Alive in America*.

10 Dan gems from the '70s—plus a forgettable ringer from Becker's recent solo album—do little to expand the listener's understanding of the band's subversive pop and jazz influences. If anything, the Steely Dan auteurs defer too much to their hired guns, who weigh down the bilious lyrics and snappy tunes with noodling fusion style vamps and—yikes!—a drum solo." Chris Willman of *Entertainment Weekly* gave the album a B+ and a more favorable review: "When the Dan quit touring in the mid-'70s, it was almost logical: Becker and Fagen's peculiar rebirth of cool had become so casually decadent that it hardly seemed in character to break a sweat on stage anymore. Their 1993–94 resumption—a big-band revue documented in 11 familiar tracks here—may have been uncharacteristically concessive, but the smooth spite in their subversive neo-Babylonian bop still sounds as contemporary as today's headlines." The album sold relatively well but only peaked at number forty on the *Billboard* 200 chart and number sixty-two in the U.K.

The *Art Crimes* Tour—1996

Steely Dan did not tour in 1995, but after a nearly two-year hiatus, they were back on the road with their longest tour to date, the *Art Crimes* tour beginning on July 5, 1996, twenty-two years since their last concert of the '70s. Over the course of a little over three months, the band played forty-four dates in the U.S., Germany, the Netherlands, Belgium, England, Scotland, Ireland, and Japan. Besides saxophonist Cornelius Bumpus and bass player Tom Barney, the band was completely different and was scaled down to eleven pieces, dropping vibraphonist Bill Ware III and having two rather than three background vocalists. Drummer Dennis Chambers was replaced by Ricky Lawson, an in-demand session player whose pocket playing was just what Steely Dan needed for this tour. Becker had met him in 1992 while producing pianist John Beasley's album *Cauldron*. Beasley, who had also played on Becker's *11 Tracks of Whack*, and guitarist Wayne Krantz, rounded out the rhythm section.

The 1996 *Art Crimes* tour would be the last for both Krantz and Beasley, although Krantz would play on Fagen's 2006 release *Morph the Cat* and would be a member of Fagen's touring band to support the album. Saxophonist Ari Ambrose was added to the horn section, and a trumpet player was brought back into the fold, Michael Leonhart. The son of noted jazz bassist Jay Leonhart, he would play on all but one (the short *Left Bank Holiday* tour of Europe in 2009) of Steely Dan's subsequent tours and would co-produce and play drums, keyboards, percussion, trumpet, flügelhorn, mellophone, mellophonium, trombonium, vibraphone, and add background vocals to Fagen's fourth solo album, 2012's *Sunken Condos*. Two new background vocalists were also added to the band, Michelle Wiley and Leonhart's sister, Carolyn Leonhart-Escoffery. Like her brother, she would also continue to take part in every subsequent Steely Dan tour except for one, 2008's *Think Fast* tour.

Not only were the personnel changes significant, the set list had changed considerably as well. *Can't Buy a Thrill* was represented not only by "Reelin' in the Years" but also by "Do It Again," sporting a jazzier arrangement with new chord changes, a horn section, a key change, and solos from guitarist Wayne Krantz and drummer Ricky Lawson. One other song was played from Steely Dan's debut album, "Midnight Cruiser," sung by original drummer Jim Hodder on the LP and by Walter Becker for this 1996 version. "My Old School" from *Countdown to Ecstasy* was still present, but "Bodhisattva" was dropped. Songs from *Pretzel Logic* had been absent, with the exception of an instrumental version of "Parker's Band" in the medley, since they dropped the title song after 1992's *New York Rock and Soul Revue* tour, but fans were now treated to powerful renditions of "Any Major Dude Will

Tell You," "Rikki Don't Lose That Number," and the only cover song Steely Dan ever committed to wax, Duke Ellington's "East St. Louis Toodle-Oo." Both "Black Friday" and "Chain Lightning" from *Katy Lied* were retired after being a part of shows since Fagen had begun playing Steely Dan songs on stage in 1990, but with the instrumental medley dropped from the show, "Bad Sneakers" was now played in full with vocals, and "Everyone's Gone to the Movies" was added as well, with Becker trading off the lead vocals with Fagen and Fagen adding a rather strange spoken-word section. "Green Earrings" and "Kid Charlemagne" from *The Royal Scam* remained in the set, and "Don't Take Me Alive" was added, the first time the song had ever been performed live. "Deacon Blues," "Josie," and "Peg" from *Aja* were still present, and "Home at Last" was added back to the set, but the title

The cover of 1996's *Art Crimes* tour program.

Becker and Fagen live on stage circa 1996.

track was dropped. In its place, a groovy version of the opening song from that album, "Black Cow," kept the crowds enthralled. "Babylon Sisters" and "Hey Nineteen" from *Gaucho* kept their places in the set, but "Third World Man" was replaced by "Glamour Profession." "FM (No Static at All)" was used as an instrumental backing for the band introductions and as an outro rather than being played in full as it had been on the '93 and '94 tours. Nothing was played from *Kamakiriad*, but Becker sang the reggae-flavored "My Waterloo" from *11 Tracks of Whack*, a song that had not been previously performed. "Green Flower Street" remained in the set, and "I.G.Y. (What a Beautiful World)" was added back to the show as well as one other track from *The Nightfly*, Jerry Leiber and Mike Stoller's "Ruby Baby," originally recorded by the Drifters in 1956 and a 1962 number two hit for Dion.

One thing in particular that made these shows different was the addition of three new songs that the audience had never heard. Only one of these would end up on a future Steely Dan album, "Jack of Speed," but for this version, Becker sang lead vocals. He introduced it as "a song that Donald and I wrote last winter that we're hoping to record in the days and years ahead for the next Steely Dan album whenever that will be finished. And this particular dysphoric ditty is entitled 'Jack of Speed.'" The announcement of the possibility of a new Steely Dan album at any time in the future always brought enthusiastic applause from the audience. The other two songs would have a more dubious fate. Although "Wet Side Story" and "Cash Only Island," which was dropped after a few shows, would be recorded during the *Two Against Nature* sessions, they remain unreleased. It's unfortunate because both songs are groove-heavy tunes, but they were too similar to the songs that ended up on *Two Against Nature*; and since they recorded so many songs during the sessions, some would have to be left on the cutting-room floor, as was often the case. If they ever decide to release expanded versions of any of their albums from the 1970s or 2000s, there would be a wealth of material that any Dan fan would be ecstatic to hear. The set list breaks down by album as follows:

Can't Buy a Thrill: "Do It Again," "Midnight Cruiser," "Reelin' In the Years"

Countdown to Ecstasy: "My Old School"

Pretzel Logic: "Any Major Dude Will Tell You," "East St. Louis Toodle Oo," "Rikki Don't Lose That Number"

Katy Lied: "Bad Sneakers," "Everyone's Gone to the Movies"

The Royal Scam: "Don't Take Me Alive," "Green Earrings," "Kid Charlemagne"

Aja: "Black Cow," "Deacon Blues," "Home at Last," "Josie," "Peg"

Gaucho: "Babylon Sisters," "Glamour Profession," "Hey Nineteen"

The Nightfly: "Green Flower Street," "I.G.Y. (What a Beautiful World)," "Ruby Baby"

11 Tracks of Whack: "My Waterloo"

Miscellaneous: "Cash Only Island," "Jack of Speed," "Wet Side Story," "FM (No Static at All)" (instrumental band intro and closer)

Although Fagen often closed the show by telling fans, "We'll probably be back next year," that wasn't the case. After playing Steely Dan songs live regularly since the 1992 *New York Rock and Soul Revue* tour, Becker and Fagen would take a break for over three years before playing live again in the new millennium.

19

There's a Room in Back with a View of the Sea

Walter Becker's Solo Career

Following the release of *Gaucho*, Steely Dan announced that they were taking a break and going on an indefinite hiatus. Walter Becker retired, for the time being, and moved to the Hawaiian island of Maui to relax, reenergize, and kick his growing narcotic addiction, something he knew he could never do if he stayed in New York. He has stated that had he stayed in New York, he would not have survived. The few years before the move had been tough for Becker beginning with the fatal overdose of his girlfriend, Karen Roberta Stanley, in their apartment on January 30, 1980, a resulting lawsuit, and being hit by a taxicab in Manhattan, resulting in a seven-month stint in a cast.

He eventually released two solo albums, 1994's *11 Tracks of Whack*, co-produced by Fagen, and 2008's *Circus Money*. Becker returned to the music business rather quietly, testing the waters as a producer in 1985 for the band China Crisis's third LP, *Flaunt the Imperfection*. Four years later, he produced the majority of their fifth LP, *Diary of a Hollow Horse*. Production work suited Becker, and he would work on records by Rickie Lee Jones, Michael Franks, Lucy Schwartz, and ten jazz albums in the 1990s.

11 Tracks of Whack

Becker's debut as a solo artist had been simmering for a while. He had been thinking of recording an album, but once he began working with Fagen, first on the *New York Rock and Soul Revue* tour and then as producer on his second solo album *Kamakiriad*, his project was put on the back burner. But there was material written. When Becker and Fagen first toured again as Steely Dan in 1993, three songs from *11 Tracks of Whack*, "Book of Liars," "Cringemaker," and "Girlfriend," were performed as well as two unreleased songs, "Our Lawn" and "Fall of '92," which was written by Becker and Fagen. When they returned to the road in 1994, Becker's vocal spotlights were "Down in the Bottom" and "Hard Up Case."

As early as May 1993, Becker had mentioned that once Fagen was finished with *Kamakiriad*, he would be playing a role on Becker's solo debut, although

Becker wasn't sure in what capacity. Once Becker released a solo LP, it made it a little easier for listeners to hear some of the differences between the two Steely Dan songwriters and what each brought to the table when collaborating. Fagen has admitted that he's a bit more of an optimist and Becker more of a realist, and although they both write with tongue firmly in cheek, Becker's lyrics tend to be darker and more sarcastic. Speaking of the lyrical content on the album, Becker explained in a 1994 interview with the *Los Angeles Times*, "I'm not as depressed as I was at the time, in the '70s and early '80s. But those are still the interesting things to write about, let's face it. That hasn't changed that much."

Harmonically, however, Fagen is more sophisticated. Becker had stated in the past that Steely Dan songs would often start with a germ of a musical idea from Fagen that would then be worked on together. It's obvious that many Steely Dan compositions were initially started on the piano, leading to many captivating chord progressions, but Fagen believed that Becker would often do something weirder than he would, harmonically speaking, and would say in a 1993 interview with *The Independent*, "nobody can make transitions from chord to chord like Walter."

Becker originally intended to record an instrumental album, since he was still not very comfortable as a lead singer. But he realized that he would be able to express more with lyrics and decided to take up the challenge. His vocal delivery is perfect for the songs, but it is an acquired taste, and some fans and critics expecting Steely Dan were let down. He initially wrote a number of songs with longtime Steely Dan guitarist Dean Parks, and while Parks ended up playing on the record, only one collaboration, "Cringemaker," made the final cut. He also attempted to record the entire album with drummer Ben Perowsky, bassist Fima Ephron, and guitarist Adam Rogers of Lost Tribe, the band he had produced the previous year,

along with Parks and keyboard player John Beasley, whom Becker had produced and who would play on Steely Dan's 1996 *Art Crimes* tour. Lost Tribe's contributions would only be heard on three songs once Becker decided to use his original demos as the basis for the other nine tracks, where he plays bass and lead guitar.

He also wrote some songs with Fagen including "Three Sisters Shaking," but none of these appeared on the final album. Without Fagen as a true writing partner for the album, Becker decided to use a minimalist approach and focus on the melody and bass

Becker released a promotional sampler CD to attract media interest before his debut album was released.

rather than a complex set of chord progressions, something he feared might be "irrelevant in the musical context of the day." When Fagen joined the project as co-producer, Becker had over twenty-five songs, or pieces of songs, and was at his wit's end. Fagen helped his partner go through the material and pick the best ones. He also played keyboards and wrote the horn and rhythm arrangements. Becker's partner was also responsible for getting him a record deal before he had even started shopping his material. While Fagen was working with Steely Dan manager, and Giant Records label head, Irving Azoff on the *New York Rock and Soul Revue: Live at the Beacon* LP, he played him some of Becker's demos, and Azoff signed him to the label on the spot. Many critics found it strange that Becker would embark on a solo career at the age of forty-four. Speaking to Christopher Hoard of *Jazziz*, he explained his reasoning behind being a solo artist. "I suppose the one thing that's driven me into having a solo career . . . is that it affords me the most control over my time and where I spend it. That at this stage in my life is as important a consideration as anything."

The Songs

The album begins with "Down in the Bottom," a straightforward rock tune based on a friend's relationship with a woman that wasn't completely equal, his friend never fully embracing their situation. The lyrics have a sense of desperation and flow beautifully, but the production is stiff and mechanical, with a snare drum that is mixed far too loudly. Becker does, however, play some exquisite lead guitar, and the song would take on a new life when played live on Steely Dan's 1994 tour.

The next track, "Junkie Girl," is a touching song about Becker's girlfriend,

Karen Stanley, who died of an overdose in their apartment in 1980. The lyrics follow Becker's train of thought through his addiction along with Stanley, his wish to die with her, and finally his realization that although he misses her, he's glad that he's alive and sober. The song includes one of the best choruses on the album, but unfortunately, this guitar-driven tune isn't nearly as dynamic as it would have been had Becker used a live drummer. Becker's solo over a complicated set of chords that only appear for that section sounds fantastic, but the backing track doesn't mimic his passion.

The cover for Becker's debut solo album 1994's *11 Tracks of Whack* co-produced with Fagen.

The third track, "Surf and/or Die," is the first with the Lost Tribe rhythm section, and from the first note it jumps out of the speakers, making one wonder why Becker had been using a drum machine up to this point. It grooves harder than anything so far, telling a true story of an acquaintance who had died in a hang-gliding accident. At his memorial service, a group of monks spoke about life, death, and the afterlife and inspired Becker to write the song. His wife at the time, Elinor, invited them to Becker's studio to bless it, and he recorded them chanting and used it during sections of the song.

"Book of Liars" is a Steely Danish shuffle with imaginative lyrics about a woman who can't tell the truth, a moving saxophone solo by Bob Sheppard, and an odd synthesized electric piano solo that doesn't really fit. One only needs to listen to the live version from Steely Dan's 1995 release *Alive in America* to hear the potential of this underrated composition.

The rhythm section from Lost Tribe returns for "Lucky Henry," an extremely intricate tune that continuously keeps the listener on the edge of his/her seat. The change from the frantic feel of the verse to the swinging beat of the chorus is extremely effective and has two disparate guitar solos, the first by Dean Parks and the second by Adam Rogers, possibly the closest to jazz fusion of any Steely Dan-related song.

"Hard Up Case" provides a good example of how programmed drums could work better than a live drummer. The groove is dark and hard and with a reggaeish horn section and deep bass line, grooves along with a threatening air. Becker turns in a menacing guitar solo over moody synthesizers, and a sweet female background vocal adds depth to this ominous-sounding tune about a man whose bad habits have caused his partner to call it quits. It does have a Steely Dan-like twist at the end when the woman gets involved with another man with similar problems to her ex. It was performed well on the 1994 Steely Dan tour.

The intro to "Cringemaker" sounds surprisingly similar to "Cousin Dupree" from 2000's *Two Against Nature*. Becker co-wrote the song with guitarist Dean Parks and was trying to recreate the sound of an old soul record, with a typical tale of a romance gone wrong after marriage. The female background vocals are also strikingly similar to "Cousin Dupree," but the production doesn't breathe, and although Becker might have been thinking of Slim Harpo's "I'm a King Bee" when attempting a single-note solo, it never reaches the peak he intended. The chord progression of the verse is clever, but not enough to save the song.

"Girlfriend" sounds incredibly dated, with a drum sound that was out of fashion when it was recorded. It's unfortunate because the melody and chord changes are arguably the most like a Steely Dan song on the album. The song's jaunty groove is another use of a joyful-sounding song with depressing lyrics. In this case, the narrator's girlfriend has left him, so he spends his time watching television and slowly losing his grip on reality. Bob Sheppard's bass clarinet solo projects that image flawlessly along with the multiple voices panned around the stereo spectrum repeating the words, "Hide in here."

"My Waterloo" is a true reggae song with a programmed side stick beat, a keyboard skank, wah-wah guitar, and a despondent lyric about loneliness that mentions Napoleon, as did "Pretzel Logic" twenty years earlier. But the song doesn't really go anywhere, and it's strange that it was played during 1996's *Art Crimes* tour as one of Becker's vocal spotlights.

Another shuffle dying for a live band, "This Moody Bastard" meanders aimlessly, and although the lyrics about a depressed man reminiscing about his younger days are more autobiographical than most Becker songs, the resulting track is weak. The chorus melody is the most interesting part of the song, but once again due to the production, the song sounds mechanized and cold, although Bob Sheppard's clarinet solo is a nice touch.

The third and final song with Lost Tribe, "Hat Too Flat" is the oddest-sounding track on the record, with the weirdest lyrics. A song about a group of aliens trying to assimilate on earth, it features an angular bass line through an envelope filter and a reggae drum groove, but the whole thing doesn't hold together, sounding more like an experiment than a fully realized song.

The album closes with the shortest song, Becker's heartfelt paean to his son Kawaii. Even when composing a song about his son, Becker is still Becker, writing about things that Kawaii has done wrong and gotten in trouble for, while explaining that nobody could possibly love him as much as he does. The song has a lilting country feel and effective female background vocals, but would have benefited from a live drummer.

The Japanese release included one additional song that should have been included on every release, "Medical Science." It's one of the funkiest tunes recorded during the sessions, and Becker's bass line grooves with the programmed drums better than any other song from *11 Tracks of Whack*, with a hooky chorus and interesting chord changes during the verse. The synthesizer and dissonant guitar parts lend a spooky quality to the track, and although Becker's vocals are laid back, you can hear the passion in his voice as he sings about drug addicts and the lives that they lead.

Circus Money

For his second solo album, 2008's *Circus Money*, Becker took a very different approach than he had for 1994's *11 Tracks of Whack*. He recruited Larry Klein to produce the record and wrote the entire album with him except for the title track. Klein began his career as a bass player performing with jazz artists Freddie Hubbard, Joe Henderson, Wayne Shorter, and Bobby McFerrin, as well as pop and rock artists Bob Dylan, Robbie Robertson, Peter Gabriel, Don Henley, Lindsey Buckingham, Randy Newman, Shawn Colvin, and Tracy Chapman. He met Joni Mitchell after playing bass on her *Wild Things Run Fast* album, and the two were married from 1982 until 1994. He produced a number of records for her including two Grammy winners, *Turbulent Indigo* and *Both Sides Now*, and also won a Grammy for Herbie Hancock's *River: The Joni Letters*, a tribute album featuring covers of Mitchell's compositions.

Becker had been a big fan of Jamaican music for years and had amassed a huge collection of records featuring the various genres from the island. He originally wanted to use authentic Jamaican rhythms and overdub music and lyrics on top, but the master tapes for many of the songs he wanted to use couldn't be located, so the idea was abandoned. Becker and Klein began writing for the album in 2005, and although Klein was originally apprehensive about collaborating with Becker due to his fear that he couldn't rise to the occasion, their partnership resulted in some incredible songs.

The rhythm section was comprised of current and future Steely Dan musicians, including Keith Carlock on drums; guitarists Jon Herington and Dean Parks; keyboard players Ted Baker and Jim Beard; saxophonists Chris Potter and Roger Rosenberg; percussionist Gordon Gottlieb; and background vocalists Carolyn Leonhart, Cindy Mizelle, and Tawatha Agee. When they began work on the album, Becker had asked Klein to play bass, but Klein convinced Becker to take care of the job himself since it was his solo album. Becker would play on every song except the title track, on which Klein would play.

Becker's vocals were once again a concern, but his delivery works perfectly for the material. Becker elaborated in a 2008 interview with the *Los Angeles Times*, "The only real strength is that I can sing things that I would not be able to explain to other people how to sing. And I can manifest the intention of the lyrics in some way, without having to be taken aback or angered or disgusted as any normal human being would be with most of the lyrics that Larry and I have written." It had a lot to do with Klein instructing Becker to sing softly rather than belt out the songs, something Becker never thought of doing.

They demoed the material using a long-discontinued sequencer that Becker still favored, Vision by Opcode, as well as a more recent sequencing program, Propellerhead's Reason, at Klein's Market Street Studio in Santa Monica. Both Becker and Klein noted that the songs changed significantly once they started working with a live band. The record was recorded extremely quickly due to Becker's more relaxed approach to recording that he had since adopted. The basic tracks were recorded live without a click track to 24-track analog tape at Avatar Studios in New York in a week and a half before vocals and overdubs were tracked at Market Street Studio. Becker's attitude was quite different than the Steely Dan days. In an interview with *Sound on Sound* magazine, he explained how

A poster for *Circus Money* that included some incredibly positive reviews.

his view on studio work had changed. "The overdubs are just for what they call sweetening. That was really important to me. To tell you the truth, I hate doing overdubs, it bores me to tears. My attention span is not there anymore to bang away at things endlessly."

Overall, the album is far superior to Becker's solo debut, with a more organic sound and top-notch playing by all of the musicians involved. Although there's a reggae lilt to the album, the material doesn't use the myriad clichés expected when one thinks of Jamaican music. The keyboards and guitars add a depth to the tracks and are extremely atmospheric, enabling the songs to breathe. Female background vocals are also used to great effect on every song and balance Becker's husky yet soulful voice. Harmonically, there are plenty of twists and turns to keep any Steely Dan Fan pleased. The title of the album comes from a comedy skit about Mahatma Gandhi entitled "The Hip Gan" by Lord Richard Buckley, a humorist who in the 1940s and 1950s created a character that was part English royalty, part hipster and anticipated aspects of the Beat Generation sensibility.

The Songs

The album opens with "Door Number Two," a sparsely arranged song that tackles a topic familiar to Steely Dan, gambling and Las Vegas. The groove is tight, with a fine tenor saxophone solo by Chris Potter and some delightful piano playing by Jim Beard on top of Ted Baker's rhythmic keyboard skank.

"Downtown Canon" fades in with some spacey keyboards and a drum machine until Keith Carlock plays a one-beat roll before launching into a full-on reggae groove. The blend of Ted Baker's Fender Rhodes electric piano, Hammond B3 organ played by Larry Goldings, and rhythm guitars by Jon Herington and Dean Parks creates the perfect vibe for a song about a New York City romance that begins with great expectations but ends in shambles. The song was edited and released as a digital single with a demo of the next song as the B-side.

The reggae influence has been apparent on the album up to this point, but "Bob Is Not Your Uncle Anymore" is the first full-blown reggae song. It even has a dub-section, delayed keyboards, guitar and keyboard skanks, wah-wah guitar, and a bass line that doesn't quit. The term "Bob's your uncle" is a British saying that infers that things are all right, but the lyrics indicate that all that could go wrong for the narrator has.

"Upside Looking Down" is a slow ballad based on an old song idea by Becker that describes a character looking back on his drug-addled life from his new perspective as a sober individual. Although it's told in the second person, it is most certainly autobiographical. Becker is in rare vocal form, singing in falsetto along with the female background vocalists on certain sections, and Dean Parks's guitar solo is tender and heartfelt.

"Paging Audrey" was also based on a song fragment Becker had long before the sessions for *Circus Money* began and was written on keyboard. This sensitive song tells the tale of a man trying to reach out to a lover who has practically vanished, possibly due to drug addiction. Becker elaborated in a 2008 interview with the *Los Angeles Times*, "It's the idea of what happens to people that disappear in various ways. You still relate to them as if they were present in ways that they may not actually be." His personal experience led him to believe that even though certain people might not exist in your day-to-day life, they could still exist in your mind. The song begins with a haunting piano played by Jim Beard, backed by Ted Baker on Fender Rhodes electric piano before the band enters with a slow jam groove. The chorus is especially poignant, with the entire band, as well as the vocalists, playing the melody while Beard adds airy piano on top, Baker dreamy Fender Rhodes, and Herington delay-infused guitar. Chris Potter takes two solos, one in the middle and one on the outro, which perfectly encapsulate the feelings of the narrator.

The title track is the only song that Becker doesn't play bass on and the only one that he wrote by himself. The New Orleans–style groove is handled with aplomb by Carlock, with Klein laying down a simple bass groove. The song is arresting, with an extremely discordant Wurlitzer electric piano part played by Beard, with piano flourishes by Baker that punctuate the uneasiness created by the groove. Potter's tenor saxophone solo is somewhat manic, and Baker adds some eerie, yet bluesy, piano fills on the fade-out. Becker has stated that he used the idea of the circus as a metaphor for life.

After "Circus Money," the sound of a calliope seems right at home for the introduction of another reggae groover, "Selfish Gene." The song is one of the simpler ones but features a stinging guitar solo by Becker, a Steely Dan-like chord progression at the ends of the verses, a hooky chorus, and a bridge sung by Klein's wife, Luciana Souza. The main character is a typical self-absorbed, L.A. type that Becker compared to Jive Miguel from "Glamour Profession."

"Do You Remember the Name" keeps the reggae flavor flowing for this story of a home wrecker who is quick to leave once she loses interest. A dazzling multi-guitar section by Herington sits alongside the skanks of keyboard players Beard and Henry Hey perfectly. The song is full of reggae devices including a rhythm breakdown, doubled bass and guitar riffs, delayed guitars, and a fabulous slide part played by Herington.

The characters of the next song have been explored many times before by Steely Dan: a desperate, drunken individual looking for a good

Becker released a digital single of the radio edit of "Downtown Canon" along with the demo for "Bob Is Not Your Uncle Anymore."

time and finding it with a girl who is just "Somebody's Saturday Night." The groove is a shuffle with some reggae influence layered on top. It's a jaunty tune for such a tale of debauchery, nothing new for Becker. Luciana Souza plays a Brazilian hand frame drum similar to a tambourine called a Pandeiro, and Becker handles the lead guitar, contributing a fiery, yet understated, solo.

The intro to "Darkling Down" is incredibly spacey, with a heavily delayed and phased Fender Rhodes electric piano playing a series of chords before the groove kicks in with a doubled bass and guitar line, a reggae keyboard skank by Baker, and Larry Golding's organ. The chorus is big, with the background vocalists in fine form before Becker rips into another solo over a series of Steely Dan-like chord changes. Always a voracious reader, Becker took the title from a 1749 poem, "The Vanity of Human Wishes" by Samuel Johnson, but the story is actually about the characters Becker met during myriad drug runs he made in the past. The lyrics are extremely poetic, and one can almost feel the depravity of the numerous places and people visited in the song.

"God's Eye View" once again begins with some lush Fender Rhodes electric piano before launching into a hard reggae groove with a bubbling bass line, skanking keyboards, and a powerful call-and-response between background vocalists Sweet Pea Atkinson and Sir Harry Bowens from Was (Not Was) and Becker. The song actually incorporates nine background vocalists, with various singers taking different roles as Becker delivers some extremely oblique lyrics. Roger Rosenberg's bass clarinet is sultry yet disturbing and adds a non-reggaeish element to what is basically a reggae song.

The last song on the album, "Three Picture Deal," begins with a moving piano intro by Jim Beard before the band kicks into this very Steely Dan-like song about a musician glomming onto his actress girlfriend's popularity. The verse melody is similar to "What a Shame About Me" from *Two Against Nature*, but the chorus is a completely different animal, with a disco groove and sultry female background vocals. Roger Rosenberg's baritone saxophone accents are a nice touch, Jon Herington plays a short but sweet, solo, and Ted Baker's organ adds some tasty blues flourishes on the outro.

The U.K. release of the album had a bonus track, "Dark Horse Dub." This reggae groove–based song about gambling is slathered in reverb, giving it a huge sound. The haunting baritone sax and distorted guitar during the verse opens up into a cheery-sounding baritone and soprano sax melody that incorporates vocals into the end of the section. The solo is an interesting combination of baritone saxophone and trombone, something that would have been nice to hear on the album proper.

20

It's the Motion in the Music

Becker and Fagen as Session Musicians, Producers, and Songwriters

Before Donald Fagen and Walter Becker were the driving force behind Steely Dan, they played on a number of sessions for several diverse artists, worked as arrangers, and wrote songs for other singers and musicians. Additionally, they would become producers in their own right and sit behind the mixing desk for a multitude of different sessions. Even after Steely Dan was formed, the duo would find time to contribute to other artists' records both together and separately. The results were not always what one would expect; therefore, their extracurricular activities in the music business are worth a bit of exploration.

Terence Boylan

Not only was Bard College the setting for Becker and Fagen's first meeting, it was also the place where the group would meet singer-songwriter Terence Boylan, the man who would hire the duo for their first studio work. Boylan began his music career in the late 1950s in Buffalo, New York. At the age of twelve, his band, the PreTeens, performed a song he wrote when he was eleven called "Playing Hard to Get" on WBNY's Buffalo Bob's Radio Show. The Buddy Holly-esque tune showed a young songwriter at work, and at age fourteen, he traveled to Greenwich Village and had a chance encounter with Bob Dylan. After spending time with Dylan and folk singer Ramblin' Jack Elliot, he returned to Buffalo and began performing in many of that city's most popular coffee-houses, including the Limelight and the Lower Level, as well as the Bell, Book and Candle, in nearby Ontario.

Boylan attended Bard College and formed a band with his older brother John, the Ginger Men, playing gigs in Greenwich Village with both the band and as a solo artist. The Night Owl Café, the Gaslight Café, the Village Gate, and Gerde's Folk City became his stomping grounds, and they shared the stage with groups such as the Flying Machine, led by James Taylor, and the Lovin' Spoonful. The Ginger Men's approach was to combine their love of folk and blues with contemporary rock 'n' roll, as so many American bands were doing at the time, but their spin was different. They signed a deal with Kama Sutra records and recorded six songs, but nothing would come of it.

Things changed for Boylan when *New York Times* critic Robert Shelton gave him a brief yet glowing mention following an appearance at the Village Gate, and the record companies showed interest in him as a solo artist. Soon after, Boylan landed a solo contract with MGM/Verve Records, but he decided to first make an experimental "rock meets theatre" album with his brother John and notable session musicians Larry Coryell, Eric Gale, Chuck Rainey, Herb Lovelle, Chuck Israels, Paul Griffin, Buddy Saltzman, Cat Mother, the All Night News Boys' drummer Michael Equine, and the Lovin' Spoonful's guitarist Zal Yanovsky. A number of these musicians would play a significant role in the recording of Steely Dan's albums within a few years. Rather than release the album as a Terence and John Boylan record, they adopted the moniker the Appletree Theatre, and the resulting LP, *Playback*, recorded in 1967 and released in 1968, was a favorite among musicians including John Lennon, who at the time stated it was one of his preferred new albums. The LP garnered critical praise, yet it didn't find a mass audience and would remain a cult classic.

After the release of *Playback*, Boylan, affectionately known as Boona, returned to Bard College and assembled the group of musicians that he would use to record his solo debut for Verve Forecast, *Alias Boona*, at New York City's Hit Factory. The LP featured three different drummers with varying degrees of studio experience. Herb Lovelle had been a professional drummer since the late '40s, playing with jazz musicians Hot Lips Page, Earl "Fatha" Hines, Teddy Wilson, Clark Terry, Erroll Garner, and others. He easily adapted to the current music scene and began playing more R&B in the late '50s, becoming a popular session musician, playing on records by Lightnin' Hopkins, Muddy Waters, Big Joe Turner, and later Bob Dylan, John Denver, B. B. King, and the Monkees, and would play drums on Steely Dan's *The Royal Scam*, although none of his tracks made the final cut. Terence Boylan produced the album and contributed guitar and vocals. He had already recorded *Playback* the year before, so he had a bit of experience in the studio; the only musicians who had never recorded an album were Walter Becker, on bass and guitar, and Donald Fagen (credited as Don Fagen), on piano and organ. They also were interested in getting a couple of their songs on the album. They wanted him to record "Who Got the Credit" and "Stone Piano," and Boylan was definitely interested. They recorded one and got halfway through the other when his label decided that he needed to rethink his album. Boylan recalled that Verve believed that due to the resurgence of the singer-songwriter, he should make an album that had more in common with James Taylor than the Band. Although Boylan understood the sentiment, he still wanted to make an album that he would be satisfied with.

The opening song on the album was Boylan's spin on his old mentor Bob Dylan's "Subterranean Homesick Blues." Dylan was so fond of *Playback* that he brought it to the attention of manager Albert Grossman. They discussed the idea of recording his sophomore LP in Woodstock, New York, where both Dylan and Grossman resided, but Boylan was already heading to the West Coast to rejoin his brother John, who had been producing some of the brightest new stars on the Los

Angeles music scene. John Boylan had already produced Rick Nelson, the Association, and the Dillards, but one of his greatest accomplishments was putting together the backing band for an artist he was managing at the time, Linda Ronstadt. The four musicians he handpicked were Don Henley, Glenn Frey, Randy Meisner, and Bernie Leadon. Within a year, they would leave Ronstadt to form the Eagles and go on to sell more records than any other American group in history. John Boylan would also co-produce Boston's debut album with guitarist and songwriter Tom Scholz. The record sold so well that he was offered the position of Vice President, West Coast for Epic Records, which he accepted.

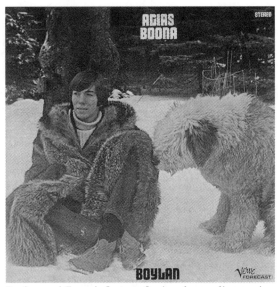

Becker and Fagen's first professional recording session was for Terence Boylan's 1969 LP *Alias Boona*, recorded at the Hit Factory in New York City.

When Terence Boylan relocated to Los Angeles, he decided to apprentice as a production assistant for John's Great Eastern Gramophone Company and assisted on several tours with the company's recording artists. After years behind the scenes in the music business, Boylan was signed to David Geffen's Asylum Records. He was in good company with label mates Joni Mitchell, Warren Zevon, the Eagles, John David Souther, and Tom Waits. He would once again cross paths with Fagen, who would play piano on two songs on his 1977 eponymous LP, "Don't Hang Up Those Dancing Shoes" and "Shame." Don Henley and Timothy B. Schmit from the Eagles were also involved as well as a number of top session musicians who had worked with Steely Dan including Jim Gordon, Jeff Porcaro, Chuck Rainey, Victor Feldman, Dean Parks, John Klemmer, Wilton Felder, David Paich, and Ben Benay. Recorded in Los Angeles at the Record Plant and Westlake Audio, the album was jazz-tinged rock, not unlike Steely Dan's catalog, and went to number one on the *Billboard* National Breakout list the week it was released. Hailed by critics, it was the most added album at radio stations for five straight weeks. By year's end, it would find itself on many end-of-the-year top ten lists in the U.S. and abroad. This led British singer Ian Matthews to cover two of the songs for his album *Stealin' Home*, and his version of "Shake It" would reach number thirteen on the *Billboard* Hot 100 chart in 1979.

A fifty-city tour with the Cate Brothers, Bonnie Raitt, and Little Feat followed to promote the album. When it was completed, Boylan found himself back on the East Coast recording the follow-up to his eponymous sophomore LP in Bearsville Studios in Woodstock. While recording at the studio founded by Albert Grossman, Boylan ended up completing two albums. One was basically a more mature jazz-rock fusion that picked up where his last album had left off, but the other was a rougher, harder-edged take on the current punk rock scene. The two albums couldn't be more different, but at the last minute it was decided to combine songs from each to create a single LP entitled *Suzy*. Fagen didn't play on this record, but once again more musicians from the Steely Dan stable took part in the proceedings, including former Dan guitarist Jeff Baxter, Larry Carlton, Ben Benay, Victor Feldman, Jim Gordon, Jay Graydon, Ed Greene, and Michael Omartian. Eagles Don Henley, Timothy B. Schmit, and Don Felder took part in the sessions, and even Chevy Chase, former drummer for Becker and Fagen's band the Leather Canary, got in on the act, playing Fender Rhodes on one song.

The reviews were once again excellent, but radio programmers were confused as to how to program the album and radio airplay fell short. Without this, the sales were disappointing and would mark the end of what should have been an illustrious career. Although he was compared to Jackson Browne, Warren Zevon, and James Taylor, Boylan would never have the success that his contemporaries did, even with fabulous reviews and the backing of a major label like Asylum. His mature songwriting, fresh lyrics, and impeccable production didn't seem to be enough in the 1970s to propel him to stardom.

Boylan continued to write and record songs for film soundtracks and other artists, and a few new compositions were released in 1999 on the CD compilation *Terence Boylan (A Retrospective)*, which paired the best material from his second and third albums along with the new material. He also owns his own record label, Spinnaker Records, and book publishing company, the River Press, and is Executive Director of the Boylan Foundation for International Medical Research, a nonprofit organization that supports biomedical research and international scientist exchange fellowships.

Jay and the Americans

Kenny Vance of Jay and the Americans played a significant role in the early Brooklyn years of the Steely Dan story. Through him the songwriting team met their future producer Gary Katz as well as engineer Elliot Scheiner. It is an understatement that without Vance the future of Becker and Fagen in the music business was dubious at best.

Although Vance felt that their songs were original and signed them to a publishing contract, the duo had a hard time placing any songs due to their odd lyrics and different sound. They were barely scraping by, so Vance hired them as string and horn arrangers for Jay and the Americans' 1969 LP *Sands of Time*, where they were credited as "You know who you are . . . thanks." Becker and Fagen were talented songwriters and musicians but hadn't done any instrumental arrangements. So they picked up a few books on arranging and gleaned a basic understanding of something that they intrinsically already knew.

They were also offered a job in Jay and the Americans' road band, but were hesitant to accept. While visiting his parents in Cleveland, Ohio, Fagen saw Jay and the Americans on *The Tonight Show*. His parents were so impressed with the fact that their son had been offered a job with a working band that was performing on television that when he returned to Brooklyn, he and Becker decided to take the job. Soon after, the duo were on the road providing bass and keyboards for the singing group and would play and arrange strings and horns for their two 1970 releases, *Wax Museum* and *Capture the Moment*.

Despite the duo's joking about their time on the oldies circuit, there were moments that they actually enjoyed. Not only did they get to tour the East Coast, they played Madison Square Garden, traveled to Florida in the wintertime, opened for the Four Seasons, and got paid in cash; not a bad situation for a fresh college graduate and a dropout.

Rather than use their real names, the duo adopted the stage names Tristan Fabriani and Gus Mahler. They would also use the nom de plume Tristan Fabriani on their 1972 debut LP *Can't Buy a Thrill*, as the writer of the liner notes. Jay Black, however, had a different pseudonym for the duo, dubbing them "the Manson and Starkweather of Rock."

Becker noted that Kenny Vance, who had gotten them the gig, was one of the more forward-thinking members of the Americans and had realized that the '60s had happened. In Becker's opinion, Jay Black was still living as if things were still like *Blackboard Jungle*, so to have these two intellectual smart-asses in the band must have been strange. Becker did, however, note that he was tolerant and that he actually liked him quite a bit. Becker elaborated in a 1995 interview with *MOJO* magazine, "Some of Jay's friends were the same guys from *Goodfellas* . . . he was married to the niece of one of the guys, which I think was a survival move: he was levering himself up into a position where he could be forgiven some debts. We would see them once in a while around the office. Some guys would come in and say, 'Hey Jay! Whyn't you get these guys to take a fuckin' haircut?' Or they'd come backstage after the show and say, 'Hey Jay, your voice sounded beautiful, but that drum, that fuckin' drum's givin' me a headache! Can you tell 'em to turn down that fuckin' drum?!'" Although Jay Black recognized their talent, in an interview in the '70s he remembered them as "cocksuckers who I may kick in the ass next time I see them."

Linda Hoover

If ever released, Linda Hoover's LP would indeed be a treat for fans of Steely Dan. Not only did Gary Katz produce it, Becker, Fagen, and Denny Dias played on it, and Becker and Fagen contributed five of the eleven songs recorded. Hoover was born May 1, 1951, in Oakland, New Jersey, to a musical family and was the youngest of three children. Her older brother Larry learned how to play keyboards and guitar, started to write songs, and taught his sister a few guitar chords, but formal study didn't interest her, so she honed her skills by learning songs by Bob Dylan and Janis Ian.

She sang in her school chorus and church choir and began performing at private parties, weddings, school concerts, and coffeehouses. She regularly won her high school talent contests at Indian Hills High School, and each year she would move on to the regional Ramsey Talent Show, where she would consistently win best soloist.

After winning the Ramsey Talent show in her sophomore year, she was approached by a woman who was interested in managing her. She recommended vocal coach Adrienne Angel in Manhattan, who was coaching a number of Broadway and television performers including Cher, Bette Midler, and Bernadette Peters, in order to assess Hoover's abilities. She had one lesson with her where she learned more about breath control, but overall she recommended that she continue on the path she was following.

Although they never signed the management deal, the same woman set up a meeting with Bobby Darin's manager Ed Burton, who ran Darin's TM Music Company, and Gary Katz, who was doing A&R work at the time using his pseudonym Gary Kannon. Although her father liked Ed Burton, a businessman in a suit, he did not feel the same way about Katz and his beatnik style. Katz soon introduced her to Bobby Darin in a hotel suite near the Copacabana in Manhattan, where she auditioned with a song that was written by her brother Larry. Nothing transpired after this meeting, but Katz eventually found somebody interested in the demo recording he had produced of Hoover: Morris Levy at Roulette Records. Hoover's father didn't trust Levy and forbade Linda from having anything to do with Levy, Roulette Records, or Gary Katz.

After graduation, Hoover moved to Florida with her parents and attended Jacksonville University to study drama, but rarely went to class. She was still in touch with Katz, and she confided in him that she could only think of one thing, making music. He promised that if she came back to New York, he would continue to shop for a deal. Hoover elaborated on the situation, "I informed my parents that I was going to go back up north to record an album with Gary Katz, which did not go over well. My mother says that she felt like I was heading into the lion's den to be eaten alive, but I would not be deterred from the dream. During the Christmas holiday of 1969 I found a ride back up north and connected with Gary again." Katz didn't actually get her a record deal when she returned; he signed her to Gary Katz Productions in the office of AVCO Embassy, where he worked as an A&R rep.

At the time, Hoover had no manager or lawyer, and although she was the artist, she had little say in the studio. At times it could be a difficult situation to be in at the age of nineteen. "I was a sensitive young woman with zero input or blessing from my parents, no management, no representation, instructors, or anyone there to honestly help me achieve what I needed to achieve. I asked Gary on several occasions if I should have a manager and his answer was always the same. 'It was too soon for management.' I did not have a manager or a lawyer I could trust, so I put my trust in all of these guys. Like a lot of young artists, I just wanted to sing, play, write and record. That was all I was concerned with at the time. I was living in Wayne, New Jersey with friends and took the bus into Manhattan. Gary met me at Port Authority as he had always done during my high school years and carried my guitar for me to the Brill Building offices of Jay and the Americans' JATA Music."

In the summer of 1970, Becker and Fagen, along with Denny Dias, entered Studio B at Advantage Sound Studio on 54th Street and Eighth Avenue in Manhattan during off hours to begin work on the LP. Jeff Baxter had stated that he worked on the album as well, but Hoover denies this: "I wish that Jeff had been involved with that album because he always treated me well. It probably would have changed the whole dynamic for me."

Hoover first met Becker and Fagen at the JATA office in the Brill Building and was impressed by their musicianship and found them friendly. "I thought they were both adorable and very cool. I did not understand at the time the relationship Donald and Walter had with JATA and Kenny Vance. I was introduced to Kenny Vance in the hallway outside of the offices, and then to Becker and Fagen where they were work-

Becker and Fagen not only contributed nearly half of the songs for Linda Hoover's unreleased album, but played on the sessions along with future Steely Dan guitarist Denny Dias.   *Courtesy of Linda Hoover*

ing next door to the main offices in a tiny room with a piano. I was so excited and happy and I liked them all very much. Walter was actually the more friendly and engaging one at first. Donald seemed more shy and reserved. It was wonderful to watch the way Donald and Walter interacted. They were the real thing and I felt honored to be working with them. I loved Donald's soft, soulful vocals, the agility of his voice. And the way he played those keys was amazing. I was not familiar with many of the jazz chords he played and they were so much more interesting and pleasing than the simple major and minor chords I usually played. I had never met anyone who could write like those two. Donald Fagen was most complimentary and helpful and never said an unkind thing to me the entire time we worked together. To this day I am a Steely Dan fan."

Not only did the duo play bass and keyboards on the album, they also contrib-uted five songs. The first song that was written especially for Hoover was "I Mean to Shine." They all held it in such high regard that it was a top contender for the title of the album. Unfortunately for Hoover, Katz, Becker, and Fagen headed to Los Angeles during the sessions, and the song was given to Barbra Streisand for inclusion on the *Barbra Joan Streisand* LP, produced by Katz's former partner Richard Perry. Hoover was especially upset when she found out that Fagen had also played organ on the recording.

The opening song, Becker and Fagen's "I Mean to Shine," has a feel and sound that would not be out of place on *Can't Buy a Thrill*, with a chord progression similar to "Brooklyn (Owes the Charmer Under Me)" and a small horn section reminiscent of "Dirty Work." The song has a middle section and outro that were dropped from Streisand's version, and some of the lyrics were changed as well, making her version a bit more generic than Hoover's, which is superior.

She follows with another song that relies on a horn section, a beautiful version of the Band's "In a Station," written by pianist Richard Manuel from the *Music from Big Pink* LP, a song whose verse melody is quite similar to Steely Dan's "Pearl of the Quarter."

Next up was another Becker and Fagen composition, "Turn My Friend Away," whose acoustic guitar and horn and flute arrangement is quite different from the duo's comfort zone. The song was the only one of the five of their compositions that was never recorded by the duo or covered by any other artist, making it a true rarity.

Hoover's own "Mama Tears" follows, an acoustic guitar ballad with not only the full band, but flute and a string arrangement in true '70s fashion. The story of a mother losing a child told by her daughter's perspective is touching, and the vibe of the playing suits the message perfectly. Hoover's second original on the album, "The Dove" is yet another acoustic guitar–driven song with the full band. This medium-tempo waltz is rather simple, with an organ part played by Fagen.

The next song, Crosby, Stills, Nash & Young's "4 + 20," was written by Stills for their 1970 album *Déjà Vu*, the second album by Crosby, Stills & Nash, and their first in the quartet configuration that added Neil Young. It topped the pop album chart for one week and generated three top forty singles: "Woodstock," "Teach Your Children," and "Our House." Unlike the original, which is purely an acoustic guitar and vocal tune, Hoover's version is another example of how different the arrangements were of the cover songs chosen for the album and how the song benefited from the addition of drums, bass, a horn section, a '60sish organ part, and an expressive lead guitar part.

The Becker and Fagen composition "Jones" follows with a country-flavored acoustic treatment of a song whose lyrics about drug addiction are the polar opposite of the sweet sound of the song. It would be recorded by Thomas Jefferson Kaye with a slightly more jaunty arrangement for his 1974 album *First Grade*, produced by Gary Katz, along with another of their compositions, "American Lovers." Becker would contribute bass to both songs and Fagen piano to another.

The next Becker and Fagen composition, "Roaring of the Lamb" was originally recorded by the duo during the demo sessions produced by Kenny Vance. The original played on piano is more disjointed than this slightly slower acoustic guitar–driven version. The song's gentle groove is peppered with a fitting horn and string arrangement and is one of the best moments of the album. They revisited "Roaring of the Lamb" when they were mining their older songs for Steely Dan albums, but for some reason, their version never saw the light of day. It would have fit perfectly on any of their early albums, and it's a shame that it wasn't released.

While working on Hoover's album, Becker and Fagen were simultaneously recording tracks for the film *You've Got to Walk It Like You Talk It or You'll Lose That Beat*. "Roll Back the Meaning" had already been recorded, and when Hoover heard the songs they were working on for the film, she flipped, commenting that it reminded her of Frank Zappa, something that thoroughly pleased Becker. They decided to record "Roll Back the Meaning" for Hoover's album. Written by the duo along with Fagen's girlfriend, Dorothy White, who helped with the lyrics,

Hoover's version dropped the Crosby, Stills & Nash three-part harmony as well as Fagen's Wurlitzer electric piano and organ, focusing on the acoustic guitar and a prominent lead guitar part, harmonized for the intro.

Hoover's least favorite song on the album was written by a friend of Kenny Vance, Richie Lifschutz. Lifschutz lived near Becker and Fagen in Brooklyn and after hearing their material decided to write a musical based on their compositions (see chapter four). The upbeat country feel of the song is augmented by some nice brushwork on the drums, a horn arrangement that would be at home on an early Steely Dan album, and a country blues lead acoustic guitar part. The album concludes with another Hoover composition, "Autumn." The song is the most stripped down of any from the album, with only Hoover's vocals, a finger-picked acoustic guitar part, and two flutes gracing the track. A suitable closing number for an album that unfortunately most people have not heard.

With her album recorded, it seemed as if Hoover was poised for success, but Morris Levy, owner of Roulette Records, expected to secure the majority of the publishing. Since Becker and Fagen were still tied up with JATA, the publishing for their songs couldn't be acquired, as was the case for the songs written by Stephen Stills, Richard Manuel, and Richie Lifschutz. Once he realized that the only songs that he would be able to publish were Hoover's three originals, he pulled the plug on the project, and the record was shelved.

Kenny Vance broke the news to Hoover, who remembers the moment clearly. "He asked me to lunch and dropped the news before dessert. It was my understanding from Kenny that the vinyl had yet to be pressed but everything else was done and ready for distribution on Roulette Records once Morris Levy gave final approval. Morris noticed the liner notes did not show that he owned the publishing on the majority of the songs. Kenny told me that Gary had told Morris that Morris' company would have all of the publishing before the project began. All of the Becker and Fagen songs were already published, as were the ones by Stephen Stills, Richard Manuel, and the one by Kenny's friend. My three songs were the only ones that were unpublished. Kenny said Morris was furious. At the same lunch on that fateful day, Kenny urged me to forget my deal with Gary and sign with his company. I was in shock as we walked back to the studio. Gary was sitting in the lobby with the guys. When I confronted him with the news Kenny had just laid on me, he confirmed that my album project was being shelved. I then asked to see the contract I had signed and wanted to see what he had signed with Morris Levy. Gary told me it was none of my business. It was like he was a different person. My heart was broken and suddenly the city of prospect and promise was the coldest place on earth. It felt like I did not really ever know any of these people at all."

Hoover stayed in New York for a while and actually had the opportunity to sing for the president of Atlantic Records, Ahmet Ertegun. She had met some musicians that had a deal with Atlantic, and they asked Hoover to sing a few songs with them for Ertegun in an attempt to secure a renewal of their contract. When he asked if they planned on having Hoover join them, they made the mistake of replying that she was only there to illustrate their ideas for some harmonies. He decided on the spot that he would not be renewing their contract.

Linda Hoover had gotten her first taste of the nasty side of the music business, something she was not prepared for, and would become a footnote in the career of Steely Dan.

Barbra Streisand

While working on the Linda Hoover album, Becker and Fagen finally had some luck placing a song with an established artist. Gary Katz's old business partner, Richard Perry, was in Los Angeles producing Barbra Streisand's twelfth album, 1971's *Barbra Joan Streisand*, and the duo's song "I Mean to Shine" was chosen as one of eleven cuts. They were definitely in good company, with Streisand recording songs by Burt Bacharach and Hal David, Carole King, John Lennon, and Laura Nyro for the album as well. Fagen played organ on the song, and countless session musicians that would play on future Steely Dan albums were part of the sessions for the album, including drummers Jim Gordon, Hal Blaine, and Jim Keltner; guitarist Hugh McCracken; and vocalists Clydie King, Venetta Fields, and Shirley Matthews. King and Matthews would appear on Steely Dan's debut LP *Can't Buy a Thrill* on three songs, Matthews would contribute background vocals to *Countdown to Ecstasy* and *Katy Lied*, and all three vocalists would participate in *The Royal Scam* and *Aja* sessions.

Perry changed some of the lyrics in the chorus and second verse and dropped the bridge and outro entirely, causing Fagen to remark that Hoover's version

of the song was much closer to what they intended. Comparing the two versions, Hoover's has more of a Dan vibe by far, and the omission of the middle section and the bland choice of lyric changes make for a rather boring version of a song that could have been better represented on Becker and Fagen's first major label release. The album peaked at number eleven on the *Billboard* pop albums chart and was certified Gold by the RIAA, but Becker and Fagen didn't see much money from the royalties. In order to move to Los Angeles to become staff writers at ABC Dunhill Records, they had to first break their contract with Kenny Vance. One of the stipulations was that Vance would retain the copyrights for "I Mean to Shine" as well as the other early songs

"I Mean to Shine" was supposed to be the name of Linda Hoover's unreleased album, but the song was given to Barbra Streisand for her 1971 album *Barbra Joan Streisand*. It was produced by Gary Katz's old partner Richard Perry, and Fagen contributed organ to the track.

he had recorded with Becker and Fagen and receive 50 percent of the publishing from their debut album, *Can't Buy a Thrill*; a small price to pay considering what they would accomplish over the next decade. The song would be covered by other artists including Barbara McNair and Diahann Carroll.

Cody Canyon

In between the sessions that would produce the unreleased Linda Hoover album and Katz's move to Los Angeles, Fagen, Katz, Dias, and Jeff "Skunk" Baxter had one more crazy idea for a recording session. They went to Amphion Studios in Boston to record as the group Cody Canyon. They recorded one song with the same name that was written by Katz and Becker and featured none other than Gary Katz on lead vocals with Linda Hoover providing the background vocals. According to Baxter, it was a ballad that told the story of how they were from deep in the hills of Cody Canyon, a strange topic for such urbane individuals.

After Hoover's album was shelved, she moved to Boston, but was convinced by engineer Mallory Earl to work with Katz, Becker, Fagen, Dias, and the newly added Baxter on the project. Although it may sound like a joke, they actually did a showcase for Warner Bros. Records and shopped their demo around but could not find a record label willing to release it, and as quickly as the band was formed, it was dissolved.

After Cody Canyon broke up, Katz asked Hoover to go to California with them, but as Hoover stated, "I did not want to go after all that had transpired. I was disillusioned. At that time I did not understand that in this life and in the world of business, things like this happen and you have to pick yourself up and keep going. Jeff Baxter tried to convince me to just let it go and move to California with them but I just could not."

Navasota

In 1972, Gary Katz, still going by the pseudonym Gary Kannon, produced his first album for ABC Records, *Rootin'* by the Southern rock band Navasota, and wasted no time in enlisting Walter Becker and Donald Fagen as session musicians, arrangers, and songwriters for the project. Recorded at the Village Recorder in Los Angeles, the album was co-produced by Dennis Collin and released in 1972. The band, which also went under the moniker Navasota-Rio, featured Dicky Sony on lead vocals, Paul Minter on bass, Lindsey Minter on drums, and Ray Pawlik and Steve Long on guitars. Although the band opened for Deep Purple, the J. Geils Band, Boston, Lynard Skynard, and others, they failed to gain a fan base outside of their home state of Texas and would be dropped by ABC records after their first and only LP.

The song that Becker and Fagen contributed was "Canyon Ladies," and although Becker wouldn't play on the album, Fagen supplied piano on three of the ten songs including "Canyon Ladies," tack piano on one song and electric piano on another. The duo also arranged horns for four songs and strings for one.

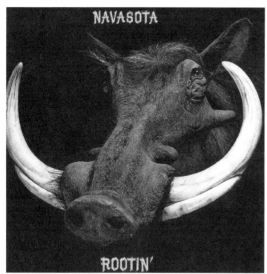

Navasota's 1972 debut album *Rootin'*, the first produced by Gary Kannon (Katz) for ABC Dunhill Records. Not only was the album produced by Kannon (Katz), but Becker and Fagen arranged horns, Fagen played piano on three songs, and the duo contributed the song "Canyon Ladies."

Not only did Becker and Fagen contribute to the album, Jeff Baxter played pedal steel guitar on two songs, and background vocals were provided by Clydie King and Shirley Matthews (listed as Sherlie Matthews), two of the singers that would appear on Steely Dan's albums. Interestingly, Mark Volman and Howard Kaylan of the Turtles (later known as Flo and Eddie) would contribute background vocals to five songs. They would also sing background vocals on an early version of "Everyone's Gone to the Movies" that saw the light of day on 1993's box set *Citizen Steely Dan*.

Thomas Jefferson Kaye

Thomas Jefferson Kontos began his career in music in the summer of 1955 when he started a vocal group, the Blaretones, in New York. They opened for Frankie Lymon and the Teenagers, Slim Harper, and others before Kontos started a new group with fellow Blaretone Bill Demarco called the Rock-Abouts. In 1958, they changed their name to the Ideals, opened for the Everly Brothers, and signed with Decca Records, releasing two singles "Annie Was a Stroller" b/w "My Girl" and "Ivy League Lover" b/w "Don't Be a Baby, Baby."

At the age of eighteen, Kontos switched career paths and joined Scepter Records as an A&R man, changing his surname to Kaye at the suggestion of label owner Florence Greenberg. During the '60s and '70s, he wrote and produced music for the Shirelles, Judy Clay, Maxine Brown, Dr. John, Chuck Jackson, the Kingsmen, Three Dog Night, Loudon Wainwright III, former Byrd Gene Clark, and the group that would initially connect him with Becker and Fagen, Jay and the Americans.

In 1969, Kaye arranged strings and horns for part of Jay and the Americans' first album, *Sands of Time*, for their JATA Enterprises. The other two arrangers for the album were Becker and Fagen. Kaye co-produced their next LP, *Wax Museum*, and served as co-producer for half of their final album, *Capture the Moment*, both of which included Becker and Fagen as horn and string arrangers and session musicians as well as Kaye, who played celeste, piano, organ, rock-si-chord, and guitar on many of the songs on the three albums.

Relocating to San Francisco, California, in the early '70s, Kaye was signed by David Geffen to produce his friend Bob Neuwirth's debut solo album, recorded in Los Angeles with myriad A-list musicians including Kris Kristofferson, Rita Coolidge, Bob Dylan, Don Everly, and Rick Danko. Kaye said of that time, "The hours are crazy, the alcohol thing is crazy, the pills are crazy, the people are crazy . . . I was just as high as everybody else and I was up for it!"

In 1973, Kaye was signed to ABC Dunhill Records as a solo artist and began working on his eponymous debut album produced by Gary Katz, an odd move after all of the experience Kaye had as a producer. Fagen sang background vocals along with soon-to-be-former Steely Dan singer David Palmer, Clydie King, and Shirley Matthews. Becker played bass on two songs, Jeff Baxter got in on the act playing guitar on one song, and future Steely Dan session players Rick Derringer and Victor Feldman played on some tracks as well. Even Gary Katz added background vocals to one song. Interestingly, one of the songs that Fagen sings on, "I'll Be Leaving Her Tomorrow," was recorded three years earlier by Jay and the Americans for their 1970 release *Capture the Moment*, produced by Kaye with American Sandy Yaguda and featuring horn and string arrangements by Becker and Fagen.

Kaye followed up in 1974 with the Katz-produced *First Grade*. Becker contributed bass to two songs, and Fagen played piano on the shortest track on the LP, the opener "Northern California," but didn't partake in the background vocals for these sessions. The duo did, however, contribute two original songs, "American Lovers" and "Jones," the ones on which Becker played. They must have thought something of "American Lovers," as they played it on their "Rarities" night at the Beacon Theatre, New York City, on September 17, 2011. Fagen introduced the song and the artist who originally recorded it. "Thomas Jefferson Kaye. A forgotten man. He's very upset. . . . he did a song that we wrote when we were working for ABC Dunhill as staff writers, and we would get in around 9:00 and pound out this crap. But we've come to like this one and Tommy Kaye liked it when he was under the influence of very powerful marijuana, and tonight it's going to be done for you. It's called 'American Lovers.' This one's not the kind of thing we write for ourselves . . . It's kind of a hippie anthem, but we were unfortunately five years too late."

Musically, the second song, "Jones," sounds less like a Steely Dan song and more like an Eagles song. Although the subject is bleak and the lyrical content has a desperate quality, the performance is rather pedestrian and doesn't hold up as well as "American Lovers." The song does, however, have some interesting chord changes and is reminiscent of other early Steely Dan songs that have a country-rock feel such as their debut single "Dallas," "Any Major Dude Will Tell You," and "With a Gun."

Becker and Fagen were not the only Steely Dan musicians to perform on Kaye's second LP. Jeff Baxter added pedal steel guitar to one song, and future Steely Dan session musicians Jim Gordon, Dean Parks, Rick Derringer, Michael Omartian, and Timothy B. Schmit all took part in the sessions as well as vocalists Clydie King and Shirley Matthews. Overall, Kaye's albums are an amalgam of blues, country, and soft rock and are unquestionably of the times, with a similar feel to many of his Californian contemporaries, such as the Eagles, Seals and Crofts, and the Doobie Brothers.

Katz enjoyed working with Kaye and has stated that he was one of his favorite artists to produce and one of the most talented musicians that he knew that never made it. Kaye's final LP wouldn't be recorded until eighteen years later in 1992, and many notable musicians took part, including Jeff Baxter, Eric Clapton, Robby Kreiger of the Doors, Dr. John, Steve Miller, Rick Danko of the Band, Joe Walsh of the Eagles, the Chicago horn section, and Timothy B. Schmit, who sang background vocals on "Rikki Don't Lose That Number," "Green Earrings," "FM (No Static At All)," "Aja," "Josie," and "Home at Last." Unfortunately, he passed away two years later from an overdose of painkillers.

John Kay

The year 1973 was a proving to be a busy one for Walter Becker and Donald Fagen. Singer-songwriter John Kay, known as the front man of the rock band Steppenwolf, released his second solo album on ABC Dunhill Records, which included a composition by the duo. For his album *My Sportin' Life*, he recorded "Giles of the River," a song that had been demoed by Denny Doherty of the Mamas and the Papas and was also given to the band Navasota. The band made it part of their live repertoire as an up-tempo country-rock song more suited to their style, but never recorded it. Kay's version has more of an easy, soft-rock feel to it and proves that Becker and Fagen could write a simpler version of their own brand of music for other artists, something that wasn't always apparent during their stint as staff writers. The record's review in *Rolling Stone* called Becker and Fagen's song "Head and shoulders above the rest of the material"; not at all surprising.

Tim Moore

Tim Moore grew up in Philadelphia, Pennsylvania, and played drums with the blues band Woody's Truck Stop, Todd Rundgren's first group. He next formed the Muffins with friend Jeff Scott, which performed originals written by Moore, often with lyrics written by Scott. They had minor U.S. success on RCA records with "Subway Traveler," but peaked in the summer of '67, opening for Lou Reed and the Velvet Underground for a week at Philadelphia's Trauma psychedelic club.

After the Muffins folded, Frank Zappa became aware of Moore as a songwriter and was interested in signing him to Bizarre Records. Moore declined after realizing that Zappa was too busy touring to produce the record himself. Moore then worked as a staff writer and session guitarist for Thom Bell, Gamble and Huff, and other producers creating the legendary Philadelphia soul sound. At the same time, he founded the band Gulliver with Daryl Hall and released one album for Elektra Records.

He signed to ABC Dunhill Records as a solo artist and began work on his eponymous debut album. He worked with producer Nick Jameson, who gave him the freedom to overdub keyboard, guitar, and bass parts over the drum tracks recorded by Russ Kunkel and future Steely Dan drummer Bernard Purdie. Moore had sung background vocals on Steely Dan's debut single "Dallas," and Donald Fagen returned the favor singing background vocals on Moore's "A Fool Like You" from his debut LP.

His next album, *Behind the Eyes*, would produce his best-known song, "Rock and Roll Love Letter," which would be a hit for the Bay City Rollers in 1976. His guitar work on the tune intrigued Keith Richards, and Moore spent a few weeks working with the Rolling Stones and Peter Tosh during rehearsals at Bearsville Studios in Woodstock, New York. Moore recorded three more solo albums, and although he has a cult following, he is truly one of the most underrated singer-songwriters of the 1970s. His songs have been recorded by Art Garfunkel, Cher, Richie Havens, Etta James, Cliff Richard, Jimmy Witherspoon, and numerous others.

Christopher Kearney

In 1975, one of the songs that Becker and Fagen demoed for the *Can't Buy a Thrill* album, "Running Child," was recorded by Canadian Christopher Kearney. Kearney was encouraged by singer-songwriter Gordon Lightfoot to pursue a career as a musician and signed with his Early Morning Production group. After a failed single for Apex Records, he signed with Capitol Records and recorded three albums for the label. His third, *Sweetwater*, included the Becker/Fagen composition written in 1972.

Poco

Poco was formed by Richie Furay, Jim Messina, and Rusty Young after the breakup of Buffalo Springfield in 1968, which counted Furay and Messina as members along with Stephen Stills, Neil Young, Dewey Martin, Jim Fielder, and Bruce Palmer at various times. There were always tensions in the band, and a number of drug busts added to the strain. Bassist Bruce Palmer was even deported twice to Canada after arrests for marijuana possession. In April 1968, Young, Furay, Messina, and Eric Clapton were involved in yet another drug bust, and the group decided to break up. After the group's breakup, Furay and Messina compiled unreleased tracks recorded between mid-1967 and early 1968 into a third and final studio album, *Last Time Around*.

Poco's initial lineup included Furay on vocals and rhythm guitar; Messina on vocals and lead guitar; Young on pedal steel guitar, banjo, dobro, guitar, mandolin, and vocals; George Grantham on drums; and Randy Meisner on bass and vocals. From the start, the group was plagued by personnel problems, and Meisner would be the first to quit after Furay refused to let anybody attend the final mix playback sessions of their 1969 debut LP *Pickin' Up the Pieces* except for himself and Messina. Meisner would be replaced by Timothy B. Schmit, who would sing background vocals and by some accounts play bass on future Steely Dan recordings. Schmit would also replace Meisner, when he quit the Eagles in 1977 after the success of their LP *Hotel California*. Poco's lineup would constantly change, with three different sets of musicians on the first four albums.

Ironically, Donald Fagen would play keyboards on Poco's twelfth studio album, 1977's *Indian Summer*, which was their second for ABC Dunhill Records and the last with Timothy B. Schmit. Fagen contributed synthesizers to two songs, the title track and "Win or Lose." Although the keyboards are relatively soft in the mix, they add a pad-like quality under the country flavor of the title track and the funk groove of "Win or Lose" and are successful in supporting the tracks in a subtle manner.

Marc Jordan

It's interesting that Fagen, who often hired session musicians to play keyboards on Steely Dan albums, would be hired so frequently as a session musician himself. In 1977, producer Gary Katz signed Canadian singer-songwriter Marc Jordan (who was also born in Brooklyn) to Warner Bros. Records and began to work on his debut LP *Mannequin*. Although he had released numerous singles in 1974 on the Canadian division of CBS Records, none of them were successful, but they did impress Katz. *Mannequin* fared much better than his previous releases and spawned the Canadian hits "Marina del Rey" and "Survival." Donald Fagen played keyboards on a number of tracks and was thanked in the credits for "all his help and time." Jordan recalled his work on the record in an interview with Don Breithaupt. "Gary was my producer, and on certain songs he would bring Donald in. Walter dropped in once or twice, but Donald would come down and actually work on stuff: play Rhodes, do synth solos, arrange on the fly. He absolutely reharmonized some of the songs, like 'Jungle Choir.' That one became clustery and dark just by virtue of Donald's voicings. He had a real musical weight to him. What he played always had this luscious darkness." Elton John's band originally cut some of the tracks, but it didn't feel right. Soon after, Steely Dan regulars took over the sessions, including drummer Jeff Porcaro, bassist Chuck Rainey, guitarists Dean Parks and Larry Carlton, keyboardists Paul Griffin and David Paich, saxophonist Tom Scott, and background vocalists Clydie King and Timothy B. Schmit.

Although Katz didn't produce Jordan's second album, another Steely Dan alumnus did. Jay Graydon, the musician who finally nailed the guitar solo on "Peg," was not only a session musician, he was a producer. He produced Jordan's second LP, *Blue Desert*, released in 1980, and went on to work with Air Supply, George Benson, Al Jarreau, the Manhattan Transfer, Patti LaBelle, Lou Rawls, Dionne Warwick, Kenny Rogers, and others. Graydon is also a prolific songwriter, and his catalog includes the Grammy winners "Turn Your Love Around" by George Benson and "After the Love Has Gone" by Earth, Wind & Fire, as well as DeBarge's "Who's Holding Donna Now" and the Dionne Warwick and Johnny Mathis duet "Friends in Love."

Although Jordan would have six top forty singles in Canada, he never charted in the U.S. As a composer, however, he has had great success, with his songs being recorded by Rod Stewart, Cher, Diana Ross, Bette Midler, Josh Groban, Bonnie Raitt, Joe Cocker, Natalie Cole, Chicago, and countless others. Today he is considered one of the most famous songwriters in Canada.

Pete Christlieb/Warne Marsh Quintet

Tenor saxophonist Pete Christlieb had already worked with Steely Dan, play-
ing memorable solos on both "Deacon Blues" and "FM (No Static at All)." They
originally hired him after hearing him play in Doc Severinsen's *Tonight Show* band.
While Christlieb was a contemporary of the duo (only three years older than
Fagen), Warne Marsh was a tenor legend and twenty-one years older than Fagen.
He studied with pianist Lennie Tristano and, along with Lee Konitz, became one
of the finest saxophonists of the Tristano-inspired "Cool School" of jazz music.
Although he followed many of the rules of the Cool School, he was a passionate
player who could burn with the best of them.

The quintet used for the album, *Apogee*, included Lou Levy on piano, Jim
Hughart on bass, and Nick Ceroli on drums. It's very possible that the album would
never have been released on Warner Bros. if Becker and Fagen hadn't produced
it. Warner Bros. was not releasing new jazz albums in the late '70s, but after the
enormous success of *Aja*, they couldn't say no to a pet project that Becker and
Fagen felt so strongly about. This would be the duo's first foray into straight-ahead
jazz, something that Becker in particular would continue to revisit as a producer
after the demise of Steely Dan. They also contributed an original composition,
"Rapunzel," based on one of Fagen's favorite songs, the Bacharach and David tune
"(In the) Land of Make Believe." The album got glowing reviews, with *Downbeat*
giving it a rare five stars. While Pete Christlieb is still with us, Warne Marsh died
on stage in 1987 at the club Donte's in Los Angeles in the middle of playing the
song "Out of Nowhere."

Far Cry

In July 1973, New York songwriter Phil Galdston met Canadian Peter Thom, and
they began writing songs together. One song, "Why Don't We Live Together," was
recorded by Barry Manilow in 1975 and was successful enough to garner interest
from Warner Bros. Records, who signed them as recording artists. Their only
album, 1977's *American Gypsies*, didn't do very well on the charts, but guitarist Jeff
Mironov, who played on Steely Dan's "Here at the Western World," appeared on
the LP.

In 1980, Galdston and Thom released an album under the moniker Far Cry.
The album, *The More Things Change . . .* , was produced by Steely Dan engineer
Elliot Scheiner, and Fagen contributed background vocals to two songs. The first,
"The Hits Just Keep Coming," also had Steve Khan on guitar and Rob Mounsey
on piano and background vocals, along with drummer Liberty DeVitto and bassist Doug Stegmeyer from Billy Joel's band. Fagen also added background vocals
to the Steely Dan-like cut "It's Not as Simple as That." Numerous musicians who
were related to Steely Dan, including guitarists Elliott Randall and Jeff Mironov;
bassist Will Lee; drummers Chris Parker, Bernard Purdie, and Ed Greene; percussionist Ralph McDonald; trumpet players Randy Brecker and Marvin Stamm;
alto and tenor saxophonist Dave Tofani; baritone saxophonist Ronnie Cuber; and

background vocalists Patti Austin, Zachary Sanders, and Frank Floyd also worked on the album.

Galdston would go on to become an extremely successful songwriter, penning hits for Ashford and Simpson, Starship, Shawn Colvin, Cher, Vanessa Williams, Aaron Neville, John Sebastian, Celine Dion, the Captain and Tennille, Marc Cohn, Yolanda Adams, Kurt Elling, Boyz II Men, Helen Reddy, and others over his forty-year career.

Rickie Lee Jones

Donald Fagen was the first of the duo to work with Rickie Lee Jones, playing synthesizer on the title track from her sophomore album, 1981's *Pirates.* Jones started her career by playing clubs in Venice, California, when she was twenty-one years old. After gaining some notice on the scene, she recorded a four-song demo of material that was heard by some important figures in the music business in 1978. Her demos came to the attention of Lenny Waronker, a producer and executive at Warner Bros. Records. Although she had a number of offers from major labels, after a bidding war, she chose Waronker and Warner Bros. due to their work with singer-songwriter Randy Newman. Waronker would co-produce her debut LP with Russ Titelman, who had produced Randy Newman, Little Feat, Graham Central Station, and James Taylor.

Her eponymous debut in 1979 included guest appearances by Dr. John, Randy Newman, and Michael McDonald and peaked at number three on the *Billboard* 200. The first single released from the album, "Chuck E.'s in Love," would be her biggest single of her career, reaching number four on the *Billboard* Hot 100 chart and number eighteen in the U.K. On April 7, 1979, one month after her debut LP was released, Jones appeared on *Saturday Night Live* and became an overnight sensation. She was so popular that her very first professional show in Boston was covered by *Time* magazine, which dubbed her "The Duchess of Coolsville." After an extremely successful tour, Jones appeared on the cover of *Rolling Stone*, at that time the largest-selling issue in the magazine's history. In 1990, Donald Fagen listed "Chuck E.'s in Love" as one of his top records on the BBC's long-running radio show *Desert Island Discs*. The success of her debut album secured four Grammy nominations, Song of the Year and Best Pop Vocal Performance, Female for "Chuck E.'s in Love," Best Rock Vocal Performance, Female for "Last Chance Texaco," as well as Best New Artist, which she won. The album also produced another top forty hit, "Young Blood."

After the success of her debut LP, Jones moved to New York City with singer-songwriter Tom Waits, her boyfriend at the time. After their breakup, she spent the majority of 1981 working on her sophomore LP, *Pirates*, partly written in reaction to this unfortunate circumstance. Drummer Steve Gadd, bassist Chuck Rainey, guitarist Dean Parks, keyboard player Rob Mounsey, saxophonist Tom Scott, trumpet player Randy Becker, and percussionist Victor Feldman, all of whom performed on Steely Dan records, contributed to this LP along with Donald Fagen, who played on the title track.

The album was a commercially successful follow-up that reached number five on the *Billboard* 200. One single, "A Lucky Guy," became the only *Billboard* Hot 100 hit from the album, peaking at number sixty-four. Jones released an EP, *Girl at Her Volcano*, in 1983 and an LP, *The Magazine*, in 1984 before taking a break from the music business.

After a five-year hiatus, Rickie Lee Jones returned with her fourth LP, *Flying Cowboys*, produced by Walter Becker. While *Flying Cowboys* wasn't as successful as her first two albums, which reached the top five in the U.S., it was an improvement on the chart success of her previous release, cracking the top forty, the last time one of her albums would achieve this feat.

Jones was initially worried about working with Becker due to the slick production of the Steely Dan albums and the fact that she considered Steely Dan "boy music." Becker was aware of her trepidation, and their polar opposite ways of making records were discussed before the project began. Becker admitted that Steely Dan made their records sound slick because of the subversive nature of the lyrics. By sugarcoating the songs production-wise, they were able to get away with topics that were not common in pop music. He realized that Jones's approach was quite different and that her songs were honest and frank, so he adjusted his production style accordingly to fit her spontaneous nature. Although at times it kept him guessing, he thoroughly enjoyed working on the project.

Becker was cognizant of how he needed to approach the production of Jones's record, and the final LP proved that he could adapt to a number of situations. They opted for simplicity and starkness rather than overproduction so as not to interfere with the songs and the vocal performances. Although he stated that the album was basically a cleaned-up version of many of her original guitar and vocal demos, his production choices shine throughout. For some songs he felt that it would be impossible to capture the spirit of the demo recordings and decided to overdub onto those tracks rather than record them from scratch. He enlisted numerous musicians that had worked with Steely Dan, on Donald Fagen's *Nightfly* album, as well as musicians that would work on Steely Dan-related projects in the future. These included drummers Jim Keltner and Peter Erskine; guitarist Dean Parks; keyboard players Greg Phillinganes and Michael Omartian; saxophonist Bob Sheppard; trumpet player Randy Brecker; and percussionists Gary B. B. Coleman and Paulinho da Costa.

The album reached number thirty-nine on the *Billboard* 200, with the college radio hit "Satellites" peaking at number twenty-three on the *Billboard* Modern Rock Tracks chart. "The Horses," which was co-written with Becker, appeared in the movie *Jerry Maguire* and became an Australian number one hit single for Daryl Braithwaite in 1991. Although *Flying Cowboys* would be Jones's last album to reach the top forty, she has maintained an illustrious career and continues to release albums to this day.

Eye to Eye

Gary Katz only worked with a handful of artists during the Steely Dan years. The first post-Steely Dan project that he would work on would be Eye to Eye. Eye to Eye was formed in San Diego, California, in 1980 by keyboardist Julian Marshall and singer Deborah Berg. Marshall and his wife, Arabella, were attending a dance performance by the San Francisco-based dance collective Mostly Women Moving, with whom Berg danced and sang. Since Berg had a knee injury, she only sang that night, and Marshall was so impressed that when he returned to London, he asked her to fly overseas to write and record together.

They signed a deal with Automatic Records and released their debut single, "Am I Normal?" which came to the attention of Katz at a Warner Bros. A&R meeting in Los Angeles. This in turn led to a contract with Warner Bros. Records. Their eponymous debut LP for the label, released in 1982, was produced by Katz and engineered by Steely Dan regulars Roger Nichols and Elliot Scheiner as well as Daniel Lazerus, who worked with Katz and Fagen on *The Nightfly*. Once again he used a number of Steely Dan alumni, including drummers Jeff Porcaro and Jim Keltner; bassist Chuck Rainey; guitarists Elliott Randall, Dean Parks, and Rick Derringer; background vocalist Timothy B. Schmit; and Fagen on synthesizer for the LP's last song, "On the Mind." He played his soon-to-be signature harmonica patch for a solo that closes the album with a very Steely Danish feel.

In an *AllMusic* review by Tim Griggs, Berg's voice is described as being "so clean that you feel as if you have taken a long bath after listening to this album." With a crack rhythm section like this, the grooves are, of course, funky yet precise, and the interpretation of the compositions by these top-tier session musicians makes the songs come alive. The album received good reviews, including one in the *New York Times* by Stephen Holden and eventually sold eighty thousand copies in the U.S., with the lead single "Nice Girls" cracking the top forty on the U.S. *Billboard* Hot 100.

A second album produced by Katz, *Shakespeare Stole My Baby*, followed in 1983 and involved a new set of Steely Dan characters, including bassist Jimmy Haslip, guitarist Larry Carlton, trumpet player Chuck Findley, and background vocalists Frank Floyd and Zack Sanders. Fagen also returned to play synthesizer on "Jabberwokky," a song with a spoken vocal/pseudo rap reminiscent of Debbie Harry's delivery on Blondie's 1980 hit "Rapture," but Warner Bros. didn't promote it, and therefore it did not sell well. After the lackluster sales of their second album, the duo decided to put the band on an indefinite hiatus while they both pursued other musical avenues and dedicated more time to their families. Until 2002, both Eye to Eye albums were only available as Japanese imports, but in 2002, they were released by independent label Wounded Bird Records on one CD.

In 2001, Marshall traveled to New York and enthusiastically began working with Berg on the third Eye to Eye album. They enlisted Roxy Music producer Rhett Davies, who had co-produced their debut single, "Am I Normal," to co-produce, and recorded in both New York City and Devonshire, England. *Clean Slate* was released on June 27, 2005, and received favorable reviews in the United Kingdom.

King of Comedy **Soundtrack**

In late 1982, Fagen and Gary Katz entered Media Sound Studios in New York City to produce the Fagen-penned song "The Finer Things" for the soundtrack for the black comedy *The King of Comedy*, directed by Martin Scorsese. The movie, starring Robert De Niro and Jerry Lewis, is a dark look at celebrity and its pitfalls, something that Fagen could definitely relate to. While the song was credited to alto saxophonist David Sanborn, Steely Dan regulars drummer Ed Greene, bassist Chuck Rainey, guitarist Steve Khan, and keyboard player Michael Omartian all played on the track. The strings were arranged by Fagen and Rob Mounsey, and Fagen joined Valerie Simpson and Leslie Miller on background vocals.

The song has a similar groove to "Babylon Sisters" and contains a number of Steely Danish harmonic tricks, but without the sardonic lyrics of a true Steely Dan song, it comes off as a little light. The soundtrack for the film also included songs by the Pretenders, Rickie Lee Jones, B. B. King. Bob James, Van Morrison, the Talking Heads, Ric Ocasek of the Cars, Robbie Robertson, and others.

Diana Ross

In 1983, Diana Ross released her third solo album for RCA Records, her four-teenth as a solo artist, and the second one entitled *Ross*. Gary Katz produced five of the eight tracks, with Ray Parker Jr. in the producer's chair for two songs and Ross producing one herself.

Katz didn't think that it was the right project for him and felt that it would have been better suited for his former partner Richard Perry. Perry is the type of producer who could find material for artists who didn't compose their own songs, while Katz worked better with artists who brought in their own compositions that he could improve. Although Katz felt that the resulting LP wasn't very success-ful, it was released shortly before Ross gave a pair of free concerts in New York's Central Park, which helped it on the charts. It reached number thirty-two on the U.S. charts, number fourteen on the U.S. R&B charts, and number forty-four in the U.K. The album's highest international chart position was in Sweden, where it reached number seven. Its first single, produced by Katz, "Pieces of Ice," peaked at number thirty-one on the U.S. charts, the only single that hit the top forty.

Fagen contributed one song, "Love Will Make It Right," on which he played synthesizer. After a rather repetitive verse, the song takes a harmonic left turn that creates tension at the perfect moment. Fagen contributes a pitch-bend-heavy synthesizer solo over the verse, which is reminiscent of some of his solos on *The Nightfly*. The song is a who's who of Steely Dan and Donald Fagen session players, with Jeff Porcaro on drums, Jimmy Haslip on bass, and keyboard player Greg Phillinganes. Other songs on the album featured more familiar names from Steely Dan albums, including Larry Carlton on guitar; Jim Horn on saxophone and flute; David Paich, Michael McDonald, and Rob Mounsey on keyboards; and Michael McDonald, Clydie King, and Shirley Matthews on background vocals. Although the song sounds a bit dated due to the drum sounds and heavy synth production, it is interesting to hear Diana Ross sing a Donald Fagen composition.

The Gospel at Colonus

In the summer of 1983, the Next Wave Festival in New York showcased *The Gospel at Colonus*, a musical based on an adaptation of Sophocles' *Oedipus at Colonus*. Fagen was so amazed by the performance that he invited engineer Daniel Lazerus, who had worked on Fagen's *Nightfly* album. Lazerus was also impressed and inquired whether anybody had approached the show's writer and arranger, Bob Telson, to record it. Telson hadn't gotten a formal offer but mentioned that David Byrne of the Talking Heads had expressed interest.

Lazerus informed Fagen, who approached Warner Bros., who gave the green light for the project, and Fagen, Lazerus, and Telson entered Clinton Studios on West 80th Street in Manhattan to begin work on the soundtrack. Due to the trio's lack of experience dealing with the financial aspect of the project, Gary Katz was soon enlisted as a co-producer. Fagen brought in Hugh McCracken to play slide guitar and harmonica on the song "Lift Me Up (Like A Dove)," and also met a number of new musicians that would work with him and Becker live and on record, including guitarist Sam Butler, drummer Leroy Clouden, percussionist Starz Vanderlocket, tenor saxophonist John Hagen, and vocalist Jevetta Steele. The performers included Clarence Fountain, the Five Blind Boys of Alabama, the Institutional Radio Choir, the J. D. Steele Singers, and J. J. Farley and the Original Soul Stirrers. Even with the Steely Dan association, Warner Bros. was unable to figure out how to market a gospel soundtrack, and the album didn't get much exposure and sold poorly.

Greg Phillinganes

Keyboard player Greg Phillinganes was a highly respected session musician who had played with countless artists including Stevie Wonder, Michael Jackson, George Benson, the Pointer Sisters, Eddie Money, Lionel Richie, Leo Sayer, Donna Summer, and Michael McDonald before he played on Fagen's *The Nightfly*. In 1984, Fagen wrote "Lazy Nina" specifically for his second solo LP, *Pulse*, a song he never recorded himself. He arranged the song with Phillinganes and received a co-production credit with Gary Katz's former partner, Richard Perry, who produced or co-produced the rest of the album.

The song is reminiscent of some of the mid-tempo numbers on *Gaucho* such as "Glamour Profession" or "Time Out of Mind," but it's a clear example of how Donald Fagen knew which songs to keep for himself and which ones to give to other people. While it has Steely Dan-style elements, it's almost like a lighter version of the band; a little more simplistic but with some of the same harmonic twists and stylistic tendencies. While Phillinganes is an outstanding keyboard player, his vocals are rather weak, and his sophomore solo album would also be his last.

Phillinganes would play the song on Soul Train on May 25, 1985, and the band Monkey House would cover the song for their 1992 debut LP, *Welcome to the Club*. The man behind Monkey House was Don Breithaupt, the author of an acclaimed book on Steely Dan's *Aja* album, part of Continuum Publishing's 33-1/3 series. When asked to describe the band's style, Breithaupt stated in a 2012 interview with the *Cashbox* Canada, "Pop songs with too many chords! There's a lot of melodic content in there and strong choruses. It was a secret of Steely Dan that if you had something that stuck as a chorus, you could get away with solos . . . I've been a Steely Dan freak since I was twelve years old. That stuff is my religion."

Phillinganes is still active on the studio scene, lending his keyboard skills to records by artists ranging from Paul Simon to Eric Clapton, Diana Ross to Whitney Houston, Kenny Loggins to Neil Diamond, Mick Jagger to the Bee Gees, Elvis Costello to Burt Bacharach, Christina Aguilera to Willie Nelson, Kanye West to Adele, and many others.

China Crisis

Walter Becker's first project as a producer—not counting Warne Marsh and Pete Christlieb's 1978 jazz album *Apogee*, co-produced with Fagen—was China Crisis's 1985 LP *Flaunt the Imperfection*. On June 21, 1981, Steely Dan announced that they were going on an indefinite hiatus following the trials and tribulations during the recording of *Gaucho*. Becker went into semi-retirement on the Hawaiian island of Maui to become "a gentleman avocado rancher and self-styled critic of the contemporary scene." He also kicked his habit, something he would never have done had he stayed in New York. He dropped out of the business completely; stopped playing bass, guitar, and piano; and had no desire to write. He began to focus on family and lost interest in the thing that had been his lifeblood for so many years. After about four years, he began to miss the studio and decided that production would be a way to get back into the business without having to move to Los Angeles. He announced his availability to some executives at Warner Bros., which was Steely Dan's label when they split up, and word spread.

China Crisis was touring in support of *Working with Fire and Steel*, and they were contemplating different producers for their next album. They told their label, Virgin Records, that they wanted to work with somebody from Steely Dan, possibly Gary Katz or keyboard player/producer Michael Omartian. They began working on songs for the album when somebody from Virgin called and told them that Warner Bros., who distributed China Crisis's records in the U.S., had heard from Walter Becker and he was interested in working on their new album. Becker had heard their second album, *Fire and Steel*, and was particularly impressed with the song "Papua," with its poppy-sounding sequenced synthesizer underpinning a lyric about nuclear holocaust, the type of juxtaposition that he and his former partner were always attracted to. They had never expected to actually work with Becker or Fagen, so they were nervous when they first met one of their musical idols, but Becker was nervous as well after nearly five years of musical inactivity.

When the band and their new producer convened at Parkgate Studios in East Sussex, U.K., some of their songs weren't finished, and they were counting on Becker to work on arrangements with them. They were so excited to be working with him that they even listed him as a band member in the credits, although he only played synthesizer on a few cuts. Becker explained his role in his usual tongue-in-cheek fashion: "[T]here were these people playing songs with three-note chords, so what I did was just went over and put the fourth finger in." Becker wanted to create a more textured sound for this album, but didn't want to spend the long, tedious hours to accomplish it as he had with Steely Dan. He elaborated on the process in a 1985 interview with Mark Leviton for *BAM*. "I had to learn that in England they do a few takes and that's it. Nobody records like Steely Dan. I started to see the value of limitations in time and money. Flaws that would bother me, they wouldn't even hear . . . Someone once said it takes two people to paint a picture: one to paint and one to shoot the guy so at some point the painting will be finished. Otherwise he'd go on painting forever. That just about sums up the producer's role on rock records, and it's something I'm comfortable with right now."

Although Becker, was by his own accord more laid-back in his new production style, China Crisis bassist Gary "Gazza" Johnson has memories of working on a bass part for four hours before being told, "We'll leave that and maybe come back and have another go at it tomorrow." He was still a taskmaster with a take-no-prisoners attitude, but the album was completed in only ten weeks.

After releasing their next album, *What Price Paradise*, with producers Clive Langer and Alan Winstanley, they began work with Becker for their 1989 LP *Diary of a Hollow Horse*. At the time, they were looking for a new producer, and their record label gave them a number of suggestions, but they decided to send Becker a tape of their demos and he loved them. This time Becker refused to record in England, so after convincing the record label that they could get a great deal on studio time at guitarist/vocalist George Benson's Lahaina Sound studio in Maui, the group flew out to begin work.

The album was originally supposed to have a horn section on more selections, but when the chart transcriber couldn't fly to Hawaii, Becker decided that it was a sign from God, and the majority of the brass arrangements were played on synthesizers. Jim Horn, who had worked with Becker in the past, was brought in to play saxophone and flute, as well as Martin Green, but these were used in a solo capacity rather than as a section. Percussionist Paulinho da Costa, who would play on Becker's *11 Tracks of Whack*, also contributed to one song.

Becker would only produce eight of the eleven tracks for China Crisis's fifth album. They initially recorded the entire album with Becker, but the record label was pressuring them for hit singles, so producer Mike Thorne was brought in to recut three tracks after the band was finished recording with Becker. Becker wasn't pleased with the record company telling him to come up with singles, because he tended to look at the recording process as a whole project. Becker also would work the band until the rhythm section parts felt right so they could achieve a dense texture without having to overdub too much, whereas Mike Thorne relied more heavily on overdubs and recorded in more of a track-by-track style. Ironically, the first two singles released from the album, "St. Saviour's Square" and "Red Letter Day," were two of the three songs produced by Thorne.

Rosie Vela

Gary Katz was responsible not only for giving Walter Becker and Donald Fagen the opportunity to create Steely Dan, but also for reuniting the duo. In 1985, he was producing an album for model turned singer-songwriter Rosie Vela when Becker stopped by the Village Recorder in Los Angeles. Vela was a classically trained piano player from age six and also studied opera as a teenager, but once she discovered the Beatles' *Sgt. Pepper's Lonely Hearts Club Band* and Frank Zappa's *Freak Out* in 1967, she began singing in a local band called Purple Haze. When her parents divorced, she relocated to Little Rock, Arkansas, with her father and brother and attended the University of Arkansas, studying music and art. She met guitarist Jimmy Roberts, whose band had some label interest, and she began to sit in and sing his brand of pop and country-rock tunes. They planned to marry in February 1974, but at Christmastime, Jimmy was diagnosed with cancer.

They still decided to get married, and when Roberts entered the hospital near the end of his life, they bought some records and took them to his hospital room with a stereo system. The last album he ever bought was Steely Dan's *Countdown to Ecstasy*. Vela recalled, "They were like the Beatles to us. We listened to them in the hospital all the time."

After Roberts's death, Vela decided that she needed to do something fast-paced to help her recover from such a devastating loss, so she moved to New York to try her hand at modeling. While in Little Rock, a photography student took some photos of her because of her wild, hippie style, and these were enough to get her a contract with the Wilhelmina Agency in 1974. After two months, she moved to the Ford Agency, and her modeling career took off. From the mid-'70s onward she graced the covers of numerous magazines around the world including *Elle*, *Harper's Bazaar*, and an astounding fourteen times on the cover of *Vogue* within a decade. She also acted in television commercials and lived with artist Peter Max for nine years until 1984. But music was still in her blood.

She built a home studio with help from her brother Chat and worked on the fifty songs that Roberts had recorded in demo form before he died. His bandmates had expressed their desire to record them as a tribute to his genius, but he was adamant that the songs were for Rosie. After a long day of photo shoots, she would return to her home studio and work on his songs, but after a while she realized that she needed to write her own material, and that decision changed the course of her life.

She recorded a demo tape and was signed by Jerry Moss to A&M records. Joe Jackson was originally the producer, but he was unable to find the time to complete the album and Gary Katz took it over. Katz was immediately impressed with her as a musician, stating in a 1986 article in *New York* magazine, "She is so talented. Her playing, singing, writing. The thing about Rosie is, she doesn't think in structures—she writes a passage because she likes it, then another and another, sometimes in the same key—and it works. For someone who started out with basically no idea what she was doing, she's very, very good—remarkable. Cool." Her debut album, *Zazu*, was comprised of eight of her original compositions, and one song, "2nd Emotion," that she co-wrote.

One day a visitor appeared, and the recording of the album took a new course. While working on the song "Tonto" at the Village Recorder in L.A., Walter Becker stopped by the studio, a visit that Katz and engineer Daniel Lazerus were expecting, but Vela was completely shocked and more than a bit nervous singing in front of one of her idols. About halfway through one particular take of the song, Becker

Becker and Fagen reunited for the first time in over five years to work with Gary Katz on Rosie Vela's debut album, *Zazu*.

began playing along on Vela's portable Yamaha keyboard. As Vela recalled in the *New York* magazine article, "He started doin' this little snaky, sexy thing that worked against the beat. I couldn't breathe." Becker was not a keyboard player, but his part ended up on the finished album. That same night he expressed his desire to play guitar on the album as well and said that his favorite song was "Interlude." When Katz played the demos for Fagen in New York, he was also quite impressed and showed an interest in playing on the album, saying that his favorite was "Interlude." Serendipity.

Katz, Becker, and Fagen reconvened at a studio in New York City called Sound Ideas, and Fagen was nervous about reconnecting with his former partner after five years. Vela was also nervous but for a different reason. She was intimidated by working with two of her musical idols. She wasn't at the next session, having been hospitalized for possible formaldehyde poisoning after drinking from a plastic bottle that had been left in the sun. That night, Becker and Fagen worked on the song that they both had said was their favorite, "Interlude." She called her brother Chat, who was in the studio while they were working on the song and he played it for her over the phone. She was so thrilled that two of her musical heroes were working on her music that she immediately perked up. Fagen played synthesizer on seven of the nine tracks, and in addition to his keyboard contribution to "Tonto," Becker played guitar on two others. Drummer Jim Keltner, bassist Jimmy Haslip, and guitarist Rick Derringer had all played on Steely Dan or Donald Fagen solo tracks, and they appeared on Vela's album as well.

It's not surprising that both Becker and Fagen liked Vela's compositions. Her jazzy chord changes, slinky melodies, funky grooves, and slick production would have been at home on *Gaucho* or *The Nightfly*. The album was released in January '86, and in 1987, Vela toured briefly in support of *Zazu* as an opening act for the Fixx. Andy Summers, the former guitarist from the Police, was also a headlining act on the tour. In the U.S., reviews were favorable, with Vela being touted as a modern-day Joni Mitchell, Rickie Lee Jones, or Kate Bush. Though the album wasn't very successful in the States, a single, "Magic Smile," peaked at twenty-seven on *Billboard*'s Adult Contemporary chart in the U.S. and was a top thirty hit on the U.K. Singles Chart. The album itself peaked at number twenty on the U.K. Albums

Chart and was certified silver by the BPI in March 1987. Katz, Becker, and Fagen thought that the single should be "Interlude," and it was released as the follow-up, but they weren't always astute at choosing the hits, and the dissonant chord changes and lack of a hook didn't resonate with the public; and although the song was promoted with a video, it went nowhere.

Soon after *Zazu* was released, Vela sang background vocals along with Joni Mitchell on Don Henley's "Who Owns This Place?" from the soundtrack to the movie *The Color of Money*. Her next job combined music and acting. In 1991, she stared as a nightclub singer in the movie *Inside Edge* and performed the bluesy ballads "Can't Walk Away from Your Love" and "Heavy Rain." She also appeared in the infamous box office disaster *Heaven's Gate* and *The Two Jakes*.

Yellowjackets

Yellowjackets were formed in 1977. Originally known as the Robben Ford Group, the band consisted of guitarist Robben Ford, keyboard player Russell Ferrante, bassist Jimmy Haslip, and drummer Ricky Lawson. Haslip would play on Fagen's "Century's End" and "Bright Lights, Big City," and Lawson would play live with Steely Dan on their 1996 *Art Crimes* tour, 2000's *Walking Distance* and *Two Against Nature* tours, and on the Grammy-winning *Two Against Nature* LP.

Ford had originally assembled this lineup to record his 1979 solo album *The Inside Story*, and the group initially combined elements of rock, blues, and fusion, with Ford contributing not only guitar but vocals. Over the next year, the group, which was becoming more democratic, eliminated Ford's vocals and moved into more of a jazz-fusion direction. They signed with Warner Bros. as Yellowjackets, but since Ford was still signed to Elektra, he had to be listed as a guest artist on the band's 1981 debut under the Yellowjackets name. Soon after the tour to support the album, Ford was replaced by saxophone player Richard Elliot, who appeared only on their second LP, *Mirage À Trois* in 1983. In 1984, he switched places with Tower of Power alto saxophonist Marc Russo before the group recorded *Samurai Samba*.

In 1986, they released the album *Shades*, named after the Donald Fagen composition. The lead-off track, "And You Know That," won a Grammy for Best R&B Instrumental Performance in 1987. Percussionist Paulinho da Costa, who would play on Becker's *11 Tracks of Whack*, added percussion to other tracks on the album.

Fra Lippo Lippi

Fra Lippo Lippi was formed in 1978 in Nesodden, Norway, by bassist Rune Kristoffersen, drummer Morten Sjøberg, and keyboardist Bjørn Sorknes. They released a 4-track instrumental EP under the name Genetic Control in 1976 but soon after changed it to Fra Lippo Lippi, derived from Robert Browning's poem about the Renaissance painter Filippo Lippi. In 1981, keyboardist Sorknes left while the band was working on material for their debut album, *In Silence*, so it was recorded as a duo and released on Uniton Records. In 1982, Per Øystein Sørensen came on board as the band's lead vocalist for their second album, *Small Mercies*, which added a pop element that was lacking from their debut, but the band faced more personnel changes while preparing for their third LP. Drummer Sjøberg and keyboardist Øyvind Kvalnes were worried about their futures as professional musicians and were unwilling to quit their day jobs, so their next LP, *Songs*, was recorded with the duo of bassist Kristoffersen and vocalist Sørensen, along with the aid of session musicians. It received positive reviews and sold five thousand copies in Norway with no single releases and little promotion. After its success in Norway, the album was rerecorded and remixed for the international market and released by Virgin Records. This version also included a new song, "Everytime I See You," which was a reworked version of the song "A Small Mercy" from their 1983 album *Small Mercies*.

For the next album, Virgin wanted to target the American audience, so the band headed to Los Angeles, where they would work with Walter Becker on their fourth LP, 1987's *Light and Shade*, with Roger Nichols engineering. The duo were augmented by Becker and some of his favorite Steely Dan/Fagen/Becker solo-era musicians including drummers Jeff Porcaro and Leroy Clouden; bassists Abe Laboriel and Jimmy Haslip; guitarist Dean Parks; saxophonist Tom Scott; and percussionist Paulinho da Costa. Becker was able to coach vocalist Per Øystein Sørensen into singing his best tracks to date, and while the album had a jazzier feel than their past releases, it still had a pop sound, and all involved were excited about the album. Unfortunately for the band, Virgin dropped a number of their acts soon after its release, including Fra Lippo Lippi.

Although the band is largely unknown throughout most of the world, Fra Lippo Lippi became superstars in the Philippines and performed to sold-out audiences in 1989. Due to their success in that country, a live album, *Crash of Light*, was prepared and manufactured for the revived Easter Productions label, but was not released due to legal difficulties. It would later be released on CD in the Philippines. After parting ways with Virgin Records, the band released two more albums, 1989's *The Colour Album* and 1992's *Dreams*, but their lack of commercial success forced the group to break up.

Michael Franks

In 1990, Becker produced three of the ten tracks for Michael Franks's *Blue Pacific* album, sharing production credits with luminaries Jeff Lorber and Tommy LiPuma. Franks had met Becker in the studio several years before and was impressed with his production work on Rickie Lee Jones's 1989 LP *Flying Cowboys*. After seeing Becker on a VH-1 special speaking about how much he enjoyed producing records, Franks called a friend at Warner Bros. Records to inquire about Becker's availability. The day before, Becker had called the same friend to ask about Michael Franks.

Franks grew up in Southern California, and although nobody in his family was musically gifted, his parents were jazz fans, and he was exposed to everybody from Nat King Cole to Peggy Lee as a child. When he was fourteen, Franks bought a Japanese Marco Polo guitar for $29.95. Six private lessons were included in the price; these would be the only lessons that he received. While in high school,

Franks began singing folk-rock, accompanying himself on guitar. He attended UCLA and earned a bachelor of arts degree in comparative literature in 1966 and a master of arts degree from the University of Oregon in 1968. He continued his studies after that and had a teaching assistantship in a PhD program in American literature at the University of Montreal before returning to teach part-time at UCLA.

While teaching at UCLA, Franks started writing songs that had a theatrical bent. He not only wrote the antiwar musical *Anthems in E-flat* starring Mark Hamill, but also music for the films *Count Your Bullets, Cockfighter,* and *Zandy's Bride,* starring Liv Ullmann and Gene Hackman. Three of his songs were recorded by Sonny Terry and Brownie McGhee for their album *Sonny & Brownie,* on which Franks played guitar, banjo, and mandolin and toured to support.

After touring with the duo, Franks released his eponymous debut LP as a solo artist. It included the minor hit "Can't Seem to Shake This Rock 'n Roll." The album would later be reissued as *Previously Unavailable* in 1983. It was his sophomore release, however, that would solidify his standing in the jazz-rock community. *The Art of Tea,* released in 1976, featured Joe Sample, Larry Carlton, and Wilton Felder of the Crusaders, all of whom had played on Steely Dan albums. It included the hit song "Popsicle Toes" and was the first of many albums by Franks released by Warner Bros. Records. Although *The Art of Tea* was actually released by Frank Sinatra's Reprise Records, Warner Bros. had bought the label in 1968. The album established his sound, a blend of smooth jazz and crossover pop. He recorded eight more albums for Warner Bros. proper and throughout the '70s and '80s enjoyed a string of hits including "The Lady Wants to Know," "When I Give My Love to You," "Monkey See, Monkey Do," "Rainy Night in Tokyo," and "Tell Me All About It." His biggest hit, however, came in 1983 with "When Sly Calls (Don't Touch That Phone)" from the album *Passionfruit.*

Becker compared Franks's voice to his former partner Fagen's, recognizing its pure tone and soulful delivery. Becker completely understood where Franks was coming from, and the challenges he often had to overcome commercially. In an interview with *SongTalk*'s Paul Zollo in 1989, Becker assessed Frank's music perfectly. "Michael's music actually exists in that ideal space between pop music and jazz that's so difficult for people to locate and be comfortable in. For Donald Fagen and myself . . . there were many times when we experimented considerably with ways of incorporating jazz things in pop music that would still give it the impact of pop but some of the harmonic sophistication of jazz . . . I think a lot of people just don't want to get involved in that challenge."

Franks knew which songs he wanted Becker to produce, "Vincent's Ear," "Crayon Sun," and "All I Need," stating that he thought that they were perfect for him, especially the mysterious "Vincent's Ear." For the album's three Becker-produced tracks, he utilized the talents of session musicians who were, or would be, involved in Steely Dan projects, including drummer Peter Erskine, guitarist Dean Parks, and keyboardist John Beasley; as well as those who would never work with the band directly: bassist Neil Stubenhaus, acoustic guitarist Buzz Feiten, percussionists Michael Fisher and Alex Acuna, and singer Livingston Taylor.

Lorber and LiPuma also used a number of Steely Dan-related session musicians including drummer Vinnie Colaiuta, bassist Freddie Washington, guitarists Larry Carlton and Paul Jackson Jr., keyboard player Joe Sample, and tenor saxophonist Bob Sheppard. The album received positive reviews and noted Franks's "return to form . . . a total rebirth . . . his best album since 1979's *Tiger in the Rain . . . Blue Pacific* is as open and beautiful as the ocean for which it is named." Franks has continued to record solo albums, and his compositions have been covered by the Manhattan Transfer, Ringo Starr, the Carpenters, Patti LaBelle, Carmen McCrae, Lyle Lovett, Kurt Elling, Diana Krall, and Shirley Bassey among others.

As a side note, Franks gave special thanks to Donald Fagen on his 1987 album *The Camera Never Lies* even though he didn't contribute to the project. Allegedly, Fagen had been stopping by the studio during the sessions and wrote the music for a song that Franks planned on writing lyrics for. By the time the music was ready, the album was completed, so it was too late to be included. Franks compared it to "The Goodbye Look" from *The Nightfly*, which makes perfect sense due to Franks's penchant for Latin-tinged grooves.

William S. Burroughs

In 1990, William S. Burroughs, whose novel *Naked Lunch* provided Steely Dan's name, released *Dead City Radio*, an album of poetry set to music provided by John

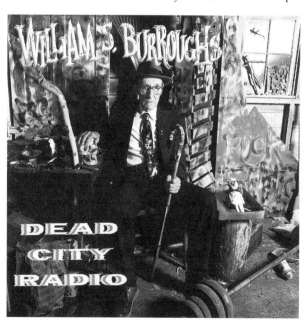

Cale, Lenny Pickett, Chris Stein, alternative rock band Sonic Youth, Frank Denning, and Donald Fagen. In 1966, Burroughs released his first spoken-word album, *Call Me Burroughs*, which included excerpts from both *Naked Lunch* and *Nova Express*. He also was a featured poet on the Giorno Poetry Systems collections in the '70s and '80s, but *Dead City Radio* was his first release to reach a wider audience.

Burroughs recorded the majority of his readings at his home in Lawrence, Kansas, between December 12 and 15, 1988, with additional recordings taking place on June 24, 1989. The material performed by Burroughs on the album included excerpts from some of his works such as *Naked Lunch*, readings from his 1989

In 1990, beat poet/author William S. Burroughs, whose novel *Naked Lunch* provided Steely Dan with their name, released the album *Dead City Radio*. Fagen contributed an avant-garde piece to accompany Burroughs entitled "A New Standard by Which to Measure Infamy."

short story collection *Tornado Alley*, excerpts from his novellas *The Cat Inside* and *Ghost of Chance*, as well as Burroughs's only commercially available recording of him singing. Although it wasn't released until 2012 as a bonus track, Burroughs sang the German standard *"Ich bin von Kopf bis Fuß auf Liebe eingestellt"* (*Falling in Love Again*), a song associated with Marlene Dietrich, during the initial sessions.

The music for the album was recorded after Burroughs laid down his readings. Fagen's contribution, the piece "A New Standard by Which to Measure Infamy," is more of an atonal, art-noise less-than-two-minute track rather than an actual song, highlighting an organ drone, spooky piano tinkling, and a wind chime-like part that adds to the overall avant-garde feel of the song. Burroughs had stated that Steely Dan was "too fancy . . . too sophisticated . . . doing too many things at once in a song." This track couldn't be further from his initial opinion.

Walter Becker's Jazz Productions

In the early '90s, Walter Becker was a busy producer. Not only was he working on Donald Fagen's *Kamakiriad*, he was also producing numerous jazz artists for two different labels, Windham Hill Records and Triloka Records, a label that counts Becker and engineer Roger Nichols as partners. The music ran the gamut from straight-ahead jazz quartets to more experimental improvisational electric work. Becker would often record a new album a day or two after finishing another, with Steely Dan engineer Roger Nichols working alongside him at Clinton Studios on West 80th Street in Manhattan. When speaking with *JazzTimes* about his new career as a jazz producer, Becker spoke of Nichols's role as particularly important, "On most pop records, you spend days getting a drum sound or experimenting. With the jazz records I've been doing, the whole record is done in two days so you're really dependent on an engineer who's going to make it happen quickly and do all the right things without a big discussion, or a trial and error type of situation. I've really come to prefer the excitement of recording live and the interplay you get with musicians. It's a much more appropriate situation for jazz records when you're looking for interplay, improvisation, freshness and fiery performances."

LeeAnn Ledgerwood

On January 4 and 5, 1991, pianist LeeAnn Ledgerwood recorded her debut album as a leader, *You Wish*, which marked the first time that Walter Becker was the sole producer of a jazz album (he had co-produced Warne Marsh and Pete Christlieb's 1978 jazz album *Apogee* with Donald Fagen). Ledgerwood had been performing in clubs in New York City for most of the '80s, and for her debut LP she called on some of the finest jazz musicians New York had to offer, including drummer Danny Gottlieb, bassists Eddie Gomez and Steve LaSpina, saxophonist Bill Evans, and flutist Jeremy Steig. The album was comprised of six originals, two from flutist Steig, and a pair of standards, Miles Davis's "Nardis" and Billy Eckstine's "I Want to Talk About You." She channels Chick Corea throughout, and the band interprets her originals well. She continues to record until the present day and has released eight albums as a leader and has played on countless sessions for other musicians, including Jeremy Steig's 1992 album, *Jigsaw*, also produced by Becker.

Andy Laverne

Five days after tracking LeeAnn Ledgerwood's debut LP, Walter Becker entered the studio from January 10 to January 12 for pianist Andy Laverne's eleventh LP as a leader, *Pleasure Seekers*. The band was on fire with drummer Dave Weckl and bassist John Patitucci, who had both played in Chick Corea's band, and Bob Sheppard on saxophone, clarinet, and flute. Pianist Andy Laverne studied at the Juilliard School of Music, Berklee College of Music, and the New England Conservatory; took private lessons from legendary jazz pianist Bill Evans; and had been recording since 1977.

Laverne's idea behind his next album that Becker produced was to play six standards and then six "originals" based on the older tunes but reharmonized with new melodic content, something that was common in the bebop era. The 1993 LP was titled *Double Standards*, and the quartet performances with Billy Drewes on tenor and soprano saxophones, bassist Steve LaSpina, and drummer Greg Hutchinson are striking, the influence of his teacher Bill Evans apparent. The album received decent reviews, but overall, most critics felt that a premise that had endless possibilities ended up being less original and more academic. Over the years, Laverne worked with Frank Sinatra, Stan Getz, Woody Herman, Dizzy Gillespie, Chick Corea, Lionel Hampton, Michael Brecker, Elvin Jones, and myriad others and has released more than fifty albums as a leader.

Bob Sheppard

In 1991, Walter Becker produced tenor saxophonist Bob Sheppard's debut LP for Windham Hill Jazz entitled *Tell Tale Signs*. Sheppard was a highly sought-after musician who had performed with numerous jazz musicians including drummer Peter Erskine and pianist Billy Childs, both of whom contributed to the album, as well as Chick Corea's Origin ensemble, Freddie Hubbard, Michael Franks, Randy Brecker, Mike Stern, Horace Silver, Lyle Mays, Dianne Reeves, Kurt Elling, Horace Silver, Nat Adderley, the Tonight Show Orchestra, and the big bands of Toshiko Akiyoshi and Lew Tabackin. He has also worked with various artists in the rock and pop world including James Taylor, Stevie Wonder, Rod Stewart, Randy Newman, Boz Scaggs, Natalie Cole, Queen Latifah, Joni Mitchell, and Rickie Lee Jones, on whose album *Flying Cowboys* he worked with Becker. Through this recording, Becker would reunite with drummer Peter Erskine and work with the pianist who had thoroughly impressed him on the Michael Franks recording dates: John Beasley. Along with Sheppard, they would all play on future Steely Dan tours.

Jeff Beal

Of all of the jazz musicians' work Walter Becker was producing in the early '90s, trumpeter/keyboard player/composer Jeff Beal's *Objects in the Mirror* was probably the most eclectic, next to the Lost Tribe LP in 1993. Beal began playing trumpet at age eight, the usual age for elementary school students to begin musical study, but the third grader would soon have the upper hand. Beal's grandmother, Irene Beal, was an accomplished pianist and professional silent-movie accompanist and introduced him to Miles Davis through his long-form work with Gil Evans, *Sketches of Spain*. The recording had a significant effect on Beal, and he would write his first long-form composition for the Oakland Youth Symphony Orchestra while a student at Castro Valley High School. The blend of improvisation with classical composition would become a trait of his future music. Beal studied composition and trumpet at the Eastman School of Music in Rochester, New York, and graduated with a bachelor of music degree in 1985.

Beal had already recorded two LPs as a leader before he worked with Becker on his 1991 release *Objects in the Mirror*. The fusion style of the album was a bit different from the more straight-ahead jazz albums he had released, but the slickness of the production is reminiscent of *Gaucho*, had Steely Dan been an instrumental fusion band. Tenor saxophonist Bob Sheppard plays alongside Beal to great effect.

Beal's true success would be as a composer for television and film. He has composed music for a number of shows, including *House of Cards*, *Monk*, *Carnivale*, and *Rome*; documentaries *Blackfish* and *The Queen of Versailles*; and the feature film *Pollock*. He has received fifteen prime-time Emmy nominations for his music, of which he won four.

Bob Bangerter

In addition to his production work for Windham Hill and Triloka Records, Becker found the time to co-produce and mix an album by freelance photographer and smooth jazz guitarist Bob Bangerter. Bangerter lived in Maui, as did Becker, and his 1991 album *Looking at the Bright Side* was released on his small Hawaiian label Don't Stop Music. It was never available in mainland stores and could only be purchased by mail order, making it a rare find. Bangerter continues to release albums in Hawaii, but his work as a photographer has found a more widespread audience. His photos have been used by Fed Ex, Mercedes Benz, the Golf Channel, Time Warner, the Turner Broadcasting Network, and several other high-profile clients.

Jeremy Steig

Becker followed the trend of 1991, and from October 14 to 16, that year, working in Manhattan's Clinton Studios, he produced yet another jazz album, flutist Jeremy Steig's *Jigsaw* LP. Becker had met Steig while producing pianist LeeAnn Ledgerwood's debut, *You Wish*, on which Steig played. Steig came from an artistic family, though not necessarily musical. His father was *New Yorker* cartoonist William Steig, and his mother, Elizabeth (Mead) Steig, was head of the Fine Arts Department at Lesley College in Cambridge, Massachusetts. He was also the nephew of American cultural anthropologist Margaret Mead, who was a popular author and speaker in the mass media during the '60s and '70s.

When Steig was nineteen, he was involved in a motorcycle accident that left him paralyzed on one side. For a number of years, he played the flute with the help of a special mouthpiece. In the '60s, he recorded with pianists Bill Evans and Danny Zeitlin, and was at the forefront of the avant-garde jazz scene. He released his first album as a leader, *Flute Fever*, in 1963 and recorded dozens of LPs as a leader, as a co-leader with Eddie Gomez, and as a sideman for jazz legends Hank Crawford, Art Farmer, Idris Muhammad, Eddie Palmieri, Lalo Schifrin, and countless others. In 1988, he played on Art Garfunkel's album *Lefty*, and in 1994, the Beastie Boys sampled the flute riff from his song "Howlin' for Judy" from his 1970 album *Legwork* for their 1994 single "Sure Shot" from the *Ill Communication* LP.

Jigsaw's personnel included a few musicians who would work with Steely Dan in the near future. Zev Katz was brought in to lay bass on some tracks on Fagen's *Kamakiriad* album, but his parts didn't make the final cut when it was decided that Becker would play bass on the entire album. Guitarist Georg Wadenius had already worked with Fagen on his 1988 track *Century's End* and would contribute to his *Kamakiriad* album, would tour with Steely Dan on the 1994 *Citizen Steely Dan* tour, and would also appear on their live album, 1995's *Alive in America*. Although pianist LeeAnn Ledgerwood played on the majority of *Jigsaw*, John Beasley, who would tour with the Dan on their 1996 *Art Crimes* tour, played piano and synthesizer on two tracks.

Dave Kikoski

Kikoski learned how to play the piano from his father and performed with him in bars in New Jersey and New York as a teenager. He studied piano at the Berklee College of Music in the early '80s before moving to New York City in 1985. He found work quickly and began touring and recording with Roy Haynes, Randy Brecker, Bob Berg, Billy Hart, and Red Rodney. In 2011, Kikoski won a Grammy Award with the Mingus Big Band for the Best Large Jazz Ensemble Album, *Live at the Jazz Standard*. He was also nominated for a Grammy for his work with Roy Haynes on his *Birds of a Feather* album.

In 1992, Kikoski released his second album as a leader, *Persistent Dreams*. Becker began work as producer on Kikoski's album the day after he finished Jeremy Steig's *Jigsaw*. He had first heard Kikoski's straight-ahead quintet a few years earlier at the Hollywood jazz club Catalina Bar and Grill. The album is a blend of more commercial-sounding originals with tracks by John Coltrane ("Satellite"), Wayne Shorter ("Toy Tune"), Rodgers and Hart ("Falling in Love with Love"), and a song made popular by Maureen McGovern from the 1972 film *The Poseidon Adventure*, "The Morning After."

Roger Nichols once again engineered the album, as he did for all of Becker's jazz productions, and Steely Dan alumnus Randy Brecker contributed trumpet and was listed as a guest artist. Becker also worked with drummer Ben Perowsky for the first time on Kikoski's album. Becker would produce the eponymous album for the band Lost Tribe, of which Perowsky was a member, in 1993, and Perowsky would play drums on three tracks on Becker's *11 Tracks of Whack*.

John Beasley

Becker was on a roll producing jazz artists, and in 1992, he produced an album for pianist John Beasley, who he had met on the Bob Sheppard sessions, entitled *Cauldron*, for Windham Hill Records. Beasley had released a live album in 1988 on Black Pearl Records, but this was his debut on a major label. Steely Dan alumnus Dean Parks played guitar, and a number of musicians that would play with Steely Dan in the future contributed to the album as well, including drummers Peter Erskine and Ricky Lawson, and Bob Sheppard, who not only played tenor saxophone but flute and bass clarinet as well. In 1993, Becker and Beasley would record the music for a children's short film, *Mose the Fireman*, narrated by Michael Keaton and illustrated by Everett Peck. Beasley also split keyboard duties with Donald Fagen on Becker's *11 Tracks of Whack* and would play keyboards on one Steely Dan tour, the *Art Crimes* tour of 1996.

In 1993, Becker would return as producer for Beasley's *A Change of Heart* LP. Sheppard returned on flute, bass clarinet, and tenor saxophone, and bassist Freddie Washington split duties with jazz legend Jon Patitucci of Chick Corea's band. Washington would play on Fagen's 2006 *Morph the Cat* album and would not only play the short tour to promote it, but would replace Tom Barney as Steely Dan's bassist on all future tours to date.

Marty Krystall

Becker met Marty Krystall while producing Rickie Lee Jones's *Flying Cowboys* album in 1989 on which he played tenor saxophone, clarinet, and English horn. Krystall had already founded the record label K2B2 with bassist Buell Neidlinger in 1979 as an outlet for their avant-garde jazz group Krystall Klear and the Buells. Their first LP, *Ready for the '90s*, was released the following year with Billy Higgins in the drum chair. They continued to release their own albums as well as those by other artists, but Neidlinger released more LPs than Krystall.

In 1992, Becker entered the studio with Krystall to record an album that was supposed to be released on Windham Hill Records, but unfortunately only one song surfaced: a cover of Thelonious Monk's "Epistrophy," which was included on the 1992 Windham Hill Sampler *Commotion 2*. Becker had quite a track record with Windham Hill at this point, so it is odd that the sampler stated that Krystall's album was due out that winter and then disappeared without a trace.

Krystall has had a successful career as a sideman, playing with Miles Davis, Bonnie Raitt; Ambrosia; Frank Zappa; Roy Orbison; Jaco Pastorius's Word of Mouth Orchestra; Aretha Franklin; Harry Nilsson; the trio of Emmylou Harris, Dolly Parton, and Linda Ronstadt; Harry Connick Jr.; Keith Moon; Randy Newman; Van Dyke Parks; Tim McGraw; and Daft Punk among others. He has also been active in the Los Angeles studio scene and has performed on the orchestral scores of motion pictures such as *X-Men*, *As Good as It Gets*, *101 Dalmatians*, *Mrs. Doubtfire*, *Minority Report*, *Forrest Gump*, *Fantastic 4 II*, *The Flintstones*, *When Harry Met Sally*, and countless others.

Glengarry Glen Ross

Although Fagen wouldn't score another film after 1988's *Bright Lights, Big City*, he did contribute the song "Blue Lou" for the soundtrack of *Glengarry Glen Ross*, a 1992 film adapted by David Mamet from his 1984 Pulitzer Prize- and Tony-winning play of the same name. The seven-minute instrumental was written as a tribute to Fagen's friend saxophonist "Blue" Lou Marino, who plays on alto along with the Joe Roccisano Orchestra. Future Steely Dan trombonist Jim Pugh also played on the song, which was included on Roccisano's 1993 album, *The Shape I'm In* as well as the *Glengarry Glen Ross* soundtrack.

Marino has been a member of Blood, Sweat & Tears, and was in the *Saturday Night Live* house band from 1975 to 1983. It was on that show that he first performed with John Belushi and Dan Aykroyd as the Blues Brothers, which led to his appearance both in the original *Blues Brothers* movie in 1980 and in the sequel, *Blues Brothers 2000*, playing the part of "Blue Lou," a name given to him by Aykroyd. He has also played with Frank Zappa, Dionne Warwick, Maureen McGovern, Deodato, James Taylor, Aerosmith, the Buddy Rich Big Band, and the Woody Herman Orchestra. Although jazz musicians consider him to be one of the finest in New York, his work with pop and rock bands has led to a lack of coverage by the jazz press. Marino would play on Fagen's *Kamakiriad* album as well as Steely Dan's comeback LP, *Two Against Nature*, in 2000.

Jennifer Warnes

Singer-songwriter Jennifer Warnes was always a talented singer and was offered her first record contract, which her father turned down, at age seven. Although she was awarded a scholarship to study opera at Immaculate Heart College after her high school graduation, she decided to focus on folk and pop music; and in 1968 signed her first record contract with Parrot Records and released the first of two albums for the label. That same year, she also joined the cast of *The Smothers Brothers Comedy Hour* and portrayed the female lead in the Los Angeles production of the musical *Hair*. Her first two albums had no chart action, and Warnes wouldn't record another until 1972, the John Cale–produced *Jennifer* LP released by Reprise Records. It would be four years until her next album.

She did, however, keep busy during those years. She met Canadian songwriter Leonard Cohen in 1971 and toured with him in 1972 and 1979 as a background vocalist and later as a vocal arranger and guest singer. She also recorded on a number of his albums spanning 1972 to 2012, including *Live Songs, Recent Songs, Various Positions, I'm Your Man, The Future, Field Commander Cohen: Tour of 1979*, and *Old Ideas*.

It wasn't until her fourth album, *Jennifer Warnes*, that she would finally have a breakthrough hit with "Right Time of the Night." The song reached number one on *Billboard*'s Easy Listening (Adult Contemporary) chart in April 1977 and number six on the *Billboard* Hot 100 chart in May 1977, but the song was not part of the original running order of the LP. Arista president Clive Davis later told *Billboard*: "If a [singer such as] Jennifer Warnes submits an album which is great but lacks a hit single, I and my A&R staff will say: 'Listen, you need a hit because you're not really going to break off FM airplay' . . . so we gave her 'Right Time of the Night.'"

The hits continued to come with "It Goes Like It Goes" from the 1979 motion picture *Norma Rae*, winning the Academy Award for Best Original Song; and her 1979 single "I Know a Heartache When I See One," which reached the top ten on the Country chart and the top twenty on both the Pop and Adult Contemporary charts.

Her biggest hit would come in 1982 when she recorded the song "Up Where We Belong" with Joe Cocker for the motion picture *An Officer and a Gentleman*. The song won the Academy Award for Best Original Song, as well as a Golden Globe Award. It also won Warnes and Cocker the Grammy Award for Best Pop Performance by a Duo or Group with Vocal. The number one single was certified platinum for over two million sales in the United States alone. She had another hit from a movie when she teamed with Bill Medley to record "(I've Had) The Time of My Life" for the 1987 film *Dirty Dancing*. The song earned Warnes her third Academy Award for Best Original Song and second Golden Globe Award in the same category. As she had done with Cocker, the number one song won Warnes and Medley the Grammy Award for Duo or Group with Vocal.

In 1992, Warnes released her seventh solo album, *The Hunter*, on which she covered a Fagen composition with lyrics by his girlfriend at the time, Marcelle Clements, "Big Noise, New York." The song was originally intended for a Spike Lee movie, but their submission was rejected. Fagen's version would appear as the B-side to "Trans-Island Skyway," but Warnes's recording would be released first. Fagen added background vocals with Frank Floyd, who sang on *Gaucho*, *The Nightfly*, and Fagen's "Century's End"; and Vinnie Colaiuta, who would play on "Negative Girl" from the *Two Against Nature* LP, played drums along with session ace John Robinson on the track. It's nice to hear Warnes's version, which has a more organic, although slick, production with real drums, guitar, a horn section, and a beautiful tenor saxophone solo in comparison to Fagen's somewhat demo-like take on the song with drum machine, synthesizers, and synth harmonica. It's also interesting to note that part of the melody of the chorus is quite similar to the title track of Steely Dan's 2003 album *Everything Must Go*, but it is more apparent on Fagen's version than Warnes's.

Lost Tribe

In 1993, Becker continued to produce interesting, artistic projects with the eponymous Lost Tribe album recorded at Becker's Hyperbolic Sound in Maui. The quintet consisted of alto saxophonist David Binney, bassist Fima Ephron, drummer Ben Perowsky, guitarist Adam Rogers, and guitarist/guitar synthesist David Gilmore, creating a sound that blended aggressive metal fusion with funk and hip-hop grooves.

The group, formed in Brooklyn in the late '80s, was the brainchild of Binney and to some degree, was an offshoot of the M-Base movement started earlier in the decade by musicians including Steve Coleman, Graham Haynes, Cassandra

Wilson, Geri Allen, Robin Eubanks, and Greg Osby. The "M-Base-concept," short for "**m**acro-**b**asic **a**rray of **s**tructured **e**xtemporization," wasn't actually a musical style but more of a way of thinking about the creation of music. As critics often do, they glommed onto the term and used it to describe the new style of jazz music coming out of Brooklyn.

Drummer Ben Perowsky was working on Dave Kikoski's record, which Becker produced, and during a break in the sessions, he began playing some speed-metal type grooves. As Perowsky recalled in an interview with the fanzine *Metal Leg*, Becker was intrigued. "Walter came in the room and asked if I knew of a crazy punk/jazz/metal/fusoid band. I had our tape in my pocket. He called me that night and said. 'I wanna produce you guys.' What was interesting was we were driving back from a gig . . . and we were trying to think of people that we could interest in this music as we had been trying for a year to assault the record business with our stuff to no avail. We were thinking, 'Wouldn't it be great if we could get a good producer.' And Walter's name came up." They flew out to Maui and recorded their 1993 debut album in thirteen days. They knew that Becker was the perfect producer for Lost Tribe because Steely Dan had raised the bar so high for pop music with their complicated harmonies and crystal-clear production. They hoped to push their own music forward as well, believing that their audience was intelligent and ready for something new and exciting.

The members of Lost Tribe were some of New York's best session musicians and have collectively played with Aretha Franklin, Maceo Parker, Medeski Martin & Wood, the Gil Evans Orchestra, Steve Coleman, the Screaming Headless Torsos, Mike Stern, future Steely Dan drummers Dennis Chambers and Vinnie Colaiuta, and several others. The majority of their debut album was instrumental, but one song had a rap and another, a chanted vocal. They released one more album for Windham Hill Records with the original lineup in 1994, and one in 1998 without guitarist Gilmore.

Perowsky, Ephron, and Rogers would return to Maui to record Becker's *11 Tracks of Whack*, but although they recorded an album's worth of material, only three songs would make the final cut. The band would re-form for a reunion concert at bassist Matt Garrison's Shapeshifter Lab in Brooklyn on June 7, 2013, the first time the original group had played together in nineteen years. Sound familiar?

Raw Stylus

In 1995, Gary Katz took on a very different role as producer for the London-based acid-jazz group Raw Stylus. The band was essentially a dance group whose core members were vocalist and composer Donna Gardier; composer, producer, programmer Ron Aslan; and multi-instrumentalist/vocalist Max Julian Brookes. In the early '90s, they released white label vinyl records, including a cover of Bill Withers's "Use Me," with original vocalist Deborah French, and distributed them directly to DJs on the London club scene.

One of their early tracks, "Pushing Against the Flow," was quite popular on the club circuit and would become the title of their only LP, produced by Katz.

The single from the album, "Believe in Me," reached number one on the U.S. Hot Dance Club Play chart and was a minor success in the U.K., reaching number sixty-six on the U.K. Singles Chart in October 1996. The album is an underrated slice of '90s acid-jazz and has similarities to fellow Brits Incognito, Jamiroquai, and Galliano.

Fagen contributed synthesizer to "37 Hours (In the U.S.A.)," along with Dan favorites, drummer Bernard Purdie, guitarist Elliott Randall, trumpet/flügelhorn player Randy Brecker, trombonist Dave Bargeron, saxophonist/flutist Lou Marini, and baritone saxophonist Ronnie Cuber. Guitarist Hugh McCracken, who had played on numerous Steely Dan, Donald Fagen, and Walter Becker albums, also contributed to the Raw Stylus LP, but this time he played harmonica on two tracks. Other Dan alumni included trumpet player Lew Soloff, percussionist Bashiri Johnson, and vibraphone player Bill Ware. The song name checks Becker and Fagen's band with the following line: "We're in town to see our favorite act, the Steely Dan reunion pack." They follow with licks from "FM (No Static at All)," and "Josie," a nice tip of the hat to a band that influenced their sound as much as the acid-jazz movement or American soul music. Raw Stylus would tour as a nine-piece band, but would break up in 1999 without ever releasing a follow-up LP. This would be the last project that Gary Katz would work on with Donald Fagen and therefore the end of his association with Steely Dan.

Mindy Jostyn

Mindy Jostyn was a vocalist and multi-instrumentalist who played violin, guitar, mandolin, harmonica, keyboards, and accordion on tours and records by Carly Simon, Billy Joel, Cindy Lauper, John Mellencamp, Joe Jackson, Pat Benatar, Shania Twain, Jon Bon Jovi, the Hooters, Laura Nyro, and several others.

She first worked with Fagen as part of the band for the New York Soul show at the Lone Star Roadhouse on September 20, 1989. She continued to perform at various New York Soul shows, and Fagen was enjoying performing live so much that he would often sit in at her Wednesday night residency at a club called Hades in Manhattan. The New York Soul shows eventually transformed into the New York Rock and Soul Revue, with Patti Austin, Michael McDonald, and Phoebe Snow sharing lead vocals with Fagen. They performed at the Beacon Theatre on April 4, 1990, with Jostyn tackling Ben E. King's "That's When It Hurts" as she had done at the Lone Star many times. She would also be a member of the band in 1991 and 1992 and would appear on *The New York Rock and Soul Revue: Live at the Beacon* LP and in the A&E television special *In Concert*. The short thirteen-date tour in 1992 would be the last time that Jostyn would play live with Becker or Fagen, but she would contribute background vocals to Fagen's *Kamakiriad* LP and harmonica and background vocals to "Confide in Me."

In 1995, Jostyn released her debut album, *Five Miles from Hope*. Not only did Carly Simon appear as a guest vocalist, the Band's Garth Hudson played accordion, and Fagen contributed melodica to the song "Too Easy." Jostyn would release four more solo albums before her death from cancer in March 2005.

Ricky Lawson

Ricky Lawson was one of the most in-demand session drummers in the '80s, '90s, and '00s. He began his career playing with Stevie Wonder in the early '70s and soon after played on sessions for Roy Ayers, Tom Waits, the Jacksons, George Duke, the Emotions, and Robben Ford. He was also a co-founder of the jazz-fusion group Yellowjackets, the band that would earn him a Grammy Award in 1987 for Best R&B Instrumental Performance for the song "And You Know That" from the album *Shades*. The album's title track was written by Donald Fagen.

Throughout the '80s, '90s, and '00s, Lawson continued to play sessions and tour with Michael Jackson, Lionel Richie, Eric Clapton, Phil Collins, Beyoncé, Babyface, Whitney Houston, Paul McCartney, Rod Stewart, Anita Baker, Aretha Franklin, Smokey Robinson, Kenny Loggins, Quincy Jones, Bette Midler, Toto, Al Jarreau, George Benson, David Sanborn, DeBarge, Sister Sledge, Teena Marie, Philip Bailey, and countless others.

His first solo album, entitled *First Things 1st*, was originally released in Japan in 1997 on the Samsung Music Label and appeared two years later in the U.S. It was a new step for Lawson, giving him the opportunity to write, arrange, produce, and perform each of the eleven tracks along with Gerald Albright, Bill Cantos, Phil Collins, George Duke, Sheila E., Nathan East, Robben Ford, James Ingram, Boney James, Al Jarreau, Kirk Whalum, Vesta Williams, and Donald Fagen. Fagen contributed acoustic piano on a song written by Phil Collins and Nathan East called "Sweet Love." The album also featured a number of Steely Dan cohorts, including bassists Jimmy Haslip and Marcus Miller, keyboard player Greg Phillinganes, and percussionist Paulinho da Costa. Lawson would release a Christmas album in 2008, but sadly passed away on December 23, 2013, of a brain hemorrhage.

Krishna Das

Krishna Das, born Jeffret Kagel, is an American vocalist known for his recordings and performances of Hindu devotional music known as kirtan. After living in India for several years he returned to the U.S. and created his own brand of music that blends kirtan with Western chord progressions. In 2005 Walter Becker not only played bass on his seventh album *All One*, but co-produced it as well. The album also features drummer Rick Allen of Def Leppard and was released on Triloka Records, a label that counts Becker and engineer Roger Nichols as partners. Das has released fourteen albums since 1996 and worked with Sting, producer Rick Rubin, and multi-instrumentalist Hans Christian. In 2013 his album *Live Ananda* was nominated for a Grammy Award for Best New Age Album.

Rebecca Pidgeon

British actress/singer-songwriter Rebecca Pidgeon has been performing since the mid-1980s originally singing for the band Ruby Blue. In 1990 she left the band shortly after their first major label release, *Down from Above*, and moved to the U.S. with her partner and future husband, playwright David Mamet. She met Mamet in the late-1980s and acted in a number of his plays and films. Although he was married at the time, they began a relationship and were married in 1991. In 2005 Becker contributed guitar to the title track of her fifth album, *Tough On Crime*, which also featured Billy Preston on keyboards. In 2008 she recorded the original, "When You Were Mine," as a duet with Brazilian singer-songwriter Luciana Souza for the soundtrack to the motion picture *Redbelt*, which was written and directed by Mamet. The Steely Dan connection? Souza is married to bassist Larry Klein, who produced Becker's second album, *Circus Money* in 2008.

Martha Wainwright

Singer-songwriter Martha Wainwright was truly part of a musical family. She is the daughter of Loudon Wainwright III, a Grammy Award-winning songwriter with twenty-three studio albums to his name, and Canadian folk singer-songwriter Kate McGarrigle, whose self-titled debut album with her sister Anna was chosen by *Melody Maker* as Best Record of the Year in 1976. Her brother Rufus Wainwright is also a celebrated singer-songwriter whose 1998 eponymous debut album, produced by Jon Brion, received critical acclaim, with *Rolling Stone* naming him the Best New Artist of the year.

In 1995, Martha sang on her father's album *Grown Man* and the following year on her mother and aunt's LP, *Matapedia*. In 1997, she released her first record as a solo artist, an independent cassette entitled *Ground Floor*. She began singing background vocals for her brother and appeared on several of his albums.

In 1999, she released two EPs, *Factory* and *Martha Wainwright*. She followed with another, *Bloody Mother Fucking Asshole*, in 2003 and *I Will Internalize* in 2005. In 2005, she recorded her debut full-length official eponymous release produced by Brad Albetta, her future husband. The album included new versions of three songs from her first two EPs along with "Bloody Mother Fucking Asshole" and nine new songs. The album reached number forty-three on *Billboard*'s Top Heatseekers chart.

Wainwright's second album, *I Know You're Married but I've Got Feelings Too*, was released in June 2008, and fared better than her debut, reaching number ten on the Top Heatseekers chart and number six in Canada. It also charted throughout Europe and Australia. Pete Townshend played guitar on two tracks, the Band's Garth Hudson contributed keyboards to one track, her brother Rufus sang on one song, and Fagen played synthesizer on the song "So Many Friends."

During Fagen's tour to support his 2006 album *Morph the Cat*, he invited Martha Wainwright to the stage at the Beacon Theatre in New York. She performed her own composition "Year of the Dragon," which had been recorded by her mother and aunt in 1998, with Fagen playing the melodica. The audience wasn't too enthusiastic, which annoyed Fagen.

Wainwright released a single with Snow Patrol in 2006, a live album that was a tribute to French singer Édith Piaf in 2009, and the studio album *Come Home to Mama* in 2012. In 2013, she recorded the soundtrack album for the fourth season of the Canadian medical drama television series *Trauma*, and in November 2015, she released the album *Songs in the Dark* with her American half-sister Lucy Wainwright Roche as the Wainwright Sisters.

Lucy Schwartz

In 2008, Becker co-produced the song "Beautiful" by artist Lucy Schwartz with Larry Klein for the movie *(It's All About) The Women*, an updated version of George Cukor's 1939 film of the same name based on a 1936 play by Clare Boothe Luce. Writer, producer, and director Diane English followed the lead of both the original play and the 1939 film making sure that no men appear on screen, even in long shots and crowd scenes. The only male character in the film is Edie's baby boy, born in the final scene of the film, and the waiter at the café seen during the credit scene. The all-star cast included Meg Ryan, Annette Bening, Eva Mendes, Debra Messing, Jada Pinkett Smith, Bette Midler, Candice Bergen, Carrie Fisher, and Cloris Leachman.

Roger Rosenberg

In 2009, Walter Becker produced his first jazz album in sixteen years, *Baritonality*, for Steely Dan's baritone saxophonist Roger Rosenberg. Rosenberg played on Steely Dan's *Two Against Nature* and *Everything Must Go*; Fagen's *Kamakiriad, Morph the Cat*, and *Sunken Condos*; and Becker's *Circus Money*; and has also toured with the band since 2006. His work in the jazz world is quite impressive; he played with artists such as Miles Davis, Buddy Rich, Phil Woods, Tony Bennett, the Bob Mintzer Big Band, and John Scofield, but his pop and rock résumé is equally remarkable, with credits including records with John Lennon, Elvis Costello, David Byrne, James Taylor, Joe Jackson, Barbra Streisand, George Michael, and Laura Nyro.

For his sophomore album as a leader, Rosenberg was joined by ex-Sonny Rollins pianist Mark Soskin, longtime Billy Taylor bassist Chip Jackson, and drummer Jeff Brillinger, who had played with Chet Baker. Besides baritone sax, Rosenberg also played bass clarinet and soprano sax on the album. The eight originals run the gamut from modal jazz to hard bop to 7/8 groove-based funk to a tender ballad. Guitarist Peter Bernstein joins Rosenberg for a duet on the only standard on the album, "Spring Can Really Hang You Up the Most." It received glowing reviews from numerous publications and was a welcome return for Rosenberg as a leader after eight years.

Clarence Fountain, Sam Butler and the Boys

Fagen first met Sam Butler when he was producing the soundtrack for *The Gospel at Colonus*, a musical based on an adaptation of Sophocles's *Oedipus at Colonus*. Fagen was so impressed with his guitar playing and vocals that he took part in the first New York Rock and Soul Revue show at the Beacon Theatre on April 4, 1990. Butler's feature spot was a duet with percussionist/background vocalist Philip Hamilton of the 1966 Sam Cooke song "Soothe Me," which was covered in '67 by Sam and Dave.

Soon after, it was rumored that Becker and Fagen had co-written seven or eight soul songs for a Sam Butler solo album to be released by Triloka records, the label that counted Becker and engineer Roger Nichols as partners. They were supposed to play on the record as well as produce it for a fall of '92 release, but nothing ever surfaced. Butler continued to work in the gospel world, but also performed on secular records by artists such as Keith Richards and Joe Cocker.

In 1972, Butler joined the Blind Boys of Alabama after fronting his family band, Little Junior and the Butleraires. The Blind Boys of Alabama have released over sixty albums, won five Grammy Awards including a Lifetime Achievement Award, and have collaborated with Solomon Burke, Peter Gabriel, Prince, George Clinton, Willie Nelson, Aaron Neville, Tom Petty, Dr. John, Ben Harper, Bonnie Raitt, Robert Randolph, Allen Toussaint, Tom Waits, Lee Ann Womack, Hank Williams Jr., k. d. Lang, Billy Preston, Lou Reed, Timothy B. Schmit of the Eagles, Mavis Staples, Susan Tedeschi, Henry Butler, Chrissie Hynde, Michael Franti, Toots Hibbert, Me'Shell NdegéOcello, Preservation Hall Jazz Band, Randy Travis, Vince Gill, John Hammond, Oak Ridge Boys, Joan Osborne, and a number of others from a variety of genres.

In 2009, Clarence Fountain, Sam Butler and the Boys released *Stepping Up & Stepping Out*, an album that walks the line between gospel and secular music. The duo made a conscious effort to keep the message spiritual, while trying to cross over and gain a bigger audience. Legendary soul artist Solomon Burke served as executive producer, and the album was co-released by Burke's One World label and Tyscot Records. Fagen not only wrote the liner notes, but played melodica on two tracks, "It's a Different World Now" and the sparsely produced, melancholy "The Birth of Jesus," proving his versatility as a musician. Other musicians from the Steely Dan camp were credited on the album as well, including drummer Leroy Clouden and bassist Lincoln Schleifer, who doesn't play bass but engineers.

Butler would finally release his solo debut in 2015, *Raise Your Hands*. Producer Brian Brinkerhoff approached Butler with an interesting concept: record an album of spirituals written by artists that are not necessarily known for that type of music. What resulted was a beautifully executed LP of songs by Bruce Springsteen, Johnny Cash, Eric Clapton, Van Morrison, Barry and Maurice Gibb, Tom Waits, U2, Curtis Mayfield, and others. The album received rave reviews and was a perfect vehicle to introduce Butler as a true force as a solo artist in the music world.

Rudimental

Rudimental are an English drum and bass band that released their debut album *Home*, which debuted at number one on the U.K. album charts, in 2013. Although not initially popular in the U.S., they won the Brit Award, the MOBO Award for Best Album, and also received nominations at the MTV Europe Music Awards for Best New Act, and Best U.K. and Ireland act. Their second single from *Home*, "Feel the Love," featuring vocals from John Newman, entered the U.K. singles chart at number one. Their fourth single from the album, "Waiting All Night" featuring Ella Eyre, also reached number one. Rudimental have achieved multiple platinum awards for record sales in several countries including the United Kingdom and Australia.

In 2015 they released their sophomore album, *We the Generation*, with guest appearances from Bobby Womack, George Clinton, Ed Sheeran, Ella Eyre, and Donald Fagen on the song "Common Emotion." The album's first single, "Bloodstream" featuring Ed Sheeran, was a reworking of the original song from Sheeran's album *x*. It reached number two on the U.K. Singles Chart.

Fagen's work with Rudimental came about rather randomly. During a meeting with their manager, the band were asked whom they wanted to work with on the new album, and as a joke, producer/multi-instrumentalist Amir Amor said Donald Fagen from Steely Dan. Surprisingly, his manager told them that it wasn't a problem, and a few weeks later they were in a studio in New York with Fagen, who was already familiar with their material and was complimentary. They were excited but nervous because of Steely Dan's reputation in the studio. In a 2015 interview with *Music Times*, Amor elaborated, "With someone like that, you never know how it will go. They might be there one day, not turn up the next. Fortunately, Donald Fagen came back. He was very enthusiastic—we were surprised at how engaged he was with electronic music . . . He was on his keyboard and we all played live . . . We recorded a couple of songs and part of what we decided to use for this record is a little spoken word piece that he did. So it's tucked away on the album on one of the songs, it'll be a little present."

21

Well, I've Seen 'Em on the TV

Steely Dan TV and Video Performances

While Steely Dan was not the most photogenic group of individuals (one magazine called them the ugliest rock 'n' roll band), they did appear on television on a number of occasions in the early '70s. Fagen would produce two videos for his 1982 release *The Nightfly*, but one was animated and the other used actors, rather than the artist himself. For *Kamakiriad* he released two videos as well, but this time he appeared in both of them. When the Dan reunited, they were far less reluctant to appear in front of the camera, so there is a wealth of video available from the later part of their career. This chapter will discuss some of the highlights.

American Bandstand

On January 27, 1973, Steely Dan made their television debut on Dick Clark's *American Bandstand* for the first time to promote their single "Do It Again" as it was climbing the charts. A week later, it peaked at number six, where it remained for three weeks, spending a total of seventeen weeks on the *Billboard* Hot 100 chart. As all bands and singers did for the show, the group had to lip-synch for this thirteenth episode of its sixteenth season.

In November 1973, Steely Dan returned to lip-synch both "My Old School" and "Bodhisattva" from their sophomore LP, *Countdown to Ecstasy*. Episode eleven from the seventeenth season gives us a rare glimpse of the first two female background vocalists to tour with the Dan, Gloria "Porky" Granola and Jenny "Bucky" Soule. Background vocalist Royce Jones, who contributed background vocals to *Countdown to Ecstasy* and would continue to tour with the group after the short-lived tenure of the "girls," also makes an appearance.

The Midnight Special

On August 19, 1972, producer Burt Sugarman premiered a late-night musical variety program that was initially produced as a one-time special. That one-off show was so successful that it became a weekly series from February 2, 1973, until May 1, 1981. The ninety-minute program followed the Friday night edition of *The Tonight*

STEELY DAN
GOING MOBILE

Screenshots from Steely Dan's 1972 appearance on *The Midnight Special* were used for the bootleg *Going Mobile*, a 1974 live recording from the Record Plant in Los Angeles that was broadcast on KMET-FM.

Show Starring Johnny Carson and showcased some of the biggest musical acts of the day.

The difference between *The Midnight Special* and *American Bandstand* was that the bands performed live on *The Midnight Special*, a definite advantage. On April 13, 1973, Steely Dan performed both "Do It Again" and "Reelin' in the Years" for the show. The band was introduced by none other than comedian Bill Cosby, whose monologue mentioned that they "have gone to college, studied music, turned on and then came through with a hit record called 'Do It Again.'" He then introduces "Reelin' in the Years." Fagen handles the lead vocals and actually seems to be enjoying himself, knowing that the chorus would be sung by the entire band.

This version of "Do It Again" is curious because although Fagen sang the hit single, he hands the lead vocals over to David Palmer, as he had for all live performances. He does, however, sing the chorus along with Palmer, but it's a bit odd that Fagen wouldn't sing the song for a television appearance, especially because it was doing so well. Ironically, Palmer would be fired within a few weeks. They play the edited single version, and Jeff Baxter plays congas. Denny Dias adds a superb solo on guitar, rather than electric sitar, and the song concludes with a short conga solo by Baxter under an extended coda.

On August 31, 1973, they returned to perform "My Old School," "Show Biz Kids," and "Reelin' in the Years." The show was hosted by singer/songwriter/keyboardist Billy Preston and is unique for a number of reasons. It's the only live television performance of "My Old School" and "Show Biz Kids," and it is also the only filmed live performance to include background singers Gloria "Porky" Granola and Jenny "Bucky" Soule.

Grammy Awards Shows

Over the years, Steely Dan and Donald Fagen as a solo artist were nominated for numerous Grammy Awards, but besides three wins for Best Engineered Recording, Non Classical for *Aja*, *Gaucho*, and "FM (No Static at All)," they wouldn't win until 2001 for *Two Against Nature*. They didn't attend every time they were nominated, but surprisingly, they showed up a few times. The list of nominations below includes presentations they attended as well as the ones that they skipped.

Steely Dan was first nominated for a Grammy at the 17th Annual Grammy Awards in 1975 for "Rikki Don't Lose That Number." The song was nominated for Best Pop Vocal Performance by a Duo, Group or Chorus and had some stiff competition. The other nominees were Paul McCartney and Wings, Quincy Jones, Dionne Warwick and the Spinners, and the Stylistics. Paul McCartney and Wings won the award for "Band on the Run."

In 1978, Steely Dan was up for three Grammys for *Aja*, Album of the Year, Best Pop Vocal Group, and Best Engineered Recording, Non Classical. While the Album of the Year award went to Fleetwood Mac for *Rumours* and the Best Pop Vocal Performance by a Group award went to the Bee Gees for "How Deep Is Your Love," Steely Dan did win the Grammy for Best Engineered Recording, Non Classical thanks to engineers Roger Nichols, Elliot Scheiner, Bill Schnee, and Al Schmitt. In 1979, Roger Nichols and Al Schmitt won the award for a second time for "FM (No Static at All)," although Steely Dan lost the Best Pop Vocal Performance by a Duo or Group to the Bee Gees' *Saturday Night Fever* soundtrack album.

Three years later at the 24th Annual Grammy Awards, their next album, and the last for nineteen years, *Gaucho*, was again nominated for Album of the Year, Best Pop Vocal Group, and Best Engineered Recording, Non Classical. Again they lost to an ex-Beatle, with John Lennon and Yoko Ono's *Double Fantasy* LP winning Album of the Year. They lost Best Pop Vocal Performance by a Duo or Group with Vocals to the Manhattan Transfer for "Boy From New York City," but once again won the Grammy for Best Engineered Recording, Non Classical.

After Steely Dan broke up, Fagen's *The Nightfly* was up for five Grammys in 1983, including Album of the Year, Best Vocal Arrangement for Two or More Voices for "Ruby Baby," Song of the Year and Best Pop Vocal Performance, Male for "I.G.Y. (What a Beautiful World)," and Best Engineered Recording, Non Classical. Fagen attended the awards show for the first time along with producer Gary Katz, but left empty-handed, losing to *Toto IV* for Album of the Year and Best Engineered Recording, Non Classical, to Toto's "Rosanna" for Best Vocal Arrangement for Two or More Voices, to Lionel Richie's "Truly" for Best Pop Vocal Performance, Male, and to songwriters Johnny Christopher, Mark James, and Wayne Thompson for Song of the Year for Willie Nelson's "Always on My Mind."

In 1994. Fagen's *Kamakiriad* was nominated for Album of the Year but lost to *The Bodyguard: Original Soundtrack Album*. The big hit from the album was Whitney Houston's number one rendition of Dolly Parton's "I Will Always Love You," a song that had also been covered by Linda Ronstadt in 1975. Parton released three versions of the song, one in 1974, another in 1982, and the third as a duet with Vince Gill in 1995. Her first two versions both hit number one on the *Billboard* Country charts, making her the first artist to earn a number one record twice with the same song. Future Steely Dan drummer Ricky Lawson played on Houston's version and stated that the one-note snare "solo" before the singer's dramatic last chorus was his favorite solo he ever recorded.

A photo from Steely Dan's second appearance on *The Midnight Special* in August 1973 was used as the back of the bootleg *Goldrush*.

In 2001, Steely Dan's first album in nineteen years, "Two Against Nature," was nominated for a number of awards. Bette Midler and Stevie Wonder presented the Album of the Year award, which Midler recognized was going to be "controversial," and Stevie Wonder jokingly referred to the Dan as "one of the angriest artists in the history of the Grammys." Steely Dan beat out Beck, Eminem, Radiohead, and Paul Simon for the honor, causing many to question the decision of the National Academy of Recording Arts and Sciences, considering the groundbreaking albums they were up against.

They also won Best Pop Performance by a Duo or Group with Vocals for the song "Cousin Dupree," although the lyrics were almost as scandalous as some of Eminem's; Best Pop Vocal Album; and Best Engineered Recording, Non Classical. When accepting the award, Fagen said, "Thanks very much. We've been around a long time. It's nice to get one of these." He would get another "one of these" in 2007 when *Morph the Cat* won a Grammy for Best Surround Sound Album, which he produced.

Old Grey Whistle Test

On July 11, 1978, the British music television program *The Old Grey Whistle Test* aired a live version of "Reelin' in the Years" that hadn't been seen on television before. The clip from 1974 begins with a rockin' guitar solo spot for Baxter before the whole band kicks in. If only we had the entire concert that this clip came from.

Television Advertisements for *Aja*

After 1973's appearances on *American Bandstand* and *The Midnight Special,* Steely Dan disappeared from the television airwaves. The next time that anything Steely Dan-related appeared on TV was to promote their sixth album, *Aja.* The first ad featured the model from the album cover, Sayoko Yamaguchi, and the voice of sultry singer, actress, and one of the two Catwomen from the '60s *Batman* television series, Eartha Kitt. They also released another advertisement that concentrated on the hit singles, with a plotline linking the movie star from "Peg" and the forgotten loser from "Deacon Blues." ABC went as far as editing both commercials together in order to create yet a third ad.

The Nightfly Videos

In 1982, Fagen created two videos for *The Nightfly.* He was definitely ahead of the curve with MTV launching only a year earlier. With so little video content for the new station, both "New Frontier" and "I.G.Y. (What a Beautiful World)" became a part of the regular playlists and were seen often. Unfortunately for Steely Dan fans, the video for "New Frontier," which was partially animated, utilized a young '50s-style teenage actor to portray Fagen, and the video for "I.G.Y. (What a Beautiful World)" was filled with vintage footage of trains and computers along with similarly vintage animated scenes of the future.

Donald Fagen and Jane Aaron Animated Shorts

In 1985 and 1987, stop-motion film director Jane Aaron, best known for her work on the PBS shows *Between the Lions* and *Sesame Street,* enlisted Donald Fagen to compose the music to accompany two of her animated short films, *Traveling Light* and *Set in Motion.* Although Fagen isn't in the videos, his quirky instrumental music is heard throughout and therefore relevant when speaking of his work in video and film.

Night Music

Between 1988 and 1990, a television show originally called *Sunday Night* and later changed to *Michelob Presents Night Music,* aired on late-night television. The show was hosted by pianist Jools Holland, of Squeeze fame, and saxophonist David Sanborn with a backing band that contained a number of musicians that had played on Steely Dan and Donald Fagen albums, including bassists Tom Barney and Marcus Miller, and guitarist Hiram Bullock. Drummers Omar Hakim and J. T. Lewis, guitarist Robben Ford, percussionist Don Alias, and keyboard players Philippe Saisse and Brenda V. Brown were also members of the band over the course of five different lineups.

For the eleventh show, Fagen was a guest along with Joe Sample, Patti Austin, and Lani Groves, who had appeared on past Steely Dan albums, and Bashiri Johnson, who would play percussion on "Brite Nightgown" from Fagen's 2006 album *Morph the Cat*. Fagen played piano with Patti Austin for her version of the standard "They Can't Take That Away from Me" and Yamaha DX7 synthesizer behind guitarist Earl Klugh for his 1977 composition "Dr. Macumba," featuring an impressive piano solo by Joe Sample. Although not on camera, he most probably played synthesizer on Sample's original "Spellbound" and on another Sample original, "When the World Turns Blue" sung by Austin. They closed the show with Fagen's "I.G.Y. (What a Beautiful World)," but unfortunately he didn't sing, he only played synthesizer, leaving the vocals for Austin to handle.

"Century's End" Video

The video for Fagen's "Century's End" from the *Bright Lights, Big City* soundtrack is curious because neither the camera-shy Fagen nor scenes from the movie are used. Instead, it is a snapshot of the nightclub and obsessive work worlds of 1980s New York City and how they meld together. I would have rather seen Fagen.

A&E's *In Concert*

On March 1 and 2, 1991, The New York Rock and Soul Revue featuring Donald Fagen, Michael McDonald, Boz Scaggs, Phoebe Snow, Charles Brown, and the Brigati Brothers was filmed at the Beacon Theatre in New York City for cable network A&E's 1992 special *In Concert*. Hosted by New Orleans legend Dr. John, shot at the Lone Star Roadhouse in New York City, with off-camera introductions by renowned New York DJ Scott Muni, the show mixed interviews with Fagen, McDonald, Scaggs, and Snow and live performances.

Charles Brown and the Brigati Brothers, however, weren't shown in the special, but the other singers all made appearances. Shot artistically in black and white, the songs featured were Steely Dan's "Pretzel Logic," and "Chain Lightning"; Boz Scaggs's take on Joe Simon's "Drowning in the Sea of Love"' Michael McDonald's stunning cover of Jackie Wilson's "Lonely Teardrops"; and Michael McDonald and Phoebe Snow's duet on Eddie Floyd and Steve Cropper's "Knock on Wood." It would be the only official film of Fagen's true return to the stage.

There was also a color trailer released to promote the show that didn't play full songs but interspersed portions of "Chain Lightning," Phoebe's Snow's take on Etta James's classic "At Last," "Drowning in the Sea of Love," "Knock on Wood," and "Lonely Teardrops," with interviews with the artists. The logo for *In Concert* was different than the final version and was titled *In Concert '91*.

Kamakiriad Electronic Press Kit and videos

To promote Donald Fagen's second solo album, 1993's *Kamakiriad* produced by Walter Becker, an electronic press kit was compiled. Interviews with Fagen and Becker, as well as actor Rick Moranis who starred in the video for "Tomorrow's Girls," were interspersed with footage from the studio with engineer Roger Nichols behind the mixing desk. The duo spoke about the concept for the album, the songwriting and recording process, and what it was like to work together in the studio after so many years. Footage from the video shoot for "Tomorrow's Girls" was also included.

Fagen produced two videos for the singles from the album, "Tomorrow's Girls" and "Snowbound," a song that Becker and Fagen initially wrote the instrumental for in 1985. Although actor Rick Moranis was hired to star in the video, Fagen finally took part as well. Filmed with Fagen singing wearing his signature shades, the footage surprisingly took precedence over the storytelling sequences. Fagen's significant contribution is interspersed with Moranis's role as the protagonist seduced by the alien women of the future.

Fagen enlisted independent film director Michel Gondry, who would win an Academy Award for Best Original Screenplay as one of the writers of *Eternal Sunshine of the Spotless Mind* in 2004, to direct the avant-garde video for the second single from *Kamakiriad*, "Snowbound." Fagen once again appears in the video in two different instances: on a television screen as an apparent leader, but also as the head of myriad underlings, expressed as animated moving parts in a never-ending rollercoaster.

11 Tracks of Whack Electronic Press Kit

Becker followed his partner's lead by releasing an electronic press kit for his 1994 debut solo album *11 Tracks of Whack*. Not only was Becker interviewed, the press kit also contained behind-the-scenes footage from the *11 Tracks of Whack* sessions.

VH1 Special

In 1995, Becker and Fagen were the focus of a half-hour special for the music network VH1. The show, shot in New York City, was incredibly enlightening, with Becker and Fagen speaking candidly about the process of songwriting, their time at Bard College, and their attempts to sell songs in the late '60s Brill Building days. They even walked down President Street in Brooklyn as they reminisced about their days on the block. Live clips from their late 1994 tour were interspersed with their interviews, making this special one of the best shows aired about the band.

The Late Show with David Letterman

In 1995, Steely Dan performed live on television for the first time since Burt Sugarman's *Midnight Special* in 1973. David Letterman was apparently a fan, and his introduction to a group that hadn't appeared on television in twenty-two years was hilarious. "You know these guys are good Paul. They got their initials on them big things over there. The Sam Donaldson Orchestra ladies and gentlemen . . . Leave the big stars alone, Paul, you're making them sick." The band kicked into their first live television show since 1973 with a striking version of "Josie" to promote the *Alive in America* LP, and as the show went to a commercial, they played "Deacon Blues."

Five years later they returned to perform "Cousin Dupree" from their first studio album in nineteen years, the Grammy Award-winning *Two Against Nature*. Fagen would also perform as a solo artist on *The Late Show*, playing "Weather in My Head" from his album *Sunken Condos* on November 15, 2012.

Classic Albums: Steely Dan Aja

In 1999, Becker and Fagen embarked on a project that would shed light on the making of what many consider their masterpiece, *Aja*. In 1992, the *Classic Albums* series debuted with a documentary on the Beatles' *Sgt. Pepper's Lonely Hearts Club Band* entitled "The Making of Sgt. Pepper." Although the *Classic Albums* moniker and title sequence weren't yet in place, the show's format was. Besides interviews with the artists, musicians, and producers involved, one of the most fascinating elements of the show was the dissection of the recordings by use of the multi-track tapes, giving the viewer the opportunity to hear singled-out tracks in a way that gives insight into the way the song was created and built layer by layer. Over the years, there have been episodes focusing on albums by John Lennon, U2, the Doors, Elton John, Phil Collins, Elvis Presley, Tom Petty and the Heartbreakers, Pink Floyd, Stevie Wonder, Queen, and countless others.

For the *Aja* installment, Becker and Fagen peel away the different layers for every song from the album except one, "I Got the News." Besides Becker and Fagen, numerous others are interviewed, including original guitarist Denny Dias; musicians that worked on the album: Michael McDonald, Chuck Rainey, Larry Carlton, Bernard Purdie, Rick Marotta, Wayne Shorter, and Dean Parks; producer Gary Katz; engineer Roger Nichols; journalist Andy Gill; and musician Ian Dury. There is also a jam session, with Becker, Fagen, Purdie, Rainey, keyboard player Paul Griffin, and

In March 2000, Eagle Rock Entertainment released the *Classic Albums: Steely Dan Aja* DVD, a fantastic "making of" documentary with footage of Becker and Fagen dissecting the songs of this groundbreaking LP.

current Steely Dan guitarist Jon Herington performing instrumental versions of "Peg," "Home at Last," and "Josie."

PBS *In the Spotlight*

One month before the February 29, 2000, release of Steely Dan's first album in nineteen years, *Two Against Nature*, Becker and Fagen entered Sony Music Studios in New York City with their band to film a PBS *In the Spotlight* special. They spent two days playing in front of a select audience for a show that would be broadcast on March 1, 2000. Not only did they play the Steely Dan classics "Green Earrings," "Bad Sneakers," "Josie," "FM (No Static at All)," "Black Friday," "Babylon Sisters," "Kid Charlemagne," "Peg," and "Pretzel Logic," they also played five songs from the new album that had not yet been released: "Cousin Dupree," "Janie Runaway," "Gaslighting Abbie," "Jack of Speed," and "What a Shame About Me." They also performed "Deacon Blues," "Do It Again," "Home at Last," and "West of Hollywood" but these songs were not broadcast. The show was released on DVD as *Steely Dan's Plush TV Jazz-Rock Party*, with the live songs interspersed with interviews with Becker, Fagen, and members of the band.

VH1's *Storytellers* TV show

Two days after filming the PBS special, Steely Dan returned to Sony Music Studios to tape an episode for the VH1 program *Storytellers*. They performed "FM (No Static at All)," "Peg," "Kid Charlemagne," "Bad Sneakers," "Josie," "Do It Again," "Cousin Dupree," and "What A Shame About Me" and fielded questions from the audience in their typical jocular manner, not giving much away with their answers. Some typical questions:

1. How did you come up with the name Steely Dan?
2. Were any songs written with a particular person in mind?

In February 2000, Steely Dan entered Sony Music Studios in New York to film a PBS *In the Spotlight* special. The show was released later that year on DVD as *Steely Dan's Plush TV Jazz-Rock Party*.

3. Who was the inspiration for "Kid Charlemagne"?
4. What kind of things did you long for in New York when you lived in Los Angeles?
5. Who was the inspiration for the lyrics to "Cousin Dupree."
6. What took you so long to release a new album?

They also turned the tables on the audience and began to ask them questions, flashing lyrics on a screen to see which audience members could name the song that contained the lyrics. This was definitely a different spin on the *Storytellers* brand.

E! Channel Network Interview

To promote *Two Against Nature*, Becker and Fagen did numerous interviews. Although this one for the E! Channel was short, rehearsal footage of the band was interspersed, making it an interesting piece.

CNN *Showbiz Today*

Another short interview from 2000 with Becker and Fagen as well as rehearsal footage of "Black Friday" and "Josie." They are as snarky as ever. When reporter Michael Okwu asked them why it took nineteen years to make *Two Against Nature*, Becker stated, "We didn't do much for the first seventeen and a half years." They closed the show with a full rehearsal performance of "Cousin Dupree."

CNN *World Beat*

CNN used their footage of the band for more than one show. *World Beat* used the "Black Friday," "Josie," and "Cousin Dupree" rehearsal footage, but they added some other video aspects. Becker and Fagen spoke of producing each other's albums, so part of the video for Fagen's "Tomorrow's Girls" was included as well as a short segment of Becker in the studio working on *11 Tracks of Whack*. A brief interview with Michael McDonald is also included. The best answer to the mundane questions was:

> Question: "Why do you think few artists rarely introduce humor to their songs?"
>
> Fagen: "No sense of humor."

The Today Show

The Today Show kicked off their early morning concert series of 2000 with a quick interview with Becker and Fagen where Katie Couric gives them a backhanded compliment by proclaiming, "You really made a point of staying consistent with . . . your original sound . . . and you didn't try to update it or change it and I think your fans are very appreciative." They followed this rather awkward interview with live versions of "Peg," "Jack of Speed," "Kid Charlemagne," and an unaired "Black Friday."

VH1 *Talk Music*

Becker and Fagen continued to make the rounds in 2000 to promote *Two Against Nature*, speaking with both print and television journalists from various networks. They were interviewed for VH1's *Talk Music* show during this period.

Steely Dan's Induction into the Rock and Roll Hall of Fame

One of the strangest things in Steely Dan's career was their induction into the Rock and Roll Hall of Fame in 2000. For some reason Moby, who seemed not only clueless about their material but also irrelevant, inducted the duo. He even seemed to be surprised himself: "I immediately asked myself a few questions, the first of these questions was 'Why are they asking me,' cause as far as I know Steely Dan seemed to hate everybody, so I was flattered but very suspicious. I wondered to myself either they like me or for some reason they really hate me and this is some sort of monstrous practical joke." Fagen thanks the musicians that have played on their albums, but Becker takes over, saying that they've already expressed their opinion about the academy, yet another dig, on their website before fielding questions. After one question, Becker responds with his own, "Who was the original drummer in the Mothers of Invention." After a quick response, they perform "Do It Again" and "Black Friday" with the house band from David Letterman's *Late Show*, the World's Most Dangerous Band with musical director Paul Schaffer. Unfortunately, the guitar solo by Queen's Brian May on "Do It Again" doesn't reach the standards of Becker's on "Black Friday."

Steely Dan Confessions

When Steely Dan's *Everything Must Go* came out in 2003, they released a special edition that included a DVD. This wasn't your typical behind-the-scenes making-of-an-album documentary or a live performance. Instead, Becker and Fagen made a short film that was a special edition of the cult HBO show *Taxicab Confessions* hosted by cabbie Rita. The duo cruise the streets of Las Vegas picking up a series of female passengers and play them tracks from the new album.

Their guests run the gamut from a ditzy blonde who loves "Reelin' in the Sheaves" to a magician with a snake named Scooby around her neck to a British girl who speaks of how fast "Essex girls" are to, guess what, a couple of "Essex girls" dressed in matching nightgowns. Rita is as funny as Becker and Fagen and has quite a few memorable lines. When asked by Rita "Whaddya do for fun?" Becker responds, "Well, there's brooding."

The twenty-two-minute film shows their sense of humor and gives us a rare glimpse of the way that they interact with people who aren't the press.

Donald Fagen Concepts for Jazz/Rock Piano

In 2003, Donald Fagen released his first instructional DVD, *Concepts for Jazz/Rock Piano*. The seventy-minute video focuses on Fagen and then-Steely Dan keyboard player Warren Bernhardt switching off between acoustic piano and Fender Rhodes electric piano as the duo analyze three Steely Dan songs, "Chain Lightning," "Peg," and "Josie," and two solo pieces from *Kamakiriad*, "On the Dunes" and "Teahouse on the Tracks." They deconstruct the tunes and discuss how although they're blues based, the altered chord changes create the harmonic sophistication that is so prevalent in Steely Dan's music. While the video might seem to appeal to musicians only, it's interesting to watch them discuss what makes these songs so special, something anybody could enjoy.

In 2003, Fagen released his first instructional DVD, *Concepts for Jazz/Rock Piano*, where he and then-Steely Dan keyboard player Warren Bernhardt analyzed a number of Steely Dan and Fagen solo compositions.

Rent Party Tour TV Special

To promote their 2009 *Rent Party* tour, Steely Dan produced an interesting thirty-minute documentary. Not only did it include interviews with Becker and Fagen, they also incorporated some behind-the-scenes rehearsal footage.

The Dukes of September

On June 14, 2012, Donald Fagen, Michael McDonald, and Boz Scaggs, billed as the Dukes of September, appeared on *Late Night with Jimmy Fallon* performing the Brothers Johnson's classic "I'll Be Good to You" to promote their upcoming tour. In November 2012, they filmed a show from their second tour at Lincoln Center in New York City. It was initially broadcast as a ninety-minute *Great Performances* special on PBS in March 2014 and released at the same time on DVD and Blu-ray discs. Their set list included classic Steely Dan numbers such as "Kid Charlemagne," "Hey Nineteen," "Pretzel Logic," "Reelin' in the Years," and "Peg";

the Michael McDonald and Doobie Brothers' hits "I Keep Forgettin'," "What a Fool Believes," and "Takin' It to the Streets"; Boz Scaggs's "Lowdown," "Lido Shuffle," and "Miss Sun"; and the soul and funk classics "People Get Up and Drive Your Funky Soul," "Who's That Lady," "Sweet Soul Music," "The Same Thing," "You Can Never Tell," "Love T.K.O.," and "Them Changes."

Donald Fagen Author Event at Barnes and Noble

To promote his 2013 book *Eminent Hipsters*, Fagen was interviewed by eminent *Rolling Stone* journalist David Fricke at the Union Square Barnes and Noble in New York City. Although some felt that the second half of the book was basically Fagen ranting about the *Dukes of September Rhythm Revue* tour, his responses to Fricke's questions kept the audience laughing.

In November 2012, Donald Fagen, Michael McDonald, and Boz Scaggs, billed as the Dukes of September, filmed a show at Lincoln Center in New York City. It was initially broadcast as a ninety-minute *Great Performances* special on PBS in March 2014 and released at the same time on DVD and Blu-ray discs.

22

The Slickest Song I've Ever Heard

Steely Dan's Return to the Studio

Two Against Nature

After Steely Dan's reunion tours of the '90s, Becker and Fagen finally released a new studio LP entitled *Two Against Nature* in 2000. It had taken them nineteen years to stage a full tour, and the same amount of time had passed since their last album, *Gaucho*, had been released. After nearly twenty years without any new product, *Two Against Nature* sold well, being certified platinum in the U.S., and won four Grammys in 2001 including Album of the Year. The inspiration for the album title came from an obscure 19th-century French novel by Joris-Karl Huysmans. The title had originally been translated as *Against the Grain* but was later changed to *Against Nature*. The book, about a French Aristocrat who retires from the world to live in a house full of gadgets that heighten one's senses inspired Oscar Wilde to write *The Picture of Dorian Gray*.

Becker elaborated on the process of making the album in an interview with Paul Zollo for *The Performing Songwriter* on March 1, 2000. "We'd been working on the album for about five months and we looked out the window and noticed that they were starting to build a large high-rise forty-story apartment house on the corner across from the studio. And we actually went back in the studio a couple of days ago to add a part to the album, and we noticed that the building was finished. And people were living in it already! And here we were still putting parts on the album!" *Two Against Nature* took three years to make. The majority of the album was written in 1997, with recording at Fagen's River Sound, Clinton Sound, Electric Lady, and additional tracking taking place at Becker's Hyperbolic Sound in Maui in '98 and '99.

It would be the last album to use a revolving set of drummers. Ricky Lawson was unavailable for most of the sessions, so he would only play on one track, the opener "Gaslighting Abbie." Drummer Leroy Clouden, who had played on Fagen's "Century's End" as well as the *Kamakiriad* album, was brought in for three songs, "Janie Runaway," "Almost Gothic," and "Cousin Dupree." Bassist Tom Barney recommended Maze drummer Michael White, who contributed to "What a Shame About Me" and "Jack of Speed," and session heavyweight Vinnie Colaiuta played drums on "Negative Girl." Earth, Wind & Fire's Sonny Emory also got involved, playing on the challenging "West of Hollywood," but it was the drummer on "Two Against Nature" that would make the most lasting impression on Becker and Fagen: Keith Carlock.

Carlock would be the sole drummer for the Dan's next album, *Everything Must Go*, as well as Fagen's *Morph the Cat* and Becker's *Circus Money*. He would also perform on every Steely Dan tour from 2003's *Everything Must Go* tour onward as well as Fagen's short *Morph the Cat* tour in 2006. Barney also recommended keyboard player Ted Baker, who in turn recommended guitarist Jon Herington, who, like Carlock, would play on every subsequent Steely Dan tour.

Herington recalls that he was initially called in to overdub rhythm guitar onto the already recorded backing tracks for one song. After a four-hour session, Becker and Fagen told him that they would call him in a week to come in and record another track. The weeks passed, and Herington began questioning his work, but after five weeks, he finally got the call from Becker. He explained that although they wouldn't be using anything from his first session, they wanted him to record on some other tunes. He's been with the band ever since. Becker and Fagen again contributed heavily to the rhythm section, with Becker handling the bass on all but three songs and guitar on every track except two, and Fagen playing keys on all but two songs along with Ted Baker and Michael Leonhart. The album also has female background vocals on every song, a first on a Steely Dan record.

The reviews for the record were generally extremely favorable. John Bungey of the *London Times* gave it eight out of ten stars, stating that, "this is one revival that has been worth the wait." In comparing it to *Gaucho*, Richard Cromelin of the *Los Angeles Times* wrote, "Brisk and biting, *Two Against Nature* shakes off the malaise and mannerism that crept into its distant predecessor, *Gaucho*." Ian McDonald realized the difference between a Becker or Fagen solo album and a Steely Dan album: "A 20-year hiatus has failed to dent the continuity of the music Becker and Fagen make together. Knowing them apart through their solo albums, we can only marvel at how the synergy between them produces stuff not only a level higher than what they do alone, but also of a different character. When they collaborate as equals, the result is Steely Dan. Separate, neither can do this trick."

The Songs

After a nineteen-year hiatus, Becker and Fagen returned with an eclectic album containing everything from R&B-flavored backbeats to complex jazz-influenced grooves. Their lyrics are as sharp as ever, and the themes do not disappoint. Whether it's a song about a nymphet and her sugar daddy, a man-child lusting after his cousin, or a self-pitying middle-aged failure running into an old college flame, the duo put a fresh spin on the subject matter, proving that their sense of humor sits perfectly in the modern world.

"Gaslighting Abbie"

The album opens with a song about a man and his mistress who scheme to make his wife think she's going insane. The term "Gaslighting" comes from the 1944 movie *Gaslight* starring Ingrid Bergman, Charles Boyer, Joseph Cotten, and eighteen-year-old Angela Lansbury in her screen debut. Ricky Lawson and bassist Tom Barney lay down a serious pocket, with Becker and Fagen adding the perfect groove on top with guitar, Fender Rhodes electric piano, and clavinet. An interesting horn arrangement with not only trumpet, tenor saxophone, and trombone, but clarinet and bass clarinet providing a nice contrast over the straight-ahead groove. Becker plays a bluesy guitar solo, and Chris Potter turns in a fierce tenor solo on the outro.

"What a Shame About Me"

Becker and Fagen once again use a light, jazz-inflected groove under an amusing but dismal story about a man who hasn't achieved the success others assumed he would. He runs into an old college flame, who is now an accomplished actress and singer, and they speak of their other friends and their spectacular career achievements. The lyrics take an unexpected turn during the last verse when the woman asks the narrator to join him at her hotel and he turns her down. Drummer Michael White lays down a sparse groove under a Fender Rhodes electric piano pad and Thelonious Monk-like piano accents played by Fagen along with some fine blues guitar licks and a ripping solo by Becker. The horn section, led by the muted trumpet work of Michael Leonhart, floats on top, adding texture while filling in the gaps.

"Two Against Nature"

Future Steely Dan drummer Keith Carlock makes his first appearance on a Steely Dan record with the intense and tricky title track. The song, in 6/4 time,

is an oddity for the Dan and includes timbales and percussion by Daniel Sadownick, additional percussion by Gordon Gottlieb, and vibraphone by Steve Shapiro. The bass part, credited to Becker, is also something different, using a bass synthesizer triggered by a sequence, the only use of a sequencer on the album. The lyrics are a hodge-podge of gruesome images about voodoo and are some of their darkest lyrics on wax. When asked if they were the two that were "gonna break the shape of things unknown" by John Sakamoto for *JAM!* magazine, Fagen responded, "Pretty much.

The first Steely Dan album in nineteen years, *Two Against Nature* was released in February 2000 and won four Grammys including Album of the Year.

That's our little self-referential piece . . . it's sort of an advertisement for ourselves." Fagen plays some angular piano and Fender Rhodes electric piano parts alongside Michael Leonhart's Wurlitzer electric piano, while Becker adds a distorted guitar solo, and Jon Herington provides chicken-pickin' rhythm guitar, his first appearance on a Steely Dan album. The horns, arranged by Leonhart, perfectly reflect the spooky nature of the lyrics, as does the equally chilling tenor saxophone solo.

"Janie Runaway"

"Janie Runaway" takes "Hey Nineteen" a step further with a tale of an underage girl who flees to New York City from Florida and finds a much older sugar daddy to take care of her. She quickly becomes part of the jet set and is even promised a European vacation, if she invites a friend along. The song is relatively simple, a mid-tempo soul groove punctuated by the horn section arranged by Fagen and a smoking alto saxophone solo by Chris Potter. "Janie Runaway" wouldn't have been out of place on Fagen's *Kamakiriad* with its uncomplicated arrangement and R&B tendencies. It was released as the album's third single, but failed to chart.

"Almost Gothic"

The easy-listening feel of "Almost Gothic" is reminiscent of "Deacon Blues," and Michael Leonhart plays a lovely trumpet solo over the sparkle of Ted Baker's Fender Rhodes electric piano and a pad-like horn arrangement, including clarinet and bass clarinet, by Fagen, who also adds Wurlitzer electric piano. Leroy Clouden and Walter Becker lay the foundation for Hugh McCracken's rhythm guitar and Jon Herington's acoustic guitar as the song grooves sweetly and effortlessly. "Almost Gothic" is a true love song, but the object of the narrator's affection has a definite personality disorder, or perhaps she's just extremely moody. Either way he is completely infatuated with her, probably more so due to her mood swings.

"Jack of Speed"

"Jack of Speed" was based on an unfinished reggaeish song that Becker and Fagen found on a twenty-year-old cassette. They played the song during the 1996 *Art Crimes* tour but with Becker on lead vocals; for the recorded version, it was slowed down, some lyrics were altered, and Fagen took over on the lead vocals about different characters flirting with madness and self-destruction. The song bounces along due to Maze drummer Michael White's hip-hopish groove along with a bubbling bass part provided by Becker. Fagen lays down a groovy Wurlitzer electric piano as Becker plays bluesy guitar licks around the vocals, horn section, and Fagen's melodica in addition to a stinging solo. "Jack of Speed" was the second single released from the album, but didn't chart.

"Cousin Dupree"

Arguably the most popular song on the album, "Cousin Dupree" was the first single released before the *Two Against Nature* album hit the stores. In 2001, it won a Grammy Award for Best Pop Performance by a Duo or Group with Vocals and was played extensively during their 2000 tours and television appearances. As Fagen would often state, the song was a "rural narrative" about a layabout who has a crush on his younger cousin. Leroy Clouden and Becker play a simple pocket, with Jon Herington adding rhythm guitar, Fagen on Wurlitzer electric piano, and Ted

Baker on Fender Rhodes electric piano. Becker once again plays an appropriately slinky guitar solo, and Fagen's stepdaughter Amy Helm adds some Theremin-like whistling during the bridge. In July 2006, Steely Dan posted a humorous letter on their website claiming that Owen Wilson stole the title of his film *You, Me, and Dupree* from their song. Owen Wilson defended himself in a similarly comical way, stating, "I have never heard the song 'Cousin Dupree' and I don't even know who this gentleman, Mr. Steely Dan, is. I hope this helps to clear things up and I can get back to concentrating on my new movie, 'Hey Nineteen.'" It was the only single from the album to chart, peaking at number thirty in the U.S.

"Negative Girl"
Recorded live in two takes that were later edited together, "Negative Girl" is the only song from the album on which neither Becker nor Fagen play. Drummer Vinnie Colaiuta lays down an almost "Aja"-like groove full of side-stick and ride cymbal while Tom Barney comes up with an incredibly innovative bass part that moves and grooves under Ted Baker's Fender Rhodes electric piano. Dean Parks and Paul Jackson Jr.'s dueling rhythm guitar parts perfectly complement each other while never getting in each other's way. Dave Schank's vibraphone is dazzling, and his solo is understated yet powerful. Fagen's vocal delivery perfectly captures the sentiment of a man in love with a toxic beauty that he knows isn't good for him, but his obsession is so strong that he continues the doomed relationship.

"West of Hollywood"
"West of Hollywood" was a rewrite of a song Becker and Fagen composed in the '80s that originally had a reggae feel. It's interesting because there is not one rhyming couplet in the entire song, and while the lyrics are oblique, a sense of doom is apparent throughout. The groove is the most rock 'n' roll on the album, played by Earth, Wind & Fire's Sonny Emory on drums, Tom Barney on bass, Jon Herington on rhythm guitar, and Ted Baker handling the piano and Fender Rhodes electric piano parts. Fagen adds a swirling Hammond B3 organ, and Becker provides another fine solo, navigating over numerous chord changes with ease. Clocking in at eight minutes and twenty-two seconds, it is the longest song on any Steely Dan studio album, the highlight being Chris Potter's four-minute solo on the outro; a true masterpiece and on a short list of the best saxophone solos on a Steely Dan record.

Everything Must Go

After the *2YK* tour concluded on September 19, 2000, in Düsseldorf, Germany, Becker and Fagen would take a break before returning to the studio to start work on their follow-up, *Everything Must Go*. The duo worked for a few weeks at Becker's Hyperbolic Sound studio before moving to Studio A at Sear Sound in New York City to begin work in August 2001. Sear Sound opened in 1970 in the Paramount Hotel on West 46th Street and in 1990 moved to the space on 48th Street that had once been used by another famous studio, the Hit Factory. The Hit Factory was where Becker and Fagen first recorded professionally when they worked on Terence Boylan's debut LP, *Alias Boona*, in 1969.

The duo originally went to Sear Sound with long-time engineer Elliot Scheiner to record the Joni Mitchell song "Carey," from her *Blue* LP, for use on a tribute album. In the drummer's chair was Mississippian Keith Carlock. Becker and Fagen had first heard Carlock at New York City's famous 55 Bar on Christopher Street in Greenwich Village as part of guitarist Wayne Krantz's trio and were immediately impressed. Not only could he play rock, funk, and soul with a deep pocket, he was also an adept jazz musician. They had used him on the title track of *Two Against Nature*, and decided to hire him as the lone drummer on *Everything Must Go*.

Steely Dan followed up the Grammy-winning *Two Against Nature* with 2003's *Everything Must Go*, their only album not to have been certified gold.

Although "Carey" was never released, Scheiner used the experience to convince Becker and Fagen to record their next album on 24-track analog tape. After working in the digital domain for their last few releases, they welcomed the warm sound of tape and decided to go back to the way they recorded their albums in the '70s. Sessions began in August 2001 at Sear Sound, where the duo also took a different approach to recording in comparison to what they had done for the last few Steely Dan albums and solo releases. Rather than try to get the perfect drum track and then overdub on top of that, they would rehearse a few songs with the band and then record the rhythm section live. They would then do the overdubs with either Roger Nichols, T. J. Doherty, or Dave Russell engineering at Skyline Studios in Manhattan, Fagen's River Sound in Manhattan, Becker's Hyperbolic Sound in Maui, or Bearsville Studios in the Catskills in upstate New York.

This was the first Steely Dan album since 1973's *Countdown to Ecstasy* that would utilize virtually the same rhythm section on every tune. Keith Carlock laid down the drums, Becker played bass and contributed guitar solos to five of the nine tracks, Fagen played keys, Jon Herington and Hugh McCracken added guitar, and Ted Baker provided piano or electric piano on all but two songs, on which Bill Charlap played. This approach gave the album more of a band feel, and the tight acoustics of the live room at Sear Sound achieved an intimate vibe.

Unfortunately, *Everything Must Go* was not as successful as the duo had hoped and was the only Steely Dan album to not achieve at least gold status, although it peaked at number nine on the U.S. album charts. The reviews were mixed, but even the ones that weren't positive weren't that bad. Robert Christgau called the material "well-turned but over familiar" in his *Rolling Stone* review, but he still gave the album three stars. Andy Gill, who had appeared in the *Classic Albums: Steely Dan Aja* documentary, wrote in *The Independent*, "There's a shortfall in the kind of bravura flourishes and knock-you-dead melodies you expect from Steely Dan." George Peterson of *Mixonline.com* praised the album: "*Everything Must Go* is a stronger album than the Dan's quadra-Grammy Award-winning *Two Against Nature*. The production is more relaxed and natural sounding; overall, the songs are better crafted, creating a more consistent package. And like other Becker/Fagen creations, *Everything Must Go* doesn't immediately grab one by the throat, but after a couple of plays, the infectious hooks on tunes such as 'Godwhacker,' 'Pixeleen,' 'Things I Miss the Most' and the two single pulls ('The Last Mall' and 'Blues Beach') are firmly locked into the listener's consciousness." Larry Wallace for PopMatters.com called the album "a summertime masterpiece," described the song "Godwhacker" as "the most ingeniously crafted pop song that will be released all year," and compared the album to 1974's *Pretzel Logic*, the LP that produced the band's highest-charting single, "Rikki Don't Lose That Number."

The Songs

Overall, *Everything Must Go* is a funkier album than *Two Against Nature*, with tight grooves and witty lyrics. The fact that the same basic rhythm section plays on every song, coupled with the use of analog tape, helped to produce a more cohesive set and a fuller sound. Although not as eclectic as their previous outing, the songs work well together, and the playing is superb by all parties involved.

"The Last Mall"

The shuffle groove of the first track, "The Last Mall," was, in drummer Keith Carlock's words, "a hard groove to get." Although the rhythm tracks on the majority of the album were recorded live, the approach for the opening song was quite different. The entire band played to a click track, and Carlock overdubbed his drums afterward, not a typical recording technique. Becker and Fagen had always been fascinated by the apocalypse, growing up during a time when bomb shelters and air raid drills were common. "The Last Mall" is set on a day when a nuclear bomb is set to go off, but makes light of the fact that people are preparing for something that they won't, and probably shouldn't want to, live through. Becker plays a cutting guitar solo full of his brand of jazz-inflected phrasing, but with a distorted tone giving it a menacing quality. It's played over Ted Baker's syncopated piano and a discordant horn arrangement by Fagen until its abrupt end.

"Things I Miss the Most"

While this tale of divorce drolly mocks the important things that the narrator misses such as "the Audi TT," "the comfy Eames chair," "the good copper pans," "the '54 Strat (which was actually stolen)," etc., it was inspired by Becker's divorce from his wife Elinor. While the chorus lyrics poke fun at the idea of divorce by the wealthy, the verses are heartfelt and show the narrator's loneliness. The breezy, easygoing groove lays the foundation for a melancholy horn arrangement but changes direction for the middle section, which gets increasingly dark before opening up for a quick Becker solo.

"Blues Beach"
"Blues Beach" is the most joyous-sounding song on the album with a "My Old School" type of groove and some tasteful Hammond B3 organ and piano playing by Fagen alongside Ted Baker's Fender Rhodes electric piano. The beat is rock solid and infectious, and Carolyn Leonhart adds multiple layers of background vocals that contribute to the party atmosphere of the song. But things aren't always so cheery on "Blues Beach." The song's hook, "And it's the long, sad Sunday of the early resigned," was a nod to social critic Paul Goodman's 1960 book *Growing Up Absurd*, which divided people into various categories, with the "early resigned" referring to beatniks. The irony is that the narrator thinks he's left his problems behind as he gets out of the city, but they follow him to his getaway.

"Godwhacker"
The subject matter of "Godwhacker" is at odds with its relentless groove, but that's nothing new for Steely Dan. Numerous journalists interpreted the lyrics as anti-Bush and anti-terrorist, but it seems more straightforward than that: a vigilante that's tracking down God to punish him for the ills of the world. Herington lays down the devious-sounding guitar line as Hugh McCracken adds some chordal elements and Becker plays sneaky lead lines on top. Jazz pianist Bill Charlap provides the groovy Fender Rhodes electric piano, as Ted Baker was unavailable, alongside Fagen's Wurlitzer electric piano to great effect. Fagen takes the first solo, playing a synth harmonica patch, followed by Becker on guitar, the first time they both take solos on a Dan record, and their intimidating approach echoes the alarming sentiment of the lyrics. With no horns, the song has a sense of space that makes the groove that much harder and deeper.

"Slang of Ages"
Walter Becker takes his first lead vocal on a Steely Dan track with "Slang of Ages." The song was originally supposed to be sung by Fagen, but since it didn't really have a vocal melody for the verse, they decided that Becker's approach to a lead vocal would work for this simple mid-tempo funk song. The lyrics are full of drug references and even a nod to the 1966 Eddie Floyd cut "Knock on Wood," played during the *New York Rock and Soul Revue* tours. Walt Weiskopf once again turns in a fantastic tenor saxophone solo before the serene bridge enters and the background vocals take the spotlight. Fagen plays Fender Rhodes electric piano, Hammond B3 organ, and synthesizer, with Ted Baker contributing the Wurlitzer electric piano that adds the dreamy part at the end of the chorus. The horns are pure soul, punctuating the tune with hits and providing pads at the ideal moments.

"Green Book"
"Green Book" is a slinky tune whose demo was originally quite a bit faster. It's a sinister-sounding track with a deep, groovy bass line by Becker; off-kilter chord changes played by Fagen on Fender Rhodes electric piano and Hammond B3 organ; and a dissonant piano part courtesy of Ted Baker. The high point of the song, however, is Becker and Fagen trading solos, with Becker playing through

an envelope filter and Fagen using an equally disturbing synthesizer patch over a series of ominous-sounding chords. Although Becker recorded his solos weeks before Fagen, they gel perfectly and sound as if they're playing off of each other. The lyrics are a postmodern imagining of a type of pornography where you can create your perfect partner, something beyond anything the modern world had experienced.

"Pixeleen"

A new topic for Steely Dan, a superhero teenage girl, from either a video game or a movie, who isn't only strong but attractive. The mid-tempo tune features Carolyn Leonhart with a solo female vocal during the choruses and the middle section, also new for a Steely Dan record. The groove bounces along smoothly, with Becker bumping along over Carlock's beat with a radiant Fender Rhodes electric piano played by Fagen as well as the subtle, yet important, Hammond B3 organ. Bill Charlap adds some piano flourishes along with a horn arrangement that fills out the tune nicely. Roger Rosenberg contributes a few short baritone saxophone solos that are unexpected due to the instrument's low register, but surprisingly suit the song perfectly.

"Lunch with Gina"

"Lunch with Gina" is yet another song about an unhinged woman, but in this case the narrator is no longer interested and is hiding from his former flame. This funk-infused tune showcases one of Becker's best bass lines and the track grooves hard from the moment the backbeat kicks in. Jon Herington and Hugh McCracken play rhythm guitar off of each other as if they've performed together forever, and Fagen and Baker take care of the Wurlitzer and Fender Rhodes electric piano parts respectively. Fagen takes his third synthesizer solo on the album during the instrumental break as well as on the fade-out and executes it fiercely. The dense vocal harmonies by Fagen and Michael Harvey add a lushness to the track as the horns interject at the ideal spots.

"Everything Must Go"

The title track, and final song on the album, is an anecdote about the dissolution of a company, similar to the Enron fiasco, but also tackles the subject of the types of "Going out of business" sales that smaller stores hold in order to con the public. The song begins with an open section for Walt Weiskopf's tenor saxophone before the pocket kicks in. The slow-burning rhythm perfectly captures the attitude of desperation mixed with a sense of reckless abandon one might feel when there's no turning back. Weiskopf not only plays over the intro but also contributes another Coltrane-like solo to the track that adds to the desperation expressed in the song's lyrics. Fagen's vocal delivery is equally distressed sounding, yet the female background vocals add a sweetness that comforts, while taking the edge off.

23

It's Even Better This Time Around

The Steely Dan Tours from 2000 to 2016

The Pre-Release *Walking Distance* Tour—2000

For three days, January 28, 29, and February 1, Steely Dan opened the doors to Sony Music Studios in New York City to film a PBS *In the Spotlight* special that would eventually become the DVD release *Plush TV Jazz-Rock Party*, and an episode of VH-1's *Storytellers*. Although it had been a little over three years since Steely Dan had toured, many band members returned for both the *Plush TV Party* dates and the *Two Against Nature* tour. Drummer Ricky Lawson and bass player Tom Barney were both back, but the other two members of the rhythm section had changed. Ted Baker, who played on *Two Against Nature*, replaced John Beasley and would tour with them again in 2003 to promote the *Everything Must Go* album, on which he also played. He would work on Fagen's 2006 release *Morph the Cat* and Becker's *Circus Money* in 2008.

The other new member of the rhythm section would prove to be one of the most important additions to Steely Dan, guitarist Jon Herington. While recording *Two Against Nature*, Becker and Fagen expressed their interest in adding another guitarist to the fold. Pianist Ted Baker was a close friend of Herington's and gave a copy of his 1992 album, *The Complete Rhyming Dictionary*, a collection of Herington original instrumentals, to Becker and Fagen. Needless to say, they were impressed and brought him into the studio to record "Two Against Nature," "Almost Gothic," "Cousin Dupree," and "West of Hollywood." He would tour to support the album and would play on every track on 2003's *Everything Must Go*. He would also appear on Fagen's *Morph the Cat* and *Sunken Condos* as well as Becker's *Circus Money*. He would not only play on every Steely Dan tour to date, he would also serve as musical director, join Fagen on his short tour to promote *Morph the Cat* in 2006, and take part in both *Dukes of September Rhythm Revue* tours.

Tenor saxophonist Cornelius Bumpus and trumpet player Michael Leonhart were back, but for the PBS and VH-1 specials, alto and tenor saxophonist Chris Potter, who had toured with the band in 1993–1994 and had contributed to the *Two Against Nature* album, was added to the horn section. A first for the tour was

The cover of the program for Steely Dan's 2000 tour supporting the release of *Two Against Nature*.

that Becker and Fagen decided to add a trombonist to the group, Jim Pugh. Becker and Fagen had jokingly boasted during their '90s shows that there would be "no trombones" on their bandstand. Pugh was the man who turned them around, and he has been a member of every Steely Dan touring ensemble since he joined the band in 2000. He also played on Fagen's *Kamakiriad* and *Sunken Condos* albums and Steely Dan's *Two Against Nature* and *Everything Must Go* LPs. Saxophonist Ari Ambrose, who had played on 1996's *Art Crimes* world tour, would be back lending his musicality to the early 2000 performances in Japan and through the first North American dates replacing Chris Potter. Bob Sheppard, a Steely Dan alumnus from the 1993–1994 tour as well as both of Walter Becker's solo albums, joined the tour in June, taking over for Ambrose. Background vocalist Carolyn Leonhart-Escoffery was the only returning background vocalist from the *Art Crimes* tour of '96. Cynthia Calhoun replaced Michelle Wiley, and a third background vocalist was added, Victoria Cave.

For the PBS special, the band played a number of songs that had been included on previous tours, including "Pretzel Logic," from the album of the same name; "Black Friday," "Bad Sneakers" and "Green Earrings" from *Katy Lied*; "Kid Charlemagne" from *The Royal Scam*; "Josie" and "Peg" from *Aja*; "Babylon Sisters" from *Gaucho*; and "FM (No Static at All)." They also played six of the nine new songs from *Two Against Nature*, which wouldn't be released for a month. These included the three singles from the album, "Cousin Dupree," "Jack of Speed," and "Janie Runaway"; plus three album tracks, "Gaslighting Abbie," "What a Shame About Me," and "West of Hollywood," although the last song wasn't included on the PBS special or the DVD release. Three other songs, "Do It Again" from *Can't Buy a Thrill* and "Deacon Blues" and "Home at Last" from *Aja*, were also performed, but were cut from the show and DVD as well.

For the *Storytellers* episode, the band played songs from every album except *Countdown to Ecstasy*, *Pretzel Logic*, and *Gaucho*, including "Do It Again," "Bad Sneakers," Kid Charlemagne" "FM (No Static at All)," "Peg," "Josie," "Jack of Speed," "Cousin Dupree," and "What a Shame About Me." Surprisingly, they took questions from the audience, but their answers, of course, did little to give insight into the meaning of their compositions.

Two Against Nature Tour—2000

The *Two Against Nature* tour, dubbed the *2YK* tour, was Steely Dan's first official world tour, traveling through Japan, the U.S., Denmark, Finland, Sweden, Norway, Germany, Scotland, England, Belgium, France, and the Netherlands over the course of four months. Although the original Steely Dan ceased touring in 1974 due to the duo's disdain for the road and Fagen's slight nervous breakdown during their short jaunt to London, the new Steely Dan seemed to love life on the road. Becker was particularly fond of the idea and enjoyed the payoff of presenting their new material, as well as old favorites, live. They were finally able to perform with a band that could interpret the music and present it in a way that satisfied the duo. They were also in a much better place financially than they were in the early '70s so the touring experience was more enjoyable and the accommodations more luxurious. As Fagen said in a February 2000 interview with the Baltimore Sun, "It's like being babies."

The set list included all of the material that they played for the PBS special with two curious omissions, "Pretzel Logic" and "Green Earrings," two songs they had been performing since they began touring again in the '90s. For the *2YK* tour, songs were added from every album and included quite a few that they had never played live before. Since the tour was supporting *Two Against Nature*, seven songs from the album were performed, including "Almost Gothic," a new addition to the set list, but it was the older songs that were most surprising.

From *Can't Buy a Thrill*, they debuted a new arrangement of "Dirty Work" sung by the female background vocalists; from *Countdown to Ecstasy*, they performed "The Boston Rag," which typically opened the show; from *Pretzel Logic*, they added the surprising choices of "Night by Night" and "Monkey in Your Soul," which was sung by Becker; and from *Katy Lied*, "Daddy Don't Live in That New York City No More," also sung by Becker. They also had a new second-set opener, "Hank's Pad," a reworked Henry Mancini instrumental originally title "Pete's Pad" from the *Peter Gunn* television series, to which Fagen added lyrics. The song featured numerous solos and concluded with a jazzy harmonized vocal by the three background vocalists. The breakdown of songs per album was:

Can't Buy a Thrill: "Dirty Work," "Do it Again," "Reelin' In the Years"
Countdown to Ecstasy: "Bodhisattva," "My Old School," "The Boston Rag"
Pretzel Logic: "Monkey in Your Soul," "Night by Night," "Rikki Don't Lose that Number"
Katy Lied: "Bad Sneakers," "Black Friday," "Daddy Don't Live in That New York City No More"
The Royal Scam: "Don't Take Me Alive," "Kid Charlemagne," "The Royal Scam"
Aja: "Deacon Blues," "Home at Last," "Josie," "Peg"
Gaucho: "Babylon Sisters," "Hey Nineteen," "Glamour Profession"
Two Against Nature: "Almost Gothic," "Cousin Dupree," "Gaslighting Abbie," "Jack of Speed," "Janie Runaway," "West of Hollywood," "What a Shame About Me"
Miscellaneous: "FM (No Static at All)," "Hank's Pad" (second set instrumental overture)

The tour reviews were generally favorable, with the *New York Times'* Jon Pareles commenting on the dichotomy between their music and lyrics: "The songs were slick and luxurious, and still disquieting." John Waters of *The Guardian* wrote enthusiastically about their London show. "As front man, Fagen has slowly developed from a morose introvert who hated the sound of his own voice to an authoritative bandleader, hunched behind his Rhodes piano like a younger Ray Charles . . . there is a sentimental mood at the heart of Steely Dan, a romantic vision of a jazz that died before they were born combined with a distaste for the decaying corpse of rock and roll. To turn this into . . . an international tour . . . playing the hits to a swaying mass of happy fans, is some kind of triumph." But others thought that Becker and Fagen lacked showmanship, and although the musicians were some of the most revered in the business, the same naysayers believed that there was a studio-like, passionless way in which the songs were delivered.

Everything Must Go Tour—2003

Six weeks after the release of *Everything Must Go*, Steely Dan hit the road for a two-and-a-half-month U.S. tour starting on July 23, 2003, in Costa Mesa, California, at the Orange County Fair and closing on October 11, 2003, in Honolulu, Hawaii. Three-quarters of their rhythm section was back, with bassist Tom Barney, guitarist Jon Herington, and keyboard player Ted Baker resuming their roles from the 2000 tour to support the *Two Against Nature* album. Once again they had a new drummer, but this one was here to stay. Keith Carlock had played on the title track from *Two Against Nature*, had been the sole drummer on the *Everything Must Go* album, and would exclusively play on Fagen's *Morph the Cat* and Becker's *Circus Money*. The 2003 *Everything Must Go* tour would be his first, but like guitarist Herington, he would go on to play on every subsequent Steely Dan tour as well as Fagen's short tour in 2006 to promote *Morph the Cat*. Steely Dan had found their new drummer.

Three of the four horn players also returned: trumpet player Michael Leonhart, tenor saxophonist Cornelius Bumpus, and trombonist Jim Pugh. The new kid on the block was alto/tenor saxophonist and clarinet player Walt Weiskopf. He played the memorable solo on "Everything Must Go," as well as four other songs from the album of the same name, and would play on every Steely Dan tour to date in addition to the *Morph the Cat* album and tour, both *Dukes of September Rhythm Revue* tours, and Fagen's 2012 solo album, *Sunken Condos*. Background vocalists Carolyn Leonhart-Escoffery and Cynthia Calhoun were back, but Victoria Cave was replaced by Cynthia Mizelle.

For the *Everything Must Go* tour, Becker and Fagen dropped a number of songs that had been added for the *2YK* tour. "Do It Again," "Dirty Work," and "Reelin' in the Years" from *Can't Buy a Thrill* were not played, so no songs from their debut album were represented. Both "Bodhisattva" and "The Boston Rag" were also cut, but "My Old School" from *Countdown to Ecstasy* survived, making it the only song played from the album. "Rikki Don't Lose that Number," "Night by Night," and "Monkey in Your Soul" from *Pretzel Logic* were all dropped from the show, but "Parker's Band" was added, and although an instrumental version had been played

A photo collage of Becker and Fagen used for the 2000 tour program.   A promo photo of Becker and Fagen used for the 2000 tour program.

during an overture on earlier tours, this was the first time it was performed in its entirety, with the three background vocalists providing the lead vocals and the sublime harmonies on the middle section. "Bad Sneakers," "Black Friday," and "Daddy Don't Live in That New York City No More" were scratched, so no songs from *Katy Lied* were played during the tour. "The Royal Scam" didn't make the cut, but both "Don't Take Me Alive" and "Kid Charlemagne" did; and two songs from *The Royal Scam* were premiered live for the first time, "The Caves of Altamira" and "Haitian Divorce." "Deacon Blues" was not played, but "Home at Last," "Josie," and "Peg" all survived, and not only did the title track from *Aja* find its way back into the set, the first time since 1994, so did "Black Cow," which hadn't been played live since 1996's *Art Crimes* tour. "Glamour Profession" was gone, but "Babylon Sisters" and "Hey Nineteen" were still performed; and one new song from *Gaucho* was premiered, "Time Out of Mind." "FM (No Static at All)" was still often played as an encore, but only one song from *Two Against Nature* remained, "Janie Runaway."

Since they were touring to promote the new album, six of the nine songs were played, although not every night, including "Blues Beach," "Godwhacker," "Lunch with Gina," "Slang of Ages," "Things I Miss the Most," and "Everything Must Go." They also had a new opening tune, a cover of one of Fagen's favorite jazz pianists, Ray Bryant's "Cubano Chant." All of the horn players and pianist Ted Baker took solos on the instrumental, and it set the stage for Becker and Fagen elegantly.

They also had a new second-set opener, an original written in 2000, "The Steely Dan Show." The song, sung by the female background vocalists and the horn section, was a tongue-in-cheek tribute to Steely Dan, written by Steely Dan. After the duo got comfortable on stage as they sauntered to their positions toward the end of the song, Fagen would acknowledge that they wrote a tribute to themselves and would add, "might as well bask in the glory such as it is." The breakdown of songs per album was:

Countdown to Ecstasy: "My Old School"
Pretzel Logic: "Parker's Band"
The Royal Scam: "Don't Take Me Alive," "Haitian Divorce," "Kid Charlemagne," "The Caves of Altamira"
Aja: "Aja, "Black Cow," "Home at Last," "Josie," "Peg"
Gaucho: "Babylon Sisters," "Hey Nineteen," "Time Out of Mind"
Two Against Nature: "Janie Runaway"
Everything Must Go: "Blues Beach," "Everything Must Go," "Godwhacker," "Lunch with Gina," "Slang of Ages," "Things I Miss the Most"
Miscellaneous: "FM (No Static at All)," "Cubano Chant" (instrumental overture), "The Steely Dan Show" (second set overture)

Donald Fagen Steps Out—*Morph the Cat* Tour—2006

On March 1, 2006, a week before the release of his third solo album, *Morph the Cat*, Fagen embarked on an eighteen-date tour with the Donald Fagen Band. He performed cuts from the album, his earlier solo work, as well as a number of classic Steely Dan favorites. Fagen cheekily dubbed it his first solo tour "since high school."

The band was a mix of Steely Dan's current touring ensemble (drummer Keith Carlock, guitarist Jon Herington, trumpeter Michael Leonhart, saxophonist Walt Weiskopf, and background vocalists Carolyn Leonhart-Escoffery and Cindy Mizelle), a guitarist and keyboard player/background vocalist from the Dan's past (Wayne Krantz and Jeff Young), and one new member (bassist Freddie Washington).

The show was quite different from a typical night with Steely Dan, focusing more on Fagen's solo career. The band played five songs from *The Nightfly*. "Green Flower Street," and "I.G.Y. (What a Beautiful World)" had been played live before, but "New Frontier," "The Goodbye Look," and "The Nightfly" were debuted on this tour. Two songs were played from *Kamakiriad*: "Countermoon," which they played briefly on their 1993 tour, and "Snowbound," which they had never played live; strange because it was the second single released from the album. Since the point of this short tour was to promote the new album, *Morph the Cat*, the band played five of the nine songs, including the title track, "Brite Nightgown," "The H Gang," "What I Do," and "Mary Shut the Garden Door."

Steely Dan fans were not disappointed, as Fagen and ensemble played "Black Cow," "Home at Last," "FM (No Static at All)," "Third World Man" (which hadn't been played since the '94 tour), "Pretzel Logic" as the first encore, and a fast, completely out of the ordinary version of "Here at the Western World" to open the show. They also played "Mis'ry and the Blues," a cover by trombonist Jack Teagarden from his last set of studio recordings before his untimely death in 1964, and closed the show with a cover of Chuck Berry's "Viva Viva Rock and Roll."

There were also a few special guests at select shows. In Chicago, Fagen sent a limo to harmonica player Howard Levy's steady gig with his band Chévere during their set break so that he could play "What I Do," which he played on the record, and still return to his gig in time for the second set. At the Beacon Theatre show in New York City, Fagen brought Canadian singer-songwriter Martha Wainwright, the sister of Rufus and daughter of Loudon, to perform what Fagen jokingly called a "scary song," her own sultry slow burner "Year of the Dragon," with Fagen playing melodica. The show was shorter than a Steely Dan show (ninety minutes) and didn't vary from night to night, besides the few special guests, but the opportunity to hear so many of Fagen's solo songs in a single evening was literally worth the price of admission.

Steelyard Sugartooth McDan (and the Fab-Originees.com) Tour—2006

This two-month summer tour of the U.S. starting on July 7, 2006, would become a somewhat regular occurrence for Steely Dan. From 2006 to 2016, Steely Dan would tour every summer (except for 2010 and 2012 when the Dukes of September would be on the road with Fagen, Michael McDonald, and Boz Scaggs) playing numerous shows across the country and the world, often with special "album" nights and other specially curated shows.

Between the 2003 tour for *Everything Must Go* and the *Steelyard Sugartooth McDan* tour of 2006, Steely Dan was dealt a terrible blow. Saxophonist Cornelius Bumpus, who had taken part in every Steely Dan tour since their second act began in 1993, died of a heart attack on February 3, 2004, while on a flight from New York to California, at the age of 58. He was scheduled to perform at the Columbia College Jazz Concert Series and although the plane made an emergency landing in Kansas City, Bumpus died before it reached the ground. He was sorely missed by all.

When Steely Dan toured in 2003, it seemed as if Becker and Fagen had finally found "the band" they wanted to work with. For the most part that was true. But for the *Steelyard Sugartooth McDan* tour, there were a few changes. Half of their rhythm section was back from 2003's *Everything Must Go* tour (Carlock on drums and Herington on guitar), but this time Tom Barney, who had been their bassist since their resurgence in 1993, was one of the two players who had left. Freddie Washington, who recently played on Fagen's *Morph the Cat* and its subsequent tour, took over the bass chair and would continue to do so to this day. He would also take part in both *Dukes of September Rhythm Revue* tours and play on one track on *Sunken Condos*.

The other rhythm section player who was absent was Ted Baker. Baker had recorded with Steely Dan since their rebirth in 2000 and had been a part of their touring ensemble since they were out to promote *Two Against Nature*. Keyboardist/background vocalist Jeff Young, however, went further back, working with Fagen since 1989's shows at Elaine's and the New York Soul shows that took place in various New York City clubs. He led the band that backed the New York Rock and Soul Revue in 1990 and 1991, and fifteen years later, he toured with the Donald Fagen Band to promote *Morph the Cat*. Fagen must have truly felt his playing because he would take over keys duty and add background vocals for the next three summer tours.

They replaced Cornelius Bumpus with baritone saxophonist Roger Rosenberg, who had participated in the sessions for *Two Against Nature*, *Everything Must Go*, *Morph the Cat*, and would later contribute to Becker's *Circus Money* and Fagen's *Sunken Condos*. He would become a regular from this tour on. Michael Leonhart was back on trumpet, Jim Pugh on trombone, and Walt Weiskopf was on saxophone. For this tour, they only employed two background vocalists, regulars Carolyn Leonhart-Escoffery and Cindy Mizelle, because not only did they have keyboardist/background vocalist Jeff Young in the band, they also had the big gun in the lead and background vocals department: Michael McDonald, who played on the double bill on thirty-one of the thirty-three dates.

Each show opened with a long set of McDonald performing a selection of Doobie Brothers hits, solo compositions, and numerous soul covers that were recorded for his previous two albums, *Motown* and *Motown Two*. The Doobies songs included "It Keeps You Runnin'," "You Belong to Me," "Minute by Minute," "What a Fool Believes," and "Takin' It to the Streets." He played three of his solo hits, "Sweet Freedom," "I Keep Forgettin' (Every Time You're Near)," and "No Love to Be Found." The songs that he had covered on the Motown albums were the Stylistics' "Stop, Look, Listen (To Your Heart)," Gladys Knight and the Pips' "I Heard It Through the Grapevine," Smoky Robinson and the Miracles' "I Second That Emotion," and two songs by Marvin Gaye and Tammi Terrell, "Ain't No Mountain High Enough" and "Ain't Nothing Like the Real Thing." He also played a song that he never recorded, Billy Preston's "That's the Way God Planned It."

After an intermission, Steely Dan hit the stage with McDonald joining in on vocals and keyboards halfway through. Many fans felt as if they got two shows for the price of one. Since both artists each played a full show, Steely Dan only played one set rather than two. For the most part, the show consisted of the songs that fans had come to expect, including "Dirty Work," "Do It Again," "Bodhisattva," "My Old School," "Black Friday," "Green Earrings," "Don't Take Me Alive," "Kid Charlemagne," "FM (No Static at All)," "Aja," "Josie," "Peg," "Hey Nineteen," and "Time Out of Mind." They did, however, add three new songs, "I Got the News" from *Aja*; "Any World (That I'm Welcome To)" from *Katy Lied*, which was played with a reggae feel and featured keyboardist Jeff Young on vocals for the second half of the song; and "Show Biz Kids" from *Countdown to Ecstasy*. During Steely Dan's third tour in 1974, McDonald had sung the song to great effect; and with the luxury of having him sit in on the tour, they couldn't resist revisiting the song with a revamped version with a new middle section rather than continuing the loop that was the basis for the recorded version. He also added background vocals to "Peg," "Do It Again," "Kid Charlemagne," and "My Old School."

As they had done on their other tours, a new intro and outro for the show was put in place. The band would open with jazz pianist Stan Kenton's "Turtle Talk," which included solos by all of the horn players. After their encore, the band would close the show with a version of Argentine tenor saxophonist Gato Barbieri's "Last Tango in Paris," a song from the film of the same title that was originally arranged by one of Fagen's favorite composers, saxophonist Oliver Nelson. The breakdown of songs per album was:

Can't Buy a Thrill: "Dirty Work," "Do It Again,"
Countdown to Ecstasy: "Bodhisattva," "My Old School," "Show Biz Kids"
Katy Lied: "Any World (That I'm Welcome To)," "Black Friday"
The Royal Scam: "Don't Take Me Alive," "Green Earrings," "Kid
  Charlemagne"
Aja: "Aja," "I Got the News," "Josie," "Peg"
Gaucho: "Hey Nineteen," "Time Out of Mind"
Miscellaneous: "FM (No Static at All)," "Turtle Talk" (instrumental overture), "Last
  Tango in Paris" (instrumental closer)

Heavy Rollers Tour—2007

From May 5 until September 24, 2007, Steely Dan embarked on their second world tour, the *Heavy Rollers* tour. The sixty-eight-date expedition was their longest to date. They spent the first two months in the U.S. and then headed to England, Belgium, France, Germany, Sweden, Norway, Finland, Denmark, Switzerland, and Italy. On August 18, they arrived in Japan for three weeks of extended engagements in Tokyo, Osaka, and Fukuoka before heading to Australia and New Zealand for two weeks to close the tour.

The band was identical to 2006, a first for the Steely Dan Orchestra, and the set list nearly was as well. The show was, of course, longer, since they were back to the two-set format without Michael McDonald; they mostly added songs that had been played on previous tours. The only new Steely Dan song added to the show was "Two Against Nature," but they did add two jazz classics. Trumpeter/arranger Gerald Wilson's "Geri" was originally recorded with his seventeen-piece big band featuring Richard "Groove" Holmes on organ for his underrated masterpiece *You Better Believe It* in 1961. The band used the song as their new overture. Trumpeter Lee Morgan's "Carolyn" was originally recorded on tenor saxophonist Hank Mobley's 1963 Blue Note album, *No Room for Squares*. The song would close the show as Becker, Fagen, and the background vocalists left the stage. The breakdown of songs per album was:

Can't Buy a Thrill: "Dirty Work," "Do It Again"
Countdown to Ecstasy: "Bodhisattva," "My Old School"
Pretzel Logic: "Pretzel Logic"
Katy Lied: "Black Friday," "Bad Sneakers," "Chain Lightning" "Daddy Don't
Live in That New York City No More"
The Royal Scam: "Green Earrings," "Haitian Divorce," "Kid Charlemagne"
Aja: "Aja," "Black Cow," "Home at Last," "I Got the News," "Josie," "Peg"
Gaucho: "Babylon Sisters," "Hey Nineteen," "Time Out of Mind"
Two Against Nature: "Two Against Nature"

Everything Must Go: "Godwhacker"
Miscellaneous: "Geri" (instrumental overture), "Carolyn" (instrumental closer)

Think Fast Tour—2008

Steely Dan was back for the summer of 2008, starting this tour in Fort Lauderdale, Florida, on June 8, 2008, and ending on August 27, 2008, in Santa Rosa, California. The only difference in the band was that background vocalist Carolyn Leonhart-Escoffery was replaced by Tawatha Agee, the only tour Leonhart-Escoffery would be absent from since she began playing with Steely Dan on the *Art Crimes* tour of 1996. Trombonist Nelson Foltz would sub for Jim Pugh on four dates, and Bob Sheppard would sub for Walt Weiskopf on the last three dates in August. They would play four additional shows in November in New Jersey and Connecticut, with keyboardist Jim Beard replacing Jeff Young and saxophonist Ari Ambrose replacing Walt Weiskopf on the last two.

The year 2008 was the third in a row that Steely Dan toured without adding much new material, so the set lists were becoming a bit stagnant. Songs would come and go, but there were many that were staples and would be heard on every tour. In 2007, Steely Dan teamed up with Michael McDonald for a double bill, and after that success, they made a change for the *Think Fast* tour that was more for themselves than for the audience: the addition of a straight-ahead jazz act as an opening band. For the Beacon Theatre dates in New York City, the Bill Charlap Trio and the Chris Creek Group entertained the audiences two nights each. Keyboard player Charlap had played on "Godwhacker" and "Pixeleen" on *Everything Must Go* when Ted Baker was unavailable, so they were familiar with his playing. They found saxophonist Chris Cheek through drummer Keith Carlock, who was a member of the group Rudder with Cheek. Catherine Russell, who took part in the 1993 and 1994 tours and would rejoin the band on the road in 2009, was a special guest for two dates at the Festival International de Jazz de Montreal in Montreal, Canada. The Sam Yahel Organ Trio joined the tour for eighteen dates, organ legend Joey DeFrancesco played thirteen dates with his trio, and Deep Blue Organ Trio played one show in Chicago. Unfortunately for the opening acts, the audience was not responsive and often talked through their set, took selfies, and waited rather impatiently for the main act. While Becker, Fagen, and all of the musicians on the stage were jazz aficionados, their audience apparently was not.

For the *Think Fast* tour the new overture was a medley of "Everyone's Gone to the Movies" and "The Fez." One new Steely Dan song was added from *The Royal Scam*, "Everything You Did," but it was revamped and played with a reggae feel. Becker had a new vocal spotlight with "Gaucho" and the female background vocalists tackled a new feature song in addition to "Parker's Band," Diana Ross and the Supremes' 1966 number nine hit "Love Is Like an Itching in My Heart." As Becker, Fagen, and the background vocalists left the stage, the band closed the show with Gato Barbieri's "Last Tango in Paris" as they had on the 2006 tour. The breakdown of songs per album was:

Countdown to Ecstasy: "Bodhisattva," "My Old School," "Show Biz Kids"
Pretzel Logic: "Parker's Band"
Katy Lied: "Black Friday," "Everyone's Gone to the Movies" (part of opening instrumental medley)
The Royal Scam: "Don't Take Me Alive," "Everything You Did," "The Fez" (part of opening instrumental medley), "Green Earrings," "Kid Charlemagne," "The Royal Scam"
Aja: "Aja," "Black Cow," "Home at Last," "I Got the News," "Josie," "Peg"
Gaucho: "Babylon Sisters," "Gaucho," "Glamour Profession," "Hey Nineteen"
Two Against Nature: "Cousin Dupree," "Two Against Nature," "What a Shame About Me"
Everything Must Go: "Godwhacker"
The Nightfly: "New Frontier"
Miscellaneous: "FM (No Static at All)," "Love is Like an Itching Heart" (Diana Ross and the Supremes cover), "Last Tango in Paris" (instrumental closer)

Rent Party and Left Bank Holiday Tours—2009

On June 9, 2009, Steely Dan embarked on the *Rent Party* tour, beginning with a show in Durham, North Carolina. After seven dates, they headed overseas for the European leg named the *Left Bank Holiday* tour. For two and a half weeks from June 25 until July 12, 2009, the Steely Dan Orchestra played the Netherlands, Belgium, Scotland, England, France, Switzerland, Italy, and for the first time, Monaco. When they returned to the states, they resumed the U.S. leg of the tour in Boston, Massachusetts, on July 22 for three dates.

For the most part, the band was the same, with Keith Carlock, Freddie Washington, and Jon Herington returning as the rhythm section, but keyboardist/background vocalist Jeff Young was no longer with them. On the four November dates that were added to 2008's *Think Fast* tour, keyboard player Jim Beard had replaced Young, and now he was back for the entire 2009 tour season. Beard had played alongside fellow keyboardist Ted Baker on Becker's 2008 release *Circus Money*, so when a keyboard player was needed for the additional dates in 2008, Becker suggested Beard. He would play on every subsequent Steely Dan tour as well as both *Dukes of September Rhythm Revue* tours. Steely Dan's rhythm section was finally in place and would play on every date to the present.

The horn section of Michael Leonhart, Jim Pugh, Walt Weiskopf, and Roger Rosenberg was back as well, but trumpet player Marvin Stamm would sub for Leonhart during the European *Left Bank Holiday* tour. Carolyn Leonhart-Escoffery was back after missing 2008's tour, and Tawatha Agee continued with the band after joining for that tour, but Cindy Mizelle was replaced for the U.S. dates by Catherine Russell, who had toured with Steely Dan in 1993 and 1994, and for the European dates by Janice Pendarvis, who had performed with Sting, David Bowie, Roberta Flack, Laurie Anderson, Peter Tosh, Philip Glass, the Rolling Stones, Nona Hendryx, the O'Jays, Jimmy Cliff, and countless others.

After touring for so many years in a row, Becker and Fagen were aware of the fact that they needed to do something special and change things up, although the first leg of the U.S. tour (seven shows) and the European leg, the *Left Bank Holiday* tour, would consist of standard set lists. Their opening act for most European dates was saxophonist Toon Roos's Quartet, and for the show in London, guitarist Elliott Randall was a special guest. Only one new song was added, "Teenie's Blues," a cover by one of Fagen's favorite musicians, saxophonist/arranger Oliver Nelson. The song was from his groundbreaking 1961 album *Blues and the Abstract Truth* and served as the new overture for the show. The closing tune was once again Gato Barbieri's "Last Tango in Paris," which was originally arranged by Nelson as well. The songs they played for this leg of the tour included:

Can't Buy a Thrill: "Do It Again," "Reelin' in the Years"
Countdown to Ecstasy: "Bodhisattva," "My Old School," "Show Biz Kids"
Pretzel Logic: "Parker's Band"
Katy Lied: "Bad Sneakers," "Black Friday," "Daddy Don't Live in That New York City No More"
The Royal Scam: "Green Earrings," "Kid Charlemagne"
Aja: "Aja," "Black Cow," "Deacon Blues," "I Got the News," "Josie," "Peg"
Gaucho: "Babylon Sisters," "Glamour Profession," "Hey Nineteen," "Time Out of Mind"
Two Against Nature: "Two Against Nature"
Everything Must Go: "Godwhacker"
Miscellaneous: "Love Is Like an Itching Heart" (Diana Ross and the Supremes cover), "Teenie's Blues" (instrumental overture), "Last Tango in Paris" (instrumental closer)

In the U.S. they continued to have an opening act as well, either organist Sam Yahel and Friends or Deep Blue Organ Trio, but the major change was the addition of special nights where they would play an album in its entirety followed by a set of select songs. The three albums they chose were *The Royal Scam*, *Aja*, and *Gaucho*. By 2009, they had played every song from *The Royal Scam* in full except for "The Fez," which had previously only been heard as an instrumental part of the overture. All songs from *Aja* had been performed live numerous times, and *Gaucho* was also well represented, with only one song being played live for the first time, "My Rival." So in essence they needed to learn two songs in order to play these three albums in full. It didn't matter because fans across the country got to hear these classic albums from first song to last, with the waggish move of "flipping the record over" on a turntable on the stage between sides. Fans were then treated to a long second set of Steely Dan material from various albums. The band also played eight "Internet Request" shows where the set lists were culled from fans' requests on the Steely Dan website. There was also a special guest at certain shows in New York City, Los Angeles, and Chicago: guitarist Larry Carlton. Hearing him play some of his original solos live was a definite plus for fans who lived in one of those three cities. Out of fifty-one shows on the second leg of the tour, they performed *Gaucho* four times, *The Royal Scam* twelve times, and *Aja* nineteen times.

They continued to use Oliver Nelson's "Teenie's Blues" as the intro to the show and closed with Gato Barbieri's "Last Tango in Paris." They did add one Steely Dan song and one cover. The Dan song was a fan favorite that Fagen never felt comfortable playing live, "Doctor Wu." That's what you get for having an "Internet Request" show. The cover that was added was the Standells' "Dirty Water." They were a garage rock band from Los Angeles and have been referred to as the punk band of the '60s. "Dirty Water" was their biggest hit, had become the anthem of several Boston sports teams, and is played following every Boston Red Sox and Boston Bruins win. The song was only performed at the three dates the Dan played in Boston at the Wang Theatre. They also played two different versions of "Reelin' in the Years," sometimes on the same night. Besides the original version, they played a reharmonized minor take on the song. The songs they played for this leg of the tour included:

Can't Buy a Thrill: "Dirty Work," "Do It Again," "Reelin' in the Years"
Countdown to Ecstasy: "Bodhisattva," "My Old School," "Show Biz Kids" "The Boston Rag"
Pretzel Logic: "Any Major Dude Will Tell You," "Parker's Band," "Pretzel Logic," "Rikki Don't Lose That Number"
Katy Lied: "Bad Sneakers," "Black Friday," "Daddy Don't Live in That New York City No More," "Doctor Wu"
The Royal Scam: "Don't Take Me Alive," "Green Earrings," "Kid Charlemagne," "The Royal Scam" (plus full album show)
Aja: full album
Gaucho: "Babylon Sisters," "Hey Nineteen," "Third World Man," "Time Out of Mind" (plus full album show)
Two Against Nature: "Two Against Nature"
Everything Must Go: "Godwhacker"
Miscellaneous: "Dirty Water" (Standells cover), "FM (No Static at All)," "Here at the Western World," "Love Is Like an Itching Heart" (Diana Ross and the Supremes cover), "Teenie's Blues" (instrumental overture), "Last Tango in Paris" (instrumental closer)

With a Little Help from His Friends: The *Dukes of September Rhythm Revue* Tour—2010

Steely Dan did not tour in 2010, the first year they hadn't hit the road since 2005. But Dan fans didn't need to worry. Donald Fagen, along with Boz Scaggs and Michael McDonald, went on the road for the *Dukes of September Rhythm Revue* tour, an extension of the New York Rock and Soul Revue shows Fagen put together from 1990 to 1993. The band was almost identical to Steely Dan's touring unit, with Jon Herington on guitar, bassist Freddie Washington, Jim Beard on keyboards, Michael Leonhart on trumpet, saxophonist Walt Weiskopf, and Carolyn Leonhart-Escoffery and Catherine Russell on background vocals. Trombonist Jim Pugh didn't participate, and the only new musicians were Jay Collins on saxophone and

Earth, Wind & Fire drummer Michael White, who had played on both "Jack of Speed" and "What a Shame About Me" from *Two Against Nature.*

Fagen, Scaggs, and McDonald had toured as part of the New York Rock and Soul Revue in August 1992, the first tour that Fagen and Walter Becker had embarked on since 1974. In 2010, it was dubbed the *Dukes of September Rhythm Revue* tour, and Walter Becker was not present. The idea was relatively similar to the shows in the '90s: play a mix of the three artists' hits with some of their favorite R&B and soul classics and B-sides, heavily weighted toward the covers rather than their hit records. They initially started out with over one hundred songs that each of them suggested. Fagen had to take the reins and constantly remind Scaggs and McDonald that they needed to narrow down their selections so charts could be written for the band. Unlike the shows from 1992, the Dukes of September Rhythm Revue wasn't only about classic soul music. They played songs by the Band, the Grateful Dead, the Beach Boys, Lee Michaels, Willy DeVille, and Thunderclap Newman alongside some of the best soul and R&B music from the '50s onward. They chose from twenty-nine songs for a twenty-four- to twenty-seven-song set list.

The show began with the band and background vocalists laying down a rollicking version of Don Covay's "Sookie, Sookie," the B-side of the 1966 reissue of his hit "Mercy, Mercy," originally released in 1964. The song featured a young Jimi Hendrix on guitar and drummer Bernard Purdie, who played on *The Royal Scam*, *Aja*, and *Gaucho*. Fagen, Scaggs, and McDonald took the stage as the overture came to a close and traded verses on Lee Michaels's controversial song from 1968, "Heighty Hi."

"Don't Mess Up a Good Thing," a 1965 Fontella Bass and Bobby McClure song, was handled with aplomb by Michael McDonald and background vocalist Catherine Russell, a song that the former Doobie Brothers singer hadn't revisited since he was fourteen. Fagen took on a very Steely Dan-sounding Grateful Dead song, "Shakedown Street," with outstanding guitar solos by both Scaggs and Herington. Fagen had been singing the song at some of Levon Helm's Midnight Rambles at his house/live venue/recording studio in Woodstock, New York. The former drummer and singer from the Band was the longtime partner of Fagen's wife, Libby Titus, and fathered a child with her.

Scaggs sang the Chuck Berry song "You Never Can Tell," with accordion by McDonald and a fierce piano solo by Fagen, proving his blues skills to all in attendance. Scaggs also sang lead on Teddy Pendergrass's "Love T.K.O." and "Cadillac Walk," written by Moon Martin and made famous by singer-songwriter Willy DeVille and his band Mink DeVille in the '70s. Martin also wrote "Bad Case of Loving You (Doctor, Doctor)," a hit for English singer Robert Palmer.

McDonald was in perfect form, tackling "I've Got News for You," a Ray Charles tune from his 1960 Album, *Genius + Soul = Jazz,* that put the spotlight on Jim Beard for some extremely inspired organ playing. Fagen, Scaggs, and McDonald would often pay tribute to the Band by playing three of their songs in a row, with Scaggs singing "Rag Mama Rag," McDonald showing his talent on the banjo and leading the band for "The Shape I'm In," and Fagen singing either "King Harvest (Has Surely Come)" or "Caledonia Mission."

The background vocalists also had their moments center stage, with Carolyn Leonhart-Escoffery taking the lead on Aretha Franklin's "Rock Steady" and Catherine Russell not only sharing the lead with Michael McDonald on "Don't Mess Up a Good Thing," but also taking control of Muddy Waters's "I Love the Life I Live, I Live the Life I Love." Not an easy task. Jim Beard added melodica, and Boz Scaggs contributed a smoking-hot guitar solo.

Fagen played three originals each night: "Green Flower Street," "I.G.Y. (What a Beautiful World)," and "Reelin' in the Years." But on a few occasional dates, "Peg" was added as an encore, along with a version of "Pretzel Logic" with Fagen and Scaggs taking the first two verses and McDonald reprising his role as the soulful singer of the middle eight from the 1974 tour. McDonald sang two Doobie Brothers hits, "What a Fool Believes" and "Takin' It to the Streets," which he performed as a duet with Catherine Russell, and one solo song, "I Keep Forgettin' (Every Time You're Near)," from his debut solo LP *If That's What It Takes*. Its similarity to an earlier song, "I Keep Forgettin'," written by Jerry Leiber and Mike Stoller and recorded by Chuck Jackson, resulted in Leiber and Stoller also being given a songwriting credit. Boz Scaggs decided to only play two of his originals, his number three hit "Lowdown," and an incredibly powerful version of his lesser-known song "Miss Sun," a duet with Catherine Russell, but many fans were surprised by the omission of "Lido Shuffle."

He did, however, close the show on a high note with an impressive take on the O'Jays' "Love Train," written by Kenny Gamble and Leon Huff. Encore numbers included the Beach Boys' "Help Me Rhonda," sung beautifully by Fagen, Scaggs, McDonald, and background vocalists Carolyn Leonhart-Escoffery and Catherine Russell, with McDonald switching from keyboards to ukulele; "Them Changes," a Buddy Miles song destroyed by Michael McDonald; and a truly deep cut, "Something in the Air" by Thunderclap Newman, a group that was formed by the Who's guitarist Pete Townshend in 1969. His concept was to create a band to perform songs composed by drummer and singer Speedy Keen, who had written "Armenia City in the Sky", the first track on *The Who Sell Out*. Townshend recruited a friend from art college, jazz pianist Andy "Thunderclap'" Newman; and a fifteen-year-old Glaswegian wunderkind, guitarist Jimmy McCulloch, who would play lead guitar in Paul McCartney's Wings from 1974 to 1977 and die of a heroin overdose in 1979 at the age of twenty-six. Fagen and McDonald shared the vocals, and their interpretation with Boz Scaggs on acoustic guitar was a surprising yet welcome addition to the set. The tour was a success, and two years later, they would embark on a new *Dukes of September Rhythm Revue* tour with an almost identical band, but a brand new set of songs.

Shuffle Diplomacy Tour—2011

For 2011's *Shuffle Diplomacy* tour, the rhythm section of Carlock, Washington, Herington, and Beard returned, as did the horn section comprised of Leonhart, Pugh, Weiskopf, and Rosenberg. Carolyn Leonhart-Escoffery and Catherine Russell were back as background vocalists, and Cindy Mizelle rejoined the band after missing 2009's *Rent Party* and *Left Bank Holiday* tours. They did have a new

A poster featuring William S. Burroughs for a 2011 show at the Tower Theater in Philadelphia, Pennsylvania, during the *Shuffle Diplomacy* tour.

name for the band, the Miles High Big Band featuring the Embassy Brats.

They once again included special shows in Los Angeles; Highland Park, Illinois; Milwaukee; Boston; and an entire week at the Beacon Theatre in New York City. Besides the three classic album nights (*The Royal Scam, Aja,* and *Gaucho)* and the "Internet Request" show, now renamed the "By Popular Demand" show, they added three additional special shows. "Dawn of the Dan" featured songs from the band's first three groundbreaking albums of the '70s, *Can't Buy a Thrill, Countdown to Ecstasy,* and *Pretzel Logic.* "21st Century Dan" focused on songs from 2000's *Two Against Nature* and 2003's *Everything Must Go.* As Becker and Fagen would put it, the "Rarities" night was chock-full of "the unreleased, the mythic, the reborn, the rarely-if-ever-heard; on this numinous Night of Nights, all will be revealed." The Beacon finale on September 23 gave the audience two shows rolled into one. Not only did they play *The Royal Scam* in its entirety, they also performed songs from the "21st Century Dan" show, plus additional selected favorites and guitarist Larry Carlton as a special guest.

The shows still had an opening act, either Sam Yahel and Friends or Deep Blue Organ Trio; and for the Dan's extraordinary seven-night run at the Beacon Theatre, several special guests sat in with the trio each night including saxophonists Mark Turner, Joe Lovano, Miguel Zenon, and Chris Potter, who had toured with Steely Dan in '93, '94, and 2000 and contributed to *Two Against Nature, Everything Must Go,* and Becker's *Circus Money.* Drummer Bill Stewart was also a special guest for one show.

Sixteen out of the fifty-three shows on the North American leg of the tour were "special shows," with seven of them taking place at New York City's Beacon Theatre, three at Boston's Wang Theatre, two at Milwaukee's Riverside Theater, two at the Greek Theatre in Los Angeles, and two at the Ravinia Festival in Highland Park, Illinois.

It's odd that with the "By Popular Demand" and "Dawn of the Dan" shows in place, only two new songs were added, although a few others that had been rarely played showed up in the set lists. The two were welcome additions, "Your Gold Teeth" and "Pearl of the Quarter" from *Countdown to Ecstasy*. "Your Gold Teeth" sounded fantastic with horns and demonstrated how advanced their songwriting was so early in their career. It was performed at almost every show on the tour, often as an opening number, so Becker and Fagen had apparently reassessed the value of this early, forgotten gem. It was one of their earliest songs that needed no reharmonization to please the two men who wrote it. "Pearl of the Quarter" had been performed at some of their shows in 1973, but if you weren't in the audience on one of those rare occasions, it would be a new experience to hear them interpret it on stage. They also played "Doctor Wu," which had only been part of the set during 2009's *Rent Party* tour because Fagen never felt that it came off well live. "Night by Night," "Monkey in Your Soul," and Duke Ellington's "East St. Louis Toddle-Oo" were three other songs only played on one tour, "Night by Night" and "Monkey in Your Soul" on 2000's *2YK* tour and "East St. Louis Toddle-Oo" on 1996's *Art Crimes* tour. Steely Dan's biggest chart hit, "Rikki Don't Lose That Number," had only been played during three tours, 1996's *Art Crimes* tour, 2000's *2YK* tour, and 2009's *Rent Party* tour, because Fagen wasn't very fond of the song, so it was a nice addition to some of the set lists. With all of these gems from *Pretzel Logic* finding a place in their show, Steely Dan had now played seven out of eleven songs from the LP. Another highlight was "You Got the Bear," a song written and recorded for the *Aja* album, but never officially released. It was first performed on the second night of the tour and was played on a handful of dates early on. It was resurrected for the "Rarities" night at the Beacon Theatre on September 17.

They opened each show with "Dizzy's Business," a tribute to bebop trumpet-playing giant Dizzy Gillespie, written by tenor saxophonist Ernie Wilkens and recorded by one of the most respected alto saxophonists of all time, Julian "Cannonball" Adderley, in 1963. They began the tour using Gato Barbieri's "Last Tango in Paris" as their closing number, as they had for the 2006, 2008, and 2009 tours, but halfway through the tour, a new closing theme was introduced. On August 15, 2011, at the Kresge Auditorium in Interlochen, Michigan, they debuted the new closer, Nelson Riddle's theme for the 1959 television series *The Untouchables*. Fagen's love of "fake, television jazz" had come full circle.

Another song that changed after fourteen shows was the incidental music used to introduce the band. They started the tour with R&B singer Lee Dorsey's "Neighbor's Daughter," with Catherine Russell singing a verse and Carolyn Leonhart-Escoffery and Cindy Mizelle providing background vocals before Becker would introduce the musicians and singers. On July 25 at Ives Concert Park in Danbury, Connecticut, they switched to James Brown's "Papa Don't Take No Mess," starting with the background vocalists singing the hook before Becker made his introductions. As they did on "Neighbor's Daughter," the vocalists returned for one more verse to close out the song.

There was one other special night, so special that it only happened once. For the one and only "Rarities" night on September 17, 2011, at the Beacon Theatre in New York City, Becker and Fagen added four of their songs that were never officially released. The first of the evening was "You Got the Bear," heard on a few select dates early in the tour. The next rarity was a song that is steeped in Steely Dan lore. While working on the *Gaucho* LP the band recorded "The Second Arrangement," a composition that in their eyes was to be a highlight of the album. Unfortunately, an engineer accidentally erased most of it, and when they attempted to rerecord it, oddly with a different drummer, they couldn't get the take they were looking for; and as Fagen stated while introducing the song, "We just didn't have the heart to do it."

The next rarity they tackled was "American Lovers," which they had given to singer Thomas Jefferson Kaye, an artist that Gary Katz produced in 1974. The song fit well in the set, with all of the classic Steely Dan devices in place: intricate chord changes, syncopated hits, unexpected turns, and a catchy hook that wouldn't have been out of place on their debut LP, *Can't Buy a Thrill*. Although both Becker and Fagen dismissed much of their early work, Fagen stated in his introduction, "we've come to like this one . . . It's kind of a hippie anthem, but we were unfortunately five years too late." Rather than sing the song himself, the Embassy Brats took over the lead vocals.

As an encore, they dusted off an unreleased song that they played to close many of their shows on the 1974 tour, "This All Too Mobile Home." The song, which has a similar groove to "Show Biz Kids," but with more complex chord changes, made quite an impression on the audience and sounded phenomenal with the added horn section and female background vocalists.

One other song played that night that could be considered a rarity was the Walter Becker-sung version of "Jack of Speed." During the 1996 *Art Crimes* tour, they performed the song that would end up on 2000's *Two Against Nature* LP, but with Becker singing rather than Fagen. After the release of the album, Fagen would always sing it live, that is, until the "Rarities" show.

In late October, the band flew to Australia to play seven dates on the continent and three dates in New Zealand. For these dates, Steely Dan shared the bill with Steve Winwood, a founding member of the Spencer Davis Group, Traffic, and Blind Faith and a musician who has had an incredibly successful career as a solo artist. His set was geared toward his band work rather than his solo material. He bookended it with two songs from his first band, the Spencer Davis Group, which he joined when he was fourteen years old. "I'm a Man," which opened his set, and "Gimme Some Lovin'," Winwood's closer, were released in late '66 and early '67 respectively; his soulful vocals cut when he was only eighteen. They were the group's best-known songs from their six-year '60s lineup. In addition to these two hits, he performed three Traffic songs; "The Low Spark of High Heeled Boys," "Light Up or Leave Me Alone," and "Dear Mr. Fantasy."

From his solo career, he only performed three songs: his number one hit "Higher Love" from his fourth solo LP, *Back in the High Life* from 1986; and "At Times We Do Forget" and "Dirty City," from his most recent album at the time, 2008's *Nine Lives*. The studio version of "Dirty City" featured Eric Clapton on guitar and reached number one on Adult Album Alternative radio for three weeks. In addition to the solo works and songs from the Spencer Davis Group and Traffic, he played "Can't Find My Way Home" from one of the first supergroups,

Blind Faith. The band was formed in 1968 and was composed of Winwood, Eric Clapton, Ginger Baker, and Ric Grech. Winwood would also join Steely Dan on stage for "Pretzel Logic" and a grooving version of Junior Walker and the All Stars' "Roadrunner" with Winwood on lead vocals. The double bill proved to be successful, and the artists would reconnect for a summer tour in 2016.

The pool of songs from which Becker and Fagen fished was deep for the 2011 *Shuffle Diplomacy* tour—more than any other tour to date, with fifty-two songs performed during the various shows. These included:

Can't Buy a Thrill: "Dirty Work," "Do It Again," "Reelin' In the Years"
Countdown to Ecstasy: "Bodhisattva," "My Old School," "Pearl of the Quarter," "Show Biz Kids," "The Boston Rag"
Pretzel Logic: "East St. Louis Toodle Oo," "Monkey in Your Soul," "Night by Night," "Parker's Band," "Rikki Don't Lose That Number"
Katy Lied: "Bad Sneakers," "Black Friday," "Doctor Wu"
The Royal Scam: "Green Earrings," "Kid Charlemagne" (plus full album show)
Aja: full album
Gaucho: "Babylon Sisters," "Gaucho," "Hey Nineteen," "Time Out of Mind" (plus full album show)
Two Against Nature: "Gaslighting Abbey," "Jack of Speed," "Janie Runaway," "Two Against Nature"
Everything Must Go: "Everything Must Go," "Godwhacker," "Lunch with Gina"
Miscellaneous: "FM (No Static at All)," "Roadrunner" (Junior Walker and the All Stars cover with Steve Winwood), "Neighbor's Daughter" (band intro), "Papa Don't Take No Mess" (band intro from July 25th), "Dizzy's Business" (instrumental overture), "Last Tango in Paris" (instrumental closer), "The Untouchables" (instrumental closer from August 15)
Unreleased Songs: "American Lovers," "The Second Arrangement," "This All Too Mobile Home," "You Got the Bear"

The *Dukes of September Rhythm Revue* Tour—2012

Steely Dan took some time off in 2012, but Donald Fagen, Boz Scaggs, and Michael McDonald were back with the *Dukes of September Rhythm Revue* tour. After a two-year hiatus, the band only had two changes: background vocalist Catherine Russell was unavailable for certain dates and would be replaced by newcomer Monet Owens for those shows, and Michael White was replaced by Nashville drummer Shannon Forrest, who had played on more top ten hits than any drummer in Nashville at the time, earning a reputation as "the hit-maker," the moniker that Steely Dan alumnus Bernard Purdie adopted in the '60s and '70s.

They once again had twenty-nine songs to choose from, but the only songs that they repeated from the 2010 tour were Steely Dan's "Peg," "Reelin' in the Years," and "Pretzel Logic"; Boz Scaggs's "Lowdown" and "Miss Sun," sung as a duet with Catherine Russell or Monet Owens; the Doobie Brothers' "What a Fool Believes" and "Takin' It to the Streets," also sung as a duet with Catherine Russell or Monet Owens; McDonald's "I Keep Forgettin' (Every Time You're Near)"; Buddy Miles's

"Them Changes," a popular final encore with lead vocals by McDonald; the Teddy Pendergrass hit "Love T.K.O.," sung by Scaggs; and Chuck Berry's "You Never Can Tell," with Scaggs on lead vocals and McDonald on accordion.

The new opening song was a cover of James Brown's "People Get Up and Drive Your Funky Soul" from the soundtrack to the 1973 movie *Slaughter's Big Rip-Off*, for which Brown composed the music. They followed with a rousing rendition of the Isley Brothers' "That Lady," a song released originally as "Who's That Lady" in 1964 and rerecorded in 1973, the more popular of the two versions. They each took a verse, with Scaggs starting off the tune, Fagen taking the second verse, and Michael McDonald bringing it home after an outstanding solo by Jon Herington. The trio of vocalists followed up with "Sweet Soul Music," a number two hit for singer Arthur Conley in 1967. The song was written by Conley and Otis Redding and was based on Sam Cooke's "Yeah Man" from his posthumous LP *Shake*. Sam Cooke's business partner, J. W. Alexander, sued both Redding and Conley for plagiarizing the melody, and a settlement was reached in which Cooke's name was added to the writer credits. Fagen introduced the song, and the first singer as Michael "White Lightning" McDonald. Scaggs took over for the second verse, and Fagen took the third verse, where he incorporated lyrics about Boz and "White Lightning." The horn section break led nicely into a bluesy guitar solo by Scaggs. Michael McDonald resumed lead vocal duties and took the song to an exciting close.

The new originals added to the set were all Steely Dan songs, except for one. Scaggs must have sensed the audience's disappointment that "Lido Shuffle" wasn't played in 2010, so for the 2012 tour, the song was added and often served as the band's first encore. Fagen dropped "Greenflower Street" and "I.G.Y. (What a Beautiful World)," but added "Kid Charlemagne" and "Hey Nineteen."

The 2012 *Dukes of September Rhythm Revue* tour focused on more popular R&B songs than 2010's tour, with songs like "Help Me Rhonda" and "Something in the Air" being dropped in favor of a more classic soul vibe. They didn't play as many obscure songs as they did on the past tour, probably figuring that their audience was happier with the more familiar material. Michael McDonald took the lead for Harold Melvin and the Blue Notes' 1972 number one hit "If You Don't Know Me by Now" sung by Teddy Pendergrass. The group initially recruited Pendergrass as the drummer for their backing band, but lead singer John Atkins quit later that year and Pendergrass was promoted.

Boz Scaggs added Willie Dixon's "The Same Thing" from 1964 to his repertoire, with a soulful vocal and hot guitar solo. The song was originally recorded by Muddy Waters and has since been performed by Dixon himself, George Thorogood, the Allman Brothers Band, the Grateful Dead, and the Band among others.

Fagen's choice of covers for 2012 were varied; he sang lead on the Lovin' Spoonful's number one hit from 1966 "Summer in the City"; and possibly the high point of the evening, Marvin Gaye's masterpiece "Trouble Man." Fagen took center stage with his melodica for a breathtaking version of this Steely Danish tune. The spacey, jazz-infused vibe of Gaye's composition, the 1972 title track to his soundtrack for the film of the same name, suited Fagen's sensibilities perfectly and demonstrated yet another influence on the Steely Dan sound.

The female background vocalists got their fair share of "star time," with Carolyn Leonhart-Escoffery covering Gladys Knight and the Pips' version of "I Heard It Through the Grapevine," Catherine Russell taking the lead for the Erma Franklin version of "Piece of Your Heart," and the two singers leading the band on the Sly and the Family Stone 1969 classic "Thank You (Falettinme Be Mice Elf Agin)," one of the songs played during the encore. They also sang a few more duets in 2012, with Leonhart-Escoffery singing the Mickey and Sylvia tune "Love Is Strange" with Boz Scaggs and the Buck Owens cover "Love's Gonna Live Here" with Fagen. Catherine Russell also sang a duet with Fagen, Ray Charles's "Tell the Truth," which in effect was a lead vocal for Russell, with Fagen and the other singers backing her up, much like Charles's original with the fabulous Margie Hendrix on vocals. In 1957, she became a member of the Raelettes singing background vocals for Ray Charles, and within a year, she was having an affair with the married singer. This led him to write two songs, one of which was "Tell the Truth," for her to sing as a duet and she became the soul of the backing vocal group she founded. In 1964, she realized that she was pregnant with his child, but he refused to divorce his wife, and the two split up soon after. Her death in 1973 remains a mystery with conflicting reports stating that she died of a heroin overdose, in a car accident, or of cancer.

In November 2012, the Dukes of September were filmed at Lincoln Center in New York City for a ninety-minute *Great Performances* special that was aired on PBS in March 2014 and released on both DVD and Blu-ray.

Mood Swings: Eight Miles to Pancake Day Tour—2013

Steely Dan took off 2012 while Fagen, Boz Scaggs, and Michael McDonald toured as the Dukes of September, but they were back in 2013 with the oddly titled *Eight Mood Swings: Eight Miles to Pancake Day* tour with the Steely Dan Bi-Polar All-Stars. According to pranksters Becker and Fagen, the title came from a sign on a restaurant stating, "Pancakes Makes People Happy." The entire band returned with only one change: background vocalist Cyndi Mizelle was replaced by a singer who had never played with Steely Dan, La Tanya Hall. Deep Blue Organ Trio was the opener for the entire tour.

After the 2009 *Rent Party* tour, where they added full album nights, and the 2011 *Shuffle Diplomacy* tour, where they not only played the album nights but added "Dawn of the Dan," "21st Century Dan," and "Rarities" nights, and played a double bill with Steve Winwood for a week, the 2013 tour fell a bit short. They did, however, add two songs from *Countdown to Ecstasy*: "King of the World" and "Razor Boy," which was sung by the female background vocalists. The only other changes to the show were the opening song and the tune used for the band introductions. For the overture, they played a fast, swinging number entitled "Blueport." Originally recorded by baritone saxophonist Gerry Mulligan, the song was written by Mulligan's bass player William Crow and was a standout track from his 1959

An advertisement for two special shows in Los Angeles during 2013's *Mood Swings: Eight Miles to Pancake Day* tour.

release *The New Gerry Mulligan Quartet*. They continued with the transition of playing an R&B song for the "band introduction" segment, and for 2013, the choice was Joe Tex's "I Want To (Do Everything for You)" from 1965. The single was his second number one on the R&B chart in the U.S. and was also his second top forty entry on the *Billboard* Hot 100. As was par for the course, the background vocalists sang a couple of stanzas before Becker's humorous introductions began.

Over the course of three months, and forty-six shows, they performed *Aja* four times and the "Greatest Hits" show twice before reaching New York. For the last week of the tour, bringing it to fifty-three dates, they spent a week at the Beacon Theatre and staged two *Aja* nights, one *Royal Scam* show, one *Gaucho* show, two "Greatest Hits" nights, and an "Audience Request" show. Although this tour didn't have many firsts, it did have one. After playing the eighth song, "Time Out of Mind," at the October 1st show at the Beacon Theatre, Becker left the stage with a fever. There were no new Steely Dan tracks introduced on this tour, so the set lists were culled from the following songs:

Can't Buy a Thrill: "Dirty Work," "Do It Again," "Reelin' In the Years"
Countdown to Ecstasy: "Bodhisattva," "King of the World," "My Old School," "Razor Boy," "Show Biz Kids," "Your Gold Teeth"
Pretzel Logic: "Pretzel Logic," "Monkey in Your Soul," "Rikki Don't Lose That Number"
Katy Lied: "Black Friday," "Daddy Don't Live in That New York City No More"
The Royal Scam: "Don't Take Me Alive," "Green Earrings," "Kid Charlemagne" (plus full album show)
Aja: full album
Gaucho: "Babylon Sisters," "Hey Nineteen," "Time Out of Mind" (plus full album show)

Everything Must Go: "Godwhacker"
Miscellaneous: I Want To (Do Everything for You)" (band intro), "Blueport" (instrumental overture), "The Untouchables" (instrumental closer)

Jamalot Ever After Tour—2014

The 2014 *Jamalot Ever After* tour was a fifty-six-date tour that broke no new ground. Besides returning to Ray Bryant's "Cubano Chant," which was last played as an overture for 2003's *Everything Must Go* tour, no changes were made to the band or set. For regular Steely Dan tour goers, these were by far the most boring of all shows, highlighting the songs that at this point had been played at most shows for the past decade. They also dropped all songs from their past two releases and played none of the deep cuts that they resurrected for the last few tours. For any fans of the opening band, they would experience a change. Those who had seen Deep Blue Organ Trio open for Steely Dan on the past tours would have been familiar with the smoking guitar work of Bobby Broom. For the 2014

On September 21, 2013, Steely Dan played the Mann Center for the Performing Arts in Philadelphia's Fairmount Park. Illustrator Alex Fine commemorated certain events during the summer concert season with baseball cards, and Steely Dan was one of the honorees.

tour, Broom returned with his new organ trio, the Bobby Broom Organi-Sation featuring Ben Paterson on organ, and Makaya McCraven and Kobie Watkins splitting drum duties on different dates. The songs represented in 2014 were:

Can't Buy a Thrill: "Dirty Work," "Reelin' in the Years"
Countdown to Ecstasy: "Bodhisattva," "My Old School," "Show Biz Kids"
Pretzel Logic: "Pretzel Logic"
Katy Lied: "Black Friday," "Daddy Don't Live in That New York City No More"
The Royal Scam: "Green Earrings," "Kid Charlemagne"
Aja: "Aja," "Black Cow," "Home at Last," "Josie," "Peg"
Gaucho: "Babylon Sisters," "Hey Nineteen," "Time Out of Mind"
Miscellaneous: "FM (No Static at All)," "I Want To (Do Everything for You)" (band intro), "Cubano Chant" (instrumental overture), "The Untouchables" (instrumental closer)

Rockabye Gollie Angel Tour—2015

It was 2015, and it was apparent that Becker and Fagen had found a rock-steady, dependable band, but that had both positive and negative results. For the *Rockabye Gollie Angel* tour, the band had returned from the year before, but the shows had become somewhat predictable, yet incredibly tight. They did, however, bring back a few songs from their most recent albums, *Two Against Nature* and *Everything Must Go*. They continued to have an opening act with the Roger Glenn Trio on the spring leg of the tour, but the most interesting, and surprising, news in the spring of 2015 was that Steely Dan would be playing two nights at hipster central, the Coachella Festival in Indio, California.

Coachella wasn't the only significant change that summer. For the second leg of the tour, Becker and Fagen decided to share a double bill with another artist. While Michael McDonald and Steve Winwood seemed like perfect cohorts due to their heavy jazz-infused soul influences, some people might have questioned their newest tour mate: Elvis Costello.

Although both acts were spawned in the '70s, their initial music couldn't be more disparate. By the time Costello, who was born Declan Patrick MacManus, released his first album, the new wave classic *My Aim Is True*, Steely Dan was on their sixth, the slick, jazz-like *Aja*. Their style of music was not compatible at the time, but lyrically, the songwriting team of Becker and Fagen and the solo songwriter Costello were light years ahead of their peers. They were all fans of Dylan and the Beatles, and were voracious readers, something that was obvious by their inherent ability to create characters and tell a compelling, and often dark, story. Costello's initial thrust on the scene was as a part of the "New Wave-Punk" camp of the late '70s, but his father, Ross MacManus, was a big band trumpeter and crooner, something that had a significant effect on Costello as a songwriter.

In 1978, Costello assembled the Attractions to back him, with Steve Nieve on keyboards, Bruce Thomas on bass, and Pete Thomas (no relation) on drums. They recorded his second album, *This Year's Model*, and continued to work as a unit with Costello at the helm for nine albums. He would experiment with a variety of different styles of music throughout his career, releasing full albums that embraced one particular genre including the Stax-influenced *Get Happy*; an album of country standards, *Almost Blue*; the Beatlesque pomp of *Imperial Bedroom* (produced by ex-Beatles engineer Geoff Emerick); the punchy, horn-heavy soul of *Punch the Clock*; the acoustic-alt-country of *King of America*, on which "Razor Boy" bassist Ray Brown played; the string quartet with vocal vibe of *The Juliet Letters*, recorded with the Brodsky Quartet; as well as full album collaborations with legendary songwriter Burt Bacharach; celebrated musician, songwriter, arranger, and record producer, New Orleans's own Allen Toussaint; and one of the most important producers and bands in hip-hop music in the past twenty years, drummer/producer Questlove and the Roots. It was apparent that Costello's musical vocabulary was extensive, so at multiple points in his career, his advanced harmonic sensibility was in perfect symmetry with Steely Dan. As songwriters, they were all interested in crafting the perfect tune and could be extremely critical of their own work. Costello would release thirty studio albums in thirty-nine years.

Unlike Steely Dan, Costello liked to change his set list from night to night. Most nights his set would contain between twelve and fifteen songs, but on two dates he performed so many encores that the set expanded to over thirty songs. Over the course of twenty-one dates as an opening act, he played fifty-seven different songs, more than the total Steely Dan songs that have ever been played live. Costello's choices covered almost every facet of his career and included compositions from an incredibly massive catalog, and he had only dipped his toe in the water. His ability and interest in covering so many different eras of his career could serve as a positive example for his elders that a varied set list would produce a more interesting concert.

For the third leg of the tour, Steely Dan continued the tradition of a one-week stand at the Beacon Theatre in New York City. This year they added an extra day, so over eight days, they staged two *Aja* nights, one *Royal Scam* night, one *Gaucho* night, one "By Popular Demand" night, two "Greatest Hits" nights, and something brand new. They continued with an opening act with the Russell Malone Organ Trio opening for four nights, the Peter Bernstein Organ Trio for two nights, and jazz guitarist Dave Stryker for one night. Singer/songwriter/guitarist Madeleine Peyroux opened the last date of the tour, advertised as "The Most Unforgettable Night of Whatever—Featuring Spectacular Musical Guests, Glorious Tunes and Riffage, and Whatever the Party Calls for! Parking Validated for First Dozen Diehard Fans." Two days before the show, neither Becker nor Fagen had set up any guest stars, so they relied on photographer, booking agent, friend, and confidant Peter Fogel to come up with a solution. A call to ex-Steely Dan guitarist Denny Dias in Los Angeles led to a one-of-a-kind night with Dias sitting in with Becker and Fagen on some of Steely Dan's seminal compositions. An appropriate finale to a different type of summer season for Becker and Fagen. In closing, in the summer of 2015, Steely Dan played thirty-one different songs during their shows, twenty-six less than Elvis Costello did in his relatively short run as an opening act. They are as follows:

Can't Buy a Thrill: "Dirty Work," "Do It Again," "Reelin' in the Years"
Countdown to Ecstasy: "Bodhisattva," "My Old School," "Razor Boy," "Show Biz Kids," "The Boston Rag," "Your Gold Teeth"
Pretzel Logic: "Monkey in Your Soul," "Pretzel Logic," "Rikki Don't Lose That Number"
Katy Lied: "Black Friday," "Daddy Don't Live in That New York City No More"
The Royal Scam: "Green Earrings," "Kid Charlemagne"
Aja: "Aja," "Black Cow," "Home at Last," "Josie," "Peg"
Gaucho: "Babylon Sisters," "Gaucho," "Hey Nineteen," "Time Out of Mind"
Two Against Nature: "Two Against Nature"
Everything Must Go: "Godwhacker," "Things I Miss the Most"
Miscellaneous: "FM (No Static at All)," "I Want To (Do Everything for You)" (band intro), "Cubano Chant" (instrumental overture), "The Untouchables" (instrumental closer)

The Dan Who Knew Too Much Tour—2016

In 2016, Steely Dan hit the road again with the same band and a similar set list. Their overture had changed, as they were now playing "November Afternoon," written by jazz trumpeters Donald Byrd and Booker Little, but the outro was still Nelson Riddle's "The Untouchables." Although the song choices hadn't changed much, they did do a few things differently. They played the New Orleans Jazz and Heritage Festival for the first time, teamed up with Steve Winwood for twenty-five dates, did four dates at the Beacon Theatre in New York with special guest Rickie Lee Jones, and continued their tradition of special album, "Greatest Hits", and "By Popular Demand" nights in New York. The one new, and incredibly surprising, change was that in addition to nights dedicated to *The Royal Scam*, *Aja*, and *Gaucho* LPs, they added *Countdown to Ecstasy* to the list. Given that Becker and Fagen have often expressed their disdain for their early albums, it's odd that they would choose the album for a new album night before *Katy Lied* or *Pretzel Logic*. The songs they played on the 2016 tour included:

Can't Buy a Thrill: "Dirty Work," "Reelin' In the Years"
Countdown to Ecstasy: "Bodhisattva," "My Old School," "Razor Boy," "Show Biz Kids," "Your Gold Teeth" (plus full album show)
Pretzel Logic: "Night by Night" (Hollywood Bowl only), "Pretzel Logic," "Rikki Don't Lose That Number"
Katy Lied: "Black Friday," "Daddy Don't Live in That New York City No More"
The Royal Scam: "Green Earrings," "Kid Charlemagne," "The Caves of Altamira" (Hollywood Bowl only), "The Royal Scam" (Hollywood Bowl only) (plus full album show)
Aja: "Aja," "Black Cow," "Deacon Blues" (Hollywood Bowl only), "Home at Last" (Hollywood Bowl only), "Josie," "Peg" (plus full album show)
Gaucho: "Babylon Sisters," "Hey Nineteen," "Third World Man" (Hollywood Bowl only), "Time Out of Mind" (plus full album show)
Two Against Nature: "Janie Runaway," "Two Against Nature"
Everything Must Go: "Godwhacker"
Miscellaneous: "I Want To (Do Everything for You)" (band intro), "November Afternoon" (instrumental overture), "The Untouchables" (instrumental closer)

Another first also occurred on the 2016 tour. On June 18 they performed at the Hollywood Bowl for their season opener with the Hollywood Bowl Orchestra. The show benefited the L.A. Philharmonic's high schooler-mentoring Composer Fellowship Program and raised $1.7 million. Nobody was quite sure how Becker and Fagen truly felt about playing with an orchestra, given that they only recorded two songs with strings in the past: "Through with Buzz" and "FM (No Static at All)." Becker's comments in a pre-show interview with the *Los Angeles Times* hinted at their lack of enthusiasm. "We feel like our band is our band. It's very solid; they can't take that away. So basically you're talking about some fiddle players, et cetera." The set list was as follows:

"Green Earrings"
"Aja"
"The Caves of Altamira"
"Hey Nineteen" (without orchestra)
"The Royal Scam"
"Deacon Blues"
"Night by Night"
"Time Out of Mind" (without orchestra)
"Third World Man"
"Home at Last"
"Josie"
"Bodhisattva"
"Kid Charlemagne"

24

Somebody Else's Favorite Song

Steely Dan Songs Covered by Other Artists

Although most fans can only imagine Becker and Fagen's compositions being played by Steely Dan, they have been covered by myriad artists in a variety of styles. Some have been successful reinterpretations; others have been odd choices by artists that had no business covering a Steely Dan song. Here are some of the best and worst that have come out over the years.

Herbie Mann

The first song that was released by Steely Dan and then covered by another artist is jazz flutist Herbie Mann's version of "Do It Again" from his 1973 album *Turtle Bay*. The original groove fits Mann's smooth jazz vibe to a tee and is a successful take on this early Dan classic. Percussionist Ralph MacDonald would play on both "Glamour Profession" and "My Rival" from the *Gaucho* LP. The dueling flute solos as well as the Fender Rhodes electric piano solo would make Becker and Fagen proud.

Charles Mann

Oddly enough, in 1973 Louisiana "swamp-pop" singer Charles Mann, no relation to Herbie, also recorded "Do It Again" for his LP *Say You Love Me Too*. This arrangement is completely different than Steely Dan's and is an early example of disco with a four-on-the-floor drumbeat, percussion, a string section, horns, and a funk groove.

Birtha

"Do It Again" was a popular cover in 1973 with ABC Dunhill Records label mates Birtha, an all-female Los Angeles rock group, releasing it as a single. Like Steely Dan, they opened for the Kinks and gained notoriety with their publicity flyers for the shows stating, "Birtha has balls."

Songbird

In 1973, guitarist Howard Leese, of the band Heart, arranged a version of "Dirty Work" with producer Mike Flicker for a single by Canadian band Songbird. It began with a beautiful guitar duet of the opening melody and followed Steely Dan's version pretty closely, with a sweet lead vocal and big harmonies on the chorus.

Eumir Deodato

Brazilian pianist, composer, record producer, and arranger Eumir Deodato recorded an exceptional instrumental version of "Do It Again" released as the A-side of a CTI single with a B-side by Brazilian drummer and percussionist Airto Moreira. It finally reached a larger audience when it was one of three bonus tracks on the CD reissue of his 1973 album *Deodato II* in 1988. Like Herbie Mann's version, the flute plays the melody, but Deodato's version hits harder, with a remarkable guitar solo and a funky Wurlitzer electric piano part. He would revisit the song for a live big band recording at the Felt Forum later that year in the wake of his hit arrangement of "2001: A Space Odyssey."

Botticelli and His Orchestra

Performing under the pseudonym "Botticelli and his Orchestra," Dutch producer Dick Bakker covered "Rikki Don't Lose That Number" for the 1974 LP *Botticelli Unlimited*. The super-easy-listening instrumental features an orchestra with a rhythm section and in a way is an absurd, yet ironic, spin on a song by the band that to many was already easy listening fare. This somewhat out-of-the-ordinary arrangement is definitely worth a listen, and luckily, the guitarist begins his solo with Jeff "Skunk" Baxter's signature lead.

Ian Matthews

In 1974, singer Ian Matthews, famous for his version of Terence Boylan's "Shakin'" (see chapter twenty), covered "Dirty Work" for his album *Some Days You Eat the Bear and Some Days the Bear Eats You*. The feel was similar to Steely Dan's version but uses a saxophone to play the intro, and the solo section goes into a funk groove, something that doesn't quite fit with the rest of the song.

José Feliciano

In 1974, another cover of "Dirty Work" was released, this one by blind singer/guitarist extraordinaire José Feliciano for his album *For My Love . . . Mother Music*. It was hard for artists to reinvent the wheel, and Feliciano, who could typically transform a song by another artist into a signature statement, follows the blueprint from Steely Dan's version but does include some strings that add little, and an intense acoustic guitar solo that seems at odds with the overall feel of the song.

Saxophonist/flutist Jim Horn and trumpet player Chuck Findley, who would both play on the *Gaucho* LP, contributed to other songs on the album.

Poco

For their eighth LP, 1975's *Head over Heels*, Poco covered the A-side from Steely Dan's first, and rarely heard, single "Dallas." Their take on the song is faster and a bit more produced, with strings, a syncopated groove, and a superior vocal performance to drummer Jim Hodder's from Steely Dan's version. They also incorporate the pedal steel guitar heard on the original, but without the intensity that Jeff Baxter brings to the table. Bassist and vocalist Timothy B. Schmit would sing background vocals and by some accounts play bass on *Pretzel Logic*, and would sing background vocals on *The Royal Scam*, *Aja*, and "FM (No Static at All)" with Eagles bandmates Glenn Frey and Don Henley.

Richie Havens

Woodstock's first performer, singer/guitarist Richie Havens, recorded a version of "Do It Again" for his eleventh LP, 1976's *The End of the Beginning*. Interestingly, Havens takes a different approach to the song and forgoes the Latin-tinged vibe of the original, opting for a funkier approach that is actually more creative than the other attempts by previous artists. The song was arranged by keyboard player William "Smitty" Smith, who had previously worked with Eric Mercury, the first artist that Gary Katz takes credit for producing. Although Jeff Baxter didn't play on Havens's take on the Steely Dan classic, he did contribute guitar and pedal steel guitar to other songs on the album.

Cornell Dupree

Session guitarist Cornell Dupree tackles "Peg" for his 1978 release *Shadow Dancing*. Percussionist Erroll "Crusher" Bennett, who would play on "Babylon Sisters" and "Gaucho," and bassist Will Lee, who would appear on Fagen's *The Nightfly* and play on "Jack of Speed" from Steely Dan's *Two Against Nature*, also contribute to the recording. His funk big-band arrangement is a little corny, and the horn harmonies are rather bland, which is curious considering that Becker and Fagen recorded Michael McDonald's closely harmonized background vocals to emulate the sound of a big band. Dupree's guitar playing, however, is, as always, impeccable.

Ahmad Jamal

Jazz pianist Ahmad Jamal recorded a version of "Black Cow" for his 1978 album *One*. He follows Steely Dan's arrangement closely, with a clavinet playing the melody except for the chorus, which adds female background vocalists that repeat the "I can't cry anymore while you run around" line twice. Jamal, known primarily as a piano player, shows his chops with an incredible solo on the clavinet, an instrument that plays a supporting role on Steely Dan's original, and Hal Blaine, who played drums on "Any World (That I'm Welcome To)," adds percussion to the track. Percussionist Paulinho da Costa, who would play on Becker's *11 Tracks of Whack*, contributed percussion to other songs on the album.

The Woody Herman Band

In 1978, world-renowned trumpet player Woody Herman was looking for material to fill out an album that he was working on. The first side was a three-part suite for big band written by keyboard player Chick Corea, but he wasn't sure what to record for the second side. A member of his band gave him a copy of *Aja*, and he became a fan immediately. Music publicist and promoter Dick LaPalm had worked with both parties and set up a meeting. Becker and Fagen, who had always been fans of Herman's, were ecstatic and along with Herman chose six songs to be recorded for side-two of the album. The album, *Chick, Donald, Walter and Woodrow*, included the songs "Green Earrings," "Kid Charlemagne," "I Got the News, "Aja," and "FM (No Static at All)." They also recorded "Deacon Blues," which would be included as a bonus track when the album was released on CD in the U.K.

Donny and Marie Osmond

Although it was never released on record, this Steely Dan cover is worth mentioning. In January 1978, brother and sister duo Donny and Marie Osmond opened an episode of their popular variety show with a version of "Reelin' in the Years." After a rubato intro, they go into a Vegas-style interpretation that is well sung and played with the familiar groove of the original, but is incredibly cheesy, especially when the "Ice Angels" begin their routine.

Pointer Sisters

In 1978, Gary Katz's former production partner Richard Perry produced a version of "Dirty Work" for the Pointer Sisters' album *Energy*. Their version uses a saxophone and slide guitar for the intro but otherwise follows the Dan's arrangement to a tee down to the Wurlitzer electric piano. They do add a stop-time section on the penultimate chorus that is quite effective. Overall, a successful cover of a song that many had attempted, but few perfected. Hearing the song performed by women puts a spin on the lyrics and demonstrates the desperation that could be felt by either gender when in a toxic relationship.

Dr. Strut

In 1979, a previously unreleased Becker and Fagen composition entitled "Canadian Star" appeared on the eponymous debut album of a jazz-funk band called Dr. Strut, released on the Motown label, which was trying to broaden its musical horizons. The album featured *Countdown to Ecstasy*'s assistant engineer Tim Weston on guitar. "Canadian Star" was the only song that was not written by the band themselves, and the instrumental track displayed some stellar guitar and sax interplay between Weston and saxophonist David Woodford. This slow burner sounds like a smooth jazz version of a song that could have been on *Gaucho* had the album included happier songs.

Dave Valentin

Apparently, "Do It Again" was a popular tune for jazz flutists, and Dave Valentin would cover the song for his 1979 LP *The Hawk*. Bassist Marcus Miller, who would play on Fagen's "Maxine," "The Goodbye Look," "The Nightfly," and "Shanghai Confidential," contributed to the track alongside percussionist Erroll "Crusher" Bennett, who would perform on "Babylon Sisters" and "Gaucho." This is one of the more interesting, and most innovative, reinterpretations of a Steely Dan song, with a heavy funk groove and some serious slap bass courtesy of Miller. It's exciting to hear an artist make the song his own rather than just follow the blueprint laid out by Becker and Fagen.

Waylon Jennings

In 1980, country superstar Waylon Jennings covered "Do It Again" for his album *Music Man*. He plays the song quite a bit faster, but the verse has a half-time feel that gives the illusion of a slower tempo. The horn arrangement would be at home at any recent Steely Dan show, and the droning effect the band achieves during the verses is hypnotic.

Norman Connors

Drummer Norman Connors's 1980 cover of "Black Cow" is hardly innovative, with a groove and horn arrangement nearly identical to Steely Dan's version, but it does feature jazz great Freddie Hubbard taking the lead on flügelhorn, which adds significantly to its appeal. Interestingly, Venetta Fields, who sang on countless Dan tracks, contributes vocals to this version that was the B-side to Connors's single "Take It to the Limit," and part of the LP of the same name.

Doc Severinsen with the National Philharmonic Orchestra of London

In 1980, *Tonight Show* band leader and trumpet player Doc Severinsen recorded a version of "Peg" with the National Philharmonic Orchestra of London entitled *London Sessions*. Becker and Fagen would hire saxophonist Pete Christlieb for "Deacon Blues" after hearing him on *The Tonight Show*. He would also play the memorable solo on "FM (No Static at All)."

Sneaker

In 1973, a West Coast band was formed by vocalist/guitarist Mitch Crane, vocalist/keyboardist Michael Carey Schneider, guitarist Tim Torrance, drummer Mike Hughes, bassist Michael Cottage, and Jim King on keyboards, synthesizers, and vibes. The band cited their main musical influences as Steely Dan, the Doobie Brothers, and the Eagles and named themselves Sneaker after the Steely Dan song "Bad Sneakers" from the *Katy Lied* LP.

They didn't release their eponymous LP until 1981 on the New York City label, Handshake Records and Tapes, but the connection to Steely Dan was more than just their admiration for the band. The album was produced by former Steely Dan guitarist Jeff "Skunk" Baxter, who not only played some guitar, but also called upon musicians who had worked with Steely Dan to augment the band's sound. These included arranger Jimmie Haskell, drummer Ed Greene, and background vocalist Shirley Matthews (listed as Sherlie Matthews).

The other Steely Dan connection was the lead-off song from the album, an early Becker and Fagen composition, "Don't Let Me In," which was demoed during their time with Kenny Vance. Sneaker had a minor hit with the song, but they're best known for their *Billboard* Hot 100 Top forty single, "More Than Just the Two of Us."

They released another studio album produced by Baxter entitled *Loose in the World*, but with the absence of a hit single, the band went their separate ways. In 2001, a Japanese record label, Cool Sound Records, released *Early On*, a collection of their early recordings, and in 2003, *Footprints in Japan*, a live recording from Osaka and Tokyo from 1982.

Yasuko Agawa

In 1983, Japanese singer and actress Yasuko Agawa released the LP *Night Line*. The album included the Becker and Fagen composition "Canadian Star," which had been recorded by Dr. Strut four years earlier. For this version, Ralph McCarthy wrote lyrics for the song, which took on a more ballad-like feel than Dr. Strut's recording. Agawa also appeared in three movies in the '70s and has released over thirty-five albums to date.

Tom Robinson

By 1984, folk-rocker turned punk-rocker turned pop-rocker released a synth-pop version of "Rikki Don't Lose That Number," which, according to John Dougan's *AllMusic* biography, has him "deftly exploring the song's homoerotic subtext." The arrangement, however, is a bland, typical '80s synth production with a solo saxophone that sounds as if it could be a Thompson Twins reject. The one interesting change is the chord progression used for the sax solo, not as good as Steely Dan's, but without doubt dissimilar.

The Four Freshmen

In 1986, the Four Freshmen, with original member Bob Flanigan, recorded two Fagen tunes from *The Nightfly* LP, "I.G.Y. (What a Beautiful World)" and "Maxine," for their *Fresh* LP. The production for "I.G.Y. (What a Beautiful World)" is somewhat amateurish, sounding like a karaoke version of Fagen's, but their version of "Maxine" is beautiful. It begins with a phenomenal solo horn section that introduces the song in a novel manner before the harmony vocals, the essence of the Four Freshmen sound, take over. I still prefer Fagen's vocals, and I don't understand why they used synthesized horns during the song after that stellar intro. The solo instrument is a trumpet rather than a saxophone, but the trumpet player cops the beginning of the solo note for note. The album also contains covers of compositions by Christopher Cross, Stevie Wonder, Duke Ellington, and Johnny Mercer, as well as songs popularized by Al Jarreau and Nat King Cole.

Hiram Bullock

Although he was a sought-after session guitarist, Hiram Bullock only worked with Steely Dan once, laying down guitar for "My Rival." He did, however, cover "Pretzel Logic" for his 1987 LP *Give It What You Got.* Bassist Will Lee, who was his former bandmate with the World's Most Dangerous Band on *Late Night with David Letterman,* had played on "Walk Between the Raindrops" from Fagen's *The Nightfly* LP, and would play on "Jack of Speed" from Steely Dan's *Two Against Nature*, contributed bass to this electro-fusion take on the song. Although the playing is top-notch, especially Bullock's harmonized guitar, his take on the song unfortunately sounds a bit dated due to the synthesizer-heavy production, a sign of the times.

Mel Tormé

In 1988, Mel Tormé released an album with the Marty Paich Dek-tette entitled *Reunion* that included Fagen's "Walk Between the Raindrops" and "The Goodbye Look." Paich was the father of Toto's keyboard player/vocalist David Paich, who had contributed to both the *Pretzel Logic* and *Katy Lied* LPs. Tormé could do no wrong with Fagen's jazzy tunes, and the band swings hard behind the singer known as "The Velvet Fog" on "Walk Between the Raindrops" and adds the ideal amount of Latin-tinged spice for "The Goodbye Look." Paich's arrangements are dense and accentuate the complexity of the chord changes of each song. I'm sure Fagen was humbled by the fact that a legend like Tormé would understand the genius of his writing and put his own spin on his material. Tormé also covered "Maxine" at a number of his live shows in the 1980s.

The Hoops McCann Band

On August 7, 1982, at the first Mount Hood Jazz Festival in Gresham, Oregon, a band at Mount Hood Community College devoted an entire set to Donald Fagen and Walter Becker compositions. Music publicist and promoter Dick LaPalm helped to put the band together, with Steely Dan stalwarts Chuck Rainey, Victor Feldman, Paul Humphrey, Ernie Watts, Jerome Richardson, Slyde Hyde, and Chuck Findley taking part in the project conducted by Joe Roccisano. The performance was recorded by Steely Dan producer Gary Katz along with producer Al Schmitt, but it was never released. Six years later, the majority of the musicians who played the live show, with the notable exceptions of bassist Chuck Rainey and multi-instrumentalist Victor Feldman (who had passed away), reconvened at the Village Recorder in L.A. to record a studio album that was released in 1988 as *The Hoops McCann Band Plays the Music of Steely Dan.*

Falco

Austrian pop star Falco, whose "Rock Me Amadeus" reached number one on the *Billboard* charts in 1985, making him the only artist whose principal language was German to score a vocal number one hit in the United States, covered "Do It Again" for his 1988 album *Wiener Blut.* The album's closing song begins with a sitar intro that leads into a synth-and-guitar-laden production with vocals that are at times sung in German and delivered in Roger Waters style, circa *The Wall*, with soulful yet corny female background vocals helping out on the chorus. Not the best interpretation of this early Dan classic.

Larry Carlton

It's interesting that Steely Dan stalwart Larry Carlton would choose "Josie" to open his 1989 album *On Solid Ground*, given that Walter Becker played the solo on the original. He sticks to the vibe of the version from *Aja* but with some added touches like harmonized guitar melodies and a completely different feel for his solo. Steely Dan regular, rhythm guitarist Dean Parks, took part in the sessions, as did bassist Abraham Laboriel, who would play on Fagen's "New Frontier," and percussionist Paulinho da Costa, who would play on Becker's *11 Tracks of Whack.*

Carlton would also base his song "Room 335," named after his recording studio (which was named after the model Gibson guitar he was famous for), on the chord changes of "Peg." The song was the lead-off track from his 1978 eponymous album, and Carlton used Jeff Porcaro on drums, Abraham Laboriel on bass, and Paulinho da Costa on percussion.

Minutemen

California punk rock group the Minutemen were the last people anybody expected to cover a song by the Dan, but they became the first to give an alt-rock treatment to a Steely Dan tune. For their 1989 album *Double Nickels on the Dime*, they cover "Doctor Wu" to great effect with a spoken-word double of the melody during part of the song, which is truncated to only 1:45.

Grover Washington Jr.

Smooth jazz saxophonist Grover Washington, Jr. was the kind of artist who would typically cover Steely Dan tunes, and in 1989, he covered "Time Out of Mind" for his album of the same name. The thing about jazz artists known for playing over funk grooves is that it was hard to bring anything new to the table. While Washington Jr. is a phenomenal player, his take on the *Gaucho* track sounds like a not-as-well-produced version of a Steely Dan song, along with female background vocals, but with a saxophone taking the melody. Not a bad version, but no real reason for it since the rhythm and horn sections basically cop the original, but without the same results. He does, however, play a nice solo on the outro.

The Manhattan Transfer

In 1989, vocal quartet the Manhattan Transfer recorded a fabulous version of Fagen's "Confide in Me" for their album *The Offbeat of Avenues*. The song was written specifically for them and would precede Fagen's own version, which would appear as the B-side to "Tomorrow's Girls," by four years. Drummer Jeff Porcaro shows up yet again on a Steely Dan cover, and the arrangement substitutes a horn section for the harmonica of Fagen's version. Also, this is the Manhattan Transfer, so there are intricate, dazzling harmonies everywhere for this take on a swinging Fagen tune that should be better known.

Howard Jones

In 1993, '80s synth-pop sensation Howard Jones released a version of Fagen's "I.G.Y. (What a Beautiful World)" as a single in Europe. The B-side was a live version of the song from a show in Philadelphia. The studio version would also be included on his 1993 compilation *The Best of Howard Jones*. The arrangement is almost identical to Fagen's, with some interesting sampled vocal pads inserted where the synth harmonica solo appeared in the original. Steely Dan session guitarist Elliott Randall plays guitar, but it's a very minor part that only appears in a few spots.

James Reyne

Australian artist James Reyne isn't well known in the U.S., but his 1994 groovy version of *Can't Buy a Thrill*'s "Only a Fool Would Say That" is worth mentioning because it's a rare cover of an underrated song. While it isn't very different from Steely Dan's version, it's sonically superior, hits harder, and features a crack rhythm section with some tasty Hammond B3 organ and a cool guitar solo reminiscent of Jeff Baxter's original.

Replicants

As we moved into the '90s, the bands that began to cover Steely Dan were more varied than those of the '70s and '80s, and their interpretations were often quite interesting. Bassist Paul D'Amour, formerly of Tool, founded Replicants with three other musicians with the plan to restrict their work to covering songs from the '70s and '80s. Although they only released one album in 1995, it included a punky power-pop version of "Dirty Work" that is arguably the best interpretation of the classic Steely Dan ballad. The album also contained songs by the Cars, Wings, John Lennon, David Bowie, Neil Young, Pink Floyd, and others.

Herbie Hancock

Jazz legend, pianist Herbie Hancock, covered "Your Gold Teeth II" for his 1996 set of pop covers *The New Standard*, but oddly it only appeared on the European release. Saxophonist Michael Brecker, who can be heard on both *Gaucho* and *The Nightfly*, swings alongside guitarist John Scofield, bassist Dave Holland, and drummer Jack DeJohnette and follows Hancock with a magnificent solo. While the composers' take on this underrated gem from *Katy Lied* had a serious swing, an incomparable bebop style guitar solo, and was harmonically complex, Hancock turns it into a true jazz reinterpretation by reharmonizing the chord changes, extending sections, and contributing an outrageous solo that plays over bar lines and switches effortlessly between blues licks and bebop lines.

Paul Hardcastle

British multi-instrumentalist and producer Paul Hardcastle offered his version of "Do It Again" for his 1997 album *Cover to Cover*. With female lead and background vocals, tenor saxophone licks, a synth vibraphone solo, and a tight backing track, it presents Steely Dan in a '90s acid-jazz setting that suits the material well.

Tori Amos

Singer/songwriter/pianist Tori Amos covered "Do It Again" in 1998 during the recording sessions for her fourth album, *From the Choirgirl Hotel*, but the song wasn't included on the LP. Instead, it can be found on the U.K. CD edition of the single "Spark" as the second track of the three-track CD single. Amos's interpretation is completely different from Steely Dan's, with reharmonizations of the chord changes and new melodic content, a welcome change in comparison to many covers of the song. It's based around a heavily distorted drum track, acoustic bass, and a haunting piano part; a superb take on a Dan song that sounds as disturbing and conniving as the lyrics.

Patti Austin

Singer Patti Austin contributed background vocals to three songs on *Gaucho*, "Babylon Sisters," "Time Out of Mind," and the title track, and would be one of the lead vocalists for the first New York Rock and Soul Show at the Beacon Theatre in 1990. Nine years later, she would cover Fagen's "I.G.Y. (What a Beautiful World)" for 1999's *Street of Dreams*, mostly comprised of some of Austin's favorite songs. Her version is a slickly produced half-time take on Fagen's originals, with a horn section atop a completely synthesized band. While there is much to be desired from the production, Austin's vocals are spot-on. She would also perform the song with Fagen on keyboards for the show *Night Music* in 1988.

Rickie Lee Jones

Singer-songwriter Rickie Lee Jones had worked with both Fagen, as a keyboard player, and Becker, as a producer, so it was no surprise that she would eventually cover one of their songs. Her choice: "Show Biz Kids" from her 2000 LP *It's Like This*. Her stripped-down version with acoustic bass, percussion, wah-wah guitar, and keyboards is initially lighter sounding than the Dan's version, but somehow is far more sinister. The fact that she repeats the infamous profanity-laden line three times in a row makes this one of the most badass covers of a Steely Dan song.

Christian McBride

Jazz bassist Christian McBride took another of Steely Dan's jazziest songs, and like Herbie Hancock, transformed it into a fully realized jazz composition. For his 2000 release *Sci-Fi*, he undertook the task of covering "Aja." He not only played acoustic bass, but Fender Rhodes electric piano. Drummer Rodney Green changes effortlessly from a swing groove to a straight feel in places one wouldn't expect; and saxophonist Ron Blake, pianist Shedrick Mitchell, and guitarist David Gilmore, who was a member of Lost Tribe, whom Becker produced, all contribute superb solos.

Joe Jackson

Singer/songwriter/pianist Joe Jackson stays true to the original for his cover of "King of the World" from his 2000 album *Summer in the City: Live in New York*. This live version is played by a trio, and Jackson plays the synthesizer solo note for note on the piano. They do, however, drop the section after the solo and return immediately to the last verse.

Jackson is apparently a big Steely Dan fan and has covered other Dan songs live over the years. His 2001 version of "Reelin' in the Years" is one of the best and spins the song in a completely different way, switching out the shuffle feel and heavy guitars for a Latin groove, piano, organ, and a Santana-ish guitar solo. He has also covered "Any Major Dude Will Tell You" with his trio, and while his take is similar to the original, he adds an impressive piano solo. During his 2006 trio tour, he even covered "Rose Darling." One thing in particular about Jackson's covers is that his voice suits them perfectly. Even when he isn't changing an arrangement drastically, he gives the songs an edge naturally, without pretension.

Me, Myself, and Irene Soundtrack

In 2000, the soundtrack for the movie *Me, Myself, and Irene*, starring Jim Carrey, included eight covers of Steely Dan songs out of the fifteen included. The songs were reinterpreted by artists from a number of different genres, the first time that the Dan would receive such fanfare. The bands that covered the songs were also at varying stages of their careers. Interestingly, they focused on songs from the early years of Steely Dan, with no songs from *The Royal Scam*, *Aja*, or *Gaucho* being covered. Out of the eight songs, three are from *Can't Buy a Thrill*; two are from *Countdown to Ecstasy*, two from *Pretzel Logic*, and one from *Katy Lied*.

"Do It Again" could not be a more perfect cover for alternative rock band Smash Mouth. Their original songs captured this same Latin-flavored, California-inspired groove, and their take on this Steely Dan classic is one of the most successful reinterpretations of the song, creating a modern version while keeping the integrity of the original intact. Indie pop band Ivy's recording of "Only a Fool Would Say That" follows the lead of the original but is smoother and loungier; imagine if "Only a Fool Would Say That" was recorded for *Aja*. Power punk band Marvelous 3's take on "Reelin' in the Years" is honestly nothing new; a harder, heavier version of the original that doesn't sound or feel as good as the original.

If anybody should cover the guitar-focused song "Bodhisattva," it should be an accomplished, fierce guitarist. Rockabilly star Brian Setzer was up for the challenge and delivered in spades not only in the guitar department but also as lead vocalist. It's not very different from the original, even copping the strummed piano strings before the first verse and certain sections of the guitar solo, but it rocks hard and is a flawless take on a song that many others couldn't even touch. Billy Goodrum was primarily a soundtrack composer, but for *Me, Myself, and Irene*, he covered "Razor Boy" with an interpretation that retains the Latin vibe of the original while adding an acoustic indie feel and a Santana-ish organ part.

It's hard to improve on Steely Dan's "Any Major Dude Will Tell You," and Wilco understands this. They stick close to the original and contribute an acoustic-heavy take on the tune with Wurlitzer electric piano front and center. The addition of the organ is definitely a nice touch, but the straight delivery of the chorus is a bit disappointing in comparison to the syncopation of the original; and the solo is nowhere near as stunning as Jeff Baxter's. Ben Folds Five covered "Barrytown" for the soundtrack, and while the feel didn't change much from the original, the bombastic intro adds something to the original and pops in throughout the song to great effect. Lyrically, the song is right up their alley, and the three-part harmony during the bridge is extremely lush.

Cambridge, Massachusetts-based band the Push Stars were never necessarily famous, but they delivered a smooth, up-tempo version of "Bad Sneakers" from *Katy Lied*. The promotion for the soundtrack landed them on the *Late Late Show with Craig Kilborn*, where they performed a noteworthy version of the song trio style.

Three additional songs were in the film that didn't make it onto the soundtrack: "Midnight Cruiser" by Nash Kato, "Monkey in Your Soul" by Freedie Johnson, and "Chain Lightning" by Leon Redbone.

Toto

Toto's eleventh studio LP, 2002's *Through the Looking Glass*, is a collection of cover songs that inspired them, including "Bodhisattva." Drummer Jeff Porcaro, who had toured with Steely Dan and played on *Pretzel Logic*, *Katy Lied*, "FM (No Static at All)," *Gaucho*, and Fagen's *The Nightfly*, had already passed, but keyboard player David Paich, who contributed to *Pretzel Logic* and *Katy Lied*, was still a member of the group when they recorded the album, which also included tracks by the Beatles, Bob Dylan, Stevie Wonder, Cream, Herbie Hancock, Elvis Costello, Bob Marley, and others. It's no surprise that the band could rock "Bodhisattva," but there's nothing new here as they cop Steely Dan's arrangement to a tee. Steve Lukather does, however, turn in an incredible solo, and the vocals are handled with aplomb by the guitarist and lead singer Bobby Kimball. The next year they would include the song on their *25th Anniversary: Live in Amsterdam* album.

INXS

In 2002, Australian record label Raven Records released a two-CD set entitled *Stay Young 1979-1982 (The Complete "Deluxe Years")* that included a live version of "Pretzel Logic" from the *Moontan Double J Concert* at Manly Vale Hotel recorded in October 1980. The INXS version forgoes the shuffle groove of the original for a straight feel, and its heavy '80s guitar interpretation and the lack of melody actually make it a bit hard to discern that it's actually a Steely Dan song.

The Royal Dan

In 2006, an album entitled *A Tribute* was released by the "band" the Royal Dan. The Royal Dan wasn't an actual band per se. Guitarist Jeff Richmond's idea was to put together a crack rhythm section and have different guitarists record their interpretations of classic Steely Dan songs. The backing band of drummer Vinnie Colaiuta, bassist Jimmy Haslip, keyboard player Peter Wolf, saxophonist Ernie Watts, and guitarist Richmond were quite familiar with Becker and Fagen's work (Colaiuta, Haslip, and Watts had worked with them before). The guitarists were some of the best from the jazz, blues, and rock world, including Al Di Meola, Robben Ford, Frank Gambale, Jimmy Herring, Steve Lukather, Steve Morse, Elliott Randall, Mike Stern, and Jeff Richmond, the musician who was responsible for the project.

Maestros of Cool

Another tribute to the band was also released in 2006, *Maestros of Cool: A Tribute to Steely Dan*. This European release was a two-CD, 24-track hipster take on twenty Steely Dan songs and four others inspired by the band. Damon Albarn from the bands Blur and Gorillaz was probably the biggest name in pop/rock music attached to the project, contributing vocals to producer Nathan Haines's version of "FM (No Static at All)." Steely Dan saxophonist Cornelius Bumpus fronted his own version of "Chain Lightning," and myriad musicians who had contributed to Steely Dan's albums, including Bernard Purdie, David Paich, Greg Phillinganes, Bob Sheppard, and John Beasley, played on some of the tracks. Beasley, who had played keyboards on Becker's *11 Tracks of Whack* and toured with Steely Dan for the *Art Crimes* tour of 1996, wrote a song, "Remember," specifically for the album credited as Stereo, on which he not only plays keyboards but sings as well.

Tommy Shaw of Styx and Jack Blades from Night Ranger

A curious cover of "Dirty Work" appeared on a 2007 album of cover songs entitled *Influence* from former Damn Yankees bandmates Tommy Shaw and Jack Blades, also veterans of Styx and Night Ranger respectively. The album features compositions by Seals and Crofts, Yes, the Mamas and the Papas, Simon and Garfunkel, and others, and while the duo turned in a fine take on Steely Dan's first hit single, it feels uninspired and breaks no new ground.

Boz Scaggs

In 2013, fellow Dukes of September and New York Rock and Soul Revue mate Boz Scaggs released his take on "Pearl of the Quarter" from his seventeenth studio album *Memphis*. Scaggs's take on the song hits harder than the original and is equal parts old-school Memphis soul and Philadelphia R&B from the heyday of Gamble and Huff. The string section is a nice touch, and Spooner Oldham's piano solo is a welcome addition that adds a bluesy element to Scaggs's version of an often forgotten Steely Dan song.

John Pizzarelli

Jazz guitarist and singer John Pizzarelli covered two songs from Fagen's *Nightfly* LP for his 2012 album *Double Exposure*. The first, "Walk Between the Raindrops," was a Fagen composition, but the second, "Ruby Baby," was a Jerry Leiber and Mike Stoller song; but Pizzarelli used Fagen's jazzier arrangement, to a certain extent, after the strikingly original introduction, for the LP. The horn arrangement that opens "Walk Between the Raindrops" is so influenced by Duke Ellington that Fagen must have been ecstatic when he first heard it. An extraordinary arrangement with a swinging piano solo and a fantastic guitar/scat solo by Pizzarelli.

The Darcys

Canadian Alternative rock band the Darcys embarked on an ambitious project in 2012 when they decided to reimagine the entire *Aja* album and record it at home on a $500 budget. They had only released two albums prior, and the decision to re-create an album that most believed could not be re-created was done to attract a buzz for their recently released second album. Band leader and drummer Wes Marskell explained their intentions in a 2012 interview with the *Daily News*. "The original album had this disparity between the mood of the music and the darkness of the lyrics. We thought, 'Wouldn't it be cool to bring those things closer together?' *Aja* just felt so far from what we do, I knew that meant we had a fighting chance to make something interesting out of it."

This is by far the most experimental set of Steely Dan covers, and they do honor the melodicism and some of the harmonic elements of the original, but that's where the similarity ends. The songs take on a dark, heavy, ominous vibe from the first track, and the album moves through a variety of feels from drum and bass to punk rock to garage rock, all with an atmosphere that truly fits the heavy nature of the lyrics. When asked about the recording of the album, Marskell remarked, "The music was so intimidating, I wish we had a legend to guide us, because so much is happening in the evolution of each song. Also, that record is so important to so many people. I had a panic attack. We put so much work into this music at times it does feel like playing our own songs."

Mark Masters Ensemble

In 2013, trumpeter/composer/arranger Mark Masters released *Everything You Did: The Music of Walter Becker and Donald Fagen*. Masters had already released a number of tribute albums to jazz heavyweights including trumpeter Clifford Brown, saxophonist Lee Konitz, trombonist Jimmy Knepper, and the Gershwin brothers, so Becker and Fagen were in good company. The Mark Masters Ensemble is essentially a big band, with a featured quartet comprised of trumpeter Tim Hagans, tenor saxophonist Billy Harper, bassist Hamilton Price, and drummer Peter Erskine, who had toured with Steely Dan on their first tour of the '90s and appeared on their only live album, *Alive in America*. Masters's arrangements completely turn the compositions on their head, with each song getting an original interpretation. Most are reharmonized in such a way that it is at times a challenge to pull the original from his idiosyncratic renditions, but this is a good thing. The tracks incorporate the essential elements of swing, Latin-jazz, and soul, giving jazz aficionados, as well as Steely Dan fans in general, an album that proves to be a fascinating listening experience.

John Wetton

Bassist and vocalist John Wetton, famous for his stints in the bands King Crimson, Roxy Music, Uriah Heep, Asia, and others, covered "Do It Again" for his live album *New York Minute*, released in 2015 but recorded in 2013. The album was recorded at the Iridium Jazz Club with the Les Paul trio and follows Steely Dan's arrangement of the song closely, but is stripped down to bass, piano, and electric guitar. Ironically, he recorded an original song with the same name, and the same keyboard riff, for a 1987 album with Roxy Music's guitarist Phil Manzanera entitled *Wetton/Manzanera*.

Madeleine Peyroux

Singer-songwriter Madeleine Peyroux began singing when she was fifteen and living in Paris with her mother. The next year she joined the Lost Wandering Blues and Jazz Band, a group of street musicians, and not only recorded two albums, but toured to support them as well. In 1996 at the age of twenty-two she released her debut album, *Dreamland*, with a who's who of jazz and session musicians including pianist Cyrus Chestnut, guitarist Vernon Reid of Living Color, guitarist Marc Ribot, saxophonist James Carter, and drummer Leon Parker. Her next album, *Careless Love*, didn't come out until 2004, but it proved to be her breakthrough album peaking at number seven in the U.K. and number five in Australia, but only reaching number seventy-one in the U.S.

For her third album, 2006's *Half the Perfect World*, she enlisted producer Larry Klein, who had worked on Becker's *Circus Money*. Becker and Klein co-wrote the album's first single, "I'm All Right," with Peyroux. The album fared better in the states peaking at number thirty-three on the *Billboard* 200. Her next album, 2009's *Bare Bones*, was also produced by Klein and once again the first single, "You Can't Do Me," involved Becker. The song was co-written with Klein and Peyroux as was the title track. Dean Parks, Jim Beard, Larry Goldings, Vinnie Colaiuta, and Luciana Souza contributed to the album and had all worked on Steely Dan related projects. The album reached number one on the Jazz charts and peaked at number twelve on the U.K. album chart. Peyroux was the opening act for two Steely Dan shows at the Beacon Theatre during their 2016 *The Dan Who Knew Too Much* tour. Dan guitarist Jon Herington and acoustic bassist Barak Mori accompanied her for a set of originals and standards and recorded an album as a trio, *Secular Hymns*, in 2016.

Luciana Souza

Brazilian singer-songwriter Luciana Souza has been in the music business since she was three years old, recording jingles for commercials. She graduated from the Berklee College of Music with a degree in Jazz Composition and received a master's from the New England Conservatory of Music. She has worked in both the jazz and classical fields and has eleven solo albums to her name. In 2007 she released *In The New Bossa Nova*, which contained the song "Love Is For Strangers," co-written by Becker and her husband, bassist/producer Larry Klein. Klein produced Becker's second album, *Circus Money* in 2008 and Souza contributed vocals and Pandeiro, a Brazilian hand frame drum similar to a tambourine. She also covered the Becker and Fagen composition "Were You Blind That Day," which was originally recorded during the *Aja* sessions but not released until they needed an additional song for *Gaucho*. The duo rewrote the lyrics and the song became "Third World Man."

In 2007 she won a Grammy Award for her work as a featured vocalist on Herbie Hancock's *River: The Joni Letters*. She has been nominated five times for Best Jazz Vocal Album and once for Best Latin Jazz Album. She has worked with countless artists including Paul Simon, James Taylor, Bobby McFerrin, Danilo Perez, Kenny Werner, John Patitucci, David Binney, and others.

25

You Were a Champion in Their Eyes

Musicians, Producers, Writers, and Others Speak About Steely Dan

azz, rock, R&B, and hip-hop musicians make up the great coterie of Steely Dan fans. The group's blend of complex chord changes, innovative melodies, and tight grooves are no doubt uniting factors. Intense, provocative, and often subversive lyrics also play a huge role in the legend of Steely Dan, so it's no surprise that writers, intellectuals, politicians, and countless others are admirers as well. In this chapter, aficionados from varied walks of life share the reasons behind their love of Steely Dan.

I love "Fun Fun Fun" and when I did that, I wanted Donald Fagen to sing it. No one would agree with me. I'm a huge Donald Fagen fan—*The Nightfly* is definitely in my top twenty. And top twenty is tough, when you love music. Fagen is my favorite, and when that didn't happen . . . I was super hurt. And most people would be like, 'What do you mean, it's *you*, they kept *you* on it,' and I'm like 'Yeah, that's what fucks it up for me!' I love [it] but imagine if Donald Fagen had sang! It'd be amazing.
   —Pharell Williams (musician/producer) ("Pharrell Williams on Surprise Hits, Daft Punk, and Watching Michael Jackson Laugh." *Vulture*, June 6, 2013)

Like most bands from before my time, I discovered Steely Dan through rap music, specifically because 'Peg' had been sampled by De La Soul on *3 Feet High and Rising*. That was about 20 years ago, and I discover new things every time I put a Steely Dan record on. I'm still discovering songs for the first time. No other band managed to let groove and intellect coexist as seamlessly. The most incredible rhythm sections with the most captivating narratives and these crazy chord changes . . . Years ago, I flew out to L.A. to visit a girlfriend who dumped me as soon as I arrived. I couldn't change my ticket so I had to stay in L.A., miserable, for five days. I bought the Steely Dan songbook and a cheap electric piano and stayed in my room for the duration of the time, teaching myself those songs. I don't often think of the girl but I use those amazing chord voicings nearly every day.
   —Mark Ronson (musician/producer) ("Icon: Donald Fagen."
   GQ, February 11, 2014)

I listen to so much Steely Dan. There is so much Steely Dan in this album (2013's *Where Does This Door Go*). My motto's always been: 'If you don't like Steely Dan, I don't like you.' Steely Dan is a great divider among music fans. Either you love it or you don't. I don't know anyone who *kind of* likes Steely Dan. It's very divisive. Fortunately everyone who I worked with on this record really appreciated it. I think even people who like Steely Dan as much as I do can admit that there's nothing sexy about Steely Dan. And so basically what I tried to do on this album was to take Steely Dan and make it sexy.

—Mayer Hawthorne (musician/producer) ("Mayer Hawthorne: 'If You Don't Like Steely Dan, I Don't Like You,'" *Spin*, July 16, 2013)

I don't think I have listened to any band more than Steely Dan. They are a bottomless pit of joy. The songs are gorgeous; the lyrics are mysterious and witty. When I was young I used those records as a gateway drug to learn about a lot of great jazz performers. I would read the credits and buy the albums of all the people who played on their records. That led to thousands of hours listening to the Brecker Brothers, Larry Carlton, Phil Woods, Wayne Shorter and countless others.

—Judd Apatow (writer/director) ("Icon: Donald Fagen," *GQ*, February 11, 2014)

Steely Dan was my favorite group even before I knew who they were. I thought they were a bunch of bikers from up north. They looked so mean and bad on the inside jacket of their album, *Can't Buy a Thrill*. But I thought they were it . . . harmonically, the lyrics, . . . Becker and Fagen blow my mind. And still to this day, they are it; they are what should be happening now. When Steely Dan's first album came out, I flipped. I thought they were the Beatles of California. I was always scared shitless playing for them. They were very demanding—not in a malicious way—but everyone respected them so much. You felt you were playing on something really special. When they were happy, it was great to see. It meant you'd accomplished something.

—Jeff Porcaro (drummer) ("Spotlight Gazette: Jeff Porcaro." *Downbeat*, Sept. 8, 1977, and "The Drummers of Steely Dan." *Modern Drummer*, November 1, 1992)

The band . . . did that part of ["Aja"] live . . . They asked for fills between the figures they already had. Back then, there were all of these stories about Becker and Fagen never being satisfied for one reason or another, but we just sort of sailed through everything. We did the song live in the studio and then Wayne overdubbed his parts after. So, I wasn't even there when he did it—unfortunately. I would have loved to have been there! I didn't even know at the time that's what was happening, but that's what it turned out to be.

—Steve Gadd (drummer) ("Steve Gadd on 'Aja,' 50 Ways to Leave Your Lover,' 'Take It Away,' others: Gimme Five." *Something Else!*, Sept. 27, 2012)

With me, they wanted something very specific. They had already recorded *The Royal Scam* with other drummers, so I had to overdub. I stuck to the original patterns, but they wanted what I could do. It was a heavy situation. I wasn't uptight about trying to impress them, I was just doing my job. They knew my earlier work, so they wanted to hear my take on their music. They were very strict to the point of super precision. Really picky. They wouldn't take no for an answer and they wouldn't accept mistakes—period. It was truly frustrating in the beginning. I come from the school that when you feel good about what you've done, it's hard to do better. It only goes downhill from there. I learned to curtail my own feelings and just wait. They wanted it their way, so you had to do many takes.

> —Bernard "Pretty" Purdie (drummer) ("The Drummers of Steely Dan,"
> *Modern Drummer* November 1, 1992)

I worked with Walter in the studio and despite whatever legends or stories have gone around . . . I found him to be a real gentlemen and lots of fun to work with. They're perfectionists. I wouldn't use the word picky. Picky somehow connotes that they focus on minuscule things that might not be so important. They are specific as to what they want and what they hear. At the same time they're very generous in letting things happen up there. So they're not control freaks. And I've worked with musicians who are control freaks.

> —Peter Erskine (drummer) ("Interview with Drummer Peter Erskine."
> *The Rhythm Section,* July 1, 1993)

A lot of people think of Steely Dan as the epitome of boring seventies stuff, never realizing this is probably the most subversive material pop has ever thrown up.

> —William Gibson (author) ("Icon: Donald Fagen,"
> *GQ,* February 11, 2014)

This is what happens when you don't construct an archetypal persona. If you're popular and melodic and faceless, you seem meaningless. [Look at] Steely Dan, a group who served as the house band for every 1978 West Coast singles band despite being more lyrically subversive than the Sex Pistols and the Clash combined. If a musician can't convince people that he's cool, nobody cool is going to care.

> —Chuck Klosterman (author) ("Icon: Donald Fagen,"
> *GQ,* February 11, 2014)

There are no finer songwriters in the country. They are kind of like the young George and Ira Gershwin; they haven't reached their peak. If they don't blow it by being assholes, they'll be around for a long time.

> —Jay Black of Jay and the Americans (singer) ("Nobody's Making
> Better Music Than an Unlikely Duo Named After a Dildo,"
> *New Times,* February 18, 1977)

I mean there are people that have read books and there's people who ain't read books. They've got a skill that make images that aren't puerile and don't make you think that you've heard it before. Very Hollywood filmic in a way. The imagery is very imaginable in a visual sense . . . *Aja*'s got a sound that lifts your heart up. It's the most consistently upful, heartwarming, even though it is a classic L.A. kind of sound . . . it's a record that sends my spirits up . . . When I listen to music that's really what I want. I don't really want to hear people moaning and I don't want to hear music that moans.

—Ian Dury (singer-songwriter)
(*Classic Albums: Steely Dan Aja*, October 21, 1999)

I'd been listening to this station on XM Radio called 'The Bridge,' the one that plays a lot of soft seventies rock. And it just started to amaze me that once upon a time, people made music like this! It's the exact opposite of rocking out. America, Seals and Crofts, Steely Dan—there's a feel to it that I'm just obsessed with.

—Fred Armisen (actor/writer/director/musician)
("Inside Bill Hader and Fred Armisen's Soft-Rock Supergroup,"
Rolling Stone, September 24, 2015)

I've worked with them enough to kind of know what I was in for. Certain words they just wanted to hear a certain way . . . Under normal circumstances . . . these are the words, here's the parts and you sang it . . . that's the phrasing. But with those guys phrasing could have such nuance . . . singing a line like 'half as much as' you'd think 'how many different ways can you say it in that phrasing, rhythmically?' But it would come down to such fine points like pronunciation and exact rhythmic; vibrato, no vibrato . . . Things like that, so it was always real challenging.

—Michael McDonald (singer-songwriter/keyboard player)
(*Classic Albums: Steely Dan Aja*, October, 21, 1999)

They are the most demanding group of people in the industry that I've worked for . . . If three of the guys are cutting the part great and one doesn't feel just right, they'll call in a whole new band and redo the whole thing . . . Donald and Walter love sophisticated harmony, but they're rock and roll guys. We're contemporaries as far as age so we all were brought up listening to the '60s. I know that they love rock and roll but they also have a passion for harmony . . . as do I. All the players they use, we love great feeling rock and roll music, but we love harmony.

—Larry Carlton (guitarist) ("Nobody's Making Better Music Than
an Unlikely Duo Named After a Dildo." *New Times*, Feb 18, 1977,
and *Classic Albums: Steely Dan Aja*, October, 21, 1999)

You gotta love 'em . . . you go in there and you're just really good friends and you'll play and you'll try to get into it and they'll say 'Yeah, that's really good,' and then the next day somebody else is doing it. A whole other band. It wasn't like they played musical chairs with the guys in the band, they played musical bands. A whole band would go and a whole incredible other band would come in.

—Rick Marotta (drummer) (*Classic Albums: Steely Dan Aja*, October, 21, 1999)

Working with Steely Dan could hardly be considered 'fun.' But it was reward-ing . . . When you worked with Gary Katz, Donald Fagen and Walter Becker, you planned on long hours and not a lot of affirming moments. When they were happy, you would pretty much hear the words, 'we got the take' and that was it. You would realize you did a good job when you got a call to do the next song . . . I know that they appreciated what the players did, but it was not something that you would feel secure about at the time of recording.

—Michael Omartian (pianist) ("Michael Omartian: Working with Steely Dan Could Hardly Be Considered Fun," *yuzu-melodies.fr*, June 9, 2012)

Even though you hear talk about tension in the studio, whenever I was with those guys it was smiles and sometimes broad belly laughs, because that's part of what the music experience is. Another curious thing is that right before I started play-ing any given solo, Donald would lean over to me and whisper: Just play the blues! He actually got that one from Duke Ellington. Ellington was absolutely one of Donald's number-one idols.

—Elliott Randall (guitarist) ("40 Years of Rocking on Reelin': Elliott Randall Interview," *Guitarist* magazine, June 2012)

I was always amazed that they pretty much heard in their heads what it was going to be like completed. So they knew right away when you get a bunch a musicians together and they're cutting the tracks and Don and Walter would be sitting in the control room going, 'No. This is not it. It's not gonna happen. So maybe we'll try this other tune with these guys.' Then they'd get another band in to try the tunes that didn't work out. And all through the project they would know, 'No. That's not it. That's not working. This is what I want.' And it was amazing that when the thing got done finally I could see what everything was gonna be like. But they knew from the very beginning.

—Roger Nichols (engineer) ("*Classic Albums: Steely Dan Aja*," October 21,1999)

They're one of my favorite groups. I like their modality, their melodicism. Their lyrics aren't bad in that vein they're working, that downer surrealism. As relaxing listening music, I'd give it a 98. One person in our band, Ruth Underwood, would give them about a 120. She really fetishes 'em. She's usually got their cassette reamed into her ear.

—Frank Zappa (musician/producer) ("Steely Dan Comes Up Swinging," *Rolling Stone*, Issue 167, August 15, 1974)

Don sort of looked like a crow most of the time. He'd walk around [the Bard campus] with this beak of a nose and he always wore black clothing and looked down with his hands in his pockets. People thought he was kind of weird and quiet. They didn't realize that he was really intelligent, a very funny, bright guy.

> —Chevy Chase (actor/writer) ("The Origins of Steely Dan—Donald Fagen Returns to Campus and Revisits the Origin of His Old Grudge," *Entertainment Weekly*, March 17, 2006)

[Fagen] hung out with some bizarre Bard students who were too dark and mysterious for some other people. They never came out of their room; they stayed up all night. They looked like ghosts . . . Absolutely no activity, chain-smoking Lucky Strikes and dope. [He was] immersed in an entirely Beat attitude.

> —Terence Boylan (musician) ("The Origins of Steely Dan—Donald Fagen Returns to Campus and Revisits the Origin of His Old Grudge," *Entertainment Weekly*, March 17, 2006)

I'm spoiled by them. They are two of the best songwriters on the planet, up there with the old Lennon/McCartney and Paul Simon.

> —Jim Hodder (drummer) ("Steely Dan Comes Up Swinging," *Rolling Stone*, Issue 167. August 15, 1974)

Vladimir (Nobokov) was the hero of Donald and Walter – they thought he was the finest writer in the West. Crazy things for little girls, though – a little twist in his personality there. (Fagen) thought Nietzsche was pretty funny. I thought Nietzsche was pretty funny. It's pretty brutal but it was a kind of humor that we had that was a little different.

> —Jeff "Skunk" Baxter (guitarist) ("Skunk Hunting in W1." *New Musical Express* July 19, 1975)

When I heard their writing, well I just stopped trying to write songs. Listening to Walter and Donald's songs was like hearing the Beatles with jazz chords. I was flabbergasted! If I hadn't met them, I'd still be back at school.

> —Denny Dias (guitarist) ("Steely Dan," *Melody Maker*, June 1, 1974)

I'll always be grateful to Donald and Walter for giving me a break and also for their musical integrity. The word 'genius' is bandied about a lot in pop music but those two are the genuine article.

> —David Palmer (singer) ("David Palmer: Q&A," *Metal Leg*, January 1, 1997)

These people are too fancy. They're too sophisticated; they're doing too many things at once in a song. To write a bestseller, you can't have too much going on. You take *The Godfather*, the horse's head. That's great. But you can't have a horse's head on every page. These people tend to have too many horses' heads.

—William S. Burroughs (author) ("Nobody's Making Better Music Than an Unlikely Duo Named After a Dildo," *New Times*, February 18, 1977)

Selected Bibliography

Books

Breithsaupt, Don. *Steely Dan's Aja (33 1/3)*. New York: Bloomsbury, 2007.

DiMartino, Dave. *Do It Again: The Steely Dan Years*. Self-published, 2009.

Fagen, Donald. *Eminent Hipsters*. New York: Viking Penguin, 2013.

O'Rourke, Stephen. *The Steely Dan File*. Lulu, 2007.

Quiggin, Thomas. *Seeing The Invisible: National Security Intelligence in an Uncertain Age*. Singapore: World Scientific, 2007.

Sweet, Brian. *Steely Dan: The Complete Guide to their Music*. London: Omnibus Press, 2004.

Sweet, Brian. *Steely Dan: Reelin' in the Years*. London: Omnibus Press, 2015.

Fanzines

Fogel, Pete, Bill Pascador, and Brian Sweet. *Metal Leg* Volumes 1–22, 1987–1993.

Magazine and Newspaper Articles

Crowe, Cameron. "The Second Coming of Steely Dan." *Rolling Stone* Issue 255 Dec. 29, 1977: 11–15.

Hopkins, Jerry. "Lou Adler." *Rolling Stone* Issue 24 Dec. 21, 1968: 18–19, 30.

Perry, Charles. "Steely Dan Comes Up Swinging." *Rolling Stone* Issue 167 Aug. 15, 1974: 32–34, 36.

Pooley, Eric. "Facing the Music." *New York* Nov. 3, 1986: 54–61.

Web Articles and Interviews

Abebe, Nitsuh. "Pharrell Williams on Surprise Hits, Daft Punk, and Watching Michael Jackson Laugh." *Vulture* Jun. 6, 2013. vulture.com/2013/06/pharrell-williams-interview.html

Bambarger, Bradley. "Sad Experiences Still a Theme in Fagen's Music." *Newhouse News Service*. Mar. 10, 2006. steelydanreader.com/2006/03/10/sad-experiences-still-theme-fagens-music

Bennington, Ron. "Donald Fagen: He's Undeniable." *theinterrobang.com* Oct. 12, 2014. theinterrobang.com/donald-fagen-when-hes-there-its-undeniable

Breskin, David. "Steely Dan Interview." *Musician* Mar. 1, 1981. steelydanreader.com/1981/03/01/steely-dan-interview

Briggs, Chris. "Showbiz Kids: Talking with Jeff Baxter, and a Critical View of Steely Dan." *ZigZag* Jul. 1974. rocksbackpages.com/Library/Article/showbiz-kids -talking-with-jeff-baxter-and-a-critical-view-of-steely-dan

Brunner, Rob. "The Origins of Steely Dan—Donald Fagen Returns to Campus and Revisits the Origin of His Old Grudge." *Entertainment Weekly* Mar. 17, 2006. steelydanreader.com/2006/03/17/back-annandale

Charlesworth, Chris. "Steely Dan: Steely Logic." *Melody Maker* Apr. 13, 1974. rocksbackpages.com/Library/Article/steely-dan-steely-logic

Cohen, Ron. "Spotlight Gazette: Jeff Porcaro." *Downbeat* Sept. 8, 1977. toto-music .net/jeff_tribute/prasa/prasa01.php

Cromelin, Richard. "Return of the Nightfly: Steely Dan co-creator Donald Fagen resurfaces after nearly a decade of silence, with new works and a new outlook on life." *Los Angeles Times* Nov., 1991. articles.latimes.com/1991-11-03/ entertainment/ca-1778_1_steely-dan/2

Cromelin, Richard. "Steely Dan: Don and Walt." *Sounds* Jun. 5, 1976. rocksback pages.com/Library/Article/steely-dan-don-and-walt

Cromelin, Richard. "Steely Dan: Excerpts from a Teenage Opera." *Phonograph Record* Jun. 1977. rocksbackpages.com/Library/Article/steely-dan-excerpts -from-a-teenage-opera

Cromelin, Richard. "Walter Becker's 'Circus Money." *Los Angeles Times* Jun. 2008 latimes.com/entertainment/la-ca-becker8-2008jun08-story.html

Deriso, Nick. "Steve Gadd on 'Aja,' 50 Ways to Leave Your Lover,' 'Take It Away,' Others: Gimme Five." *Something Else!* Sept. 27, 2012. somethingelsereviews .com/2012/09/27/steve-gadd-on-aja-50-ways-to-leave-your-lover-take-it-away -others

Dias, Denny. "The Buzzing of the Field." steelydan.com/dennys2.html

Dias, Denny. "Steely Dan, Men and Machines." steelydan.com/dennys.html

Dias, Denny. "Katy and the Gremlin." steelydan.com/dennys3.html

Dickson, Jamie. "40 Years of Rocking on Reelin': Elliott Randall Interview." *Guitarist* Jun. 2012. elliott-randall.com/2012/06/guitarist-magazine-interview-june-2012

Farber, Jim. "The Darcys Put a New Spin on Steely Dan's Classic '70s album *Aja*." *The Daily News* Mar. 1, 2012. nydailynews.com/entertainment/music-arts/ darcys-put-new-spin-steely-dan-classic-70s-album-aja-article-1.1030693

Fear, David. "Inside Bill Hader and Fred Armisen's Soft-Rock Supergroup." *Rolling Stone* Sept. 24, 2015 rollingstone.com/tv/news/inside-bill-hader-and-fred -armisens-soft-rock-supergroup-20150924

Ferguson, Euan. "Steely Dan: Named After a Giant Dildo, and Still Stimulating After a 20-Year Break." *The Guardian* Feb. 20, 2000. steelydanreader.com/2000/ 02/20/smart-enough-like

Fogel, Pete. "Interview with Chris Parker." *Metal Leg* Issue 22 Aug. 1993. steelydan reader.com/1993/08/01/metal-leg-22/#8

Gardner, Eriq. "Steely Dan Sued by Former Singer David Palmer Over Digital Royalties." *Billboard* Mar. 1, 2014. billboard.com/biz/articles/news/ legal-and-management/5923015/steely-dan-sued-by-former-singer-david -palmer-over

Giles, Jeff. "Anatomy of a Song: Jay Graydon Discusses Steely Dan's 'Peg.'" *Popdose.com* May 14, 2010. popdose.com/anatomy-of-a-song-jay-graydon-discusses-steely-dans-peg

Gill, Andy. "The Return of Steely Dan." *MOJO* Issue 23 Oct. 1995. rocksbackpages.com/Library/Article/steely-dan-the-return-of-steely-dan

Hichak, Paul G. "Interview with Drummer Peter Erskine." *The Rhythm Section* Jul, 1, 1993. steelydanreader.com/1993/07/01/interview-with-drummer-peter-erskine

Hoskyns, Barney. "Steely Dan: Librarians on Acid." *Guardian* Jan. 2000. rocksbackpages.com/Library/Article/steely-dan-librarians-on-acid

Hoskyns, Barney. "Curbing Their Enthusiasm." *Uncut* Jun. 2003. rocksbackpages.com/Library/Article/curbing-their-enthusiasm-steely-dan

Houser, Kristen. "Interview with Gary Katz: Legendary Producer and A&R Man!" *LA Music Blog* Jul. 26, 2010. lamusicblog.com/2010/07/interview/interview-with-gary-katz

Hutchinson, Lydia. "The Dark Humor of Donald Fagen." *Performing Songwriter* Jan. 9, 2011. performingsongwriter.com/happy-birthday-donald-fagen

Ingham, Chris "Steely Dan and Jazz." *Jazzwise* Dec. 2000. rocksbackpages.com/Library/Article/steely-dan-and-jazz

Ingham, Chris "Steely Dan: Joined at the Hip." *MOJO* Jan. 2000. rocksbackpages.com/Library/Article/steely-dan-joined-at-the-hip

Jones, Dylan. "Icon: Donald Fagen." *GQ* Feb. 11, 2014. gq-magazine.co.uk/article/donald-fagen-steely-dan-aja

Kaplan, Fred. "What Rhymes with Orange Alert?" *New York Times* Feb. 26, 2006. nytimes.com/2006/02/26/arts/music/what-rhymes-with-orange-alert.html

Leviton, Mark. "Walter Becker: Breaking the Silence." *BAM* Dec. 1985. rocksbackpages.com/Library/Article/walter-becker-breaking-the-silence

Lubow, Arthur. "Nobody's Making Better Music Than an Unlikely Duo Named After a Dildo." *New Times* Feb. 18, 1977. steelydanreader.com/1977/02/18/fancy-dan

Mejia, Paula. "Mayer Hawthorne: 'If You Don't Like Steely Dan, I Don't Like You." *Spin* Jul. 16, 2013. spin.com/2013/07/mayer-hawthorne-where-does-this-door-go-interview

Mervis, Scott. "Uncovering the Mysteries of Steely Dan." *Pittsburgh Post Gazette* Aug. 7, 2014. post-gazette.com/ae/music/2014/08/07/Crunching-on-Steely-Dan-s-Pretzel-Logic/stories/201408070131

Micaleff, Ken. "The Drummers of Steely Dan." *Modern Drummer* Nov. 1, 1992. *steelydanreader.com/1992/11/01/the-drummers-of-steely-dan*

Molenda, Michael. "Guitar Talk, a Session Roundtable of the Guitarists on Donald Fagen's *Sunken Condos*." *Guitar Player* Mar. 6, 2013. guitarplayer.com/miscellaneous/1139/guitar-talk-a-session-roundtable-of-the-guitarists-on-donald-fagens-sunken-condos/23084

Morse, Steve. "Steely Dan Reelin' Again." *Boston Globe* Aug. 20, 1993. steelydanreader.com/1993/08/20/steely-dan-reelin

Myers, Marc. "How Steely Dan Got Wayne Shorter." *JazzWax* Jul. 8, 2011. jazzwax.com/2011/07/how-steely-dan-got-wayne-shorter.html

Myers, Marc. "Interview: Donald Fagen." *JazzWax* Jul. 15, 2011. jazzwax.com/2011/07/interview-donald-fagen.html

Norman, Tony. "The Once-Reclusive Members of Steely Dan Now Seem Happy to Step into the Public Eye." *Pittsburgh Post-Gazette* Jun. 30, 2000. old.post-gazette.com/magazine/20000629steely2.asp

Obrecht, Jay. "GP Flashback: Jeff Baxter, December 1980." *Guitar Player* Dec. 1980. guitarplayer.com/miscellaneous/1139/gp-flashback-jeff-baxter-december-1980/13402

Plantier, Boris. "Michael Omartian: Working with Steely Dan Could Hardly Be Considered 'Fun.'" *yuzu-melodies.fr* Jun. 9, 2012. yuzu-melodies.fr/Michael-Omartian-Working-with-Steely-Dan-could-hardly-be-considered-fun_a1240.html

Regen, Jon. "Donald Fagen: Inside the Process." *Keyboard* Mar. 7, 2013. keyboardmag.com/artists/1236/donald-fagen-inside-the-process/29102

Rosen, Steven. "Counting Down to Headline Status: Steely Dan." *Los Angeles Free Press* Aug. 1973. rocksbackpages.com/Library/Article/counting-down-to-headline-status-steely-dan

Sakamoto, John. "The Steely Dan Q&A." *JAM! Music* Feb. 29, 2000. steelydan.com/2vnjam.html

Salewicz, Chris. "Skunk Hunting in W1." *New Musical Express* Jul. 19, 1975. rocksbackpages.com/Library/Article/skunk-hunting-in-w1

Shteamer, Hank. "Walter Becker." *Time Out New York* Jun. 11, 2008. timeout.com/newyork/music/walter-becker

Simmons, Sylvie. "Steely Dan." *Sounds* Oct. 22, 1977. rocksbackpages.com/Library/Article/steely-dan-2

Smith, Giles. "From Nought to 40 in 11 Years: Donald Fagen Has Been Away a Long Time, Desperately Avoiding Work." *The Independent* May 19, 1993. independent.co.uk/arts-entertainment/music/interview-from-nought-to-40-in-11-years-donald-fagen-has-been-away-a-long-time-desperately-avoiding-2323998.html

Stevenson, Jane. "Fagen on New Disc, Steely Dan Return." *Toronto Sun* Mar. 13, 2006 *steelydanreader.com/2006/03/13/fagen-new-disc-steely-dan-return*

Sweet, Brian. "Roger Nichols Interview." *Metal Leg 21* Apr. 1993. steelydanreader.com/1993/04/01/metal-leg-21/#5

Tingen, Paul. "Larry Klein and Helik Hadar: Recording Circus Money." *Sound on Sound* Nov. 2008. soundonsound.com/sos/nov08/articles/becker.htm

Tingen, Paul. "Recording *Morph the Cat.*" *Sound on Sound* Aug. 2006. soundonsound.com/people/donald-fagen

Welch, Chris. "Steely Dan." *Melody Maker* Jun. 1, 1974. rocksbackpages.com/Library/Article/steely-dan

Willman, Chris. "The Reinventing of Walter Becker." *Los Angeles Times* Sept. 14, 1994. articles.latimes.com/1994-09-14/entertainment/ca-38521_1_steely-dan/1

Yaffe, David. "Shanah Tova from Donald Fagen." *Tablet* Oct. 16, 2012. tabletmag.com/jewish-arts-and-culture/music/114035/shanah-tova-from-donald-fagen

Zollo, Paul. "Steely Dan Continues the Battle." *CDNOW.com* Jan. 2000. rocksbackpages.com/Library/Article/steely-dan-continues-the-battle

Zollo, Paul. "Walter Becker Interview." *Song Talk* Winter 1989. steelydanreader.com/1990/10/15/metal-leg-14/#4

Audio and Video Interviews and Documentaries

Classic Albums: Steely Dan Aja. Dir. Alan Lewens. Eagle Rock/Image Entertainment Oct. 21, 1999.

McNamara, Dennis. "Song by Song with Gary Katz." *WLIR-FM* Jan. 1979. transcribed on steelydanreader.com

Wilber, Jason. "In Search of a Song: Gary Katz." *PRX* Aug. 2, 2014. https://beta.prx.org/stories/126440

Websites

Allmusic.com
Billboard.com
Canadianbands.com
Discogs.com
Interzone: Steely Dan—broberg.pp.se
Jayandtheamericans.net
Steely Dan Database—steelydan.nl/index.htm
SteelyDanReader.com
Somethingelsereviews.com—Steely Dan Sunday
Terenceboylan.com

Index

THE FAQ SERIES

Nirvana FAQ
by John D. Luerssen
Backbeat Books
9781617134500...................... $24.99

Pink Floyd FAQ
by Stuart Shea
Backbeat Books
9780879309503...................$19.99

Elvis Films FAQ
by Paul Simpson
Applause Books
9781557838582.................... $24.99

Elvis Music FAQ
by Mike Eder
Backbeat Books
9781617130496...................... $24.99

Pearl Jam FAQ
*by Bernard M. Corbett and
Thomas Edward Harkins*
Backbeat Books
9781617136122 ....$19.99

Prog Rock FAQ
by Will Romano
Backbeat Books
9781617135873 .... $24.99

Pro Wrestling FAQ
by Brian Solomon
Backbeat Books
9781617135996...................... $29.99

**The Rocky Horror
Picture Show FAQ**
by Dave Thompson
Applause Books
9781495007477 ....$19.99

Rush FAQ
by Max Mobley
Backbeat Books
9781617134517 ....$19.99

Saturday Night Live FAQ
by Stephen Tropiano
Applause Books
9781557839510...................... $24.99

Seinfeld FAQ
by Nicholas Nigro
Applause Books
9781557838575.................... $24.99

Sherlock Holmes FAQ
by Dave Thompson
Applause Books
9781480331495.................... $24.99

The Smiths FAQ
by John D. Luerssen
Backbeat Books
9781480394490.................. $24.99

Soccer FAQ
by Dave Thompson
Backbeat Books
9781617135989...................... $24.99

The Sound of Music FAQ
by Barry Monush
Applause Books
9781480360433.................. $27.99

South Park FAQ
by Dave Thompson
Applause Books
9781480350649.................. $24.99

Bruce Springsteen FAQ
by John D. Luerssen
Backbeat Books
9781617130939.......................$22.99

Star Trek FAQ
(Unofficial and Unauthorized)
by Mark Clark
Applause Books
9781557837929.......................$19.99

Star Trek FAQ 2.0
(Unofficial and Unauthorized)
by Mark Clark
Applause Books
9781557837936...................... $22.99

Star Wars FAQ
by Mark Clark
Applause Books
978480360181 .... $24.99

Quentin Tarantino FAQ
by Dale Sherman
Applause Books
9781480355880.................. $24.99

Three Stooges FAQ
by David J. Hogan
Applause Books
9781557837882....................$22.99

TV Finales FAQ
*by Stephen Tropiano and
Holly Van Buren*
Applause Books
9781480391444 ....$19.99

The Twilight Zone FAQ
by Dave Thompson
Applause Books
9781480396180 ....$19.99

Twin Peaks FAQ
*by David Bushman and
Arthur Smith*
Applause Books
9781495015861.......................$19.99

The Who FAQ
by Mike Segretto
Backbeat Books
9781480361034 .... $24.99

The Wizard of Oz FAQ
by David J. Hogan
Applause Books
9781480350625 .... $24.99

The X-Files FAQ
by John Kenneth Muir
Applause Books
9781480369740................... $24.99

Neil Young FAQ
by Glen Boyd
Backbeat Books
9781617130373.......................$19.99

Frank Zappa FAQ
by John Corcelli
Backbeat Books
9781617136030.......................$19.99

HAL•LEONARD®
PERFORMING ARTS
PUBLISHING GROUP

FAQ.halleonardbooks.com